HIGHER EDUCA

Higher Education for Good

Teaching and Learning Futures

Edited by
Laura Czerniewicz and Catherine Cronin

https://www.openbookpublishers.com

©2023 Laura Czerniewicz and Catherine Cronin (eds). Copyright of individual chapters is maintained by the chapter's authors.

This work is licensed under a Creative Commons Attribution-NonCommercial 4.0 International (CC BY-NC 4.0). This license allows you to share, copy, distribute and transmit the text; to adapt the text for non-commercial purposes of the text providing attribution is made to the authors (but not in any way that suggests that they endorse you or your use of the work). Attribution should include the following information:

Laura Czerniewicz and Catherine Cronin (eds), *Higher Education for Good: Teaching and Learning Futures*. Cambridge, UK: Open Book Publishers, 2023, https://doi.org/10.11647/OBP.0363

Copyright and permissions for the reuse of many of the images included in this publication differ from the above. This information is provided in the captions.

Further details about CC BY-NC licenses are available at http://creativecommons.org/licenses/by-nc/4.0/

All external links were active at the time of publication unless otherwise stated and have been archived via the Internet Archive Wayback Machine at https://archive.org/web

Digital material and resources associated with this volume are available at https://doi.org/10.11647/OBP.0363#resources

ISBN Paperback: 978-1-80511-127-6
ISBN Hardback: 978-1-80511-128-3
ISBN Digital (PDF): 978-1-80511-129-0
ISBN Digital ebook (EPUB): 978-1-80511-130-6
ISBN XML: 978-1-80511-132-0
ISBN HTML: 978-1-80511-133-7

DOI: 10.11647/OBP.0363

Cover image: George Sfougaras, *Hope*, CC BY-NC-ND
Cover design: Jeevanjot Kaur Nagpal

Contents

List of Artwork	ix
About the editors	1
About the authors and artists	3
List of peer-reviewers	23
Acknowledgements	25
Foreword	27
Jonathan Jansen	
Preface	31
Carolina Guzmán-Valenzuela	

Section I
Finding Fortitude and Hope   35

Higher education for good	37
Catherine Cronin and Laura Czerniewicz	
1. Writing from the wreckage: Austerity and the public university	53
Robin DeRosa	
2. Counters to despair	81
Sherri Spelic	

Section II
Making Sense of the Unknown and Emergent   89

3. On public goods, cursing, and finding hope in the (neoliberal) twilight zone	91
Su-Ming Khoo	
4. Imagining higher education as infrastructures of care	111
Leslie Chan, Mona Ghali, and Paul Prinsloo	

5. Why decolonising "knowledge" matters: Deliberations for
educators on that made fragile   137
Dina Zoe Belluigi

6. Closing the factory: Reimagining higher education as commons   161
Jim Luke

7. Fostering the gift: On property regimes and teaching pedagogies
in higher education   183
Andreas Wittel

8. A meditation on global further education, in haiku form   199
Jess Auerbach Jahajeeah

9. Artificial intelligence for good?
Challenges and possibilities of AI in higher education from a data
justice perspective   239
Ekaterina Pechenkina

10. HE4Good assemblages: FemEdTech Quilt of Care and Justice in
Open Education   267
*Frances Bell, Lorna Campbell, Giulia Forsythe, Lou Mycroft,
and Anne-Marie Scott*

**Section III
Considering Alternative Futures   291**

11. Calm in the storm   293
Paola Corti and Chrissi Nerantzi

12. Visioning futures of higher education for the common good   303
Mpine Makoe

13. Speculative futures for higher education: weaving perspectives
for good   317
*Elizabeth Childs, George Veletsianos, Amber Donahue,
Tamara Leary, Kyla McLeod, and Anne-Marie Scott*

14. "Vibrant, open and accessible":
Students' visions of higher education futures   335
*Sharon Flynn, Julie Byrne, Maeve Devoy, Jonathon Johnston, Rob Lowney,
Eimer Magee, Kate Molloy, David Moloney, Morag Munro, Fernandos
Ongolly, Jasmine Ryan, Suzanne Stone, Michaela Waters, and Kyle Wright*

15. Vulnerability and generosity: The good future for Australian
higher education   353
Kate Bowles

Section IV
Making Change through Teaching, Assessment and Learning Design   371

16. A design justice approach to Universal Design for Learning: Perspectives from the Global South   373
Aleya Ramparsad Banwari, Philip Dambisya, Benedict Khumalo, and Kristin van Tonder

17. Humanising learning design with digital pragmatism   397
Kate Molloy and Clare Thomson

18. Advancing 'openness' as a strategy against platformisation in education   421
Tel Amiel and Janaina do Rozário Diniz

19. Imagination and justice: Teaching the future(s) of higher education through Africanfuturist speculative fiction   445
Felicitas Macgilchrist and Eamon Costello

20. One-one coco full basket — on the value of critical pedagogy of caring for learning and teaching in higher education   473
Carol Hordatt Gentles

21. Critical data literacies for good   491
Caroline Kuhn, Judith Pete, and Juliana E. Raffaghelli

22. Collaboratively reimagining teaching and learning   509
Flora Fabian, Jonathan Harle, Perpetua Kalimasi, Rehema Kilonzo, Gloria Lamaro, Albert Luswata, David Monk, Edwin Ngowi, Femi Nzegwu, and Damary Sikalieh

23. The only way is ethics: A dialogue of assessment and social good   533
Tim Fawns and Juuso Nieminen, but not necessarily in that order

Section V
(Re)making HE Systems and Structures   555

24. Cultivating sustainable blended and open learning ecosystems   557
Patricia Arinto, Primo Garcia, and Ana Katrina Marcial

25. Making higher education institutions as open knowledge institutions   575
Pradeep Kumar Misra and Sanjaya Mishra

26. "It's about transforming lives!": Supporting students in post pandemic higher education 591
Vicki Trowler

27. Who cares about procurement? 603
Anne-Marie Scott and Brenna Clarke Gray

Afterword: Higher education for good 623
Raewyn Connell

The last word: "Making noises through our work" 627
Jyoti Arora

Index 635

List of Artwork

Hope   35
George Sfougaras

Old Tree   89
Alex Abrahams

Vessels of Hope   291
Giulia Forsythe

Little Me   371
Sheila MacNeill

The Right to Flourish   555
Niamh McArdle

About the editors

Catherine Cronin is an independent scholar whose work focuses on critical and social justice approaches in digital, open, and higher education. Born in the Bronx and now living in the west of Ireland, Catherine has interwoven work in higher education, community education, and activism for 40 years in multiple countries and contexts. She recently completed a three-year strategic role in Ireland's National Forum for the Enhancement of Teaching and Learning in Higher Education where she led sector-wide projects in digital and open education. She has master's degrees in systems engineering and women's studies and a PhD in open education (University of Galway). She received a GO-GN Fellowship in 2022 for *Just Knowledge*, her research on equity-focused, community-based, open knowledge. Catherine has published widely and openly on critical and social justice approaches, digital and open education, and intersectional feminism. She serves on the editorial boards of several journals, is an active member of FemEdTech, and contributes regularly to collaborative projects within Ireland and globally. Catherine blogs and shares scholarship at http://catherinecronin.net.

Laura Czerniewicz has worked in education throughout her professional life as a teacher, teacher educator, publisher, strategist, researcher, and scholar. She is professor emerita at the University of Cape Town, South Africa. With personal links to South Africa, Zimbabwe, France, Poland, New Zealand, and Germany, she considers herself a world citizen. Laura's work has been underpinned by an enduring concern about digital and social inequities; this has manifested recently in research on changing forms of teaching and learning provision and in the datafication of education. She has a long-standing commitment to open education and serious unease about the corporate capture of higher education. She serves on the editorial boards of many national and international journals; has been an interested contributor and participant at relevant events on every continent; and is an active reviewer of pertinent articles, books, proposals etc. and blogs at https://czernie.weebly.com.

Larry Erhuvwuoghene Onokpite is from Agbarha-Otor, Delta State, Nigeria. He is a registered member of the Professional Editors' Guild of South Africa and has copy edited journal articles, dissertations, fiction writings and a book, as well as all chapters in *Higher Education for Good: Teaching and Learning Futures*. Larry is currently a doctoral student at Ohio State University with research interests in dyslexia education and educational neuroscience. Larry enjoys road running, photography, and cooking. https://editors.org.za/user/larry-onokpite

About the authors and artists

Alex Abrahams (b. 1991) is a trained curator and artist from Cape Town (South Africa). Alex is pursuing his art career with great commitment. He participated in seven group exhibitions in 2021, which was his debut year. His work can be viewed at www.alexrabrahams.com

Tel Amiel is an adjunct professor at the School of Education at the University of Brasília (Brazil) where he coordinates the UNESCO Chair in Distance Education, and is also an adjunct professor at the University of Nova Gorica (Slovenia) in the Master in Leadership in Open Education program. Co-founder of the Open Education Initiative: an activist research group. More information can be found at: https://amiel.net.br
https://orcid.org/0000-0002-1775-1148

Patricia Arinto is a former dean of the Faculty of Education at the University of the Philippines (UP) Open University, and currently dean of UP Tacloban College (Philippines). Her research interests include teacher professional development in blended and online learning, learning design, and open educational practices. She has a doctorate in education from the Institute of Education at the University of London; a postgraduate certificate in Technology-Based Distributed Learning from the University of British Columbia; an MA in Comparative Literature from UP Diliman; and a BA in Communication Arts from UP Visayas Tacloban College.
https://orcid.org/0000-0003-4452-9283

Jyoti Arora is a PhD Scholar at the Zakir Husain Centre for Educational Studies in the School of Social Sciences at Jawaharlal Nehru University (India). Her research interests include higher education, teacher education, and educational policy.
https://orcid.org/0000-0003-1196-0966

Jess Auerbach Jahajeeah is an associate professor at the Graduate School of Business in the University of Cape Town (South Africa). She is director for the MPhil in Inclusive Innovation. Jess has lived and worked in Angola, Brazil, Mauritius, Mozambique, the UK, the US, and Zambia. In Mauritius she was founding faculty at a start-up university. She is the author of two books, and currently writing a third on digital infrastructure. She holds a PhD in anthropology from Stanford University.
http://jessauerbach.net
https://orcid.org/0000-0001-9064-1474

Frances Bell, since her retirement from Salford Business School (UK) in 2013, has enjoyed the freedom to pursue learning textile arts and conducting independent research with valued others. Some of her treasured achievements since retirement include being part of FemEdTech, a feminist network of those associated with education technology, and being part of the project that is a material-digital expression of FemEdTech values, the FemEdTech Quilt of Care and Justice in Open Education.
http://francesbell.com
https://orcid.org/0000-0002-7543-6832

Dina Zoe Belluigi is a reader at Queen's University Belfast (Northern Ireland) and affiliated with Nelson Mandela University (South Africa). Her work relates to the conditions for the agency and ethico-historical responsibility of academics and artists in contexts undergoing transitions in authority and in the shadow of oppression. She has been honoured to participate in research and practice in South Africa, India, Northern Ireland, and England, as well as with displaced Syrian academics.
https://pure.qub.ac.uk/en/persons/dina-belluigi
https://orcid.org/0000-0003-4005-0160

Kate Bowles is a narrative researcher in the social history of cinema-going and the patient experience of illness. She is the Associate Dean International in the Faculty of the Arts, Social Sciences and Humanities at the University of Wollongong (Australia), on Dharawal Country.
http://musicfordeckchairs.com

Julie Byrne is assistant professor in Online Education & Development at Trinity College Dublin (Ireland). She was Trinity's academic lead (2019–2021) on the national Enhancing Digital Teaching and Learning (EDTL) project and is a current member of the Leading European Advanced Digital Skills (LEADS) consortium, funded by the European Commission. She was director of Trinity's first fully online postgraduate programme and is a contributor to Trinity's first micro-credential programme where she offers an online course, Digital Technologies in Human Services.
https://orcid.org/0000-0002-5913-1158

Lorna Campbell is a learning technologist and open education practitioner with a longstanding commitment to supporting open knowledge, open education, and OER. She is an active member of the FemEdTech network and a senior certified member of the Association for Learning Technology (ALT). Lorna is based in Scotland and currently works at the University of Edinburgh, where she is manager of the university's OER Service. She blogs about openness, knowledge equity, feminism, and digital labour at Open World:
http://lornamcampbell.org
https://orcid.org/0000-0001-6767-856X

Leslie Chan is associate professor in the Department of Global Development Studies and director of the Knowledge Equity Lab at the University of Toronto Scarborough (Canada). He studies the role and design of knowledge infrastructure and their impact on local and international development, and in particular the geopolitics of academic knowledge production and the uneven power relations embedded in this production.
https://knowledgeequitylab.ca
https://orcid.org/0000-0001-7779-2059

Elizabeth Childs is a professor in the School of Education and Technology at Royal Roads University (Canada). She is interested in the design, creation and implementation of flexible learning environments that incorporate the affordances of technologies and provide learners with increased choice, flexibility, and opportunities. Dr. Childs' research interests include online and blended learning, openness and open

pedagogy, online learning communities and digital habitats, design thinking and participatory design approaches.
https://malat-coursesite.royalroads.ca/malat
https://orcid.org/0000-0003-2654-1705

Raewyn Connell is professor emerita at the University of Sydney and a Life Member of the National Tertiary Education Union (Australia). She has published widely in the areas of class dynamics, social theory of gender relations, masculinity, transsexuality, poverty and education, and higher education. She has been an advisor to United Nations initiatives on gender equality and peace-making. Her most recent book is *The Good University* (2019).
http://www.raewynconnell.net

Paola Corti is a project manager and instructional designer at Politecnico di Milano (Italy). She works on international projects, MOOC design and development, and professional development courses for faculty and researchers on open education and innovative pedagogical approaches. She is the open education community manager of the European Network of Open Education Librarians (ENOEL), supporting librarians in taking action to implement the UNESCO OER Recommendation. She is a facilitator for Creative Commons certificate courses.
https://orcid.org/0000-0001-8506-7148

Eamon Costello is an associate professor of Digital Learning in Dublin City University (Ireland). He is deeply curious about the ways in which we can actively shape our world so that we can have better and more humane places where we can think, work, live and learn. He is an advocate of using the right tool for the job or sometimes none at all, for not everything can be fixed or should be built.
https://www.dcu.ie/researchsupport/research-profile?person_id=14193#tab-research
https://orcid.org/0000-0002-2775-6006

Philip Mbulalina Dambisya is a trainee learning designer at the University of Cape Town's Centre for Innovation in Learning and Teaching (CILT) (South Africa). With qualifications in Audiology, Health Professions Education, and Public Health, he is passionate about exploring the nexus of health, social justice, and education. Viewing

education as one of many vehicles towards the uplifting of others, Philip is a believer in and proponent of quality open education.
http://orcid.org/0000-0003-0571-2667

Robin DeRosa is director of Learning and Libraries at Plymouth State University, a public university in New Hampshire (USA). While her academic training was originally focused on early American literature and history, she now researches and writes about higher education and is an advocate for open, public, and sustainable futures for learning.
http://robinderosa.net
https://orcid.org/0000-0002-4375-3307

Maeve A. Devoy is the author of *A City Symphony* and *The Tell Tale Collection*. She has an MA in Literary Journalism and a BA in Journalism. She spends her time teaching creative writing across the country (Ireland).

Janaina do Rozário Diniz is a teacher at the University of the State of Minas Gerais (Brazil). She develops research on free software in education, platformisation in education, and disinformation.
https://orcid.org/0000-0001-7993-5447

Amber Donahue is proud to be a teacher and advocate of public education, whose 17 years as a K-12 educator have taught her about the power of kindness, human connection, and critical thinking. She is keenly interested in exploring technology's impact on society and how education systems can rise to the challenge of preparing students for life in the digital age.

Flora Masumbuo Fabian is professor of Biomedical Science, focusing on transformative teaching-learning in higher education. Co-author of *Gender Mainstreaming in Higher Education Toolkit* (INASP, 2016), Fabian is a champion in embedding gender responsive pedagogy in HE and promoting equal opportunities for females and males in economic participation. Former University of Dodoma director of research, current Mwanza University (Tanzania) vice chancellor, Fabian has over 40 publications in peer reviewed journals.
https://www.inasp.info/staff/flora-fabian
https://orcid.org/0000-0002-4880-1021

Tim Fawns is an associate professor at the Monash Education Academy, Monash University (Australia). His research interests are at the intersection between digital, clinical, and higher education, with a particular focus on the relationship between technology and educational practice. He has recently published a book titled *Online Postgraduate Education in a Postdigital World: Beyond Technology*.
http://timfawns.com
https://orcid.org/0000-0001-5014-2662

Sharon Flynn was project manager of the Enhancing Digital Capacity in Teaching and Learning (EDTL) project (2019–2022) in Ireland, working with academic leaders across seven universities. The project aimed to enhance the digital competencies and learning experience of Irish university students, with a particular focus on academic staff development. She was Assistant Director of the Centre for Excellence in Learning and Teaching at the University of Galway (Ireland) for 13 years.
https://www.linkedin.com/in/sharonlflynn/
https://orcid.org/0000-0002-5755-7147

Giulia Forsythe is the director, Teaching and Learning at the Centre for Pedagogical Innovation at Brock University in Ontario (Canada).
https://gforsythe.ca/
https://orcid.org/0000-0001-9669-9706

Primo G. Garcia is the Vice Chancellor for Academic Affairs and a professor of Research and Development Management at the University of the Philippines Open University. He holds a PhD in Organization Studies from the University of Melbourne. His research interests include organisation and management, e-learning, and management of distance education.
https://orcid.org/0000-0002-8693-3746

Mona Ghali is an independent researcher based in Toronto (Canada). Her eclectic studies cut across disciplinary fields including global education policy, conflict and peace studies, international development, and feminist and critical theories. At present, she is interested in understanding how radical discourses are co-opted in mainstream politics, policies, and practices.

Brenna Clarke Gray holds a PhD in Canadian Literature and is a tenured coordinator in Educational Technologies at Thompson Rivers University in Kamloops, BC (Canada), where she is part of the Learning Technology and Innovation team. Brenna's research interests include the history and future of open tenure processes, scholarly podcasting, and educational technology support as care work. She is powered primarily by righteous indignation and lattes.
http://brennaclarkegray.ca
https://orcid.org/0000-0002-6079-0484

Carolina Guzmán-Valenzuela is interested in the study of higher education. For the last 12 years, she has been conducting research on the role of universities in the twenty-first century. Currently, she is leading a national project on knowledge production in the social sciences and the humanities in Latin America financed by Fondecyt Chile (1200633).
https://www.researchgate.net/profile/Carolina-Guzman-Valenzuela
https://orcid.org/0000-0002-7974-762X

Jonathan Harle is director of programmes at INASP and lives and works in Berlin (Germany). He works with educators, researchers, and universities to find new ways to strengthen capacity, confidence, and leadership in research, teaching, and learning. He convened and co-leads the Transforming Higher Education for Social Change in East Africa (TESCEA) partnership.
https://www.inasp.info/staff/jonathan-harle
https://orcid.org/0000-0001-6804-2969

Carol Hordatt Gentles is a senior lecturer with the School of Education, University of West Indies (Jamaica). Her research focuses on improving teacher quality through teacher education and teacher development in the Caribbean region where she has worked as a consultant for the World Bank and UNESCO on several projects. She currently serves as president of the International Council of Education for Teaching. She is also chief editor for the *Caribbean Journal of Education*.
https://orcid.org/0000-0001-5744-7231?lang=en

Jonathan Jansen is distinguished professor of Education at the University of Stellenbosch (South Africa). He is currently president of the South Africa Academy of Science and Knight-Hennessey Fellow at

Stanford University (USA). He has published widely in the areas of education, democracy, and human rights. His most recent books include *Corrupted: A Study of Chronic Dysfunction in South African Universities* (2023) and *The Decolonization of Knowledge: Radical ideas and the Shaping of Institutions in South Africa* (with Cyrill Walters, 2022).
https://www.jonathanjansen.org
https://orcid.org/0000-0002-8614-5678

Jonny Johnston is an educational developer at the Centre for Academic Practice at Trinity College Dublin (Ireland), where he leads on a range of teaching enhancement interventions. Jonny has been formally working in academic development since 2019. His original background and research training is in modern languages and literatures (PhD Germanic Studies, Trinity College Dublin). His current interests lie in curriculum and in structured approaches to teacher education and development in higher education.

Perpetua Joseph Kalimasi is a senior lecturer in Educational Management and Policy Studies at Mzumbe University (Tanzania). She is currently the head of Teaching Skills and Distance Learning at Mzumbe University. Her research and supervision interests include graduate employability, gender, lifelong learning, entrepreneurship education, inclusive education, school management, and vocational education. She is currently the coordinator for gender and inclusive education for the World Bank HEET programme for Higher Education Transformation implemented at Mzumbe University.

Su-Ming Khoo is associate professor and head of Sociology at the University of Galway (Ireland) and visiting professor in Critical Studies in Higher Education Transformation (CriSHET) at Nelson Mandela University (2022–2027) in South Africa. She researches, teaches, and writes about human development, rights, public goods, public activism, global learning, and development education, decoloniality, higher education, and transdisciplinarity.
https://orcid.org/0000-0001-8346-3913

Benedict Khumalo is a trainee learning designer and disability researcher, currently enrolled for an MPhil Disabilities Studies at the

University of Cape Town (UCT) (South Africa). His research focuses on special schools' educators' perceptions of inclusive education in South Africa. He has three postgraduate qualifications: Social Development and Social Anthropology from the University of the Western Cape and a postgraduate diploma in Disability Studies from UCT. He is interested in discourses of inclusive education, including online learning and curriculum design.

Rehema Kilonzo is a senior lecturer and director of Internationalisation, Convocation and Continuing Education at the University of Dodoma (Tanzania). She teaches at the intersection of sociology, policy analysis, and development. Her current research focuses on private managed cash transfers, funded by DANIDA. She was a TESCEA project lead at the University of Dodoma.
http://www.udom.ac.tz

Caroline Kuhn came from Venezuela to Europe to pursue a PhD. Now a senior lecturer based at the School of Education in Bath Spa University (UK), her research focuses on the intersection of sociology, philosophy, technology, and education. She has a particular interest in open education and social justice framed under a critical pedagogy approach. She is also interested in issues of data justice and how technology can be meaningfully integrated into resource-constrained contexts so that different ways of knowing and being are respected, and agency is fostered.
https://www.bathspa.ac.uk/our-people/caroline-kuhn/
https://orcid.org/0000-0003-0393-6093

Gloria Lamaro is a lecturer in Education Management, Faculty of Education at Gulu University (Uganda). She is a member of the editorial board of the *Journal for Common Research Network*. Her research interests include gender equity, empowerment of women in the workplace, and HE in Africa. She oversees development programs in capacity building and training for academic staff, MA training, and establishment of higher education qualifications for academic staff in Uganda. She is a programme assessor for the Uganda National Council for Higher Education.

Tamara Leary is an associate professor, teaching in the MA in Higher Education Administration and Leadership program at Royal Roads University, Victoria, BC (Canada). Prior to becoming a full-time faculty member, Tamara occupied administration roles within Student Affairs. Her research interests include higher education administration and leadership, student affairs, and organisation culture within higher education.

Rob Lowney is an academic developer (Digital Learning) in the Teaching Enhancement Unit at Dublin City University (Ireland). He is a Senior Certified Member of the Association for Learning Technology and Senior Fellow of Advance HE. He works with university teachers to develop their teaching excellence, including with technologies. He is interested in staff-student pedagogical partnerships and leads the university's Students as Partners in Assessment project.
https://www.dcu.ie/teu/people/rob-lowney
https://orcid.org/0000-0002-8866-4367

Jim Luke is professor of economics and former Open Learning Faculty Fellow at a community college in Michigan (USA), where he created the Open Learning Lab, a web-based pedagogy innovation incubator. Jim has expertise in strategic planning, organisational development, innovation, technology, open education and open pedagogy, economic history, and institutional economics. His current research interests include commons as alternative economic systems and diversity in higher education.
https://econproph.com
https://orcid.org/0000-0002-8584-4442

Albert Luswata is a senior lecturer and director of the Institute of Ethics at Uganda Martyrs University. He has trained faculty in online and transformative teaching at his university and other African universities through the PedaL and TESCEA projects. His research interests are ethics, higher education partnerships, transformative teaching/learning, and gender responsive pedagogies.
https://orcid.org/0000-0003-4276-3682

Felicitas Macgilchrist is Professor of Digital Education and Schools at the University of Oldenburg (Germany). Her research explores the cultural politics of educational technology, taking up critical and speculative approaches. She is currently thinking about how design justice can be centred in edtech development, school practice and public discourse. She is co-editor of *Learning, Media and Technology* and toots occasionally at @discoursology@social.coop.
https://orcid.org/0000-0002-2828-4127

Sheila MacNeill is an artist and independent digital learning consultant based in Glasgow (Scotland). Open educational practice is a central part of Sheila's professional educational practice. Sheila works with a range of HE providers and educational organisations both in the UK and internationally.
https://howsheilaseesit.net

Eimer Magee was a student on the MEngSc in Biopharmaceutical Engineering at University College Dublin (Ireland) in 2021–2022, and a student associate intern for the Enhancing Digital Teaching and Learning (EDTL) project with the Irish Universities Association.

Mpine Makoe is the executive dean of the College of Education at the University of South Africa (UNISA) and a Commonwealth of Learning chair in Open Education Resources/Practices. She has published extensively in open and distance learning related fields and in the futures of higher education. She worked on numerous commissioned research projects for Commonwealth of Learning, UNESCO, British Council, and the Council for Higher Education.
https://orcid.org/0000-0003-4192-1781

Ana Katrina Marcial is an assistant professor teaching in the undergraduate and graduate programs at the Faculty of Education, University of the Philippines Open University. She is currently the chair of the graduate certificate and MA in Distance Education programs at UPOU. She also served as chair of the graduate diploma and MA in Language and Literacy Education programs and head of the Office of Academic Support and Instructional Services. Her current interests relate to language teaching, learning design, and continuing professional development for teachers.
https://orcid.org/0000-0001-6744-3023

Niamh McArdle is a graphic designer and occasional artist based in Dublin (Ireland). Originally from a very small village in Galway, she is interested in emotive storytelling through the use of typography, language, and image-making. She creates work with the intention of prompting emotion from whoever happens to see it.
https://www.linkedin.com/in/niamh-mcardle-493451186

Kyla McLeod is the director of student services and an associate faculty member within the School of Education and Technology at Royal Roads University (Canada). She has worked in student affairs for over 25 years and enjoys the challenges associated with supporting the learning experiences of a consistently changing student demographic. Her recent research interests are in understanding how non-Indigenous student services practitioners can effectively respond to the calls-to-action that were made through the final report of Canada's Truth and Reconciliation Commission.

Sanjaya Mishra is Director, Education at Commonwealth of Learning, Canada and promotes open education and open access to information and knowledge for all. As a staff developer, instructional designer and practitioner of distance learning, Dr Mishra has developed several award-winning platforms and courses for increasing access to quality education. His current focus is on supporting Sustainable Development Goal 4 (SDG 4) through the use of open and distance learning, especially by creating an enabling policy environment for ethical use of technology for improving the quality of lifelong learning opportunities for all.
https://www.col.org/members/dr-sanjaya-mishra
https://orcid.org/0000-0003-3291-2410

Pradeep Kumar Misra is professor and director of the Centre for Policy Research in Higher Education at the National Institute of Educational Planning and Administration, New Delhi (India). He has received several prestigious international research scholarships, published widely in journals of international repute, authored reference books, including his popular book *Learning and Teaching for Teachers*, completed research and development projects, developed educational media programs, and visited many countries for educational purposes.
http://cprhe.niepa.ac.in

https://orcid.org/0000-0002-9164-6071

Kate Molloy is an instructional designer at Atlantic Technological University (Ireland) and was previously a learning technologist in CELT, University of Galway. She was the university lead on the Irish Universities Association Enhancing Digital Teaching and Learning (EDTL) project from 2019 to 2022. Her work focuses on the informed and ethical use of technology, learning design, inclusion, and open practice. Kate is secretary national executive of the Computers in Education Society of Ireland (CESI).
https://kate-molloy.net/about/
https://orcid.org/0000-0003-3544-3170

David Moloney works as digital skills development lead in the Centre for Transformative Learning (CTL), University of Limerick (Ireland).
https://daveymoloney.com/
https://orcid.org/0009-0005-5763-3778

David Monk is a lecturer in the faculty of Education and Humanities at Gulu University (Uganda), honorary assistant professor in the School of Education at Nottingham University (UK), affiliate faculty of Education University of Victoria (Canada), special advisor to the UNESCO Chair Lifelong Learning Youth and Work, and coordinator for the Gulu Hub of the UNESCO Chair Community Based Research and Social Responsibility in Higher Education.
https://orcid.org/0000-0002-9178-6576

Morag Munro is Maynooth University's (Ireland) EDTL institutional lead, and lecturer on the postgraduate diploma in HE Teaching, Learning, and Assessment. Prior to this, Morag was learning technologist and head of the Learning Innovation Unit at Dublin City University. She has also worked at the University of Strathclyde and in the commercial eLearning sector. Her research interests include critical perspectives on educational technologies and educational policy, education for global citizenship and sustainability, and student-staff partnerships.
https://www.maynoothuniversity.ie/people/morag-munro
https://orcid.org/0000-0002-3131-8981

Lou Mycroft is an educator, changemaker and social entrepreneur. Inspired by nomadic posthuman professionalism, she works pan-organisationally, anti-competitively and pro-socially with changemakers and policymakers across further education to enact new values-led possibilities. This takes graft, and there are still people looking out for magic bullets, but change is in the air.
https://loumycroft.substack.com

Chrissi Nerantzi is an associate professor in education in the School of Education at the University of Leeds (UK). Her research interests include creativity, open education, cross-boundary collaborative learning, networks, and communities. She has initiated a range of open professional development initiatives that have been sustained over the years, bringing educators, students, and the wider public together.
https://essl.leeds.ac.uk/education/staff/2085/dr-chrissi-nerantzi
https://orcid.org/0000-0001-7145-1800

Edwin Ngowi is a senior lecturer in the department of Development and Strategic Studies at Sokoine University of Agriculture (Tanzania). Dr Ngowi has specialities in socioeconomic impact research; development policy analysis; livelihoods, climate change, and variability impact analysis; and sustainable development analysis. In this book, he shares an experience of a project consortium Transforming Employability for Social Change in East Africa (TESCEA) developed by a group of academics, learning designers, and social entrepreneurs.
https://www.cssh.sua.ac.tz/developmentstudies/edwin-estomii-ngowi/
https://orcid.org/0000-0003-3655-8973

Juuso Henrik Nieminen is an assistant professor at the University of Hong Kong and an Honorary Fellow at Deakin University (Australia). Dr Nieminen's research concerns the social, cultural, and political dimensions of assessment in higher education. Dr Nieminen is particularly interested in how assessment shapes student identities and how it could be designed inclusively for a diversity of learners.
http://juusonieminen.com
https://orcid.org/0000-0003-3087-8933

Femi Nzegwu is assistant professor of Monitoring, Evaluation, and Learning at the London School of Hygiene and Tropical Medicine (UK). She is a social researcher, MEL and international project management specialist with 30 years of experience in these fields, including institutional learning, institutional and national capacity development, and sharing and institutional strategy development. She is highly multidisciplinary and holds degrees in post-colonial studies, public health, sociology, and economics.
https://orcid.org/0000-0003-2208-4498

Fernandos Ongolly is a doctoral research student at the Business School at University College Dublin (Ireland). He is a Kenyan anthropologist based in Ireland interested in research on how people evolve and adapt to new technologies in many aspects of life such as education, health, and business, among others. He previously worked at the Irish Universities Association's (IUA) Enhancing Digital Teaching and Learning (EDTL) project as a student associate intern and is currently a portal administrator at Euraxess Ireland based at the IUA.
https://www.linkedin.com/in/fernandos-ongolly-89927b32

Ekaterina (Katya) Pechenkina is a cultural anthropologist, teaching and learning scholar, and award-winning lecturer at Swinburne University of Technology (Australia). Her research focuses on impact and evaluation in education, as well as on understanding how educators and students experience technological change. She is also a published fiction author and supervises a number of Creative Writing PhDs by artefact and exegesis.
https://www.swinburne.edu.au/research/our-research/access-our-research/find-a-researcher-or-supervisor/researcher-profile/?id=epechenkina
https://orcid.org/0000-0001-6997-6974

Judith Pete has been an educator in higher education institutions in East Africa for 13 years. She was regional director for Africa for ROER4D and is currently Uniservitate regional coordinator for Service Learning Hub for Africa at Tangaza University College (Kenya). She holds a PhD from the Open University (Netherlands) and MBA from Catholic University

of Eastern Africa. She won the 2021/22 Researcher of the Year Award and is a member of UNESCO University Network and alumnus of GO-GN.
https://scholar.google.com/citations?hl=en&user=kJPx3lsAAAAJ.
https://orcid.org/0000-0003-0971-5945

Paul Prinsloo is a research professor in Open and Distance Learning in the Department of Business Management, College of Economic and Management Sciences, University of South Africa (Unisa). His research interests include, inter alia, the ethics of (not) collecting and using student data. Paul was born curious and in trouble and, since then, nothing has changed. His Twitter and Mastodon aliases are @14prinsp.
https://opendistanceteachingandlearning.wordpress.com
https://orcid.org/0000-0002-1838-540X

Juliana Elisa Raffaghelli is an assistant professor in educational research and experimental pedagogy at the University of Padua (Italy). She actively practices the values of open science and education, exploring the impacts on educators' professional identities. Juliana is also an associated researcher of the research group Edul@b (Universitat Oberta de Catalunya, Spain) and associated researcher to the TIC-CIAFIC department at the Center for Research in Philosophical and Cultural Anthropology, National Commission of Science and Technology (Argentina).
https://jraffaghelli.com
https://orcid.org/0000-0002-8753-6478

Aleya Ramparsad Banwari is an entrepreneur, activist, and social innovator who is passionate about social justice, community-based activism, and creating a better African future for tomorrow through driving digital transformation. Aleya is a co-director and co-founder of GrabAGrad, a graduate-led innovation and consulting firm specialising in disruptive solutions, staffed entirely by previously unemployed graduates. Aleya is currently pursuing a Masters in Public Health at the University of Cape Town. Aleya's academic credentials also encompass a Bachelor of Social Science in Political Science, Industrial Sociology, and Social Anthropology in 2018, followed by their Honours in Social Anthropology in 2019 (University of Cape Town), and certifications in Design Thinking and Change Management.
https://www.linkedin.com/in/aleya-ramparsad-banwari-they-she-35bb2b7b
https://orcid.org/0000-0003-2871-1907

Jasmine Ryan was a final year BA student of Politics and International Relations with Philosophy at the University of Limerick (UL) (Ireland) in 2021 to 2022, and a student associate intern for the Enhancing Digital Teaching and Learning (EDTL) project with the Irish Universities Association. She played a pivotal role in the LevUL Up Student Digital Skills and Competence Development Programme, enhancing student experiences. Jasmine currently works as a Leadership & Representation administrator in UL Student Life.

Anne-Marie Scott has worked in higher education senior digital leadership for over 20 years in the UK (University of Edinburgh) and Canada (Athabasca University), with a particular interest in open educational technologies. She is Board Chair of the Apereo open-source software foundation, board member of the Open Source Initiative, and advisor to the OpenETC (Canada). She has an MA in Literature and a postgraduate diploma in E-Learning from the University of Edinburgh. www.ammienoot.com
https://orcid.org/0000-0003-4769-1577

George Sfougaras makes work that exists at the intersection of art, history, politics, and culture. His topics are drawn from personal experiences, family histories, and contemporary events. His work engages others at an emotional level and encourages dialogue, healing, and reconciliation, within the self and the world beyond. His art serves to extend life beyond our time through its magic and infinite ways of validating the human experience. www.georgesfougaras.com

Damary Sikalieh is a professor of Management and Entrepreneurship Education at the United States International University–Africa. Professionally, she has over 50 publications with immense experience in curriculum development and transformative teaching and learning. In consultancy, she has served on different project teams with the university and the Association of Faculty Enrichment in Learning and Teaching (AFELT). Her research interests are in the broader areas of management, entrepreneurship with a bias to inclusivity, and resilience.
http://www.afelt.org
https://orcid.org/0000-0002-3953-5024

Sherri Spelic teaches elementary physical education at an international school in Vienna (Austria). She has written extensively on topics related to education, identity and power and among other things publishes a monthly social justice newsletter for educators: *Bending The Arc*. Check out her book of essays, *Care At The Core* or find her on Twitter @edifiedlistener.

Suzanne Stone has over ten years' experience working in the higher education sector as a learning technologist and more recently as an academic developer. With specific expertise in learning technologies and the development of staff digital capabilities, Suzanne has collaborated on a range of research projects relating to technology for teaching and learning. Her current research focuses on digital wellbeing, digital assessment, and the use of ChatGPT in assessment design.
https://www.dcu.ie/teu/people/suzanne-stone

Clare Thomson is an assistant professor of Digital Pedagogies and Course Design at Heriot-Watt University (Scotland), and previously a digital education consultant in the Office for Digital Learning at Ulster University (Northern Ireland). Clare is also currently a part-time doctoral student at the University of Edinburgh, researching reflective practice. Inclusion, creativity, collaboration, and care are her cornerstones.
https://www.lostandfoundinedtech.org
https://orcid.org/0000-0002-8608-4801

Vicki Trowler has been unable to escape the gravitational pull of higher education and has spent almost her entire adult life studying at, working at, or researching universities in South Africa and the UK. Vicki has a M.Ed in Higher Education Studies from the University of the Western Cape (South Africa) and a PhD from the University of Edinburgh (UK). She is currently a postdoctoral researcher at the University of Huddersfield (UK).
https://www.linkedin.com/in/vicke
https://orcid.org/0000-0001-7050-099X

Kristin van Tonder is an educator, curriculum developer, and policy advocate with a passion for accessible and equal education. She is currently a Master's candidate in Education at the University of Cape Town (South Africa), where her research interests include instructional and curriculum design, cognitive development and inclusive education in K-12 and higher education contexts.
https://www.linkedin.com/in/kristin-van-tonder-5a326875
https://orcid.org/0000-0002-3709-5838

George Veletsianos is professor and Canada research chair in Innovative Learning and Technology at Royal Roads University in Victoria, British Columbia (Canada). His research agenda focuses on three strands: design, development, and evaluation of online and blended learning environments; the study of learning experiences and participation in emerging online environments; and learning futures.
http://www.veletsianos.com
https://orcid.org/0000-0002-6579-9576

Michaela Waters was a final year BBS student of Business Studies and Accounting at Maynooth University (Ireland) in 2021 to 2022 and a student associate intern for the Enhancing Digital Teaching and Learning (EDTL) project with the Irish Universities Association.

Andreas Wittel teaches and researches at the School of Arts and Humanities, Nottingham Trent University (UK). His research explores the political economy of digital technologies and alternatives to capitalism. More recently his research explores questions of political ecology and possibilities to prevent environmental collapse, such as a political ecology of commoning in degrowth.
https://orcid.org/0000-0002-4680-6670

Kyle Wright was a third-year Creative Digital Media student in Technological University Dublin Blanchardstown (Ireland) in 2021–22. He has a passion for technology and the creative arts, hoping to move into graphic design and cinematography after graduation. Outside of class, Kyle is part of a Dublin-based rock band.
http://kylewrightmedia.com

List of peer-reviewers

Each chapter in this book has been reviewed by esteemed scholars in higher education. Most reviews were openly shared with respective authors. The editors and authors are grateful to the following reviewers for their expertise, time, and care in providing valuable feedback:

Ishan Abeywardena, University of Waterloo, Canada

Jane-Frances Agbu, Commonwealth of Learning, Canada, Nigeria

Najma Aghardien, University of the Witwatersrand, South Africa

Ibrar Bhatt, Queens University Belfast, Northern Ireland

Carina Bossu, The Open University, UK

Cheryl Brown, Te Kaupeka Ako, Canterbury University, New Zealand

Linda Castañeda, Universidad de Murcia, Spain

Manuel João Costa, University of Minho, Portugal

Alison Farrell, Maynooth University, Ireland

Jairo Fúnez-Flores, Texas Tech University, USA

Peter Goodyear, University of Sydney, Australia

Himasha Gunasekara, Te Kaupeka Ako, Canterbury University, New Zealand

Sandhya Gunness, University of Mauritius, Mauritius

Melissa Highton, University of Edinburgh, Scotland

Phil Hill, Mindwires, USA

Mandy Hlengwa, Rhodes University, South Africa

Cheryl Hodgkinson-Williams, University of Cape Town, South Africa

Petar Jandrić, Zagreb University of Applied Sciences, Croatia

Christopher Knaus, University of Washington Tacoma, USA

Allison Littlejohn, University College London, UK

Tristan McCowan, University College London, UK

Gita Mistri, Durban University of Technology, South Africa

Erick Montenegro, Pell Institute for the Study of Opportunity in Education, USA

Marcela Morales, Open Education Global. Mexico

Hoda Mostafa, American University Cairo, Egypt

Simbarashe Moyo, University of the Witwatersrand, South Africa

Jackline Nyerere, Kenyatta University, Kenya

Larry Erhuvwuoghene Onokpite, Ohio State University, USA

Luci Pangrazio, Deakin University, Australia

Rubina Ramparsad, University of Mauritius, Mauritius

Shikha Raturi, University of the South Pacific, Fiji

Jen Ross, University of Edinburgh, Scotland

Bonnie Stewart, University of Windsor, Canada

Marwan Tarazi, Berzeit University, Palestine

Melody Viczko, Western University, Canada

Ben Williamson, University of Edinburgh, Scotland

This book has also been peer-reviewed anonymously by experts in their field according to OBP's own peer-review processes. We thank them for their feedback.

Acknowledgements

Our warm gratitude extends to so many:

First and foremost, to all 71 authors without whom there would be no book—for dedication, imagination, and commitment to the future of higher education.

To all foreword and afterword authors: Jyoti Arora, Raewyn Connell, Carolina Guzmán-Valenzuela, and Jonathan Jansen, for generous and provocative contributions that we are honoured to include in the book. And to Simon Marginson, for an inspiring global list of young scholars of the future.

To all potential authors who took time to conceptualise a long abstract, who invested in writing but had to withdraw for a range of good reasons. Please keep writing; we will keep reading. This journey isn't over!

To thoughtful reviewers, for taking on this work during tough times, for committing and keeping to deadlines, and especially for deep, constructive reviews, most of which were openly shared.

To the talented artists who responded so generously to our call and who expressed, in beautiful form, unique yet aligned visions for the future.

To colleagues who played essential and appreciated mentoring roles, including Cheryl Hodgkinson-Williams, Nokthula Vilakati, and Michelle Willmers.

To copy-editor Larry Erhuvwuokhene Onokpite for outstanding and indefatigable work in copy editing all 27 chapters of the book.

To Open Book Publishers' Alessandra Tosi for expressing enthusiastic interest right from the start and for impressive professionalism all the way through.

To everyone on social media and other networks who disseminated our call for proposals and answered our questions, including the FemEdTech and Continuity With Care networks.

To our dear friends and colleagues who supported and believed in the work, and to our families, especially Rick and Hamish, for continual support and for cheerfully living with this project from the seed of an idea to its fruition.

And finally, to those who gave us breath and give us hope. To our foremothers who imagined and fought for the futures that are our present, to our forebears in critical education and activism, to all who imagine better futures for/on this precious planet, and to all who work to create them.

Thank you.

Foreword

Jonathan Jansen

In the daily churn of university operations, it would appear as though the question of *purposes*: "What are universities for?" has been settled. Students are clients. Teaching is inputs. Publications are outputs. Curriculum is (unit) standards. Measurement is accountability. Assessment is performance. Scholarship is metrics. Graduates (oven-ready) are for the labour market. Leadership is management.

The language of critique that targets these narrowed down purposes for the university is by now familiar to those who study higher education: the neoliberal university, managerialism, the new public management, academic capitalism and more. But does a critical language that routinely describes these tendencies in the modern university do anything to even begin to shift institutional practice? In other words, have the critics reckoned with the power of what we call the institutional curriculum — that ensemble of rules, regulations, values, and processes that keep official knowledge sheltered in place?

Recent South African experience is instructive in this regard. In 2015, our universities experienced massive disruptions through student revolts against the colonial imprint and consequences of higher education. The curriculum was too white, the professors too pale, and institutional cultures too exclusive. The students started with the radical descriptor *decolonisation* that later formed part of a couplet of demands for "a free, decolonised education". On the face of it, this was a powerful moment in student resistance that seemed to enjoy support from "management" across the 26 public universities. Did anything change?

Our study on the uptake of decolonisation in the curriculum of public universities showed that little changed beyond the official performance of participation and support (Jansen & Walters, 2022) because the institutional curriculum did its job domesticating, marginalising, and subverting any attempts at radical incursion into settled knowledge inside universities.

The authors in this stunning new book are not unaware of the power of institutions labouring under the weight of a political economy that reduces academic work to market value. What, then, about the "pockets of freedom" (Raaper, 2019) in universities that can be exploited to do the work of resistance and generate alternatives to teaching, learning, assessment, and the making of curriculum?

This understanding of change is vital if a politics of hope — what Kate Bowles in this book calls "small hope-building practices" — rather than despair is going to emerge from under the crushing authority of the neoliberal university. The writers are aware of broader, democratic commitments to openness, participation, inclusion, and "infrastructures of care" (Chan et al., this volume). I have worked in those crevices as a university leader in a university which gained notoriety for racism. My colleagues created social and physical spaces on campus, such as the Institute for Reconciliation and Social Justice at the University of the Free State, where students could gather for both informal interactions and formal events on topics like race, identity, and our shared humanity. It was also a generative space for creative works from art, music, history, drama, and politics that gave expression to student struggles and ideals.

The downside of these enclave initiatives in large institutions is that systemic or system-wide change is not possible. Our study of enclave curricula found not only considerable institutional resistance on the one hand but also benign neglect on the other. Enclave initiatives are often the result of the activism of one or more scholars who fight for resources on an ongoing basis. They work hard to mobilise allies within their universities in the struggle for a pedagogy or assessment that is more socially just. They demonstrate alternative ways of teaching and leading at seminars and workshops on their own and other campuses. In other words, there is a considerable personal investment in sustaining an engaged and transformative pedagogy on the campus.

What is intellectually fascinating is how exactly academics with an enlarged agenda for pedagogy and assessment work in these institutional crevices such that they satisfy institutional demands, while at the same time widening those pockets of freedom. Here are hard lessons to be learnt that are sometimes ignored in the optimistic, breezy accounts of alternative education; that kind of naivete is not only poor analysis but also weak strategy when it comes to the politics of change. One example will suffice.

At my current university, I encouraged staff in student support to develop a core curriculum for undergraduates that deals openly with issues of race, identity, power, and history. This was important since thousands of first years enrol annually from very diverse schools in terms of race and resources, and some constitute a threat to the wellbeing of black students on a formerly white university campus. The university management generously funded a pilot of the core. The students who attended voluntarily were exceptional and greatly enriched the core. But they were generally open-minded, progressive black and white students, not the ones you wanted to target for this kind of curriculum. We made the case for system-wide implementation, but the argument was that some of the deans did not feel there was time for an addition to the curriculum. This, by the way, is a nonsense argument in curriculum theory.

There is always time given the highly selective tradition of curriculum decision-making. Still, the pilot was funded every year, a curriculum enclave of sorts. Until a white student in a brazenly racist attack in 2022 urinated onto the laptop and other belongings of a black student. There was intense and widespread reaction on and beyond the campus which led to the appointment of a judicial commission of inquiry into racism at the university. In the meantime, the student was suspended pending an investigation and eventually expelled. It was at this time that the university took seriously the plea for an institution-wide core curriculum that will now be implemented. What is the point of this account? That rare, enclave curricula or other projects can sometimes break through because of an institutional crisis or burst of conscience on the part of university leadership. By the time of this crisis at my university, there was a fully trialled core curriculum in place ready for implementation.

And finally, when there is the opportunity for deep thinking about "higher education for good" we should always ask, "good for whom?" (Childs et al., this volume). One of the most devastating consequences of the pandemic is that lockdown arrangements led to great learning losses for those with little to no access to bridging technologies and, in the process, widened the inequality gap between students of the middle classes and the poor. Put differently, when reimagining the neoliberal university, we must constantly and consciously pose the question as to the differential impacts of newly envisaged institutions. That reimagination has implications for everything from infrastructure to pedagogy and to forms of assessment.

This courageous book works with an unspoken proposition, that we cannot wait for the neoliberal university to transform itself. Universities can change "because of their capacity for challenge, critique, invention and intellectual growth... but it has to be fought for" (Connell 2019, p. 10).

References

Connell, R. (2019). *The good university: What universities actually do and why it's time for radical change*. Zed Books

Jansen, J. D., & Walters, C. A. (2022). *The decolonization of knowledge: The shaping of institutions in South Africa and beyond*. Cambridge University Press

Raaper, R. (2019). Assessment policy and "pockets of freedom" in a neoliberal university. A Foucauldian perspective. In C. Manathunga & D. Bottrell (Eds), *Resisting neoliberalism in higher education* (pp. 155–75). Palgrave Macmillan.

Stellenbosch, South Africa, 18 August 2022

Preface

Carolina Guzmán-Valenzuela

Higher Education for Good: Teaching and Learning Futures presents us with a formidable effort about ways in which higher education institutions can be thought of as organisations that consider, promote, and produce the good. Although this might be seen as a simple declaration of intentions or even as a straightforward task, both the editors and the chapter contributors indicate that, without an individual and collective will, careful thought, strategic planning, key partnerships, and innovative initiatives, this task is difficult to pull off. But this book goes much further, offering new ways of thinking about universities, their missions, and values and how to put into practice concrete initiatives in specific contexts to deal with the challenges of the current world.

Nowadays, universities operate in very complex environments. Ecological and climate crises, the COVID-19 pandemic, wars and armed conflicts, financial crises affecting the poorest, refugee and migratory movements, extreme populist movements, growing inequities (especially between wealthy countries in the Global North and countries with fragile economies in the Global South), violence, racial and sexual discrimination, labour division, little care for Indigenous groups and their knowledges and practices, and a host of other problems make us think about the world as a very difficult place in which to live, especially for the most fragile and vulnerable. Amid these crises, challenges, and problems, the book contains an urgent call to think about the role of universities and how they can help in addressing these challenges in an active and committed way.

Unfortunately, all too often, universities are encased in their own problems and challenges so that producing the good becomes even more challenging. As noted by most chapter authors of this book, higher education systems and universities are trapped in a series of narratives and practices that are dominated by financial drivers, reputational aspiration, and performance indicators. Income and reputation have become desirable assets for which higher education institutions compete by changing their structures, missions, values, and practices. Productivity and measures of quality have become goals in themselves.

As a result, higher education is seen too often as a set of goods with economic and prestige value that are traded in the market. This vision of higher education has shaped every sphere of universities and their practices. At global and national levels, universities are seen as economic engines of progress able to produce effective workers for the labour market and consequently boosting the economy. Universities are also seen as producers of profitable knowledge and research that can be commercialised rather than as producers of knowledge for the public good.

At an institutional level, many of these commercial narratives and practices shape universities' missions and values. This promotes a university that operates under competitiveness and business-like principles and a cognitive capitalism paradigm. In the classroom, these discourses are reflected in the ways in which teaching and learning processes are practised with an emphasis on grades, skills, and certifications.

Both academics and students have come to form a pedagogical relationship that is shaped by market principles. On the one hand, many academics experience precarity and insecurity in their jobs, increasing demands to perform, or are pushed to generate income and reputation through academic publications and research grants. On the other hand, students become consumers of credentials with an overvaluation of grades and skills for the labour market. On top of this, recently, the COVID-19 pandemic brought not only disastrous economic consequences for universities, academics, and students, but it also challenged the ways in which teaching and learning had taken place. The pandemic also made evident inequities within and across countries and regions and put technologies and online learning as top priorities.

Although universities have not produced these problems, challenges, and powerful narratives by themselves, they have become complicit and even have been reinforcing marketised practices and inequities and promoting values that clash with the principles of the common good. In this milieu, what do universities have to offer? How can universities contribute to the good despite these rather gloomy and dark times, narratives, and practices?

This is the great contribution of this edited book and its 27 chapters by authors from all around the world who have given much careful thought about what the "good" looks like. Drawing on critical reflections about the challenges and problems affecting the world and the role and responsibility that universities have in countering these problems, the authors offer creative insights about what some of them call tactics of resistance and collective and collaborative actions across different levels and dimensions. These include initiating policy changes, promoting certain types of teaching and learning practices and assessment, forging partnerships between universities and other kinds of organisations of society nationally and internationally, working with local communities to solve concrete problems, producing and using technologies that facilitate learning in creative ways, and so on.

What is seen clearly throughout the chapters is a need for a new set of values for universities across the world, hindered by discourses and practices focused on economic aspects, reputation, and indicators. The reader will see, for example, how the reflections, initiatives, and strategies proposed in the book advocate for social justice, inclusion of the different and the most vulnerable, plurality, generosity, care for others, reparation, democracy, concern for the environment and the climate crisis, hope, equity, creativity, critical thinking and reflection, engagement with communities, higher learning and open access, and reduction of poverty. The promotion of these values, as shown throughout the chapters, can be fulfilled through multiple ways and at different orders of scale — such as participatory approaches (including teachers, students, and communities) — by exercising critical pedagogies and pedagogies of care, promoting antiracist practices and decolonising teaching methods and the curriculum, acknowledging Indigenous lands, creating partnerships and working collaboratively with students, rural communities and/ or with other universities or organisations, through critical data literacy, and using new technologies to promote online and blended learning or even artificial intelligence.

All these initiatives aim to overcome an overemphasis on metrics, assessment, control, and performance.

Another aspect that makes this book unique is that of creatively thinking about the university — beyond traditional academic practices. In many chapters, the reader will find rather unusual ways of writing in an academic book (for example, poetry, a tale, narrative, co-written pieces, science fiction, visual essays, and the description of a quilt weaving). These new forms of communicating ways in which universities may produce goods are not only creative, but bring fresh air to stimulate academia, teachers, students, and communities to think about what universities can do amid the several crises in which they are immersed.

As the editors of the book stated in the call for chapters, what authors bring in their chapters are glimmers of optimism and hope for the future. Many of these glimmers provided by the authors emerged because of the pandemic in combination with all the challenges and problems affecting universities. As such, these glimmers of hope may help to change not only universities but the world.

Arica, Chile, 11 August 2022

Section I
Finding Fortitude and Hope

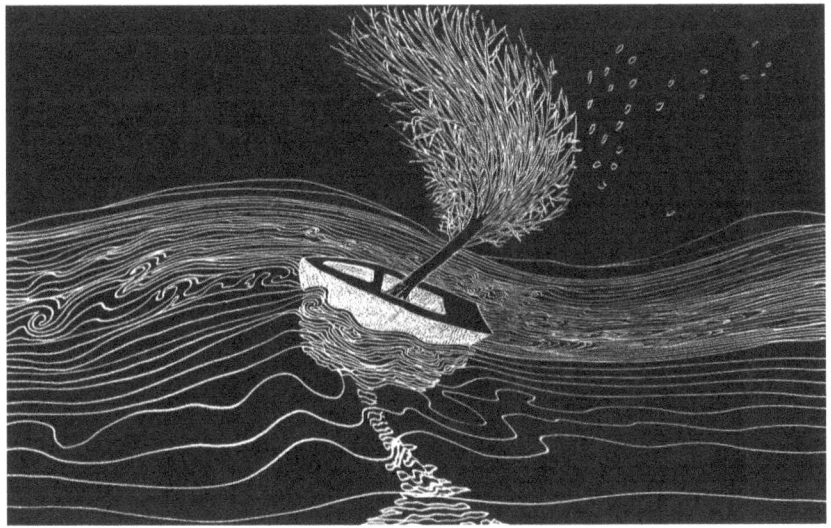

'Hope' by George Sfougaras (CC BY NC-ND)

Note from the artist

The print 'Hope' was inspired by the exodus of refugees and the images of people sailing across the Mediterranean from Turkey to the Greek islands. The news was and is saturated with shocking pictures of little boats and uprooted people, desperately seeking a better life, leaving all they had and all that sustained them behind.

Early on the day when the original idea was conceived, I was walking to my studio through Victoria Park in Leicester. The trees had shed their last autumnal leaves and stood in a bitter breeze which bent and swayed their thin branches. They stoically faced their circumstances in the hope of a new spring and new life. The image of the tree made me think of how hope survives and sustains us — even guides us — when we face insurmountable odds. The tree on the boat is a metaphor. The three components of the print, the boat, the tree, and the sea are simple and universally understood, but their juxtaposition makes us look again and reflect. The tree symbolises a person who has been displaced or uprooted and through life-changing events, forced to become a refugee. Anyone in that position cannot survive long without putting roots down somewhere. When they do, will they survive and thrive, create a meaningful life for themselves and their children, and bear fruit?

Every displaced person is sustained in their search for a better life through their hopes and dreams. For immigrant families, the education of the children was seen as the way to succeed in a new country. It was certainly the case for me, coming to the UK as an adolescent with basic English. I vividly recall wanting to master the language, to integrate and be seen as capable and competent in my school and later in the workplace. Having come to a rather insular and xenophobic 1970s England, I saw education as my way to demonstrate my capacity for hard work, but, more than that, to address the perceptions of 'foreigners' as less capable, less educated, less emotionally literate, and somehow less than. Higher education gave me a way to gain qualifications, which allowed me to progress and, in some ways, overcome the barriers of prejudice, at least professionally. Towards the end of my career as the head teacher of a school, I realised that the hope education gave me was still a powerful currency, and in my discussions with displaced or disenfranchised young people, I was able to turn to the hope that education offers, to escape difficult circumstances, and to create a better world through knowledge and insight.

On a deeply personal level, the image reminds me of my own family's tortuous path to safety, when they escaped war and ethnic violence. My mother's family followed a route from their home in Smyrna (Izmir) in 1922 to the island of Chios, which a century later is the same route taken by refugees from the Middle East and Asia. They rebuilt their lives in Greece, the 'home' country they had never seen. It seems that they were destined to uproot again, this time during the troubled Greek Junta period. History is, for all of us, a bigger part of our lives than we like to acknowledge.

Higher education for good

Catherine Cronin and Laura Czerniewicz

"There is a crack, a crack in everything. That's how the light gets in."[1] This book is about the light in higher education, a sector that was already fragmenting and fragile before the pandemic began, and since then has been addressing and resisting foundational challenges. Rare are the academics and professionals who are not dispirited, even demoralised. In the face of such despair, it feels hard to know what to do, to believe that it is possible to do anything at all, or even to find the energy to act. Yet change *is* possible, both change responding to flaws in the sector and proactive change aiming to prioritise values that are just, humane, and globally sustainable.

Using the Igbo word "nkali" to describe power structures in the world, Adichie (2009) has persuasively explained how there is never a "single story". A single story stereotypes and risks promoting a hegemonic universal discourse. A single story pretends that "one size fits all". In this book, the reflections, analyses, and expression of principles in context mean multiple stories, in multiple realities, even within similar physical locations. The book is a commitment to the importance of context and intersectionality.

We co-editors, Laura and Catherine, are academics committed to social justice and open education. We are colleagues and we are friends. Together, in 2021, we chose to take a journey of radical hope; the result is this book.[2] We consciously take inspiration from those fighting for justice globally — those who came before us and those whom we walk

---

1 Cohen, L. (1992). Anthem [Song]. On The Future. Columbia.
2 We share the frustrations of many of the authors of this book with the limitations of ordering author names which don't allow for the representation of genuine collaboration. This chapter — and this book — is forged in trust and mutual

alongside, including the authors and artists in this book and the many scholars cited within it. At the start of this book project (in June 2021), each of us was employed full-time in higher education — Laura as professor of education at the University of Cape Town in South Africa and Catherine as digital and open education lead at Ireland's National Forum for the Enhancement of Teaching and Learning in Higher Education. As this book goes to press, we occupy different professional positions as professor emerita and independent scholar, respectively, and remain as committed as ever to work which enacts the principles driving this book. The decision to seek answers regarding what higher education (HE) for good would look like, and what can be done, has been driven by our own experiences in a turbulent sector as well as by the global picture.

What to expect from this book

The chapters in *Higher Education for Good: Teaching and Learning Futures* offer ways of thinking, conceptualising, and creating real possibilities for making and remaking HE for good, with a particular but not sole focus on teaching and learning. Throughout the book is a vision of universities re/claiming their roles of "serving society as a change agent and empowering people across different sections of society" (Misra & Mishra, Ch. 25). Even to imagine such a move, let alone to lobby for and enact it, is to plant a sapling in our imagination: "And now that we have thought of it, it is already growing, and might yet come to be seen for miles" (Bowles, Ch. 15).

The book brings to fruition 27 chapters written by 71 authors in 17 countries.[3] Authors include established academics and researchers, learning professionals, and early career scholars, as well as students, those in academic leadership positions, and educators working outside higher education but with valuable perspectives on it. Responding to our invitation to consider all forms of creative expression, including but extending beyond the usual academic genre, chapters are written in a variety of forms: critical reflections,

---

overlays of writing and editing. We "resolved" this conundrum by alternating authorship order for book and chapter.

[3] Adding the peer reviewers brings the number of countries to 26.

conceptual essays, dialogues, speculative fiction, poetry (including haiku), graphic reflection, image, and audio. Each chapter was peer reviewed by at least one scholar external to the book project (see the list of external peer reviewers), and at least one fellow book author. Chapters directly related to teaching, learning and students were also reviewed by student reviewers.

In addition to these diverse chapters, we wanted to acknowledge the role of artists in "seeding resistance and providing the tools for us to imagine otherwise" (Davis et al., 2022, p. 8). Artwork relevant to the book's themes is included in the book, together with reflections from the artists.

The book is organised into five sections, enabling readers to focus on particular areas of interest. Section I, *Finding Fortitude and Hope*, contains foundational ideas for the book, elucidating current dilemmas and looking to the future with conviction and hope. Section II, *Making Sense of the Unknown and Emergent*, offers a range of theoretical lenses and imaginaries by which we can make sense of and reconsider our present, unfolding dilemmas. In Section III, *Considering Alternative Futures*, authors offer various ways to vision and imagine better futures, as a step towards bringing such realities into being. Section IV, *Making Change through Teaching, Assessment and Learning Design*, contains a collection of diverse and creative ways that educators and students have used to make changes in the broad area of teaching and learning, with examples from HE sectors in eleven countries. Finally, the chapters in Section V, *(Re)making HE Structures and Systems*, take a broad view, describing ways to embed long-term change through systemic and structural changes at institutional and national levels.

Towards a manifesto for higher education for good

Considered together, the chapters and artwork in the book coalesce into an agenda for higher education for good that responds directly to our opening question, "What is to be done"? Overall, the book represents an invitation to hope, identifies avenues for thought and action, and provides inspiration towards a possible manifesto(s) for "higher education for good" which could be tailored to specific contexts. The book's five tenets of action, inspiration, and hope are:

1. Name and analyse the troubles of HE
2. Challenge assumptions and resist hegemonies
3. Make claims for just, humane, and globally sustainable HE
4. Courageously imagine and share fresh possibilities
5. Make positive changes, here and now

As we elaborate on each of these tenets below, we provide illustrative examples from the book. Most chapters exemplify several tenets, so these examples are far from exclusive.

Tenet One: Name and analyse the troubles of HE

Naming and analysing the troubling problems of HE are necessary in order to challenge and to change them: "Not everything that is faced can be changed, but nothing can be changed until it is faced" (Baldwin, 1962). Thus, a book about HE for good must inevitably begin by analysing "the bad". As Fricker (2013) writes of studying *injustice* in her work on epistemic justice, the "negative imprint reveals the form of the positive value" (p. 1318).

The chapters in this book attest to the need to both confront the overt challenges and excavate the covert ones because, as Auerbach Jahajeeah (Ch. 8) contends, universities "take for granted and are taken for granted". It is by "challenging, scrutinising, and problematising what seems natural and commonsensical" (Kuhn et al., Ch. 21) that a foundation can be laid for uncovering the troubles of HE and for illuminating the good which exists nevertheless. Undertaking this work requires a kind of "radical acceptance that the status quo is neither desirable nor acceptable... there is nothing that is 'normal' about current systems" (Childs et al., Ch. 13).

What are the troubles of higher education?

This book makes blindingly clear the damage wrought to higher education by the evolving permutations of **neoliberalism**, not only economically through continuous state underfunding but also politically and culturally through the transfer of free market thinking into educational practices and language. Almost all chapters begin with the consequences of neoliberalism in HE, the dominance of which is critiqued as being treated in a matter-of-fact way "as ahistorical, apolitical and value-neutral" (Hordatt Gentles, Ch. 20). DeRosa (Ch. 1) maps out in detail and in despair the particularities of the "pervasive austerity logic that constricts not just our budgets, but every facet of what we do"; Khoo (Ch. 3) emphasises that "neoliberalism continues to evolve its uncanny non-death... [that] broad and deep economic and sociopolitical crises have continued, spreading the slow violence of structural harm, inequity and precarity".

Related to neoliberalism is **coloniality**, arguably two sides of the same coin. While colonialism is time and place bound, its logic endures in ongoing systems and practices, patterns, and structures of power premised on extraction and exploitation, echoing colonial forms of engagement. In higher education, coloniality is manifest in many ways including economically, culturally, and epistemologically. Coloniality persists "in the unjust politics of knowledge legitimation" which infiltrate the academy and the curriculum and indeed "creates absence where there is presence" (Mbembe in Belluigi, Ch. 5). A point affirmed by many authors, Belluigi explains why the decolonisation of knowledge is a critical endeavour for educators, academic developers, and learning professionals in terms of questioning knowledge formations of the self, the social, and the ecological in education.

Intrinsic to both neoliberalism and coloniality and threaded through many of the chapters are the risks of **data extraction** to students and academics through the business models of big tech companies which became particularly entrenched in the sector during the pandemic. In different ways, several chapters explore data extraction and sovereignty. Amiel and do Rozário Diniz (Ch. 18) address these risks through educators' efforts to offer alternative practices and understandings of extractive platform logics. Scott and Gray (Ch. 27) make overt the hidden politics, ethics, considerations, and implications of software choices for teaching and learning. The urgency of data literacies and the need for data justice are articulated in several chapters.

Interwoven throughout are the many forms of **inequity** and levels of **exclusion** expressed in and contributed to by HE. Macgilchrist and Costello (Ch. 19) sum up how performance metrics generate hierarchical rankings of universities, amplifying uneven global access to essential infrastructure, while surveillance technologies disproportionately penalise students of colour and predictive analytics systems can block the paths of students whom the system predicts to be unlikely to succeed. Furthermore, digital education concerns mirror material realities where exclusions "such as perpetuated language barriers and ableism permeate the fabric of higher education… [and where] being unheard and underrepresented can cause students to feel alienated in their educational journey" (Ramparsad Banwari et al., Ch. 16).

Tenet Two: Challenge assumptions and resist hegemonies

Awareness and anger at the status quo can spur action and there are numerous examples in the book of both calls to and enactments of resistance. Khoo (Ch. 3) eloquently shows the power of "cursing the darkness" of colonial legacies in the sector, while also arguing that darkness can be "an interruption that serves to foster creativity and imagination".

To change knowledge and understanding in the sector means **centring** and bringing in from the margins voices and views. It means intentionally **crossing borders** of all kinds: geographic, disciplinary, status and "accepted genre". This may take effort, given how hegemonies in HE rest on socialisation and reward systems, but such efforts to move past acquired familiarity yield enrichment in the form of wider and deeper intellectual resources and insights. We concur that "there's really no such thing as the 'voiceless'. There are only the deliberately silenced, or the preferably unheard" (Roy, 2004). We hope in our own way that this book, in form and content, demonstrates how knowledge is deepened for everyone when boundaries are crossed.

Challenging assumptions is both hard and possible. In their chapter on openness as a strategy against HE corporate capture and associated platform models, Amiel and do Rosário Diniz (Ch. 18) push back against the dominant Silicon Valley narratives of education, recounting their practical efforts to resist big tech's extractive surveillance demands inside classrooms, and offer alternatives of both practice and thinking. And in her chapter employing a data justice perspective on the use of AI in higher education, Pechenkina (Ch. 9) provides frameworks which see "learners as leaders directing AI action within complex educational terrains".

Several chapters are built on profound challenges to knowledge, economic, and cultural hegemonies; they affirm educator agency despite limited room to manoeuvre and the structural constraints outlined above. Attention is focused on "trying to disrupt the technical rationality that erodes our [educators'] capacity and confidence for professional autonomy" (Hordatt Gentles, Ch. 20). That disruption includes moves towards "care" and moves towards the "social". It is the social that Fawns and Nieminen (Ch. 23) emphasise in their provocative conversation on assessment, explaining how "assessment for good means social, not just individual good... requir[ing] an epistemological shift from the measurement of individual competencies and abilities against known standards, to collective and communal ways of knowing".

Tenet Three: Make claims for just, humane, and globally sustainable HE

Making legitimate and explicit claims to better futures is necessary, both to fuel resistance to dominant narratives and to inspire the production of new visions. A key element in resisting and moving beyond the status quo is to "stake claims to improving conditions and society" (Phoenix, 2022). Considered together, the chapters in HE4Good make specific and powerful claims for higher education that is just, humane, and globally sustainable.

One bias within large systems is to assume that stated good intentions (HEI mission statements advocating equity, diversity, and inclusion, for example) translate into good practice. More pernicious is the masking of bad practice with statements of commitment to laudable ideals. Forestalling or resisting this tendency towards diverse forms of "washing" (e.g. equity-washing, green-washing, open-washing) requires continual attention and the persistent assertion of values consonant with justice, humanity, and global sustainability in order to manifest these values in HE systems, structures, policies, and practices. This is as true at global, regional, and national levels as it is for individual higher education institutions.

Across the 27 diverse chapters in this book, all authors articulate specific **values** which could characterise "good" higher education in context. These include equity, justice (social, economic, environmental, epistemic, data, and design justice), sustainability, pluriversality, mutuality, generosity, creativity, and collectivism — all underpinned by ethics including affirmative ethics, relational ethics, environmental ethics, and ethics of care.

To further articulate these characteristics, authors draw on a wealth of **theory** and theory-informed practice to conceive of "good". Authors describe different forms including moral and cultural goods (Fawns & Nieminen, Ch. 23) and "good" as grounded in different cosmologies/spiritualities centred on human interconnection and our "radical interdependence" with the earth (Chan et al., Ch. 4). Authors also interrogate various inter-related theoretical concepts such as public good, common good, social/societal good, and economic good; some seek to disentangle the concepts of public and common good.

For many scholars, "good' means conceptualising different **structures** and **governance** for HE. Luke (Ch. 6) theorises the knowledge commons as the community of scholars that establishes rules and norms, managing the use, creation, and sharing of a common pool resource which is the intangible sum of human knowledge. He makes the case for universities as part of a polycentric network of smaller commons within the larger knowledge commons and for educators' role as stewards of the knowledge pool. Wittel (Ch. 7) takes a Marxist perspective to argue for a higher education commons, explaining that it would provide the best context to foster higher education as a gift, emphasising that such a political economy can only be made sustainable in a post-capitalist world. He makes the case for the pedagogical principles of resonance, relevance, and imagination for educators to foster the gift. Furthermore, Chan et al. (Ch. 4) propose an alternative "communal-based exchange model" for HE to align with a "growing understanding of the importance of land-based pedagogy as practised by many Indigenous communities around the world, while calling for the validation of Indigenous knowledge, epistemology, and ontology within the hegemonic structure of higher education."

Reconceptualising good requires an **epistemological shift**: a commitment to higher education for good means promoting a pluriversality of knowledge, embracing a horizontal strategy of openness to dialogue among different epistemic traditions, and addressing the underlying structures that prevent such transformation from taking place (Luckett & Shay, 2017; Mbembe, 2015).

The **characteristics of good** in higher education as explored in this volume align in many respects with Raewyn Connell's (2019) five characteristics of the "good university", i.e. democratic, engaged, truthful, creative, and sustainable.[4] In addition, there is agreement that "goodness" is both relational and contextual, deeply interwoven with our ideological, political, and social realities. As Auerbach Jahajeeah (Ch. 8) expresses in her inspiring haikus:

> pursuit of a good
> future. we must remember
> that the good does not
>
> rest in the tables
> of university ranks
> or the shininess
>
> of lecture theatres.
> rather the good nestles in
> amongst between us

Making claims to better HE futures is essential, helping not just to sustain resistance but also to articulate narratives of hope and inspire new visions.

Tenet Four: Courageously imagine and share fresh possibilities

In a time when previously anticipated HE futures may be fading and new futures are projected by technocorporate actors committed to profit-making, we in higher education are called to imagine alternatives. As Davis et al. (2022) wrote of the brilliant Octavia Butler: "we will dream our way out; we must imagine beyond the given" (p. 16). Treating the future as a site of "radical possibility" (Facer, 2016), we can bravely imagine and share fresh possibilities and alternative HE futures, beyond existing realities and hegemonic discourses.

In our call for chapters for this book, we invited all contributors to share "glimmers of **alternative futures**" of higher education for good. This requires grappling with the future in ways that keep possibilities open rather than closing them down. We are compelled to ask, for example: What alternative visions of HE would prioritise dignity, wellbeing, and

---

4   See Raewyn Connell's afterword in this book.

flourishing for all who are engaged with HE? What alternative visions of HE would extend possibilities for all who are currently excluded, particularly marginalised individuals and communities? What alternative visions of HE would hold and extend possibilities for future generations and for our planet?

One approach to addressing these complex questions is to use **speculative methods** for researching, analysing, designing, and teaching, i.e. asking "what if" instead of "what is". Speculative approaches enable working with the future as a space of uncertainty, collaborative and creative imagining/reimagining, deepening our understanding of the present, and bringing capacious realities into being (Houlden & Veletsianos, 2022; Ross, 2022). Authors of three chapters in the book detail their use of speculative approaches. Macgilchrist and Costello (Ch. 19) describe using Africanfuturist speculative fiction (Okorafor, 2019) to invite students to imagine a university far beyond contemporary colonialist institutions, intentionally opening generative spaces "for students and lecturers to reflect on their (our) own positions in the academy, to critique the reproduction of classed, raced, gendered inequities in higher education… and to generate futures that are oriented to justice". Childs et al. (Ch. 13) used a speculative scenario to evoke responses from colleagues with very different roles in higher education, and Flynn et al. (Ch. 14) invited students to write their own speculative imaginaries of HE futures.

Audre Lorde (1984) wrote that **poetry** is "the way we give name to the nameless so it can be thought" (p. 37). Two authors used the medium of poetry to "name the nameless", unsettling both what and how we think and talk about HE. Spelic (Ch. 2) offers a collection of five short, powerful poems, preceded by a short meditation on hope. Auerbach Jahajeeah (Ch. 8) explores the present and possible futures of HE in a dramatically different form: the haiku, supported by extensive footnotes. Other authors used different **imaginative forms** to invite readers to "imagine beyond the given" (Davis et al., 2022). Corti and Nerantzi's chapter (Ch. 11), in the form of a landscape photograph, audio podcast and transcript, invites readers (and potentially educators and students) to "see the higher education landscape with fresh eyes" and to imagine alternative futures themselves. Trowler (Ch. 26) uses the format of a graphic reflection to give voice to "non-traditional students'" views of what "good" education looks like.

What counts as a fresh possibility is shaped by **context**. Some changes may seem small from the outside, or already accepted practice in a different context, yet revolutionary in a particular environment. At the same time, HE hegemonies mean that educators everywhere are weighed down by similar pressures and their imaginative interventions are of universal interest. This book is awash with extraordinary examples, offering fresh approaches, practices, and ways of thinking in a variety of contexts. Ramparsad Banwari et al. (Ch. 16) critically analyse and apply a universal design for learning (UDL) approach to course design in South Africa. They highlight how social and design justice can be attained by expanding conceptions of access and equity to explicitly address "barriers that are faced by students who have been excluded, marginalised, or diminished because of their skin colour, language, ethnicity, gender, and/or sexual orientation". Molloy and Thomson (Ch. 17), from their standpoints as learning designers in Irish/UK universities, explain how aspirational values are implemented in the work of learning designers who offer "good help" in ways that are generative, iterative, and positive, guiding towards achievement in small steps and eventually leading to "transformational changes". These and other examples of locally grounded work provide insights into their unique contexts, as well as bringing new insights, inspiration, and avenues for change-making to other HE contexts.

Tenet Five: Make positive change, here and now

An overriding message across all chapters in this book is that change is indeed possible, and that now is the time. The chorus of voices in this book only amplifies de Sousa Santos's (2012) invocation: "In my mind we are at a juncture which our complexity scientists would characterise as a situation of bifurcation. Minimal movements in one or other direction may produce major and irreversible changes. Such is the magnitude of our responsibility" (p. 12).

Change means looking to the past as well as to the future. Moving forward often requires taking care to **repair the past** in meaningful ways. Exploitations of the past live on in the present and universities are complicit, criticised for perpetuating past injustices and for failing to address colonial and apartheid pasts (Makoe, Ch. 12). In HE locations such as Australia, Canada, and the United States, for example, acknowledging the past means acknowledging the land stolen from Indigenous peoples for universities to be built. Important steps to heal the past can be taken in different ways. Change can take the form of redress, moving beyond "sitting on our hands" to think practically about "back rent" (Bowles, Ch. 15). Indeed, Connell (2019), the author of the afterword of this book, has made practical suggestions for taxes to be paid to developing countries for the "international" students who bolster the coffers of universities in the Global North (as Bowles points out).

Making change also means recognising that **streams become rivers**: small changes matter and genuine change is possible. In this book are many examples of seemingly small changes, having affected one individual, one class, or one course. Hordatt Gentles (Ch. 20) describes a conscious decision to adopt a pedagogy of care in her teaching. Kuhn et al. (Ch. 21) describe a class studying social change who made and shared lists of indigenous trees in English, Swahili, and other local languages. Small changes can be contagious and inspiring; they can have ripple effects, in both intended and unintended ways, oftentimes unknown. The students who developed lists of trees shared openly decided to plant trees in the community around the university, making impossible-to-measure changes to university-community relationships and indeed to climate change mitigation. Work done locally can have huge consequences, "no matter how far we think we are from each other and how different from the 'other', we are all very intimately interconnected" (Gebru, 2022).

Large-scale changes can grow from a multitude of small changes and can also happen in both planned and unplanned ways. Indeed, as Wittel (Ch. 7) points out so aptly: "The most astonishing realisation about changes due to lockdown was the fact that many well-established procedures could not only be changed, but they could also be changed with lightning speed. Furthermore, these changes all handed over power to university teachers, or more precisely, the changes handed power back to university teachers."

Planned large-scale changes are complex, as Arinto et al. (Ch. 24) show, using the framework of an ecology with biotic and abiotic nodes and components to illustrate the intentional design of a national and very diverse HE sector, requiring several modalities across 7,000 islands and 182 ethnolinguistic groups. Misra and Mishra (Ch. 25) explore specific challenges within a national higher education sector, outlining specific recommendations towards making (or remaking) HEIs as open knowledge institutions (OKIs).

Effective progressive change is strengthened by **communality**, the condition of belonging to a community, the condition of being communal. It is most powerful when forged through **coalition**. After all, "it is in the many acts, small and large, acting in constellations and collectivities, over time and place that bear results" (Sultana, 2022).

Calls for and enactments of community and coalition are rich threads through the book, with authors writing of the importance of engaging collectively, in partnership, in communities of practice, in prosocial communities, in open communities, and in networks — within HEIs, across HEIs, between HEIs and wider communities, beyond HEIs, and across borders of all kinds. The work of creating this book has been a communal and border-crossing act. In seeking to share diverse perspectives, in every sense, and to affirm openness in the process, we have taken inspiration from Mounzer (2016): "The only way to make borders meaningless is to keep insisting on crossing them… For when you cross a border, you are not only affirming its permeability, but also changing the landscape on both sides".

Manifesting communal change is not easy in cultures that reward individualism and competition, yet such change is possible. For example, Fabian et al. (Ch. 22) describe a complex university project that entailed an intentional effort to create something that none of the seven organisations involved could have achieved alone, resulting in a "way of working together… which centred on principles of mutual respect and trust, of valuing each other's knowledge and expertise, of collaborative working practices and consensus-based decision making". In writing of the FemEdTech Quilt project as a communal activity, Bell et al. (Ch. 10) draw on Braidotti's (2022) work on posthuman feminism, espousing affirmative ethics "stressing diversity while asserting that we are in this posthuman convergence together" and relational ethics "assum[ing] one cares enough to minimise the fractures and seek for generative alliances" (p. 237). Communal change in HE, though often exceptionally challenging, can bring unique rewards: "The process of becoming, exemplified by both the quilts and the FemEdTech network, has been a sustaining joyful practice of what happens in the spaces of coming-together (care, joy, hope, awe) in the face of crisis and the pressure of advanced capitalism" (Bell et al.).

Dwelling in hope

The delineation of the five tenets listed above does not imply a sequence or flow, any idea of completion, or even a single manifesto. Rather, the contributors to this book, individually and together as a diverse chorus, offer ways forward towards "good" higher education through imagination, openness, heart, and hope.

As the traditional saying goes: the best time to plant a tree is twenty years ago, the second-best time is now. Through its ideas, this book seeds many trees in both fertile and seemingly barren soil; they will grow through commitment and hope.

In our work and thinking, prior to and during the process of editing this book, we have been inspired by numerous perspectives on and analyses of hope — practical, critical, radical, epistemic, and existential hope (Butler, 2000; Facer, 2016; Freire, 1994; Ojala, 2017; Schwittay, 2021; Solnit & Lutunatabua, 2023). We conclude, however, with our own understanding of hope, galvanised by the contributors to this book and specific to the work of (re)making higher education for good.

Hope is firmly rooted in the belief that it is never too late.

Hope is practical. It means taking action, being disciplined, making plans.

Hope is impractical. It means dreaming, being undisciplined, being open-ended.

Hope is strengthened when practised in solidarity with others. It means building and strengthening alliances, coalitions, communities.

Hope is contested and contradictory. And yet whatever its form, it is essential.

Without hope, there would be no future worth living.

Depending on the challenges, the context, the timing, the resources available, and the will of all involved, the creative and critical work of building a just, humane, and globally sustainable higher education is always beginning — as beautifully expressed in one of Sherri Spelic's poems (Ch. 2):

> If my students and I build anything at all
> we must build imaginations
>
> If my students and I build
> a city of care
>
> a province of justice
> a nation of acceptance
>
> We are never done
> and always beginning.

References

Adichie, C. N. (2009). *The danger of a single story* [Video]. TED Conferences. https://www.ted.com/talks/chimamanda_ngozi_adichie_the_danger_of_a_single_story?language=en

Baldwin, J. (1962, January 14). *As much truth as one can bear*. The New York Times. https://www.nytimes.com/1962/01/14/archives/as-much-truth-as-one-can-bear-to-speak-out-about-the-world-as-it-is.html

Braidotti, R. (2022). *Posthuman feminism*. Polity.

Butler, O. E. (2000). A few rules for predicting the future. *Essence, 31*(1), 165. https://commongood.cc/reader/a-few-rules-for-predicting-the-future-by-octavia-e-butler/

Connell, R. (2019). *The good university: What universities actually do and why it's time for radical change*. Zed Books.

Davis. A. Y., Dent, G., Meiners, E. R., & Richie, B. E. (2022). *Abolition. Feminism. Now*. Hamish Hamilton.

de Sousa Santos, B. (2012). The university at a crossroads. *Human Architecture: Journal of Self-Knowledge, X*(1), 7–16. https://www.boaventuradesousasantos.pt/media/University%20at%20crossroads_HumanArchitecture2011.pdf

Facer, K. (2016). Using the future in education: Creating space for openness, hope and novelty. In H. E. Lees, & N. Noddings (Eds), *The Palgrave international handbook of alternative education* (pp. 63–78). Palgrave McMillan. https://doi.org/10.1057/978-1-137-41291-1_5

Freire, P. (1994). *Pedagogy of hope: Reliving pedagogy of the oppressed*. Continuum Publishing. (Original work published in 1970.)

Fricker, M. (2013). Epistemic justice as a condition of political freedom? *Synthese, 190*, 1317–1332.
https://doi.org/10.1007/s11229-012-0227-3

Gebru, T. (2022, May 26). Timnit Gebru to UC Berkeley graduates: Work collectively for a better future for all. *Berkeley School of Information*.
https://www.ischool.berkeley.edu/news/2022/timnit-gebru-uc-berkeley-graduates-work-collectively-better-future-all

Houlden, S., & Veletsianos, G. (2022). Impossible dreaming: On speculative education fiction and hopeful learning futures. *Postdigital Science and Education*, 1–18.
https://doi.org/10.1007/s42438-022-00348-7

Lorde, A. (1984). *Sister outsider: Essays and speeches*. Crossing Press.

Luckett, K., & Shay, S. (2020). Reframing the curriculum: A transformative approach. *Critical Studies in Education, 61*(1), 50–65.
https://doi.org/10.1080/17508487.2017.1356341

Mbembe, A. (2015, n.d). *Decolonizing knowledge and the question of the archive* [PDF]. The Wits Institute for Social and Economic Research.
https://wiser.wits.ac.za/system/files/Achille%20Mbembe%20-%20Decolonizing%20Knowledge%20and%20the%20Question%20of%20the%20Archive.pdf

Mounzer, L. (2016, October 6). *War in translation: Giving voice to the women of Syria*. Literary Hub.
https://lithub.com/war-in-translation-giving-voice-to-the-women-of-syria/

Ojala, M. (2017). Hope and anticipation in education for a sustainable future. *Futures, 94*, 76–84.

Okorafor, N. (2015). *Binti*. Tor Books.

Phoenix, A. (2022). (Re)inspiring narratives of resistance: COVID-19, racisms and narratives of hope. *Social Sciences, 11*(10). https://doi.org/10.3390/socsci11100470

Ross, J. (2022). *Digital futures for learning: Speculative methods and pedagogies*. Taylor & Francis.

Roy, A. (2004, November 8). *The 2004 Sydney peace prize lecture* [Video]. University of Sydney.
https://sydneypeacefoundation.org.au/peace-prize-recipients/2004-arundhati-roy/

Schwittay, A. (2021). *Creative universities: Reimagining education for global challenges and alternative futures*. Policy Press.

Solnit, R., & Lutunatabua, T. Y. (Eds), (2023). *Not too late: Changing the climate story from despair to possibility*. Haymarket Books.

Sultana, F. (2022). The unbearable heaviness of climate coloniality. *Political Geography*, 99.
https://doi.org/10.1016/j.polgeo.2022.102638

1. Writing from the wreckage: Austerity and the public university

Robin DeRosa

> I came to explore the wreck.
> The words are purposes.
> The words are maps.
> I came to see the damage that was done
> and the treasures that prevail.
>
> (Adrienne Rich, "Diving into the Wreck")

As do many of us who identify as lifelong English majors, I start most of my writing projects by reading. Of course, there is focused research — quite a lot of which went into my preparation for this chapter. But there is also the reading that English majors do around the edges of any writing project: to procrastinate, to find inspiration in others who have managed to somehow put together a coherent story, to feel the hefty weight of a thick book instead of the glaring vacantness of a blank screen. I knew this chapter would centre on the ravaging effects of austerity on higher education and I felt instantly overwhelmed by the fatigue that the topic generates in my brain, by the anxiety it generates in my stomach, by the existential tickle that it generates in my soul that there is no choice but to find a glimmer of hope in the wreckage. So, I reached not for my keyboard, but for a book to distract or, if I were lucky, catalyse me. Eddie S. Glaude Jr's biography of James Baldwin, *Begin Again*, was on my desk waiting for this moment. I opened it and read the epigraph from James Baldwin (quoted by his brother, David):

> I pray I have done my work… when I've gone from here, and all the turmoil, through the wreckage, and rubble, and through whatever, when someone finds themselves digging through the ruins… I pray

that somewhere in that wreckage they'll find me, somewhere in that wreckage that they use something I've left behind. (Glaude, 2021)

The quote reminded me of Adrienne Rich's "Diving into the Wreck" — a poem that is at least partially responsible for making me a college English major. At the crossroads of these two writers, each one offering up the shards of broken systems that had almost broken them, I found the fortitude to begin this chapter. Baldwin and Rich catalyse my work here not just because of how they specifically wrote against the racist, sexist, heteronormative contexts that surrounded them and which deeply inflect higher education today, but also because I came to their work through the study of literature. As literature degrees are accused of failing to train students for the realities of today's labour market (nobody is advertising for a *humanist* after all!), it seems to me both ironic and not coincidental that literature degrees are also excellent at equipping students with the critical thinking skills we need to see through that absurd accusation.

Across many parts of the world, we are being spoon-fed a dominant narrative about higher education: that we need to cut institutional spending, that public funding is never returning, that universities are rigid and outdated, that learning that serves markets is always best for learners, that teaching has given way to indoctrination. However, a close reading will demonstrate that these are parts of a calculated grift. In this chapter, in the spirit of the poets, playwrights, readers and humanists who have inspired me, I hope to lay out the detritus of a deeply broken system and refuse the easy solutions that would package it all up into something we do not need, something that we pay for with our humanity.

23 years ago, I started teaching as an adjunct at my regional public university in a small, rural town in New Hampshire, United States. I was finishing my dissertation at a university near Boston when I moved up here as a trailing partner to Phil, who had a one-year position as a sculpture professor. Within a year, Phil had secured a tenure-track position in art, and within three years, I was on the tenure-track in English. We loved our colleagues! We loved our students! We built a house in the mountains, adopted a dog, and had a daughter who grew up on campus. It feels now like that was another era.

This year, at the age of 59, Phil left our university in a massive buyout that ended up in a 25% reduction in the college's full-time faculty. We are not sure we will be able to afford his early retirement, but he was not sure he would physically or mentally survive the pressure to innovate his program into something newer and shinier (newer and shinier than art!). I go to work now, and it feels lonelier there without him and without so many of my other colleagues who have left. Some of their own choosing, and others — especially staff — due to being "right-sized" out of their jobs. The sculpture major was abandoned when Phil left. As programs get cut, I worry that one day we will have only criminal justice, nursing, and business courses left.

Despite it all, this little university has phenomenal caring faculty and staff and its earliest history as a teachers' college probably has much to do with its persistent belief that education is core to a community. But in the shadows of our teaching-focused mission and our bucolic mountain views, harsh realities are lurking. You can count on one hand the faculty of colour at this predominantly white institution. BIPOC students here can feel surveilled and unsafe, as locals with confederate flags on their trucks cruise up and down Main Street. Students with mobility-related disabilities cannot manage the deteriorating walkways, especially in winter when they are not shovelled promptly. Almost every student I talk to is facing money-related issues: high tuition, student debt (both of which are among the highest in the nation), food insecurity, juggling a job on top of school, and on and on. In 2020, when COVID-19 came calling, professors like me lamented how hard life suddenly became, but for many of my students (and contingent faculty and undercompensated staff), the general message I heard was: "yeah, it's harder now, but for the most part, we were already just barely getting by".

How have public higher education systems, not just in America but in so many places around the world, devolved into such a gut punch? Or perhaps more accurately, how have public higher education systems always contained within themselves the seeds of the gut punch that is right now, at this moment, bringing so many of us to our knees? I am writing this to/for/with the gut punched. Maybe you are like Phil and you were forced into an early retirement as your college's budget contracted. Maybe you aren't that lucky, and you are an underpaid contingent faculty member working at four different institutions, hoping you don't get COVID-19, because you have no health insurance. Maybe you teach in the liberal arts, and you fear retrenchment. Maybe you are a staff member who has absorbed the jobs of two other people who were let go, so you have three times the workload even though you haven't had even a cost-of-living raise in years. Maybe the lab you manage can't afford to replace broken microscopes, or maybe the last time it rained, the ceiling of your library collapsed just a short distance away from your desk (yes, it happened to me a few weeks ago). Maybe you teach at Harvard, and you have no idea what I am talking about. But probably you don't teach at Harvard. Since most faculty don't teach there, and most students don't go there.

You can get a sense of just how engulfing this austerity is of faculty, staff professional, and personal wellbeing as you read the interspersed boxed quotations from people working, struggling in colleges and universities, who shared their experiences with me as I prepared to write this piece. My own experience is situated in the United States, but the voices that reached out to me in response to my call about labouring under austerity were from multiple countries including the UK, India, Canada, Mexico, and Australia. Unfortunately, while the contexts and details are distinct, there are many common threads in the stories I hear from colleagues around the world.

> I worry that the 20% of my salary going into retirement savings won't be enough because my body and brain will be broken far before their time. I worry that I will not be able to survive. In times past, money was tight but people cared about one another. And that's what's different about the austerity logic of today--it's not just that money must be saved, it is that administrators cannot even bring themselves to admit how their choices and words hurt the real people around them.

I likely don't have to tell you what "austerity" is. Those of us labouring under austerity know in our bones that it goes far beyond anaemic budgets and endless bean counting, and that there is a pervasive austerity logic that constricts not just our budgets, but every facet of what we do. It permeates our bodies and our minds and changes our experience of working in higher education. But to begin to deconstruct the logic of austerity, we must look to the framework that surrounds it.

The vocabulary of austerity

The word "neoliberal" has an odour of jargon about it; it is part of neoliberalism's insidiousness that every time you bring it up, someone will roll their eyes because the term feels so very *academic*. My goal here is to try to break it down in plain language, because austerity describes what it's like to labour and learn at most colleges and universities these days. But neoliberalism tells us *why*.

Broadly, the principles that guide neoliberal logic cohere around (Mintz, 2021):

> the efficiency of the free market and the deregulation and privatization of the public sector that markets require; tax reduction; abandoning the welfare state; and replacing the notion of the public good with a personal responsibility for one's own welfare. (para. 2)

Despite these broad commonalities, the manifestations of neoliberalism are historically and geographically specific. As an American writer who is most familiar with the US context, I am mindful not only of how Americentric analyses can colonise other analytical possibilities, but also of how US influence has colonised educational systems in ways that serve to engender neoliberal trends in other countries. In 2010, one UK report called the privatisation of UK universities the "Americanization of higher education", explaining that both the Labour and Tory parties envision the emergence of a system more like that in the US (University and College Union, 2010). In other parts of the world, the privatising forces of the United States are less merely influential than they are violently colonising. In the 1980's, the US had stated policy (as did the IMF and World Bank) advocating for privatisation in sub-Saharan Africa and tying aid missions to activities that cultivated privatisation (Fenske, 2007). Today, Bridge International, an American company, has more than four hundred "innovative" schools in Kenya and Uganda. In January 2016, the Liberian education minister announced that the entire pre-primary and primary education system would be outsourced to Bridge (Tyre, 2017).

Whether it is India's shift from funding educational institutions with government grants to funding them with "resources from the market on the basis of equity from individuals or corporate entities through bonds" (Parey, 2019), the rise of the for-profit university industry in

Switzerland (Lanci, 2022), or the fact that over 70% of college students in some countries in Latin America (Chile, El Salvador, Peru) are educated in private universities (Internacional de la Educatión, 2020), across many parts of the world, there is a shift from public infrastructure to private. With this shift comes a shifting of funding away from direct instruction, increasing inequities, and a troubling confusion about the role and value of "public" institutions worldwide.

The words "public" and "private" become murky when we use them to talk about neoliberalism in education. Certainly, one obvious example of neoliberalism at work in a US context is with school vouchers, which allow parent-taxpayers in many states to use tax funds that would normally go to public schools to fund private educations for their own children instead. This is what Ball and Youdell call "exogenous" privatisation, where private interests — represented as partnerships or initiatives — absorb public dollars and infrastructures. It contrasts but shares core values with "endogenous" privatisation, where public schools use organising principles and strategies from business, where academic leaders explicitly claim that their schools and colleges indeed *are* businesses because they require the logic of business to operate (Ball & Youdell, 2008, p. 18). It works both ways: transfer resources from public to private investments or transfer operational models from private to public organisations. Either way you slice it, you've got a lot of slippage between two words that most people think of as antonyms.

Proponents of both exogenous and endogenous privatisation obscure the fact that they are replacing the public good with private interest. Instead, neoliberalism depends upon a fundamental belief (or ruse) that capitalism is indeed good for society. But free market capitalism, where consumers get to decide how to spend their money, and their decisions control prices and drive innovation as different products compete for their attention, is not as well suited to some "products" as it is to others. When you are not talking about products at all, but processes that undergird quality of life (education, health, communication, safety, justice), it can be problematic to apply the logic of markets.

The cuts in education are not made because education is too costly but because capitalism demands continuous growth and (un)naturally encroaches on systems and relationships that are not a good match for market logic. There are dramatic parallels to be made between for-profit hospitals, for-profit prisons, and for-profit education (I would posit that it is not coincidental that two of the more robust majors at my precarious public college are nursing and criminal justice). But it is not just the exogenous examples like this where profit is the point. It is the endogenous examples as well, where our non-profit and public *organisations* in health care, in criminal justice, in education, begin to behave like for-profit organisations. This is capitalism not as an economic system, but as an organising logic, and this is why austerity is not only about cutting costs, but also about measuring what matters by using metrics that come from the world of business.

> *Our team has grown by 50% while our responsibilities have grown by 200% and our pay has stagnated—and this was before the added stress of Covid. Students notice how busy we are and apologize for taking up our time. Everyone is just constantly in a state of near burnout while earning low wages in a high cost-of-living location. I know we could do amazing things to transform the learning experience if we just had a bit more invested in us, both as individuals and as a profession.*

Counting beans is not just a way of doing more with less, being efficient, lean, or frugal. Counting beans is most notably about calling things that are not beans, "beans", so that they can be counted. A parallel in teaching might be when you quantify a student's learning in a course on American literature as an 87.25 — whatever scientific rubrics you might have used to assign that grade. I think we can agree that student learning or performance cannot be quantified so precisely. The neoliberal university insists on grades not so much because it is unenlightened, punitive, rigorous, or objective, but because grades are the logical outcome of a system that is essentially a widget factory that launders complex relationships, processes, and ideas (learning) into a commodity.

From the public good to private goods

For-profit colleges in the US have recently taken a lot of heat for how they exploit students looking to invest in themselves and their own learning. They are persuasive illustrations of what Giroux (2016) calls "casino capitalism" which he describes as "driven by an unchecked desire to accumulate capital at all costs" fully apart from any kind of social responsibility. Tressie McMillan Cottom demonstrates the grift of the for-profits in her 2017 book, *Lower Ed*. But for-profit colleges are just the most explicit layer of a larger neoliberal pattern, which now insidiously undergirds the entire US higher educational system — a system in which the burden of educational costs is transferred from public communities to individual private consumers. In a 2022 opinion piece for *The New York Times*, Cottom (2022) tells the story of how a group of benefactors paid off all past due tuition bills in collection for graduates of Bennett College, a historically Black non-profit women's college:

> We knew that student loan debt was most expensive for the families who had the most to lose, and we kept offering the loans with the same cheerful promise: It's worth it. When you are scammed by a friend, it is a shame. When your country scams you, it is a fraud.

In discussing the benefactors' gift, Cottom (2022) writes:

> The biggest deal is not the cash that forgiveness might free up and which could be spent on rising housing costs or used to pad their savings. The Bennett leaders I spoke with say the most tangible benefit is that students who owe the college money can now get access to their academic transcripts, proving that they have in fact attended school.

The withholding of transcripts is a telling marker of how commodified education has become. Its value inheres as much in the credential as in the learning that the credential symbolises. As learning is shifted from a process to a transaction, and students are shifted from learners to consumers, public funding can be reduced, because why should the "public" pay for a private good?

Despite the amount of time that journalists spend reporting on the Ivy League or online private behemoths, 80% of all college students in the US attend public institutions that are, in fact, not even close to being fully publicly funded (National Center for Education Statistics, 2022). Welch (2015) reports that the state share of revenues for Michigan State, the University of Illinois, and the University of California at Berkeley "reduced by more than half between 1987 and 2012, and state support for the University of Oregon plummet[ed] in that period from 36 percent to 9 percent."

This defunding often dovetails with fiscal crises such as the 2008 global financial crisis. But even during periods of economic recovery, funding in most places still looks like a downward spiral. California demonstrates this pattern: "In the early 1990s, California contributed 78 percent of the total cost per student, a number that had shrunk to 37 percent by the 2015–16 academic year." This adds to a decidedly non-public bottom line for the public university budget:

> In 2019–20, state contributions were only around 10 percent of UC core operating funds, which provide permanent support for the mission of the university and the administrative and support services needed to carry it out. Other revenue came primarily from private sources, especially tuition and fees. (Hamilton and Nielsen, 2021)

As public funding declines, the burden to cover a college's operating expenses falls more and more to students and their families. Similar cycles of public defunding, economic crisis, failed recovery, and the transition of costs to students and their families are playing out across the globe. In India, both the centre and the states have divested from public higher education, and expenditure on higher education has declined from 0.86% of the GDP in 2011 to just 0.52% in 2020 (Qamar, 2022a). In 2022, the union minister of higher education, Dharmendra Pradhan, advised the Indian people that they should let go of the idea that universities must be funded only by the government (Qamar, 2022b). In South Africa, the 2022 academic year began with significant student protests, as public universities faced ZAR10 billion (US$650 million) student funding shortfall (Naidu, 2022). Even China, which from 2006 to 2013 saw massive increases in public funding of higher education, has seen public funding allocations increase by less than 2% per year since 2013, meaning that on a per student basis, public funding in China is declining (Usher, 2022).

The ramifications of public defunding are sometimes clear, as in the case of American student loan debt — an obvious display of the transfer of college costs to individual student consumers. Still, we don't talk as much about institutional debt which combines with public defunding to promote institutional corporatisation: "Between 2003 and 2016, institutional debt at public and community colleges more than doubled, rising from $73 billion to $151 billion. In that time, interest payments on this debt nearly doubled as well" (Schirmer, 2021). The effect of this kind of debt on the public mission of our colleges is severe:

> These loans are not innocuous sources of financing for our institutions. Legally binding debt service obligations stipulate that repayments must be an institution's first budgetary priority; debt covenants constitute powerful drivers of university austerity. Thus, when institutions encounter financial troubles (such as a global pandemic), they must respond first and foremost to their obligations to creditors before addressing the needs of the educational communities they serve. Debt financing creates an asymmetrical power relation between creditors (big banks) and debtors (colleges and universities). This relationship subjects public higher education to free-market evaluations of a school's risk and value, often reinforcing racist and classist ideas. Because securing funds depends on an institution's credit rating, credit rating agencies operate as universities' shadow governors. These private financial institutions are anything but democratic. They are not elected or even appointed by elected officials. Their chief concerns are not the public good but returns on investments. (Schirmer, 2021)

Schirmer asserts that from 3% to 10% of institutions' total revenue goes to the interest and fees for private creditors. She cites this whopper of a statistic about the City University of New York: "37 percent of students' tuition and fees goes to paying CUNY's annual debt service" (Schirmer, 2021).

As institutional debt rises and public funding shrinks, it's imprudent to spend time criticising the one or two desperate "lazy rivers" that have been installed by colleges looking to make themselves more attractive to student consumers. The dominant narrative of our institutions is not gross overspending, it is that nothing is safe from tactics that could make anything, even direct instruction cheaper. The overreliance on contingent faculty is the starkest example of the under-resourcing of instruction. Welch (2015) notes:

> While 75 percent of US college and university faculty at the start of the 1970s had the security of long-term tenure-track employment, today more than 75 percent of instructional faculty are classified 'contingent', teaching on contracts as short as a single semester, typically without healthcare, disability, and retirement benefits.

Between 1990 and 2012, "part-time faculty employment increased 121 percent, with adjunct positions in the public 4-year sector increasing the most" (Anthony et. al, 2020). And while it is hard to meaningfully compare percentages between systems in different countries, the casualisation of postsecondary faculty is an escalating trend across Africa, Asia, Australia, Europe, and North and South America.

> Positions like this are the reason so many young(ish—I'm 40), excellent scholars and teachers are leaving the academy. If you're going to bargain with our lives and livelihoods—and quality of life, because good luck getting a mortgage on a temporary contract and good luck having kids if you don't know whether you'll have health insurance in a year—you don't get our loyalty, excellence, or expertise.

Cuts to instruction are coupled with a focus on the generation of new revenues. While this can sometimes look like splashy, consumer-targeted spending (lazy rivers, million-dollar scoreboards, extravagant dorms), more common are clever partnerships that shift funding models from public to private sources. This is a double-edged endeavour where students shoulder costs, but the private market promises a return on investment. For example, "workforce development" is a model where private companies spur public colleges to create curriculum that essentially outsources the training of the future employees to the educational system, and colleges in turn can promise their graduates that they will be in-demand by the labour force when they complete their degree. The casino is open, and we are laying down bets fast and furious to keep the lights on.

If casino capitalism is about selling degrees and debt, another way that learning is commodified is what Welch (2015) calls academic capitalism, where a "new army of academic administrators carries out a long-term project of repackaging education and research as profitable commodities in an economy presumed to depend on the production of services and ideas rather than the production of durable goods" (Welch, 2015). This is less about fast profits and more about turning a knowledge commons into a knowledge economy, where education itself — not just its credentials and certificates — operates to serve markets that depend on information, skills, and innovation. We can even promise preparation for jobs that have not even been invented yet, a "futureproofing" of graduates by exposing them to hi-tech makerspaces filled with robotic equipment that will likely be outdated in eight months.

And of course, what matters most here are our students, whose very bodies are poised on a precipice above this public-private riptide. This is no more painfully evident than in discussion of "the demographic cliff". While some regions face growing higher education enrolments (even as public funding still contracts), many areas of the United States, including in the Northeast where I work, are facing the shrinking of the college-aged population. Many scholars foresee these declines continuing. There is really no way to overstate the intense panic this produces amongst enrolment managers and the extent to which that panic tightens the academic budgets they influence. The "student body", then, is transformed from a collective body (that generates collective benefits through education) into individual bodies (that are valued by their tuition dollars and competitive earning potential). As consumers and products, students in this scenario are targets of both investment (the customer is always right!), and exploitation (hobbled by debt and often years shy of graduation, many students leave college cheated out of the returns they were promised).

Enjoying the view from the top of the demographic cliff that helped to make him famous is economist Nathan D. Grawe, whose 2018 book *Demographics and the Demand for Higher Education* supplanted many contributing factors to the enrolment crisis (public defunding, student debt, tuition limits, mismanagement, rampant financialisation) with just one overdetermined variable (demographics). This turned a complex landscape into "a technical problem with only technical fixes" (Nemser & Whitener, 2021). A slew of consulting companies quickly stepped in to help clarify the demographic trends and offer enrolment management solutions. This seems to me to be a pattern worth paying attention to — when solutions are sold

> Our university has moved toward a decentralized budget model called "Responsibility-Centered Management" in which individual schools are awarded funds based on class enrollments and number of majors, basically a "butts in seats" model. It runs the risk of pitting colleagues against each other in the pursuit of growing enrollments and can provide motivation to water down curriculum to appease students looking to maintain a high GPA with little time or effort.

by the same source that shapes the problem, there is cause for scepticism. It reminds me of what open education advocate, Rajiv Jhangiani (2019) says about trusting textbook companies to solve the problem of high textbook costs through programs like automatic textbook billing or inclusive access: "It's like leasing a fire extinguisher from a serial arsonist." This is a cycle that inflects higher education under neoliberalism. It is very hard to locate a starting point or separate cause from effect because the problems and the solutions are mixed.

This "devolutionary cycle" explains how public defunding and public universities' privatising solutions are enmeshed in a dysfunctional symbiosis (Newfield, 2016). It is impossible to disconnect the cultural faith we have in private solutions from the pressing need our public institutions require to seek them out. Thought leaders like Grawe (2018) are not only recognising a problem (demographic challenges); they are generating one (public higher education is broken). Naomi Klein called out this phenomenon in her 2007 book, *The Shock Doctrine*. She charted how "disaster capitalism" manufactures crises to open opportunities for austerity and market-oriented solutionism.

On March 23, 2020, days after COVID-19 pushed a majority of higher education institutions online (the "remote pivot", which sounds like a lovely *pas-de-deux* instead of the chaotic horror story that it was for most faculty and students), the lead story on Yahoo Finance was positively giddy: "Amid novel coronavirus outbreak, for-profit education stocks are expected to gain manifold as online educators are viewing shutdowns as an opportunity to increase its reach among students" (Zacks Equity Research, 2020). A headline on *Inside Higher Ed* stated it matter-of-factly: "Ed-Tech Vendors Confront Sudden Opportunity and Risk" (Seltzer, 2020). The diction of opportunity and risk demonstrates how crisis functions to drive capitalism. The opportunities here are not about

> *For me the nightmare has been of being on short-term contracts for almost two decades. The longest contract was three years - that was incredible. Sometimes there was a break of a few months between contracts which meant that the regulations stopped applying to me because when I started the next contract it was considered to be starting all over again.*

serving learners; they are about profit margins. The risks here are not about global pandemic and death; they are about unrecouped financial investment. How can we understand the needs of students and serve learning goals when our "solutions" are solving a problem that is not shaped by either?

Pandemics, changing demographics, recessions, wars, natural disasters, climate change, shifting labour markets — I don't know, take your pick. They are real, difficult, many of them are undeniably awful, terrifying, and could be called a "crisis" by any reasonable person. However, there is also a slippage where the object of the crisis is blamed for the crisis itself. As in any situation where a victim is blamed for crimes against them, public colleges and universities are characterised not as healthy systems that need to respond to a challenge but as broken systems whose failures are at least in part responsible for the state of crisis itself.

Yet, instead of sounding alarm bells, most colleges and universities are obscuring the ideological effects of austerity by adopting a pretence of agency, as if it is an empowering choice to pull our institutions up by our bootstraps and innovate our way to sustainability: "Terminologies of right-sizing, student-centred, restructuring and reimagining are being used to create committees that recommend the elimination of disciplines, programs and majors that no longer serve the market-driven corporate universities that are built on revenue-generating enterprises" (Dutt-Ballerstadt, 2022). As public institutions, we mix public-oriented diction (togetherness and needs) with privatising diction (right-sizing, brands, value propositions, consumers), reflecting the way that we have internalised privatisation, allowing our missions to be shaped by forces that are more aligned with the corporate world than with public education. So, when "partnerships" with

> I was "asked" to manage a campus-wide retention intervention with no financial resources, a lack of campus buy-in, and no staffing. I was doing the role of three people plus part of my old role, all while being a first-time parent of a newborn. It became clear that it was no longer healthy nor safe for me to function in this environment. I left that role, and was not replaced. The division was dissolved, and my work was split off onto others...who did not receive any title changes or compensation.

corporate America come knocking, we open the doors wide because these partnerships are perfectly aligned with the academic capitalism of our institutions, where we seek solutions to fix what we are told (by corporate influence) is broken.

We might think about whether we are using the word "broken" as an adjective or a verb. Does it describe the condition of public higher education itself, or what is being done to it? One clue comes from the fact that the demographic cliff hitting my public university in New Hampshire — which has caused us to cut several long-standing liberal arts majors and minors in the last couple of years — is not hitting Ivy League Dartmouth, just an hour down the road. Welch (2015) argues:

> In the neoliberal reordering of higher education, students at elite private and state flagship universities may still major in...women's studies, Africana studies, German, music performance, public history, and linguistics; it is from campuses meant to produce skilled workers that such programs are cut. (Welch 2015)

One of the "problems" with the liberal arts, in fact, is that its purpose is not primarily tied to economic markets. Busteed (2019) calls this out as "collusion in the growth of an intellectual oligarchy in which only the very richest and most prestigious institutions preserve access to liberal arts traditions."

The devaluation of the liberal arts is directly related to the increase in public-private partnerships that are changing the ideological dimensions of colleges and universities, and not, I should add, in the way that the extreme right is claiming. One key stage of this process has been the explosion of OPM (Online Program Management) deals which can be anything from technical infrastructure to help schools offer online courses to a complete outsourcing of everything related to delivering an online degree, e.g. "all-inclusive distance-learning programs rebranded under the institution's name" (Mattes, 2015). In 2011, the US Department of Education issued guidance that permitted a new profit-sharing model, where OPM companies which are not accredited as schools, assume the bulk of the financial risk in launching online offerings, but also the bulk of the financial rewards if the program is successful. Today, at least 550 US colleges have such arrangements, and the OPM industry has global revenue of an estimated $8 billion, with much of that money flowing directly from federal student loans (Bannon & Smith, 2022). Students sometimes enrol in courses at public universities such as the University of Oregon or the University of Central Florida and never realise that none of the curriculum or instruction is coming from the school listed at the top of their course website (Bannon & Smith, 2022). What this means is not that the door to corporate influence is open but that there are essentially no walls at all between the corporate world and public education.

It should surprise no one when the University of Nike emerges. Joshua Hunt's 2018 book, *University of Nike: How Corporate Cash Bought American Higher Education*, tells a sordid story about how the University of Oregon bent to the will of corporate mega donor, Phil Knight. However, the tale implicates neoliberalism itself as much as it critiques Knight and the university leadership that got in bed with him to enrich the military industrial complex during the Cold War (Crepeau, 2018). At Brown University (my alma mater), faculty recently voted against the creation of a new Center for Philosophy, Politics and Economics. The student newspaper reports:

> For those opposing the PPE Center, the principal concern lies with the influence of dark money in higher education… PPE and similar centers at other universities, such as Duke and the University of North Carolina at Chapel Hill, have been funded by…billionaire and conservative political mega-donor Charles Koch. (Cigarroa, 2022)

I remember being an undergrad at Brown. I can almost imagine myself teaching there, seated at a fancy seminar table underneath a ceiling that is caving in on me. It would probably be easy to walk away from even a billion-dollar Koch check. But at Flagler College, a private liberal arts school in Florida with a graduation rate in the 50% range, it will likely not be so easy to pass up the five-million-dollar gift offered for an "Institute of Classical Education", championed by a college trustee who also chairs the board of a nationwide charter school network created by Hillsdale College — a private Christian college that has become a major player in America's culture wars. Kathryn Joyce (2022) describes the trend: "Big-money conservative interests are proposing and creating a roster of educational centers dedicated to conservative ideology or laissez-faire economics, often wrapped in the language of 'classical education', 'civics' or 'freedom'."

It's more than fair to see a distinction between smash-and-grab for-profit universities and struggling public colleges forced into difficult cuts. The American for-profit FastTrain College allegedly enrolled 1300 students lacking eligibility requirements (like high school diplomas) so they could take in $6.5 million in federal student grants and loans. The CEO hired "the sluttiest girls he could find" to act as admissions reps (Quandt, 2015). It's so hideous, it's hard to believe!

> My director decided to "right-size" our library. Five out of five librarians left, and he replaced them with one: me. I cannot cover everything which needs be done, and I end up feeling so guilty. I've had panic attacks before work, cried myself to sleep. The stress has exacerbated my chronic illnesses; I'm afraid some of these issues will end up being with me for the rest of my life. I understand that everyone is coping with financial binds, but surely there are less damaging ways. I love academia, but it's trying to kill me.

On one level, it's nothing like the painful erosion of the Women's Studies program at my own public university, which year by year lost more faculty and courses due to budget cuts and declining enrolments. But the neoliberal logic that drives FastTrain also drives cuts to publicly funded Women's Studies programs. The misogyny that lurks inside each of these examples is not a bug but a feature of neoliberalism, eroding not just public universities but the "public" as a citizenry. This is neoliberalism as corrosive to social justice and to democracy itself.

Call it what it is

Across the globe, fascism, authoritarianism, neo-Nazism, and populism are all on the rise. In Europe, far right parties have participated in coalition governments (Finland, the Netherlands, Switzerland, Estonia, Latvia), become major political players (Italy, Sweden, Spain, France), and infiltrated formerly moderate parties (Poland) (Freedman, 2022). The Assistant Commissioner of Australia's national police agency warned in 2021 that far right extremism is the country's fastest-growing threat (Xinhua, 2021). In recent years, conservative governments or governments with significant anti-democratic elements have gained increasing political power in Japan, India, the Philippines, Thailand, and Cambodia (Chacko & Jayasuriya, 2018). Brazil is leading a "third wave" of the Latin American far right shaped by neoliberalism and military power illustrated by the presidency of Jair Bolsonaro (Goldstein, 2022). (Lula's defeat of Bolsonaro just as this book goes to press changes that landscape somewhat.) Though the particulars shift by year and by region, this is a disturbing political trend.

The United States, basking in the frightening afterglow of the Trump presidency, makes for an apt case study in the relationship between neoliberalism and the rise of authoritarianism. Donald Trump, educated at elite private institutions from kindergarten through college, once gloated at a political rally "I love the poorly educated! We're the smartest people, we're the most loyal!" ("Trump", 2016). While popular author and political conservative J. D. Vance exclaims that because they indoctrinate young people, "professors are the enemy" (Reichman, 2021). It is not scholars or teachers who are rapidly indoctrinating the masses. Whether it is Trump "making America great again" or Akesson "making Sweden good again", there is a correlation between the oppressive politics — xenophobic, homophobic, transphobic, racist, misogynistic, ableist — of rising conservative extremists and neoliberalism. Oppressive politics cannot help but develop when dehumanising systems place profits over people. Nevertheless, the free market logic of neoliberalism is being supplanted by a more politically pointed goal. What people like Trump and his counterparts around the world are pushing now is illiberalism or "the destruction of liberal democracy, in order to create a theocratic-based state with controlled elections, education, and culture" (Sexton, 2022). This landscape produces anti-trans legislation in schools, "divisive concepts" laws that bar class discussions about systemic racism, and an ironic backlash of accusations against educators for their "woke" indoctrinating curriculum.

> *We recently saw our administration slow down the implementation of a "Race, Equity and Inclusion" General Education requirement and make optional a first-year book (previously a requirement) that was related to the history of racism in our country. The fear was that such activities on our campus would draw the ire of the state and they would punish us by further decreasing our funding. So the less the state supports us financially, the more control they have.*

The neoliberal university has not led us to these oppressive politics as much as the history of oppression has been built into our higher education systems since their beginnings. In the United States, it is an (un)settling fact that 99% of the land "granted" to our land-grant institutions by the 1862 Morrill Act came from violence-backed land cessions, where Indigenous people were forced to give up land that would become the basis of the public university system in the U.S. (Lee & Ahtone, 2020). Scholars such as Adam Harris have probed how historically Black colleges and universities (HBCUs) have accommodated students of colour displaced by racism from our "public" institutions that denied them admission and educated them with just a fraction of the public funds that have flowed to predominantly white schools. The current neoliberal thrust is a *return* to the historical root of American education, not a departure. Similarly, in Canada, where seemingly every month the bodies of more First Nation children are unearthed from residential school grounds, educational systems have literally been built on a foundation of violence and oppression. Again, this is a complicated cycle or spiral, not a linear course that we could easily correct; it's as much a horrifying backslide as it is a frightening new reality.

Diving for hope

One of the troubling features of this neoliberal backslide into the socially unjust world that spawned our current systems is that every "solution" makes the problem worse. As we work to save our institutions, we accept the terms of the debate that dictate *why* they need saving. But what's breaking us is not a budget shortfall or a demographic cliff. It's not that there's no market for Art History or that faculty haven't been innovative enough in our uses of technology in our teaching. Rich, powerful people are still sending their children to residential universities where they can study Engineering, yes, but also Philosophy and Painting. Some people who are not rich and powerful will also be admitted and supported at these elite schools, so that the facade of the meritocracy can be preserved. However, the other 80% of students will find they are being sold a different bill of sale: far fewer (but more costly) options, all of them designed only to provide the labour pool for the preservation of a broken world.

I am wary (and weary) of the fact that if I try to offer a solution, I would be offering something that would quickly be co-opted and repackaged by a nefarious system that is far more cunning than I could ever be. Instead, I will take a page from scholars, artists, writers, and activists who, before me, have recognised that the systems that enveloped them were causing such harm and violence. I offer the wreckage, exposed for what it is. For me, as it was for James Baldwin and Adrienne Rich,

> *Some say I am resilient, I don't see it that way. I am a survivor. More layoffs are coming, this will be the third go round at the institution. It is uncertain how I will fare. I have done this work because I believe in the good in people. I am tired yet hopeful. Thank you for reading this. It is my story and I have lived it.*

diving into this wreckage is a gesture of hope. Throughout my writing of this piece, I have been reading Glaude's biography of Baldwin. Towards the end of the book, Glaude (2020) quotes part of a speech that Baldwin gave less than a year before he died of cancer: "Liberation from the languages and categories that box us in requires that we tap the source of it all, free ourselves from the lie, and start this whole damn thing over" (p. 200). It is not above the wreckage but into it and through it we must go. We must use all our critical reading skills to free ourselves from the lies we are being told and sold and tap into our humanity to design what comes next. Every day at my own school, I am struck repeatedly by the care, hope, and joy that infuses the daily work that my colleagues do with students and with each other. They exercise this care, express this hope, and uplift me with their joy even as they wonder out loud how long they can continue at a job that is also killing them.

I will close with a nod to Paulo Freire, who inspired so many of us to think of education not as a series of answers to be banked, but as a series of problems to be posed. I don't have answers, but I feel empowered for posing the problems, and I commit to being creative and collaborative as I address them every day with my colleagues: faculty, staff, students, and those who hope to see a future that is the opposite of extractive, exploitative, and exhausting. It is not too much to ask: we must ask it not of this wreckage, but of each other. This is why this collection matters to me. The authors who have carried each other along in the process of working across our individual pieces are mapping the future. I think it is a map that looks unlike anything we have seen before. It is not a straight line to a destination, with carefully calculated mileages and driving times that maximise efficiency. It is a detrital map, shards spread into a million possible patterns by those of us who see clearly what is happening and who know for certain that anything can still happen.

Acknowledgements

I would like to acknowledge the contributions that the following people made to this chapter. All shortcomings here are my own, but I am extremely grateful to these scholars and colleagues (some of whom are friends and others of whom I know only through their work) for the way they have helped to shape this piece. Thank you to Nancy Welch, Ted Weiland, Leslie Chan, Ben Williamson, Cathy Germano, Kate Mullaugh, Mikaila Mariel Lemonik Arthur, Mickey Fitch-Collins, Caitlin Archer-Helke, Tressie McMillan Cottom, Christopher Newfield, Matthew Cheney, Larry Onokpite, Laura Czerniewicz, Catherine Cronin, Jim Luke, Su-Ming Khoo, Rajiv Jhangiani, Philip Trostel, and Kate Bowles.

References

Albertson-Grove, J. (2022). *Class of 2022 graduating with hope – and heavy debt*. New Hampshire Union Leader.
https://www.unionleader.com/news/education/class-of-2022-graduating-with-hope----and-heavy-debt/article_1031bcaf-5a5f-58e9-8f59-138060068f3c.html

Anthony, W., Brown, P. L., Fynn, N., & Gadzekpo, P. (2020). The plight of adjuncts in higher education. *National Organization for Student Success, 8*, 3–10.
https://files.eric.ed.gov/fulltext/EJ1246736.pdf

Ball, S. J., & Youdell, D. (2008). *Hidden privatisation in public education* [PDF]. Institute of Education, University of London.
https://www.right-to-education.org/sites/right-to-education.org/files/resource-attachments/Education_International_Hidden_Privatisation_in_Public_Education.pdf

Bannon, L., & Smith, R. (2022, July 6). That fancy university course? It might actually come from an education company. *The Wall Street Journal*.

https://www.wsj.com/articles/that-fancy-university-course-it-might-actually-come-from-an-education-company-11657126489

Brühwiler, C. F. (2018). "We'll manage"? European public universities and the refugee crisis. *Expositions, 12*(2), 191–205.
https://expositions.journals.villanova.edu/index.php/expositions/article/view/2363

Busteed, B. (2019, December 15). *Importance of college drops nearly 50% among young adults in just six years*. Forbes.
https://www.forbes.com/sites/brandonbusteed/2019/12/15/importance-of-college-drops-nearly-50-among-young-adults-in-just-six-years/

Chacko, P., & Jayasuriya, K. (2018). Asia's conservative moment: Understanding the rise of the right. *Journal of Contemporary Asia, 48*(4), 529–40.
https://doi.org/10.1080/00472336.2018.1448108

Cigarroa, E. (2022, February 1). *Faculty members express concern over proposed PPE Center*. The Brown Daily Herald.
https://www.browndailyherald.com/article/2022/02/faculty-members-express-concern-over-proposed-ppe-center

Cottom, T. M. (2017). *Lower ed: The troubling rise of for-profit colleges in the new economy*. The New Press.

Cottom, T. M. (2022, May 21). *America turned the greatest vehicle of social mobility into a debt machine*. The New York Times.
https://www.nytimes.com/2022/05/21/opinion/cancel-student-loan-debt.html

Crepeau, R. (2018). *University of Nike: How corporate cash bought American higher education* [Review of the book *University of Nike: How corporate cash bought American higher education*, by J. Hunt]. New York Journal of Books.
https://www.nyjournalofbooks.com/book-review/university-nike

Donald Trump. (2022, May 27). In *Wikipedia*.
https://en.wikipedia.org/w/index.php?title=Donald_Trump&oldid=1090130150

Dutt-Ballerstadt, R., & Louis, B. M. J. (2022, May 4). *It's time to challenge the corporate university*. Truthout.
https://truthout.org/articles/its-time-to-challenge-the-corporate-university/

Fenske, K. (2007). Public acceptance of privatisation in Malawi over time. *Africa Insight, 36*(3).
http://doi.org/ 10.4314/ai.v36i3.22482

Fjellman, A. M., & Haley, A. (2021). The plague of privatization: A futures analysis of the zombification of education. *Policy Futures in Education, 21*(5), 1–20.
https://doi.org/10.1177/14782103211029491

Freedman, S. (2022, April 23). *The rise of the far right in Europe*. Comment is Freed. https://samf.substack.com/p/the-rise-of-the-far-right-in-europe

Freire, P. (2000). *Pedagogy of the oppressed*. Continuum. (Original work published in 1970).

Giroux, H. (2016, February 19). *The mad violence of casino capitalism*. CounterPunch. https://www.counterpunch.org/2016/02/19/the-mad-violence-of-casino-capitalism/

Glaude, E. S. (2020). *Begin again: James Baldwin's America and its urgent lessons for our own*. Crown. https://www.penguinrandomhouse.com/books/575725/begin-again-by-eddie-s-glaude-jr/

Goldrick-Rab, S. (2016). *Paying the price: College costs, financial aid, and the betrayal of the American dream*. The University of Chicago Press.

Goldstein, A. (n.d.). *Brazil leads the third wave of the Latin American far right*. Center for Research on Extremism. https://www.sv.uio.no/c-rex/english/news-and-events/right-now/2021/brazil-leads-the-third-wave-of-the-latin-american-.html

Grawe, N. D. (2018). *Demographics and the demand for higher education*. Johns Hopkins University Press. https://search.ebscohost.com/login.aspx?direct=true&scope=site&db=nlebk&db=nlabk&AN=1501196

Hamilton, L., & Nielsen, K. (2021, June 1). *Our broke public universities*. The Chronicle of Higher Education. http://www.chronicle.com/article/our-broke-public-universities

Hanford, E. (Director). (2022). *Some college, no degree* [Audio documentary]. American Public Media. http://americanradioworks.publicradio.org/features/tomorrows-college/dropouts/

Harris, A. (2021). *The state must provide: Why America's colleges have always been unequal — and how to set them right*. Ecco.

Higher Ed Dive Team. (2022, April 22). *A look at trends in college consolidation since 2016*. Higher Ed Dive. https://www.highereddive.com/news/how-many-colleges-and-universities-have-closed-since-2016/539379/

Horton, S. (2010, June). *Not for profit: Six questions for Martha Nussbaum*. Harper's Magazine. https://harpers.org/2010/06/_not-for-profit_-six-questions-for-martha-nussbaum/

Hunt, J. (2018). *University of Nike: How corporate cash bought American higher education*. Melville House.

Hursh, D. (2017). The end of public schools? The corporate reform agenda to privatize education. *Policy Futures in Education, 15*(3), 389–99. https://doi.org/10.1177/1478210317715799

Internacional de la Educacíon. (2020). *Privatisation and commodification of university in Latin America* [PDF]. https://issuu.com/educationinternational/docs/debate_sobre_la_privatizacion_english__digital_

Jhangiani, R. (2019, December 4). *Supporting Open Educational Practices from the Library* [Webinar]. Kwantlen Polytechnic University. http://www.carl-abrc.ca/wp-content/uploads/2019/12/RJianghianin__webinar_Dec2019.pdf

Johanna, F., & Vujnovik, M. (2021, December 7). *Shared governance unionism and the right against austerity in the age of COVID-19.* AAUP. https://www.aaup.org/article/shared-governance-unionism-and-fight-against-austerity-age-covid-19

Joyce, K. (2022, May 31). *Now the far right is coming for college too: With taxpayer-funded "classical education".* Salon. https://www.salon.com/2022/05/31/exclusive-now-the-far-right-is-coming-for-college-too--with-taxpayer-funded-classical-education/

Klein, N. (2007). *The Shock Doctrine: The Rise of Disaster Capitalism* (1st edition). Metropolitan Books.

Komljenovic, J. (2020). Higher education industry expansion: Commodification versus assetization. *Science, Technology, & Human Values, 45*(1), 3–33. https://doi.org/10.1177/0162243919829567

Komljenovic, J., & Robertson, S. L. (2016). The dynamics of 'market-making' in higher education. *Journal of Education Policy, 31*(5), 622–36. https://doi.org/10.1080/02680939.2016.1157732

Kraus, N. (2021, September 25). *Talk of austerity is destroying public higher education: And that's the point.* The Cap Times. https://captimes.com/opinion/column/opinion-talk-of-austerity-is-destroying-public-higher-education-and-that-s-the-point/article_59a416f3-efb0-5ac5-a959-79c378be51e5.html

LaCasse, A. (2021, July 15). *"Divisive concepts" ban is New Hampshire law: Will it affect the way teachers discuss race and diversity*? Yahoo News. https://news.yahoo.com/divisive-concepts-ban-hampshire-law-171818828.html

Lanci, C. (2022, August 9). *Geneva private universities come under the spotlight.* Swissinfo. https://www.swissinfo.ch/eng/business/swiss-private-universities-issuing--unrecognised--degrees/47786510

Lee, R., & Ahtone, T. (2020, March 30). Land-grab universities. *High Country News*.
https://www.hcn.org/issues/52.4/indigenous-affairs-education-land-grab-universities

Marginson, S. (1997). Imagining Ivy: Pitfalls in the privatization of higher education in Australia. *Comparative Education Review, 41*(4), 460–80.
https://doi.org/10.1086/447465

Mattes, M. (2017). The private side of public higher education. *The Century Foundation*.
https://tcf.org/content/report/private-side-public-higher-education/

Mintz, B. (2021, October 27). *Neoliberalism and the crisis of higher education*. Marxist Sociology Blog.
https://marxistsociology.org/2021/10/neoliberalism-and-the-crisis-of-higher-education/

Mungai, C. (2016, April 1). *An Africa first! Liberia outsources entire education system to a private American firm. Why all should pay attention.* AboveWhispers.
http://abovewhispers.com/2016/04/01/an-africa-first-liberia-outsources-entire-education-system-to-a-private-american-firm-why-all-should-pay-attention/

Naidu, E. (2022, February 3). *Institutions brace for protests as funding cuts loom.* University World News.
https://www.universityworldnews.com/post.php?story=20220130175151981

Nassirian, B. (2022, August 8). It's time to end higher ed's gimmicky sales tactics. *The Chronicle of Higher Education*.
http://www.chronicle.com/article/its-time-to-end-higher-eds-gimmicky-sales-tactics

National Center for Education Statistics. (2022). *Undergraduate Enrollment. Annual Reports*.
https://nces.ed.gov/programs/coe/indicator/cha

Nations, J. M. (2021). How austerity politics led to tuition charges at the University of California and City University of New York. *History of Education Quarterly, 61*(3), 273–96.
https://doi.org/10.1017/heq.2021.4

Nemser, D., & Whitener, B. (2021). Demographic realism and the crisis of higher education [Review of the books *The agile college: How institutions successfully navigate demographics changes & Demographics and the demand for higher education*, by N. D. Grawe]. *Los Angeles Review of Books*.
https://lareviewofbooks.org/article/demographic-realism-and-the-crisis-of-higher-education/

Newfield, C. (2016). *The great mistake: How we wrecked public universities and how we can fix them*. Johns Hopkins University Press.

Newfield, C. (2022). Suboptimal by Design [Review of the book *Broke: The racial consequences of underfunding public universities*, by L. T. Hamilton & K. Nielsen]. *Los Angeles Review of Books*.
https://lareviewofbooks.org/article/suboptimal-by-design-on-laura-t-hamilton-and-kelly-nielsens-broke-the-racial-consequences-of-underfunding-public-universities/

Pasquerella, L., Davis, D. A., & Skorton, D. J. (2022). *What we value: Public health, social justice, and educating for democracy*. University of Virginia Press.

Pushkar (2021, May 25). *The pandemic will accelerate higher education's privatisation in India*. Times Higher Education.
https://www.timeshighereducation.com/opinion/pandemic-will-accelerate-higher-educations-privatisation-india

Qamar, F. (2022a, September 5). *India needs more investment in higher education*. The Hindu.
https://www.thehindu.com/opinion/op-ed/india-needs-more-investment-in-higher-education/article65853546.ece

Qamar, F. (2022b, September 12). *Public investment needs political will*. Deccan Herald.
https://www.deccanherald.com/opinion/comment/public-investment-needs-political-will-1144542.html

Quandt, K. R. (2015, November 17). *Some of America's worst for-profit colleges are taking billions in taxpayer funds*. Slate magazine.
http://www.slate.com/articles/news_and_politics/education/2015/11/for_profit_colleges_on_the_heightened_cash_monitoring_list_are_taking_billions.html

Reichman, H. (2021, December 14). *"The professors are the enemy": Right-wing attacks on academic freedom have real repercussions*. The Chronicle of Higher Education.
http://www.chronicle.com/article/the-professors-are-the-enemy

Rich, A. (1973). *Diving into the wreck: Poems 1971–1972*. WW Norton.

Sandel, M. J. (2021). *Tyranny of merit*. Picador Paper.

Schirmer, E., Wozniak, J. T., Morrison, D., Levy, R., & Gonsalves, J. (2021, April 15). *American universities are buried under a mountain of debt*. The Nation.
https://www.thenation.com/article/activism/universities-student-debt-reveal/

Seltzer, R. (2020, March 16). *Ed-tech vendors confront sudden opportunity and risk*. Inside Higher Ed.
https://www.insidehighered.com/news/2020/03/16/coronavirus-closures-force-colleges-move-students-online-ed-tech-experts-see

Sexton, J. Y. [@JYSexton]. (2022, February 9). *Neoliberalism found purchase on both sides of the aisle. Democrats joined Republicans in an economic consensus that prioritized markets while carrying out austerity.* [Tweet]. Twitter. https://twitter.com/JYSexton/status/1491435412883185670

Spitalniak, L. (2022, February 9). *Public colleges offer highest chance of positive ROI to students, report finds.* Higher Ed Dive. https://www.highereddive.com/news/public-colleges-offer-highest-chance-of-positive-roi-to-students-report-fi/618531/

Stich, A. E., & Case, C. (2022). [Review of the book *Broke: The racial consequences of underfunding public universities*, by L. T. Hamilton & K. Nielsen]. *The Review of Higher Education, 45*(3), 409–14. https://doi.org/10.1353/rhe.2022.0004

Tauscher, T. (n.d.). *UNH reacts to HB2 regulations on teaching race.* The New Hampshire. https://tnhdigital.com/19351/news/unh-reacts-to-hb2-regulations-on-teaching-race/

Trepanier, L. (2022, August 15). *The Public Value of Higher Education.* VoegelinView. https://voegelinview.com/the-public-value-of-higher-education/

Trostel, P. (2012). *It's not just the money: The benefits of college education to individuals and to society* [PDF]. Lumina Foundation. https://www.luminafoundation.org/files/resources/its-not-just-the-money.pdf

Trump, D. J. (2016, February 24). *Trump: "I love the poorly educated".* The Daily Beast. https://www.thedailybeast.com/cheats/2016/02/24/trump-i-love-the-poorly-educated

Tyre, P. (2017, June 27). *Can a tech start-up successfully educate children in Africa?* Pulitzer Center. https://pulitzercenter.org/stories/can-tech-start-successfully-educate-children-africa

University and College Union (2010). *Privatising our universities. UCU February 2010* [PDF]. https://www.ucu.org.uk/media/3791/Privatising-our-universities-Feb-10/pdf/ucu_privatisingouruniversities_feb10.pdf

Usher, A. (2022, March 9). *A closer look at Chinese higher education.* HESA. https://higheredstrategy.com/a-closer-look-at-chinese-higher-education/

Welch, N. (2015). Educating for austerity. *International Socialist Review, 98*. https://isreview.org/issue/98/educating-austerity/index.html

Williamson, B., & Hogan, A. (2021, March 12). *Code acts in education: Pandemic privatization and digitalization in higher education.* National Education Policy Center.
https://nepc.colorado.edu/blog/pandemic-privatization

Xinhua. (2021, October 8). *Australia's right-wing extremism fastest-growing threat: Federal police.* XINHUANET.
http://www.news.cn/english/2021-10/08/c_1310231828.htm

Zacks Equity Research. (2020, March 23). *Coronavirus outbreak to offer opportunities to online educators.* Yahoo Finance.
https://finance.yahoo.com/news/coronavirus-outbreak-offer-opportunities-online-153203022.html

2. Counters to despair

Sherri Spelic

When I proposed the title of this chapter, "Counters to despair", I believed that I was choosing words carefully. In fact, they are borrowed from Catherine and Laura's original call for chapters of #HE4Good. *Counters*, as in, *actions against a negative or encroaching force*, I thought. Nevertheless, I continued to picture *"a level surface (such as a table, shelf or display case) over which transactions are conducted or food is served or on which goods are displayed or work is conducted."*[1] Kitchen, lunch, and display counters refused to leave my mind.

Here's what I know: you needn't work directly in the realm of post-secondary education to be worried about its future. You need not hold a PhD to recognise that higher education in many places remains deeply beholden to oppressive structures including (but not limited to) white supremacy, patriarchy, and unchecked neoliberalism. You and I, as citizens, as learners, as members of society, need not accept these threats to higher education as inevitable or insurmountable.

There are barriers between the futures we most dread and the current realities we inhabit. Let's call them counters. What are they made of? How do we build them?

Which counters exist to separate us from despair? Over which counters must we negotiate conditions that prevent and/or alleviate despair? Which counters appear freshly constructed and which ones seem ancient and everlasting? What must we do to resist an understandable leaning toward despair?

---

1 Merriam-Webster, Incorporated. (2022). Counter. https://www.merriam-webster.com/dictionary/counter

I place these words, poems, and meditations on the counter before us. I pile these words between us and despair. Despair remains distinctly possible, tangible, and real. Even as we sit or stand at the counter, we can observe and contemplate despair without becoming it. How we do that will vary, as will the ways despair presents itself to us at different times. To counter despair requires that we acknowledge its existence, its reality. We can do that and still hold ourselves separate.

Choosing words feels easier than choosing a state of mind. And when we can, we choose anyway.

Give me hope, please.

It would be so nice to talk about what gives me hope. In fact, I would love for someone, *something* to come over here and give me some hope. "Look, here's something you can feel good about. It might happen again. There's hope!" Or "Hey, did you hear about this initiative, it's going to be funded for another academic cycle! That's something to make us hopeful, right?"

Just imagine if we could walk through our campuses, down the halls of our institutions exchanging bits of tangible hope with each other. Hope on a lanyard, hope in notebooks, hope in the library stacks, hope on cafeteria napkins, hope in coffee cups, hope as a marching band, hope on sports jerseys, t-shirts, and baseball caps, hope as an administrator, hope as a raise for custodial and cafeteria workers, hope in the all-gender bathrooms, hope as instructor equity. Imagine all those sources and outlets for hope!

Picture this: hope circulating back and forth, round and round! We can feel it, right? I mean, hope in abundance generates its own wild energy. It's like you can smell it in your morning coffee. It's practically rising off your device as you compose that affirming email. People are talking about the mood, the vibe — all this hope in the air, on the ground — showing up like a flash mob in the most unlikely places: in the mental health centre, in the IT department meeting, in the provost's and registrar's offices. Unbidden, hope just strides in, inserts itself seamlessly into the conversation as if it had been there all along. And that's the thing, hope seems to have arrived and spread, just like that!

You know, however, that's not how this story works.

Hope is/was around because some folks are/were about the business of growing and cultivating it. Not focused on scaling up and turning a profit, we're talking about folks shaping hope for themselves and their loved ones, for friends and close colleagues. We're not talking about a perpetually renewable resource either. It's quite possible to run out of hope, to have your hope snatched away in broad daylight. So, if you're in the habit of cultivating hope, you learn to hold it close, to protect it. You don't skip around tossing it to anyone you meet. That said, it's not beyond you or me to build our own pockets of hope to draw from. You know, start small and keep going. Apply where necessary, share some where you can. Pooling hope can open fresh perspectives. Won't know until you try it. Sure, not every plan is going to work, but give your hope some practice and it gets stronger, more robust: also more savvy. Bear in mind that homegrown hope is not a superhero, it doesn't swoop, fly, or rescue. It's strategy and compassion; brass tacks and long-range vision; stubborn support and healthy resistance. Hope is a teacher who is still curious.

Hard is

What's hard is
what's hard is reaching an understanding. We say
r e a c h an understanding like walking over a bridge,
a bridge over troubled water, perhaps,
to reach an understanding.
But the bridge
collapses
right under our feet.
We are no longer standing
we can no longer reach
we have fallen down
and that's what's hard.

What's hard about people
What's hard about people is trying to
understand them.
What's hard about people is trying to understand
why on god's green earth
they are not more like us.
What's hard about people is trying to understand
why in the world
we can't be more like them.
What's hard about people is trying to understand
why on god's green earth
it's so damn difficult to be a person.

What's hard about knowing
What's hard about knowing is realising
It's not the same, it's not enough
To change outcomes, attitudes, the climate
Or even the premise of survival
Because... power
What's hard about knowing is that power
Does not care what you feel
Holds no interest in your growth
What's hard is we say knowledge is power
When we mean
That we wish it were so.
Wishing is easy and knowing, insufficient.
That's what's hard.

Alysa chooses to PhD[2]

Motivations?
Program focused on my area of study: social justice in education
Needed space to deepen my thinking
Most drawn to programs where my professors
Were doing more community centred action research
Going where I hoped to feel more supported
In radical dreaming

Thoughts on #HigherEd then and now?
Saw it as elitist actually; worried about how I would navigate it.
Aspects of the system that seem like a pyramid scheme
Ha!
I've really had to sit with how two truths can coexist:
Several things that maintain academia as exclusionary and
I can also pursue big questions; embrace an iterative ongoing process.
I'm here and also hope to work against the parts that cause harm.

Future of #HigherEd and potential for liberatory ed?
Actively still navigating my role, wondering how I will make it out
On the other side
Feel most hopeful when researchers challenge
The researcher/researched binary structure which
Positions the researcher as "expert" or "discoverer" of knowledge
— Can be incredibly colonising;
also positions participants as somehow less knowledgeable.
I see potential to work collaboratively with communities in authentic ways
where we really use these spaces to challenge and change power structures —
the glorification of the written word is heavy in higher ed.
I see potential for liberatory ed, when a more arts driven approach
is accepted.

---

2   Based on an email interview with Alysa Perreras, Inclusion, Justice and Antiracist Consultant and Researcher, Bogota, Colombia; Doctoral Student, Education for Social Justice, University of San Diego.

Never done, always beginning[3]

What I'm learning, what I'm seeing is that
Just one thing
Is hardly a thing
Because it cannot serve
All of our needs today
Or tomorrow

Just one thing
Is hardly a thing
Because we need more tools
For many tasks
Both seen and unseen

If I try to build something
I hope my students will want

It doesn't mean that they
should never learn to struggle

It doesn't mean that they
should never learn to protest

It doesn't mean that their
wants won't change shape or direction

If I try to build something
I hope my students will want

It means I'm striving to
champion their independence

It means I'm striving to
help them choose wisely

It means I'm striving to
let go of my need to control the outcome

If my students and I build something
we find useful

If my students and I build anything at all

---

[3] "Never done, always beginning" is the final poem in my keynote for the OTESSA Conference, May 16–19, 2022. https://edifiedlistener.blog/2022/05/17/hide-and-seek-on-kids-power-and-resistance-in-education-otessa-22-keynote/

we must build imaginations

If my students and I build
a city of care

a province of justice
a nation of acceptance

We are never done
and always beginning.

Assessment

We laugh to keep from crying. We laugh again.

The dream revisited

Once upon a time, I was able to dream.

I said,[4]

"In my dreams my children and grandchildren will not go to college; they will give birth to one."

I wonder now if I still mean it.

In my dreams my children and grandchildren will remain voracious learners, willing to share their curiosity and expertise generously and wholeheartedly.

In my dreams my children and grandchildren will recognise both a need to help and be helped; to build in community and develop a healthy capacity for solitude.

In my dreams my children and grandchildren will know love — how to give and receive it, how to spread and apply it, how to celebrate and rekindle it, how to mourn its loss and nurture its beginnings.

In my dreams my children and grandchildren understand freedom and responsibility and the tensions these produce; they can recognise themselves in society and its making.

In my dreams my children and grandchildren may or may not go to college.

In my dreams my children and grandchildren give birth to a fresh understanding.

In my dreams my children and grandchildren and their grandchildren have vision that extends beyond the known; imaginations that stretch the universe. They blossom with promise.

Still I dream.

---

4   "How Much Higher, Education? https://edifiedlistener.medium.com/how-much-higher-education-653b6b5707c7

Section II
Making Sense of the Unknown and Emergent

'Old Tree' by Alex Abrahams. All rights reserved: used with artist's permission.

Note from the artist:

The branches of the tree tangled over my head and I struggled to find my way. Where is the path? In which direction do I go? As a young student, I looked for the sun rays in the thicket of higher education, but often it was dark and clammy. "Keep chopping," they said, "you will find the opening and the light of learning." Higher education is for good, for your good, for life's good. Just beat down the thorns and you will be there.

3. On public goods, cursing, and finding hope in the (neoliberal) twilight zone

Su-Ming Khoo

> To solve political problems becomes difficult for those who allow anxiety alone to pose them. It is necessary for anxiety to pose them. But their solution demands at a certain point the removal of this anxiety (Bataille, G. The Accursed Share, 1991, p. 14)

This chapter traces the predicaments of public higher education in the neoliberal "twilight zone", stuck with the choice between neoliberal globalism and global neoliberalism (Khoo, 2017; Schuurman, 2009). Confronting a rising sense of darkness (Fleming, 2021) and dread (Goldberg, 2021), this chapter reverses the aphorism that "it is better to light a candle than to curse the darkness". Cursing the darkness that neoliberalism visits on HE might be a critically generative thing to do, as it surfaces the normative foundations that are otherwise occluded by a pervasive sense of dread. The chapter discusses the importance of hope in the face of dread, turning to gentler educational darkness and generative aspects of dark pedagogies. To dare to think about what we mean by public good, educational good, or higher good requires more than the lighting of candles. It calls for energetically rejecting the cursed times that we are living through and opening the possibility of reclaiming reality.

Introduction

Why has higher education become stuck in a twilight zone of boring choices between global neoliberalism or neoliberal globalism? Discussing the fate of critical futures, Schuurman (2009) suggests that we need more "middle-range" theorising to address "the new imperialism" of neoliberal globalisation from the ground up. Such middle-range thinking should engage with empirical situations and search for "pertinent questions" instead of "correct answers" (Schuurman, 2019, p. 847). The pertinent questions trouble the efficacy of critical thinking itself. How far can critique really go? We are not sure if it is possible for critiques of neoliberalism to escape the iron laws of oligarchy, the iron cage of bureaucracy, or the relentless drive for efficiency that expresses the power of governmentality in myriad ways. This chapter provokes these critical questions, even if it cannot fully answer them, and thinks through their implications for the possibility of social democracy.

Alternatives to neoliberalism should have gained ground following the 2008–2009 global financial crisis, when global neoliberalism arguably lost its triumphal claims (Gerbaudo, 2016; Khurana & Narayan, 2021). And yet, alternatives have not gained ground and neoliberalism continues to evolve its uncanny non-death (Crouch, 2011). Existing broad and deep economic and sociopolitical crises have continued, spreading the slow violence of structural harm, inequity, and precarity, starkly illustrated by the distribution of losses and harms of the global COVID-19 pandemic, ongoing since early 2020.

In this chapter, I address a sense of rising darkness and dread brought by neoliberalism in higher education. Instead of "lighting a candle" to optimistically wish that things will turn out well, I discuss the rise of neoliberal darkness and dread in higher education and its voiding of public things. I curse the darkness to expose foundational assumptions and assaults that work to void the public good, erode public "somethings" and turn them into "nothings". As the poet, Seamus Heaney, remarked while reflecting on the challenge of transformation facing South Africa after apartheid, hope is not merely optimism that things will turn out for the best, hope is a sense of service, commitment, and readiness to work for a common "something": "… hope is something that is there to be worked for, is worth working for, and can work" (Johnson, 2002, para. 11). I explore the critical alternatives offered by dark pedagogies and negative capability as well as a substantive alternative economics of publicness and public good that resists the cruel optimism of liberal public good theory. Theories of the gift economy and performative assembly against the cruelties of neoliberal austerity and hope for a more liveable life offer hope for a public and socially democratic higher education beyond the neoliberal twilight zone. Not all forms of darkness result in the voiding of public good. Dark pedagogies and educationally generative darkness may serve the regeneration of public things. However, the regeneration of public things requires decolonial demands for restitution and restoration to be taken seriously, if hope for the public good is not to founder on the rocks of colonial-imperial legacies that continue to trouble democratic societies as they currently exist.

Darkness and dread

My starting point was a sense of rising darkness and pervading dread. I had no idea when starting to write this chapter that "Dark Academia" was a meme, a social media trend engineered for millennials born in the strangely specific timeframe of 1997 to 2012 (Brinkhof, 2022). The Dark Academic responds to the brutalist modernity of marketised neoliberal higher education with solitary romanticism. Rejecting the modern world and other people, Dark Academics are nostalgic for a lost world of higher education, a world of cosily special, elite, and privileged places of distinction (Horgan, 2021). But Readings (1997) admonishes that a return to a past state of innocence is impossible. Academics today already dwell and work "in ruins". Dwelling in the ruins is neither a cosy nor comfortable experience, but it offers more real, if ambivalent hope.

The title of Peter Fleming's (2021) book *Dark Academia: How Universities Die* is hardly optimistic. The neoliberalisation of higher education is linked to many examples of psychological, social, and bodily harms and deprivations, including the absence of the basic decencies of health insurance, and, tragically, even death by suicide. Academic death has been spurred on by the pressures of commercialisation, managerialism, competitive individualism, bureaucracy, and acceleration — all of which have transformed once-privileged academic jobs into hellish dystopias and put an end to ideals of autonomy, craft, intrinsic satisfaction, and vocational motivation. Fleming's complaint is that traditional academic values based on these ideals have become irrelevant or reduced to nostalgic quirks and eccentricities. One review dismisses Fleming's complaints as nostalgic, unwarranted, and based on a fantasy that never lived up to its own ideals. Perhaps academia was never worth saving in the first place? (Guo, 2021). This move from suspicion to surrender confirms, with resignation and sadness, that the failure of the ideal is only too real. Little can be done about the misfit between academic ideals and the "brave new world" of higher education (Fleming 2021, pp. 5 & 7). Dark academia's complaints list many ills — degraded and precarious working conditions, wage theft, authoritarianism, and callous behaviour by senior management who seem to inhabit an entirely different reality — "La-la Land", in Fleming's words. Ordinary staff and student experiences of the "edufactory" and metrics nightmare are jarringly at odds with the blandly aspirational cheerfulness conveyed by marketing departments. Corruption, the corrosion of character, bad faith, acceleration, and declining trust characterise this dark affect, accompanied by pathological states of egotism and anxiety (Mahon, 2022).

The academic "collegium of peers" that Fleming mourns may never have existed for many in the first place. Yet merely confirming that top-down, command production economy has replaced the collegium of peers represents a tacit acceptance of a new reality ruled by censorship, suppression of dissent, and the remediation of bad news with public relations. Accounts of exhaustion and burnout are feeding a new academic genre, "quit-lit" (Shreve, 2018), recommending exit as the only sane choice. The only way for academics to survive is to quit the "factories of knowledge" and "industries of creativity" (Raunig, 2012), leaving the captains of industry to do what they will.

Dread is the sense of futures becoming futureless, social screws turned, social fabric torn apart (Goldberg, 2021). Structural transformations underpin this growing sense of dread: the individualisation, displacement and precaritisation of employment, eroding work benefits and pensions, intrusive surveillance and monitoring, and a continuous stream of mediatised news and comment, bringing either bad tidings or nauseating corporate spin. Low intensity conflict and slow violence feed this sense of dread, increasing anxiety and unsettlement, which Goldberg (2021) describes as "a tightening knot in the social stomach", the social fraying at the seams, with "nothing but quicksand all the way down" (pp. 13 & 19). We sit in dread like frogs brought to the boil, only with some awareness that our environment is getting more and more uncomfortable. Are resistance and hope even possible to counter the social life of dread? As the writer, Franz Kafka said to his friend Max Brod (1960), there is plenty of hope, hope abounds... "but not for us". Can we even hope against hope that things will not worsen? Perhaps things might just stay good enough, even if we cannot hope for improvement? Is public higher education already trapped in Kafka time, with no hope for us?

Cursing the darkness

"It is better to light a candle than to curse the darkness", or so the saying goes. But is it? Lighting a candle is a gesture of hope and mourning across many different cultures, symbolising grief, and satisfying the need to commemorate. Hope looks for signs of reprieve, and a flicker of light may feel like a welcome gift of a moment of contemplation as darkness descends.

Cursing the darkness, however, is different. To curse the darkness is to name that which you curse and engage in an everyday form of resistance. A curse is more than just an expletive or a complaint (Ahmed, 2021), it is to employ a weapon of the weak (Scott, 1985), to respond to the adversity of powerlessness with word magic. This chapter curses neoliberalism in higher education at twilight. "At twilight" is not necessarily the same as "in twilight". "At" twilight is a temporal moment, not an intrinsic condition, inviting speculation about the point between fading light and falling darkness.

The magic of cursing is psychologically and psychosomatically potent, perhaps because it is ambivalent. Cursing serves to intimidate, attack and haunt — to counter one form of dark power with another, but it also can heal, invigorate, and inspire. Considering the violently occult nature of academic darkness, does it not make sense to respond to one occult attack with another? To curse the dark side of working and studying in the neoliberal university is to call out the falling darkness, to refuse to surrender to dread and resignation. Cursing refuses the marketing hype, with its forced celebration of problem-free success, and rejects the endless insistence that we must substitute our work of teaching, learning, or researching with pseudo-competitions for publicity and funding.

Cursing is a pragmatic attempt at human communication with forces that seem incapable of listening to us. What makes a curse a curse is the cultural distinction between acceptable versus taboo. This line is never self-evident since offensiveness is always a property of a very particular context. Of course, I write from Ireland, where the proclivity to curse goes back for millennia. Unlike in other places, where cursing may function as an incantation to bring future harm or to make an offensive utterance, in Ireland, cursing is far more flexible and ambiguous, considered to be a righteous art, honed, and practised against occupiers and their intermediaries (Waters, 2021).

Cursing's word magic lies in the testing of the limits of the cultural context, and in testing the limits, it lays bare the norms that are operating behind the veil of taboo. This is why Mona Eltahawy (2020) encourages feminists to practise cursing as one of the seven "sins" that should be committed to resist and overcome the oppression of a "universal and normalized" order. Maybe it is not enough to "forget neoliberalism" and to decide that we don't need it. No. One should "fuck neoliberalism. Fuck it to hell" (Springer, 2016, p. 289). In this moment, at least, cursing releases psychic energy, breaking through the relentless normalisation of the accursed and dread-inducing neoliberal twilight. At that moment, the world is opened for remaking and re-inhabitation. Springer asks, *what if cursing is a call for enactive agency that goes beyond mere words, combining theory and practice into the beautiful praxis of prefiguration?*

Cursing is physically like laughing and it is often followed by laughing. It causes an intake of breath and a turn of the mind that may otherwise continue on a trajectory of thoughtlessness. Thoughtlessness is an absence of thought, an absence that is at the root of what Hannah Arendt (2013) called the "banality of evil". Who has not faced powerful bureaucrats' clichéd protestations that they are merely "doing their job"? Cursing, like laughing, interrupts this deadly train of thoughtlessness with a "sudden expulsion of air" and shows, a little fiercely, with "the fence of your teeth" an unwillingness to put up with something (Knott, 2013, p. 19). The apparent lightness of cursing and laughter does not indicate a lack of seriousness. Thought, effort, rumination, and courage may have gone into that sudden expletive, cackle, or curse. The dogged continuity of banality and resignation are interrupted, space is cleared, norms are laid bare, the scene is oxygenated, and, suddenly, possibility may emerge for something and somewhere being returned to, with the possibility of the present being inhabited differently, perhaps even with a future.

Voiding publicness: From somethings to nothings

One main reason we should curse neoliberalism is for the way it transforms goods by processes of voiding. Neoliberal policies and procedures mandate the transformation of specific "somethings" into generic "nothings" (Ritzer & Ryan, 2002). This *nothingification* contravenes the three axiomatic dimensions of publicness, i.e. public procedures, institutions, and services. Public things are eroded and corroded when they become less procedurally democratic, when distributional inequity is deepened, and when broadly beneficent characteristics such as health, safety (Khoo, 2014), scientific integrity, and/or respect are compromised.

Honig (2015) defines "public things" as things that equalise relations among people and wonders if they can survive the onslaught of neoliberal austerity. She argues that people must fight for public things by gathering publicly as diverse equals in opposition to austerity, inequality, and privilege hoarding. The regeneration of social democracy depends on the regeneration of its public things (Honig, 2022). Public things are things that, by their very existence, serve a kind of psychological-developmental role necessary to the maintenance of democratic life (Honig, 2015). Combining Arendt's theories about the "common world" and Winnicott's developmental psychology centred on transitional objects, Honig (2015) argues that public goods' durability is under threat and this erosion diminishes the prospects for public life.

Brown (2015) echoes Honig's warning about the undoing of the demos as neoliberalism's stealthy revolution. Arendt (2013/1958) characterises the public as the *space of appearance* that enables a sense of political freedom and equality to come into being whenever citizens act in concert through speech and persuasion. Likewise, in *The Public and its Problems*, Dewey (1927) defines publicness as a collective communicative response to shared problems. A "public" does not exist until a problem brings a public together to solve the problem by deliberating about it as a community. Honig uses Arendtian concepts to defend public things as things that help the public to define and enact social democracy. This is like the collective enactment that Dewey has in mind — democracy as constituted by people acting in concert to solve problems as shared public concerns.

Higher education descends into darkness when neoliberal mechanisms appropriate public goods and surrender the obligations to publicly provide them with other "fixes" of markets, financing, and technology. Neoliberal market fixes are distinct from liberal axioms as they involve dark forms of surveillance, disciplinary control, and authoritarian and summary exercises of power. Marketisation and the introduction of "new public management" into what was previously public higher education erodes it as a public good, while barbarising its enactment of public life. This barbarisation is what we mostly cannot see but can still sense as dread (Goldberg, 2021), a sense of public life and the public good becoming hollowed out, and transformed into something futureless (Brown, 2015; Honig, 2015). In a previous era of public goods thinking, the 1950s-60s, hopes for higher education to serve common good, equitable social provisioning, and the remediation of social injustice were answered with promises of economic and social mobility. The theoretical, conceptual, and empirical impasse of the 1980s replaced Keynesian fixes with a much darker zeitgeist. In the subsequent era, yawning inequalities of absurd wealth and callous welfare austerity have been "fixed" by promoting xenophobia and the murderous borderisation, a determined rehabilitation of patriarchal misogyny and racism, a resort to imperial nostalgia, and re-militarisation (Giroux, 2005). Neoliberal barbarisation can justly be described as necropolitics — the power and capacity to dictate who (or what) may live and who (or what) must die (Keval & Wright, 2021; Mbembe, 2003, 2019).

Privatisation is a dark process because it pursues the neoliberal globalisation of nothing in the name of efficiency, relevance, and "global" positioning. "Nothing" involves the substitution of local forms of life having distinct content with globalised, empty forms: templates that are centrally controlled, standardised, and lacking in distinctive content. *Nothingification* produces something — property — and privatisation enacts a historical technique of segregation that divides and diminishes the publicness of education (Harris, 1993; Honig, 2022). In the United States, racial segregation of children in public schools was deemed unconstitutional by the Brown v. Board of Education ruling in 1954. This ruling catalysed white collectivisation of investments in private schooling and their subsequent withdrawal from public education in some states, thwarting the formation of integrated education as a public good that could bring people together in an integrated, democratic manner. The strategy of privilege hoarding, in tandem with the withdrawal and destruction of public schooling assets, amounts to nothing less than violent "democracide" (Honig, 2022).

Dark pedagogies

Although the darkness brought by neoliberal voiding dominates the sector, higher education's "darkness" is heterogenous, not homogenous. The voiding, corruption, and corrosion of public higher education and the pathological states and harms documented by Fleming (2021) should not be minimised. But higher education's darkness is more than just neoliberal darkness. "Darkness" also offers the possibility of change, that the world might be other than what it currently is (Barnett & Bengtsen 2021, 2022).

"Dark pedagogies" imply a pivot to embrace darkness when Enlightenment goals and expectations are found wanting. Lysgaard, Bengtsson and Laugerson (2019, 2020) suggest that darkness should be constructively engaged with, within, and for an environmentally threatened world. Dark pedagogies embrace uncertainty, catastrophe, and terror, by taking an affective turn to add urgency to shared ethical commitments in an already broken world (Mulgan, 2014). Indeed, the dread situation of the current planetary crisis including, of course, the climate crisis, may necessitate the power of dark pedagogies to face planetary darkness and effect a necessary turn towards different, more bearable futures. Educational darkness is a "thing" that exceeds the didactic slog, harnessing aesthetic and affective aspects to spark learning and transformation (Lysgaard et al., 2019).

Darkness is a complex with inner tensions (Barnett & Bengtsen, 2021) that also stands intrinsically for pedagogical aspects of education, including considerations of pedagogy's own limitations, constraints, contradictions, ironies, and contingencies. The tasks of higher education acknowledge and enact being-with ontological darkness. However, higher education's pedagogical tasks also simultaneously include that of emancipation — freeing students, the wider public, and academics from over-dependence on epistemological, phenomenological, and ideological darkness. Darkness can be an interruption that serves to foster creativity and imagination. A significant tension remains between dark pedagogies and the neoliberal darkness of profit-motivated domestication and commodification, turning higher education into "factories of knowledge and industries of creativity" (Raunig, 2012). As educators, we strive to move ourselves and our students out of the neoliberal twilight zone and yet remain caught within it. We also harbour the hope of thrusting them (and ourselves) back into the kinds of darkness that foster a certain cluster of pedagogical virtues, goods, and necessities. These include Keatsian negative capability, being capable of inhabiting a zone of uncertainties, mysteries, and doubts without immediately needing to fall back upon the answers that are already rehearsed and incanted.

The cruel optimism of liberal publicness

Can anyone dare to speak about public higher education and hope for public good when the public realm in almost every context has never *not* been constituted by imperial, colonial, racialised, and sexist forms of exclusion, dispossession, and erasure? Today, it seems almost impossible to imagine public higher education that is not thoroughly neoliberal, by which we mean "capitalist" and, by the same token, inegalitarian and imperialist in its extractivist tendencies, since that is what neoliberalism is — the reconstitution of capitalism and imperialism in a new form (Khoo 2022; Patnaik & Patnaik, 2021).

Public good as it is currently constituted may be incommensurable with demands for decolonisation and the necessity of reckoning with the colonial legacies of higher education. Restitution and reparation are required to remedy structural inequities if postcolonial public goods are to become more inclusive and legitimate. This does not, however, resolve the objection that the liberal public sphere is incommensurable with different, decolonial epistemologies and ontologies "beyond the abyssal line" (de Sousa Santos, 2007) — the abyssal line being an onto-epistemic divide instituted within Euro-Western thinking that radically divides social reality into "this side of the line" replaying colonial-modern ordering, with a supplement of social fascism from its radical negation. The "other side of the line" constitutes emancipation from abyssal ordering, through the formation of a counter-hegemonic subaltern cosmopolitanism. Subaltern cosmopolitanism is characterised by a deep and enduring incompleteness, ecologism, radical co-presence, diversity, and attention to the sociology of ignorances and absences. Some decolonial critiques (Stein, 2022) warn that decoloniality and the "public" and "public good" may be incompatible, since irreducibly different ontologies and epistemologies are involved (p. 79). Besides, many public goods including those of higher education have been and continue to be accumulated through racialised processes of exploitation, accumulation, and extraction, in much the same way as "private" goods. These decolonial critiques question whether the very notion of public goods can ever be made benevolent. I agree that the claim of incommensurability and past exploitative foundations trouble, yet do not think that these critiques entirely cancel out the potential of publicness. Critical-decolonial claims of incommensurability can be accommodated in an open and imperfect conception of a contingently constituted public good. Public goods are not necessarily incompatible with a beyond-abyssal "ecology of knowledges" as outlined by de Sousa Santos (2007). It is precisely the function of the public sphere to hold different and possibly conflicting perspectives without being annihilated by the existence of differences. In terms of public things, public higher education can provide space for disputes and function as a holding environment for such legitimate disputes.

Is it even desirable or possible to try to bring different theoretical and praxiological traditions to bear on a commitment to the public good? In New Public Goods theory (Khoo, 2014), I outline an axiomatic approach to public goods that is open-ended without demanding absolute convergence. Yet, criteria of equity and beneficence limit how far disputes can be resolved by relativist or nihilist claims that difference is always the trump card. New Public Goods theory requires the plurality of democratic participation to be triangulated with possibly clashing goals of equitable consumption and generalised public benefit such as safety or public health. The three axioms of democratic deliberation, equitable enjoyment of goods, and broad beneficence can offer support and counter threats to an achievable ecology of knowledges.

Conclusion: Enacting alternative publicness beyond the neoliberal twilight zone

Public goods and gift economies offer alternative ideas about economics and the economies of higher education in the spirit of recreating an alternative social imaginary to that of neoliberal higher education (Khoo, 2016). These alternatives offer a ground for world-making in ways that better articulate social democratic and human concerns while critically challenging and rejecting ongoing neoliberal reforms.

Judith Butler's (2015) concept of performative assembly offers a banister to lean on when thinking about the possibilities of a public good without guarantees. Lives may be incommensurable but all lives are always already public and social, situated in a larger social, economic, and infrastructural world that exceeds individualised perspectives and ethics. Butler notes that the public presently defines the human and life in contradictory terms, treating some human lives as grievable and others not. Tuck and Yang (2012) reject non-performative decolonisation with their assertion that decolonisation is not a metaphor when there are concrete demands to restitute Indigenous rights, lands, and sovereignty.

Social and economic concerns are grounded in the body and cannot be fully dissociated from the infrastructural and environmental conditions within which bodies live and act (Butler, 2015). Under conditions of precarity, performative politics (assembly) require bodies to act together, facing the precarious conditions that undermine the very conditions of acting. Gatherings enacted by bodies under duress give rise to a form of solidarity that is both mournful and joyful, where the gathering itself signifies persistence and resistance (Butler, 2015). As struggles continue for fair treatment at different points of entry, progression and attainment, workers and students in higher education also struggle with worsening work conditions and declining earnings, increasing fees, and rising costs. These worsening conditions increasingly necessitate hardship funds, food, and hygiene banks to maintain the basic needs of students, academics, and other higher education workers. It has become more crucial than ever to keep fighting against worsening conditions for the least securely employed and the worst-paid, against overwork and the theft of time and health, and to secure wages, wellbeing and even life itself. It is becoming increasingly difficult to maintain such basic bodily needs for food, shelter, and healthcare, both inside and outside higher education, due to the broader devastation of public ways of life. In the face of the neoliberal erosion of joint and public welfare, bodily needs come up time and again, to make moral and political claims for fair treatment and the just distribution of public goods.

Thus, while the ideals of the public good may be criticised for being partial, exclusionary, and failing to gain universalising voice, the precarity wrought by the destruction of redistributive mechanisms and public services may still galvanise an assembly of protesters to secure a more liveable life for themselves, but also for all (Butler, 2015, p. 183). Butler advocates for nonviolent protest to constitute a different world from the one that people encounter and resist. Collectives of protesters may encounter violence from the state and other authorities, but Butler argues that they must refuse to reproduce the terms of violence. Butler poses a similar question to that of Adorno — can one act as if a good public life is possible while living in a bad public life? Adorno pithily pronounces that "wrong life cannot be lived rightly" (Butler 2015, p. 193). This is echoed by those who point to the structure of inequality, exploitation, and effacement that continue to persist and the cruel optimism (Berlant, 2011), haunting the people who continue striving to improve this bad structure which keeps on structurally and systematically closing itself to so many.

The public sphere as we currently know it is a space in which higher education is deeply contested. All around the world, students and staff are mobilising against conditions and policies that have continuously disadvantaged certain types of bodies and persons, deeming their work and lives to be less than human, less intelligible, less rewardable, and less grievable. All body politics must begin by recognising interdependency, and this establishes a relation between precarity and performativity, vulnerability, and performative politics (Butler, 2015). When people gather to rally against neoliberalism-induced conditions of precarity, they are assembling and acting performatively against that precarity. The performativity of protest politics emerges from conditions of precarity, with an overarching demand for a liveable life. Shared vulnerability makes it both necessary and possible to demand that bodies have what they need to survive, and survival is surely a precondition for all the other claims that might be made (Butler, 2015). The imperative of survival brings into focus how principles of equality and interdependency might be fairly realised in opposition to the unfair distribution of precarity.

The "higher" aspects of higher education relate to its educational economy beyond the restriction of production. Publicness can be linked to "good" by reference to academic integrity, the proper exercise of autonomy afforded by the principle of academic freedom, but also to its function as a "holding environment" in Honig's terms. The alternative economy of higher education includes aspects of darkness and the pedagogical possibilities that they bring. The educative "obstinacy" and "higher" characteristics remain in tension with myriad and insistent demands that higher education serve society (specifically, employers), be "engaged", have "relevance" and "impact". The gift of time and space (Williams, 2012) and the resistant and "obstinate" nature of the pedagogical activity and the educative enterprise (Biesta, 2019) are crucial to the development of democratic and epistemic capabilities, fostering generative "negative capabilities" to entertain "uncertainties, mysteries, doubts", without immediately having to reduce understanding down to bald forms of fact and reason.

Aine Mahon's delightful collection *The Promise of the University: Reclaiming Humanity, Humility, and Hope* gestures towards a dawning of a very different sort of higher education as "a humane, humble and hopeful project whose unique potential is staked on a very delicate trust between participating parties" (Mahon, 2021, p. 1). This delicate hope feels like an unexpected balm. Perhaps we have become too used to rough treatment. I began this essay with malediction because higher education's falling darkness sometimes feels to me like a mentally and physically violent assault. At other times, it feels like a bucket of voided waste being tipped onto my head. Sometimes I feel like higher education is trying to kill me, so it wasn't surprising when the words and metaphors to describe higher education were dark and violent — attack, corrosion, even death. None of these descriptions of darkness harbour the gentler sense of anticipated darkness, the darkness of regular, cyclical crepuscular descent, boding rest and restoration with the anticipation of dawn.

This chapter has cursed the darkness of neoliberalism and considered the uses of public things. We may conclude by moving from occult darkness to dwelling within darkness' more gentle ethos. The insightful, restful, restorative, and regenerative aspects of darkness may prove invaluable for sustaining public things and continuing the social-democratic, educational, and research work of higher education in dark times. As darkness falls, we may curse it because we are not ready to surrender to neoliberalism's voiding. We need public higher education to persist as a repository of transitional objects that offer a holding environment for the generation of social democratic possibilities (Honig, 2015). Liveable lives, health, and public higher education are ideas to postpone the end of the world. Instead of pushing the disadvantaged further into a zone of difference marked by discrimination and deprivation, public things keep alive the possibility of building back a common, social-democratic shared world. Returning to Heaney's hope, that "hope is something that is there to be worked for, is worth working for, and can work" (Johnson, 2002, para. 11), perhaps we can still harbour hope for higher education as a public and democratic something — fostering a sense of commitment and readiness to work towards possibilities for a shared and more socially just world to come.

Acknowledgements

Irish Research Council project grant Coalesce/2019/88 provided opportunities that contributed towards the writing of this chapter.

References

Ahmed, S. (2021). *Complaint!* Duke University Press.

Arendt, H. (2013). *The human condition*. University of Chicago Press. (Original work published in 1958).

Barnett, R., & Bengtsen, S. (2021). Into or out of the light? Four shades of pedagogical darkness. In A. Mahon (Ed.), *Debating higher education: Philosophical perspectives: The promise of the university* (pp. 147–58). Springer.

Bataille, G. (1991). *The accursed share* (H. Robert, Trans.). Zone Books.

Berlant, L. (2011). *Cruel optimism*. Duke University Press.

Bhambra, G. (2021). Colonial global economy: Towards a theoretical reorientation of political economy. *Review of International Political Economy, 28*(1), 307–22. https://doi.org/10.1080/09692290.2020.1830831

Biesta, G. (2019). *Obstinate education: Reconnecting school and society*. Brill.

Brinkhof, T. (2022, January 22). *What is "Dark Academia," and why is it trending on social media in 2022?* BIG THINK. https://bigthink.com/high-culture/dark-academia/

Brod, M. (1960). *Franz Kafka: A biography* (R. Winston & G. H. Roberts, Trans.). Schocken Books

Brown, W. (2015). *Undoing the demos: Neoliberalism's stealth revolution*. Princeton University Press.

Butler, J. (2015). *Notes toward a performative theory of assembly*. Harvard University Press.

Crouch, C. (2011). *The strange non-death of neoliberalism*. Polity Press.

de Sousa Santos, B. (2007, 29 June). *Beyond abyssal thinking: From global lines to ecologies of knowledges*. EUROZINE. https://www.eurozine.com/beyond-abyssal-thinking/

Dewey, J. (1927). *The public and its problems*. Holt Publishers.

Eltahawy, M. (2020, December 18). *Why I say "Fuck"*. FEMINIST GIANT. https://www.feministgiant.com/p/essay-why-i-say-fuck

Fleming, P. (2021). *Dark academic: How universities die*. Pluto Press.

Gerbaudo, P. (2016, November 4). *Post-neoliberalism and the politics of sovereignty*. Open Democracy. https://www.opendemocracy.net/en/post-neoliberalism-and-politics-of-sovereignty/

Giroux, H. (2005). Cultural studies in dark times: Public pedagogy and the challenge of neoliberalism. *Fast Capitalism, 1*(2), 75–86. https://doi.org/10.32855/fcapital.200502.010

Goldberg, D. T. (2021). *Dread: Facing futureless futures*. Polity.

Guo, C. (2021, September 2). Book review: Dark academia: How universities die by Peter Fleming. [Review of the book *Dark academia: How universities die* by Peter Fleming] *LSE Review of Books*. https://blogs.lse.ac.uk/lsereviewofbooks/2021/09/02/book-review-dark-academia-how-universities-die-by-peter-fleming/

Harris, C. (2020). Reflections on whiteness as property. *Harvard Law Review, 134*(1), 1–10.
https://harvardlawreview.org/wp-content/uploads/2020/08/134-Harv.-L.-Rev.-F.-1-2.pdf

Honig, B. (2015). *Public things: Democracy in disrepair*. Fordham University Press.

Honig, B. (2022, January 18). *Maid in America: Whiteness as property*. Politics and Letters.
http://politicsslashletters.org/commentary/maid-in-america-whiteness-as-property/

Horgan, A. (2021, December 19). *The "dark academia" subculture offers a fantasy alternative to the neoliberal university*. Jacobin.
https://jacobin.com/2021/12/instagram-tumblr-humanities-romanticism-old-money-uk

Johnson, M. (2013, April 7). *Bataille's "the accursed share" and Absence: An analytical approach to data, decision and economics*. Improvisation Blog.
http://dailyimprovisation.blogspot.com/2013/04/batailles-accursed-share-and-absence.html

Johnson, S. (2002, October 31). *Seamus Heaney: "Hope is something that is there to be worked for"*. Independent.
https://www.independent.co.uk/arts-entertainment/books/features/seamus-heaney-hope-is-something-that-is-there-to-be-worked-for-141727.html

Jones, P., & Stokke, K. (Eds), (2005). *Democratising development: The politics of socio-economic rights in South Africa*. Martinus Nijhoff Publishers.

Keval, H., & Wright, T. (2021). Necropolitical constructions of happiness, COVID-19 and higher education. *Critical Studies on Security, 9*(2), 169–73.
https://doi.org/10.1080/21624887.2021.1978644

Khoo, S. (2014). Public goods: From market efficiency to democratic effectiveness. In R. Andrews (Ed.), *Commonwealth governance handbook 2013/14* (pp. 97–100) Commonwealth Secretariat.

Khoo, S. (2016). Public scholarship and alternative economies: Revisiting democracy and justice in higher education imaginaries. In T. Shultz, & M. Viczko (Eds), *Assembling and governing the higher education institution democracy, social justice and leadership in global higher education* (pp. 149–74). Palgrave Macmillan.

Khoo, S. (2017). Engaging development and human rights curriculum in higher education in the neoliberal twilight zone. *Policy and Practice: A Development Education Review, 25*, 34–58.
https://www.developmenteducationreview.com/issue/issue-25/engaging-development-and-human-rights-curriculum-higher-education-neoliberal-twilight

Khoo, S. (2022). Decolonising political economy: Reading: "Capital and imperialism" at neoliberalism's crisis conjuncture. *Policy and Practice: A Development Education Review, 34*, 76–94.
https://www.developmenteducationreview.com/issue/issue-34/decolonising-political-economy-reading-capital-and-imperialism-neoliberalism%E2%80%99s-crisis

Khoo, S., & Floss, M. (2022). Surviving necropolitical developments amidst democratic disinformation: A pandemic perspective from Brazil. In G. McCann, N. Mishra, & P. Carmody (Eds), *COVID-19, the Global South, and the pandemic's development impact* (pp. 9–23). Bristol University Press. https://doi.org/10.51952/9781529225679.ch001

Khurana, I., & Narayan, J. (2021). (After) Neoliberalism? Rethinking the return of the state. *Discover Society: New Series, 1*(4).
https://doi.org/10.51428/dsoc.2021.04.0003

Knott, M. L. (2013). *Unlearning with Hannah Arendt*. Penguin Random House.

Krenak, A. (2020). *Ideas to postpone the end of the world*. House of Anansi Press.

Lysgaard, J. A., Bengtsson, S. H., & Laugesen, M. H. L. (2019). *Dark pedagogy: Education, horror and the Anthropocene*. Palgrave MacMillan.

Lysgaard, J. A., & Bengtsson, S. (2020). Dark pedagogy, speculative realism and environmental and sustainability education. *Environmental Education Research, 26*(9–10), 1453–65.
https://doi.org/10.1080/13504622.2020.1739230

Mahon, A. (2021). The gift of an interval? Revisiting the promises of higher education. In A. Mahon (Ed.), *The promise of the university: Reclaiming humanity, humility, and hope* (pp. 1–13). Springer.

Marks, S. (2011). Human rights and root causes. *The Modern Law Review, 74*(1), 57–78.
https://doi.org/10.1111/j.1468-2230.2010.00836.x

Mbembé, J. A. (2003). Necropolitics (L. Meintjes, Trans.). *Public Culture, 15*(1), 11–40.
https://muse.jhu.edu/article/39984

Mbembé, J. A. (2019). *Necropolitics*. Duke University Press.

Meer, N. (2022). *The cruel optimism of racial injustice*. Policy Press.

Mulgan, T. (2011). *Ethics for a broken world: Imagining philosophy after catastrophe*. Cambridge University Press.

Patnaik, P., & Patnaik, U. (2021). *Capitalism and imperialism: Theory, history and the present*. Monthly Review Press.

Raunig, G. (2012). *Factories of knowledge, industries of creativity* (A. Derieg, Trans.). MIT Press.

Readings, B. (1997). *The university in ruins*. Harvard University Press.

Ritzer, G., & Ryan, M. (2002). The globalization of nothing, social thought & research. *Postmodernism, Globalization, and Politics, 25*(1/2), 51–81.
https://www.jstor.org/stable/23250006

Schuurman, F. J. (2009). Critical development theory: Moving out of the twilight zone. *Third World Quarterly, 30*(5), 831–48.
https://doi.org/10.1080/01436590902959024

Scott, J. C. (1985). *Weapons of the weak: Everyday forms of peasant resistance*. Yale University Press.

Shreve, G. (2018, April 4). *"Quit lit" then and now*. Inside Higher Ed.
https://www.insidehighered.com/views/2018/04/04/comparison-quit-lit-1970s-and-today-opinion

Springer, S. (2016). Fuck neoliberalism. *ACME: An International Journal for Critical Geographies, 15*(2), 285–92.
https://acme-journal.org/index.php/acme/article/view/1342

Stein, S. (2022). *Unsettling the university: Confronting the colonial foundations of US higher education*. Johns Hopkins University Press.

Tuck, E., & Yang, K. W. (2012). Decolonization is not a metaphor. *Decolonization: Indigeneity, Education and Society, 1*(1), 1–40.
https://jps.library.utoronto.ca/index.php/des/article/view/18630

Waters, T. (2020). Irish cursing and the art of magic, 1750–2018. *Past & Present, 247*(1), 113–49.
https://doi.org/10.1093/pastj/gtz051

Williams, K. (1989). The gift of an interval: Michael Oakeshott's idea of a university education. *British Journal of Educational Studies, 37*(4), 384–97.
https://www.tandfonline.com/doi/epdf/10.1080/00071005.1989.9973826

4. Imagining higher education as infrastructures of care

Leslie Chan, Mona Ghali, and Paul Prinsloo

Universities are rarely characterised as extractive, having largely evaded critiques levelled commonly against extractive industries like mining. The COVID-19 pandemic has amplified extractive processes due to the increased reliance on digital platforms and infrastructure controlled by corporate players known for extractive business models built on surveillance, technocratic control, and non-transparent governance. This essay is an exercise in reimagining the "good" university as an institution enabled by infrastructures of care in contradistinction to extractive infrastructures.

We begin by laying out why an infrastructural lens is essential for revealing extractive infrastructure's deep history and politics and how they became entangled with higher education institutions (HEIs). By taking an infrastructural approach, we suggest care is highly contingent upon infrastructures that predispose persons and groups within higher education institutions to embody and enact care. Then, we use a variety of historical and contemporary examples centred around three themes of land, bodies, and data, including land grant universities, slave economies, internationalisation strategies, labour precarity, and learning management systems (LMS) — to show how extractive logics operate, who benefits, and who suffers harm. We then reflect on educational infrastructures as complex socio-techno-political systems that are continually captured by iterations of colonial relations and racial capitalist logic. Finally, we discuss the principles integral to reimagining universities as infrastructures of care.

We authors include an independent education researcher and two long-time educators and education researchers situated in prominent HEIs in the North and the South. We share a common concern for how higher education policies, procedures, and practices reinforce a technocratic infrastructure of extraction and exclusion; how they manifest in the prolific use of performance metrics, surveillance technologies, inequitable assessment practices, asymmetrical private-public partnerships, discourses of work readiness and employability as well as in the precarity in academic employment and beyond.

Why an infrastructural lens?

Infrastructures are fundamentally socio-techno-political in that technical components are embedded in social relationships, institutions, and practices that contribute to their persistence (Franklin, 1990). At the same time, infrastructures co-constitute social and political practices. In this way, infrastructures define the conditions for possible actions while at the same time precluding or foreclosing other possibilities of social practices and relations (Coutard & Shove, 2018). A crude example is a school building with no accessibility features that would likely preclude or impede the participation of students with disabilities.

Infrastructures also assume multiple forms. As material infrastructures, universities facilitate the flow of persons and ideas across time and space (Larkin, 2013). As knowledge infrastructures (Bowker, 2018), HEIs are sites where knowledge is classified, disciplined, (re)created, (in)validated, and disseminated, and where epistemic and social relations of power are subtended and reproduced. Infrastructures are also affective and summon emotions tied with dualisms of self-other, human-nature, success-failure. Selfies of ebullient graduates against some iconic campus structures are not just Instagram-worthy posts, they are declarative statements of success that are linked to both their location and identity. Places have stories, though dominant stories by the powerful often erase the real and deep history of places and the original inhabitants.

These three infrastructural forms — material, knowledge, and affective — inform social relations that can be located along a spectrum spanning from purposefully extractive to generative and caring practices. We focus on infrastructures that orient or predispose individual and organisational behaviours toward extractive or caring relations and actions, as shown in Figure 4.1, and we focus on three broad and intersecting themes of Land, Bodies and Data to illustrate how extraction logic operates in contradistinction to the infrastructure of care. While we understand that HEIs will never be free of extractive practices, our aspiration is to encourage practices and designs that increasingly centre the principles of care.

Figure 4.1

Spectrum of infrastructures

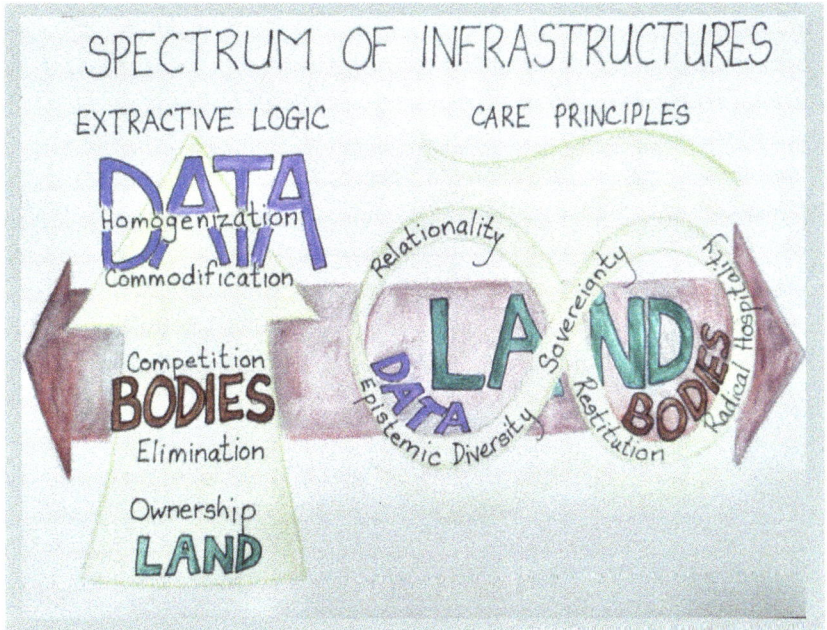

Infrastructures of care and extraction are governed by different logics. Extraction is characterised by colonial logics of elimination, ownership, commodification, and homogenisation that contribute to the erasure, dispossession, and marginalisation of certain groups based on hierarchical relations of power. In contrast, infrastructures of care are governed by logics of reciprocity, reparation, gifting, sovereignty, hospitality, and epistemic pluralism that support a deep relationality and respect for the land and non-human life forms (Simpson 2014;

Tallbear & Willey, 2019). Notions of "the good" grounded in different cosmologies/spiritualities are centred on human interconnection and our "radical interdependence" with the earth (Escobar 2018; Mignolo, 2014). By extension, the "good" university is entangled with the land (water and air) on which it exists, faculty members, administrators, and students, academic and non-academic partners, support workers, and surrounding communities.

In making this argument, we examine how infrastructures affect the capacity of individuals and groups to exercise autonomy in relation to land, bodies, and data. We focus on these material, corporal, and data fields because the evolution of higher education systems has been contingent on the allocation of lands, the expansion of higher education through cheap and unpaid labour, internationalisation, and assetisation of data for measuring productivity and institutional effectiveness (Dijck et. al. 2018; Komljenovic, 2021; Williamson, 2017; Williamson et al., 2020). At the same time, these three domains are interconnected since place shapes knowledge, knowledge is embodied, and bodies are sites for extraction. While data is the most recent frontier, the evolution of universities suggests that extractive infrastructures date to the origins of higher education institutions through land grants, the "gift" of land by settler colonial governments to incentivise the development of HEIs in newly acquired territories through "treaties" designed to dispossess Indigenous people from their land while deeply enriching the new landlords.

Land

It is now common across Canadian, US, New Zealand, and Australian universities to open public meetings, lectures, and ceremonies with a land acknowledgement, "a formal statement recognising the unique and enduring relationship that exists between Indigenous peoples and their traditional territories."[1] While such acknowledgements are meant to honour and express gratitude to past and present Indigenous peoples connected to the lands on which the university is built, they

---

1 For an example, see https://indigenous.utoronto.ca/about/land-acknowledgement/

rarely acknowledge the expulsion of peoples and the dispossession of Indigenous lands. This practice also leaves unproblematised the violent colonial histories, policies, and legal frameworks of settler colonial governments that "othered" Indigenous peoples and attempted to erase their culture and epistemologies.

Land-grant universities, in countries like Canada and the United States, wherein "public" lands were donated to establish higher education institutions, conformed to a "logic of elimination" (Wolfe, 2006). Apart from the use or threat of use of force to control land, settler colonial governments incentivised homesteading of European settlers and provided social infrastructure such as schools and universities for newcomers and growing communities. These policies resulted in the erasure of Indigenous peoples through forcible transfer and territorial displacement to reserves and attempted cultural assimilation through Indian residential and day schools (Truth and Reconciliation Commission, 2015).

Variations of the logic of elimination were enacted across settler colonial states. The University of Auckland (New Zealand) benefited directly from the oppression of the Ngati Awa people, whose land was confiscated in 1865 for the university (Kuokkanen, 2011). In the US, the Morrill Land-Grant Acts of 1862, involving almost 11 million acres, established land-grant colleges from proceeds of the sale of federally owned land, often obtained from tribal nations through treaty, cession, or expropriation (Busch & Lucy, 2019; Lee & Ahtone, 2020). Following the land transfer, these universities continued to profit from their land holding through leasing and other financialisation arrangements (Valverde et al., 2020). As historian Caitlan Harvey (2021) calculates, the territoriality of land grant universities covers three continents, over 15 million acres, and implicates settler universities in the process of Indigenous dispossession and the subversion of Indigenous sovereignty.

Beyond their material infrastructure, land grant institutions constitute centres of knowledge production and innovation. These universities established new disciplinary fields like agricultural sciences and engineering that altered human relations with the land. Commercial farmers and plantation owners supported agricultural research institutes and extension services to raise production and efficiency and were early adopters of new technologies (Busch & Lacy, 2019). The spread of agricultural technologies transformed settler landscapes by replacing Indigenous knowledge systems that valorised human-nature relations with an extractive model of exploitation that now risks our planetary boundaries (Harvey, 2021).

The worldview of seeing the land as an infinite resource to be exploited and extracted has been at the core of Western expansionism and the ethos of modern science, positioning "man" above "nature", which is to be controlled and reconfigured to serve capitalism's insatiable need for raw materials and above all, cheap labour (an important topic, and the focus of the next section). Many higher education institutions are not only complicit in this form of racial capitalism but active in the ongoing extraction of land and bodies. As Mzileni and Mkhize (2019) noted, the "colonial nature of the university in South Africa is directly linked spatially to the historic land question of dispossession in South Africa" (p. 104). This preoccupation leaves little room for an ethics of care; and the respect, responsibility, and relationality with the land that are central to Indigenous ways of knowing and being have largely been dismissed by the institutions that continue to extract and benefit from the land, without any thought of giving back to what gives life and well-being in the first place. (Simpson 2014; Tuck and Yang 2012; Tynan 2021).

Sámi scholar, Kuokkanen (2007), detailed the limitations and harms caused by settler expectations and proposes in resonance with other Indigenous scholars and knowledge keepers, a different episteme, which she terms "the logic of the gift". This entails moving away from market-based exchanges that expect the transfer of value for value, or thing for other thing, which is founded on hegemonic standards of rationality, especially rational self-interest, and on the ideals of individual freedom. This market-based exchange economy model is so normalised within the academy that we seldom question its validity, "but it is this mentality of exchange, ownership, and competition, that has made it possible for the university and the 'value' it produces to be made to conform more and more to neo-liberal monetarist expectations" (Lange, 2010, p. 89).

The "gift logic" and its call for a communal-based exchange model resonates with the growing understanding of the importance of land-based pedagogy as practiced by many Indigenous communities around the world, while calling for the validation of Indigenous knowledge, epistemology, and ontology within the hegemonic structure of higher education (Fraser, 2022; Simpson, 2014). Escobar (2022) reminds us that throughout history and across cultures, human experience has largely been place-based and communal, enacted at the local level, and with deep respect for the land, the source of all life's gifts:

> This condition of existence is an important dimension of relationality and responds to the symbiotic co-emergence of living beings and their worlds, resulting in "communitarian entanglements" that make us kin to everything that is alive. Oaxacan activists refer to this dynamic as the *condicion nosótrica de ser*, the we-condition of being. If we see ourselves *nosótricamente*, we cannot but adopt the principles of love, care and compassion as ethics of living, starting with home, place and community — this not in order to isolate ourselves but to prepare for greater sharing rooted in autonomy, for communication and *compartencia* ("sharingness"). (para. 2)

Along with other Afro-Indigenous communities in Latin America, Escobar and other activist scholars call for new design thinking to transition our world of brutal extraction to a pluriverse, where many other worlds coexist in harmony and peace with the earth. In the final section of this paper, we explore how some of these design principles can inform how we nurture infrastructures of care in higher education.

Bodies

Extractive infrastructures commodify human bodies based on social constructions of difference (Bowker & Star, 2000). Due to space considerations, we limit the conversation to "bodies" differentiated by race, class, and precarity, while acknowledging that bodies othered by abilities and other dimensions have also been subject to harm and invisibility in the academy. With respect to race, economic historians document the association of higher education institutions with slave economies and racial capitalism (Robinson, 1983). In tandem with Black and Indigenous protest movements for racial justice like Black Lives Matter, Rhodes Must Fall, and Curriculum So White, archival searches of university records have made visible institutional ties to slavery.

While not directly involved in British slavery (1600–1838), British universities benefited from the unpaid labour of enslaved peoples. Some university founders, benefactors, and faculty were slave owners and traders, or trustees and family members of persons involved in the slave economies in the Caribbean (Draper 2018; Mullen, 2021). For example, Codrington Library at All Souls College Oxford was gifted books valued at £6,000 upon the death of Christopher Codrington in 1710, a sugar plantation owner and former governor of Barbados (Williams, 2021, p. 71).

In the United States, enslaved peoples who laboured on plantations contributed to the wealth of the white slaveholding class and, by extension, university endowments. In the case of Georgetown University, the Jesuits of Maryland sold 272 enslaved men, women, and children who worked on Jesuit plantations in 1838 for about $400 per person (Georgetown Slavery Archive, n.d.). Harvard University acknowledged its leadership, faculty, and staff enslaved at least 70 Black and Indigenous peoples. Its benefactors amassed their wealth through slave trading and the unpaid labour of slaves on plantations in the American South, northern textile industries, and the Caribbean. Their donations enabled the college to expand its faculty, buildings, student residences, and professorships (Harvard University, 2022). In other words, the commodification of black bodies enabled universities to amass endowments and fund research projects. At the same time, the social construction of racial hierarchies, endorsed by what Frederick Douglass called "scientific moonshine" legitimated slavery, segregation, the denial of Black people's access to formal education, and other racist practices (Harris et al., 2019).

Some social movements upset the status quo, disrupt self-other constructions, and dismantle extractive infrastructures with discourses of abolition, resurgence, or other expressions of resistance and solidarity. In the context of 21st century #IdleNoMore, #BlackLivesMatter and #RhodesMustFall protests, statues were felled or trucked away, building names were vetted, anti-racism policies were rolled out at higher education institutions, often framed as diversity, inclusion, and equity. The latter typically include actions to expand representation of underrepresented groups at all levels, including governance bodies, faculty, and student enrolment.

It remains unclear whether such reforms will make space for epistemic pluralism based on the lived experience and situated knowledge of groups historically subjected to systemic discrimination, or if inclusion will be thin and measured with facile metrics (Stein, 2017). Thin inclusion like liberal multiculturalism emphasises tolerance and fails to problematise both meritocracy and selection criteria established by the dominant group that makes invisible alternative forms of knowledge. The concept of meritocracy emphasises individual responsibility and minimises historical, political, economic, and legal practices that privilege white faculty and students over others (Sandel, 2020). These include legacy admission practices, historical and ongoing systemic violence including land expropriation, institutional slavery, mass incarceration, and denial of property, civil, political, and social rights that disqualified e.g. non-European, non-Christians, and women from accessing education. Here again, we see evidence how infrastructures are not static; they morph in response to resistance and may be reinvented to reinforce underlying logics and unequal power relations.

Internationalisation and academic precarity

Since the 1990s, new forms of commodification have arisen with internationalisation policies in the context of demographic shifts in western states. This is accompanied by increasing domestic student debt levels commensurate with rising tuition fees. Since economic growth rates selectively enabled the expansion of a middle and upper middle class in China, India, and elsewhere capable of paying a premium for study abroad, universities compete for these elite populations. In some cases, Canada for example, inbound student mobility is conjoined with immigration policies that offer youthful, foreign graduates a pathway to citizenship to generate "work-ready" newcomer Canadians in the context of demographic transition. In Canada, international students contributed more to the country's economy than auto parts, lumber, and aircraft exports. They spent $CDN 21.6 billion on tuition, accommodation, and other educational expenditures in 2018, and international graduates filled 170,000 jobs in 2016 (Government of Canada, 2019).

Increased competition for international students links universities with other extractive infrastructures. These include student recruitment and immigration agencies, private tutoring services, SAT, IELTS, and TOEFL test preparation companies. Competition also reinforces the use of national, regional, and global university ranking systems as universities seek positional advantage in league tables to signal higher education excellence (Hazelkorn, 2015). These rankings and their composite indicators inform institutional policies and resource allocation decisions, data sharing with private data analytics companies, actions that ensure better conformity to standards, and translate into improved results in league tables (Chen & Chan, 2021). Moreover, these standards elicit behaviour in ways that are not necessarily visible. Shahjahan et al. (2021) claim that rankers like Times Higher Education (THE) and Quacquarelli Symonds Ltd (QS) use their social media platforms as an affective infrastructure to evince certain emotions and desires among their audience including parents, students, and HEIs that help sustain, diffuse, and normalise global university rankings. Storytelling by tweets, hashtags, and reactions enables rankers to create feedback loops with HEIs through congratulatory remarks to top scorers and positive chart movers, and to convince students that it is a trusted and compassionate source for information to support decision-making.

While the use of contract staff predates internationalisation policies, universities have scaled up the recruitment of part-time teaching staff concurrent with expansion of international students and cuts in public spending. For example, sessional lecturers and part-time instructors hired to teach a specific course vary in motivation for academic contract work. Some may enjoy teaching and have full-time employment or alternative sources of income. In these cases, sessional teaching supplements income. Others, including recent graduates and post-doctoral researchers, use it as an interim phase while searching for a full-time teaching position to obtain teaching evaluations necessary for tenure-track positions or long-term contract academic work (Field & Jones, 2016).

Extraction largely affects the latter group, an unlikely segment of the "precariat", which is characterised by unstable labour and insecurity, undervalued or unpaid work, as well as the erosion of rights, including economic rights (Standing, 2011). With the expansion of enrolment at all levels, the surplus pool of applicants has outstripped the number of open full-time faculty positions, contributing to hardship and disaffection for some unsuccessful candidates. For university administrators, this surplus provides an opportunity to recruit overqualified persons for positions that do not require specialised knowledge, research, and analytical skills, thereby intensifying competition for those roles with MA degree holders. Moreover, while precarity may be a condition of this class of instructors, the decision to exit academia cuts across early to late-stage academics. This is due to the increased demands for productivity that disproportionately affect females because of the feminisation of child and elder care, poor work-life balance, and implicit biases that sway promotions and tenure away from persons from ethnic and racialised groups (Gewin, 2022).

This discussion conveys the extraordinary reach of extractive infrastructures, their embeddedness in historical and contemporary forms of capitalism, and complicity in global inequality.

Data

A growing number of scholars (Benjamin, 2019; Browne, 2015; Dhaliwal, 2022; McIlwain, 2019; Noble, 2018) and research initiatives document how surveillance practices, datafication of bodies, and algorithmic governance are well rehearsed colonial practices now encoded into digital infrastructure, both computational hardware and software architectures. They are continually reshaping our cultural imaginaries, political-economic frameworks, and epistemic beliefs about education and its purpose in accordance with market and capitalist logic. Accordingly, it is important to explore digital platforms such as Learning Management Systems (LMS) that have become part of the standard operating procedures of HEIs in pandemic times. As universities adjusted to the COVID-19 lockdowns and governments increased spending on digital solutions, the pandemic presented an opportunity for enterprising, cloud-based, learning platform providers and digital education consultants to expand their market share in response to surging demand.

We focus here on LMSs because they constitute socio-political-technological infrastructures for organising the flow of student bodies by structuring courses, storing teaching and learning materials, managing communications, and monitoring academic performance. Providers like Canvas, Blackboard, D2L, and Moodle constitute more than technical solutions for translocating curricular materials from the physical to the virtual environment. Knowledge managed in learning management platforms and stored in digitised and data-field forms on institutional servers or in "the cloud" is characterised by several features that differentiate today's storage systems from historical depositories like archives and libraries. Yet, like earlier knowledge depositories, it does not escape epistemic violence, the imposition of hegemonic epistemic frameworks that establish and entrench practices of domination while erasing other ways of seeing and making sense of the world (Fricker, 2009; Spivak, 1988).

First, it is crucial to understand and interrogate "the cloud" as much more than a convenient storage for data but as linked to the previous discussions of land, bodies, and (academic) precarity. Far from being placeless and ethereal, "the cloud" is deeply embedded in the imperial and colonial history of the West, as its transglobal infrastructure of server farms, cables, and routers largely depend on colonial occupation (Hu, 2015). We cannot talk about "the cloud" without considering how it acts as a superstructure disembodying land and bodies, and presents data-as-resource to be used, reused, cleaned, massaged, and cooked.

Second, learning management platforms make possible a myriad of ways of analysing and extracting knowledge not just with unprecedented speed, but also remoteness from the site of learning — thereby decontextualising the data and stripping it of its sovereignty. Third, data can be mobilised to generate "objective" representations of academic achievement (such as percentile ranking) and recommendations on pathways for completion based on past academic performance, effectively streaming students without regard for contributing factors not measured. Fourth, designing for interoperability allows platforms to use third-party apps and the extraction of data far beyond the LMS, thus expanding the highly profitable surveillance edtech economy (Marachi & Quill, 2020). The array of these vendors suggests that they not only provide a service or product, but they also define the rules of the game in terms of educational objectives (Williamson 2020, 2022).

These features of the new digitised containers are the product of the confluence of factors internal and external to the university. They include the failure of academic institutions to invest adequately in research and development of independent open-source learning platforms and cybersecurity systems (see also Amiel & do Rozário Diniz, Chapter 18, this volume). When combined with fiscal constraints due to downward pressures on public investment in higher education, HEIs have tended to outsource infrastructure provision to save on capital investment.

We also see the rise of philanthropic foundations integrated in global educational governance systems promoting specific socio-technical imaginaries in a post-pandemic world (Tompkins-Strange, 2020). These imaginaries respond to concerns about student success, retention, and employability. Under these circumstances, it comes as no surprise that edtech companies offer data as "prosthetic vision" (Beer, 2019, p. 7), and a particular imaginary of the affordances of data. Student data is a "data frontier" where data can be extracted and the student experience colonised (Beer, 2019; Prinsloo, 2020). In exchange for extraction, they offer analytics as *"speedy, accessible, revealing, panoramic, prophetic* and *smart"* (Beer, 2019, p. 22). This imaginary is ultimately realised through algorithmic decision-making.

Recent contributions by Birch et al. (2021) and Komljenovic (2021) adopt the concept "data rentiership". They suggest that personal data, when aggregated, can be mined and sold to generate rents that share similarities with extractive industries producing commodities, like oil, minerals, and illicit goods. Data rentiership entails the generation of revenue from ownership and control of a data asset due to constructed value of the data (Birch et al., 2020). While it is important not to overstate the parallels between rentier states and data rentiership in HEIs, nonetheless the comparison is worth exploring. Commercial LMS providers negotiate agreements with a small cadre of managers typically not inclusive of student or faculty representatives. Like mining companies, they offer a reciprocal, if unequal exchange, providing technologies, maintenance, and upgrades for operating platforms in return for licensing fees and far more important, data assets. These assets are turned into analytics that are then sold back to the HEIs and a multiple of buyers at much higher costs. But these costs far exceed monetary terms.

Rentier state theory is instructive in highlighting the potential risks in the absence of social mobilisation that checks the power of private companies on the one hand (i.e. land grabs, environmental degradation, and labour exploitation), and incentivises conflict on the other hand. These risks in HEIs include the potential (mis)use of learning analytics like user engagement metrics to create new products that address poor academic performance among "at-risk" students. They may use metrics to inform university policies and practices regarding admission criteria and program offerings to improve graduation and employability rates, hence gaming performance-based financing systems wherein government accountability mechanisms peg financing levels to results. Finally, they may exercise influence to lobby for loosening data privacy regulations to enable more intrusive data collection and mining systems.

While the full downstream impact of data extraction in HEIs may only become clear in the future, we can learn from other harmful surveillance technologies such as proctoring software using facial recognition technologies and plagiarism software based on text matching (Caines & Silverman, 2021; Gilliard & Selwyn, 2022). So far, learning management and financial systems operate on separate platforms. If these were merged, then data analytics would combine students' social-economic status with academic performance. With the concentration of platform providers, a relatively small number of companies would control a volume of global data and generate predictive analytics with machine learning that could conceivably influence decision making including admissions, thereby reducing students to economically productive individuals dislocated from place and history.

Resource-poor institutions might be forced to open their platforms to commercial advertisers and private companies, and buy pre-packaged course content to offset costs. If rentier state theory has predictive value, it suggests that institutional policies and practices might be driven by short-term decision making designed to improve enrolment, retention, graduation rates, and ranking positions within global ranking systems, and to curate disciplinary forms of knowledge that contribute to "work-ready" graduates. In other words, the private firms that own the LMS platforms might begin to guide decision-making on course provision based on selective judgements regarding valuable/superior versus worthless/inferior forms of knowledge in relation to the marketplace. Epistemic violence will no longer be enacted in spectacular bonfires, but in opaque algorithmic decision making. At its extreme, the rentier university is a dystopian imaginary of institutions with selective memory, coupled tightly to capitalist forms of production, and wayward from its missional purpose as a public good.

Critical explorations of data colonialism (Couldry & Mejias, 2019), surveillance capitalism (Zuboff, 2019), digital serfdom (Fairfield, 2017), and technoscientific capitalism (Birch et al., 2020) bespeak the risks of data collection, aggregator platforms and using data for profiteering. Like historical colonialism, data colonialism changes the evolution of economic and social relations, distributes benefits from resource appropriation unequally, and normalises datafication of all aspects of life to support capitalism (Couldry & Mejias, 2019). Data extraction is not only intensified, but also expanded to "data frontiers" — *terra nullius* spaces (geopolitical, personal, social, and private) — ripe for the picking (Prinsloo, 2020). The parallel between data colonialism and land-grab universities are becoming clear. Just like the universities benefit from land grants, while ignoring Indigenous land claims and epistemologies, the ownership, control, and use of personal student and faculty data erases the situated knowledges and claims to data sovereignty.

In the context of this chapter, we must consider how to move from data extraction and data colonialism to data as in service of care. It is, however, crucial that in the context of data-as-care, we distinguish between current practices where the extraction of data is portrayed as care, e.g. learning analytics to support students, data-as-care distanced from capitalist accumulation, and colonial and patriarchal relations (Ricaurte, 2022). Data sovereignty is a multidimensional concept encompassing much more than the right to know *why* individuals' data are collected, *by whom* and *combined* with other databases, and *reformatting* for other purposes, but rather to have full control about the scope and purpose of collection as well as ownership of data (Hummel et al 2021). Linked to the notion of data sovereignty is the notion of data-as-repair, emerging from commitments of restitution, reparation, and repair (e.g. Zolkos, 2020).

In moving towards data-as-care, we must acknowledge and account for how data emerges from and perpetuates structural inequalities, erasure, and intergenerational trauma. Data-as-care means data sovereignty and repairing its inequalities means acknowledging the situated knowledge(s) of women and girls, racialised groups, Indigenous communities, immigrants, refugees, persons with disabilities, non-binary people, and rural communities to understand algorithmic harms (D'Ignazio & Klein 2020; Costanza-Chock 2020; Ricaurte, 2022).

Glimpses of infrastructure as care: Data sovereignty and epistemic pluralism

Several projects offer insights into how infrastructures of care can be imagined and defined. The Papa Reo project (Papa Reo, n.d.), located in Māori, envisions the enabling of "smaller indigenous language communities to develop their own speech recognition and natural language processing capabilities, ensuring that the sovereignty of the data remains with them and the benefits derived from these technologies goes directly to their communities." The project arises from the reality that minority languages and the communities who speak these languages are "largely invisible and unheard in the digital world", and due to the absence of large data sets required for machine learning, peoples speaking minority languages cannot engage and participate fully in a digitally networked world. In this project, Indigenous land and culture intersect with language, making different bodies possible using a different digital infrastructure. Significant in the context of this article is the undertaking that the data used in the Papa Reo project will not be owned by the initiative but "cared for under the principle of *kaitiakitanga* [guardianship] and any benefit derived from data flows to the source of the data" (Papa Reo, n.d.). This implies guardianship instead of ownership of the data. Those undertaking the initiative are seen as "caretakers of the data and seek to ensure that all decisions made about the use of that data respect its mana and that of the people from whom it descends" (Papa Reo, n.d.).

Other examples of data-as-care include the *CARE Principles for Indigenous Data Governance* and the *Indigenous Protocol and Artificial Intelligence* (Carroll et al., 2020; Lewis, 2020). Both affirm the centrality of Indigenous knowledge and self-determination in the governance, design, and use of data systems. CARE principles of Collective benefit, Authority of control, Responsibility, and Ethics, affirm Indigenous control of data and mitigate harm from data appropriation and misuse (Lewis, 2020, p. 4). The Protocol provides guidelines for the ethical design, use, role, and rights of artificial intelligence (AI) entities, which include acknowledging locality (specific territories), relationality (to humans, non-human species, and the earth), responsibility, awareness of cultural and social systems, and data sovereignty. The guidelines indicate that AI should be co-designed with and responsive and accountable to local communities and connect to global contexts. Rather than uniformity and standardisation, the protocol acknowledges variation between specific communities. These principles indicate that AI system designers need to be aware of their cultural biases and accommodate other cultural and social frameworks in decision-making. Every component of the AI system hardware and software stack should be considered in the ethical evaluation of the system given that their raw materials are extracted from the earth and may one day return there. Indigenous communities must control how their data is solicited, collected, analysed, and operationalised, and decide when to protect and share it, where the cultural and intellectual property rights reside and to whom those rights adhere, and how these rights are governed.

These projects conceived by Indigenous and Non-Indigenous peoples are instructive for the "good" university in both how they were developed through consultative processes, and their articulation as a set of principles grounded in Indigenous knowledge systems that value guardianship over ownership, and life rights over human rights (Mignolo, 2014). In much the same way, the "good" university cannot assume that data governance systems will protect the rights of students, staff, and faculty, communities, or the environment. Norms and rules regulating the reuse and dissemination of the knowledge produced, disseminated through learning management systems, and other data platforms must affirm the control and sovereignty of academic faculty, staff, and students. To this end, negotiations must be inclusive of representatives from these groups and transparent. Given the concentration of power among platform providers, universities might find common purposes and create codes of conduct to regulate contractors and establish principles that affirm data and epistemic sovereignty (see also Pechenkina, Chapter 9, this volume). These should be the minimum duty of care when negotiating with vendors on infrastructural provision.

Discussion

Thus far, we outlined how infrastructures of extraction have become the default at higher education institutions. Only with active resistance and its inversion (Bowker, 2018) do infrastructures of care emerge to expose shortcomings and contest inequities. At each reversible turn to care from extraction, persons or groups once labelled as non-human beings or problems wilfully demand recognition, access, reparation, and justice. But even when more inclusive and just spaces are established, whether through selective recruitment of faculty, accommodative practices, affirmative action programs, protection of data privacy, pluriversal learning or other means, still, there may be efforts to subvert, diminish or otherwise steer reforms.

So, infrastructures of care can be differentiated into weak and strong forms spanning thin inclusion to decolonisation, from restorative to regenerative. They are always emergent, historically contingent, and subject to a clash of infrastructural mindsets, because there is no consensus around what constitutes "care" and a "good university". If framed mainly by efficiency and productivity, it produces extractive infrastructures that fetishise quantifiable and transactional relations. Care in this context simply means getting students to graduate on time and finding employment in their field.

Conversely, if the "good" university is framed by a relational ethic, then it leans toward material, epistemic, and affective infrastructures that are reparative insofar as they acknowledge complicity in historical and ongoing racial injustice, and act to atone with reforms in admission policies, scholarship programs and transitional pathways for racialised youth and adults, and provision of adequate academic support systems. Blanco (2021) writes on radical hospitality, which begins with exercising empathy. As applied here, care infrastructures that follow a logic of radical hospitality acknowledge a shared humanity, are redistributive, and affirm the public good. Hospitality is not solely governed by wealth; even resource poor institutions can practice hospitality. This can include decommodifying international students and making visible data on student drop out, suicide rates, and wellbeing that remains undocumented and anecdotal. Universities can extend the radical hospitality offered to Ukrainian refugee students following Russia's war in Ukraine in 2022 to other non-European refugee groups. But hospitality can be performative and patronising, just like thin inclusion. Guarding against thin hospitality demands attention to epistemic pluralism in design choices, including the design of holistic technologies, giving control and freedom to the users for flexible processes, not prescribed outcomes (Franklin, 1990). Such care infrastructures allow social actors or learners to be in charge, to strive in a non-hierarchical environment that is free from patriarchy, racial biases, and toxic competitiveness.

In our journey of collaborating on this chapter, we grappled with how forms of extractive infrastructures are entangled with one another. This involved two steps. First, peeling them apart to better understand the logics that underlie their durability and their differentiated impact on land, bodies, and data. Then we reassembled them to see the whole but not to create a roadmap for transformation from A to B packaged in a series of discrete moves. This might disappoint some. As extractive infrastructures are not specific to universities but are co-constituted by relationships beyond the academy, infrastructures of care may seem like dreamscapes. But both extractive and care-full infrastructures described in this chapter coexist in tension. Universities are never fully extractive, nor can they become totally caring; this is an obvious statement. On balance, based on the limited examples provided here, universities tend to bend toward extraction and constitute "sites for social reproduction and conquest denial" (Moten & Harney, 2013). Our injunction to reimagine the good university is offered with the qualification that there are no ready-made solutions to the complex problems of care and its provision in our institutional infrastructure. We take solace in the words of Ursula Franklin: "For your own sanity, you have to remember that not all problems can be solved. Not all problems can be solved, but all problems can be illuminated."[2] Still, our chapter, alongside others in this collection, is an invitation to reflect on the infrastructures that govern higher education institutions, their underlying logics, and intergenerational consequences in terms of who is harmed and, conversely, who benefits. Reflection is necessary but not sufficient. The next phase is to (re)design infrastructures — material, epistemic, and affective — governed by care principles. Already, such work is evidenced in distributed, decentralised initiatives involving faculty, students, community groups, and bottom-up networks (see examples in Hall & Tandon, 2021). This may include local organisations proximate to campus, as well as distal, transnational, and diasporic communities that seek to collaborate, learn, and find common purpose with differentiated

---

2   Quoted by M. Meredith. *All problems can be illuminated; not all problems can be solved. BB9.* http://bb9.berlinbiennale.de/all-problems-can-be-illuminated-not-all-problems-can-be-solved/

pathways and rebuff efforts to scale and speed up. These are not the same as "maroon communities" in the sense that they do not seek refuge separate from the wider, extractive university infrastructures. On the contrary, they seek to subvert these infrastructures, as groups engage across disciplinary and national boundaries, ethno-cultural and racial identities and other forms of difference with care.

References

Beer, D. (2019). *The data gaze: Capitalism, power and perception*. Sage.

Benjamin, R. (2019). *Race after technology: Abolitionist tools for the New Jim Code*. Polity books.

Birch, K., Chiappetta, M., & Artyushina, A. (2020). The problem of innovation in technoscientific capitalism: Data rentiership and the policy implications of turning personal digital data into a private asset. *Policy Studies, 41*(5), 468–87.
http://doi.org/10.1080/01442872.2020.1748264

Blanco, G. L. (2021). Higher education and the enduring value of hospitality: Reflections for the 21st century. In H. van't Land, A. Corcoran, & D. Iancu (Eds), *The promise of higher education: Essays in honour of 70 years of IAU* (pp. 175–79). Springer.
https://doi.org/10.1007/978-3-030-67245-4_27

Bowker, G. C. (2018). Sustainable knowledge infrastructures. In N. Anand, A. Gupta, & H. Appe (Eds), *The promise of infrastructures* (pp. 203–22). Duke University Press.
https://doi.org/10.1515/9781478002031-010

Bowker, G. C., & Star, S. L. (2000). *Sorting things out: Classification and its consequences*. MIT Press.
https://doi.org/10.7551%2Fmitpress%2F6352.001.0001

Browne, S. (2015). *Dark matters: On the surveillance of blackness*. Duke University Press.
https://doi.org/10.1215%2F9780822375302

Busch, L. M., & Lacy, W. B. (2019). *Science, agriculture, and the politics of research*. Routledge.
https://doi.org/10.4324/9780429305467

Caines, A., & Silverman, S. (2021). Back doors, trap doors, and fourth-party deals: How you end up with harmful academic surveillance technology on your campus without even knowing. *The Journal of Interactive Technology and Pedagogy, 20.*
https://jitp.commons.gc.cuny.edu/back-doors-trap-doors-and-fourth-party-deals-how-you-end-up-with-harmful-academic-surveillance-technology-on-your-campus-without-even-knowing/

Carroll, S. R., Garba, I., Figueora-Rodríguez, O. L., Holbrook, J., Lovett, R., Materechera, S., Parsons, M., Raseroka, K., Rodriguez-Lonebear, D., Rowe, R., Sara, R., Walker, J. D., Anderson, J., & Hudson, M. (2020). The CARE principles for Indigenous data governance. *Data Science Journal, 19*(43), 1–12. https://doi.org/10.5334/dsj-2020-043

Chen, G., & Chan, L. (2021). University rankings and governance by metrics and algorithms. In E. Hazelkorn & G. Mihu (Eds), *Research handbook on university rankings: Theory, methodology, influence, and impact* (pp. 425–43). Edward Elgar Publishing.
https://doi.org/10.4337/9781788974981.00043

Costanza-Chock, S. (2020). *Design justice: Community-led practices to build the worlds we need.* MIT Press.

Couldry, N., & Mejias, U. A. (2019). *The costs of connection. How data is colonizing human life and appropriating it for capitalism.* Stanford University Press.
https://doi.org/10.1515%2F9781503609754

Coutard, O., & Shove, E. (2018). Infrastructures, practices and the dynamics of demand. In E. Shove, and F. Trentmann (Eds), *Infrastructures in practice* (pp. 10–22). Routledge.
https://doi.org/10.4324/9781351106177

D'Ignazio, C., & Klein, L. F. (2020). *Data feminism.* The MIT Press.
https://data-feminism.mitpress.mit.edu/

Dhaliwal, R. S. (2022). The cyber-homunculus: On race and labor in plans for computation. *Configurations, 30*(4), 377–409.
https://doi.org/10.1353%2Fcon.2022.0028

Draper, N. (2018). British universities and Caribbean slavery. In J. Pellew & L. Goldman (Eds), *Dethroning historical reputations: Universities, museums and the commemoration of benefactors* (pp. 93–106). University of London Press.

Dijck, J. van, Poell, T., & Waal, M. de. (2018). *The platform society.* Oxford University Press.

Escobar, A. (2022). *Five axes of transition: Imagining "alternatives" for the post-pandemic future.* Radical Ecological Democracy.
https://radicalecologicaldemocracy.org/five-axes-of-transition-imagining-alternatives-for-the-post-pandemic-future/

Escobar, A. (2018). *Designs for the pluriverse: Radical interdependence, autonomy, and the making of worlds*. Duke University Press.

Fairfield, J. A. T. (2017). *Owned: Property, privacy, and the new digital serfdom*. Cambridge University Press.
https://doi.org/10.1017/9781316671467

Field, C., & Jones, G. (2016). *A survey of sessional faculty in Ontario publicly-funded universities* [PDF]. Toronto: Centre for the Study of Canadian and International Higher Education, OISE, University of Toronto
https://ciheblog.files.wordpress.com/2016/08/full-report.pdf

Franklin, U. M. (1990). *The real world of technology*. Anansi.

Fraser, A. (2022). A critical approach to Indigenous pedagogy – Aina-based (land-based) learning. *Ngoonjook: Australian First Nations' Journal, 36*, 44–50.
https://search.informit.org/doi/epdf/10.3316/informit.437217003009981

Fricker, M. (2009). *Epistemic Injustice: power and the ethics of knowing*. Oxford University Press.

Georgetown Slavery Archive (n.d.). *Sale of Maryland Jesuit's enslaved community to Louisiana in 1838*.
https://slaveryarchive.georgetown.edu/collections/show/1

Gewin, V. (2022). Mid-career mass exodus: A 'great resignation' wave among academics has many researchers stepping off the tenure track. *Nature, 606*, 211–13.
https://media.nature.com/original/magazine-assets/d41586-022-01512-6/d41586-022-01512-6.pdf

Gilliard, C., & Selwyn, N. (2022). Automated surveillance in education. *Postdigital Science and Education*.
https://doi.org/10.1007/s42438-022-00295-3

Government of Canada (2019). *Building on success: International education strategy (2019–2024)* [PDF].
https://www.international.gc.ca/education/assets/pdfs/ies-sei/Building-on-Success-International-Education-Strategy-2019-2024.pdf

Hall, B. L., & Tandon, R. (Eds), (2021). *Socially Responsible Higher Education: International Perspectives on Knowledge Democracy*. Brill.
https://doi.org/10.1163/9789004459076

Harris, L. M., Campbell, J. T., & Brophy, A. L. (Eds.) (2019). *Slavery and the university: Histories and legacies*. University of Georgia Press.

Harvard University (2022). *The report of the presidential committee on Harvard & the legacy of slavery* [PDF].
https://legacyofslavery.harvard.edu/report

Harvey, C. P. A. (2021). The wealth of knowledge: Land-grab universities in a British imperial and global context. *Native American and Indigenous Studies 8*(1), 97–105.
https://doi.org/10.5749/natiindistudj.8.1.0097

Hazelkorn, E. (2015). *Rankings and the reshaping of higher education: The battle for world-class excellence*. Palgrave Macmillan.
https://doi.org/10.1057%2F9781137446671

Hill Collins, P. (1990) *Black feminist thought: Knowledge, consciousness and the politics of empowerment*. Unwin Hyman.

Hu, T. H. (2015). *A prehistory of the cloud*. MIT Press.

Hummel, P., Braun, M., Tretter, M., & Dabrock, P. (2021). Data sovereignty: A review. *Big Data & Society, 8*(1).
https://doi.org/10.1177/2053951720982012

Kuokkanen, R. (2007). *Reshaping the university: Responsibility, indigenous epistemes and the logic of the gift*. UBC Press.

Komljenovic, J. (2021). The rise of education rentiers: Digital platforms, digital data and rents. *Learning, Media and Technology, 46*(3), 320–32.
https://doi.org/10.1080/17439884.2021.1891422.

Lange, L. (2010). Review of reshaping the university: Responsibility, indigenous epistemes, and the logic of the Ggft. *Studies in Social Justice, 4*(1), 87–91.
https://doi.org/10.26522/ssj.v4i1.1010

Larkin, B. (2013). The politics and poetics of infrastructure. *Annual Review of Anthropology, 42*(1), 327–43.
https://doi.org/10.1146%2Fannurev-anthro-092412-155522

Lee, R., & Ahtone, T. (2020). *Expropriated Indigenous land is the foundation of the land-grant university system*. High Country News.
https://www.hcn.org/issues/52.4/indigenous-affairs-education-land-grab-universities

Lewis, J. E. (Ed). (2020). *Indigenous protocol and artificial intelligence position paper. Honolulu, Hawai'i: The Initiative for Indigenous Futures and the Canadian Institute for Advanced Research (CIFAR)* [PDF].
https://spectrum.library.concordia.ca/id/eprint/986506/7/Indigenous_Protocol_and_AI_2020.pdf

Marachi, R., & Quill, L. (2020). The case of Canvas: Longitudinal datafication through learning management systems. *Teaching in Higher Education, 25*(4), 418–34.
https://doi.org/10.1080/13562517.2020.1739641

McIlwain, C. D. (2019). *Black software: The internet and racial justice, from the AfroNet to Black Lives Matter*. Oxford University Press.

Mignolo, W. D. (2014). From life rights to human rights. In C. Douzinas and C. Gearty (Eds), *The meanings of rights: The philosophy and social theory of human rights* (pp. 161–80). Cambridge University Press.

Mignolo, W. D. (2018). On pluriversality and multipolar world order: Decoloniality after decolonization; dewesternization after the Cold War. In B. Reiter (Ed.), *Constructing the pluriverse: The geopolitics of knowledge* (pp. 90–116). Duke University Press. https://doi.org/10.1515%2F9781478002017-006

Mullen, S. (2021). British Universities and transatlantic slavery: The University of Glasgow case. *History Workshop Journal, 91*(1), 210–33. https://doi.org/10.1093%2Fhwj%2Fdbaa035

Mzileni, P., & Mkhize, N. (2019). Decolonisation as a spatial question: The student accommodation crisis and higher education transformation. *South African Review of Sociology, 50*(3–4), 104–15. https://doi.org/10.1080/21528586.2020.1733649

Noble, S. U. (2018). *Algorithms of oppression: How search engines reinforce racism.* NYU Press. https://doi.org/10.2307%2Fj.ctt1pwt9w

Papa Reo (n.d.). Kaupapa – our mission. https://papareo.nz/#kaupapa

Prinsloo, P. (2020). Data frontiers and frontiers of power in (higher) education: A view of/from the Global South. *Teaching in Higher Education, 25*(4), 366–83. https://doi.org/10.1080%2F13562517.2020.1723537

Ricaurte, P. (2022, March 4). *Artificial Intelligence and the feminist decolonial imagination.* BotPopuli. https://botpopuli.net/artificial-intelligence-and-the-feminist-decolonial-imagination/

Robinson, C. J. (1983). *Black Marxism: The making of the Black radical tradition.* The University of North Carolina Press.

Sandel, M. J. (2020). *The tyranny of merit: What's become of the common good?* Farrar, Straus and Giroux.

Shahjahan, R. A., Grimm, A. & Allen, R. M. (2021). The "LOOMING DISASTER" for higher education: How commercial rankers use social media to amplify and foster affect. *Higher Education*, 1–17. https://doi.org/10.1007/s10734-021-00762-z https://link.springer.com/content/pdf/10.1007/s10734-021-00762-z.pdf

Simpson, L. B. (2014). Land as pedagogy: Nishnaabeg intelligence and rebellious transformation. *Decolonization: Indigeneity, Education & Society, 3*(3), 1–25. https://jps.library.utoronto.ca/index.php/des/article/view/22170

Spivak, G. C. (1988). Can the subaltern speak? In C. Nelson & L. Grossberg (Eds), *Marxism and the interpretation of culture* (pp. 21–78). University of Illinois Press.

Standing, G. (2011). *The precariat: The new dangerous class*. Bloomsbury Academic. https://doi.org/10.5040/9781849664554

Stein, S. (2017). The persistent challenges of addressing epistemic dominance in higher education: Considering the case of curriculum internationalisation. *Comparative Education Review, 61*(S1), S25–S50. https://doi.org/10.1086/690456

Tallbear, K., & Willey, A. (2019). Critical relationality: Queer, Indigenous, and multispecies belonging beyond settler sex & nature. *Imaginations: Journal of Cross-Cultural Image Studies, 10*(1), 5–15. https://doi.org/10.17742%2Fimage.cr.10.1.1

Tuck, E., & Yang, K. W. (2012). Decolonization is not a metaphor. *Decolonization: Indigeneity, Education & Society, 1*(1), 1–40. https://jps.library.utoronto.ca/index.php/des/article/view/18630

Tompkins-Stange, M. E. (2020). *Policy patrons: Philanthropy, education reform, and the politics of influence*. Harvard Education Press.

Truth and Reconciliation Commission of Canada (2015). *Honouring the truth, reconciling for the future: Summary of the final report of the Truth and Reconciliation Commission of Canada* [PDF]. https://ehprnh2mwo3.exactdn.com/wp-content/uploads/2021/01/Executive_Summary_English_Web.pdf

Tynan, L. (2021). What is relationality? Indigenous knowledges, practices and responsibilities with kin. *Cultural Geographies, 28*(4), 597–610. https://doi.org/10.1177/14744740211029287

Valverde, M., Briggs, J., Tran, G., & Montevirgen, M. (2020). Public universities as real estate developers in the age of "the art of the deal", *Studies in Political Economy, 101*(1), 35–58. https://doi.org/10.1080/07078552.2020.1738781

Williams, E. E. (2021). *Capitalism and slavery*. The University of North Carolina Press.

Williamson, B. (2017). Educating Silicon Valley: Corporate education reform and the reproduction of the techno-economic revolution. *Review of Education, Pedagogy, and Cultural Studies, 39*(3), 265–88. https://doi.org/10.1080/10714413.2017.1326274

Williamson, B. (2020). New pandemic edtech power networks. *Code Acts in Education*. https://codeactsineducation.wordpress.com/2020/04/01/new-pandemic-edtech-power-networks/

Williamson, B., Bayne, S., & Shay, S. (2020). The datafication of teaching in higher education: Critical issues and perspectives. *Teaching in Higher Education, 25*(4), 351–65.
https://doi.org/10.1080/13562517.2020.1748811

Williamson, B. (2022). The future of datafication in education? Clouds, bodies and ethics. In L. Pangrazio, & J. Sefton-Green, J. (Eds), *Learning to live with datafication: Educational case studies and initiatives from across the world* (pp. 209–15). Routledge.

Wolfe, P. (2006). Settler colonialism and the elimination of the native. *Journal of Genocide Research, 8*(4), 387–409.
https://doi.org/10.1080=14623520601056240

Zolkos, M. (2020). Restitution and the Politics of Repair: Tropes, Imaginaries, Theory. Edinburgh University Press.

Zuboff, S. (2019). *The age of surveillance capitalism: The fight for a human future at the new frontier of power*. PublicAffairs.

5. Why decolonising "knowledge" matters: Deliberations for educators on that made fragile

Dina Zoe Belluigi

Reimagining teaching, learning, belonging, and curricula design are all very important. However, when their relation to knowledges and the interests such knowledge formations serve is marginalised from the re-membering required of such imagination, it is deeply problematic. This chapter grapples with the question of why decolonising "knowledge" matters for teaching and learning. It shares a selection of important considerations at this point in time. It draws inter-textually to deliberate about (a) why "knowledge" (singular) should be decolonised within the modern western-oriented university; (b) why the decolonisation of knowledges matters, with consideration of their relation to the formations of the self, political, social, and ecological in education; and (c) what the potential act(s) of decolonising knowledges through education holds for engendering critical and generative roles which educators should occupy. As a way into this deliberation, the chapter begins with observations of the phenomenon of what seems like either educators' avoidance, ignorance, or passing-the-buck on the question of the transformation of knowledges in the university in post-colonial contexts.

Introduction

Central to the authority and functions of the university are the politics of knowledge recognition, legitimation, production, and reproduction. The calls to decolonise "knowledge" and to decolonise the curriculum remind us that education should not be passive dissemination of "knowledge". Educators for the common good have a duty to rise to this challenge. Thus, while this chapter's focus is on why decolonising "knowledge" matters for those operating at the micro-curriculum, the acts of decolonising necessitate extending beyond the safe spaces of teaching and learning, and beyond the university if there is indeed a commitment to serving the global common good.

The chapter is written by an educator and a researcher of higher education. The process of composing this text was one where I thought about, and for, educators' agency in relation to the larger conditions of possibility for the decolonisation of "knowledge". While I too have engaged in related struggles within a university in the Global North, the layers of narration in this text are underpinned by an Afropolitan orientation informed by critical personal, professional, and academic deliberations as a person who is South Africa-born and educated.

A central thematic, around which the chapter is shaped, is ethico-political responsibility. Due to the scope and focus of this chapter, this is primarily concerned with educators' agency. This critical dialogue about the conditions of possibility is not to be confused with a transference of blame or of deficit onto educator communities who are always already overburdened and often decapacitated. Rather, threaded throughout are concerns about conditions at the meso- and macro- level; and critiques about *that* and *those* which constrain such agency, and constrain educators' imaginaries of their agency and practices of collective resistance to such constraints. These critical discursive deliberations are informed by the sources I include in this chapter — observations and realisations from my research and learning from the scholarship of others. The resultant chapter is thus an intertextual offering to this anthology, made humbly as an homage to the works of the many educators it references, from whose contributions I believe there is much value for learning, critique, and, in turn, space for further contributions by educators.

Relinquishing of transformative agency when related to "knowledge" within teaching and learning

I begin with observations from recent research projects which asked questions about how academics situate and construct the locus of their agency to contribute to the transformation of the university. During interviews, my collaborators and I noticed that most participants would often avoid discussing the meso and macro levels of higher education, even when prompted (Belluigi et al., 2020; Dhawan et al., 2021). Sociocultural considerations of collegial relations, academic development, governance and management of institutions, research-teaching dynamics, and issues of "knowledge" were rarely included. Where the participants of our studies demonstrated their capacity to articulate, reflect, and be critical about their agency to affect change, was at the level of micro-curriculum, that is, about the teaching-learning-assessment-methods-topics-relations within the classes that they taught. While I do not refute the importance of initiatives, documentation, and scholarship to do with the micro-curriculum, it takes joined-up approaches to academic practice and academic structures to effect substantive change across the ecologies of higher education.

Questions of agency, transformation, and the university are important because academic freedom is premised on academics' engagement in matters related to the professional freedoms of education, research, governance (Hoffmann & Kinzelbach, 2018), socially-engaged academic freedom (Zavale & Langa, 2018), and the human rights of freedom of expression (International Labour Organisation and UNESCO, 2008). However, context plays a role in the conditioning of agents. The participants of the research projects to which I refer above were situated in South Africa and India. These are two contexts with undeniable academic unfreedoms in their histories, and where the majority of their populations were excluded from the publics of the so-called public good(s). Institutional interventions and policies were created in response to democratic constitutional obligations to address such legacies. Thus, one might expect these changes in conditions to have engendered critical consciousness of academics' transformative agency; and that, due to such conditions, current academics would situate the locus of their agency in a number of spaces across the ecology of the university. One might hope that this would be particularly enabling for academics from social groups which were structurally recognised as historically unprivileged, marginalised, or excluded. However, this is not what was observed. Participants almost exclusively constructed the micro-curriculum as the primary legitimate arena for them to exhibit their creativity, benevolence, and occasionally vulnerability. For those minoritised, such as Black academics in "historically white institutions" in South Africa and Adivasi academics in India, the micro-curriculum offered a retreat from the fractious dynamics of the other spaces of the university where many continued to face discrimination and misrecognition. Many expressed frustration that their transformative agency was limited to literally "embodying" compliance to employment affirmative action quotas. The majority of all the participants who were interviewed seemed to take the relinquishing of their responsibility for granted — passively entrusted to researchers, learned societies, and publishers validated by established traditions of the global institution. Of concern is that such resignation cut across both those critical and those uncritical of global inequalities in universities and in terms of knowledge production.

This is a paradox for praxis. On the one hand, most of the educators interviewed were challenging of ivory tower constructions of the (campus and virtual) classroom as a white cube where the outside world is othered. Some of these acted on their commitment to conscientise their students about aspects of the political, historical, ethical, economic, cultural, social relations, oppressions, and injustices of their societies and global dynamics. They often facilitated their students' actions for change when facing outside of the university. On the other hand, for various reasons, they omitted utilising their academic agency to affect the ecology of higher education, and from their students' critical consciousness. In such ways, they reproduced the dulling of active academic citizenry.

There may be many reasons for, justifications of, and influences on such avoidance of the agency to engage with structural issues — be they ignorance, collusion, self-preservation et cetera. Much academic "development" reinforces artificial distinctions between the questioning of content and form, by focusing on the professionalisation and quality assurance of teaching, assessment and (micro)curriculum design. This may be the result of the segregations between academics' development for teaching as distinct from that for research. However, knowledges move and morph within, and well beyond, the boundaries of the classroom. As alluded to above, "knowledge" was rarely identified by participants as a consideration for *transformation*, and even less rarely discussed with confidence when discussing their transformative agency. Perhaps the stay-in-your-lane enculturation dynamics enforced by current neoliberal employment practices had imposed borderlines on the increasingly sessional, precarious, teaching-only educator's practice and imaginaries. Such meso-level dynamics school academics through "institutional curriculum" (Lange & Parker, 2019) norms and values, and/ or through disciplinary curricula.

Conditions such as these have impoverished constructions of academic freedom and minimised its relation to the longer struggles for freedom from such systems as colonisation, patriarchy, and local and global hegemonies (Sall, 1997). The tasking and inspiring of educators to enact their transformative leadership, to challenge inappropriate uses of power and work with collectives, including students, against structural injustices has been informed by the contestations of various proponents and traditions across time. Social movements often begin well beyond the academy, their lenses and understandings have infused various critical traditions within it, including from curriculum theory, feminisms, queer theory, post-colonialisms, and post-modernisms. This chapter is situated within the current renewal of decolonisation, and grapples particularly with *why* the decolonisation of "knowledge" matters for teaching and learning for the common good.

Why "knowledge"?

Knowledge stratifications are commonplace within contemporary higher education. These stratifications are explicitly and implicitly practiced by those who teach, albeit with some challenge exerted by educators and scholars, as I discuss in this section. For instance, it is not uncommon that inherited value judgments about *which* knowledges matter become most visibly imposed within summative assessment regimes. Examples include penalising students for the use of first person writing or for using "non-academic" qualifiers as external referends such as work experience.[1] Such practices are in part informed by the devaluing of *a posteriori* knowledges gained from experience, and privileging of *a priori* "knowledge" independent of experience. The dominant construction of the former in the modern, western-oriented university is that it is limited because it is gained subjectively and is situated in context. The latter is lauded as universal and objective. This Kantian (2007) distinction informed the denigration of value ascribed to knowledges gained from the informal education of social institutions (family, religion, group identities such as through racialisation, genderisation, minoritisation etc), from the non-human (including the so-called natural world and spiritual realms), and from individual life experience.

Against these is the elevation of knowledges gained through so-called "disinterested" enquiry undertaken for a good greater than one grouping (i.e. a public good) legitimised through academic communities (peer review, publication, etc.). That "knowledge" is then explicitly reproduced (and taught) by those given authority (i.e. teachers) through the formal micro-curriculum. Another dominantly recognised distinction of knowledges is that of the influential ancient Greek thinkers, such as Aristotle (2004), who constructed "knowledge" in terms of its appropriateness for its purpose (or "ends"/ telos), creating distinctions between enquiry as theoretical (for its own sake), productive (instrumental towards making something, involving planning, functional creativity and skills or mastery), and practical (a moral disposition or wisdom for judgement-making in ethical and political life that involves a relation between the two dimensions of theory and practice). The latter has informed much debate about how "knowledge" is acquired, learnt, honed et cetera.

---

1   Indeed, the academic language used in this paper parallels these constructs. For the most part in this text, I have chosen not to use first person pronouns and foreground explicit discussions of how my biography and experience (as a person and as a practitioner) has come to bare on the knowledges I bring to what, to my mind, is a mostly inter-textual conceptual piece. The absence of a positionality statement related to my sociodemographics will probably be taken as grounds for critique, as has become somewhat of a convention at this point in time (Abu Moghli & Kadiwal, 2021; Macfarlane, 2021; Secules et al., 2021). I made this decision because I felt it would overshadow the argument, which is that one's authorial choices should be informed and active, and that educators can play a role in developing their students' and colleagues' critical capacity in making curricular choices, as well as their own.

A reoccurring question that underpins these attempts at stratifying knowledges is *what "knowledge" should be valued in the formal curriculum?* Less acknowledged are the dynamics of power that determine who is asking, whose responses to that question are heard, the impositions of appropriateness in "should", and the singularity of the construction of "knowledge". Ethical contestations, about the effects on those and that un/undervalued that have raised by those within, and those beyond the university, seem to have had negligible impact.

The renewed calls to decolonise "knowledge" as part of the larger process of decolonising the university are calls to action underpinned by long asserted concerns about the unjust politics of "knowledge" legitimation. The relation of "knowledge" to power under-girdles the legitimacy of the university as a gatekeeping institution. It is that relation which ascribes it authority, and by implication, those who teach, and research become authorities and trustees of "knowledge". Written acknowledgements of the association between power and "knowledge", and wealth and legacies, are old:

> Knowledge is power and it can command obedience. A man of knowledge during his lifetime can make people obey and follow him and he is praised and venerated after his death. Remember that knowledge is a ruler and wealth is its subject. Those who accumulate wealth though alive yet are dead to realities of life and those who gather knowledge will remain alive through their knowledge and wisdom even after death; though their faces may disappear from the community of living beings, yet their ideas and knowledge which they left behind and their memory will remain in the minds of men... (Imam Ali (559–661) in al-Radi, 1989, p. 552)

The de/legitimation of certain knowledges is an assertion of power. Those decisions, about what (in)forms the archive and the cannon (misspelt purposefully), impact on the hierarchical selections of included excluded, centred-marginalised, un-privileged. Questions that arise are: *In whose interests are these acts? Which knowledges are misrecognised and unvalued, and why? How is this problematic rooted in binaries of colonial/ Indigenous, scientific evidence/ belief system, dominant/ oppressed?*

In raising such questions, solidarities extend across time and beyond the decolonial interest to those whose "voice" (read: expression, participation, authority) has been repressed by various systems of oppression. These solidarities include questioning patriarchy, whiteness, ableism, heteronormativity, authoritarianism, etc., including cultural imperialism and colonialism. The global imaginary that emerged through European modernity and colonialism (Stein et al., 2019) exerted hegemonic spheres of influence through the university's various forms and functions. These influences acted on the character and politics of subordinated human and non-human subjects and contexts, for the purposes of creating or maintaining power relations of inequality and oppression. The supposed "goods" of progress and civilisation were a convenient mirage masking the gains of empires. While occupation of land, extraction of natural resources, physical violence, and the removal of language rights and freedom of belief are the more obvious forms of such hegemony, their exertion *through* the educational function and often *with* the collusion of education is of particular consideration for this chapter. The modern university, its fundamentals forged through Western Europe's aesthetic relation to the Enlightenment, enacted its subjugations, accumulation, and relations of conquest in various ways. Examples of its formalisation extend from the settler colonial university in Canada (Stein, 2020) to the apartheid's university in South Africa (Lalu, 2007).

In the contemporary global neoliberal HE order, such hegemony is most obviously visible in the material power exerted by US higher education that reproduces cultural and linguistic conformity that is particularly in that nation's interests (Marginson, 2008), while continuing to solidify and extend the interests of European whiteness. Obfuscation of the complicity of the minority world in the inequalities and suppression of the majority world was also prevalent in the goods of "development" discourses in the decolonisation period post-WWII (Kapoor, 2014), some of which continues in the positioning of those of the majority world as "lesser than" (if not explicitly "deficit") through the Sustainable Development Goals and the tasking of universities to "drive" that global agenda.

Why the decolonisation of "knowledge" matters

Recognising these distinctions and their ramification, in what ways might the decolonisation of "knowledge" matter to teaching and learning? There is a myriad of answers to this question, depending on context and conceptualisation. Within this section, several points raised by fellow scholars are discussed as openings for the consideration of those of us who are educators.

The first is that the decolonisation of "knowledge" is central to the conditions for academic freedom. While the decolonisation of the curriculum/university should not be seen as a metaphor which displaces the reckoning for the material restitution of and rights for land, self-determination, and sovereignty (Tuck & Yang, 2012), African intellectuals have recognised that the struggle for epistemic freedom (Ndlovu-Gatsheni, 2018) and academic freedom (Sall, 1997) is a continuation of the long struggle for freedom, from which emerges much of the current decolonisation drive. A fundamental ethical impetus underpins these contestations towards alterity, plurality, and democracy, as means to push against the dominant violence of marginalisation, negation, exclusion, and enslavement.

This is because the concern with decolonisation is not only to do with hegemony (as I discussed in the last section), but also its creation of absence when there is presence. Mbembe (2015) articulated this when he spoke about how:

> This hegemonic tradition has not only become hegemonic. It also actively represses anything that actually is articulated, thought and envisioned from outside of these frames. (p. 10)

This is the epistemic injustice of the disciplines of the modern university, which "renders the collective interpretive resources required for epistemic justice structurally prejudiced" (Keet, 2014, p. 23). Such a meso-curriculum may problematically reproduce the skewed faculties or dulled consciousness of students, academics, and collectives. De Sousa Santos (2007) offers metaphors to evoke that which characterises colonialist social regulation/emancipation, and which continues in re-presentations of knowledges. The metaphors are abyssal "lines" and "gazes" of dominant thinking. They map the sub/human by invisibilising entire knowledge systems out of the imaginary of the modern western university. The implications for the majority world, its knowledge systems, ways of being and material realities are at the core of de Sousa Santos' interest — what he suggests is that this ordering system persists in current times and implicates us all. Beyond the period of colonisations, such abyssal thinking colludes perversely in ways where "human principles don't get compromised by inhuman practices" (de Sousa Santos, 2007, p. 45). Such perversions inform various formations, subjectifications, subjugations, social divisions, and stratifications. They impose subject-object relations of the "self", to the human "other", the individual and collective. They shape relations of the human to non-human animals, and constructions which distinguish and prioritise the human from "nature". They are enacted through local and global stratifications of power, through such mechanisms as the state and "soft power", elites and hegemony. They also impact on delineations of good(s) and (the) common(s) within HE discourses.

Such problematic formations play out within the factory of the university and related culture industries, including education and research. Harm, obliteration, and misrecognition of the knowledges that are "othered" by the modern university and by the political, religious, and economic systems with which it has colluded, have entailed appropriation and extraction without mutual benefit. An example is how the more explicit colonialist appropriations of Indigenous knowledges of the social and natural world have morphed in the current times of the global "knowledge economy". Capitalist systems of subordination and of exploitation of African intellectual workers, for instance, were recently dubbed the "Black Market" of the current "research industry" by those positioned as "research assistants" in post-conflict research (Mwambari & Owor, 2019, n.p.). Similarly, those from the majority world primarily provide the invisible labour behind many of the large, profit-making academic publishers, whose authors, editors, and editorial boards continue to be primarily peopled by those based in the minority world. This economy continues to practice the "intellectual marginalisation" of those in the majority world (Obeng-Odoom, 2019), operating in the interests of the minority world rather than the global common good.

Contestations and agential negotiations are exerted by such intellectual workers (Connell et al., 2017). Working from the perspective of sociology in England, Bhambhra (2020) posits that it is insufficient to only point to the unjust gaps, omissions and silences created by the politics of knowledge production by the modern university and its culture industries. She argues that what must be engaged with is *why* knowledges are excluded and *what difference* their inclusion would be for understanding. This is not the type of superficial "added value" reasoning for "diversity". It is about "accounting for the connected histories" (Bhambra, 2020, p. 455) of imperialism across the geographical contexts and projects which have produced divisions and stratifications in knowledges. However, Stein and da Silva (2020) assert that where decolonisation differs to many other critiques of the university and modernity, is in its emphasis on knowledges (plural) and in the insistence of pushing against the continuation of colonial dynamics which benefit the modern western-oriented university:

> [Decolonial critiques] refuse the notion that the primary violence of colonization is the exclusion of certain populations and communities from the supposedly universal promises offered by modern institutions. To name exclusion as the primary violence of this system is to 1) invalidate other ways of knowing and being, by assuming that everyone desires access to the same promised futures and direction of social change; and, 2) invisibilize the fact that these modern institutions do not simply exclude 'othered' populations, but rather are made possible at the expense of violence against those populations. (p. 549)

Clustered around the decolonisation of "knowledge" is critique: for justice, to destabilise the philosophical foundations of Western modernity, to problematise the politics of representation and authority within the webs of knowledge formation and legitimisation. As important to the critical project are those projects which are generative: of plural knowledges, for reclamation, repair, and recognition of what has continued despite, independent of, against or alongside the dominant "knowledge" *cannonised* and often weaponised by university. Thus, a central purpose underpinning what decolonising knowledges does, is re-membering against the problematic construction of subject-object relations *within* knowledge formation. This is the endeavour to

> unsettle modernity's dominant ontological and epistemological foundations by seriously engaging the conceptual potential of thinking with (ethical dimension) alterity and from (geopolitical dimension) exteriority. (Fúnez-Flores, 2022, p. 21)

Such re-membering involves de-membering what colonialism did and does, which is not about memory but a re-location in history (Ndlovu-Gatsheni, 2022) that entails recovery and reclamation of authors (in the broad sense of those who generate and represent knowledges), authorship (as an agentially creative and responsible role), and authority (to hold the influence to inform, produce and reproduce). In addition to the possibilities within research and relations with non-academic citizens and spaces, education offers space to disrupt reproduction of "knowledge" and to foster such re-membering through critical and generative social and knowledge formations. I turn briefly to these possibilities in the next section.

Why the educator matters for decolonising "knowledge"

A renewed call to democratise knowledge production and legitimation has been heralded to which we are asked to respond. Recognising the concerns identified in the prior section, and how avoiding decolonising "knowledge" may mis-educate students and reproduce unjust, hegemonic, and harmful subjectifications of their relations to themselves and others (human and non-human), what roles might educators play in this endeavour at the level of the micro-curriculum?

The machinations of the modern, western-oriented university come with a set of processes, many of which are assumed. First, that knowledges produced (i.e. discovered or created) by the university and legitimated through various assessment processes can then be disseminated as "knowledge". The educational project (at university and school levels) then becomes about reproducing that produced by the university as if universal and value-neutral, with contextualisation, translation and engagement being the purposes of learning. This construction between academic research and the content taught within educational institutions is a top-down imposition of that which is validated by the powers that be within the modern university's machinations. Presented as such, it seems to offer little agency or influence in terms of what occurs at the micro-level within the classroom, and often too its relations to the academic and non-academic world (including that related to the "third mission", i.e. the university's contribution to and engagement with society).

Scholarly attention has been given to how values of "knowledge" are structured, and given some wiggle room, for the teacher and student within the micro-curriculum. The tools offered to researchers by Bernstein (1973, 1990) is one such example, looking at the relation between content and form at the micro-curricula level. He termed these "classification" (i.e. the imposition of structure, boundaries or insulation on the content of education), and "framing" as the degree of agency which teachers and students have over the form of their engagement with such "knowledge". There has also been recognition of what de Carvalho and Florez-Florez (2014, p. 122) call the "thematic and theoretical sectarianism" of knowledges by disciplinary structuring. This follows the pattern of disciplining knowledges through the rejection of theories that belong to the canon of other disciplines and the embrace of a small group which encloses and delineates it as a distinct discipline.

Some have framed the role of the teacher as the mediator or guide to the discourse conflicts on what is powerful "knowledge" (including the author, see for instance Belluigi, 2017; De Vos & Belluigi, 2011). In such formulations, the teacher as facilitator takes on the role of making explicit the enculturation of the tacit or hidden curriculum around the politics of assessment and of "knowledge". In the name of academic "success", they reproduce the dominant order as a means of epistemological access for students. In many cases, this is educational development aka industrial psychology: we know the system is skewed, but for individuals to pragmatically cope, the rules of the game are made "transparent" for the purposes of being complied with. Critiques abound, pointing to the dangers of discourses of access for success (Belluigi & Thondhlana, 2022) and of product promotion (White, 2019). Pragmatically, many equity approaches limited by political will may take on such approaches to be affirmative. However, they cannot claim to be transformative (McKenna et al., 2022) if focused on the micro-curriculum without acknowledging the scale of the problematics in the ecology of HE, the institutions' relation to its publics, and the politics of the "knowledge" project. Dominant notions of "access for success" within the disciplines threaten to ossify the norms and logics of academia and knowledge dissemination as all powerful. Indeed, even when new areas of enquiry arise, they are hailed back into the knowledge structures of the minority world through resource inequalities, workforce mechanisms and intellectual framing (Connell et al., 2018).

Despite these machinations, power dynamics, and the dominant discourses of the modern university, counter-narratives about the agency of educators are being increasingly asserted. For instance, research on the hegemony of the global metropole in domains of knowledges by Connell et al. (2017) points to how negotiations by academics and institutions can reshape knowledge production. Once structured by colonialism and minority-majority world inequalities, trade routes of the global economy of knowledges can be criss-crossed for solidarity, learning and resistance. In their arguments for the decolonisation of universities in Latin America, de Carvalho and Florez-Florez (2014, p. 122) posit academic practice as transgression. They hold that the rules and logics which transdisciplinarity follows are not always already inscribed by those of modern academic cannons. De Sousa Santos (2007), as with others, has attempted to capture this zeitgeist and to also indicate the collective nature of the struggle:

> The complexity of this movement is difficult to unravel as it unfolds under our eyes, and our eyes cannot help being on this side of the line and seeing from the inside out. To capture the full measure of what is going on requires a gigantic decentering effort. No single scholar can do it alone, as an individual. Drawing on a collective effort to develop an epistemology of the South, I surmise that this movement is made of a main movement and a subaltern countermovement. The main movement I call the return of the colonial and the return of the colonizer, and the countermovement I call subaltern cosmopolitanism. (pp. 21–22)

At the level of the micro-curriculum, educators connect knowledges with learning, enquiry, critique and with the experiential and representation, in ways which can be dialogic and disruptive. For those who still have the agency to develop curricula, a paper by Andreotti et al. (2011) offers a visualisation of two lenses. On either side of the abyssal line, the lenses are related to universal knowing and relational knowing, in reference to interpretations related to the introduction of different epistemologies in higher education. They argue that when engaging with such knowledges, educators should grapple with political, ontological, and metaphysical questions.

What many working on this assert, is the importance of deliberation and of resistance. In the quotation below (Connell et al., 2017), the educator is re-membered as a "knowledge worker" who is well placed to engage in several sites of struggle from micro- to macro-levels:

> Movement in a democratic direction, then, is not ordained by history. If it occurs it will be through social and intellectual struggle, as well as political and economic shifts. The approach we have suggested helps identify necessary sites of struggle. One is the situation of the knowledge workforce, always partly casualized, currently subject to increasing pressure from neoliberal governments and managements. Another is the scientific communication system, currently being commodified and concentrated in the hands of a small group of corporations, but challenged by a popular open-access movement. A third is the formation of intellectual workers, in education systems increasingly privatized and homogenized on a world scale but also active sites of cultural contestation. A fourth is the production of knowledge in social movements such as environmentalism, challenging both the disinformation spread by the fossil fuel industry and the hierarchies of knowledge in mainstream science. (p. 32)

Operative criticism (Belluigi, 2017) may be of value for educators. This is an umbrella term for various approaches of reflexive criticism which are concerned with what scholarship and authorship *signify*, by observing (and being responsive to) their reception, translation, and impact in context. Keet (2014) argues that epistemic justice is key to disrupting the epistemic injustice within disciplines. As with decolonisation, such conscientisation is a process rather than an ending, but it is of fundamental importance for critical consciousness to develop and to inform action. It is the educator's role to facilitate operative criticism with communities of learning and academic practice. In dialogue with students in the micro-curriculum and colleagues in the meso-curriculum, such praxis holds potential to destabilise prevailing mythologies and doxa, and to recognise the contradictions and oppressions enacted through knowledge formation and social formation, where some (humans, non-humans, and aspects of the environment) are objects of others' will and consumption.

This praxis is more radical than "access", "equity", technocratic critical thinking "skills", or units of content. The intellectual, political, and moral elements of such impetus must not be reduced, simplified, or dehistoricised. There are already claims that this has happened to the radical impetus of the decolonisation drive in South Africa (Madlingozi, 2018), and in the standardisation, domestication, depoliticisation, and commodification of decolonisation discourses in parts of Western Europe (Abu Moghli & Kadiwal, 2021). Similar dulling occurred within the South African higher education system when the discourse of constitutional "transformation" was institutionalised. Reflecting on this latter phenomenon, Lange (2014, p. 5) argues this was because of the insufficient examination of "knowledge for transformation (the knowledge that needs to be produced in order to make change possible)" over and above the "knowledge of transformation (which is the knowledge we generate about transformation itself)". Shahjahan et al. (2022) offer directions for the possibility of a field of solidarities, growing from knowledges produced through educational research on decolonising curriculum and pedagogy. They base this on a critical analysis of over 200 hundred texts using a geopolitics of knowledge framework. What they found was that the themes that emerged were *contextual* when it came to meanings of decolonisation, of actualising decolonisation, and of the challenges which that posed in HE. Situated within and operating across contexts, educators are uniquely placed to enable such as field of solidarities by engaging students, academic and non-academic fellow educators in decolonising "knowledge".

There is creative agency in representation, writing and acts of narration. These common-place modes of doing within the university can be enabling of the development of voice, authorship, and knowledges. The literary-academic presence is one such locus for change. Larson (2018, p. 521) described this as "an author's textual expression of cultural, regional, linguistic, and scholarly orientation" which is disciplined within hegemonic educational processes for students, and further within academic representational processes. In addition to how educators re-present, a directly generative educational role can be played in creating the conditions for students to experience the power of counter-narratives of knowledges, to contribute to their formation and legitimation, and to extend the responsibility of authoring and authorship for the common good.

The decolonial turn offers potential for a future pluriversity that does not alienate, minoritise, or "other". To challenge the ideology of Eurocentrism that "seeks to universalize the West and provincialize the rest" (Zeleza, 2009, p. 133), African intellectuals have been exploring Afropolitanism as one approach which positions "Africa at the centre of things, not existing as an appendix or a satellite of other countries" (Mbembe, 2021), or disciplinary fields (such as in "African Studies"). Such de-/re-centring acts as a means for African researchers to see ourselves, and our relations to others, creatively, critically, and ethically before radiating outwards. Within this is the ethical injunction for the university's knowledges and ways of being to not be alienating to the life experiences of Africans (Ratele, 2019).

Limitations to the agency of individuals and constraints on curriculum design are many. In contexts where political will and a critical mass can exert collective action and urgency, more openings are possible. In some contexts, this is happening through the access of first-generation students, and in turn first generation academics. Such conditions are being seized for cultivating academic citizens' responsibilities to end the miseducation of the mis-recognition of the modern, western university to engage with just knowledges, and for educators to enact their roles as stewards and trustees of knowledges for the common good.

Conclusion

The relation of the curriculum to *which* knowledges are selected, foregrounded, and thereby (re)produced through what is taught and what is learnt is not a marginal concern. In a time when the social justice imperatives of "public good" have been all but emptied out and reduced to only a few publics within nation-bound stratifications and geopolitical priorities, there is too much importance to avoid engaging with the common good of knowledges. While many dominant voices in decolonisation drives are understandably concerned with the human, these too must not be separated from the entanglements of the university's knowledges with the violences done to non-human animals and environments which have led to the age of the Anthropocene and environmental melancholia (Lertzman, 2015). Decolonisation thus extends dominant notions of the common:

> It is about humankind ruling in common for a common which includes the non-humans, which is the proper name for democracy. (Mbembe, 2015, p. 10)

The common goods of knowledges are situated, extended, delineated, and connected in their relations to the human and non-human subjectivities impacted in the classroom and beyond, across the globe.

The call to "decolonise the curriculum" is inclusive of the formal, informal, and hidden aspects of the micro, meso and micro-curriculum, particularly when calls are linked to "decolonising the university". This chapter has argued that the segregation of the micro-curriculum of teaching-and-learning from these wider relations is a cause for concern. Decolonising endeavours can be too easily compartmentalised, creating gaps in our academic practices which allow for the domestification of academic practice and even the commodification of this discourse. Such individual or institutional profit is gained to the detriment of decolonisation serving the global common good.

This chapter offers some deliberations about why *teachers* should actively engage their critical and generative agency within higher education when it comes to the decolonisation of "knowledge". Creating the environments to critique "knowledge" by facilitating the development of critical consciousness within students', colleagues' and one's own processes of enquiry and learning about the university, is within educators' sphere of influence. Doing so would contribute to destabilising the reproduction of the hegemonic ordering of knowledge delegitimation within the micro-curriculum. It would open space to engage with knowledges marginalised, misrecognised, excluded, or destroyed without requiring their appropriation or assimilation, but rather relations of curiosity, desire, doubt, and recognition.

Academics have power (and responsibility) as trustees of education and of knowledges. Exercising this with ethical humility may better serve to build the critical consciousness of academic citizens to the injustices of that/those harmed, to recognise and assert what should be reclaimed from that appropriated, to commemorate that which has resisted or continued despite the modern university, and to work with those (within and beyond HE) who can strengthen that made fragile.

Acknowledgements

I am grateful to the reviewers of my chapter, Jairo Fúnez-Flores, Chris Knaus and Cheng-Wen Huang, for their challenges of my blind spots and appreciations of my struggles with this chapter. Thank you also to my institutional colleagues and fellow migrant academics, Amanda Kramer and Mel Engman, for sharing questions about the quandaries of the 'why' raised in this chapter, when considering our selves within our current context in Northern Ireland. The final cycle of peer review by the editors was invaluable — thank you Laura and Catherine.

References

Abu Moghli, M., & Kadiwal, L. (2021). Decolonising the curriculum beyond the surge: Conceptualisation, positionality and conduct. *London Review of Education, 19*(1), 1–16.
https://doi.org/10.14324/LRE.19.1.23

al-Radi, M. ibn al-H. S. (1989). *Nahjul balagha: Sermons, letters, and sayings of Imam Ali*. Ansariyan Publications.

Andreotti, V., Ahenakew, C., & Cooper, G. (2011). Epistemological pluralism: Ethical and pedagogical challenges in higher education. *AlterNative: An International Journal of Indigenous Peoples, 7*(1), 40–50.
https://doi.org/10.1177/117718011100700104

Aristotle. (2004). *The nicomachean ethics* (J. A. K. Thomson, Trans.). Penguin Classics.

Belluigi, D. Z. (2017). The significance of conflicting discourses in a professional degree: Assessment in undergraduate fine art practice. *Discourse: Studies in the Cultural Politics of Education, 38*(2), 209–21.
https://doi.org/10.1080/01596306.2015.1075961

Belluigi, D. Z., Dhawan, N. B., & Idahosa, G. E. O. (2020, December 2). Sustainability is based on the faith we have towards the work that we are doing: The conditions of academic citizenry in South Africa and India [Panel]. In M. van Winden, K. Wimpenny, C. Hagenmeier, & J. Beelen (Chairs), *Panel H50, Africa Knows! It's time to decolonise our minds*, Leiden African Studies Association.
https://nomadit.co.uk/conference/africaknows/paper/57778

Belluigi, D. Z., & Thondhlana, G. (2022). In whose interest is training the dog? Black academics' reflection on academic development for access and success in an historically white university in South Africa. In D. Thomas & J. Arday (Eds), *Doing equity and diversity for success in higher education: Redressing structural inequalities in the academy* (pp. 265–76). Palgrave Macmillan UK.
https://doi.org/10.1007/978-3-030-65668-3_20

Bernstein, B. (1973). On the classification and framing of educational knowledge. In R. Brown (Ed.), *Knowledge, education, and cultural change* (pp. 85–115). Routledge.

Bernstein, B. (1990). *The structuring of pedagogic discourse*. Routledge.

Bhambra, G. K. (2020). Introduction – Roots, routes, and reconstruction: Travelling ideas/theories. *The Sociological Review, 68*(3), 455–60.
https://doi.org/10.1177/0038026119899361

Carvalho, J. J. D., & Flórez-Flórez, J. (2014). The meeting of knowledges: A project for the decolonization of universities in Latin America. *Postcolonial Studies, 17*(2), 122–39.
https://doi.org/10.1080/13688790.2014.966411

Connell, R., Collyer, F., Maia, J., & Morrell, R. (2017). Toward a global sociology of knowledge: Post-colonial realities and intellectual practices. *International Sociology, 32*(1), 21–37.
https://doi.org/10.1177/0268580916676913

Connell, R., Pearse, R., Collyer, F., Maia, J., & Morrell, R. (2018). Re-making the global economy of knowledge: Do new fields of research change the structure of North–South relations? *The British Journal of Sociology, 69*(3), 738–57.
https://doi.org/10.1111/1468-4446.12294

de Sousa Santos, B. (2007). Beyond abyssal thinking—Boaventura de Sousa Santos from global lines to ecologies of knowledges. *Review, XXX*(1), 1–66.
https://www.jstor.org/stable/40241677

De Vos, M., & Belluigi, D. Z. (2011). Formative assessment as mediation. *Perspectives in Education, 29*(2), 39–47.
https://journals.ufs.ac.za/index.php/pie/article/view/1682

Dhawan, N., Belluigi, D. Z., & Idahosa, G. E. O. (2021). *Disrupting the new middle class space of Indian public universities. Proceedings of the International Conference on Globalisation of Professional Legal Education*. Queen's University, Belfast Digital Library.
https://pure.qub.ac.uk/en/publications/disrupting-the-new-middle-class-space-of-indian-public-universiti

Fúnez-Flores, J. I. (2022). Decolonial and ontological challenges in social and anthropological theory. *Theory, Culture & Society, 39*(6), 21–41.
https://doi.org/10.1177/02632764211073011

Hoffmann, F., & Kinzelbach, K. (2018). Forbidden knowledge. Academic freedom and political repression in the university sector can be measured. This is how. *Global Public Policy Institute*.
https://www.gppi.net/media/Kinzelbach_Hoffmann_2018_Forbidden_Knowledge.pdf

International Labour Organisation and UNESCO. (2008). *The ILO/UNESCO recommendation concerning the status of teachers (1966) and The UNESCO recommendation concerning the status of higher-education teaching personnel (1997)* [PDF].
https://unesdoc.unesco.org/ark:/48223/pf0000160495

Kant, I. (2007). *Critique of pure reason*. Penguin Classics.

Kapoor, I. (2014). Psychoanalysis and development: Contributions, examples, limits. *Third World Quarterly, 35*(7), 1120–43.
https://doi.org/10.1080/01436597.2014.926101

Keet, A. (2014). Epistemic othering and the decolonisation of knowledge. *Africa Insight, 44*(1), 23–37.
https://www.ajol.info/index.php/ai/article/view/110048

Lalu, P. (2007). Apartheid's university: Notes on the renewal of the enlightenment. *Journal of Higher Education in Africa / Revue de l'enseignement Supérieur En Afrique, 5*(1), 45–60.
https://www.academia.edu/2888623/Apartheid_s_University_Notes_on_the_Renewal_of_the_Enlightenment_

Lange, L. (2014). Rethinking transformation and its knowledge(s): The case of South African higher education. *Critical Studies in Teaching and Learning (CriSTaL), 2*(1), 1–24.
https://hdl.handle.net/10520/EJC179307

Lange, L., & Parker, G. (2019). The institutional curriculum, pedagogy and the decolonisation of the South African university. In J. D. Jansen (Ed.), *Decolonisation in universities* (pp. 79–99). Wits University Press.

Larson, J. (2018). Other voices: Authors' literary-academic presence and publication in the discursive world system. *Discourse: Studies in the Cultural Politics of Education, 39*(4), 521–35.
https://doi.org/10.1080/01596306.2016.1278357

Lertzman, R. (2015). *Environmental melancholia: Psychoanalytic dimensions of engagement*. Routledge.

Macfarlane, B. (2021). Methodology, fake learning, and emotional performativity. *ECNU Review of Education, 5*(1), 140–55.
https://doi.org/10.1177/2096531120984786

Madlingozi, T. (2018, November 1). *Decolonising decolonisation with Mphahlele*. New Frame.
https://www.newframe.com/decolonising-decolonisation-mphahlele/

Marginson, S. (2008). Towards a global university hegemony. *Critique internationale, 39*(2), 87–107.
https://www.cairn-int.info/revue-critique-internationale-2008-2-p-87.html

Mbembe, A. (2015). *Decolonizing knowledge and the question of the archive* [PDF]. The Wits Institute for Social and Economic Research
https://wiser.wits.ac.za/system/files/Achille%20Mbembe%20-%20Decolonizing%20Knowledge%20and%20the%20Question%20of%20the%20Archive.pdf

McKenna, S., Hlengwa, A., Quinn, L., & Vorster, J. A. (2022). From affirmative to transformative approaches to academic development. *Teaching in Higher Education, 27*(8), 1005–17.
https://doi.org/10.1080/13562517.2022.2119077

Mwambari, D., & Owor, A. (2019, June 8). *The black market of knowledge production*. Convivial Thinking.
https://convivialthinking.org/index.php/2019/06/08/the-black-market-of-knowledge-production/

Ndlovu-Gatsheni, S. (2018). *Epistemic freedom in Africa: Deprovincialization and decolonization*. Routledge.

Ndlovu-Gatsheni, S. (2022). *Lecture on Grappling with complex contemporary politics of knowledge and contested meaning(s) of decolonization in Africa*. Personal collection of S. Ndlovu-Gatsheni, University of Johannesburg, Johannesburg Gauteng.

Obeng-Odoom, F. (2019). The intellectual marginalisation of Africa. *African Identities, 17*(3–4), 211–24.
https://doi.org/10.1080/14725843.2019.1667223

Ratele, K. (2019). *The world looks Like this from here: Thoughts on African psychology*. Wits University Press.

Sall, E. (Ed.), (1997). *Women in academia: Gender and academic freedom in Africa*. CODESRIA.

Secules, S., McCall, C., Mejia, J. A., Beebe, C., Masters, A. S., L. Sánchez-Peña, M., & Svyantek, M. (2021). Positionality practices and dimensions of impact on equity research: A collaborative inquiry and call to the community. *Journal of Engineering Education, 110*(1), 19–43.
https://doi.org/10.1002/jee.20377

Shahjahan, R. A., Estera, A. L., Surla, K. L., & Edwards, K. T. (2022). Decolonizing curriculum and pedagogy: A comparative review across disciplines and global higher education contexts. *Review of Educational Research, 92*(1), 73–113.
https://doi.org/10.3102/00346543211042423

Stein, S. (2020). A colonial history of the higher education present: Rethinking land-grant institutions through processes of accumulation and relations of conquest. *Critical Studies in Education, 61*(2), 212–28.
https://doi.org/10.1080/17508487.2017.1409646

Stein, S., Andreotti, V. de O., & Suša, R. (2019). Beyond 2015, within the modern/colonial global imaginary? Global development and higher education. *Critical Studies in Education, 60*(3), 281–301.
https://doi.org/10.1080/17508487.2016.1247737

Stein, S., & Silva, J. E. da. (2020). Challenges and complexities of decolonizing internationalization in a time of global crises. *ETD – Educação Temática Digital, 22*(3), 546–66.

https://doi.org/10.20396/etd.v22i3.8659310

Tuck, E., & Yang, K. W. (2012). Decolonization is not a metaphor. *Decolonization: Indigeneity, Education&Society, 1*(1), 1–40.
https://jps.library.utoronto.ca/index.php/des/article/view/18630

White, J. (2019). The end of powerful knowledge? *London Review of Education, 17*(3), 429–38.
https://doi.org/10.18546/LRE.17.3.15

Zavale, N. C., & Langa, P. V. (2018). African diaspora and the search for academic freedom safe havens: Outline of a research agenda. *Journal of Higher Education in Africa / Revue de l'enseignement Supérieur En Afrique, 16*(1/2), 1–24.
https://www.jstor.org/stable/10.2307/26819626

Zeleza, P. T. (2009). African studies and universities since independence: The challenges of epistemic and institutional decolonization. *Transition, 23*(101), 110–35.
https://doi.org/10.2979/trs.2009.-.101.110

6. Closing the factory: Reimagining higher education as commons

Jim Luke

Learning is essential to human survival, but opportunities for advanced education have historically been limited. With the invention of the printing press, the proliferation of literacy, the adoption of technology to automate production, and the need for more educated workers, societies have become increasingly motivated to extend longer and longer periods of education to more and more of its members. In this unprecedented process of expanding access to education, the organising structures, and the imaginaries that inform them, have transformed over time.

This chapter, like this book, is explicitly about higher education and the good it provides. The author invites the reader to explore concepts such as "higher education", "good", "imaginary", "commons", and "knowledge commons" which may have varying connotations and are worthy of discussion to arrive at a shared understanding.

My perspective is a global, macro, historically informed economic perspective. By "economic", I do not mean market, capitalist, or any specific economic system. Rather, I mean higher education is in significant ways an economic institution. It uses real resources, and people engage in economic activity: producing, consuming, enjoying, and accumulating. The economics of higher education considers how these activities are to be organised and governed and their purpose or function in society. It is a macro perspective, because it is concerned with the degree to which the society supports higher education and why, and the ways that education benefits society.

The chapter encompasses the evolution of three imaginaries of higher education, two of which have repeated historically across the globe. In the early 21st century, an opportunity for a third imaginary has emerged, one that holds great promise and I propose needs the attention and efforts of both academics and the larger society.

The first describes how the social imaginary of higher education has been remarkably similar across civilisations. I will call this the "elite knowledge commons". The specifics of the membership of the elite, the organisation, support, subjects, traditions, and even pedagogies may differ, but there has been a shared imaginary, which has been socially beneficial albeit limited and inequitable.

The second involves the broadening of higher education beyond the historically elite due to economic development, much of it resulting from the Industrial Revolution and its accompanying production and communication technologies. This expansion of participation, itself a social good, brought with it a major alteration in the imaginary of higher education, which I call the "knowledge factory". This imaginary is illustrated by the experience of higher education in the US over the past 150 years. However, the emergence of this second imaginary is not unique to the US. As areas of the world have become industrialised, the knowledge factory imaginary extended its influence.

Current developments, such as internet technology, open pedagogy, OER, and open access publishing are creating the conditions to realise a third imaginary. Societies cannot and should not return to the elite knowledge commons because of its inequitable, undemocratic, and exclusive characteristics. Instead, I invite the reader to imagine a new knowledge commons, encompassing an open and equitable higher education. I do not provide a specific design for that commons because the rules and structure of a commons must arise from the community it serves. Rather, I identify the tasks and work needed to create that imaginary.

Terms

Higher education

In *The Origins of Higher Learning*, Lowe and Yasuhara (2017) provide a sweeping history of how humankind first evolved centres of higher learning from ancient times onward, throughout the eastern hemisphere. They use the term "centers of higher learning" as an umbrella term for what today we call higher education institutions (HEIs). Their term embraces a variety of different institutional arrangements across centuries and cultures, including the predecessors to today's universities and colleges.

Although I will use the term "higher education" and the acronyms HE and HEIs (higher education institutions) in keeping with the general practice of this book, I am referring to the broad conception of "centers of higher learning" referenced by Lowe and Yasuhara. This corresponds to the UNESCO (2012) concept of tertiary education, which encompasses all organisations that build on secondary education including advanced academic education, but also advanced vocational or professional education.

Imaginary

Charles Taylor (2004) defines a social imaginary as

> the ways people imagine their social existence, how they fit together with others, how things go on between them and their fellows, the expectations that are normally met, and the deeper normative notions and images that underlie these expectations. (p. 23)

The social imaginary of higher education represents the "normative notions and images" of what people expect the social role and purpose of HEIs to be. Imaginaries are important because they form the background or presumption of how things work that in turn drives the development of specific institutions, behaviours, and even language.

David Foster Wallace (2005 as cited in Clear, n.d.) frequently told a story of

> ... these two young fish swimming along and they happen to meet an older fish swimming the other way, who nods at them and says "Morning, boys. How's the water?" And the two young fish swim on for a bit, and then eventually one of them looks over at the other and goes "What the hell is water?" (para. 1)

The imaginary of higher learning is the water in which academics swim. The size, organisation, access, topics, and motivations for study in HEIs are driven by the imaginary. The imaginary shapes how we think about HEIs and higher learning as a pursuit. To better understand the imaginary, to see the water, it is helpful to examine:

- What good does higher learning provide? For whom?
- Who is higher learning for? Who determines the scope of what is to be learned? Just a few or many?
- What are the metaphors and language we use to describe higher learning and HEIs?
- Why sustain higher learning? What stories or theories do we tell to justify or explain it?
- How are the people involved to be organised? How is the endeavour structured or governed?

Lowe and Yasuhara discerned a common pattern from ancient times and across civilisations, geography, and cultures regarding these questions and more. What they found in the origins has been quite consistent and forms an imaginary for HEIs that persists today. I call that imaginary the elite knowledge commons. The elite knowledge commons provided society with great good by furthering civilisation and social, domestic, and political order, but was limited. A primary effect was to entrench and perpetuate the power of ruling classes. In little more than a century, a new imaginary has emerged to overcome the flaw but has also had its flaws and limitations.

Good

Higher learning develops technologies and knowledge that improve and extend lives. But beyond the practical, it provides meaning. Lowe and Yasuhara (2017) describe it as "sustained interest in questions that went beyond daily survival" (p. xiii). HE nurtures culture, governance, religion, arts, and science. It helps people make meaning of life. It is common to all civilisations in some fashion, and we may consider it essential to civilisation.

However, being essential to civilisation does not mean universally applicable. In addition to the content and extent of knowledge created and stewarded by HEIs, I explicitly consider the extent of participation in higher learning. Access, more participation by more people, is itself an important dimension of goodness to be considered.

There are numerous examples of the ways higher education, by extending the collective pool of human knowledge and technology, has provided social good. Let us consider just one, the example of longevity and health. Less than 150 years ago, the average human life expectancy throughout the world, across all cultures and throughout history, hovered between 26 and 40 years. Then in the past 150 years, the knowledge created and shared, most often via HEIs, triggered a great transformation. According to *Our World in Data*, "Since 1900 the global average life expectancy has more than doubled and is now above 70 years" (Roser, Ortiz-Ospina, & Ritchie, 2019). The authors explain there is still inequality between countries but all countries have improved. The nations with the shortest life expectancies today have longer life expectancy than existed in the best countries before 1900. This more than doubling of life expectancy at birth, primarily from reduced child mortality, in a mere century and a half has benefited humanity. Entire diseases have been eradicated and sanitation greatly improved. The solutions that extended life arose from communal knowledge pools created and shared by scholars working together in HEIs.

Learning is literally an economic good in the sense that people and society demand more of it. These benefits are mostly externalities. Yes, learning provides individual benefits for the scholar involved, but the greatest portion of the benefits accrue to people who are not directly involved in a particular learning activity. This existence of externalities is critical to acknowledge since it means that imaginaries that rely on market-oriented decision-making by individuals will not achieve a social optimum.

Commons

By commons I mean a communal-based economic institution designed to resolve collective action problems with respect to a shared resource pool that is valuable but limited. I follow the guidelines and definitions of Elinor Ostrom and related scholars (Caffentzis, 2013; Hess, 2012; Hess & Ostrom, 2007; Nordman, 2021; Ostrom 1990, 2005). They identify conditions for commons, making it clear that a commons is not just a collection of things. There must be a "common pool resource" (CPR), a collection of resources that people share. Contrary to popular understanding, a commons is not the CPR itself. The community of people and the rules, norms, and mechanisms they evolve to govern and steward the CPR constitute the commons. For example, the fish in a particular river may be a CPR. The community comprises the fishery and the people who do the fishing, extract, and possibly consume those fish from that CPR. The community evolves norms and mechanisms for self-governance and stewardship of the CPR. In our fishery example, this may include limits on sizes of the catch or times to fish. Fish are not a commons; fisheries are.

Key elements of any commons are that it is (1) neither state-owned nor private, (2) neither centralised nor totally decentralised, (3) not hierarchical. A very large commons typically has a polycentric, nested structure that comprises many smaller networked commons, each of which determines its own norms and governance.

Further, there must be some collective action problem associated with the community's use of the common pool. Typically, a collective action problem is a conflict between individual choices and community benefit or sustainability. Can individuals be prevented from making choices that benefit themselves at the expense of the community? Can the individual be protected from abuse by the community? In a commons, the community transparently and democratically organises itself, establishes behavioural norms or rules, and then enforces those norms. In other words, it creates its own governance. Governance is not imposed from outside or above. It may be informed by networked knowledge of other commons — what is called polycentricity but must govern itself. Transparency and communication are usually key to self-governance.

Ostrom (1990) also determined empirically that a commons, particularly the longest lasting and most sustainable, is strongly bounded. A bounded commons is clearly defined in both membership and the scope of activity or CPR involved. Behaviour is transparent and observable by other members of the community. Intra-commons communication is easy. The issue of boundedness will prove central to our story of the changing imaginary of higher education. Ostrom and the scholars of the Ostrom Workshop in their empirical studies of commons throughout the world have found that, contrary to the popular fallacy of the tragedy of the commons, many well-organised commons are among the most sustainable and long-lasting social and communal structures known, outlasting most governments, nation-states, empires, and businesses (Nordman, 2021).

Knowledge commons

In recent decades, many scholars, including Elinor Ostrom herself (Caffentzis 2012; Hess 2012; Ostrom & Hess, 2007), began work to define and analyse higher education and the knowledge commons. One of those scholars, Caffentzis (2012), observed that knowledge is "a vast communal product being produced prodigiously on a daily basis... knowledge is both an end and a means to an even higher end" (p. 31). This communal product, this knowledge commons, has been a boon to humanity.

Caffentzis (2012) makes a powerful case for thinking of knowledge, which is the product of learning, as a commons. The tangible artefacts of higher learning, the journal articles, books, and other writings, are not the knowledge commons. These artifacts aren't even the sum of the common pool resource. The common pool resource is the intangible sum of human knowledge. Knowledge is intangible. It is in the knower, a human being for whom it is meaningful. However, human knowledge is ephemeral, and we humans long ago invented texts and other means of more permanently encoding that knowledge so that others may share in it. The CPR is both what the scholars know and what the library encodes for the learner.

The commons, then, is the community of scholars that establishes the rules and norms and that navigates and manages the use, creation, and sharing of this CPR, this shared pool of human knowledge. Caffentzis (2012) suggests that universities:

> ...are the institutions that present themselves both as providing the preliminary training required to access knowledge and as expanding the dimensions of the knowledge commons through scientific and scholarly research and artistic creations. (p. 35)

I will expand Caffentzis' assertion in two ways. First, we should consider all institutions of tertiary education not as separate institutions, but as a polycentric network of smaller commons within the larger knowledge commons. Second, teaching and research are two facets of the same activity: stewardship of the knowledge pool.

The past and still present imaginary: The elite knowledge commons

HEIs have roots in commons structures, as is evident in Lowe and Yasuhara's (2017) survey of the origins of higher learning. They describe a pattern that holds across cultures and societies including Europe, the Islamic world, India, China, Persia, Korea, Japan, and Vietnam, summarised as follows:

- Libraries, a collection of artifacts, developed first, to accumulate and preserve human knowledge. These libraries attracted groups of scholars to study the texts, forming small communities.

- Higher learning was and is communal and social. Even a solitary reading of an old text is social. The scholar is still engaged in dialogue, albeit across time and space. As scholars learn, they generate artifacts of their learning and creativity. They write and add to the pool.

- Stewardship of the pool of knowledge was the mission. This occurred through scholars' own study, their additions to the pool, and the dissemination of their learning through documents or teaching.

- Teaching at these centres of higher learning became powerful mechanisms of dissemination of knowledge, distributing the benefits of the pool of knowledge to the larger society.

- Higher learning has powerful, positive externalities and benefits for the larger society. Indeed, these social benefits have nearly always been the primary motivation for a society's funding and support of higher learning centres, rather than the benefits to individual learners. While the mass of people indirectly benefited from the pool of human knowledge, it was the elites of power structures, the rulers, religious leaders, and aristocrats, who benefited most, leading to their willingness to economically support the centres.

- Long-term scholars at these centres evolved their own rules and governance. External economic support often came with restrictions on topics of study, but in general internal norms and conventions were set by each centre in a manner consistent with a commons. Eventually, with the advent of universities, the scholars came to be seen collectively as "the faculty" with rights to self-governance.

- To realise the benefits to society, scholars have had to be supported. Higher learning centres have nearly always been funded or supported by governments, large religious organisations, or wealthy patrons. Stewarding a knowledge commons does not feed the scholars unless they were previously endowed with land. HEIs are not self-supporting.

In the early examples of higher learning, the elements of commons are present. There is a CPR: the pool of knowledge, in the libraries' collections of texts and the collective learned knowledge of the scholars. There is a defined and bounded community: the scholars that evolved to become known as faculty. There is shared self-governance. There is polycentricity in the existence of networks of HEIs each with their own idiosyncratic self-governance and CPR yet sharing and communicating between the different HEIs.

There is also a collective action problem. The metrics that shape HE encourage and reward recognition and reputation, resulting in a perpetual choice between cooperation and competition amongst scholars. When the community is small and the faculty all know one another, the collective action problem is manageable. The stronger norms are communicated and shared with other commons. Strong norms, such as the prohibition on plagiarism, evolve to handle the collective action problem.

But who are the scholars? Who is included in the knowledge commons? How many are there? Historically, it has consisted of a small number of elite scholars in any society or civilisation. Until the twentieth century, enrolment in higher education was typically limited to a tiny percentage of the population aged 14 and over, regardless of nation or culture. Membership as a full scholar, a professor or equivalent, was even rarer. The specifics of who or what types of individuals were privileged to pursue higher education varied widely with culture and the society. Some societies valued religious scholarship, some valued the potential for administrative arts, yet others valued artistic merit, and some valued science.

The restriction to a very small number of participants — an elite — had multiple causes, most of which changed in the twentieth century. First, from a practical standpoint, agricultural productivity and economies simply could not produce the economic surplus to support any but a very small number of scholars. Second, the rulers and patrons providing the support often did not want expanded access. Finally, expanded access to higher learning depends on prior access to elementary (basic literacy) and secondary education. Those preconditions were not widely met in many countries until after they had experienced the Industrial Revolution.

Limiting access to higher education was socially a two-edged sword. By bounding and limiting access and membership in HEIs, the sustainability of the elite knowledge commons was enhanced. Few HEIs were self-supporting (other than by initial charitable endowments). Higher education has long been dependent on patrons, sovereigns, governments, and religious institutions for economic support, and the relationship was interdependent. HEIs provided the learned advisors and administrators who supported the powerful in return for financial support and the freedom to pursue their scholarly interests. Limitations on higher education access also served to limit HEIs' claims on the limited economic resources of society.

The limited access did not always result in social good for individual citizens. The greatest individual benefits were concentrated among the ruling classes. Much of society lacked the formal education necessary to achieve a better quality of life. In some cases, higher education became a conservative force perpetuating social injustice by supporting oppressive power structures.

Nonetheless, the elite knowledge commons proved a sustainable imaginary for millennia across cultures and nations. It remains today most clearly in a small number of centuries-old universities, the self-styled elite universities of today.

Opening access to knowledge: The knowledge factory

In roughly the same period as the great transformation of life expectancies, social and economic forces have been at play that would form a new imaginary, the knowledge factory.

In the late nineteenth century and early decades of the twentieth century, the US experienced dramatic economic growth and development. Technological, communication, and organisational innovations, themselves often (though not always) the product of HEIs or highly educated individuals, drove a need for a larger, better educated population. This economic growth, particularly when driven by improved agricultural productivity, enabled society to support a vastly larger class of scholars, either temporarily as students preparing for entry to the labour force or as permanent scholars working in HEIs. Improved living conditions and survivability naturally also led to a greater desire for learning among larger numbers of the population. In 1897, there were 386 HEIs in the US with the typical institution enrolling less than 780 students (Goldin & Katz, 1999, p. 41–44). By 2010, there were over seven thousand HEIs enrolling, on average, more than 3,075 students each (NCES [National Center for Education Statistics], 2019). The bulk of this growth happened between 1920 and 1970 (Goldin, 1999). This expansion gained momentum in the US around the beginning of the twentieth century. As the century progressed, new colleges and universities were created, and new forms of HEIs and new structures were developed. Two-year schools emerged, called junior colleges or community colleges. Colleges added professional schools and degrees, as well as graduate programs. When the twentieth century dawned, most colleges and universities were small, flat organisations with perhaps a president, a registrar, and the faculty. What is currently considered administrative work was divided among faculty members. As complexity grew, so did the need for more management and an apparent need for specialisation.

Economic development drove a need to increase both access to and the scope of HEIs. In the popular parlance, HEIs had to scale-up to handle vastly larger enrolments. This phenomenon started in, but was not limited to, the US; rather, as economic development spread across the globe, the pattern repeated. The examples I cite are from the US, but they are relevant to most economically developed countries and have been adopted as a model by many developing countries.

We should consider the increased access to HE as most definitely good because it corrected a flaw in the elite knowledge commons imaginary. Increased access enables improved opportunities, quality of life, and democratic participation. However, organising and coordinating this explosion of knowledge production and dissemination called for a new imaginary, as did the number and variety of forms of higher education.

A new imaginary for organising productive work was already available: the mass production and bureaucratic structure of the modern capitalist corporation — visible, praised by leaders, and intuitively understood by many. Alfred Chandler's (1977) revolutionary history and analysis of the modern corporation, *The Visible Hand*, recounts the formation of large-scale corporate enterprises during this period as part of the industrialisation process. Chandler details the increased demand for educated managers, engineers, and other professionals that it entailed. The connection to mass production is explicit. He describes the new managerial-focused imaginary of the multi-unit corporate enterprise as built upon the earlier work on bureaucracy by Max Weber in the previous century.

Chandler's managed multi-unit organisation is based on hierarchy, bureaucracy, a division of labour, plans, and defined, measurable, and repeatable objective outcomes. Production is the goal, and processes must be well-defined. The organisation is independent of the people involved. Metrics, plans, standardisation, objectification, defined lines of authority, and decision-making are essential.

HEIs in the US rapidly adopted this new bureaucratic, hierarchical structure built to achieve scale. As a practical matter, they couldn't adopt the use of accounting profits as the supreme goal or metric of success since most HEIs were financially supported by religious organisations, charitable contributions, endowments, or government funding rather than the fee-for-product/service characteristic of a capitalist firm. Explicit financial profits are not necessary to the adoption of the organisational paradigm; HEI leaders in the mid and late-twentieth century adopted the concept and language of mass production via an organisation that resembles a modern industrial enterprise. Clark Kerr (2001), the president and chancellor of the University of California, an advocate and architect of a massive publicly funded university system, compared the modern university to a corporate holding company. He said that a university was just the owner of a series of different entrepreneurial knowledge-producing enterprises to be managed by a professional manager for efficiency and effectiveness.

Words have power: The semantics of the knowledge factory

The adoption of the knowledge factory imaginary is visible in the semantics frequently used today. The imaginary itself is a metaphor. In a commons, there is little distinction between production and other activities such as consumption or appreciation. A household is a commons, yet we don't consider it exclusively a production facility. In the new imaginary, instead of centring learning as the core activity with all its implications, we have imagined a production process, a factory. We do not learn. We produce knowledge.

The new imaginary, unlike a commons, focuses predominantly on production, outcomes, and measurement of productive activities. The production must be objectively observable and countable. But what does higher education produce? How can it be measured? How is knowledge measured? What is success in learning?

The knowledge factory objectifies, commodifies, and reifies metrics as evidence of production. Production must have defined outcomes and plans so that the defined objects can be counted. The knowledge factory focused obsessively on institutional rankings, degrees and credentials granted, materials created and published, grade point averages, success, retention, and completion. HEIs seek to help students "acquire" job skills. I am sure the reader can add more.

Multi-unit corporate organisations have well-defined processes for production managed by engineers, often separate from the production workers themselves. Division of labour predominates. The knowledge factory has its own version of these processes. It has its own specialised administrative staff units/departments for human resources, facilities, legal, and accounting. There are research and lab specialists. It also has evolved instructional design, a group of specialists to define and manage the learning process and resources for maximum effectiveness to achieve preset learning outcomes.

The theory behind the knowledge factory imaginary: Human capital and intellectual property

Starting in the 1950s, economists led by Theodore Schultz (1981) and Gary Becker (1975) of the University of Chicago, developed "human capital theory" (HCT) (Blaug, 1976). Originally conceived to reconcile empirical wage differences with orthodox "free market" theory, HCT was soon embraced by policymakers as a normative principle. HCT defined the value of education in strictly individualistic economic terms: higher wages for educated workers due to higher market productivity. Widespread embrace of HCT and the language of HCT helped to reframe the purpose of higher education.

HCT in the HEI-as-mass-producer imaginary easily penetrated the consciousness of higher education, at least at the leadership and policy maker level, because HCT aligned well with the goals of neoliberal political forces in developed countries in the 1970s and 1980s.

HCT analogises the individual to capital. Education is an "investment" in an individual's future ability to produce marketable output. In HCT, what matters is individual financial gain and what can be traded in the market. The output of HEIs is now split. The "teaching" side of the enterprise produces valuable college graduates, with value measured by the increase in the earnings that the labour market assigns. The "research" side produces new knowledge as measured by publications, citation counts, and monetisable inventions, all created in a publish-or-perish environment. The broad social benefits of higher education, largely the result of economic externalities and human lived experience, are no longer considered.

Equally important as HCT was the emergence of the concept of "intellectual property" (IP). IP locates knowledge not in the scholar or the learner but in the tangible artefacts produced: the writings, publications, and inventions. Capitalist-oriented governments were increasingly willing to bestow market monopoly privileges to the creators of these artefacts via copyrights and patents. Instead of recognising knowledge as accumulated learning known and shared by scholars, knowledge was reduced to a tangible, measurable product.

HCT and IP together redefined knowledge and learning in the higher education imaginary and helped to create a new division of labour.

Teaching produced graduates and research produced knowledge products: journal articles, patents, inventions, and books. Between HCT and IP, the reimagination of higher education as purely a production enterprise was complete, and, in theory at least, measurable. All that was missing now in the imaginary of the knowledge factory were the engineering or design components embodied in standardisation of courses, assessment metrics, the role of instructional design as separate from the instructor, and increased division of labour. Education's value could be measured as return-on-investment (ROI). The society-wide benefits of higher education became the higher GDP growth rate resulting from the sum of the individuals' ROIs.

A contested imaginary

The imaginary of the knowledge factory continues to animate higher education in the US and many other countries today. It is successful if measured by the number, size, or growth in number of HEIs that implicitly have adopted it. However, it is not widely popular. The older HEIs of the elite knowledge commons have, unsurprisingly, long resisted the call for widespread access. Wide access is anathema to elite-ness. Elite institutions have largely responded by adopting factory tactics: rankings and competition. The elites can maintain their elite-ness by establishing that they are the best and the others are all lesser.

Knowledge factories enable enclosure of the CPR since knowledge is no longer a common pool. It is property to be privately-owned for the generation of profit, deriving its profits from redirection of the economic resources devoted to supporting higher learning. To the neoliberal supporters of IP, HCT, and the knowledge factory imaginary, this is a feature not a bug. But to thousands of scholars worldwide, it has been the trigger for a world-wide movement advocating open education and open educational resources (OER).

Nor is the knowledge factory popular even among its own scholars. The knowledge factory imaginary improves upon the knowledge elite imaginary by improving access, a beneficial effect. However, it does so by promoting bureaucracy, competition, and the reduction of scholars and scholarship to commodities in a corporate enterprise. Meaningful scholarship is likely to be diminished in the drive for increased productivity. These forces limit our collective ability to imagine and create beneficial solutions to compelling social problems today, such as climate change, inequity, global public health, poverty, and others. We have a pressing need for a different imaginary.

An open knowledge commons

The great good of the knowledge factory imaginary is dramatically expanded access, i.e. the value of bringing higher learning to masses of people instead of a small elite. Yet it appears that the factory imaginary is not sustainable. Kate Raworth (2017) in *Doughnut Economics*, her popular book on reimagining economics, identifies four realms of provisioning for people's needs: the state, market/firms, households, and commons. The large hierarchical bureaucracies of the knowledge factory make it appear that HEIs must belong to either the realm of the state or the market/firm, depending on direct funding source and ownership. Raworth reminds us that there is a proven alternative for education: the commons. Our challenge then is to reimagine and find ways to implement a sustainable knowledge commons as open to all.

What would such a knowledge commons look like? The commons, its norms, and its governance mechanisms must evolve from the community itself, not be imposed from a central authority, whether by state or private capital. There is no panacea, as Ostrom (1990) quite frequently preached. There are, however, clear principles which can be used, and are being used, as alternatives to the predominant knowledge factory imaginary.

Scope not scale, humanocracy not bureaucracy

HE leaders often refer to increasing access as "scaling up"; this language, adopted from capitalist mass-production oriented corporations, misleads. Strictly speaking, higher education cannot scale in the economic sense, rather it can increase scope or proliferate (Luke, 2018). Economically and organisationally speaking, scale means to produce the same thing, the same way, repeatedly until a high volume is achieved.

Education is different. Teaching and learning are not so much scalable, rather they are expandable in scope via networks.

By reframing increasing access as expanding the network of HEIs, by increasing scope instead of the size of each HEI, the commons can be protected while expanding the numbers reached. This is a viable alternative to scaling. In addition, polycentricity supports respect for self-determination and differences between entities. The same network principle can help us to redesign existing HEIs as flat enterprises instead of hierarchical bureaucracies (Hamel & Zanini, 2020).

Focus on the social, not the individual

HEIs are not self-sustaining. The current embrace of HCT and IP discourages social and public support of higher education. HCT reduces the public support question to a financing mechanism for what is assumed to be solely private, individual benefits. At one time, the social and public benefits of higher education were commonly acknowledged, such as an informed and discerning electorate, a functional infrastructure, a stable, sustainable, and equitable economic system, acknowledged universal civil rights, optimal public health and longevity, and the opportunity to engage in leisure, self-development, and personal growth. Scholars and HEIs must return to a focus on public, social benefits.

Resist new forms of enclosures

Private enterprises, in particular publishers, edtech vendors, land developers, and finance firms, extract their revenue and profits from the flow of resources intended to support HEIs, often under a demonstrably false assumption of greater efficiency. This is a form of enclosure of the commons and represents a failure to effectively solve the collective action problem. Such enterprises have used new technologies to effectively breach the bounds of the commons and siphon off resources. Many of these firms are creating a new version of the knowledge factory in which knowledge production is privatised and managed by investors outside the HEIs (Williamson, 2022). An alternative imaginary, the new open knowledge commons, must be disseminated and protected at least as effectively and persistently as these privatisation narratives.

The various "open" movements including open access publishing, OER, open pedagogy, and free, open-source software provide a promising beginning. They need not only greater participation and support by HEIs and academics, but also better explication of their role in forming an open knowledge commons rather than just being a cheaper alternative to for-profit firms and vendors. An alternative imaginary requires academics to spend more time and effort building networks across both HEIs and education-adjacent organisations such as libraries and museums, and less time or effort on hierarchies and rankings. Such a shift in effort entails the willingness to forego the knowledge factory paradigm in HEI governance.

Resolving the collective action problem by cooperating, not competing

Corporations are built on competition between institutions and between people in the institution. Competition creates collective action problems and sub-optimal choices. Institutional rankings, for example, are destructive and less than zero-sum: most lose — and the winners gain little. A restoration of the commons would require a change in our language, our behaviour, and agreed norms to restore cooperation at all levels, from individual scholars to institutions. Structures and roles need to be reimagined internally to reduce division of labour and bureaucracy, focusing instead on building teams and networks both within existing HEIs and between organisations. Research already happens at the cross-institution level, but such collaboration and sharing could be expanded to pedagogy and support functions.

To restore cooperation requires more communication and more perspectives. It requires listening and trust. Both result from more active communication and human connections. While it sounds daunting and idealistic, it is possible through the communications technologies now available based on the internet and the open web. The difficulty of communication between physically distant groups has long been a major barrier to collaboration, whether in HE or the rest of the economy. The existence and continued development of the internet and web, themselves the creation of academic collaboration and sharing, make a dream of a global networked knowledge commons feasible.

Conclusion

Two imaginaries have dominated higher learning, both of which have produced some good, but both have flaws. The elite knowledge commons created and stewarded human knowledge and higher learning for millennia across the world, delivering broad social benefits, but allowing the elite and their sponsors or patrons to retain power and control of society.

In the past century or so a new imaginary, the knowledge factory emerged to mass produce knowledge and spread the good of higher education to millions, even billions, more people — a good thing indeed. But the knowledge factory itself is not sustainable and is not a good steward. It objectifies and commodifies knowledge, leaving it lifeless and separated from the humans who would know it. It values possession and accumulation, not learning, living, knowing, and sharing.

HEIs are not knowledge factories. Learning is individual and knowledge is not a commodity to be mass produced. When learning is structured as mass production — as a factory — the power to control learning and ultimately people's future lives is concentrated in just a few leaders. The people in higher education: students, educators, scholars, and administrators are not interchangeable parts in a production process. Rather, knowledge is a living pool stewarded by people, each unique but connected to others. Collectively, the pool is a profound good from which all humanity can draw creative solutions.

As a species, we humans face daunting challenges today. Our technology connects us across the globe but has not yet overcome our divisiveness. Our planet is rapidly burning up due to our own activities, yet we haven't been able to stop it. Even our signature accomplishment of the past century and a half, the lengthening of our very lives themselves, appears to have reversed in some countries as we struggle with a pandemic and diseases of despair. The key to our collective survival is our collective knowledge and our willingness to collaborate in good faith. To unlock and utilise the great and growing pool of knowledge, we need to reimagine higher education as an open commons. Scholars are not cogs in a capitalist knowledge factory. We need stewards of the public knowledge commons.

Acknowledgements

I'd like to acknowledge Sue-Anne Sweeney, my wife, partner, and colleague for her constant support, inspiration, assistance, and patience. Without her, my ideas and words would still be stuck in my brain. I'd also like to thank Laura Czerniewicz and Catherine Cronin, Robin DeRosa, Su-Ming Koo, Kate Bowles, and many others for their insistent encouragement to pursue my research on the commons in higher education.

References

Becker, G. S. (1975). *Human capital: A theoretical and empirical analysis, with special reference to education.* University of Chicago Press.

Blaug, M. (1976). The empirical status of human capital theory: A slightly jaundiced survey. *Journal of Economic Literature, 14*(3), 827–55. https://www.jstor.org/stable/2722630

Caffentzis, C. G. (2012). From lobsters to universities: The making of the knowledge commons. *St Antony's International Review, 8*(1), 25–42. http://www.jstor.org/stable/26229085 Chandler, A. D. (*1993*). *The visible hand: The managerial revolution in American* business. Harvard University Press.

Clear, J. (n.d.). "This is water" delivered by David Foster Wallace. *James Clear.* https://jamesclear.com/great-speeches/this-is-water-by-david-foster-wallace/

Goldin, C. (1999). *A brief history of education in the United States.* National Bureau of Economic Research. https://doi.org/10.3386/h0119

Goldin, C. & Katz, L. (1999). The shaping of higher education: The formative years in the United States, 1890 to 1940. *Journal of Economic Perspectives, 13*(1), 37–62. https://doi.org/10.1257/jep.13.1.37

Hamel, G. & Zanini, M. (2020). *Humanocracy: Creating organizations as amazing as the people inside them.* Harvard Business Review Press.

Hess, C. (2012). The unfolding of the knowledge commons. *St Antony's International Review, 8*(1), 13–24. https://www.jstor.org/stable/10.2307/26229084

Hess, C. & Ostrom, E. (Eds), (2007). *Understanding knowledge as a commons: From theory to practice.* MIT Press.
https://doi.org/10.7551/mitpress/6980.001.0001

Kerr, C. (2001). *The uses of the university.* Harvard University Press.

Lowe, R., & Yasuhara, Y. (2016). *The origins of higher learning: Knowledge networks and the early development of universities.* Routledge.
https://doi.org/10.4324/9781315728551

Luke, J. (2019, May 20). *Scale and scope.* Econproph.
https://econproph.com/2019/05/20/scale-and-scope/

NCES. (2019) *Digest of education statistics.* National Center for Education Statistics.
https://nces.ed.gov/programs/digest/2019menu_tables.asp

Nordman, E. (2021). *The uncommon knowledge of Elinor Ostrom: Essential lessons for collective action.* Island Press.

Ostrom, E. (1990). *Governing the commons.* Cambridge University Press.

Ostrom, E. (2005) *Understanding institutional diversity.* Princeton University Press.
https://doi.org/10.1515/9781400831739

Roser, M., Ortiz-Ospina, E., & Ritchie, H. (2019). *Life expectancy.* Our World in Data.
https://ourworldindata.org/life-expectancy

Raworth, K. (2017). *Doughnut economics: Seven ways to think like a 21st-century economist.* Chelsea Green Publishing. https://doi.org/10.1525/9780520318540

Taylor, C. (2004). *Modern social imaginaries.* Duke University Press.
https://doi.org/10.1215/9780822385806

UNESCO. (2012). *Standard classification of education 2011.* UNESCO Institute for Statistics.
https://doi.org/10.15220/978-92-9189-123-8-en

Williamson, B. & Komljenovic, J. (2022). Investing in imagined digital futures: The techno-financial "futuring" of edtech investors in higher education. *Critical Studies in Education,* 64(3), 234–49.
https://doi.org/10.1080/17508487.2022.2081587

7. Fostering the gift: On property regimes and teaching pedagogies in higher education

Andreas Wittel

Let us begin this chapter with a story of hope. As for all parts of society, the COVID-19 lockdown had profound implications for higher education in the United Kingdom. I want to point to one of the most surprising implications regarding bureaucracy, processes, procedures, and regulations. Such procedures are products of strictly hierarchical decisions that are imposed, as in all corporations, by managerial staff. The most astonishing realisation about changes due to lockdown was the fact that many well-established procedures could not only be changed, but they could also be changed with lightning speed. Furthermore, these changes all handed over power to university teachers, or more precisely, the changes handed power back to university teachers. With the commodification of higher education and the transformation of formerly public institutions into profit-making corporations, the autonomy of university teachers had become significantly reduced over the last decades. Suddenly, however, this autonomy returned. Shortly after the introduction of lockdown, university teachers found themselves free to make crucial decisions about adapting teaching to the requirements of the sudden shift to online education. They were asked to improvise and find flexible solutions. They did not have to justify their decisions. University teachers were the only ones who could rescue the academic year for students and therefore, for the university. They were given a carte blanche for this rescue.

To give an example: assessments are one of the most scrutinised areas of quality control in higher education. They are scrutinised by the united efforts of managers, teachers, and external examiners.

Making changes to assessments is a complex procedure, one that takes time. While the duration of this process differs across universities, applications for changes are usually made many months before the start of a new academic year. This means that often more than a year can pass between the initial application for a change of assessment, and the actual period in which the assessment is carried out. The scrutiny of assessments is so vigorous that there is no room for spontaneity. It is also difficult to introduce a new assessment from a perspective of sheer curiosity, from a trial-and-error position that can reverse things if the changes do not work well. With the introduction of lockdown, some assessments had to be changed. This affected student presentations, which had to be moved to an online mode. Applications for extensions were granted without evidence or any questions asked. What mattered were not established procedures but finding a way to complete the academic year so that students could move on.

This period of increased power and autonomy for university teachers did not last long. Soon management took back control and bureaucratic procedures were re-established. Still, this is a story of hope. It demonstrates that alternatives exist, that neither the bureaucratic procedures nor the hierarchical power structures within the university are set in stone. It also demonstrates that it is important, even imperative, to imagine an alternative university and an alternative form of higher education. The invitation to reflect on good education is a challenge that demands imagination. It is in this spirit that I will address the theme of this book: good education.

In the first part, *Higher education as a gift*, I argue that higher education is a gift, like art, or better, that it can be a gift. For the gift to emerge we need to explore the political-economic context in which higher education operates. We also need to examine teaching pedagogies that provide fertile soil for the gift. I examine the potential of the gift to shine from these two angles. The first angle (property regimes or political economies) will be explored in the second part of this chapter — *From public to private to common good*. In the third part, *Higher education for life*, I explore good pedagogies. I argue that in times of multiple and existential crises, three pedagogical principles are particularly important to create the gift.

Higher education as a gift

Hyde (2007) develops an innovative approach to gift theory. He explores art as a gift and explains the connection between the gift and art through a comparison of art with non-art. Using the example of a specific line of romantic novels that are mass-produced "according to a formula developed through market research" (Hyde 2007, p. xv), Hyde explains their form of mass production published within fixed formulaic parameters. Hyde (2007) argues that this series of romantic novels is not perceived as art since it has been written with only one intention: for it to be sold on the market:

It is the assumption of this book that a work of art is a gift, not a commodity. Or, to state the modern case with more precision, that works of art exist simultaneously in two 'economies', a market economy and a gift economy. Only one of these is essential, however: a work of art can survive without a market, but where there is no gift there is no art (p. xvi).

For Hyde, the notion of the gift refers on the one hand to the creation of the artwork, to the gift or talent of the artist. But it also refers to an audience, to those who get challenged, touched, moved, inspired, or transformed by a work of art. The inner world of the gift is the inner world of the artist, the creator of the gift. The outer world refers to the recipients of the gift. While most anthropologists, starting with Mauss (1954), explore the gift from the perspective of social relations, Hyde has his starting point with the gift as an object. From this perspective of the gift as an object, he then explores its social dimensions. These social dimensions, Hyde insists, are not just the bond between the gift giver and its receiver. Ultimately, they are about a community of people who circulate gifts.

Hyde's interest in the immaterial aspects of the gift is particularly relevant to my argument. A painting in a gallery exists obviously in a very material form, often with a frame that marks its physical space. However, the gift of this painting does not travel in its material form, as the painting does not leave the gallery. The gift that the visitor of a gallery receives by being drawn to the painting is completely immaterial: a thought, a feeling, an experience, an understanding, a memory, a connection, or a vision.

For Hyde, the cardinal difference between gift exchange and commodity exchange is the fact that a gift establishes a bond, whereas the commodity does not. The commodity might have value (in the sense of exchange value), but the gift has worth: "We do not deal in commodities when we wish to initiate or preserve ties of affection" (Hyde 2007, p. 85). For this reason, we associate the gift with community and with obligation, whereas we associate commodities with alienation and freedom. The bond creating nature of the gift is also the reason why some gifts must be refused.

Perhaps the most important point Hyde makes about gifts is their tendency to circulate. He uses various examples to illustrate their circulation in gift communities. Scientific knowledge blossoms much more in a gift environment compared to a market environment that treats scientific knowledge as a commodity. This is also true for material gifts which leave the binary of giving and taking, often travelling from one person to the next. The gift increases its worth as it moves from the second to the third person. Hyde (2007) posits that "While gifts are marked by motion and momentum at the level of the individual, gift exchange at the level of the group offers equilibrium and coherence, a kind of anarchist stability" (p. 97). Indeed, Hyde sees strong connections between anarchist theory and practices of gift exchange. Ultimately, he understands gifts as an "anarchist property" (Hyde 2007, p. 120). Both gift exchange and anarchism share the assumption that community appears at its best when parts of the self are not restrained but given away.

Higher education is a gift and not a commodity, just as art is a gift and not a commodity. It can exist in two economies — in a market economy and in a gift economy. However, only one of these is essential. Education can survive without a market, but where there is no gift, there is no education. The gift in education is something that lies beyond economic rationality: it refers to a specific form of pedagogy. Similar to art, the gift in education refers to a gifted teacher and to a student who becomes enriched, inspired, challenged, moved, or transformed. For the gift in higher education to emerge, certain conditions must be met. These conditions refer to both property regimes (or to political economies) and to pedagogical principles. Let us begin with the exploration of the political-economic context of higher education.

From public to private to common good

There is little disagreement in the literature that the transformation of the public university into a corporate institution, and the transformation of academic work into academic labour, is not a development to be applauded. The many downsides are all too clear, starting with the obvious fact that students begin their adult life with the burden of a huge amount of debt which they will have to repay for years and decades to come. Particularly problematic is the integration of education into consumer culture and the transformation of an educational interaction into a service industry, where students are turned into customers and teachers into facilitators.

This raises the question: which political economy of higher education can protect or even foster the gift? I argue that the status and the nature of the gift in education changes according to the political-economic regime in which higher education is provided. These political-economic regimes refer to different forms of property: public property and private property. In both regimes, the public university and the commodified university, the gift is obscured.

In regimes of education as a private good (the commodified or corporate university), the gift becomes so obscured that it is nearly invisible. We do not perceive something to be a gift that we pay for. Considering that fees in higher education are often life-changing investments, it is no wonder that students expect a good return for their investment. What happens when students are turned into consumers of education? For Stiegler (2010), consumerism produces impoverished and passive subjects, leading to a destruction of "savoir vivre with the aim of creating available purchasing power" (p. 27). He describes consumerism as a form of proletarianisation. While he does not connect his critique of consumerism to the field of education, such a link is rather illuminating. Students who define themselves as consumers of education become impoverished as all positive aspects of learning (including the work, dedication, commitment, and energy that is required to learn) are overshadowed by an ideology that equates the purchase of education with the ownership of knowledge. After all, consumption is the opposite of production and work. It is safe to say that the market intensifies experiences of alienation for both the teacher and the student. Ultimately the market suffocates the gift-giving and gift-receiving nature of education.

However, this does not mean that a return to the public university is necessarily the most desirable option. In regimes of education as a public good, the gift gets obscured by the provision of a service by the state, a provision that is free for students and paid for by taxes. Nostalgia for education as a public good tends to ignore the critique that this regime has generated. Nearly half a century ago, Bourdieu (1986) argued convincingly that class and social distinctions are predominantly upheld through education and the public university. Willis (1977) and Collins (1979) have developed similar arguments about university education as a space of privilege. For this reason, I have much sympathy with the position of the Edu-factory collective (2009) which states the following:

> The state university is in ruins, the mass university is in ruins, and the university as a privileged place of national culture — just like the concept of national culture itself — is in ruins. We're not suffering from nostalgia. Quite the contrary, we vindicate the university's destruction. (p. 1)

It is only in a third regime, in the political economy of the commons that the gift in higher education can truly shine. Obviously, this does not mean that every higher education commons is per se an idyllic site. Issues of power and domination will not go away, but the common ownership of higher education does provide the most fertile ground for the gift to unfold.

A commons is generally understood as a set of natural or cultural resources that can be used by all those members who are part of a commons. The members of a commons are stakeholders with an equal interest in the resources that are being shared. The resources are created or administered by the commoners. The enemy of the commons is the market. Processes of privatisation, marketisation, and commodification of common property are an enclosure or a dispossession of the commons. Together with the state, the market aims to destroy the commons.

Liberal concepts of the commons (Ostrom, 1990) emphasise the sharing of resources. My understanding of a commons is more influenced by Marxist concepts of a commons as a social system. De Angelis (2017) makes an important distinction between endogenous and exogenous dimensions of the commons. While Ostrom is mostly concerned with the internal aspects of the commons (with the social system between commoners), Marxian theorists are more interested in how the social system of a commons is influenced by external factors, by capital. The Marxian perspective is vital for an understanding of the difficulties to create a higher education commons.

To explore the possibility of a higher education commons, we need to start with the relation between education and a commons. The notion of an education commons is rather problematic. If we apply the definition of liberal commons theorists such as Ostrom's, the shared resource in an education commons would be knowledge. However, contrary to the definition, knowledge is not equally shared in a community of education commoners. In fact, it cannot be equally shared as the very process of education is fundamentally hierarchical, with teachers more likely to be on the giving end (delivering knowledge and deciding on the form of pedagogy), and students more likely to be on the receiving end of the educational process. A similar problem arises with the self-organisation and the governance of an education commons. It is difficult to imagine a setting that gives students the same influence as teachers in the organisation, and the normative framework in educational processes.

Still, there are numerous examples of education commons. For this, we should turn to anarchist and libertarian theories and practices of education (Suissa, 2010). Most anarchist educators see an anarchist school as an embryo of a future anarchist society. Therefore, anarchist education must embrace and reflect core anarchist values and principles such as equality, autonomy, brotherhood, solidarity, mutualism, non-coercion, generosity, and collective forms of decision-making. One of the key challenges for anarchist education is to translate these values and principles into the practicalities of the relationship between teachers and students. The challenge is to make this relationship as equal and non-hierarchical as possible. Famous anarchist schools such as the Escuela Moderna in Barcelona, the Ferrer School in New York, and the Walden Center in Berkeley have put their emphasis on a more spontaneous, child-centred, anti-authoritarian pedagogy, on learning-by-doing, and on communal and co-operative learning. Students are included in decision-making processes about the curriculum and encouraged to organise their own work schedules. Rigid timetables are to be avoided, and students allowed to come and go as they wish. Last, but not least, such schools insist on a form of teaching that does not make use of grades, awards, or punishments.

Another example of an education commons is the much younger tradition of homeschooling or home education communities. While homeschooling is as old as humankind, the modern homeschooling movement started in the 1960s as a reaction to state education. It is not an anarchist invention but has received much support from anarchist educational philosophers. Homeschooling initiatives are neither organised by the market nor by the state. They are run by parent-commoners and function according to the time and labour they invest. All parents who are part of a homeschooling network invest more or less in such a project and have an approximate influence in the governance of the network.

What does this mean for higher education? Due to the highly specialised nature of higher education, an arrangement like homeschooling is difficult to set up in capitalist societies. Nevertheless, a tradition of a higher education commons does exist in the form of free and autonomous universities. Free and autonomous universities such as the Free and Autonomous University of San Francisco in the US, or the Social Science Centre in the UK are neither organised by the market nor by the state.

Although free and autonomous universities have a long historical tradition, their recent surge is very much a response to the commodification of higher education. Free and autonomous universities are an activist approach to higher education that aims to create a non-alienated framework for teaching and learning. These institutions usually do not have formal recognition. They are not able to offer certification comparable to public or private universities. However, this is not seen as a problem. On the contrary, it gives them a great amount of freedom with respect to both organisational structures and pedagogical approaches.

While organisational structures and pedagogical approaches vary between these institutions, there is a good deal of common ground. Most of them avoid or aim to reduce hierarchical structures between teachers and students. Most of them operate based on collective decision-making processes. They also share much common ground with respect to pedagogy and the meaning of education. They reject a vision of university education that prepares students for work in capitalist economies. Instead, they aim to transform higher education. They see education as a social and political project, as a crucial steppingstone for the creation of another society. Indeed, free and autonomous universities share most of the values of the anarchist theories of education.

Free and autonomous universities have emerged in many geographical locations all over the world in the last two decades, but most of them are or were in the strongholds of neoliberal capitalism, namely in the UK and the USA. It should also be noted that many of these initiatives have had a rather short lifespan. To understand why it is so difficult to develop sustainable institutions of autonomous higher education, we need to turn our attention to labour. Educational labour takes place predominantly in the interaction between teacher and student. While this educational labour is voluntary and non-paid labour, therefore a non-alienated form of labour, it is nonetheless intense and time-consuming. It requires a significant and sustainable enthusiasm from those who provide it. It is in these settings that the gift of higher education can shine especially bright and clear. However, as this is a gift that does not generate an obligation to return the gift — like art — it is fragile and vulnerable, because it comes with a high price for those who teach without getting paid for their work. One of the longest initiatives in the UK was the Social Science Centre in Lincoln, which opened in 2011 and was closed in 2019.

Higher education for life: On resonance, relevance, and imagination

The third and final part of this chapter engages with pedagogies that help to assert the gift in higher education. I focus on three pedagogical principles: resonance, relevance, and imagination. Resonance is about the relationship between the teacher and the student. Relevance is about the content that is taught. Imagination is about a learning objective.

Resonance

Let us inspect closer the educational gift that emerges in the interaction between student and teacher. For this, I will introduce Hartmut Rosa's concept of resonance. Rosa (2013) analyses contemporary social transformations mainly through the lens of acceleration. Rosa identifies three forms of acceleration that have changed the speed of modern life. The first one, technological acceleration, refers to transport technologies, communication technologies, and technologies of production. The second form is the acceleration of social change which refers to things such as cultural knowledge, social institutions, and personal relationships. The third form is the acceleration in the pace of life and a chronic lack of time: even though technological change should free up time for individuals (as we can travel, communicate, and produce at ever-increasing speed), our pace of life is still accelerating. These three forms and their internal connection is what Rosa calls "social acceleration". The discrepancy between technological acceleration and organisation efficiency, and the acceleration of our pace of life is what Rosa (2013) defines as growth: "the average rate of growth (defined as the increase of the total quantity of things produced, communicated, distances covered, etc.) exceeds the average rate of acceleration" (p. 68–69). To put it simply, the more we try to save time via technological means, the less time we have. However, this does not mean that technological innovations are the culprit. These innovations do not make our life faster. They are rather a consequence of an experience of a scarcity of time. The real culprit is capitalism, a system that turns time into money and acceleration into profit. In the logic of capital, social acceleration turns into an unavoidable compulsion.

From this perspective, Rosa develops a new critique of alienation. If changes in the pace of our lives occur at an ever faster rate, it becomes difficult to maintain strong feelings, convictions, and connections — social, institutional, personal, and intimate connections. What is required instead is flexibility and adaptability to change. There is no need for depth and authenticity anymore. All attempts to intimately familiarise with the status quo, and all attempts to create stability, stand in direct contrast to the need to keep up with change. Rosa understands alienation as a loss of autonomy and self-determination, as an experience of life under the condition of frenetic acceleration.

For Rosa (2016), the opposite of alienation is resonance. We are non-alienated when we manage to build non-instrumental, responsive, and transformative relationships. These are relationships with people, but also with nature and with art. They are not about domination, manipulation, and control. Instead, they are about a form of interaction that is based on mutuality, on the dialogical nature of listening and answering. Relationships resonate when our interactions are important and meaningful, when we are touched and affected by them. We travel to the sea because the sea can speak to us, because we become transformed by our interaction with the sea. We listen to live music because we want to be affected and transformed by this experience. Rosa insists that resonance does not mean a harmonious relationship. Complete harmony does not generate dialogue and resonance. Resonance is as much about dissonance, about the discerning of difference. Thus, disagreement, even conflict, is one important ingredient of resonance. But resonance also needs convergence and the building of bridges. Otherwise, the transformation would be impossible.

Rosa's concept of resonance has much in common with Hyde's concept of the gift. Obviously higher education depends on the principles of interaction, dialogue, mutuality, and reciprocity. It cannot be a one-way street. Concepts of the "pure gift" (Derrida, 1994), a gift that is based on altruism, do not apply here. The pure or altruistic gift does not create social obligations, and does not produce any bonds. It does not produce resonance. The concept of education as a gift is about mutuality. For higher education to work as a gift, it must generate feedback. No response, no resonance, no gift. A visitor of an art gallery who remains unaffected by a work of art in front of her will hardly perceive this work as a gift. The same is true in education. Students who remain unaffected by the interaction with their teacher do not receive a gift.

Relevance

Relevance is about linking one topic to another one in a way that helps to improve an understanding of the first topic. Relevance refers to the content of education. It is about themes and topics. How can we decide which topics matter or matter perhaps more than others? How can we privilege some themes over others? How can we develop hierarchies of relevance? After all, what is relevant is profoundly subjective. It is subjective because it is a reaction to the conditions and contexts within which we experience life and the world. What is relevant depends on our geographical (local, regional, and national), political, social, economic, cultural, and spiritual contexts.

Furthermore, the notion of relevance depends on whether our contexts, circumstances and environments are relatively stable or characterised by rupture, transformation, and/or crisis. In times of relative stability, the question of relevance might be less contested and perhaps less urgent than in times of transformation. In times of crisis, the question of relevance moves to centre stage. Hall and Schwarz (1985) tell us that "crises occur when the social formation can no longer be reproduced on the basis of the preexisting system of social relations" (p. 9). There is little disagreement that we are confronted with multiple crises, among others a crisis of social justice, a crisis of democracy and political legitimacy with growing and intensifying social exclusions and divisions, and a crisis of capitalism with rapidly increasing economic inequality on a global scale. We are also confronted with the threat of intensifying global conflict and possibly an increase in global wars. The most important crisis we must address is climate change and environmental collapse.

We are living in the age of extinction. Extinction is not a singular event; it is a process, and it has already begun. Both animal species and plant species have significantly decreased over the last half century. The Intergovernmental Panel on Climate Change (IPCC), which has a history of underestimating the real pace of climate change, predicts in their *Sixth Assessment Report* that from 2022, it is likely that global temperatures will exceed by 1.5 degrees preindustrial levels in the next two decades, and that this will likely lead to a further extinction of 20% to 30% of the remaining animal and plant species. The report also makes clear that climate change has already harmed human physical and mental health and has increased human mortality and morbidity. Even though there is a possibility to avoid human extinction, it is too early to make assumptions. After all, this question will depend on how we (humans) will act during the coming decades. It will depend on the decisions we take to overcome extinction, it will depend on our ability to create a new global system of social relations, and a new system of relations with non-human life that can slow down and ultimately halt extinction.

In such a situation, education can only be relevant if it makes connections that help to address and to overcome the multiplicity of crises that humanity is facing. Technocratic approaches will not help. In such a situation good education is education that understands relevance most of all from a moral perspective. To say this loud and clear, good education is education that values all life.

Imagination

For very good reasons, the concept of critical thinking is a key learning objective in the social sciences and the humanities. Critical thinking is a core skill concerned with the development of persuasive arguments, the assessment of credible evidence to support an argument and the exploration of weaknesses in the argument of others. It is an academic skill which is based on the premise that the stronger argument wins.

To explain why critical thinking needs to be complemented with the fostering of imagination, I want to turn to a famous quote by Antonio Gramsci (1971):

> The crisis consists precisely in the fact that the old is dying and the new cannot be born; in this interregnum a great variety of morbid symptoms appear (p. 276)

Written nearly 100 years ago while being imprisoned by Mussolini, this quote could hardly be more relevant today. Today's morbid symptoms, to name a few, are the continuous rise of social and economic inequalities, the attack on democratic institutions and practices, and environmental collapse on an accelerating scale. The question needs to be raised whether critical thinking is sufficient to equip students with the skills they need to overcome the interregnum and to be able to contribute to the birth of the new.

Critical thinking is a fundamental skill to foster analysis and understanding. It does not foster a way of thinking that creates alternatives. Imagination is needed as a core learning objective. Imagination is about possibilities, different systems and structures and a different way to live. For imagination to be productive, it needs to align the present with a different future. It needs to make suggestions on how to get from the old to the new. For imagination to be productive, it needs to be aware of power and class, it needs to be aware of the interests of those who benefit from the old and oppose the new. For imagination to be productive, it needs to reflect on forms of organisation that can bring about change. Finally, for imagination to be productive, it needs to be based on hope for a better future, on optimism of the will, to borrow again from Gramsci.

Paolo Freire's *Pedagogy of the Oppressed*, published in 1968, is an invaluable starting point for such an educational journey. More recently, Henry Giroux's *Pedagogy of Resistance* (2022) provides a timely reengagement with Freire's work, revisiting his *Pedagogy of Hope*. Giroux argues that a pedagogy of resistance needs to be built around a vision that is based on hope. Indeed, the recent surge of academic literature that emphasises the value of hope in dark times is a very hopeful development.

Conclusion

I have argued, building on Hyde's concept of art as gift, that higher education can similarly be a gift. However, for this gift to unfold, we need to engage with two things: the political economy of higher education and a set of teaching pedagogies that can foster the gift. With respect to the political economy, I have argued that the commodification of higher education is not a helpful context for the gift to shine. While a higher education commons would provide the best context to foster the gift, such a political economy can only be made sustainable in a post-capitalist world. With respect to teaching practices, I have made a case for three pedagogical principles that are particularly important in this moment of crises. Teachers who create resonance, reflect on the relevance of their content, and stimulate imagination as a learning outcome are more likely to bring out and foster the gift.

References

Bourdieu, P. (1986). *Distinction: A social critique of the judgement of taste*. Routledge.

Collins, R. (1979). *The credential society: An historical sociology of education and stratification*. Academic Press.

De Angelis, M. (2017). *Omnia sunt communia: On the commons and the transformation to postcapitalism*. Zed Books.

Derrida, J. (1994). Given Time: I. Counterfeit Money. University of Chicago Press.

Edu-factory Collective (2009). *Toward a global autonomous university: Cognitive labor, the production of knowledge and exodus from the education factory*. Autonomedia.

Freire, P. (1994). *Pedagogy of hope: Reliving pedagogy of the oppressed*. Continuum. (Original work published in 1992).

Freire, P. (2010). Pedagogy of the oppressed. Continuum. (Original work published in 1970).

Giroux, H. A. (2022). *Pedagogy of resistance: Against manufactured ignorance.* Bloomsbury.

Gramsci, A. (1971). Selections from the prison notebooks of Antonio Gramsci (H. Quintin & G. Nowell-Smith, Eds.). Lawrence and Wishart.

Hall, S., & Schwarz, B. (1985). State and society, 1880–1930. In M. Langan & B. Schwarz (Eds), *Crises in the British state: 1880–1930* (pp. 7–32). Hutchinson.

Holt, J. (1976). *Instead of education: Ways to help people do things better.* Dutton.

Hyde, L. (2007). *The gift: How the creative spirit transforms the world.* Canongate Books Ltd.

Illich, I. (1971). *Deschooling society.* Harper & Row.

IPCC Working Group (2022). *Climate change 2022: Impacts, adaptation and vulnerability.* https://www.ipcc.ch/report/sixth-assessment-report-working-group-ii/

Mauss, M. (1954). *The gift: Forms and functions of exchange in archaic societies.* Cohen & West Ltd.

Ostrom, E. (1990). *Governing the commons: The evolution of institutions for collective action.* Cambridge University Press.

Rosa, H. (2013). *Social acceleration: A new theory of modernity.* Columbia University Press.

Rosa, H. (2016). *Resonanz: Eine Soziologie der Weltbeziehung.* Suhrkamp.

Stiegler, B. (2010). *For a new critique of political economy.* Polity Press.

Strathern, M. (2000). *Audit cultures: Anthropological studies in accountability, ethics and the academy.* Routledge.

Suissa, J. (2010). *Anarchism and education: A philosophical perspective.* PM Press.

Willis, P. (1977). *Learning to labour: How working class kids get working class jobs.* Ashgate.

8. A meditation on global further education, in haiku form

Jess Auerbach Jahajeeah

Note to Readers

Universities take for granted and are taken for granted. The forms and structures they use to present, contest, and create knowledge are rarely interrogated. Their specificity to the places in which they operate is often lost in the uniformity of ranking, global branding, and translatable structure. Political imperatives such as inequality, changing governments, and the growing awareness of a planet in peril do sometimes lead to structures-of-knowledge scrutiny. Most academics have little time for this, however, as they race in the hamster-wheels of neoliberal knowledge production and consumption.

Yet knowledge practices — its imbibing, its fermentation, its reproduction — have radically altered since the emergence of the internet as a tool of individual and collective thinking. The structures of learning, teaching and hierarchies that shape lives from kindergarten through to retirement are struggling to make sense of the sudden change.

In this piece I write in haiku form with the arguments elaborated in footnotes. I have never been to Japan, do not speak Japanese, and do not have the deep cultural knowledge that might enable me to engage the medium with the reverence that it deserves. I use it here with the greatest respect and a full acknowledgment of my limitations. Like millions of other children around the world, I learned it in school poetry.

As a school student, I saw intuitively the value of distilling arguments, and turned haikus into a study tool for my exams. These were my rafts on

© 2023 Jess Auerbach Jahajeeah, CC BY-NC 4.0   https://doi.org/10.11647/OBP.0363.08

which my memory attached linkages, and in moments of high pressure I found I could use them as boats with the details unfolding in my mind from the poetry's wake.

I have used this method since my teens, and they have carried me from high school through study and teaching engagements in learning spaces in South Africa, the UK, the USA, Angola, Brazil, Mauritius and beyond. I use them here with great gratitude for the connections between worlds they have enabled.

Heuristically, I think it is helpful to demonstrate how an arbitrary structure of argument with a very particular history quickly becomes so expected as to flow invisibly. The structure also makes visible the reality that statements are the proverbial tips of (rapidly melting) icebergs, and when excavated and explored open into knowledge histories.

Furthermore, it points to our increasing skill at reading on multiple levels at once, brought to the fore largely through engagements with hyperlinkages and digital texts and video — often all simultaneously. This chapter is limited in scope by the requirement of publication in the format of a page: if one were to assume readership online, the structure could be very different.

Teaching today — whether with tiny children or adults in one of the many folds of contemporary careers — is more complex than ever before. The expertise of the educator is constantly held up against the light of all information online, emotional and cognitive personal realities, as well as the vastly divergent norms that exist across intersectional knowledge traditions.

Some learning spaces incorporate new tools and offer students opportunities to weave their own knowledge tapestries, with the instructor as guide or facilitator. Others still treat the professor as a priest with the unique ability of translating the Latin in the bible to the illiterate masses thereby saving their souls. The origins of the contemporary global university structure lie in the Christian priesthood — knowledge, empire and capitalism all entangled.

Some students need a priest for their learning; others find guidance via different paths.

An average class of students anywhere in the world includes a mix of students needing both — sometimes the same person thrives with one or the other depending on the particularities of a moment.

One of the challenges facing today's universities is that most of us working in further education (which we usually call "higher" education in the university sector as a matter of privilege and status) are also in jobs that depend on the status quo.

How do we think outside of that, with our students and an unpredictable future at the forefronts of our minds? How do we imagine the "good" of further education, or keep conscious the vocational pull that brings many into its orbit? This chapter is a meditation in flow and aims to open into a deeper discussion about what we know, what is internalised, and how we (those of us working in further education) evaluate our own realities.[1]

Part I: Entry

My rule for reading
is: distil the argument
into a haiku[2]

if i can't, i missed
the real intervention is
the essential point[3]

the point of this piece:
curating information
is our task, our work[4]

---

1 Here I thank the editors of this collection for providing this space. I also thank Robin DeRosa, Sandhya Gunness and Rubina Rampersad for their thought-provoking engagement as peer-reviewers. With their support the chapter has been strengthened considerably.

2 We all have rules for reading that we acquire in our basic education. Before beginning a new task of understanding, it is valuable to interrogate our earliest memories of reading. Where did we learn? How did we learn? How did symbols on a page or screen transform into meaning? How are characters linked to and in our imagination? If our first written language is the Chinese script, we might think in pictures, for example (Mcbride-Chang et al., 2000). But for those of us bereft of such a powerful imaginative guide, how do we make pictures in our minds from the Roman script, for example? How do such pictures become meaning?

3 What is the takeaway from anything we read? As we increasingly also think in and with pictures (on social media, TV, film, and meme), how do we distil meaning and build that into our knowledge of the world? Writing is only one system, and context matters: the same information on Twitter (or X?) as in an academic essay will often be internalised in radically different ways (Olagbaju & Popoola, 2020).

4 I suggest in this chapter that universities are increasingly spaces of knowledge distillation, curation, and guidance. The unique skill of academic practitioners is to

"our" being those of us
whose livelihoods manifest
as knowledge makers[5]

whether full time with
benefits, or part of the
vast precarity[6]

of post-docs, contract
academics, of content
moderators, of[7]

all those who train the
tools: algorithms of mass
consent: discontent.[8]

Part II: Proposition

Universities
no longer hold the keys to
knowledge. Google has[9]

changed information
hierarchies: where we experts
now grow on platforms[10]

---

      be able to make sense of vast fields of information and to place these within relevant societal contexts that students can then navigate without becoming overwhelmed.

5   The imagined audience of this specific text are those who work in the formal academy in any way. Here I do not just include academic faculty, but the individuals who administer and guide students through complex systems, as well as those who bolster critical skills such as writing, digital capability, computer literacy, social awareness, and/or political inclusion (Breakstone et al., 2021).

6   (Brankovitch, 2021).

7   (Kerr, 2022).

8   (Altenried, 2020).

9   I name Google here, though of course, I am aware of the multiple alternatives to google as a noun and as a verb. It is important to interrogate what infrastructures of knowledge become invisible by virtue of sheer market force, however, and the terms of the exchange we enter when we provide data traces for supposedly free services. A growing literature speaks to the danger of offering up our data for free (Barassi, 2020; Benjamin, 2019) whilst at the same time Google and the other "big five" tech companies — Apple, Meta, Microsoft, and Twitter — become ever more ubiquitous and ever capable of suppressing opposition (Orlowski, 2020; Ziegenbalg & Thalheim, 2021; see also Amiel & do Rozário Diniz, Chapter 18, this volume).

10   The COVID-19 pandemic, amongst many other events, highlighted the extent to which decentralised systems of knowledge have the capacity to create and maintain

> like money on trees
> what of the livelihoods we
> whose bread depends on[11]
>
> knowing much more than
> anyone else can think of
> flows and boundaries[12]
>
> here is one vision
> for the changes we must make

---

    multiple alternative realities. Philosophically, this can be a good thing, and much of this chapter argues for a multitude of knowledges to be recognised as important (Trisos et al., 2021). Cultural relativism, however, is not a refined enough tool for the information environment that we now live in, where the costs of certain knowledge claims may well be the death of millions (Posetti et al., 2018). The South African government's early response to the HIV pandemic was highlighted in a pre-social media era, however, this is not unique to the current moment. As Ian Goldin has argued (Goldin & Kutarna, 2016) we are simply at a moment in history where the speed of knowledge cycles is gathering momentum such that we urgently need new tools at the level of global politics to address the crises these information contestations provoke.

11 One of the many challenges of online content is that it is devoid of context. In a video about Google in Africa, current minister of small businesses, Ms. Stella Ndabeni-Abrahams, informed the viewer that "we [South Africans] must Google our way out of poverty" (Google, 2021). Yet what does Google understand about the lived experience of hunger? The smell of inadequate sanitation in South African townships? The cost of data and the difficulty of determining fact from product-placement on an internet that is very far away from neutral?

12 Academia provides occupations like any other. In South African universities, the majority within the system are privileged to receive good salaries that remunerate us for our time, though many experience deep exclusion from the South African further education space due to what Andre Keet calls "epistemic othering" and the deep violence of apartheid that continues (Habib 2019; Jansen 2017; Keet, 2014; Monatshana, 2020). South African professional academic salaries remain far less than in the corporate sector, shaping the profession as vocational. Just like those who market products, we must convince people that our work holds value. At a 2022 research awards ceremony of the South African National Research Foundation, the director, Dr. Fulufhelo Nelwamondo, urged award recipients to be mindful that in the national fiscus, research monies were in direct tension with the R350 (approximately US$20) monthly grant given by government to prevent starvation of the majority of the country's citizens. South Africa, as a microcosm of global capitalism, makes visible dynamics that are present around the globe, and in wealthy countries such as the USA, these dynamics have become even more pressing and precarious. Academic labour is increasingly outsourced into the gig economy.

for education[13]

to work, hold and lift
in universities that
open up futures:[14]

(too long didn't read:
the answer is don't look North
for validation)[15]

validation is
complex, and often
politically[16]

informed. Where there are
resource constraints people fight
much more over crumbs.[17]

---

13 This suggestion draws on my unusual journey from non-traditional schooling in South Africa through the relatively privileged undergraduate institution of UCT (University of Cape Town). After working in a refugee camp in Mozambique, I was trained at Oxford and Stanford where I lived in constant awareness of the many contradictions of global further education. During my PhD years, I lived, worked, and taught in Angolan and Brazilian higher education, and when I finished, I spent three years doing the same in Mauritius. Then I moved between three very different South African universities: Stellenbosch, North-West, and recently back to UCT in the "adult" role of associate professor and program director for the MPhil in inclusive innovation.

14 There's a lot of good that we can maintain across these spaces, but I also think some changes would take us a very long way. I draw on many thinkers and writers in this space, and appreciate the mentorship of, amongst others, Jonathan Jansen (Jansen, 2002; Jansen et al., 2020), Saleem Badat (Badat & Sayed, 2014; Badat, 2020), Laura Czerniewicz (Czerniewicz et al., 2019, 2020; Gourlay et al., 2021), Pamela Maseko (Kaschula & Maseko, 2014; Maseko, 2017) and others.

15 "TLDR" meaning 'too long didn't read' flies often across the screens of undergraduates, much to the exasperation of many of those who teach them (Lahiri, 2017). Yet as I have argued elsewhere in an article on the pedagogy of hyperlinkages (Auerbach, 2022a), students now read *differently*, not necessarily less. Here I also nod to popular culture, and the 2021 film *Don't Look Up!* (McKay, 2021).

16 Let me add here that "looking North" can be a tremendous source of inspiration and insight for many scholars and that is not a bad thing — the challenge is that the sightline (and cite line) rarely goes in both directions. This is what Steve Biko's *Black consciousness* aimed to address, but even his significant insights are rarely engaged outside narrow — in this case South African — circles (Biko, 2002).

17 As a result, scholars in poor countries *feel* they are inferior, and scholars in rich countries generally believe they are "the top of the field" without either being able to perceive and reflect on the system holistically and looking consciously in all directions.

Part III: Starting Point

I know so little
should be our starting point to
think with our students[18]

#TogetherWeCan
trace histories of ideas
who taught whom and why[19]

and where and with what
consequences. This is how
the world has been made.[20]

Part IV: Argument

I have argued for
a pedagogy of hyper
linkages designed[21]

to use lateral
reading and the insights of
passion, exploring[22]

---

18 The internet gives us an illusion of knowing a lot, but it is helpful to undertake exercises that highlight knowledge limits. Who can navigate across their city? Who can divide 1498 by three in their heads? How have our memories changed and how do we excavate the contours of what we know, what is available to know, and what it is that Google and ChatGPT cannot answer?

19 Understanding the technologies of hashtags, for example, is a helpful tool of contemporary knowledge management (Nyabola, 2018), but one we cannot take for granted in our students (Lembani et al., 2020). What more power might student research have when it is explicitly political, grounded in contemporary debates and documenting fleeting realities?

20 Understanding the flows of knowledge through what we might consider the kinship charts of academia is a helpful first step (Overing et al., 2015; Peletz, 1995). Who taught whom (and is married to whom) matters because ideas principally flow and are carried through people (Levine, 2013; Philips, 2019). As Bruno Latour reminds us, "science" is not devoid of politics (Latour, 2004), and the creation of canons has been the amplifying of certain intellectual ancestors, and the silencing of others (Nyamnjoh, 2005, 2016, 2020). The silenced ancestors increasingly grow tired of being ignored, and wish to speak (Estes, 2019).

21 A pedagogy of hyperlinks is a pedagogy that acknowledges the multiple levels of linked reading with which students engage (Auerbach, 2022a). It encourages them to move from one source to another, drawing connections and consciously exploring a multitude of diverse sources that move from the broad to the very particular.

22 Lateral reading is a technique whereby one reads *around* a source online, rather than through it. For example, if students google the University of Cape Town, they

> across platforms and
> citational politics
> towards useful truths[23]
>
> useful truths will more
> and more become what defines
> us — we must curate[24]
>
> the stories with which
> our students work, guide their dreams
> reading, viewing, thoughts[25]
>
> through miasmas of
> possible material.
> what is relevant?[26]

---

      don't read its home page, but rather read *about* the institution on other sources. This allows students to develop discernment regarding the quality and positionality of sources — an online encyclopaedia versus a product page or marketing. Lateral reading has been argued to be essential as a skill towards democracy (Brodsky et al., 2021; McGrew & Byrne, 2022).

23 Truths most often have objectives and help student's parse data and information to understand *why* a given truth holds salience and when is helpful. That Mauritius is on a cyclonic belt is much more relevant if you live on the island in February than if you read about it in a geography textbook, for example! In an interview I did with a Mauritian doctor many years ago, he said: "but imagine now if everyone hears a cyclone is coming and instead of preparing, they shout "fake news!" Imagine the consequences!" (Auerbach, 2020).

24 It is impossible to keep up with all information. Every day, terabytes are added to the internet in English alone (https://ourworldindata.org/internet). No human mind can keep up, so we rely on other human minds, and on algorithms. But it is us who program the algorithms, and what they see depends on how we train them (O'Neil, 2016).

25 What are the stories the internet knows? How do we ensure our students can write into being the Wikipedia that does not exist? How do we ensure they are confident to make, not just consume, emerging materials? When teaching undergraduates today, I feel an essential writing exercise is the assignment of a Wikipedia post created on a topic that is not there. For students in less wealthy countries, much of their knowledge is not reflected online — from their hometowns to the local soccer club. For students who occupy places of power, much that needs to be said has already been written, but always from specific points of view. This is a valuable point of departure.

26 To discern what is relevant, university knowledge curators must gaze into the future and find ways to teach students how they, themselves, can access emerging materials and make use of them to build systems that are currently invisible, nascent, or inaccessible. In a primary school where I taught in Angola, children learned to recycle, although there were no recycling facilities in the country (Auerbach, 2020b). Further education must constantly engage in similar processes of knowledge guidance if our students are to be at home in the coming worlds.

it is not to leave
thinking for the sake of thought
behind us. Thinking[27]

is critical, yes
but in a world on fire, floods
wash screens, pulp ink, sear[28]

into futures that
need new tools of learning. Now.
How do we respond?[29]

Part V: People

Here are three people
from three African countries
three learning systems[30]

we meet them now to
explore the "skills" they need to
survive in this time.[31]

---

27 Far from being anti-intellectual, this work is a serious intellectual, political, and social endeavour. It highlights the complexity of preparing for a changing world, and in this way South Africa has much to teach. With great imperfection, with the arrival of democracy, a generation of South African academics embraced teaching students of wildly different backgrounds to themselves for a future that none of them could envision. Though South African democracy limps and often stumbles, it is also an example of a miraculous transition. Critique must be made, but it is also valuable to keep sight of what has been achieved, and for others to learn from it (Keet & Swartz, 2015).

28 The climate catastrophe increasingly shapes every single person's lived reality (IPCC, 2022).

29 Writing in early 2023, as the world faces a global food crisis arguably created by outdated international institutions incapable of inclusive problem-solving, it is obvious that the longer we wait, the more people die. The four horsemen of the apocalypse already exist in many homes, but their fate has not yet been sealed (Roy, 2020).

30 One of the challenges of South African education is the tendency of its handservants to think themselves exceptional. Indeed, apartheid was a particular kind of aberration, but the systems it represented exist unfettered in the world, and many of our northern neighbours in the rest of Africa have dealt with similar challenges to ours for many years (Nyamnjoh, 2011, 2012, 2013). Whilst the world can learn from South Africa, South Africa too has a great deal to learn from the world — the rest of continental "Africa" included (Mamdani, 2016). Multiple perspectives are possible at once.

31 As Yuval Harari (2018) has argued, where you live does shape what your future will hold, unless you are part of a miniscule few with geographic mobility (Heiman

one reviewer of
these poems asked about cliché
a valuable[32]

intervention. Yes
there's risk: to tell stories
is to simplify[33]

and to perhaps hit
up against the limits of
the readers' world view[34]

these are real students
whom I have taught and thought with.
each of our lives has[35]

elements of the
everyday, and of cliché:
this is of value[36]

please read further in
deep micro-realities
to make sense of them:[37]

---

et al., 2012). Even then, the bonds of love often hold one fixed in powerful ways (Sichone, 2008) or are broken at tremendous personal cost (Patel, 2010). A "global education" usually means one in which those from wealthy countries feel comfortable (Ferguson-Patrick et al., 2018; Fuller & Stevenson, 2019). This term should be changed to "elite education" and the realities of a truly *global* population in terms of struggle and exclusion should be centred. How do you thrive in a system designed to exclude you? When we reflect on "global education" in resource poor environments, this question should arguably be the focus (Glass et al., 2021).

32 (Canagarajah, 2011).
33 "Our concern with history… is a concern with preformed images already imprinted on our brains, images at which we keep staring while the truth lies elsewhere, away from it all, somewhere as yet undiscovered."(Sebald, 2014, p. v), *Austerlitz* in Zia Haider Rahman (2014) *In the Light of What We Know*.
34 (Jain, 2019).
35 How to write about one another with respect and care is a question that has long challenged fiction and anthropology (Clifford & Marcus, 1989). The same questions are now pushing themselves into digital spaces, where not just words but visual or three-dimensional imagery can be used with varying degrees of what scholars' call "informed consent".
36 Grimm & Grimm (1800/2011) Grimm's Complete Fairy Tales
37 My personal preference is to read the great novelists of each country to gain a sense of the emotional and structural palette with which lives are painted and experienced in each place. For Angola, I recommend Ondjaki, Pepetela, and Jose Eduardo Agualuso. For Mauritius, Nathacha Appanah, Lindsay Collen, and Sabah Carrim. South Africa's canon is vast but perhaps Zakes Mda, Johann Coetzee, and

8. A meditation on global further education 209

of Angola, South
Africa and of Brazil
Much to learn from each.

*

Buhle's twenty-three
he grew up poor in North-West
South Africa. He[38]

walked to school, took a
taxi down to study more
had never switched on[39]

a computer when
he got to my class to start
his degree. Sent half[40]

of his scholarship
money home every month to
feed the family[41]

      Imraan Coovadia are starting points. Alternatively go onto a streaming service near you and play the country's music — this guides insight just as well, IMO.

38 The names I use here are not real, and in each case represent what in anthropology we call "composite characters" (Berry, 2021). Though certain details have been changed or disguised, each person represents students I have taught, and the realities and constraints that they bring to the classroom. Post 1994, South Africa has seen a phenomenal rise in the number of what in the US are called "first generation" students — the first in their family to attend tertiary education. As for "poor" versus "wealthy", I do not mince my words here. I did once, using the term "economically marginalised" in the draft of a book that I shared with undergraduates for critical comment (it was a teaching and learning book, and that seemed only fair). The students told me they experienced the phrase as patronising, they commented: be honest and don't hide it in fancy academese just to make yourself feel less uncomfortable. Their input and good sense is acknowledged in the publication (Auerbach, 2020b, p. 197).

39 South Africa's rural villages are often largely cut off from global knowledge infrastructure. Buhle's village had one road going through the middle, and a small shop, with scattered rural homesteads on either side. There was nowhere with wi-fi, no recreational facilities, and his school was six kilometres away and served several villages, not just one. He had never been to the city that the university was in before he arrived and was helped to settle in through a network of connections made via a national church.

40 Over the years I have met many students who have arrived at university without digital skills. In this case, I asked him if his high school had not had a computer lab, and he said yes it had, but to use it you had to pay R20 (at the time of writing, US$1.28, CNY 85.6) a month and his family could not afford that cost.

41 His parents had been impacted deeply by the many structural violences of South African society, and social grants (Dawson & Fouksman, 2020; Ferguson, 2015)

university
left him hungry and angry
overqualified[42]

for manual labour
under-supported to risk
another degree[43]

he learned referencing
and academic writing
but you can't eat words[44]

and he is at home
where he began, just older
with much wider dreams[45]

---

were their only source of income. Realising the importance of skills like computing, Buhle sent as much money as he could from his government student grant to his siblings in the hope that they would find themselves facing different realities (Pillay et al., 2021; Yende, 2021).

42 He had wanted to study engineering, but his marks were not high enough to gain admission, so he landed up in the humanities. He liked some of the content, but he also couldn't see the point of a lot of it because it seemed so removed from his lived experience. Much of the time he was hungry — in part because he could only afford to live far away from the main university campus, walked far into the city each day, and could not afford to eat-to-fullness at the student cafeterias (see for example, Mabharwana, 2022).

43 His expectations changed dramatically as his exposure widened, but he graduated with huge gaps in terms of how to take his literary knowledge and turn that into a career. He understood the value of postgraduate training and had attained the marks for it, but the level of support he needed, particularly for the fourth year of study which in South Africa is called Honours, was not forthcoming, from either the university or the state.

44 How do majority white faculty, largely from South Africa's suburbs, prepare majority black students — at this institution largely from rural areas — for the workforce, particularly when most have always followed an academic path? Most South African universities have radically underfunded and understaffed career offices — this is a pain point and an opportunity because it can so easily be changed.

45 This student is one of a significant number of unemployed graduates who, after three years of study, remain in much the same position they were in when they started, but now with the added psychological burden of feeling that they have failed (Botha & Botha, 2022). Deeper connections need to be made between the humanities and the workforces that our graduates enter across the world. A professional degree provides a pathway to a particular future that is usually financially secure, but the "openness" of the humanities is one of its challenges, particularly for those who do not move in privileged circles. This sense of constantly failing our students was a large part of what led me to leave a career in anthropology and join the faculty at a business school. Understanding the dynamics of system failure and where we

students like Buhle
need our universities
to open them doors[46]

but often inside
them, the teaching staff don't know
which doors to think with[47]

our institutions
need permeable doors, light
instead of solid[48]

they must understand
their responsibility
to youngsters like him[49]

graduation sans
work spells a brutal future
mental health crisis[50]

---

might be able to intervene to improve student's life trajectories is a large part of my now ongoing research.

46 This is, however, a fixable problem. Universities could easily strengthen their work readiness programs, and develop parallel courses that give students internship experience, prepare them for interviews, provide access to networks, career counselling, and support with planning their futures. Many academics shy away from "skills" but this is out of sync with the urgency of contemporary life, and the weight of duty so many students carry. As academics themselves are often disconnected from professional fields, they do not have the necessary capabilities to train students in this way. Both students and staff, therefore, must be supported towards a different reality of learning.

47 Academics cannot afford to be so removed from the world as to not articulate the substantive ways they create good (Young, 2020). At the same time, it is worth focusing on the great power that those working in contemporary structures of learning still have over their students' thinking. Those who act with compassion and integrity in thousands of everyday moments can shape futures in powerful ways, and this is work that should be valued and treasured by society even though it is often slow to bear fruit. It may take an undergraduate ten years to understand information presented to them in university.

48 Permeable in the sense of being linked to the localised economies in which they are located so that students can gain work experience along the way and apply their insights as they learn them.

49 Universities serve society, and though I said earlier that South African universities have done a lot, I don't think it's enough. I do think many, many students fall through the cracks. That is a challenge of institutional structures, however, so to resolve it the structures will have to change.

50 As elsewhere, students in South Africa know exactly what they are missing out on as they see through their cellphone's daily updates all that they might never reach — particularly if they are unemployed. This contributes to a mental health

South Africa can't
add more trauma to our long
long list. We must do[51]

better. Work matters
regardless of the content:
qualification[52]

is empty without
a pathway into the next
phase, stage, bright future.[53]

*

Marianna is
a fourth-year economics
student, Angolan[54]

she studies for free
at a university
built after the war.[55]

---

crisis that we do not yet have solid data for, but that texts like Whabee Long's that explore the impact of a lack of dignity on a human psyche (Long, 2021) suggest has far reaching consequences.

51 Lesley Green has argued that South African history has unfolded as a series of traumas (Green, 2020). The impact has left the country shaken and must be interrupted.
52 Learning for learning's sake is valuable and I believe that option should be maintained. But learning on an empty belly is impossible. In non-professional fields, I believe much more attention needs to be given to where our students land in their first years after graduation. How do we link "learning" to 'living", particularly in resource-scarce environments where the margins of survival are very thin? Learning that is decontextualised is as empty as search-data on a glowing screen (DeSouza & Leite, 2008).
53 The term "bright future" becomes empty political rhetoric if it is not realised. In this story, I have described the many challenges facing one student. That life continues though, and hopefully will be re-told as a story of overcoming as things continue to unfold for him. When he "makes it" and is employed and later installs the first wi-fi router in a public facility, he will be hailed as a hero and no doubt the university will congratulate itself for enabling class mobility. Both stories can be true at the same time.
54 Here I draw on two years of ethnographic research in Angola in 2013 and 2014, and an ongoing relationship with the higher education sector (Auerbach, 2022b).
55 Angola's public universities are free to attend, though there is rarely additional stipend money for living expenses, such as is routinely covered in South Africa through NSFAS (National Student Financial Aid Scheme). However, demand far exceeds capacity, and a burgeoning private university sector has filled that gap. Some institutions, such as the Catholic University in Luanda, offer programs that are recognised around the world and carry significant status. Others have much less

8. A meditation on global further education 213

where she studies is
a collection of pre-fab
classrooms, concrete paths[56]

wi-fi only for
staff, a library with just
three hundred odd books[57]

Marianna's placed
in a class of just thirty
that's how many chairs[58]

fit into the room.
her university is
so competitive[59]

few chairs, they study
for free. An economy
that gapes with space for[60]

---

rigorous accreditation but meet the pragmatic demands of students working in an economy that is rapidly complexifying (Faria, 2009).

56 The Universidade Katyavala Bwila (UKB) in Benguela hosted me for the duration of my initial fieldwork. For years they have been promised permanent facilities but continue to operate out of prefabricated classrooms that limit the institution's reach and expansion. Classroom capacity is approximately 30 students, which has a radical impact on feasible enrolments.

57 In 2023 I returned to Angola after a break extended by the pandemic. Much has changed, but the university sector continues to struggle and at the time I visited was in the midst of a prolonged faculty strike. My most recent trip to Benguela province where UKB os located was in 2018. UKB, like others, increasingly caters to a student body who prefer their material in digital form. Angolan universities also benefit from the Brazilian government's commitment to open access scholarly publications, and therefore have access to huge quantities of peer-reviewed scholarship at no cost. All you need is to read Portuguese and know where to look, because like so many learning structures, the Brazilian system is not easily legible to Google Scholar algorithms nor do outsiders easily comprehend the vast available knowledge that the national system *Lattes* makes accessible to readers of Portuguese (de Brito et al., 2016; Gouveia, 2019; Costa & Leite, 2008).

58 See Footnote 58.

59 To gain placement, students write competitive entrance exams that are typically exponentially over-subscribed in terms of student-potential seat rations. I have argued elsewhere that by the sheer arithmetic of admissions ratios, these make the institution arguably as competitive as Stanford (Pusumane & Auerbach Jahajeeah, 2024). That thinking in such terms is often challenging (*does more competitive mean "better?"*) and reveals much about the structures of thinking (Williams, 1977) that shape knowledge hierarchies worldwide.

60 Angola experienced almost 40 years of conflict. A struggle for independence from Portugal began in the 1960s, morphed into a Cold War proxy conflict and civil war,

skilled, and connected
there are many options for
graduates with her[61]

social capital
knowing who you know matters
getting into the[62]

right political
party. The card you carry
opens up pathways[63]

Marianna has
a two-year-old daughter who
she hopes will one day[64]

---

and ended only in 2002. There followed a period of oil-related economic boom (Soares de Oliveira, 2015) that came to a juddering halt when the commodity price crashed in December 2014. Since then, huge strides have been made in diversifying the Angolan economy, but the country faces significant challenges in the areas of health, education, employment, and infrastructure.

61 In such an environment, however, qualified individuals are quickly snapped up by potential employers, with the proviso that, sometimes, political party membership is a prerequisite of employment, regardless of technical fit.

62 Elsewhere I have referred to this process as the "trafficking of influence" and suggested that it is by no means unique to Angola (Auerbach, 2020b). It is worth remembering that given Angola's role in the Cold War, then-youth who now run the country were trained on both sides of the "iron curtain" and subject to contradictory ideological influences (Auerbach, 2022b). This means that Angola today is a remarkable space of ideological plurality and possibility, and that the model of cadre deployment in the professional sector — public but to some extent also private — is marked by policies and practices much closer to those experienced in contemporary China (Mok, 2016).

63 Many Angolans I worked with described the importance of putting one's political party membership specifically to the ruling *MPLA* party on the top of any pile of documents one handed to the authorities, to even be considered. It is worth noting, however, that there have already been significant changes in popular and political expression in Angola (Pearce et al., 2018) The national elections of 2022 saw a significant erosion in the MPLA's voter support. Though they won the elections, they did so by a hair's breadth and are unlikely to govern unquestioned going forward.

64 Today's young Angolans live in a context where for those with education, housing, and transportation, it is not unreasonable to have very different life expectations to those of their parents. That said, everyday life continues to carry a heavy mental load (Emma, 2018), and most young Angolans exposed to the many comforts of the contemporary global consumer economy have very different aspirations for the material circumstances of their own children.

study in English
outside Angola, wider
expanses for her.[65]

Their family is
one of growing means, they build
their business, work[66]

together across
three generations and she
is the golden child[67]

who will visit France
climb the Eiffel tower and
survey the city.[68]

*

Kushal's shirt lies close
to his body from the heat;
he works in transport[69]

---

65 Many Angolans who go abroad study in either Brazil or Portugal, though the latter is much more expensive and requires success in the complex visa processes of the European bureaucracy (Agência, 2013; Alfredo, 2012; Faria, 2009). Studying in English-speaking countries provides high status and valuable networks but requires the extra expenditure of a year spent learning a language. Increasingly, rather than making this investment in the anglophone sphere, Angolan parents are opting to send their children to China for higher education (though this process was interrupted in significant ways by the COVID-19 pandemic).

66 Marianna's father studied in Cuba as a child and remained there for 17 years — long enough to obtain a university degree. In addition to his work as a governmental administrator, he opened a successful transportation business which Marianna helped to manage.

67 As the first in her family to be the *child* of one who is university-educated, Marianna has benefitted from incredible social mobility within the family that she herself can continue. She dreams of visiting Paris, but unlike her parent's generation, this dream was entirely feasible and was part of her personal savings plan.

68 Before the COVID-19 pandemic, horizons had changed in significant ways for billions of people worldwide. As was quickly documented (Kochhar, 2021), much of this progress was rapidly undone in 2020 and 2021, and the ongoing conflict in Europe seems likely to set back a more equitable world order.

69 The contexts of students' physical environments are an important consideration in developing localised curricula. Often academics assume that the buildings that comprise universities neutralise the uneven effects of environmental conditions, but this is rarely the case, and when it is, only applies to the short periods of time that students learn on campus. The COVID-19 pandemic highlighted the importance of reflection on and in the physical environment: what kinds of desk do students use, and where? Is the roof insulated to muffle the sound of rain in an online lecture?

middle management
he likes the sound of it: soon:
Kushal: PhD[70]

two children study
in Australia so he
spends mostly on them[71]

but he's got to climb
the ranks, and just one degree
from the national[72]

university
won't cut it these days so he
enrolled from his life[73]

twenty years of long
experience written up
in academese[74]

in his class, others
of similar ambitions:
career progress and[75]

How might bodily comfort or discomfort shape the emotional association with learning?

70 Aspirations and motivations are complex, but we should not disallow our student's vanity as well! It can be a highly motivating resource to draw upon!

71 Students such as Kushal are often referred to in academic literature as "non-traditional". As researchers, of course, we must question whose tradition is the invisible norm in this case, and why. If the wealthiest parts of Europe and North America were not positioned as centres of the universe, it's clear that Kushal is much closer to the norm in higher learning than a nineteen-year-old with no financial dependents could ever be.

72 Increasingly in the so-called "knowledge economy", an undergraduate degree has become the starting requirement, and further progression requires at least a master's degree.

73 Recognition of prior learning structures are critical interventions that allow students to gain acknowledgement for work they have already done. These could be strengthened and supported more across the continent, but a critical component to that work would be lobbying for recognition of such incentives by privileged gatekeepers who assess the "quality" of specific degrees.

74 Translating knowledge into academese is a complex process that relies on a willingness not to master content but to master conventions of communication.

75 In the university in Mauritius in which Kushal studied, he was, as suggested, absolutely normal in terms of both the experiences he brought into the room, and the expectations he had for his future.

8. A meditation on global further education 217

vanity, hopes for
money, recognition, praise
locally grown, and[76]

seeded, and nurtured
long distance education
on this African[77]

island. Kushal looks
up, sees digital knowledge
economy, knows[78]

the papers matter
after work, after food he
writes. One paragraph[79]

and another. One
citation towards his plan
of graduation[80]

---

76 What is the point of a university degree? In an environment so full of options, all institutions can strengthen their offerings by interrogating exactly why students choose them.

77 Of all the available canons, what were the accidents of history that led to the consolidation of each of our own? Mauritius is unusual because it lies in the middle of the Indian Ocean. As a former colony of the Netherlands, France, and England, and as a space whose population descends mostly from South Asia and contemporary China, it is a country of highly contested ancient knowledge systems. In this context, the Open university that Kushal attends has many canons to draw upon when structuring its curriculum.

78 Mauritius has a remarkable history of educational success. From high rates of illiteracy in the early 1960s, it has transformed itself into Africa's most educated population relying on a complexified economy in the service sector supported by free education, healthcare, and food subsidies (Dookhitram et al., 2018; Eriksen, 1998; Zafar, 2011). Though not without significant challenges, Mauritius demonstrates that it is possible to radically alter the lives of most of the population despite scarce material resources. Kushal's grandparents were indentured labourers, his parents were agricultural workers who gained literacy later in life, but he himself was able to go to university and his own children now study abroad. Like Marianna, there has been tremendous change within the course of two generations that South Africa and other countries might also do well to acknowledge and think with.

79 So much work in contemporary further education takes place before dawn and after dark, but this is often left out of public discourse of education. This institution has a model that four accepted papers equate to a PhD, so many students simply focus on journal articles right after they finish data collection.

80 The politics of citation are important to reflect upon and openly address in furthering education in this region. Who is cited, which voices are amplified, what knowledge becomes the gold standard for the field? These are all questions of paramount political and psychic importance. Movements such as #RhodesMustFall in South

Part VI: Questions

How do we serve them?
Buhle, Marianna, and
Kushal? They are our[81]

"African uni-
versity students!" they each
walk such unique paths[82]

the people teaching
them, are not in high profile
places, their branding[83]

is muted; impact
vast, and sometimes, limited
glorified high schools,[84]

Africa gave some attention to this work, but by 2022 it already feels that much of this has faded into an echo and is no longer front and centre of university collective minds. This is arguably even more important for those like Kushal who are there for the certificate rather than to interrogate knowledge structures themselves. Knowledge curation in this context can build, nourish, and empower or it can serve to make him feel that he is only the most insignificant spot on the edge of the great knowledge empire.

81 Much ink has been spilled on the purpose of universities in the world, and of course that purpose is multiple and multidimensional. I write in this way simply to keep front and centre of mind the very real lives that are at the core of educational work, however it is parsed politically and sociologically.

82 The diversity of higher education worldwide is perhaps part of what makes it such a difficult sector to manage or on which to comment meaningfully. Emerging institutions such as Minerva, the London Interdisciplinary School, and the African Leadership College challenge the model of brick-and-mortar institutions, building on centuries of similar push-back from distance learning institutions such as UNISA or inclusive access education via community colleges in the United States or the Open universities worldwide.

83 Yet despite this diversity, conversation about the university sector continues to be led by a handful of wealthy brands in the US, UK and slowly an emerging number in China (Sharma, 2022).

84 It is widely accepted that university ranking tables such as that of *Times Higher Education* do not capture the impact of institutions of higher education in *localised* spaces. This is part of why three "high profile" Chinese universities have recently opted to leave the ranking system (see below). But what of universities such as those in Angola and Mauritius that never even try to "make" the rankings, but contribute significantly to the transformation of localised economies and the radical shifting of millions of lives?

though, are not what is
needed. The education
industry complex[85]

must beat to new tunes.
Buhle, Marianna and
Kushal all think with[86]

the internet, their
minds plug in to collective
insight, exploring[87]

truths: both fake and real
surely universities
are the place to learn[88]

---

85 The Education industrial complex builds on work that comes from war: how do we build factories of ammunition, production lines of human workers? Rufalow (2020) has demonstrated that technology itself can be co-opted in schools to prepare students to be knowledge workers, knowledge receivers, or knowledge makers depending on the structure of thinking (Williams, 1977) that is instilled in the school and by the teachers. He writes about one small school district in California. What are the implications for the world?

86 The COVID-19 pandemic had uneven and, in many cases, disastrous consequences for students around the world, and has widened global learning inequality. Yet for a moment, it also compelled institutions to force staff to engage with new technologies that enabled learning and to consider in concrete ways the material conditions in which their students lived and learned. In South Africa, it was particularly striking, and as so often South Africa highlights systems that manifest around the world: a majority privileged, middle-class faculty were forced to engage with the material circumstances of their students, not just abstractly but in practical terms. This enabled significant leaps in understanding.

87 New visual literacies now shape the ways that knowledge is internalised by billions of people. Universities, however, for the most part continue to rely on text as a primary tool of inquiry. My teaching has suggested that the same students who struggle to write a simple undergraduate essay are often capable of making sophisticated videos in which they articulate complex theoretical points and communicate with classmates and outside audiences highly successfully. Is it fair to penalise them because their knowledge skills are *different* to that of previous generations? Personally, I don't believe it is, but university structures have for the most part failed to recognise these emerging skills and ways of communicating.

88 Yet discernment of the quality of digital content is something that must be actively taught (Rufalow, 2020). Some people gain access to such teaching through parents and teachers in school, or through national digital policies that land unevenly. Many of us, however, are not formally trained in how to parse the many kinds of information so easily available online. I am convinced that teaching this will become the primary task of universities.

> the difference? If not
> universities then who?
> who teaches the new[89]
>
> literacies and
> capabilities of new
> knowledge work? New forms[90]
>
> must be mastered by
> students, but also by staff.
> Today's status quo[91]
>
> serves the interests
> of empire unabated.
> how do we now change?[92]

---

89 In an already highly differentiated global schooling system, can we expect this work to happen at school? That seems unrealistic. There is, however, a real opportunity for the global higher education sector to take on this challenge collectively.

90 Learning to read, watch and listen with discernment whilst parsing multiple forms of online information is today's knowledge *work*. Depending on the storytelling skill, genre and personal preference, individuals now have multiple ways to communicate their insights and understandings, and even gaining a working comprehension of what knowledge already exists often requires the use of algorithmic or human-network based tools.

91 How do permanent academic staff adjust to such a seismic shift? Must they, or do the old systems of knowledge regulation remain important to teach? For example, during the COVID-19 pandemic, many of us encountered colleagues who were uncomfortable using basic digital tools and insisted that the only place for pedagogy was in a lecture theatre. I found it easy to empathise with them as human beings, but much more problematic given the very real needs of very real students already up against a global emergency. Should a university require technological capabilities of its staff, and if so, how to address the systematic privileges that tenure systems enable? I remember watching Amanda Peet and Annie Wyman's US Netflix series *The Chair* (2021) during this time and cringing: though our learning contexts were far apart, the series was wholly relatable.

92 Whilst the early internet promised liberation and equality, global hierarchies of knowledge have simply been reinforced and reinscribed in new ways (Bratton, 2016). Paywalls make it impossible for even Africa's "top" university (UCT claims the spot, but it depends which table you look at) to have daily access to newspapers such as *The New York Times*. Relative currency strength means people in New York can easily afford to read South African news. Even open access publishing now comes with fees so eye-wateringly expensive to those not earning in dollars or euros that only some academics in wealthy countries can afford to publish that way. These are two of thousands of examples of knowledge hierarchy reinstatement with an iron fist clad in open clothing.

Part VII: Propositions for Good

reading, writing, and
arithmetic remain the
bedrock of human[93]

communication.
in an era of climate
catastrophe, we[94]

must add: empathy
resilience, ethics and
compassion. Students[95]

must leave with the doors
open: education will
be there whenever[96]

---

93 I remember being told by a senior experimental-university manager that these were "20th century skills". I understood what he meant but vehemently disagree. How we read and write and count has changed, but the skills remain even more critical. To make sense of 21st century data, we all need sophisticated analytic skills based on numeracy and literacy that go beyond what is presented on the page and into the "black box" (O'Neil, 2016) of argument creation.

94 As worldwide weather systems change and predictability breaks down, effective communication that bridges partisan and political divides is critical. How do we communicate such that the people who need to believe us, believe us? How do we teach this to the students we are entrusted to educate in a meaningful way? Most countries now have a sense of what lies on the horizon: how do we use knowledge systems to adequately prepare?

95 This comes down to the ability to build direct personal relationships of trust and accountability. What is missing from digital information are the critical skills of humanity. For those able to study at in-person institutions, relationships with academic staff become morally loaded in significant new ways. Some scholars rage against the incursion of "identity politics" into the scholarly arena, but arguably miss the point that what students are seeking is less information and more guidance on how to navigate the cacophony of a world where everyone — all nine billion of us and some of the non-human — have a voice.

96 Further education in this context becomes a revolving door through which students should feel able to enter whenever they need. Some of this might happen through online learning and short courses, but if the sector was to imagine itself as a site of civil service towards the public, its entire structure could radically alter towards the good of society. In this imagination, the university becomes a site of expertise accessible to the public. A website shares knowledge expertise as a form of public consultants. Instead of universities choosing which issues their researchers are interested in addressing, communities approach the university to ask for help with what they are already doing (see Misra & Mishra, Chapter 25, this volume).

it's needed. They must
return to fill in new gaps
to resource themselves.[97]

make a video
edit Wikipedia
influence anyone[98]

everything that we
can find online we do not
need to teach. Instead[99]

the time we used to
give to content can go to
that which separates[100]

knowledge producers
from knowledge consumers and
enables insight.[101]

our students need to
have advanced digital skills
whatever field, they must[102]

---

97 In a rapidly changing world, all of us need to constantly upskill ourselves with new technologies and forms of communication (Doxdator, 2017). A revolving door policy at universities would make this much easier. The system, including the concept of degrees, needs reformulation and reconceptualisation.

98 As mentioned earlier, in my experience, teaching students how to edit Wikipedia is a far more effective writing intervention than teaching them how to write an essay. When working on Wikipedia, students engage systems of knowledge production, peer review, the politics of knowledge work as well as structure, language, grammar, referencing and so on. In addition, many feel empowered, and the pool of available knowledge expands to include parts of the world and life experience that may be invisible to the gaze of the typically white, typically "Northern" editors of Silicon-Valley platforms (Davidson, 2017; Giannella, 2015). Marking a Wikipedia entry is a lot more difficult than marking an essay, but the question remains, which is the structure that needs to change?

99 Teaching how to find information and making sure students have time and the ability of focus to process it is the key, not the contents.

100 Time is a precious resource — perhaps the most valuable in our distracted, diffuse economy.

101 In my opinion, this is the critical distinction that differentiates groups in the 21st century. This is the transformation that universities can facilitate for their constituents.

102 I am saying the same thing in multiple ways, so the point is clear here: knowledge work matters.

8. A meditation on global further education

parse data for its
quality, integrity.
they must be taught how[103]

power plays into
a fractured internet that
is shaped by firewalls[104]

they must make content
that changes collective views.
using emerging[105]

tools now no longer
a negotiable skill.
these tools come to life[106]

with baggage: loaded
intellectual property
and algorithms[107]

they may make their own.
feel ready to shape new and
expansive stories[108]

digital skills need
knowledge histories grounded
in storytelling[109]

---

103 If a student has never used a computer before arriving at university or has used one but never interrogated how it works, they need to be taught how, why, and politics all at once. When this happens, the effects are transformative on just as many levels.
104 (Hillman, 2021; Starosielski, 2015).
105 The power of storytelling has never been as critical as when shaping imagination (Adichie, 2016).
106 This is an active process. Pasi Välaiho refers to this as the use of "biopolitical screens" — drawing on Michel Foucault, he points out how screens *make* life as well as reflect it (Välaiho, 2014).
107 In *Weapons of Math Destruction*, O'Neil (2016) explores how algorithms uphold unequal systems that privilege elite interests in schooling, healthcare, incarceration, and a host of other areas.
108 I often hear colleagues decry the aspiration of young people to become "influencers". I think that this desire to shape narrative is a powerful force that universities can tap into as a motivation and as a project of global political reform.
109 Knowledge-histories are part of the literacy needed to parse contemporary information. Where do ideas come from? How do we trace them? Who are the guiding intellectual ancestors?

in mental health. There
is no sense guiding a new
cohort if we[110]

fail them at finish
line of working within their
own minds: strengths and pain[111]

disciplinary
boundaries will slowly melt
in the face of the[112]

crises must confront
we can't afford the ego
of existing shapes[113]

nibble this structure
open the blocks into air
fill the gaps with the[114]

work we know we must
do. Buhle has rage and he
will not wait too long[115]

Marianna has
choices — so many paths lead
to gentler futures[116]

---

110 I also hear many colleagues acknowledging the mental health catastrophe so many of us and our students confront daily. What could be a clearer signal that our processing systems are broken, and that we need new tools and new approaches to ensure that we are healthy?

111 Academics lead by example. What if we ourselves modelled mental health practices with the same pragmatism that we share insights into article and data generation?

112 Most of us still teach in disciplinary silos created for the needs of empire. These are not effective for solving global and local crises.

113 The egos in academia are astonishing. Petty chiefs of micro-kingdoms unwilling to acknowledge that the emperor so often has no clothes. "Let them eat cake" she says while she strides up the corridor and slams the door. Many academics are married to and only socialise within academic circles, so often don't even *know* how unusual much of our collegial behaviour is! The system reinforces itself partly because there are so few spaces of exit and re-entry.

114 (Nyamnjoh, 2016).

115 Growing inequality will only lead to crisis. The curve must be corrected as a matter of urgency on every level.

116 With so many options, contemporary higher education is not a given first choice. Academia relies, in its current funding model, on classroom numbers — but what if these decline?

Kushal needs a piece
of paper, and paper's made
from trees. As long as[117]

there are trees, Kushal
will be just fine. So, do we
wait for the boards to[118]

review our curry-
culums? Our stews of knowledge
in empirical[119]

pots? Or do we look
to the sky at the edge of
our horizons and[120]

recognise that we
must take our students so much
further than we can[121]

ourselves, in this time
even see? As we move to
uncertain futures.[122]

"the pedagogy
of care" is way too easy
universe branding[123]

training scholars and
admin who care: we should talk
remuneration.[124]

---

117 Pragmatism is part of the inertia that limits systemic reform.
118 COVID-19 showed that we can change systems quickly — we usually simply don't.
119 What are the ingredients of education? Who does it nourish? Should everyone be eating the same food? What of those whose stew is made of bones?
120 I think that we must go further.
121 Going further is the work of the *good*.
122 4IR is the term most often used to capture this, but it usually assumes acceptance of the exigencies of existing technologies of control.
123 The COVID-19 pandemic saw a multitude of universities around the globe embracing a "pedagogy of care" in different ways — including the one in which I worked at the time. I do believe that a lot of people enter further education *because* they care, and so there is a certain truth to many of these claims. Yet without systemic analysis that addresses both staff and student burnout, industrial labour and thinking, and overwork, it is difficult to experience sincerity in high-level slogans.
124 This is where the proverbial rubber hits the road. Payment, job security, promotion, and other benefits are almost never linked to the key performance indicator: "how

Education for
Good life. Good future. Good plans
it is captured in[125]

these stories of three
young Africans. each one of
them quietly in[126]

pursuit of a good
future. We must remember
that the good does not[127]

rest in the tables
of university ranks
or the shininess[128]

of lecture theatres.
rather the good nestles in
amongst between us[129]

in unseeable
spaces, (if the lens used is
Harvard <--> Nullius.)[130]

---

have you demonstrated a pedagogy of care in your teaching or work with students?" Until this changes, the "good" is individual choice in a system that is interested in citation scores.

125 For the brief period in human history that comprises the past 500 years, education in western industrial societies has been seen as an investment to be made in children and young people that pays dividends later. However, this is atypical of humanity-wide experiences of learning through deeper histories, where "life-long" learning has been experienced and valued in the way that those educated in the "west" now seem increasingly invested in.

126 Just as tools of technology now zoom effortlessly between eye-level and the macro-picture, those in further education must constantly grapple with the multiple scales of teaching and planning that may shift in salience depending on the micro-subject at hand.

127 The everyday actions of everyday people are ultimately what shapes lived experience (Stanton, 2015).

128 This is not the place for a critique of university world rankings, but it is worth noting that as with so many systems that shape how quality is evaluated, the structure was developed to be used with western tools to make sense of western realities (Jöns & Hoyler, 2013).

129 (Tempest, 2016).

130 The mental models most of us are trained to accept make anything that does not at least *try* to look like Harvard seem all but invisible.

across Africa
across much of the planet
learning's happening[131]

it is not dressed in
the robes of elite courses
the classrooms often[132]

have mildew and rust
on the walls, but nonetheless
serve their students well.[133]

What is the image
of the good that is pursued?
we do not need a[134]

thousand Stanfords here
we need spaces of learning
linked to everyday[135]

---

131 Given the complexity of most learning spaces, it is not unsurprising that even governments rarely have full records of all learning institutions that operate on their territories — particularly, when extra-curricular and religious education are also factored in. What learning looks like, feels like, and sounds like, varies dramatically from place to place.

132 At one of the universities, I have worked in, we had some power to shape the way the first class graduated. I remember the horror expressed by a colleague from South America who observed that if our students were allowed to graduate in robes reflecting the European 18th century judiciary, we would have failed at our work of decolonisation. They graduated in those robes, with Kenti cloth from Ghana as a decoration, ironically speaking to Europeans and African American traditions rather than the many available options in the country in which the university was located. We felt we had failed.

133 How "well" is understood is of course the critical issue here. I personally believe that if students see value in what they are learning and enrol year after year, finding ways to make their studies improve their lives or open new doors, perhaps outsiders should be cautious about judging too fast.

134 Success or failure depends largely on personal internalised reference points. Beauty is in the eye of the beholder (and perhaps in particular the eye of influencers) (Nuttall, 2006; Taussig, 2012).

135 I have such gratitude for Stanford and all it gave me personally, but I found myself continually bewildered by the disconnect between institutional grappling with privilege and claims of excellence. In one public meeting with the president, I remember standing up and asking why, if Stanford was as committed as it said it was to educational inclusion and equity, it didn't give some of its budget to Berkeley. Unsurprisingly, the president didn't know how to respond to my sentiments, but the point could be made beyond the national as well.

realities, that
hold up mirrors to leaders
give students new tools.[136]

It is not to build
New, but rather to strengthen and
bolster those who are[137]

already doing
this work, already meeting
challenges that are[138]

visible at ground
level; entwined with hope, aspiration, and tiny[139]

steps. For good, include
them. university change
with small places, small[140]

campuses outside
ranking agencies' purview
engage with what is[141]

---

136 Just as Stanford and Berkeley are both products, most of all, of different streams of US policy towards higher education, the Catholic University of Luanda and Augustino Neto speak to the same in Angola. Recognising the ideological, political, and social imbrication of higher education in local realities is an important component of thinking with and for higher education for good.
137 The expansion of institutions of learning across Africa and across the globe makes sense given growing populations, but it also runs the risk of segregating populations further based on financial capital. There is great importance in the reality that South Africans from all walks of life meet at national universities. If these options are removed through the proliferation of private streams for learning, we run a serious risk of deepening segregation and losing some of the few opportunities we currently have for building genuine social networks based on shared experience.
138 Again, so much work towards the goals of better futures is already going on. The challenge is those doing the work are often simply not invited to the tables at which it is discussed, praised, or planned for.
139 If a tree falls in a forest and nobody hears it, does it make a sound? If a professor does not have a Google Scholar profile, does she really write?
140 It is currently infinitely easier for a South African postgraduate student to go on exchange to Europe than for the same student to go to Mozambique. This is not an inevitability, however, but a result of choices. Change the choices.
141 If our evaluation of prestige rests on internalised assumptions of what is and is not excellent, we are unlikely to learn from examples that fall outside of that internalisation. But what if we are wrong?

8. A meditation on global further education 229

actually goes
on, actually making
change, actually[142]

transformational.
It requires learning new tools
language, context, form[143]

requires suspending
internalised visions of
what education[144]

should be. Requires forms
of listening, of seeing
through double sided[145]

glass, then opening
wide the doorways crossing in
between in entries[146]

we find solutions
waiting in plain sight if we
use sense, not tables[147]

expand the frame of
vision and clear listening;
reference markers[148]

---

142 In most of my meetings with "global" higher education foundations, I have found Angola and Mozambique left out, simply because they operate in Portuguese. Portugal and Brazil do engage but they too operate in very particular ambits of influence, and there are few points of intersection (Cesarino, 2011; Ribeiro, 2020).
143 When I have incentivised undergraduates to learn the languages of neighbouring African countries, I have found the uptake positive and enthusiastic. These undergraduates' curiosity can be molded, and the benefits of exchanges with Africa can be powerfully shaped. However, that's only possible if those teaching them have done this work.
144 If nothing else, my hope is that this text provokes a meditation on what these are.
145 Here I reiterate the value of a deep engagement with literature outside of academic publishing. Novels often reveal far more than scholarship in terms of how things were, how they are, and how they might become (Ghosh, 2008).
146 (Ghosh, 2020).
147 Angola is unlikely to become like Portugal in the next 40 years, but it could much more conceivably operate much like Brazil. Instead of looking North, it makes a difference to teach us to look left and right instead.
148 Many of us in higher education are deeply ignorant about academic institutions in neighbouring countries and regions, whilst simultaneously being very conscious of "how things are done" at Oxford or Yale.

that are closer to
home; futures that are much more
realistic. And to[149]

assume the good is
not already here in the
labour of thousands.[150]

Recognise them all.
Value the work of education. Leave space be-[151]

Yond the algorithm.
Syllables to go far with[152]
Openings to grow.[153]

References

Adichie, C. N. (2016). *The danger of a single story*. National Geographic Society.

Agência, B. (2013). *Estudantes estrangeiros buscam oportunidades no Brasil*. O Globo https://oglobo.globo.com/brasil/educacao/estudantes-estrangeiros-buscam-oportunidades-no-brasil-7565288

Alfredo, A. (2012). *Aventuras de um estudante Angolano no Estrangeiro*. Mayamba Editora.

Altenreid, M. (2020). The platform as factory: Crowd work and the hidden labour behind artificial intelligence. *Capital and Class, 44* (2), 145–58. https://doi.org/10.1177/0309816819899410

---

149 This is not to suggest that we settle for "less", but rather to reframe the discussion so that we ourselves are not always found wanting.
150 The deep commitment and powerful work of so many people cannot be in vain.
151 As a lot of wise people have observed, hitting the same rock again and again with the same stick is unlikely to yield new results, until the stick breaks. We should be careful not to try to address 21st century crises in the same way.
152 I've been moved by the reactions to this piece so far. It seems many of us are short of breath, perhaps other forms of expression might support us differently.
153 In as many directions as there are thinkers, teachers, practitioners in further education: forests of fresh imagination and care that are needed to revive the failing planet.

Auerbach, J. (2020a). *Dimunn ki pou dir? An analysis of social cohesion in contemporary Mauritius* [Unpublished manuscript]. Centre for Intercultural Studies, Open University of Mauritius.

Auerbach, J. (2020b). *From water to wine: Becoming middle class in Angola*. University of Toronto Press.

Auerbach, J. (2022a). The pedagogy of hyperlinkages: Knowledge curatorialism and the archive of kindness. *South African Journal of Higher Education, 36*(1), 76–95.
https://hdl.handle.net/10520/ejc-high_v36_n1_a5

Auerbach, J. (2022b). Expanding available futures: Ideological contestation in Angola's emerging higher education sector. *Comparative Education Review, 66*(1), 142–60.
https://doi.org/10.1086/717552

Badat, S. (2020). Reproduction, transformation and public South African higher education during and beyond Covid-19. *Transformation: Critical Perspectives on Southern Africa, 104*(1), 24–42.
https://doi.org/10.1353/trn.2020.0030

Badat, S., & Sayed, Y. (2014). Post-1994 South African education: The challenge of social justice. *Annals of the American Academy of Political and Social Science, 652*(1), 127–48.
https://doi.org/10.1177/0002716213511188

Barassi, V. (2020). *Child, data, citizen: How tech companies are profiling us from before birth*. MIT Press.

Benjamin, R. (2019). *Race after technology: Abolitionist tools for the New Jim Code*. Polity Press.

Berry, M. (2021). Linking digital wayfaring and creative writing: True fictions from ethnographic fieldwork. *New Writing, 18*(2), 239–50.
https://doi.org/10.1080/14790726.2020.1797821

Biko, S. (2002) *I write what I like: Selected writings*. University of Chicago Press.

Botha, P. A., & Botha, A. (2022). Investigating the self-perceived acquired competencies of humanities graduates at a South African university. *South African Journal of Higher Education, 36*(2), 25–45.
https://doi.org/10.20853/36-2-4170

Bratton, B. H. (2016). *The stack: On software and sovereignty*. MIT Press.

Brankovitch, J. (2021, March 21). *Welcome to Germany – the country where most academic careers expire before they start*. Escher Blog.
https://echer.org/welcome-to-germany-95vswisszeitvg/.

Breakstone, J., Smith, M., Connors, P., Ortega, T., Kerr, D., & Wineburg, S. (2021). Lateral reading: College students learn to critically evaluate internet sources in an online course. *Harvard Kennedy School Misinformation Review, 2*(1), 1–17.

https://doi.org/10.37016/mr-2020-56

Brodsky, J. E., Brooks, P. J., Scimeca, D., Todorova, R., Galati, P., Batson, M., Grosso, R., Matthews, M., Miller, V., & Caulfield, M. (2021). Improving college students' fact-checking strategies through lateral reading instruction in a general education civics course. *Cognitive Research: Principles and Implications, 6*(1), 1–18.
https://doi.org/10.1186/s41235-021-00291-4

Canagarajah, S. (2011). Codemeshing in academic writing: Identifying teachable strategies of translanguaging. *The Modern Language Journal, 95*(3), 401–17.
https://www.jstor.org/stable/41262375

Cesarino, L. (2011). Anthropology of development and the challenge of South-South cooperation. *Vibrant: Virtual Brazilian Anthropology, 9*(1), 197–293.
https://doi.org/10.1590/S1809-43412012000100017

Clifford, J., & Marcus. G. (1989). *Writing culture: The poetics and politics of ethnography*. University of California Press

Czerniewicz, L., Agherdien, N., Badenhorst, J., Belluigi, D., Chambers, T., Chili, M., de Villiers, M., Felix, A., Gachago, D., Gokhale, C., Ivala, E., Kramm, N., Madiba, M., Mistri, G., Mgqwashu, E., Pallitt, N., Prinsloo, P., Solomon, K., Strydom, S.,... Wissing, G. (2020). A wake-up call: Equity, inequality and Covid-19 emergency remote teaching and learning. *Postdigital Science and Education, 2*(3), 946–67.
https://doi.org/10.1007/s42438-020-00187-4

Czerniewicz, L., Trotter, H., & Haupt, G. (2019). Online teaching in response to student protests and campus shutdowns: Academics' perspectives. *International Journal of Educational Technology in Higher Education, 16*(1), 1–22.
https://doi.org/10.1186/s41239-019-0170-1

Davidson, C. N. (2017). *The new education: How to revolutionize the university to prepare students for a world in flux*. Basic Books.

Dawson, H. J., & Fouksman, E. (2020). Labour, laziness and distribution: Work imaginaries among the South African unemployed. *Africa, 90*(2), 229–51.
https://doi.org/10.1017/S0001972019001037

de Brito, A. G. C., Quoniam, L., & Mena-Chalco, J. P. (2016). Exploração da plataforma lattes por assunto: Proposta de metodologia. *Transinformacao, 28*(1), 77–86.
https://doi.org/10.1590/2318-08892016002800006

de Souza Costa, S. M., & Leite, C. L. F. (2008). Brazilian open access initiatives: Key strategies and challenges. In *Proceedings of the ELPUB 2008 conference on electronic publishing, Toronto, Canada*.
https://www.researchgate.net/publication/30864934

Dookhitram, K., Bokhoree, C., & Chitoo, H. (2018). Mauritius: Unlocking educational sustainability's hidden value. In H. Letchamanan & D. Dhar

(Eds), *Education in South Asia and the Indian Ocean islands* (pp. 293–304). Bloomsbury Academic. https://doi.org/10.5040/9781474244329.0021

Doxdator, B. (2017, July 8). *A field guide to jobs that don't exist yet*. Edtech in the Wild. https://edtechbooks.org/wild/jobs_that_dont_exist.

Emma. (2018). *The mental load: A feminist comic*. Seven Stories Press.

Eriksen, T. H. (1998). *Common denominators: Ethnicity, nation-building and compromise in Mauritius*. Berg Books.

Estes, N. (2019). *Our history is the future: Standing rock versus the Dakota Access Pipeline and the long tradition of Indigenous resistance*. Verso.

Faria, M. L. de. (2009). Cooperação no âmbito do ensino superior: Ser estudante angolano em universidades portuguesas. *Pro-Posições, 20*(1), 45–63. https://doi.org/10.1590/S0103-73072009000100004

Ferguson, J. (2015). *Give a man a fish: Reflections on the new politics of distribution*. Duke University Press.

Ferguson-Patrick, K., Reynolds, R., & Macqueen, S. (2018). Integrating curriculum: A case study of teaching Global Education. *European Journal of Teacher Education, 41*(2), 187–201. https://doi.org/10.1080/02619768.2018.1426565

Fuller, K., & Stevenson, H. (2019). Global education reform: Understanding the movement. *Educational Review, 71*(1), 1–4. https://doi.org/10.1080/00131911.2019.1532718

Ghosh, A. (2008). *Sea of poppies*. John Murray.

Ghosh, A. (2020). *The nutmeg's curse: Parables for a planet in crisis*. University of Chicago Press.

Giannella, E. (2015). Morality and the idea of progress in Silicon Valley. *Berkeley Journal of Sociology, 59*, 70–77. https://berkeleyjournal.org/files/2022/04/2015-BJS-Vol-59-screen-optimized.pdf

Glass, C. R., Streitwieser, B., & Gopal, A. (2021). Inequities of global mobility: Socioeconomic stratification in the meanings of a university education for international students. *Compare, 51*(1), 43–60. https://doi.org/10.1080/03057925.2019.1590180

Goldin, I., & Kutarna, C. (2016). *Age of discovery: Navigating the risks and rewards of our new renaissance*. St Martin's Press.

Google. (2021, October 6). *Google for Africa* [Video]. YouTube. https://www.youtube.com/watch?v=GJw_gOAnAtE

Gourlay, L., Rodríguez-Illera, J. L., Barberà, E., Bali, M., Gachago, D., Pallitt, N., Jones, C., Bayne, S., Hansen, S. B., Hrastinski, S., Jaldemark, J., Themelis, C.,

Pischetola, M., Dirckinck-Holmfeld, L., Matthews, A., Gulson, K. N., Lee, K., Bligh, B., Thibaut, P.,... Knox, J. (2021). Networked learning in 2021: A community definition. *Postdigital Science and Education, 3*(2), 326–69. https://doi.org/10.1007/s42438-021-00222-y

Gouveia, F. C. (2019). Altmetric studies in Brazil: An analysis from the curricula on the Lattes Platform-CNPq. *Transinformacao, 31,* 1–10. https://doi.org/10.1590/2318-0889201931e190027

Green, L. (2020). *Rock, water, life: Ecology and humanities for a decolonial South Africa.* Duke University Press.

Grimm, J., & Grimm, W. (1800/2011). *Grimm's complete fairy tales.* Canterbury Classics.

Habib, A. (2019) *Rebels and rage: Reflecting on #FeesMustFall.* Jonathan Ball

Harari, Y. N. (2018). *21 lessons for the 21st Century.* Spiegel & Grau.

Heiman, R., Liechty, M., & Freeman, C. (Eds). (2012). *The global middle classes.* School of Advanced Research.

Hillman, J. (2021). *The digital silk road: China's quest to wire the world and win the future.* Harper Collins.

Jain, L. (2019). *Things that art: A graphic menagerie of enchanting curiosity.* University of Toronto Press

Jansen, J. (2017). *As by fire: The end of the South African university.* NB Publishers

Jansen, J. D. (2002). Political symbolism as policy craft: Explaining non-reform in South African education after apartheid. *Journal of Education Policy, 17*(2), 199–215.
https://doi.org/10.1080/02680930110116534

Jansen, J., Phillips, H., Ajam, T., Metz, T., Benatar, S., Auerbach, J., Mesthrie, R., Pityana, B., Habib, A., Madonsela, T., & Reddy, V. (2020). Special compilation: What the social sciences and humanities allow us to see and do in response to Covid-19. *South African Journal of Science, 116*(7/8), 1–16
https://doi.org/10.17159/sajs.2020/8501

Jöns, H., & Hoyler, M. (2013). Global geographies of higher education: The perspective of world university rankings. *Geoforum, 46,* 45–59.
https://doi.org/10.1016/j.geoforum.2012.12.014

Kaschula, R. H., & Maseko, P. (2014). The intellectualisation of African languages, multilingualism and education: A research-based approach. *South East Academic Libraries System, 13,* 8–35.
http://vital.seals.ac.za:8080/vital/access/manager/Repository/vital:27548

Keet, A., & Swartz, D. (2015). A transformation barometer for South African higher education [Unpublished manuscript]. Draft discussion document, André Keet and Derrick Swartz with the TMF/TSG.

Kerr, P. (2022). Academic pipeline of academic treadmill? Post-doctoral fellowships and the circular logic of development. *South African Journal of Higher Education, 36* (3), 72–90.
https://orcid.org/0000-0003-4257-6078

Kochhar, R. (2021). *The Pandemic stalls growth in the global middle class, pushes poverty up sharply*. Pew Research Center.
https://www.pewresearch.org/global/2021/03/18/the-pandemic-stalls-growth-in-the-global-middle-class-pushes-poverty-up-sharply/

Lahiri, M. (2017). The view from here: Too long; didn't read. *English, 66*(252), 1–5.
https://doi.org/10.1093/english/efw065

Latour, B. (2004). Whose cosmos, which cosmopolitics? *Common Knowledge, 10*(3), 450–62.
http://www.bruno-latour.fr/node/209.html

Lembani, R., Gunter, A., Breines, M., & Dalu, M. T. B. (2020). The same course, different access: The digital divide between urban and rural distance education students in South Africa. *Journal of Geography in Higher Education, 44*(1), 70–84.
https://doi.org/10.1080/03098265.2019.1694876

Levine, S. (2013). *Medicine and the politics of knowledge*. HSRC Press.

Long, W. (2021). *Nation on the couch: Inside South Africa's mind*. Melinda Ferguson Books.

Mabharwana, N. (2022). *Food security at the University of the Western Cape: an exploration of actions and programmes to address student hunger* [Unpublished master's thesis]. University of the Western Cape.

Mamdani, M. (2016). Between the public intellectual and the scholar: Decolonization and some post-independence initiatives in African higher education. *Inter-Asia Cultural Studies, 17*(1), 68–83.
https://doi.org/10.1080/14649373.2016.1140260

Maseko, P. (2017). Exploring the history of the writing of isiXhosa: An organic or an engineered process? *International Journal of African Renaissance Studies, 12*(2), 81–96.
https://doi.org/10.1080/18186874.2017.1400218

Mcbride-Chang, C., Suk, C., & Ho, H. (2000). Developmental issues in Chinese children's character acquisition. *Journal of Educational Psychology, 92*(1), 50–55.
https://doi.org/10.I037//0022-0663.92.1.50

McGrew, S., & Byrne, V. L. (2022). Conversations after lateral reading: Supporting teachers to focus on process, not content. *Computers & Education, 185*, 1–13.
https://doi.org/10.1016/j.compedu.2022.104519

McKay, A. (Director). (2021). *Don't look up*. [Film]. Netflix.

Mok, K. H. (2016). Massification of higher education, graduate employment and social mobility in the Greater China region. *British Journal of Sociology of Education, 37*(1), 51–71.
https://doi.org/10.1080/01425692.2015.1111751

Monatsha, B. (2020). *Molapo o tlatswa ke meltaswana: Re-existence in the context of remote learning and Covid-19* [Unpublished honours dissertation]. North-West University.

Nuttall, S. (2006). *Beautiful ugly: African and diaspora aesthetics*. Duke University Press.

Nyabola, N. (2018). *Digital democracy, analogue politics: How the internet era is transforming politics in Kenya*. Zed Books.

Nyamnjoh, F. (2005). Madams and maids in southern Africa: Coping with uncertainties, and the art of mutual zombification. *Africa Spectrum, 40*(2), 181–96.
https://www.jstor.org/stable/40175071

Nyamnjoh, F. (2011). Cameroonian bushfalling: Negotiation of identity and belonging in fiction and ethnography. *American Ethnologist, 38*(4), 197–293.
https://doi.org/10.1111/j.1548-1425.2011.01331.x

Nyamnjoh, F. (2016). *#RhodesMustFall: Nibbling at resilient colonialism in South Africa*. Langaa.

Nyamnjoh, F. (2020). A post-Covid-19 fantasy on incompleteness and conviviality. In C. Besteman, H. Cabot & B. Kalir (Eds), *Post-Covid fantasies* [Website]. American Ethnologist.
https://americanethnologist.org/online-content/collections/post-covid-fantasies/post-covid-fantasies-an-introduction/

Nyamnjoh, F. B. (2012). Potted plants in greenhouses: A critical reflection on the resilience of colonial education in Africa. *Journal of Asian and African Studies, 47*(2), 129–54.
https://doi.org/10.1177/0021909611417240

Nyamnjoh, F. B. (2013). *Insiders and outsiders: Citizenship and xenophobia in contemporary southern Africa*. Zed Books.

Olagbaju, O. O., & Popoola, A. G. (2020). Effects of audio-visual social media resources-supported instruction on learning outcomes in reading. *International Journal of Technology in Education, 3*(2), 92–104.
https://doi.org/10.46328/ijte.v3i2.26

O'Neil, C. (2016). *Weapons of math destruction*. Crown/Archetype.

Orlowski, J. (Director). (2020). *The social dilemma*. [Film]. Netflix

Overing, J., Fortis, P., Margiotti, M., Giminiani, P. di, & Gonzalez Galvez, M. (2015). Kinship in anthropology. In J. Wright (Ed.), *International Encyclopedia of Social and Behavioural Sciences* (pp. 36–43). Elsevier.
https://www.academia.edu/20079615/Kinship_in_Anthropology

Patel, S. (2010). *Migritude*. Kaya Press.

Pearce, J., Péclard, D., & Soares de Oliveira, R. (2018). Angola's elections and the politics of presidential succession. *African Affairs, 117*(466), 146–60. https://doi.org/10.1093/afraf/adx045

Peletz, M. G. (1995). Kinship studies in late twentieth-century anthropology. *Annual Review of Anthropology, 24*, 343–72. https://www.jstor.org/stable/2155941

Philips, H. (2019). *UCT under apartheid: From onset to sit in*. Fanele/Jacana.

Pillay, N., Bhorat, H., & Asmal, Z. (2021). Higher education outcomes in South Africa: The role of the national student financial aid scheme. In W. Pearson, & V. Reddy (Eds), *Social justice and education in the 21st century* (pp. 171–94). Palgrave.

Posetti, J., Ireton, C., Wardle, C., Derakshan, H., Matthews, A., Abu-Fadil, M., Trewinard, T., Bell, F., & Mantzarlis, A. (2018). In C. Ireton, & J. Posseti (Eds), *Journalism, fake news and disinformation: Handbook for journalism education and training* (pp. 1–122). UNESCO. https://unesdoc.unesco.org/ark:/48223/pf0000265552

Pusumane, O., & Auerbach Jahajeeah, J. (2024 forthcoming). Using transformative leadership to 'nibble at resilient colonialism': An autoethnographic account of student-faculty experiences. (Chapter 14). In S. Swartz, T. De Kock, & C. Odora Hoppers (Eds), *Transformative leadership in African contexts: Ideas and actions to bring about just social change*. HSRC Press.

Rahman, Z. (2014). *In the light of what we know*. Farrar, Strauss and Giroux

Ribeiro, A. B. (2020). *Modernization dreams, lusotropical promises: A global studies perspective on Brazil-Mozambique development discourse*. Koningklijke Brill.

Roy, A. (2020). *The pandemic as a portal*. The Financial Times. https://www.ft.com/content/10d8f5e8-74eb-11ea-95fe-fcd274e920ca

Rufalow, M. H. (2020). *Digital divisions: How schools create inequality in the tech era*. University of Chicago Press.

Sharma, Y. (2022, May 11). Three major universities quit international rankings. *University World News*. https://www.universityworldnews.com/post.php?story=20220511170923665

Sichone, O. (2008). Xenophobia and xenophilia in South Africa: African migrants in Cape Town. In P. Werbner (Ed.), *Anthropology and the new cosmopolitanism: Rooted, feminist and vernacular perspectives* (pp. 197–293). Routledge.

Soares de Oliveira, R. (2015). *Magnificent and beggar land: Angola since the civil war*. Hurst.

Stanton, B. (2015). *Humans of New York*. St Martin's Press.

Starosielski, N. (2015). *The undersea network*. Duke University Press.

Taussig, M. (2012). *Beauty and the beast.* University of Chicago Press.

Tempest, K. (2016). *The bricks that built the houses.* Bloomsbury.

Trisos, C. H., Auerbach, J., & Katti, M. (2021). Decoloniality and anti-oppressive practices for a more ethical ecology. *Nature Ecology & Evolution, 5*(9), 1205–12. https://doi.org/10.1038/s41559-021-01460-w

Välaiho, P. (2014). *Biopolitical screens: Images, power and the neoliberal brain.* MIT Press.

Williams, R. (1977). *Marxism and literature.* Oxford University Press.

Yende, S. J. (2021). Funding opportunities and challenges: A case of South African institutions of higher learning. *Journal of Public Administration, 56*(1), 70–79.
https://hdl.handle.net/10520/ejc-jpad-v56-n1-a6

Young, R. (2020). *Australian universities: Thriving in a changing world.* National Security College of Australia.
https://nsc.crawford.anu.edu.au/publication/18199/australian-universities-thriving-changing-world

Zafar, A. (2011). *Mauritius: An economic success story* [PDF]. World bank Africa success stories.
https://www.un.org/esa/socdev/egms/docs/2016/AliZafar.pdf

Ziegenbalg, O., & Thalheim, R. (Writer & Director). (2021, October 7). Episode 1.4 [TV series Episode 1.4]. In A. Benz, R. Thalheim, & O. Ziegenbalg (Executive Producers), *The billion dollar code.* Kundschafter Film Produktion; Sunnysideup Film Produktion.

9. Artificial intelligence for good? Challenges and possibilities of AI in higher education from a data justice perspective

Ekaterina Pechenkina

Artificial intelligence technologies and methods have long been gaining traction in higher education, with accelerated growth in uptake and spread since the COVID-19 pandemic, including the 2023 rise of generative AI. However, even before the rapid evolution currently unfolding, AI-powered bots have already been widely used by universities, fielding student inquiries and delivering automated feedback in teaching and learning contexts. While this chapter acknowledges the groundbreaking changes currently wrought by generative AI technologies in HE, in particular in relation to assessment, it is primarily concerned with overarching principles and frameworks rather than with capturing the current rapidly-changing state of the tech industry. Among specific interests of this chapter is the use of AI tools by universities to predict students' academic outcomes based on demographics, performance, and other data. The chapter explores whether and how AI brings benefits in the areas of student support and learning, and whether and how AI, as a symptom of HE's massification, further complicates justice and equity issues. Drawing on scholarship dedicated to data justice and ethics of care, the chapter seeks to answer urgent questions associated with the proliferation of AI in HE: (a) how can AI be used in HE for good, (b) how can this rapidly growing industry be regulated, and (c) what would a conceptual framework for data justice and fair usage of AI in HE look like?

Introduction

My first experience with artificial intelligence (AI) in higher education (HE) dates to 2008 when I was employed on a short contract to work at a university administration. In my first week, my new manager came back excited and inspired from an overseas conference. There was one particular presentation that excited her the most: the one discussing how learning analytics and similar "automated" tools can identify students "at-risk" as early as the first day of the semester based on data students provide at enrolment, such as their postcode, whether they are first in the family to attend a university, and whatever other demographic data they are required to give throughout the application process (e.g. ethnicity, place of birth, whether they come from a refugee background or self-identify as Aboriginal and/or Torres Strait Islander — a collective term used by the Australian government for Australia's First Nations peoples). Hearing this, I blurted out: "so, we will be racially profiling students?". The manager did not react well to the remark. Long story short, my contract was not renewed. Naturally, the incident stayed with me over the years.

When over a decade later I responded to an invitation to contribute a chapter to the #HE4Good book, AI immediately came to mind. As a scholarship of teaching and learning (SoTL) researcher interested in the various ways technologies impact on and change teaching and learning practice and student experience, I am continually concerned with equity, justice, integrity, digital surveillance, and other salient issues associated with the proliferation of AI across the spheres of life.

A useful UNESCO publication offers an extensive list of possible applications of AI in HE, with a specific focus on generative AI. Among these possibilities are using AI as a guide, collaborative coach, motivator, assessor, and co-designer (Sabzalieva & Valentini, 2023). The same report also identifies a number of challenges such as academic integrity, accessibility, cognitive bias, and lack of regulation. None of these challenges are new. It is the latter issue in particular that this chapter is concerned with as it asks how we — educators, administrators, university leaders — can ensure that the inevitable propagation of AI technologies in our classrooms and wider HE spaces is indeed "for good".

Drawing on scholarship around data justice (Dencik et al., 2019; Hoffmann, 2019; Taylor, 2017), ethics of care (Prinsloo, 2017; Prinsloo &

Slade, 2017) and other relevant works, I analyse the phenomenon of AI in universities through the lens of social justice and in the wider context of datafication and massification of HE. I then make an argument for a data justice framework and principles that universities can — and should — use to guide their AI efforts to ensure that AI is indeed used for good. This chapter focuses on the superset of AI systems and tools on the conceptual level, rather than specifically on LLM (such as ChatGPT) as the matters of regulation and governance apply to a variety of AI applications.

Part critical review, part reflective piece, this chapter proposes an evidence-based roadmap for the future of AI governance in HE. It reiterates the urgent need for regulation and data justice in this field and proposes specific ways to enable AI practices that maximise the good for students, educators, universities, and communities.

Artificial intelligence is here to stay

Defined as "computer systems that undertake tasks usually thought to require human cognitive processes and decision-making capabilities" (Riedel et al., 2017, p. 1), AI technologies and methods entered HE's lexicon about 30 years ago (Zawacki-Richter et al., 2019), yet AI is still positioned as an "emerging" field in HE. A recent Horizon report (Pelletier et al., 2021) identified AI among the six top technologies and practices expected to have a significant impact on the future of teaching and learning in tertiary education. The 2022 report (Pelletier et al., 2022) made a similar prediction. None of these predictions, however, truly accounted for the evolutionary leap that AI technologies took in 2023, with the rise of generative AI and large language models (LLMs) such as ChatGPT (What's the next work in large language models?, 2023).

While AI technologies have much in common with the field of learner data measurement, collection and analysis collectively known as learning analytics (LA), AI in HE is swiftly evolving into a field of its own, encompassing a variety of methods and approaches, from machine learning to neural networks (Zawacki-Richter et al., 2019). Universities already use AI systems and methods in a variety of ways, such as administrative support provision (Sandu & Gide, 2019). Despite concerns around chatbots' limited capacity to solve complex issues, combined with issues around privacy and exposure of personal information, the main selling point of chatbots to universities is that these technologies promise improved productivity and streamlined communications (Sandu & Gide, 2019).

There are other implied promises of "good" associated with AI integrations in HE. When seen through the lens of techno-optimism, defined as a consistent belief that science and technology can solve the various issues faced by our society (Alexander & Rutherford, 2019), such promises are typical of the edtech sector. And so, AI systems come to HE bearing "gifts": from automating repetitive tasks that may not require human intervention, such as certain types of marking and assessing, providing feedback, responding to student queries (Zawacki-Richter et al., 2019), to such alleged benefits to teaching and learning as enhanced interactivity and personalised experiences for students in asynchronous online environments (Tanveer et al., 2020). This "automation is good" discourse is not new. In a 2021 book chronicling the history of so-called "teaching machines", programmed devices designed to offer students personalised learning in the 1950s in accordance with B. F. Skinner's controversial behaviourist theory, Audrey Watters outlines how Skinner's (and Pressey's before him) "innovations" in teaching and learning did not quite live up to their hype.

Other alleged benefits are associated with LA-centric applications of AI, which are tasked with helping educators and administrators understand how student online behaviour may be indicative of their academic outcomes (Herodotou et al., 2019). However, using AI for predicting human behaviour comes with loaded, and well-founded, concerns around equity and ethics (Kantayya, 2020; Lee, 2018), as well as data privacy and exploitation (Ouyang & Jiao, 2021; Schiff, 2021).

While the promise of automation and prediction may be appealing, such as for educators tasked with teaching large cohorts, faced with high student attrition or dealing with significant volumes of administrative work, the possibility of outsourcing such vital tasks as marking or feedback-giving to machines/algorithms may not sit well. Perhaps, some types of marking (e.g. multiple choice quiz or a highly structured essay) can indeed be automated, but as much as I would love to delegate my overflowing emails and student queries to an AI assistant, there remains a deep-seated sense of dread. sava saheli singh (2021) rightly points out that so-called "smart" technologies in education (where "smart" refers to the ability of a technology or a device to "make the decision so the person doesn't have to think") can "tak[e] away the ability of a teacher to connect meaningfully with their students" (p. 262–63). Even with its offer of a rapid response, can AI ever provide the same level of care to a student that a human educator would? And what about the various possibilities of misuse of these technologies, such as a recent case surrounding chatbot ChatGPT, with its use detected in one-fifth of student assessments (Cassidy, 2023b) or an even more recent example of an educator using AI software incorrectly to detect cheating, resulting in false accusation and withholding of grades (Klee, 2023)?

Despite mounting concerns, AI presence in universities is becoming ubiquitous, affecting multiple aspects of experience for students and staff. While some universities decided to ban the use of certain types of AI altogether, many others looked for smooth integration and effective usage while slowly revising their policies and governance frameworks. But as universities compete for students and resources, especially in the augmented post pandemic terrain characterised by shrinking budgets and austerity measures, it is not surprising if they turn increasingly to AI solutions. However, will this happen at the expense of student and staff privacy and digital rights? Chris Gilliard and other scholars working in this field issue legitimate warnings, including in relation to digital redlining — a digital equivalent of "historical form of societal division… that enforce class boundaries and discriminate against specific groups" (Gilliard, 2017, p. 64). The 2023 UNESCO report (Sabzalieva & Valentini, 2023) cites privacy concerns, commercialisation and, again, governance, as central challenges to overcome.

Issues around data ownership concerned with liability and accountability require extensive investigation, as many universities around the world use US-based educational technologies (such as learning management systems, or LMS). Similarly, the ongoing investment into AI technologies is also in the hands of 'big tech', which is dominated by US firms. This means student and staff data are likely to be stored on overseas servers, creating a legislative conundrum in cases of leaks and breaches, as well as issues associated with power relations.[1] Further, there are related matters of accessibility, commercialisation and

---

1 See the Amiel & Deniz chapter "Advancing 'openness' as a strategy against platformization in education" for a detailed discussion of these issues.

equity, given AI as an industry is profit-driven, and while its products may be free of cost at first they will likely end up behind paywalls eventually. Although non-for-profit alternatives to the likes of ChatGPT do exist, the lack of overarching governance policy and regulations creates many risks for universities, potentially allowing questionable practices to proliferate. However, such regulations are on the rise. Despite several countries banning or blocking ChatGPT (Sabzalieva & Valentini, 2023) and the CEO of OpenAI himself testifying in favour of regulation (Bhuiyan, 2023), these are far from widespread and many issues of uneven protections and access remain unaddressed.

In light of the rapid changes outlined, there is an urgent need for critical research, with practitioners and scholars coming together to provide evidence and inform regulation and governance design. In-depth understandings of AI's impact on students and staff are essential. Maximum impact will be gained if theorists and practitioners work together to continue building this body of knowledge.

How AI is used in higher education

In their systematic review of research over the period 2007–2018, Zawacki-Richter et al. (2019) identify four main types of applications of AI in HE:

- Profiling/prediction,
- Assessment/evaluation,
- Adaptive systems/personalisation, and
- Intelligent tutoring systems.

The review outlines an assortment of possibilities afforded by AI, from using machine learning to predicting the likelihood of a student dropping out to providing just-in-time feedback to detecting plagiarism (Bahadir 2016; Luckin et al., 2016; Zawacki-Richter et al., 2019). A more recent review by Crompton and Burke (2023) offers a similar list of types of AI applications in HE, with the only new category added being AI assistants. "Self-supervised learning" which draws on the ability of AI systems to "learn from raw or non-labeled data" is touted as one of the most important relevant advances of AI relevant to HE (Mondelli, 2021, p. 13; Zhang et al., 2021). In a related conceptual discussion, Prinsloo (2017) proposes categorising the ways universities collect, analyse, and use student data as a matrix of seven dimensions: "automation; visibility; directionality; assemblage; temporality; sorting; and structuring" (p. 138).

AI systems can also be categorised based on tasks they perform across HE domains such as proctoring, office productivity, and admissions, and can be integrated into institutional learning management and student information systems and mobile apps used by students and staff (Pelletier et al., 2021). There are many specific examples of AI systems in action. A predictive algorithmic model tested by Delen (2011), for instance, demonstrated an accuracy of 81.19% when determining a student's likelihood of dropping out, with factors such as previous academic achievement and the presence of financial support being key to determining their chances of success. It is not clear what happens next, but presumably with this information at their disposal, universities can "intervene" early and offer "at risk" students the help they need to stay enrolled. Whether students would accept such help and how effective it would be is less certain. My concern about using LA for racial profiling that in 2008 essentially cost me my job becomes salient again; my PhD research into the drivers of academic success of Indigenous Australian students revealed that "support" from the university was perceived very differently by Indigenous students depending on the way it was offered. When students felt singled out for "support" because of their Indigeneity, they rejected such offerings, finding them tokenistic and even stigmatising (Pechenkina, 2014, 2015).

In another predictive application of AI in HE, "sentiment analysis" using AI algorithmic capabilities can determine negative and positive attitudes in student social media posts about a particular course and based on that, make judgements about student experiences (Pham et al., 2020). Perhaps a less controversial example, AI systems and capabilities can also be used to understand how students self-regulate learning — their metacognition skills — and ways to scaffold and facilitate those in personalised ways (Pelletier et al., 2021).

AI technologies can be used to evaluate the content of student assignments (automated marking), identifying topics covered in essays, engaging students in a dialogue about their learning progression, and offering support and resources to help them achieve their learning goals.

Pelletier et al. (2021) provide several examples of the latter, including various chatbots that can enable student language practice with a virtual avatar which delivers "natural responses" to students.

Other examples of utilising AI in HE have to do with latent semantic analysis or semantic web technologies which can "inform personalised learning pathways for students" by evaluating and verifying recognition of prior learning (RPL) and converting credits and credentials obtained by students elsewhere to count toward their degree (Zawacki-Richter et al. 2019, p. 17). It is argued that in addition to saving time and money, these affordances of AI may increase students' employability by helping them match their skills and competencies with requirements of the workplace. Similar to intelligent tutoring systems, AI tools used as digital assistants can support student learning by posing diagnostic questions and guiding students toward accessing resources relevant to their needs (Crompton & Burke, 2023).

At the time of writing, the media discourse surrounding AI tools in HE, specifically generative AI, has been both alarming and alarmist, with a torrent of articles outlining the documented or alleged misuse of bots like ChatGPT by students. Commonly used by copywriters, lawyers, and other professionals to generate website content, legal briefs and so on, bot-generated text has been detected in university students' written assignments (Cassidy, 2023b). However, the discourse quickly shifted to discussing practical steps forward, such as assessment redesign and re-thinking the matter of governance around academic integrity and the use of AI.

Concerns around assessment are not new, with Pelletier et al. (2021) arguing for the need to re-think assessment to "better serve 'generation AI'" (p. 13). Assessment could be redesigned to reduce opportunities for students to use text-generating bots and to rely on their critical thinking and reflection skills instead, while the way examinations are run would also need change, with some universities already reverting to "pen and paper" exams (Cassidy, 2023a). Considering this, it is troubling that of the sample analysed by Zawacki-Richter et al. (2019), only two out of 146 articles (1.4% of the sample) engaged critically with issues relating to ethics and risks that come with AI applications in HE. This apparent scarcity of critical perspectives in practitioners' research suggests a prevalence of techno-centric, uncritical implementations of AI technologies in HE, which can produce more harm than good.

In addition to the issues outlined above, there are many more serious risks associated with AI in HE, ranging from those posed to students and educators due to unconscious bias affecting the fairness of algorithmic decisions and the misuse of private data, to potential loss of academic and administrative/professional support jobs. Further risks include harm to workers as well as climate effects. Lack of algorithm transparency constitutes an ongoing challenge, likely to disproportionately affect those who may already be vulnerable and disempowered (Kantayya, 2020; Lee, 2018), as Gilliard's (2017) work on surveillance and digital redlining highlights. Further, Buolamwini and Gebru (2018) note the potential of machine learning algorithms to discriminate based on race and gender among other classes, offering ways to alleviate these biases.

Pedagogically-led implementation of AI in teaching and learning remains an underexplored area in peer reviewed literature (Zawacki-Richter et al., 2019), indicative of a divide that persists between practitioners' drive for technological innovation and the pedagogical rationale behind it. These and other challenges associated with AI in HE are discussed in the next section, which brings to light important criticisms before offering a way forward.

Challenges and risks of artificial intelligence in higher education

Ethics, privacy and other issues associated with AI practices in HE were rarely foregrounded in the studies reviewed by Zawacki-Richter et al. (2019), with rare exceptions (Li, 2007; Welham, 2008). Li (2007), acknowledging that when using automated systems to deliver support or teaching, students might be worried about possibilities of discrimination when their personal data was accessed, while Welham (2008) was primarily concerned with the cost and affordability of AI applications for publicly funded universities which may not be able to compete with their wealthier counterparts.

However, there is a promising rise of diverse, critical voices that challenge the techno-centric and techno-optimistic accounts which exalt the technical affordances and possibilities of AI (and edtech more generally) while brushing over (or wilfully ignoring) the deeper concerns over privacy, equity, profiling and other serious risks and challenges. For example, contrasting the earlier promises of increased productivity and freeing up of educators' time via automating "routine" tasks, Mirbabaie et al. (2022) highlight how the integration of AI systems into day-to-day university life may also have legal implications for workloads and enterprise bargaining agreements which are designed to protect staff and jobs. Further, when it comes to students, the central narrative maintained by edtech companies that sell surveillance and other AI-powered products to universities is that cheating is on the rise and students cannot be trusted (Swauger, 2020). While the evidence behind such trends is not so clear-cut (Newton, 2018), it is suggested that the increase in student cheating observed over the decades "may be due to an overall increase in self-reported cheating generally, rather than contract cheating specifically" (p. 1). What is more concerning, however, is how bodies and behaviours of students are categorised by the AI surveillance systems. As Swauger (2020) observes, "cisgender, able-bodied, neurotypical, [male, and] white" bodies are "generally categorized… as normal and safe" by these technologies, hence there is little risk of jeopardising such bodies' academic or professional standings. Bodies that do not share these characteristics, however, may not fare so well.

Analysing the dilemmas surrounding AI, surveillance and algorithmic decision-making in education, Prinsloo (2017) warns that ethical considerations must be prioritised and negotiated in this complicated terrain where human and nonhuman actors interact. Other scholars also employ critical perspectives to argue that antiracist, equity, and privacy principles must be embedded into any policies concerned with using AI systems in HE to reduce harm and not to disenfranchise and disempower students and/or educators (Ouyang & Jiao, 2021; Schiff, 2021). Discussing what it means for AI to truly empower human actors, Ouyang and Jiao (2021) theorise empowerment as a conceptual movement from the dominant paradigm in which learners are *recipients* of AI-directed teaching and support, toward a paradigm which sees learners as leaders *directing* AI action within complex educational terrains. The importance of ethical considerations in the latter scenario is implied.

Among the most significant challenges associated with the use of AI in HE are those related to teaching and learning. Analysing AI applications in so-called intelligent tutoring services, Zawacki-Richter et al. (2019) located four main types of their use:

- Teaching/delivering content,
- Diagnosing strengths/gaps in students' knowledge; providing automated feedback
- Curating resources and materials based on student need, and
- Facilitating collaboration.

An alarming finding of this review indicates a scarcity of research that mindfully applies educational theories and pedagogical foundations to inform AI decisions in teaching and learning. Only a handful of studies were identified where educational theory and pedagogical thinking were apparent in AI designs. Among these were the two Barker (2010, 2011) studies, which drew on Bloom's taxonomy and cognitive levels when designing automated feedback systems for adoptive testing modelling. Other examples discussed developing AI solutions to enable learning progression support with intelligent tutoring systems. Arguably, these and similar practices can benefit immensely from robust theorising, for example, by bringing Vygotskian ideas about learning and development into online and hybrid spaces (Hall, 2007). Ouyang and Jiao's 2021 review reinforces this need, highlighting that many of the above-mentioned issues persist and pedagogical theories underpinning AI-based learning and instruction are still rare to find in AI-focused HE studies.

A specific set of challenges associated with AI in HE relates to the use of chatbots and similar mechanisms to resolve student inquiries, provide feedback, assess students' work, and perform other types of automated or semi-automated tasks. While a deeper understanding of costs and "return on investment" is needed, there is perhaps a potential for bots to save universities time and money, for example, by using bot-enabled apps to understand student experiences (and challenges) and use this knowledge to reduce attrition (Nietzel, 2020). However, the increasing use of bots may also be indicative of massification and commercialisation of HE, where students are "customers" or "users" rather than learners. This is troubling as, I would argue, it further increases the distance between students and learning and between students and educators, potentially isolating and disenfranchising some students and further marginalising those who might already be disadvantaged. Peer reviewed research into bot-assisted support and teaching, especially from a student perspective, remains scarce, while challenges associated with using AI bots in student support require serious exploration, with quality (Pérez et al., 2020) and security (Hasal et al., 2021) being particularly salient issues.

While scholars of AI and educational technologies more generally (Facer & Selwyn, 2021; Ferguson, 2019; Selwyn & Gašević, 2020) argue in favour of prioritising ethical and pedagogically-sound approaches to designing and deploying AI tools in HE, prior to the rise of generative AI, university leadership appeared overly preoccupied with using AI for surveillance and student outcome prediction, focusing on early identification of "students-at-risk". While these goals are still very much present, the current discourse has shifted to deal with regulating the use of generative AI by students and staff. Relevant discussions can be found in scholarship dedicated specifically to LA, with Guzmán-Valenzuela et al. (2021) and other authors warning of a divide that persists between practice-based and management-oriented applications of LA in HE. With AI's proliferation across HE, challenges and risks associated with ethics, privacy and related issues deserve a deeper exploration — and with the possibilities of generative AI, these concerns are more important than ever.

Ethics, privacy, and data justice

Data justice discourses highlight important privacy and digital surveillance concerns, such as the potential misuse of data and the quality of services and teaching provided to students. These issues become particularly problematic when juxtaposed with the idea of HE as a "public good" (Marginson, 2011) along with its stated noble goals, such as students' personal development, reducing inequality, and tackling other societal challenges (Bowen & Fincher, 1996).

Specific risks to student privacy are associated with the use of AI-enabled surveillance in examination and proctoring practices (Pelletier et al., 2021). Chin (2020) and Clark (2021) chronicle one such case of digital proctoring, where a university staff member faced litigation after publicly raising concerns about the practice and the software. At the heart of the case is the evidence-based concern that using an AI software to proctor online examinations caused students emotional harm by tracking their private spaces using built-in cameras, deploying abnormal eye movement function as well as other invasive technologies to determine when students were not looking at their test. Such student behaviours were labelled problematic, indicating signs of cheating. However, the software did not account for neurodivergent students and those with physical and learning disabilities, raising the concerns of discrimination. While teachers could choose not to use the software, it was not clear what alternative methods of remote proctoring were available to them. It was also not clear whether students could opt out from this practice without harming their standing in the university. It comes as little surprise that students are speaking up against automated proctoring, online tracking, and other types of surveillance (Feathers & Rose, 2020), calling it out as ableist, discriminatory, and intrusive (Chin, 2020; Gullo, 2022).

Text-matching platforms used by universities to detect plagiarism and other misconduct offer another example of automated surveillance that has become ubiquitous in HE. Mphahlele and McKenna (2019) decode several myths surrounding one such platform widely used by universities (at the time of the study's publication, it was being used by 15,000 HE institutions in over 140 countries). The most common myth alarmingly has to do with the software's perceived core function: while it is a misconception that it detects plagiarism, this myth continues to popularise this text-matching product among universities and beyond. Software like this is used primarily to police student behaviour rather than for educational or developmental purposes. I argue that such uncritical, routine use of surveillance software on students feeds into the overall culture of surveillance that has become normalised at universities and other workplaces.[2]

While specific university policies guide institutional efforts relating to academic integrity and so-called contract cheating, as Stoesz et al. (2019) point out, these policies often lack "specific and direct language", their principles are not clearly defined, and overall, such policies are often underdeveloped. Whether or not universities mandate the use of such platforms, the choice of usage is often left with individual teaching academics. Once activated, one widely used text-matching platform

---

2   See, for example, this article in review: Bowell P., Smith G., Pechenkina E., & Scifleet, P. 'You're walking on eggshells': Exploring subjective experiences of workplace tracking. *Culture and Organization*, 29(6), 1-20.

automatically produces a colour-coded "similarity score" students can preview. Academics can view a "similarity report" once the assignment is submitted, indicating where text in the student assignment matches text published elsewhere. All submissions processed in this way are digitally stored in a repository owned by the company that owns the software.[3] It is ironic that tools meant to uphold academic integrity in turn collect students' work and sell it for profit (Morris & Stommel, 2017). While students and academics can request that individual papers be removed, this process can take time. At the same time, academics can request to see relevant assignments submitted elsewhere to analyse a piece under investigation for cheating. Depending on a university's academic misconduct policy, students can face penalties, such as suspension or exclusion.[4] While similarity checks may be beneficial to students, helping them develop a stronger sense of integrity and become better writers, they come with risks and punishments in stock. Student consent is implied here but it is not fully informed — throughout their studies students remain largely unaware of what data generated by their actions is gathered, how it is used, or how they can opt out.

Considering the threat of lawsuits and persecution of whistle-blowers and critics (Chin, 2020), clear university-level frameworks to govern the use of AI are necessary if universities are serious about their promises in relation to students' and faculty's wellbeing. Moreso, such frameworks must go hand in hand with protection offered to staff and students who speak up about their experiences and offer critiques, holding those in power accountable.

Professional development and upskilling of staff, as well as students, is another critical challenge to tackle alongside ethical AI integrations into the HE. In such a task, principles of data justice informed by empathy, antiracist philosophy, ethics of care, and trauma-informed teaching must take centre stage to ensure AI technologies do no harm.

---

3   Notably, the leading text-matching company was recently sold in some of the biggest edtech acquisitions in the history of the industry (see https://www.edsurge.com/news/2019-03-06-turnitin-to-be-acquired-by-advance-publications-for-1-75b)

4   See, for instance, Swinburne University of Technology's student academic misconduct regulations 2012: https://www.swinburne.edu.au/about/policies-regulations/student-academic-misconduct/#academic_misconduct_regulations_4

A data justice framework for artificial intelligence in higher education

Data justice is an important dimension of the debate surrounding the ethics of using AI in HE. Explored by Dencik et al. (2019), Prinsloo and Slade (2017), Taylor (2017) and others, data justice can be understood as a dimension of the broader social justice discourse, concerned specifically with datafication and digital rights and freedoms in the context of datafied society. Data justice presents a useful framework "for engaging with... challenges [associated with datafication] in a way that privileges an explicit concern for social justice" (Dencik & Sanchez-Monedero, 2022, p. 2) as data-driven discrimination can take place whenever data is collected (Kantayya, 2020). A "fairness in the way people are made visible, represented and treated as a result of their production of digital data" Taylor (2017, p. 1), as explained earlier in the chapter, data justice is urgently needed in HE the same way it is needed in all other domains of datafied society.

Student and staff anxieties around intrusive surveillance and data-based profiling should be centred when designing fair and equitable AI solutions. This is particularly important in online and hybrid environments which attract large and diverse cohorts and where personalised student experiences are not always possible without technological interventions.

The establishment of specialised institutes and advisory groups tasked with producing ethical frameworks and policies for governance of AI in HE, like the UK's now-defunct Institute for Ethical AI in Education,[5] Germany's state-funded project AI Campus,[6] Australia's Data61, Hong-Kong-based Asia-Pacific Artificial Intelligence Association,[7] and other similar formations, indicates a concerted move toward a unifying approach in this field, at least at national levels.

---

5 The Institute is no longer operating; www.buckingham.ac.uk/research-the-institute-for-ethical-ai-in-education/
6 According to its website, AI campus is "the AI Campus is a not-for-profit space where research, start-ups and corporates come together and collaborate on Artificial Intelligence."; www.aicampus.berlin/
7 According to its website, AAIA is "an academic, non-profit and non-governmental organization voluntarily formed 1074 academicians worldwide"; https://www.aaia-ai.org/

The framework and principles presented below (see Figure 9.1) are a synthesis of recommendations developed by other scholars and practitioners. It is proposed that universities use these principles when developing institutional policies for AI, to ensure that all implementations of AI are fair, transparent, and just.

Figure 9.1

Conceptual framework for principles for AI governance in HE[8]

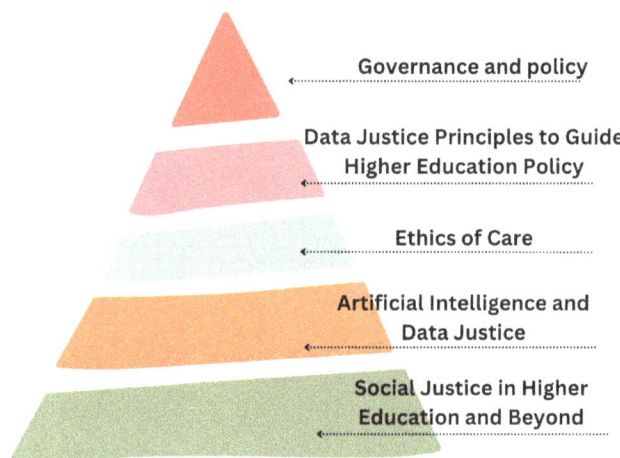

Data justice-based principles for AI governance in HE:

- *Transparency*: to offer upfront information to students and staff about *what* data is collected and *how* it will be used.
- *Clarity*: to spell out rationale (pedagogical and/or otherwise) for all AI solutions affecting students and staff and explain in plain language *why* this data is collected.
- *No harm*: to embed into AI designs measures against harmful profiling, e.g. data about students' ethnicity, for example, could be hidden/not made available to algorithms unless there is a strong rationale for its inclusion.

---

8   This image was inspired by Emeritus Associate Professor Cheryl Hodgkinson-Williams's peer review.

- *Agency*: to allow students and staff to actively exercise their right to *opt out* and withdraw their data without prejudice.
- *Active governance*: to set up a meaningful institutional entity to handle complaints and other issues of relevance to AI. A dedicated ethics committee could be set up and populated by members who are up to date on these issues. Any such committee must include student representatives and social justice advocates.
- *Accountability*: to consider AI's expected benefits against estimated risks, with mitigation strategies put in place as well as reporting processes embedded to ensure accountability and transparency to the public.

Ethical principles currently found in peer reviewed research are primarily concerned with LA and using data for prediction of outcomes, such as principles developed by Corrin et al. (2019), which include privacy, data ownership, transparency, consent, anonymity, non-maleficence, security, and access. An excellent example of university-level framework for the ethical use of student data comes from Athabasca University, highlighting such principles as Supporting and Developing Learner Agency, Duty of Care, Transparency and Accuracy, and others.[9] However, most of these, like the OECD principles,[10] are non-binding recommendations, which limits their reach and impact. Importantly, with some exceptions (Jones et al., 2020), meaningful staff and student voices tend to be missing from these important discussions altogether.

Among the conceptual works informing the proposed framework is Prinsloo's (2017) matrix explaining four main AI-performed processes in education and which focuses on the shifting responsibility between algorithmic and human actors. The matrix is presented as a spectrum of possibilities based on the presence of human agency, starting from tasks performed solely by humans and ending with tasks performed fully by algorithms without human oversight and intervention. Two in-between

---

9   Principles for Ethical Use of Personalized Student Data are available here: https://www.athabascau.ca/university-secretariat/_documents/policy/principles-for-ethical-use-personalized-student-data.pdf
10 G20/OECD Principles of Corporate Governance; www.oecd.org/corporate/principles-corporate-governance/

possibilities included tasks shared between humans and machines and tasks performed by algorithms with human supervision.

Commissioned by the Australian Government, Dawson et al.'s (2019) discussion paper is also relevant to the above framework and principles. It identifies *trust* as a key principle when integrating AI solutions and systems, regardless of industry. The paper solicited feedback regarding AI ethics, receiving 130 submissions from government, business, academia, and the non-government sector and from individuals. As a result, the following eight principles emerged as important:

- Wellbeing
- Human-centred values
- Fairness
- Privacy protection and security
- Reliability and safety
- Transparency and explain-ability
- Contestability
- Accountability

These principles are voluntary, offered as guidance for businesses and other stakeholders wishing to exercise high ethical standards in their work with AI. The main consequence of this is that it is left to the discretion of organisations whether to follow these guidelines or not, which makes it difficult to assign responsibility and accountability. Among the case studies submitted in response to Dawson et al. (2019), none came from HE or the wider education sector. Among the recommendations produced were formation of advisory groups and review panels tasked with guiding the organisation's leadership in responsible AI use, reviewing sensitive cases and complaints, and championing ethical use across smaller teams. The overall need for training and useful exemplars was also identified as essential (Dawson et al., 2019).

Among the case studies in Dawson et al. (2019) was one by Microsoft,[11] which focused on the ethical and safe use of chatbots. Key practices of

---

11   See Australia's Artificial Intelligence Ethics Framework for further information: www.industry.gov.au/data-and-publications/australias-artificial-intelligence-ethics-framework/testing-the-ai-ethics-principles/ai-ethics-case-study-microsoft

operationalising the above-mentioned ethical principles included clearly defining chatbots' purpose, informing customers/clients about the bot's non-human status, designing the bot and interactions to redirect customers to a human representative when needed, emphasising respect for individual preferences, and seeking views on bot usage and experiences from customers. The principle of transparency of data collection and usage emerged as the most important to make explicit. This principle was implemented in the chatbot design by including a "an easy-to-find 'Show me all you know about me' button, or a profile page for users to manage privacy settings" (Australian Government, n.d.), including an option to opt out, where possible.

Another useful consideration comes from the 2022 concept note developed by Research ICT Africa, which critiques existing Global-North-centred governance frameworks and proposes an approach informed by a positive regulation model rather than a more typical negative regulatory perspective. The authors argue that the governance approach needs to actively redress inequality and injustice and to follow such principles of rights-based AI as "(in)visibility [or representation]; (dis)engagement with technology; and (anti)discrimination" (Research ICT Africa, 2022, p. 3).

Principles such as those discussed above do not imply a one-size-fits-all approach, but rather customisation and tailoring to fit specific HE contexts. Further, having principles as guidance-only would not put the necessary pressure of accountability on universities. A real commitment is needed from university leaders, for example, by embedding these principles in HE policy and procedures. Further, HE-specific AI solutions would need to be guided by a set of industry-relevant standards, inclusive of built-in pedagogical rationale for AI technologies used in teaching and learning scenarios.

Conclusion

Data without context, stripped of in-depth understanding of human experience, is close to meaningless. With cases of AI algorithmic discrimination based on race (Kantayya, 2020), gender (Buolamwini & Gebru, 2018), and religious clothing (Chin, 2020), and with Google notoriously firing AI ethics researchers (Schiffer, 2021; Vincent, 2021), it is urgent that questions and critiques around AI ethics be taken seriously. The focus of any AI endeavour in HE must be on human experience and actual human needs, rather than on predictive technologies, student surveillance or detection of cheating.

While issues around the ethics of AI usage, such as those concerned with privacy and data capture may be similar in other sectors, the specific nature of HE requires context-specific principles to be devised and implemented. Considering how quickly AI systems develop and mature, policies and regulations governing AI must go beyond "catch-up" mode, pre-emptive regulation is required. The development of governance policy and related frameworks should be a cyclical process that considers the fast-evolving nature of AI technologies, allowing for amendments and clarification of "grey areas" as new information emerges. Agile advisory bodies need to provide clarifications and interpretations, hence keeping policy relevant and responsive. Ideally, resultant AI policies would acknowledge existing biases and implement ways to minimise those, recognising the complexity of factors influencing student academic success. A positive regulation model must drive such efforts.

National (and even international) regulation, arrived at via negotiations between industry and sectoral bodies, researchers, and governments, could govern the use of AI systems in HE. While scholars increasingly engage with this topic, important questions around data ownership, privacy, transparency, and ethics are far from resolved. Principles in existence are largely proposed as recommendations, and with rare exceptions, staff and student voices are missing from these processes and recommendations. Although there are several social groups that lobby for the ethical use of technology in wider society, there is an obvious absence of a united HE-focused voice that starts at the universities' level and is powered by evidence-based research to help advocate for meaningful adoption of ethical principles.

Despite ongoing 'breakthroughs' concerned with visual art and writing produced by AI bots that regurgitate content, amid concerns with plagiarism and IP theft, "robots" are not going to take over HE jobs just yet. However, trust and transparency where AI decisions are concerned are still missing. Students and staff are rarely privy to important developments around AI that may directly affect their work and study. The use of AI needs to be rigorously supervised and written into enterprise bargaining agreements, with possible implications for workload and day-to-day functions of professional and academic staff considered. Likewise, AI algorithms used for identifying "students-at-risk" should be critically interrogated and re/designed in a way that does not harm. Clear options must be provided for staff and students to opt out, or at the very least make informed decisions about their involvement and usage. Lastly, the governance of AI, in particular generative AI like ChatGPT, must be solidified in relevant university policies concerned with academic misconduct, plagiarism and so on. Relevant staff require training, tools, and resources, including examples of redesigning assignments to maximise students' critical thinking, problem solving, and collaboration. One such example was proposed by a peer reviewer of this chapter who suggested the following approach: using a tool like an AI essay generator or text-matching software in class together with students. An auto-generated essay draft could be critiqued, individually or in groups, with students invited to identify issues and gaps and offer improvements. Such an exercise could help demystify these tools and processes as well as help students to critically reflect on the assumptions such tools are making about writing and referencing. Similarly, students could be guided in using tools like ChatGPT in generating responses to essay questions and then critiquing together the limitations. Again, assessment would need to be redesigned in ways that encourage students to use critical thinking and produce unique responses to scenarios. I welcome readers to propose other approaches that make use of AI tools in scenarios that do no harm.

If universities are truly serious about their mission statements centring student experiences, then a data justice framework for AI in HE is non-negotiable. Currently, the use of AI in HE is not always "for good". Vigilance is essential and it is important to call out risks and problems. At the same time, the extraordinary power of AI can also be harnessed for good. Such opportunities deserve equal attention and resourcing so that AI can serve the ends of social justice in education.

References

Alexander, B., Ashford-Rowe, K., Barajas-Murph, N., Dobbin, G., Knott, J., McCormack, M., Pomerantz, J., Seilhamer, R., & Weber, N. (2019). *EDUCAUSE horizon report*. EDUCAUSE.
https://library.educause.edu/-/media/files/library/2019/4/2019horizonreport.pdf

Alexander, S., & Rutherford, J. (2019). A critique of techno-optimism: Efficiency without sufficiency is lost. In A. Kalfagianni, D. Fuchs, & A. Hayden (Eds), *Routledge handbook of global sustainability governance* (pp. 231–41). Routledge.

Australian Government. (n.d.). *AI ethics case study: Microsoft*. Australia Government Department of Industry, Science and Resources.
https://www.industry.gov.au/data-and-publications/australias-artificial-intelligence-ethics-framework/testing-the-ai-ethics-principles/ai-ethics-case-study-microsoft

Bahadır, E. (2016). Using neural network and logistic regression analysis to predict prospective mathematics teachers' academic success upon entering graduate education. *Kuram ve Uygulamada Egitim Bilimleri, 16*(3), 943–64.
https://doi.org/10.12738/estp.2016.3.0214.

Barker, T. (2010). An automated feedback system based on adaptive testing: Extending the model. *International Journal of Emerging Technologies in Learning, 5*(2), 11–14.
https://doi.org/10.3991/ijet.v5i2.1235.

Barker, T. (2011). An automated individual feedback and marking system: An empirical study. *Electronic Journal of E-Learning, 9*(1), 1–14.
https://www.learntechlib.org/p/52053/.

Bhattacharya, A. (2021, September 3). How Byju's became the world's biggest ed-tech company during the Covid-19 pandemic. Scroll.in.
https://scroll.in/article/1004404/how-byjus-became-the-worlds-biggest-ed-tech-company-during-the-covid-19-pandemic

Bhuiyan, J. (2023, 17 May). OpenAI CEO calls for laws to mitigate 'risks of increasingly powerful' AI. *The Guardian*.
https://www.theguardian.com/technology/2023/may/16/ceo-openai-chatgpt-ai-tech-regulations

Bowen, H. R., & Fincher, C. (1996). *Investment in learning: The individual and social value of American higher education*. Routledge.

Buolamwini, J., & Gebru, T. (2018). *Gender Shades: Intersectional Accuracy Disparities in Commercial Gender Classification Proceedings of the 1st Conference on Fairness, Accountability and Transparency*, Proceedings of Machine Learning Research, *81*, 77–91.
http://proceedings.mlr.press/v81/buolamwini18a.html?mod=article_inline

Cassidy, C. (2023a, January 10). Australian universities to return to pen and paper exams after students caught using AI to write essays. *The Guardian*.
https://www.theguardian.com/australia-news/2023/jan/10/universities-to-return-to-pen-and-paper-exams-after-students-caught-using-ai-to-write-essays

Cassidy, C. (2023b, January 17). Lecturer detects bot use in one-fifth of assessments as concerns mount over AI in exams. *The Guardian*.
https://www.theguardian.com/australia-news/2023/jan/17/lecturer-detects-bot-use-in-one-fifth-of-assessments-as-concerns-mount-over-ai-in-exams

Chin, M. (2020, October 22). An ed-tech specialist spoke out about remote testing software – and now he's being sued. *The Verge*.
https://www.theverge.com/2020/10/22/21526792/proctorio-online-test-proctoring-lawsuit-universities-students-coronavirus

Clark, M. (2021, April 9). Students of color are getting flagged to their teachers because testing software can't see them. *The Verge*.
https://www.theverge.com/2021/4/8/22374386/proctorio-racial-bias-issues-opencv-facial-detection-schools-tests-remote-learning

Crompton, H., & Burke, D. (2023). *Artificial intelligence in higher education: the state of the field*. International Journal of Educational Technology in Higher Education, *20*(1), 1–22.
https://doi.org/10.1186/s41239-023-00392-8

Corrin, L., Kennedy, G., French, S., Buckingham Shum, S., Kitto, K., Pardo, A., West, D., Mirriahi, N., & Colvin, C. (2019). *The ethics of learning analytics in Australian higher education*. www.melbourne-cshe.unimelb.edu.au/__data/assets/pdf_file/0004/3035047/LA_Ethics_Discussion_Paper.pdf

Dawson, D., Schleiger, E., Horton, J., McLaughlin, J., Robinson, C., Quezada, G., Scowcroft, J., & Hajkowicz, S. (2019). *Artificial intelligence: Australia's ethics framework (a discussion paper)*. Commonwealth Scientific and Industrial Research Organisation, Australia.
https://www.csiro.au/en/research/technology-space/ai/ai-ethics-framework

Delen, D. (2011). Predicting student attrition with data mining methods. *Journal of College Student Retention: Research, Theory and Practice*, *13*(1), 17–35.
https://doi.org/10.2190/CS.13.1.b

Dencik, L., & Sanchez-Monedero, J. (2022). Data justice. *Internet Policy Review*, *11*(1), 1–16.
https://doi.org/10.14763/2022.1.1615

Dencik, L., Hintz, A., Redden, J., & Treré, E. (2019). Exploring data justice: Conceptions, applications and directions. *Information, Communication & Society*, *22*(7), 873–81.
https://www.tandfonline.com/doi/full/10.1080/1369118X.2019.1606268

Editorial Board. (2023, April). *What's the next word in large language models? Nature Machine Intelligence, 5,* 331–32.
https://doi.org/10.1038/s42256-023-00655-z

Facer, K., & Selwyn, N. (2021). *Digital technology and the futures of education: Towards non-stupid' optimism.* UNESCO.
https://unesdoc.unesco.org/ark:/48223/pf0000377071

Feathers, T., & Rose, J. (2020). *Students are rebelling against eye-tracking exam surveillance tools.* Vice.
https://www.vice.com/en/article/n7wxvd/students-are-rebelling-against-eye-tracking-exam-surveillance-tools

Ferguson, R. (2019). Ethical challenges for learning analytics. *Journal of Learning Analytics, 6*(3), 25–30.
http://dx.doi.org/10.18608/jla.2019.63.5

Gilliard, C. (2017). Pedagogy and the logic of platforms. *Educause Review, 52*(4), 64–65.
https://er.educause.edu/-/media/files/articles/2017/7/erm174111.pdf

Global Market Insights (2022). *Artificial intelligence (AI) in education market.*
https://www.gminsights.com/industry-analysis/artificial-intelligence-ai-in-education-market

Gullo, K. (2022, March 25). *EFF client Erik Johnson and Proctorio settle lawsuit over bogus DMCA claims.* Electronic Frontier Foundation.
https://www.eff.org/deeplinks/2022/03/eff-client-eric-johnson-and-proctorio-settle-lawsuit-over-bogus-dmca-claims

Guzmán-Valenzuela, C., Gómez-González, C., Rojas-Murphy Tagle, A., & Lorca-Vyhmeister, A. (2021). Learning analytics in higher education: A preponderance of analytics but very little learning? *International Journal of Educational Technology in Higher Education, 18*(1), 1–19.
https://doi.org/10.1186/s41239-021-00258-x

Hall, A. (2007, August). *Vygotsky goes online: Learning design from a socio-cultural perspective* [Workshop paper]. Learning and socio-cultural Theory: Exploring modern Vygotskian perspectives international workshop 2007, Australia.
https://ro.uow.edu.au/llrg/vol1/iss1/6

Hasal, M., Nowaková, J., Ahmed Saghair, K., Abdulla, H., Snášel, V., & Ogiela, L. (2021). Chatbots: Security, privacy, data protection, and social aspects. *Concurrency and Computation: Practice and Experience, 33*(19), 1–13.
https://doi.org/10.1002/cpe.6426

Herodotou, C., Hlosta, M., Boroowa, A., Rienties, B., Zdrahal, Z., & Mangafa, C. (2019). Empowering online teachers through predictive learning analytics. *British Journal of Educational Technology, 50*(6), 3064–79.
https://doi.org/10.1111/bjet.12853

Hoffmann, A. L. (2019). Where fairness fails: Data, algorithms, and the limits of antidiscrimination discourse. *Information, Communication & Society*, 22(7), 900–15.
https://doi.org/10.1080/1369118X.2019.1573912

Jones, K. M., Asher, A., Goben, A., Perry, M. R., Salo, D., Briney, K. A., & Robertshaw, M. B. (2020). "We're being tracked at all times": Student perspectives of their privacy in relation to learning analytics in higher education. *Journal of the Association for Information Science and Technology*, 71(9), 1044–59.
https://doi.org/10.1002/asi.24358

Kantayya, S. (Director). (2020). *Coded bias*. [Documentary]. 7th Empire Media.

Klee, M. (2023, 17 May) *Professor flunks all his students after ChatGPT falsely claims it wrote their papers*. Rolling Stone.
https://www.rollingstone.com/culture/culture-features/texas-am-chatgpt-ai-professor-flunks-students-false-claims-1234736601/

Lee, N. T. (2018). Detecting racial bias in algorithms and machine learning. *Journal of Information, Communication and Ethics in Society*, 16(3), 252–60.
https://doi.org/10.1108/JICES-06-2018-0056

Li, X. (2007). Intelligent agent-supported online education. *Decision Sciences Journal of Innovative Education*, 5(2), 311–31.
https://doi.org/10.1111/j.1540-4609.2007.00143.x

Luckin, R., Holmes, W., Griffiths, M., & Forcier, L. B. (2016). *Intelligence unleashed: An argument for AI in education*.
http://discovery.ucl.ac.uk/1475756/

Marginson, S. (2011). Higher education and public good. *Higher Education Quarterly*, 65(4), 411–33.
https://doi.org/10.1111/j.1468-2273.2011.00496.x

Mascarenhas, N. (2022, March 10). *Course Hero scoops up Scribbr for subject-specific study help*. Join TechCrunch+.
https://techcrunch.com/2022/03/10/course-hero-scribbr/

Matthews, C., Twaddle, J., Cashion, G., & Wu, S. (n.d.). *Redefining the role of EdTech: A threat to our education institutions, or a strategic catalyst for growth?* PwC.
https://www.pwc.com.au/government/government-matters/education-tech-edtech-revolutionise-education-institutions.html

Mirbabaie, M., Brünker, F., Möllmann Frick, N. R., & Stieglitz, S. (2022). The rise of artificial intelligence: Understanding the AI identity threat at the workplace. *Electronic Markets*, 32(1), 73–99.
https://doi.org/10.1007/s12525-021-00496-x

Morris, S. M., & Stommel, J. (2017, June 15). *A guide for resisting edtech: The case against Turnitin*. Hybrid Pedagogy.
https://hybridpedagogy.org/resisting-edtech/

Mphahlele, A., & McKenna, S. (2019). The use of Turnitin in the higher education sector: Decoding the myth. *Assessment & Evaluation in Higher Education*, 44(7), 1079–89.
https://doi.org/10.1080/02602938.2019.1573971

Newton, P. M. (2018). How common is commercial contract cheating in higher education and is it increasing? A systematic review. *Frontiers in Education*, 3(67), 1–18. https://doi.org/10.3389/feduc.2018.00067

Nietzel, M. T. (2020, March 12). *How colleges are using chatbots to improve student retention*. Forbes.
https://www.forbes.com/sites/michaeltnietzel/2020/03/12/how-colleges-can-chatbot-their-way-to-better-student-retention/?sh=496f12b26b34

Ouyang, F., & Jiao, P. (2021). Artificial intelligence in education: The three paradigms. *Computers and Education: Artificial Intelligence*, 2, 1–6.
https://doi.org/10.1016/j.caeai.2021.100020

Pechenkina, E. (2014). *Being successful. Becoming successful: An ethnography of Indigenous students at an Australian university* [Doctoral dissertation, University of Melbourne, Faculty of Arts].
https://minerva-access.unimelb.edu.au/items/1856f614-cf78-5700-a1a4-64c8f6360455/full

Pechenkina, E. (2015). Who needs support? Perceptions of institutional support by Indigenous Australian students at an Australian University. *UNESCO Observatory Multi-Disciplinary Journal in the Arts*, 4(1), 1–17.
https://www.unescoejournal.com/volume-4-issue-1/

Pelletier, K., Brown, M., Brooks, D. C., McCormack, M., Reeves, J., Arbino, N., Bozkurt, A., Crawford, S., Czerniewicz, L., Gibson, R., Linder, K., Mason, J., & Mondelli, V. (2021). *EDUCAUSE horizon report*. EDUCAUSE.
https://library.educause.edu/resources/2021/4/2021-educause-horizon-report-teaching-and-learning-edition

Pelletier, K., McCormack, M., Reeves, J., Robert, J., Arbino, N., Dickson-Deane, C., Guevara, C., Koster, L., Sánchez-Mendiola, M., Bessette, L. S., & Stine, J. (2022). *EDUCAUSE Horizon Report*. EDUCAUSE.
https://library.educause.edu/-/media/files/library/2022/4/2022hrteachinglearning.pdf?la=en&hash=6F6B51DFF485A06DF6BDA8F88A0894EF9938D50B

Pérez, J. Q., Daradoumis, T., & Puig, J. M. M. (2020). Rediscovering the use of chatbots in education: A systematic literature review. *Computer Applications in Engineering Education*, 28(6), 1549–65.
https://doi.org/10.1002/cae.22326

Pham, T. D., Vo, D., Li, F., Baker, K., Han, B., Lindsay, L., Pashna, M., & Rowley, R. (2020). Natural language processing for analysis of student online sentiment in a postgraduate program. *Pacific Journal of Technology Enhanced Learning*, 2(2), 15–30.
https://doi.org/10.24135/pjtel.v2i2.4

Prinsloo, P. (2017). Fleeing from Frankenstein's monster and meeting Kafka on the way: Algorithmic decision-making in higher education. *E-Learning and Digital Media, 14*(3), 138–63.
https://doi.org/10.1177/2042753017731355.

Prinsloo, P., Slade, S. (2017). Big data, higher education and learning analytics: Beyond justice, towards an ethics of care. In B. K. Daniel (Ed.), *Big data and learning analytics in higher education* (pp. 109–24). Springer, Cham.

Research ICT Africa (2022). *Concept Note, From Data Protection to Data Justice: Redressing the uneven distribution of opportunities and harms in AI.*
https://researchictafrica.net/publication/from-data-protection-to-data-justice-redressing-the-uneven-distribution-of-opportunities-and-harms-in-ai/

Riedel, A., Essa, A., & Bowen, K. (2017, April 12). *7 Things you should know about artificial intelligence in teaching and learning.* EDUCAUSE.
https://library.educause.edu/resources/2017/4/7-things-you-should-know-about-artificial-intelligence-in-teaching-and-learning

Sabzalieva, E., & Valentini, A. (2023). *ChatGPT and artificial intelligence in higher education: quick start guide.* United Nations Educational, Scientific and Cultural Organization Digital Library.
https://unesdoc.unesco.org/ark:/48223/pf0000385146

Sandu, N., & Gide, E. (2019). Adoption of AI-Chatbots to enhance student learning experience in higher education in India. *Proceedings of the 18th international conference on information technology based higher education and training* (pp. 1–5). IEEE.
https://doi.org/10.1109/ITHET46829.2019

Schiff, D. (2021). Out of the laboratory and into the classroom: The future of artificial intelligence in education. *AI & Society, 36*(1), 331–48.
https://doi.org/10.1007/s00146-020-01033-8

Schiffer, Z. (2021, February 20). *Google fires second AI ethics researcher following an internal investigation.* The Verge.
https://www.theverge.com/2021/2/19/22292011/google-second-ethical-ai-researcher-fired

Selwyn, N., & Gašević, D. (2020). The datafication of higher education: Discussing the promises and problems. *Teaching in Higher Education, 25*(4), 527–40.
https://doi.org/10.1080/13562517.2019.1689388

singh, s. s., Davis, J. E., & Gilliard, C. (2021). Smart educational technology: A conversation between sava saheli singh, Jade E. Davis, and Chris Gilliard. *Surveillance & Society, 19*(2), 262–71.
https://doi.org/10.24908/ss.v19i2.14812

Stoesz, B. M., Eaton, S. E., Miron, J., & Thacker, E. J. (2019). Academic integrity and contract cheating policy analysis of colleges in Ontario, Canada. *International Journal for Educational Integrity, 15*(1), 1–18. https://doi.org/10.1007/s40979-019-0042-4

Swauger, S. (2020, April 2). *Our bodies encoded: Algorithmic test proctoring in higher education*. Hybrid Pedagogy. https://hybridpedagogy.org/our-bodies-encoded-algorithmic-test-proctoring-in-higher-education/

Swinburne University of Technology. (2012). *Student academic misconduct regulations 2012*. https://www.swinburne.edu.au/about/policies-regulations/student-academic-misconduct/#academic_misconduct_regulations_4

Tanveer, M., Hassan, S., & Bhaumik, A. (2020). Academic policy regarding sustainability and artificial intelligence (AI). *Sustainability, 12*(22), 1–13. https://doi.org/10.3390/su12229435

Taylor, L. (2017). What is data justice? The case for connecting digital rights and freedoms globally. *Big Data & Society, 4*(2), 1–14. https://journals.sagepub.com/doi/full/10.1177/2053951717736335

Vincent, J. (2021, April 13). *Google is poisoning its reputation with AI researchers*. The Verge. https://www.theverge.com/2021/4/13/22370158/google-ai-ethics-timnit-gebru-margaret-mitchell-firing-reputation

Watters, A. (2021). *Teaching machines: The history of personalized learning*. MIT Press.

Welham, D. (2008). AI in training (1980–2000): Foundation for the future or misplaced optimism? *British Journal of Educational Technology, 39*(2), 287–303. https://doi.org/10.1111/j.1467-8535.2008.00818.x.

Zawacki-Richter, O., Marín, V. I., Bond, M., & Gouverneur, F. (2019). Systematic review of research on artificial intelligence applications in higher education – where are the educators? *International Journal of Educational Technology in Higher Education, 16*(1), 1–27. https://doi.org/10.1186/s41239-019-0171-0

Zhang, D., Mishra, S., Brynjolfsson, E., Etchemendy, J., Ganguli, D., Grosz, B., Lyons, T., Manyika, J., Niebles, J. C., Sellitto, M., Shoham, Y., Clark, J., & Perrault, R. (2021). *The AI index 2021 annual report*. Stanford University. https://aiindex.stanford.edu/ai-index-report-2021/arXivpreprint arXiv:2103.0631

10. HE4Good assemblages: FemEdTech Quilt of Care and Justice in Open Education

Frances Bell, Lorna Campbell, Giulia Forsythe, Lou Mycroft, and Anne-Marie Scott

Introduction

Quilting has always been a communal activity and, most often, women's activity. It provides a space where women are in control of their own labour: a space where they can come together to share their skill, pass on their craft, tell their stories, and find support. These spaces stand outside the neoliberal institutions that seek to appropriate and exploit our labour, our skill, and our care. The FemEdTech-quilt assemblage has provided a space for women and male allies from all over the world to collaborate, to share their skills, their stories, their inspiration, and their creativity. We, the writers of this chapter, are five humans who each has engaged with the FemEdTech Quilt of Care and Justice in Open Education (Figure 10.1) in different ways, and who all have been active in the FemEdTech network.

Figure 10.1

Four quilts hung together. Image by Frances Bell, adapted by Giulia Forsythe (2022), Flickr, https://www.flickr.com/photos/francesbell/52437074543, CC BY-NC-SA 4.0

FemEdTech describes itself as "a reflexive, emergent network of people learning, practising and researching in educational technology".[1] As the name suggests, the network converges on the intersections of feminism, education, and technology. The FemEdTech Quilt of Care and Justice in Open Education was a collaborative quilting project emerging from FemEdTech, developed over many months in 2019 and 2020 in connection with two international open education conferences: OER19 (Recentering Open: Critical and global perspectives[2]) and OER20 (Care

---

1 FemEdTech Open Space https://femedtech.net/
2 OER19 Conference website, https://oer19.oerconf.org/

in Openness[3]). From the start, the quilt was identified as an activist undertaking (Bell, 2019c):

> Our quilt project is not only a Feminist project and an Open Education project but also a form of Activism in itself. Together we can create a quilt that can inspire during and after its creation; acknowledge all contributions and their history; and make a difference to Care and Justice in Education and Technology contexts. Most of the work will be done before OER20 and there is no need to be a delegate at the conference to participate. (para. 4)

The call for participation emphasised a variety of modes of participation that aimed to enable participants to decelerate and contribute within their capabilities and comfort zones (Bell, 2019c). Participants answered the call by sending (to an address in England) 6 and 12-inch quilt squares that they had stitched, knitted, and occasionally glued together; and fabric, to be used for backing the quilt. Those who created quilt squares could optionally submit the story behind their contribution to a website. The quilts were assembled in their physical forms and quilted, after which photographs were taken to create the digital quilt,[4] where submitted stories were linked to images of the relevant squares. The assembly of the quilt took place against the unravelling backdrop of the COVID-19 pandemic. The anticipated launch and display of the FemEdTech Quilt at the OER20 conference in London in April 2020 never happened, as the conference moved online. FemEdTech practice changed in response to the impact of COVID-19, as described throughout this chapter.

In this chapter, we articulate the lives and purposes of the quilt that became four quilts, using makers' stories of their quilt squares, images, and Markov Chain poetry, alongside "unseen" contributions such as the thoughts, feelings, readings, and memories we shared as authors during "Thinking Environment" conversations (Kline, 2020). This is a posthuman account, in that it uses posthuman thinking as an analytic lens, drawing on a genealogy which brings together five years within a slow ontology of FemEdTech feminist praxis (Beetham et al., 2022), and the process of creating material and digital quilts. Posthumanism

---

3 OER20 Conference website, https://oer20.oerconf.org/
4 Digital Quilt, https://quilt.femedtech.net/quilt

takes many forms. We draw on the "accountabilities of posthuman research" summarised beautifully by Thompson and Adams (2020). To express the extent of the assemblage of humans and non-humans associated with the quilt emerging from FemEdTech, we refer to it as the "FemEdTech-quilt assemblage". We acknowledge the inevitable incompleteness of our (and any) account. We strive to include and account for multiple forms of subjectivity, inspired by Braidotti's (2022) relational approach to engaging with issues of power within a "heterogenous assemblage of embodied and embedded humans" (p. 6).

Though the scope of our exploration of the material and digital artefacts associated with the FemEdTech-quilt assemblage is limited by the availability of full histories of elements such as fabrics and squares with untold stories (and by the time at our disposal), we explore in more detail the story of four squares and the motivations and experiences of each maker. The stories of the selected squares speak for themselves through a Markov Chain poem. We also reflect on two communal events in the life of the FemEdTech quilts.

Our multiple subjectivities

We are the posthuman FemEdTech-quilt assemblage, in that, though partially manifest as material artefact(s) — crafted by human hands — technologies, stories and desires are woven through our conception, execution and differing perceptions of *us* as a posthuman assemblage.

The quilt exists in differing material and digital forms, but of course these are not fixed products: squares, stories, and quilts are only part of the FemEdTech-quilt assemblage. Squares are made from fabric, thread, and various embellishments such as buttons, labels, badges, and 3D printed objects; created by human and non-human labour. Assemblages are a process of becoming. Beetham et al. (2022) characterise the FemEdTech quilt as emerging from entanglements (in physical and virtual spaces) that include thinking together, stitching separately, and values development:

> ... the textile squares and textual stories refer to one another in a variety of ways, both narrative and spatial. The quilt can be seen variously as the rematerialisation of virtual connections, as a geography of the FemEdTech network, as a rebuke to the conventional authorship of the blog post or conference presentation, and as a desire to write fully with and not merely alongside other feminists. (p. 150)

Writers and artists (human and non-human) assist in telling the story: art, fabric, artefacts, images, and stories bear the work of communicating beyond the humans, known or unknown, who may be involved. The humans include the authors of this chapter, makers of squares of the quilt, donors of fabric, words, and ideas. The quilts would not exist without nameless voices, non-human artefacts, collective thinking, and labour. The importance of assemblage is to counter the acceleration of our times when humans are kept busy (and both humans and non-humans exploited) in the service of capitalism. We are the result of a "praxis, a collective engagement to produce different assemblages" (Braidotti, 2019, p. 52), one of which is this chapter. Braidotti goes on to write: "We are not one and the same, but we can interact together." (Braidotti, 2019, p. 52). The material and digital quilt-making required not only slow practice but a slow ontology (Ulmer, 2017) — a process, rather than just a space. So far, throughout the lifetime of the material and digital quilts, the humans involved (materially, digitally, affectively, cognitively) in the quilts' creation were compelled by the process to decelerate, helping them to curate, to stitch, to draw, to write, and to think. We acknowledge the pressures of the time: being creative in neoliberal times is itself a form of resistance. As they look back, some makers may remember the stress of completing the square, particularly if they weren't experienced quilters, but all will remember the satisfaction of being part of a constellation of contributors who sent in squares, fabric, and stories. A sense of collective achievement and awe was expressed at the OER20 virtual session that explored the possible future of the quilts.

We, who are not one and the same, use posthumanism in a Braidottian sense of *more-than-human* (Braidotti, 2019). Decentring the human allows us to present an account of the FemEdTech-quilt assemblage as a more representative whole. The quilts are inanimate but enlivened by the activist energy of those who contribute to the assemblage around the quilts. The "grammar of animacy" (Kimmerer, 2021) vitalises the quilts as equals amongst humans.

The many intentional practices which comprise the ever changing and partially known history of the quilts subvert the conventional power relations that dominate our lives in HE. Ulmer (2017) and Braidotti (2019), like many posthuman thinkers, draw on the work of 17th century Dutch Jewish philosopher, Baruch Spinoza, who writing in Latin used two words for power: *potestas* and *potentia*. *Potestas* is what we know as power-as-usual, power-over, status and "clout". Composition of the material quilt had to be planned and managed. Inevitably, there was some measure of "power over" people's natural wish for freedom of expression. For example, the squares had to be a certain size, and a similar material weight. *Potentia*, on the other hand, is conceptualised as a joyful, affirmative activism, a power-with that operates at the collective level, rhizomatic in nature, as the assemblage is always open-bordered with no single goal in sight. Braidotti (2019) correlates Spinoza's potentia with *zoe*, the power of life itself, present in all life-forms, including stories. A life, our individual lives, play our part and are subsumed in the assemblage.

The assemblage emerged from two powerful sites of *potentia*, the FemEdTech network and the culture of concern for care and justice in open education, demonstrated via the commitment to prosocial, anti-competitive curation practices and in other ways, before and during COVID-19 (Beetham et al., 2022). Like posthumanism, feminism takes many forms, evident in FemEdTech practices such as a slow ontology that enables acknowledgement of the history of feminism, and reflection on the shorter history of the FemEdTech network (Beetham et al., 2022); and in the "material turn" to which feminists have contributed (Atenas et al., 2022, p. 2). The FemEdTech quilt is an example of the material turn as *potentia* in praxis.

Ulmer (2017) asserts that "writing… is constituted in the entanglement of being, creating, and producing in qualitative research." In the context of the FemEdTech quilt (a project of material and qualitative research involving making and writing), working with slow principles balances the requirements humans may otherwise experience of work-related *potestas*, with the embodied, post-anthropocentric energy of *potentia*. Ulmer (2017) calls it "differently productive". We, the posthuman FemEdTech-quilt assemblage exist, and will continue to exist, as a *potentia* process. No human owns the assemblage, but many humans will continue to be involved in the stewardship of our material-digital-affective *life*.

The story of 'we': the posthuman FemEdTech-quilt assemblage

The idea of the FemEdTech quilt project emerged from various sites: conversations at OER19 and much else that emerged from open education/FemEdTech circles in 2018 and 2019. It is rooted deeply in historic, ongoing values development conversations and FemEdTech feminist practice: writings on the FemEdTech website and tweets/replies/curation at the #FemEdTech hashtag and @FemEdTech Twitter account. Much remains invisible, "forgotten" yet still present as we continue the work, intentionally including multiple subjectivities as a feminist practice of counter-memory which Braidotti (1996, p. 312) describes as "forgetting to forget".

As part of her curation of the @FemEdTech Twitter account in 2018 and inspired by #WorldValuesDay, Mary Loftus (@marloft) tweeted a provocative question: "Does the #femedtech community have some shared values? What might they be? Answers in a tweet ;) #WorldValuesDay". The Twitter activity is described in a FemEdTech blog post (Bell, 2019a) and summarised in Figure 10.2.

Figure 10.2

Summary of the #FemEdTech values activity, October 2018. Image by Giulia Forsythe (2022), Flickr, https://www.flickr.com/photos/gforsythe/52415660369, CC BY 2.0

In her keynote at OER19 titled *A quilt of stars: Time, work and open pedagogy*, Bowles (2019) brought quilts into the minds of conference delegates as she explored issues such as precarity and academic time in the context of open pedagogy. Bowles (2019) identified a quilt as something that can encompass many things. These ideas are reflected in Beetham's (2019) observations in her blog post opening a values development activity a few weeks later. Beetham (2019) linked values development in FemEdTech to the collective repair work needed in higher education (HE) to deal with issues of "marketisation, precarity and audit", writing of threads, repair, and reuse. Throughout 2019, FemEdTech values development and the quilt project developed in tandem, influencing each other.

Conversations about the quilt project continued during the summer of 2019 in the context of values development activities in April/May (Beetham, 2019) and August/September (Bell, 2019b) of that year.[5] The intention was always that the quilt would exist in a material-digital form. As explained in the chapter introduction, the quilt is an activist project with a particular focus on openness and social justice (Campbell, 2020): feminist collective action is important (Mountz et al., 2015). The call for participation (Bell, 2019c) acknowledged Lambert's (2018) framework (Three principles of social justice applied to open education) — redistributive, recognitive and representational justice. Lambert built on Fraser's (2007) work which strongly argues that the lenses of economic redistribution (linking to Marxist approaches) and cultural recognition (often called identity politics) are complementary rather than opposed: "Only by looking to integrative approaches that unite redistribution and recognition can we meet the requirements of justice for all." (Fraser, 2007, p. 34).

The pivot online (Weller, 2020) and successive lockdowns meant that the quilt did not travel to OER20, as the Association for Learning Technology (ALT) sensibly and sensitively lifted the attendance fee and ran a reduced programme online. The quilt was presented in a 30-minute session followed by a discussion of its possible future;

---

5   FemEdTech Values Activity April/May, August/September 2019, https://femedtech.net/about-femedtech/femedtech-values-activity/

its outlet for activism took place via the digital version. Meanwhile, activities at FemEdTech changed in response to experiences of network members as education pivoted online during the pandemic. Shared curation of the Twitter account was paused; the call for papers for a Feminist Special Issue of *Learning, Media & Technology* was postponed from April to June 2020 (Bell et al., 2020); and a letter was written to journal editors (FemEdTech, 2020) calling on the editors and editorial boards of scholarly journals to acknowledge and mitigate the disproportionate impact of the COVID-19 pandemic on women researchers and scholars. Activism persisted in the unfamiliar context of HE during a global pandemic.

It was always envisaged that people across the world who were not delegates could be present at OER20 in a material sense via their quilt contribution. The current quilt includes squares made by people across Australia, Canada, several countries in Europe, and also in New Zealand, South Africa, and the United States. Contributions arrived slowly at first: intentions to submit accelerated in January 2020 and squares arrived by post before and after the 31 January 2020 deadline. The work of completing the quilts progressed as the phenomenon of a global pandemic emerged, a material process to hold onto as HE moved online. Relationships that emerged from the making of quilt squares were powerfully connecting during the difficult months of 2020, visible in FemEdTech writings, e.g. Campbell (2020).

Conceiving the quilt, project, fabrics, thread, people, connections, and technology as an assemblage that emerged before and during COVID-19 can offer us insights into the materiality of connections that are based on physical and online work and objects, locally and globally; a branch of posthumanism often referred to as "new materialism" (Braidotti, 2000). These include environmental ethics and the sustainability of materials. The history of quilting includes repurposing of scraps, worn clothes imbued with memories, and feed sacks, all of which are present in the FemEdTech quilts. The paradox is that quilting is big business in neoliberal times. People accumulate freshly purposed "stashes" of fabric purchased and not always used: the principle of reuse is often forgotten.

Four squares, a poem and two events

Conscious that much remains invisible and forgotten in our attempt to tell the stories of the FemEdTech-quilt assemblage, we dive deeper to examine four of the squares made for the FemEdTech quilt project via their stories (Haxell, 2020; Lambert, 2020; Thomson, 2020; Wright, 2020) and a Markov Chain poem generated from those stories; and two events related to the quilt project: the online webinar at OER20, and the informal event at ALTC22, held in September 2022 at Manchester, when the quilt was displayed publicly for the first time. Although the quilt stories were openly licensed for reuse and adaptation, we as authors have engaged with the makers/writers as we have developed this chapter, especially on how we have interpreted their stories. We draw on reflections from two authors and an editor who took part in these events, as well as relevant blog posts. We acknowledge the partiality of what we can learn from squares and events but draw out what might be learned for future, more detailed and extensive, funded research. There are currently around fifty quilt square stories and many quilt squares without articulated stories; and numerous impacts of, and connections to, the FemEdTech-quilt assemblage that remain beyond our gaze.

Themes from four squares

We chose four quilt squares whose authors had supplied stories. One author read and reread the stories in conjunction with posthuman readings (Braidotti, 2019, 2020, 2022), identifying themes from one or more of the stories, and associating them with relevant posthuman concepts. Three general themes were identified in the stories. These are outlined along with their connections to posthuman theory in Table 1.

Table 1

Linking themes from squares/stories to posthuman concepts/lens

Themes from squares/ stories	Posthuman concepts/lens
Technology including sewing machines (used/ avoided), plane, Wikimedia, Twitter	Xenofeminists: "Adopting a materialist stance, they focus on mundane technologies such as domestic labour-saving devices, as well as larger infrastructural technological systems, to raise key issues of alienation and reproductive labour. Xenofeminism aims at concrete political interventions upon society, following the slogan 'If nature is unjust, change nature!'. This is a critical, affirmative and upbeat response to the challenges of the posthuman times." (Braidotti, 2019b, pp. 88–89)
Care/justice/hope	Affirmative ethics: "Posthuman feminism creates connections without amalgamations, stressing diversity while asserting that we are in this posthuman convergence together. It thus proposes a relational ethics that assumes one cares enough to minimise the fractures and seek for generative alliances." (Braidotti, 2022, p. 237)
Environment/ reuse/ language/ culture	Learning from cultures and environment: "Respectful learning from the oldest guardians of the earth is a good place to start; 'we' differ but are in this together." (Braidotti, 2019b, p. 49) "Indigenous expressivism" — the speaking as a country "that includes people, rocks, birds, animals and the weather". Indigenous philosophies do not separate humans from non-humans: all have agency, subjectivity and "humanity". (Braidotti, 2022, pp. 133–34)

In our chosen squares, the stories tell of encounters with technologies ranging from sewing machines and a plane, to Wikimedia and Twitter. Sewing machines were avoided in favour of the more portable hand-stitching, or embraced and adapted to programme the stitching of a poem, whilst noting the absence of support for the Māori language. One story celebrated the design, build, and flying of a plane by one, if not the first, woman aviator — the story author later contributed to a related Wikipedia article. Another story acknowledged the role of Twitter and YouTube in individual and networked learning. The story authors may not see themselves as Xenofeminists (Table 1), but their affirmative ethos is in tune with this approach to feminism.

The stories from the squares we have chosen are also imbued with themes of care and justice. This is not surprising as the squares were made in response to a call for participation in a Quilt of Care and Justice in Open Education (Bell, 2019c) that was developed in tandem with values development at FemEdTech. Social justice was explicitly mentioned in the call (Bell, 2019c) through the principles referenced. Hope features, explicitly or implicitly, as a theme of all four of the stories.

Affirmative ethics (Table 1) aligns with the concept of the quilt as a vehicle for activism and could form part of a useful framework for a more detailed posthuman account of the FemEdTech quilt assemblage and inform ongoing values development for FemEdTech.

One story draws on Māori culture and language as it illustrates a powerful proverb that demonstrates the need for sustainable practice and care for all others. All four stories, in one way or another, emphasise the value of reusing textiles/fabrics in the creation of the squares, revealing learning from the early history of quilting and from Indigenous cultures (Table 1).

Keep hope alive: a Markov Chain poem

One of the challenges that we faced as authors was in imagining how the quilt itself could "speak". We were concerned not to fall into the trap of anthropomorphism and given that the quilt contains several different languages in both the stories and the squares themselves, it was difficult to even imagine what words it might use. We took some inspiration from the concrete poetry and scrapbook works of the Glaswegian poet, Edwin Morgan (The Edwin Morgan Trust, 2020) and after some experimentation, the digital voice of the quilt was mediated by a Markov Chain engine[6] generating an output from four stories associated with digital quilt squares. Whilst we still cannot quite remove our human subjectivity from the voice of the quilt, the algorithmically generated sentences, we suggest, create something closer to the quilt's own voice, and invite a new form of interpretation

---

6   Markov Chain Text Generator — Online Sentence Prediction https://www.dcode.fr/markov-chain-text

and interrogation. By analysing the distribution of probability that certain word elements will follow other words from the text sample, a new assemblage of the FemEdTech quilt has been generated, entangling the posthuman and the algorithmic. The techno-mediated voice to the quilt allows the multiple different voices and languages, human and posthuman, woven into the physical and digital fabric of the quilt, a chance to speak out and to keep hope alive. It is interesting to read the generated voice in conjunction with the human told stories from which the poem emerges. This is the poem from the stories of four squares: a poem from fifty stories would look quite different.

> Keep hope had shape us a new ideas we are all the harvesting
>
> Hope self-care and carry the large pocket treasures to go out on
>
> Alive thanks to advocate right it was a border between the message is
>
> Received a relatively small island that I'd be compelled to believe the
>
> Lovely cabin and then of sacred buildings they have written behind bars our
>
> Email from different countries and adversity losing her achieve she had capacity for
>
> From my final touches for Reza broken hearted and her plane in our
>
> Frances contacted me Behrouz's song these blocks together in the walls of
>
> Latter part of fabric shops for Reza broken hearted and our processes often
>
> Part of others was the years for open mind the large pocket is
>
> Asking me to capture whilst I initially tweeted and cultures by our lives
>
> Interested in my partner and setbacks is as I have had shape us
>
> This website squeezing in this Whakatauki Maori proverb is very limited but with
>
> Project which we didn't see in our hearts are out into her

> Which was therefore that spans the physical and quilting techniques the years for
>
> Inspired by twitter bird but went I can the general atmosphere what
>
> Many expressed the idea of nuns in our ideas we ourselves can the
>
> Justice focussed contributions at snail's poetry and locally you all our own
>
> Focussed contributions at OER including wearing trousers which had voluntarily embraced an inspiration
>
> Contributions at this website squeezing in all our busy busyness on us and...

Engaging with the FemEdTech Quilt — two events

We look at two events as part of the FemEdTech-quilt assemblage: the online webinar at OER20 and the informal in-person event at ALTC22, held in Manchester in September 2022. Three observers (referred to as Observers 1/2/3 at events 2020/2022) supplied observations via structured reflections on the two events.

A 30-minute webinar in April 2020 replaced the planned 60-minute OER20 session *Femedtech Quilt of Care and Justice in Open Education: Final Touches*[7] that would have enabled face to face conference participants to contribute to the completion of the material quilts. In the webinar, the quilts were visible via a link to the digital quilt and a link to a video that traced the process of the quilts to date. Participants watched the video on YouTube and then returned to a discussion via webinar chat, audio, and/or video. The workshop interaction focused on the question: "How can the FemEdTech quilt make a difference to care and justice in open education?"

The expectation at that time was that the quilts could be displayed at an event in the autumn of 2020 when "things got back to normal". Although the closest connection to the material quilts was a low tech video comprising narrated slideshows of images of the quilts in

---

7   FemEdTech Quilt of Care and Justice in Open Education: Final Touches https://oer20.oerconf.org/sessions/o-127/, including webinar recording and link to process video https://youtu.be/TyKBalbVRjA

progress, the conversation in the webinar following viewing of the video revealed surprisingly strong emotions: "it's safe to say that there wasn't a dry eye in the house after watching it. Like the quilt itself, the upswell of collective emotion was *beautifully imperfect, imperfectly beautiful.*" (Observer 2, 2020 event). It is difficult to explain the materiality of the webinar experience. For those who were already involved in the quilt as makers/supporters, an emotional response is understandable, but the video and experience seemed to draw in newcomers to the FemEdTech-quilt assemblage. Responses to the video came at a time when, although the conference was postponed, most of us had little idea of all that the pandemic would bring to our lives.

The second event came two and a half years later, after several lockdowns and the slow return of face-to-face conferences. This time, the quilt did not appear as part of the scheduled conference programme but rather as an informal presence on the second day of ALTC22 (FemEdTech, 2022a) in a space outside the main lecture theatre. The quilts were spread out across tables. Observer 2 (2022 event) noted: "It was especially lovely to see people finding and reconnecting with squares they had created, pointing out this or that square: 'That's my daughter's dress!' 'That's my mother's earring.'"

In the informal space, we offered the chance for delegates to contribute to squares that would later be added to blank squares on the quilt by sewing on a button or adding a few stitches of embroidery: "… it was wonderful seeing people taking a quiet moment out of the busy conference schedule and becoming absorbed in the shared task of making" (Observer 2, 2022 event). There was a tangible sense of joy from the few makers present, seeing their contributions in the context of the material quilts. Makers from a group were delighted to locate their group's squares spread across the four quilts, differently located from their memory of being made and sent together (Observer 1, 2022 event). Some delegates coming across the quilt project for the first time were interested to think about whether they could do a similar project in their own communities (Observer 1, 2022 event).

A highlight was an informal hanging of the quilts from a balcony at the end of day (Figure 10.3). A group of people closely connected to the quilts held them for others to view, as had been intended in 2020. Observer 3 (2022 event) narrated: "Physically carrying, displaying and touching the quilt at ALTC22, alongside good friends and engaging with many others was to *be* FemEdTech in a new and deep way."

Figure 10.3

Quilts hung informally from balcony at ALTC22. Image by Kerry Pinny (2022), used with permission

MacNeill (2022) reflected in her blog after the conference: "In quite a magical way, the presence of the quilt provided a way to bind many of us together by providing a safe, open, space to have long overdue catch ups, to share experiences and allow time for reflection and just 'being'."

The first event, unexpectedly moved online, provoked emotions that are not easily explicable. The second event, informal but face-to-face, offered a material encounter with the quilts that was unexpected and emotional. These events and the role of the FemEdTech-quilt assemblage over the last three years raise questions about materiality associated with this assemblage.

Contribution to HE for Good

The FemEdTech-quilt assemblage was a coming together of physical and digital material, memories, words, hopes, conversations, and the embodied labour of stitching: a process of "becoming-quilt" and another step in the always "becoming-FemEdTech". From the experience of the OER20 online event, and subsequent activity at the FemEdTech Open Space, it can be argued that the quilt assemblage contributed to FemEdTech during COVID-19 through the *connections* of the makers and others. The activism planned for the quilt was diverted as some FemEdTech quilt square makers turned to the writing of open letters (FemEdTech, 2020), and editing a special issue in 2020 and 2021 (FemEdTech, 2022b).

Our examination of two events, the first at OER20 where the quilts, makers and others were present virtually, and the second at ALTC22 where the quilts and a few makers were physically present, both raise questions about what materiality and co-presence mean in differently hybrid events. OER20 was planned as a face-to-face event that became fully virtual once the London conference was cancelled due to COVID-19. ALTC22 was a face-to-face event in Manchester with virtual elements being part of the ALT conference website and social media channels/hashtags. Of course, both events were experienced differently, and sometimes emotionally, by participants, raising questions about the relationships between material artefacts, and digital stories and images, in human collaboration and activism. As we begin to glimpse some of the connections, human and non-human, FemEdTech-quilt assemblage has something to say for good in HE, summarised in Figure 10.4. We have made a start in this chapter: a more substantial (funded) posthuman study could take time to look beyond four squares' stories to those by as many authors as were willing to be involved; and reach beyond the reactions of people at two events to identify and explore human and nonhuman connections to the FemEdTech-quilt assemblage. In designing such a study, researchers (not necessarily the authors of this chapter) could take an experimental approach that takes account of the dynamics that Thompson and Adams (2020) recommend:

> ... three dynamics which could serve as an initial lens for holding posthuman research work accountable: (1) explain how the researcher speaks with things; (2) actively engage in weaving and fusing of human and nonhuman storylines; and (3) acknowledge the liveliness of posthuman research work in the performativity of difference. (p. 344)

Within the scope of this chapter, we have endeavoured to address these dynamics but we acknowledge that an extended scope could say and show much more.

Figure 10.4

HE4Good quilt assemblage. Image by Giulia Forsythe (2022),
Flickr, https://www.flickr.com/photos/gforsythe/52416155101/, CC BY 2.0

The hope for the material quilts travelling widely were thwarted by COVID-19 (for now) but learning from the conception of the quilts is not limited to being physically co-present with them. The quilts' reality resists the overwhelm and velocity of university life under neoliberalism; it withstands the *"naturalisation of misery"* in the HE workforce (Moten & Harney, 2013, p. 117). Each stitch in the composition of the material quilts is an act of resistance. They would not have been possible in any form without a constellation of humans contributing to their creation. The quilts are an expression of community — prosocial, anti-competitive, and therein lies a learning that many in HE already know: we can only do this together, and we are already here. "We" are Moten and Harney's *undercommons*: an unseen, invisible constellation of *potentia* coming together to hold a line of resistance through our slow, side-stepping practices of creation. No one person could have created the whole, or if they had, that whole would have been something quite different. Human makers, no matter what your workload, your despair, your overwhelm, you stitched your sorrows into joy when you collectively created the quilts. An innumerable number of "minor gestures" (Manning, 2016).

Braidotti (2022, p. 237) identifies posthuman feminism as "a political praxis that supports feminist commons and community-based experiments with what 'we' are capable of becoming". Both the FemEdTech network itself, and the FemEdTech quilt can be regarded as feminist commons and as community-based experiments. We have articulated how we see FemEdTech contributing to HE for good. Our posthuman account of the FemEdTech-quilt assemblage demonstrates how themes from our selected squares can connect with posthuman concepts. If that works for four squares, more themes and connections could emerge to contribute to a posthuman account that includes fifty squares, and the Markov Chain poem would be quite different. The FemEdTech-quilt assemblage has many more human and non-human connections than we have been able to reach in this chapter. Although no account could find all those connections, a more extensive posthuman account could be generative in exploring the range of connections in the assemblage.

In a recent podcast, Helen Beetham and Sheila MacNeill reflected on the impact that the pivot online during COVID-19 had on perceptions of the "real world co-located classroom" (Knight, 2022). They gave an example of moving from "dislocation" during lockdown to a co-location enabled by digital technology and observe that concepts of co-location and dislocation merit further exploration. The concept of moving between dislocation and co-location is reminiscent of twenty years of thinking that has conceptualised virtual work by avoiding a binary opposition of online and offline, continuity and discontinuity, and instead classifying work environments (from published research) based on the types of discontinuities involved (Watson-Manheim et al., 2002). There is a growing volume of research on what presence, co-location and dislocation mean in differently hybrid education events (Raes, 2022). A more detailed posthuman account of the FemEdTech-quilt assemblage could contribute to a framework that makes sense of research into educator and student practices in hybrid education events.

The FemEdTech-quilt assemblage shows that within relational, affirmative ethics, resistance is possible. The process of becoming, exemplified by both the quilts and the FemEdTech network, has been a sustaining joyful practice of what happens in the spaces of coming-together (care, joy, hope, awe) in the face of crisis and the pressure of advanced capitalism. Resistance requires radical rest (rest for health, rest for hope) (Ginwright, 2022). The slow ontology of the assemblage required waves and pauses (Kline, 2020) which allowed space to think. This may be the most crucial resistance of all in an industrialised HE which fills every potential pause with compliance activity. Feminists create, feminists resist, and feminists celebrate difference.

Acknowledgements

We acknowledge FemEdTech supporters, activists, and quilt-square makers; and the insightful feedback from HE4Good reviewers and editors. Thanks for being part of the assemblage and for enabling us to transform this chapter far beyond our initial conception.

References

Atenas, J., Beetham, H., Bell, F., Cronin, C., Vu Henry, J., & Walji, S. (2022). Feminisms, technologies and learning: Continuities and contestations. *Learning, Media and Technology*, 47(1), 1–10.
https://doi.org/10.1080/17439884.2022.2041830

Beetham, H. (2019, May 1). *Threads*. FemEdTech.
https://femedtech.net/published/threads/

Beetham, H., Drumm, L., Bell, F., Mycroft, L., & Forsythe, G. (2022). Curation and collaboration as activism: Emerging critical practices of #FemEdTech. *Learning, Media and Technology*, 47(1), 143–55.
https://doi.org/10.1080/17439884.2021.2018607

Bell, F., Atenas, J., Beetham, H., Cronin, C., Vu Henry, J., & Walji, S. (2020, June 10). *Call for papers – Special issue: Feminist perspectives on learning, media and educational technology*. FemEdTech.
https://femedtech.net/current-projects/call-for-papers-special-issue-feminist-perspectives-on-learning-media-and-educational-technology/

Bell, F. (2019a, May 10). *Values activity facilitated by @marloft in October 2018*. FemEdTech.
https://femedtech.net/published/values-activity-facilitated-by-marloft-in-october-2018/

Bell, F. (2019b, August 24). *Data, dialogue and doing in FemEdTech values development*. FemEdTech.
https://femedtech.net/published/data-dialogue-and-doing-in-femedtech-values-development/

Bell, F. (2019c, November 12). *Call for participation in our project – the FemEdTech Quilt of Care and Justice in Open Education*. Association for Learning Technologies.
https://quilt.femedtech.net/call-for-participation/

Birhane, A. (2021). Algorithmic injustice: A relational ethics approach. *Patterns*, 2(2), 1–9.
https://doi.org/10.1016/j.patter.2021.100205

Bowles, K. (2019, April 10). *A quilt of stars: Time, work and open pedagogy* [Video]. YouTube.
https://www.youtube.com/watch?v=ff1NBTLjWj8&t=120s

Braidotti, R. (1996). Nomadism with a difference: Deleuze's legacy in a feminist perspective. *Man and World*, 29, 305–14.
https://doi.org/10.1007/BF01248440

Braidotti, R. (2000). Teratologies. In I. Buchanan & C. Colebrook (Eds), *Deleuze and feminist theory* (pp. 156–72). Edinburgh University Press.

Braidotti, R. (2019a). A theoretical framework for the critical posthumanities. *Theory, Culture & Society*, 36(6), 31–61.
https://doi.org/10.1177/0263276418771486

Braidotti, R. (2019b). *Posthuman knowledge*. Polity.

Braidotti, R. (2020). We are in this together, but we are not one and the same. *Journal of Bioethical Inquiry*, 17, 465–69.
https://doi.org/10.1007/s11673-020-10017-8

Braidotti, R. (2022). *Posthuman feminism*. Polity.

Campbell, L. M. (2020, March 12). *Sharing the Labour of Care*. FemEdTech.
https://femedtech.net/published/sharing-the-labour-of-care/

FemEdTech. (2020, May 1). *Open letter to editors/editorial boards*.
https://femedtech.net/published/open-letter-to-editors-editorial-boards

FemEdTech. (2022a, August 31). *FemEdTech Quilt at ALTC 2022.* https://femedtech.net/published/stories/femedtech-quilt-at-altc-2022/

FemEdTech. (2022b, November 30). *Feminist perspectives on learning, media and technology.* https://femedtech.net/special-issue-of-learning-media-technology-feminist-perspectives-on-learning-media-and-educational-technology/

Fraser, N. (2007). Feminist politics in the age of recognition: A two-dimensional approach to gender justice. *Studies in Social Justice, 1*(1), 23–35. https://doi.org/10.26522/ssj.v1i1.979

Ginwright, S. A. (2022). *The four pivots: Reimagining justice, reimagining ourselves.* North Atlantic Books.

Haxell, A. (2020, February 12). *If the heart of the flax was removed, where would the bellbird sing?* FemEdTech. https://quilt.femedtech.net/2020/02/12/if-the-heart-of-the-flax-was-removed-where-would-the-bellbird-sing/

Kimmerer, R. W. (2021). *The democracy of species.* Penguin Books.

Knight, S. (Host). (2022, September 6). *Beyond the technology: The education 4.0 podcast* [Audio podcast]. Jisc. https://www.jisc.ac.uk/podcasts/beyond-the-technology-reviewing-learning-and-curriculum-design-06-sep-2022

Lambert, S. R. (2018). Changing our (dis)course: A distinctive social justice aligned definition of open education. *Journal of Learning for Development, 5*(3), 225–44. https://doi.org/10.56059/jl4d.v5i3.290

Lambert, S. R. (2020, April 11). *Keep hope alive!* FemEdTech. https://quilt.femedtech.net/2020/04/11/keep-hope-alive/

Lawlor Wright, T. (2020, March 21). *Openness is a state of mind.* FemEdTech. https://quilt.femedtech.net/2020/03/21/openness-is-a-state-of-mind/

MacNeill, S. (2022, September 12). Transcending the digital and physical at #altc22 – the #femedtechquilt. *HOWSHEILASEESIT.* https://howsheilaseesit.net/oer/transcending-the-digital-and-physical-at-altc22-the-femedtechquilt/

Manning, E. (2016). *The minor gesture: Thought in the act.* Duke University Press.

Moten, F., and Harney, S. (2013). *The undercommons: Fugitive planning & black study.* Minor Compositions. https://doi.org/10.5070/H372053213

Mountz, A., Bonds, A., Mansfield, B., Loyd, J., Hyndman, J., Walton-Roberts, M., Basu, R., Whitson, R., Hawkins, R., Hamilton, T., & Curran, W. (2015). For slow scholarship: A feminist politics of resistance through collective action in the neoliberal university. *ACME: An International Journal for Critical Geographies, 14*(4), 1235–59. https://acme-journal.org/index.php/acme/article/view/1058

Raes, A. (2022). Exploring student and teacher experiences in hybrid learning environments: Does presence matter? *Postdigital Science and Education, 4*(1), 138–59.
https://doi.org/10.1007/s42438-021-00274-0

Thompson, T. L., & Adams, C. (2020). Accountabilities of posthuman research. *Explorations in Media Ecology, 19*(3), 337–49.
https://doi.org/10.1386/eme_00050_7

Thomson, C. (2020, February 19). *Strength*. FemEdTech.
https://quilt.femedtech.net/2020/02/19/strength/

Ulmer, J. B. (2017). Writing slow ontology. *Qualitative Inquiry, 23*(3), 201–11.
https://doi.org/10.1177/1077800416643994

Watson-Manheim, M. B., Chudoba, K. M., & Crowston, K. (2002). Discontinuities and continuities: A new way to understand virtual work. *Information Technology & People, 15*, 191–209.
https://psycnet.apa.org/doi/10.1108/09593840210444746

Weller, M. (2020, March 12). *The COVID-19 online pivot: Adapting university teaching to social distancing*. LSE.
https://blogs.lse.ac.uk/impactofsocialsciences/2020/03/12/the-covid-19-online-pivot-adapting-university-teaching-to-social-distancing/

Section III
Considering Alternative Futures

'Vessels of Hope' by Giulia Forsythe (CC0)

'Vessels of Hope' by Giulia Forsythe (CC0)

Note from the artist

"It is the story that makes the difference" wrote Ursula Le Guin (1989, p. 168). Not the killer story of arrows, bombs, and destruction, but the life story of care and survival. The shape of the story is the sling for the child, the basket for gathering food, the vessel to carry water. HE4Good is a container to explore the "good" higher education can bring; it is the hope in a storm, the light beacon to guide towards safe harbour as successive waves of crises pummel the most vulnerable.

References:

Le Guin, U. K. (1989). *The carrier bag theory of fiction*. Ignota Books. (Original work published in 1986).

11. Calm in the storm

Paola Corti and Chrissi Nerantzi

Note for readers and suggestions for use

This chapter is in the form of a photograph, an audio podcast, and a transcript of the podcast, referenced at the end of the chapter. Paola and Chrissi speak in alternate turns in the podcast; this is noted in the transcript.

We propose that our contribution could be used as an alternative conversation trigger, in whole or in part. The use we make of both audio and written visual language offers alternative ways to uncover and discover novel connections. The format we have chosen is an open invitation to immerse the listener and/or reader with us and our thinking and to encourage conversation. Readers/listeners can use a range of metaphors from nature and the world around you to explore, discuss and debate challenging issues and opportunities with other educators and students. The metaphors can be linked to higher education experiences and practices to better understand what is important, to see the higher education landscape with fresh eyes, and to identify and embrace positive ways forward.

Introduction

Chrissi: Close your eyes.

Get comfortable.

And relax.

Take a deep breath in.

Release it.

Take another one.

Release it.

Now breathe normally.

Feel the air travelling through your whole body.

Now open your eyes.

Look at the photo in front of you. (Figure 11.1)

Figure 11.1

Valtellina valley, Italy. Photo by Paola Corti.
https://pxhere.com/it/photo/1667214, CC0

What do you see?

Where are you in this landscape?

What paths do you see?

Look at the open areas.

And the steep mountains.

Look at the light and the darkness.

Where would you like to be in this landscape?

Teleport yourself there, into the picture.

How do you feel being in this landscape?

Is it a familiar space?

Is it in any way different from what you know?

What would you be in this landscape?

What will you bring with you?

How could you feel connected with everything that surrounds you?

Keep breathing naturally.

What do you imagine?

This place

Paola: In this photograph, the sun has just risen from behind a mountain on the right but is partially hidden behind beautiful white fluffy morning clouds. So, the light is not harming the eyes as it is not too direct. The effects of the sunlight on the surroundings are truly amazing: it highlights the profile of the mountains, it reaches the bottom of the valley, making fields shine, and it reflects on the waters of the river and the lake. You can see their beauty and their potential. All the elements of the landscape together make it beautiful. It's a mixture of elements; none of them alone would create the same effect.

One of the details I love most is the light that changes according to the profile of the mountains: you see these lines in between light and shadow, and you can perceive the direction of the rays, but you don't see them directly. You can't touch it; you see its effect on the rest. As if the light, even if you can't look at it in itself, can make everything else matter in your eyes.

This valley went through floods, avalanches, and landslides over time.

It is not only an image of calm, peace, and beauty.

The weather can change quite quickly and become stormy or windy. It can start raining at any moment. Also, the temperature might rise or fall at any time.

A long time ago, when the Romans arrived, they had built terracing to cultivate the sunniest side.

Historical, social, cultural, and natural events are coming together.

It can get incredibly hot in the summer and incredibly cold in the winter.

People there help each other to maintain the valley as it is, let it evolve naturally, and preserve it while living in it.

Some people are there day after day, all year; others come just for the weekend, for work or for fun, to relax or to reenergise.

Some of them cultivate the fields, and others have shops and offer services.

Some people climb, run, cycle, or simply enjoy exploring the surroundings.

To let this valley develop sustainably means balancing logistic solutions (like new roads to the skiing areas), with the needs of a territory that "holds together" with a precise — and sometimes fragile — balance.

Being respectful of this balance makes a real difference.

Chrissi: Now, you...

Where would you be in this landscape?

Would you choose to be on the peak of the mountain, climbing to the top with a lot of energy, and technical skills, engaging with your whole body, feeling the cold and the chill wind but proceeding notwithstanding all challenges? Would you be there as a mountain guide, taking care of others, or with your peers, caring for each other, or as a solitary climber?

Or do you see yourself in the plain, looking around you in a peaceful and restful moment, taking a pause while all other people around you are working in the field and you can observe them carefully, but just looking around?

Or maybe you could be in an Italian bar, along the street, starting your day with an espresso and getting ready to dive into work?

What about travelling from one side to the other?

Or sailing on the water, in a boat?

Or even swimming?

How does it feel being there?

What do you see nearby?

And in the distance?

What helps you feel calm?

Can you sense the excitement?

Where does it come from?

Considering higher education for good

Paola: The valley you see is called Valtellina, and it is in the Lombardy region, in the north of Italy, close to the Alps and the Swiss border. It runs from west to east. When I thought about higher education for Good (HE4Good from now on), I immediately went back to this particular photo. I have thousands of photos taken in the mountains. I immediately felt a great connection with the book's theme, and I went looking for it. I talked with Chrissi about it, and we are here now, sharing with you why we feel like this landscape, as a whole and as a collection of small parts, possibilities, and activities instantly stopped in the shot, but relentlessly ongoing, can somehow represent the higher education landscape.

Imagine all forms of life in this valley. From the smallest insect, or bacterium, to the largest tree and herds of roe deer. Small and big animals, including humans, small blades of grass and centennial trees, diversity in its full glory represented and needed to keep the ecosystem balanced.

Imagine people living and working there. All facilities, services, spaces, and their use all change over time. The fastest and the slowest changes. Every day. Overtime. While the light — in this specific case, the sunlight — and the weather change continuously in a flow that experts can try to foresee but could not 100% guess.

Let's think about HE4Good now.

As in this valley, in HE4Good, people can come and go. The entrance is open, and students of all ages move through it freely, taking opportunities to learn from others and from each other. Sometimes, they have to pay for specific services. Sometimes, they can be autonomous in picking what is available for free. They can also stay for a little bit longer. They can enjoy what HE4Good has to offer in terms of experience, knowledge, exchange with other people, explorations, and learning new skills. Moreover, they can contribute to all of it. They can make plans here, they can and have to take good care of what they touch, taste, use. Otherwise, the somehow fragile balance it relies on can fall apart and can consequently fail to maintain its offer as good as it is or become even better than it is now.

People living in the valleys are known to welcome those joining them for a while. Still, sometimes, they prefer them to return to where they came from, which resonates with the anti-immigration attitude of some countries and some universities. This is part of their idea of sustainability: the valley cannot physically host everyone, it has room for a certain amount of people, and that's it. More than that would not be sustainable. With HE4Good, as expanded as it can be, with more people than ever before virtually studying at university and with online resources and open resources, practices, and communities available, there is potentially no limit to access in terms of sustainability. Even if we are not there yet at present and even if the required infrastructure needs to be sustainable too, in itself. There are still hurdles, significant hurdles, regarding making these precious learning opportunities accessible to all, and we mean *all*. Finding imaginative ways to embrace all humans and helping them grow and flourish is so important. In a similar way, the valleys are open and embracing.

What about making connections?

In the valley, as in HE4Good, covering distances and reaching out to the place or the people you are headed to is not always easy. It largely depends on the path you walk and how many mountains, rivers, and other challenges are in your way. Sometimes it's a brand-new street, just renewed and recently enlarged, with good signals and linked to well-funded opportunities of political importance. Sometimes they are single tracks with steep climbs and descents, and some scary places to cross. But they have been built with care and commitment by people who see the need and want to contribute to creating passages for small groups of users, not necessarily for large numbers. These paths are less visible. Sometimes, they are very well indicated but not as mainstream as a highway. Some tracks are entirely new, nobody has gone there before, and they are a space of pure exploration, between risks and opportunities, and the agency is totally in the hands of the explorers. All are needed. All work to create access opportunities. All have to respect and preserve the others to keep the whole valley *and the entire university* sustainable.

Constantly keeping an eye on the needs of the other living beings involved in the valley, as in higher education, is fundamental to preserving the very existence of the whole ecosystem. Resources are limited in some areas, and they should be responsibly used with priorities agreed upon based on responsibility for the greater good. On the other hand, peer support and shared efforts can be key solutions to specific challenges through coordinated actions that can be beneficial for more than one issue at a time. In the valley, all the terraces on the sunny side both make it easier to grow vineyards and, at the same time, prevent avalanches from falling freely and violently to the bottom of the valley. Similarly, there are actions in HE4Good that can be beneficial for more than one stakeholder at a time. Consider open practices: an example where students, educators and researchers can build experiences together and produce outputs that serve different purposes while providing visibility to the institution. Sometimes these are also beneficial for citizens at large through the outcomes.

The river Adda flows through the valley and pours its water into Lake Como. The same happens in the academic context: stimulations, information and knowledge created and shared can flow outside the boundaries of the university and continuously, relentlessly get mixed into the civil society with other knowledge belonging to different contexts. No degrees of separation in the end. Through the water cycle, the mixed waters will return to the highest peaks and pour down in another form, like rain or snow, when the moment comes. This is nature's circle, and we must be mindful of the harmful disruptions we may cause…

We are describing these ecosystems in parallel to help us see the value of different elements and their links. In HE4Good, we also see the power of virtuous examples, even when small and situated, contextual, as something that can be inspiring for others to act elsewhere, maybe with change to adapt them to a different context. Also, we see the beauty of handcrafted solutions where mainstream ones do not reach the same results, and sometimes, the power of scaling down and having more focused outputs instead of choosing one-size-fits-all solutions. Adaptation to specific needs is more valuable/more effective as a long-term strategic approach when looking at diversity as a rich opportunity to be preserved.

Before we reach the end and wrap up after reflecting out loud, let's go back to the adjective in the acronym HE4Good: let's talk about "good". "Good" doesn't necessarily mean pleasant or riskless or even reassuring, or stable. As it happens in the valley, work is needed, and things that seem to be stable are stable just for a little while or a bit longer. Risk is around the corner not only when you decide to climb. It can accompany you while you start your new activity on the plain! The same happens in higher education, with more visible projects or small or new activities that can make change happen from the ground up. Also, "good" can be restless, fatiguing, sometimes fearful, and somehow constantly changing even when not visible or evident.

But… aren't change and learning viscerally linked to each other? "Good" embeds all these adjectives altogether. HE4Good relies on our attitude to embrace them all, deal with them, manage to go beyond their consequences and be mindful of others struggling with the same challenges together.

We would like to invite you to consider the following in reference to HE4Good:

1. **Be patient**: the growth of a system is often very slow and not immediately visible. Commitment, persistence, and teamwork are key.

2. What is sure, **change happens** all the time; it happens to you, as an individual, and as a member of a changing community; be ready.
3. Remember, you will, at times, **feel discomfort**. It is OK; it's part of change and learning.
4. Be mindful that **you are not alone**: share resources, expertise, and spaces.
5. Work with others... act **together.**

Moving forward

Chrissi: Now close your eyes again.

Breathe naturally.

Take a deep breath and focus on the landscape you were just in.

What do you remember?

If you could bottle something you found there, what would it be?

Think about it.

Which three things would you take with you?

Take them with you, in your bottle.

Now create your own landscape.

How does it look?

How does it feel?

What do you see?

Teleport yourself into your landscape.

Place yourself somewhere in your landscape that makes you feel energised... empowered.

What will you explore?

Where are your curiosity and imagination taking you?

What about the landscape around you?

Your companions?

The whole ecosystem?

How will you embrace otherness, hope and care?

Thank you for listening and for being willing to move forward.

Acknowledgments

We would like to thank (in chronological order): Professor Margy MacMillan, Valeria Baudo, Margherita Ferrario, Adam Frank, Dr Sadia Afroze Sultana, Marta Bustillo, Bianca Gregori, and our reviewers and editors for providing valuable feedback and suggestions for our chapter. It wouldn't have been the same without their ideas and thoughts.

References

Corti, P. & Nerantzi, C. (Co-hosts). (2022, October 27). CALM IN THE STORM [Audio podcast.] *#HE4Good*. Google Drive. https://drive.google.com/file/d/1UEPFL2_TithAr9FUBKGDJCCfWi6TVncg/view?usp=sharing

12. Visioning futures of higher education for the common good

Mpine Makoe

The process of thinking about the future is vital. It encourages us to critically examine our assumptions of higher education to identify features that may assist us in developing a desirable higher education for the future. This chapter describes how a group of higher education experts and policymakers used a visioning process to construct images of a desirable higher education system. The systematic use of a visioning process resulted in "common good" as a visionary lens. Although it may be difficult to change higher education practices, systems and structures for the students who will be studying in 2050, it is achievable if we start with the aim of the common good. It is important that the higher education sector, not only universities, think and act strategically to address the outcomes that they want to achieve for the benefit of future generations. Higher education that is committed to the common good can cultivate human capacities to solve social, economic, environment, and development challenges, especially in developing countries such as South Africa.

Introduction

The fundamental aim of higher education is to prepare citizens to contribute to society through knowledge, understanding, critical thinking, and innovative ideas — developing and advancing society as a community. As a result, higher education institutions need to continually engage in thinking about how to ensure that they achieve this aim. Toffler (1974) argued that "unless we understand the powerful psychological role played by images of the future for a resilient higher education sector, we cannot effectively overhaul our schools, colleges or universities, no matter what innovation we introduce" (p. 19). It is crucial that higher education policymakers, researchers, and academics engage in a visioning process. Without this engagement, higher education institutions risk being "the Cinderella sector of the technology world — constantly receiving the hand-me-downs from the business, defence and leisure industries and then trying to repurpose them for educational goals" (Daanen & Facer, 2007, p. 4).

Higher education has been disrupted in many ways in recent years, e.g. the pervasiveness of technology, the high demand for access to higher education, astronomical growth of unemployment rates and global inequality. The higher education sector is challenged now more than ever to proactively shape more just and inclusive futures (UNESCO, 2021). It is important that higher education is viewed as central to human rights and human dignity. Higher education promotes the full development of human capability, fosters self-reliance, facilitates economic growth, and shapes the culture that enables the world to be a better place for all. Globally, people look to higher education to address issues such as poverty, health, climate change, job creation, social cohesion, and other social and political challenges. Supporting the 1948 *Universal Declaration of Human Rights* must be foundational: higher education must be "available, accessible and adaptable" to all groups irrespective of their background (UNESCO, 2015). In this chapter, higher education institutions refer not only to universities, but to all institutions of higher learning including technical and vocational education training, research institutes, and formal learning networks.

In recent years, higher education has been criticised for failing to address its colonial and apartheid past. Legacies of this past persist and have led to deep dissatisfaction amongst higher education students and those that cannot find employment after graduating. Higher education students in South Africa, for example, took to the streets to register their frustrations in protests against a colonised education system that does not adequately prepare them for the future. Colonialist narratives of education have been used to relegate Indigenous cultures and traditions to a subservient space. African people did not have authority to claim their identity over the education system that was handed down to them.

Higher education in South Africa, as in most African countries, was introduced by colonisers with a clear "imperial mission" of providing education to the colonial administrators and later to Indigenous people who were able to speak and write in English (Tait, 2008). Colonial higher education was created with a clear vision "to serve the Empire with its oppression of people all around the world" (Tait, 2008, p. 86). The Afrikaner government, which ascended to power in 1946, used education to drive their vision of a racially compartmentalised society, ensuring that white people had preferential access to higher education while black people received an education that limited their potential (Cross, 1986). Despite numerous post-colonial and post-apartheid education policies that were meant to address this unequal education system, these core values remain embedded in South African higher education systems. What is urgently needed is a transformed higher education system based on the social justice principles of equity, access, and inclusivity.

Thus, it is critical to think about how higher education can ensure that all people have equitable access to quality education in the future. The process of thinking about the future helps people to critically examine their assumptions, to reject what stands in the way of progress, and to strengthen what needs to be taken forward. To study the future is to analyse potential change that is likely to make a systemic or fundamental difference over the next 30 years or more, and to empower stakeholders to function in the future (Inayatullah, 2013). It is on these bases that this chapter describes how a futures research method was used for visioning the desired futures of higher education. Visions of the future are powerful rhetorical devices, enabling us to work on problems that current systems cannot address (Facer & Sandford, 2010; Vlasman, Quist & Van Mansvelt, 2004). The intentional use of the plural words such as "futures" and "knowledges" challenge the assumption of a single predictable future (UNESCO, 2021). The aim is to validate multiple plausible and desirable images that enable the higher education sector the freedom to choose what works best in their context.

Visioning HE futures

Futures research provides a set of methodologies, from a range of disciplines, to identify and understand a range of possible futures — whether desirable or not (Bell, 1997; Dator, 2009; Inayatullah, 2008; Puglisi, 2001). Some futures research methods use mapping processes (futures triangle, futures wheel), anticipation (emerging issues analysis, trends analysis), creating alternatives (scenarios, Delphi), and transformative methods (visioning, causal layered analysis, backcasting) (Inayatullah, 2013, 2018; Puglisi, 2001). The purpose is to imagine futures to create new policies and strategies that will enable us to operate effectively when the new futures emerge (Dator, 2009). Daanen and Facer (2007) commented: "It is not possible to make decisions about the future of education in a vacuum" (p. 29). We need to systematically provide knowledge about possible and desired futures that could be used by different stakeholders in the education sector. This process needs clear values that underpin the visions it is presenting (Masini, 1999).

Visioning is a methodology that focuses on images that draw society towards a goal meant to overcome current crises. The aim of visioning is not to predict or anticipate the future, but to imagine desirable futures (Gümüsay & Reinecke, 2022). Through the visioning process, individuals' aspirations and hopes are merged into a vision, making wishes for the future explicit (Bell, 1997; Puglisi, 2001). Visioning assists the process of thinking through the consequences of the "what-if" to "decide upon more desirable pathways that make communities work" (Gümüsay & Reinecke, 2022, p. 240). Visioning can enhance the imagination to build images of a desirable and ideal higher education, i.e. improving, overcoming, and radically transforming the current situation.

In July 2021, 25 policy makers and experts in higher education participated at a virtual workshop commissioned for the 2022 UNESCO World Higher Education Conference (WHEC) (Makoe, 2022). Participants with skills and expertise in higher education policy environments were asked to "imagine what communities and higher education will look like in 2050" and then asked to consider the steps needed to reach these desirable futures. More than half of the participants came from the Global South, while less than 40% came from the Global North. Most world regions were represented except the Middle East. The aim of the workshop was to bring together higher education experts and policymakers to engage in constructing images of the desirable higher education of 2050.

The process of visioning was organised in four phases: identify present problem/s, recognise past successes, explore wishes of the future, and construct images of desirable futures. Below are the outcomes of this process as generated by the participants in the UNESCO (WHEC) workshop.

1. Identify present problems

The first phase of the visioning process was to identify the complex problems and challenges of the current higher education sector. According to workshop participants, these include inadequate funding from the state, growing demand for high level qualifications, curriculum that does not adequately address the job market, high numbers of unemployed graduates, and more. Participants were also concerned about financialisation and neoliberalisation practices which lead to privileging certain types of knowledges, degrees and jobs that continue to preserve inequalities. In some countries, the government has silenced the voices of academics by taking over the governance structures of higher education. Many emphasised the need to include higher education leaders and staff members, as well as students in decision making processes. In this exercise, one participant described universities as mirrors, which reflect the current problems in society. All of these challenges need to be addressed if we are to transform higher education.

The lack of investment in higher education from both the public and private sector is the root cause of many problems as identified in the workshop. In most countries in Africa and many elsewhere, higher education institutions receive insufficient funds from their respective governments. To survive, universities have had to appeal for funding from the private sector, pushing universities to prioritise cost-cutting and fundraising measures. Those who tend to benefit from this system are students who are financially well-off, leaving behind thousands of students who are poor: "treat[ing] education as just another service to be delivered to those who can afford to buy it" (Ochwa-Echel, 2013, p. 3). What this illustrates is that the public good approach that assumes that the state's role is to represent the interest of all its citizens is no longer credible. Many governments, especially in developing countries, have been unable to meet the education demands and needs of their citizens (Quilligan, 2012).

2. Recognise past successes

Recognising past successes enables us to strengthen them as we visualise the future. Despite the myriad challenges faced by higher education, participants expressed the need to celebrate the transformations adopted during the COVID-19 pandemic, i.e. development of skills such as global citizenship, empathy, critical thinking, technological skills and others that assist people with functioning in a highly digitalised world. The increased use of digitalisation has made it possible for communities to form connections, which enhances collaboration amongst students, researchers, instructors, academics, and other learning communities.

This higher education role of servicing a public is grounded on an understanding of interconnectedness between and amongst humans, their relationship with one another, the lived beings in the planet and the knowledges of those worlds (Barnett, 2021; Razak, 2020). This deeply social view of working together for the common purpose is embodied in humanising education that reflects social and cultural practices that engender participation, cooperation, reciprocity, and empathy (Locatelli, 2018; Ng, 2009). After all, the nature of education is sharing. Therefore, higher education should cease to elevate one type of knowledge over the others and focus on "developing imagination and creativity to restore cultural values and knowledge drawn from Indigenous wisdom and experiences seriously" (Razak, 2020, p. 410). These Indigenous-inspired values have deep roots which are still valuable today. It is important to strengthen these values as we visualise the futures of higher education.

3. Explore wishes for the future

In responding to the question on the futures of higher education, participants expressed the need for tangible actions to be taken as steps towards achieving the "higher education we want" in 2050. What higher education needs in 2050 is an education that prepares students not only for livelihood but also teaches them to be ethical moral human beings who work together for the good of the community and the planet. This need requires higher education to reinvent itself, not merely focusing on disciplinary knowledge, but on other knowledges that develop capacities for integrity, diligence and resilience for responsibility and service (Razak, 2020; Sarango, 2021). These values will go a long way in addressing some of the challenges faced by higher education. Teaching about values and articulating ideals of recognising one's responsibilities to the community and the planet is key to education (Barnett, 2021; Sarango, 2021). Higher education institutions are expected to take this role seriously and help develop capacities for integrity, morality and resiliency to serve others with a sense of higher purpose (Boyadjieva & Ilieva-Trichkova, 2019; Mino, 2020; Ng, 2009).

The workshop participants determined that higher education should aim to produce humanised innovators, leaders, and citizens —noting that one area that has been ignored by higher education has been the nurturing of the human that begins with the heart instead of the head (Razak, 2021). The aim of humanising education can be traced back to many Indigenous knowledge systems. Values such as Ubuntu are based on one's relation to others: *umuntu ngumuntu ngabantu* — "I am what I am because of others". Applying the principles of cooperation and sharing amongst people can motivate higher education institutions to collaborate and work together in the same way that African communities have done when raising and educating children, hence the saying: "a child is raised by a village". This concept of communing is not unique to African contexts; some of its principles can also be found in other cultures. For example, the foundation of the education paradigm in the Abya Yala continent (known as America) is that "human beings (both men and women) learn, in fulfilling themselves in community, from life, with life, and for life" (Sarango, 2014, in Sarango, 2021).

Many participants imagined connected communities of people living together, learning, and sharing knowledge in a communal environment. In their imaginations, they saw an environmentally friendly world where the planet and the people co-exist. In this world, higher education was envisaged as more open, diverse, flexible, inclusive, and accessible to many including those with limited financial resources. In their vision, the 2050 higher education is trusted by stakeholders and seen as relevant to the communities it serves.

Overall, the visions identified by policymakers were rooted in communities working together to develop education systems that address the needs of a common society. Better futures are only achievable if we start by creating a different type of higher education that humanises education and embraces the concept of common good by encouraging the co-construction of knowledges foregrounded in relational and collective aspects of teaching and learning (Sarango, 2021).

The "common good" concept positions education at the centre of collective societal endeavour. Through common good, education is considered as part of the domain of the public where transparent and participatory processes can take place and human beings can benefit from education which is centred around people and their connections (Deneulin & Townsend, 2006; Locatelli, 2018). The difference between common good and public good is that the former requires some form of collectivity in terms of how they are produced and shared, while the latter can be enjoyed as individual goods (Locatelli, 2018). It is common good when the resources are produced by the community for the benefit of all, and it is public good if the state manages the public resources (Quilligan, 2013). What this means is that one can use the goods or services that are made available by the government without directly contributing to its provision (Deneulin & Townsend, 2006). While the recipients of public good may remain passive, common good requires active participants (Locatelli, 2018). Although the characterisation of both public and common goods may be different, they are both bound by the principles of human rights that promote accessible education to all groups irrespective of their background. Gilchrist (2018) explained that "to deny someone with capacity access to higher education is to deny them their potential as human beings"

(p. 647). Visioning education as a common good will enable us to have a shared vision of the community that will be supported by higher education of the future.

4. Construct desirable images of futures

The last phase of the visioning process was to construct desirable images of futures, i.e. images that can draw us forward as higher education stakeholders. Participants determined that nations cannot continue with higher education systems that exclude people based on their financial status or their home address, but rather, should ensure that every citizen has unimpeded access to education. Acknowledging that education is a human right, requires the state to continue financing, delivering, monitoring, and regulating higher education (Locatelli, 2018). Likewise, higher education leaders must continue to define and create different types of higher education that will ensure that no one is left behind.

The images identified by policy makers were in line with the common good principles based on communities working together. It is not only the "good life" of an individual that matters (Deneulin & Townsend, 2007), but the good of the world in which humans live. This vision is based on the values that need to be reinforced to create an education system guided by the common good principles of solidarity towards a shared vision of the community. Visions such as this "inspire us by stating what we are striving to become, why we do what we do, and what higher contribution flows from our efforts" (Bezold, 2009, p. 84). These visions can motivate us to take action towards better futures.

Higher education for the common good

Using common good as a foundational principle can enable policymakers and leaders to design context-specific scenarios of higher education in 2050. Higher education that is committed to the common good can be an environment that cultivates human capacities to solve social, economic, environmental and development issues, especially in developing countries. According to the policy makers in the workshop, the aim should be to design a development-driven higher education system that is based on the common good principles of bringing different players together to share ideas and use home grown Indigenous knowledge systems that will address the needs of communities and societies (Makoe, 2022). This approach addresses the social justice mandate of higher education — closely linked with common good principles that support accessible, inclusive and affordable higher education that gives every person a chance to develop to their full potential in a community. To address social injustices that have been fuelled by past and present practices, higher education must address maldistribution of resources and economic inequality to enable access to education in an equitable way. Redistributive justice directly addresses access issues, especially for people who have not had access to higher education resources in the past. (Lambert, 2018). However, access without success is not an opportunity, and therefore not a common good.

Institutionalised hierarchies that prioritise the cultural values of dominant groups have denied other cultures from participating fully in the higher education sector. Redistributive justice recognises that people's cultures and practices should be valued and respected, regardless of their status (Hodgkinson-William & Trotter, 2018). In countries that were formally colonised, such as South Africa, western-oriented epistemic perspectives feature prominently in the curriculum (Adefila et al., 2021). Framing knowledge in this way excludes many people who are participating in higher education: "when people do not have a voice they also do not have an opportunity to decide what is really important educationally in order to avoid becoming an "object of charity or non-persons with respect to justice" (Hodgkinson-William & Trotter, 2018, p. 208). Students need to be given tools and capabilities to question the knowledge provided to them. The knowledge base acquired in higher education should not only be about finding a job; it should also provide the ground to access new knowledges, to understand, to develop as a person with a solid value base, and to acquire intercultural knowledge, including valuing others. Common good encourages students to reflect on their moral beliefs as well as enabling them to understand the real-world implications of those values (Ford, 2016). According to UNESCO (2015), the "common good, encompassing ethical and political concerns, provides a principle to rethink the purpose of education" (p. 80).

Conclusion

A visioning process helped us to construct images of futures that can influence human behaviour in the present, thus helping to contribute to shaping the futures to which we aspire (Bell, 1997). This method is not meant to imply the identification of one's actual future, but to build images of an ideal world in a systematic way. In the example described in this chapter, the different phases of the visioning process provided a systematic way of identifying "common good" as a visionary lens for higher education in 2050. The vision of a common good represents a compelling expression of the image of a desired future that is equitable and just. The principle of common good provides a powerful lens to imagine communities in 2050 and to co-create the higher education required to serve it. By so doing, policymakers and leaders will be able to design, strategise, plan, and develop pathways towards higher education in 2050. Although it will be difficult to change higher education practices, systems, and structures, it is achievable if we work to commit to the principles of common good. The entire higher education sector, not only universities, should think and act strategically to address the outcomes that will benefit all students and future generations.

References

Adefila, A., Teixeira, R. V., Morini, M., Teixeira Garcia, M. L., Zanotti T. M., Delboni, G. F., Spolander, G., & Khalil-Babatunde, M. (2021). Higher education decolonisation: #Whose voices and their geographical locations? *Globalisation, Societies and Education, 20*(3), 262–76. https://doi.org/10.1080/14767724.2021.1887724

Barnett, R. (2021). *Towards the ecological university* [PDF]. UNESCO-IESALC. https://www.iesalc.unesco.org/en/wp-content/uploads/2021/02/Barnett-EN.pdf

Bell, W. (1997). Futures studies comes to an age: Where are we now and where are we going?, *Futures Research Quarterly*, 13, 37–50. https://www.researchgate.net/profile/Wendell-Bell/publication/253441407_FUTURES_STUDIES_COMES_OF_AGE_WHERE_ARE_WE_NOW_AND_WHERE_ARE_WE_GOING/links/55786d3108ae75363755b2ff/FUTURES-STUDIES-COMES-OF-AGE-WHERE-ARE-WE-NOW-AND-WHERE-ARE-WE-GOING.pdf

Bezold, C. (2009). Aspirational futures. *Journal of Futures Studies, 13*(4), 81–90.
https://jfsdigital.org/articles-and-essays/2009-2/vol-13-no-4-may/articles-essays/aspirational-futures/

Boyadjieva P., & Ilieva-Trichkova, P. (2019). From conceptualisation to measurement of higher education as a common good: Challenges and possibilities. *Higher Education, 77*(6), 1047–63.
https://doi.org/10.1007/s10734-018-0319-1

Cross, M. (1986). A historical review of education in South Africa: Towards an assessment. *Comparative Education, 22*(3), 185–200.
http://www.jstor.org/stable/3099112

Daanen, H., & Facer, K. (2007). *2020 and Beyond: Future Scenarios for Education in the Age of New Technologies*. Futurelab.
http://www.futurelab.org.uk/resources/documents/opening_education/2020_and_beyond.pdf

Dator, J. (2009). Alternative futures at the Manoa School. *Journal of Futures Studies, 14*(2), 1–18.
https://jfsdigital.org/wp-content/uploads/2014/01/142-A01.pdf

Deneulin, S., & Townsend, N. (2007). Public goods, global public goods and the common good. *International Journal of Social Economics, 34*(1–2), 19–36.
https://doi.org/10.1108/03068290710723345

Facer, K., & Sandford, R. (2010). The next 25 years?: Future scenarios and future directions for education and technology. *Journal of Computer Assisted Learning, 26*, 74–93.
https://doi.org/10.1111/j.1365-2729.2009.00337.x

Ford, M. P. (2016). *Education for the common good: The goal of education needs to be more than individual success*. American Association of University Professors.
https://www.aaup.org/article/education-common-good#.Y4R924LP2z5

Gilchrist, H. (2018). Higher education is a human right. *Washington University Global Studies Law Review, 17*(3), 645–76.
https://papers.ssrn.com/sol3/Delivery.cfm/SSRN_ID3770157_code865180.pdf?abstractid=3100852&mirid=1&type=2

Gümüsay, A. A., & Reinecke, J. (2022). Researching for desirable futures: From real Utopias to imagining alternatives. *Journal of Management Studies, 59*(1), 238–52.
https://doi.org/10.1111/joms.12709

Hodgkinson-Williams, C. A., & Trotter, H. (2018). A social justice framework for understanding open educational resources and practices in the Global South. *Journal of Learning for Development, 5*(3), 204–24.
https://doi.org/10.56059/jl4d.v5i3.312

Inayatullah, S. (2008). Six pillars: Futures thinking for transforming. *Foresight, 10*(1), 4–28.
https://doi.org/10.1108/14636680810855991

Inayatullah, S. (2013). Futures studies: Theories and methods. In F. G. Junquera (Ed.), *There's a future: Visions for a better world* (pp. 36–66). BBVA.
https://www.bbvaopenmind.com/en/books/there-is-a-future-visions-for-a-better-world/

Inayatullah, S. (2018). Foresight in challenging environments. *Journal of Futures Studies, 22*(4), 15–24.
https://doi.org/10.6531/JFS.201806.22(4).0002

Lambert, S. R. (2018). Changing our (dis)course: A distinctive social justice aligned definition of open education. *Journal of Learning for Development, 5*(3), 225–44.
https://doi.org/10.56059/jl4d.v5i3.290

Locatelli, R. (2018). *Education as a public and common good: Reframing the governance of education in a changing context* [PDF]. UNESCO.
https://unesdoc.unesco.org/ark:/48223/pf0000261614/PDF/261614eng.pdf.multi%20Locatelli.R.2018.Educationasapublicandcommongood%20(1).pdf

Makoe, M. (2022). *The futures of higher education. Reimagining the futures of higher education: Insights from a scenario development process towards 2050. Paper commissioned for the World Higher Education Conference 18–20 May 2022* [PDF]. UNESCO. Paper commissioned for World Higher Education Conference, 18–20 May 2022.
https://cdn.eventscase.com/www.whec2022.org/uploads/users/699058/uploads/dfe1d89e49b8371b7e3e067af7bf405496d9c2dccdd006a1af610c3c1c17a29e11b3d10a924b6d30748bc781046650d35b4f.6283359689ca7.pdf

Mannermaa, M. (1986). Futures research and social decision making: Alternative futures as a case study. *Futures, 18*(5), 658–70.
https://doi.org/10.1016/0016-3287(86)90038-8

Masini, E. B. (1999). Rethinking futures studies. In Z. Sardar (Ed.), *Rescuing all our futures* (pp. 36–48). Adamantine Press. Republished in *Futures, 38*(10), 1158–68.
https://doi.org/10.1016/j.futures.2006.02.004

Ng, R. M-C. (2009) College and character: What did Confucius teach us about the importance of integrating ethics, character, learning, and education? *Journal of College and Character, 10*(40), 1–7.
https://doi.org/10.2202/1940-1639.1045

Mino, T. (2020). Humanizing higher education: Three case studies in Sub-Saharan Africa. *International Journal of African Higher Education, 7*(1), 69–95.
https://ejournals.bc.edu/index.php/ijahe/article/view/11249

Ochwa-Echel, J. R. (2013). Neoliberalism and university education in Sub-Saharan Africa *Sage Open, 3*(3), 1–8.
https://doi.org/10.1177/2158244013504933

Puglisi, M. (2001). The study of the futures: An overview of futures studies methodologies. In D. Camarda & L. Grassini L. (Eds), *Interdependency* between agriculture and urbanization: Conflicts on sustainable use of soil and water (pp. 439–63) [PDF]. CIHEAM-IAMB. https://om.ciheam.org/om/pdf/a44/02001611.pdf

Quilligan, J. B. (2012). Why Distinguish Common Goods from Public Goods? In: Bollier, D. & Helfrich, S. (Eds), *The wealth of the commons: A world beyond market and state* (pp. 73–81). Levellers Press.

Razak, D. A. (2021). The disruptive futures of education – Post-COVID-19 pandemic. In H. van't Land, A. Corcoran, & D-C. Iancu (Eds), *The promise of higher education: Essays in honour of 70 Years of IAU* (pp. 407–12). Springer.

Sarango, M. L. F. (2021). *Project: Futures of higher education* [PDF]. UNESCO. https://www.iesalc.unesco.org/eng/wp-content/uploads/2021/03/Sarango-Macas-EN.pdf

Tait, A. (2008). What are open universities for? *Open Learning: The Journal of Open, Distance and e-Learning, 23*(2), 85–93. https://doi.org/10.1080/02680510802051871

Toffler, A. (1974). *Learning for tomorrow. The role of the future in education*. Vintage Books.

Vlasman, A., Quist, J., & van Mansvelt, J-D. (2004). Future visions and visioning for sustainability in higher education: Results and examples from the Netherlands. In D. Ferrer-Balas, K. F. Mulder, J. Bruno, & R. Sans (Eds), *Proceedings in the second international conference on engineering education in sustainable development*, (pp. 1–14). International Centre for Numerical Methods in Engineering, Barcelona (CIMNE).
https://www.researchgate.net/profile/Jaco-Quist/publication/285745435_Future_visions_and_visioning_for_sustainability_in_higher_education_Results_and_examples_from_The_Netherlands/links/5caf17734585156cd78f91e7/Future-visions-and-visioning-for-sustainability-in-higher-education-Results-and-examples-from-The-Netherlands.pdf

UNESCO (2015). *Rethinking education: Towards a global common good?* UNESCO. https://unesdoc.unesco.org/ark:/48223/pf0000232652

UNESCO (2021). *Reimagining our futures together: A new social contract for education*. UNESCO.
https://unesdoc.unesco.org/ark:/48223/pf0000379381

13. Speculative futures for higher education: weaving perspectives for good

Elizabeth Childs, George Veletsianos, Amber Donahue, Tamara Leary, Kyla McLeod, and Anne-Marie Scott

Much has been written and speculated about the future of teaching and learning, recently brought to the forefront by calls to "reimagine" the future of education and to explore a "new normal" emerging from the COVID-19 pandemic (UN 2020; UNESCO 2021). In our service as co-leaders of the Digital Transformation (DT) working group at Royal Roads University (RRU) Canada, we (Veletsianos and Childs) were asked to advise our institution on the ways we believe it could, and ought to, respond to the challenges and opportunities that this moment offers. In doing so, we grounded our recommendations both in the long-standing and far-reaching literature on online and distance education and educational technology, as well as in the critical possibilities that speculative methods offer (Veletsianos 2020; Veletsianos et. al., 2022). Speculative methods are "research approaches that explore and create possible futures under conditions of complexity and uncertainty" (Ross, 2018, p. 197) to "inform us about what matters now in the field, what issues and problems we have inherited, and what debates define what can or cannot be currently thought about or imagined" (Ross, 2017, p. 220).

Recognising that future systems are grounded in the realities of what we have in front of us, it can be difficult to reimagine new systems from scratch. For example, in the absence of a national department of education and in the context of a provincial funding model in Canada, the credit hour is hard to move away from as it drives the legislated funding formulas for post-secondary institutions (BC Government, n.d.). Needing to expand the ability of the DT working group to explore possibilities, a speculative narrative of the experience of one learner (Magda) was created to guide our work. Magda's narrative and persona shouldn't be taken as representative of students in general or RRU students in particular: it served as a provocation for the DT working group as we examined what digital transformation could look like at RRU. The narrative was intended to be open-ended, discipline agnostic, and somewhat closely understood by people within the system in order that it would invite them to reflect and think creatively about some of the opportunities and issues for RRU post-pandemic.

The DT working group used the narrative of Magda's speculative future to advance the idea that digital transformation designed to serve student and societal needs requires transformation at multiple systemic levels. Such transformation goes beyond technological and pedagogical changes at the teaching and learning level. While this idea is not new at RRU — indeed RRU has a long history of innovation (Harris et al., 2018; Harris et al., 2021), like every institution of higher education, our institution faces systemic challenges that constrain its possibilities and its ability to do good in the world. By way of an example, some systemic challenges experienced locally during the work of the DT working group, and in the writing of this chapter, include the review of current post-secondary provincial funding allocations (BC Government, n.d.), Indigenous reconciliation and decolonisation of knowledge (Truth and Reconciliation Commission of Canada, 2015), lack of affordable housing (CBC, 2022), and an increasing number of climate emergencies including historic fires, floods and droughts (Little, 2021) which have impacted the overall ability of the British Columbia HE sector and RRU to access adequate resources to enact its mission of "Inspiring people with the courage to transform the world" (Royal Roads University, 2022, para. 1). All under the backdrop of a global pandemic.

Within this complex context, questions of "who" HE is good for and why were tangential, yet implicit questions raised by the working group. Given that RRU has a Learning, Teaching and Research model (LTRM) (Harris et al., 2021), a signature pedagogy that informs all aspects of how the institution operates, the working group implicitly held that a notion of "good" was embodied in RRU's approach to learning, teaching and research as compiled in the LTRM document (RRU, 2019):

> The LTRM can be distilled to three core categories of values, or attributes of practice...applied and authentic, caring and community-based, and transformational. Situated in its wider context, the LTRM expresses how we work at RRU and connects to both what we learn, teach and research (common threads running through our work, such as leadership, social innovation, and sustainability), and most importantly, why we work at RRU, to help to create life changing learning experiences in service of positive social change. (pp. 1–2)

Drawing from the base provided by the LTRM (Harris et al., 2021), and the process of weaving knowledge systems together that is used by some to place Indigenous knowledge systems on par with the Western scientific paradigm (Henri et al., 2021; Johnson et al., 2016; Kimmerer, 2002), we used a metaphor where "good" could be viewed as a weaving, where the warp and weft include practical, pedagogical, contextual, societal, and critical aspects.

In this chapter, we invited colleagues holding multiple roles within the larger Canadian HE system to respond to the speculative narrative of Magda used by the digital technologies working group to further grapple with the question of "goodness" given a specific context and situation, rather than with the question of "goodness" in universal terms. Given this specific future, suspending disbelief for a moment, and imagining that this future is a reality, colleagues were asked to contemplate: Is this a good future? Who is it good for? What are the implications of this future for your role? What tensions and opportunities does such a future entail for your role? The chapter therefore serves as a container for an exchange amongst co-authors to examine perspectives and implications of a change in teaching and learning as captured in the narrative of Magda and reflected on by participants. In doing so, the chapter attempts to cross theory-practice-policy lines to provide a contextualised, systemic examination of a possible iteration of the higher education experience. As the speculative future of Magda was hypothetically set before Fall/Autumn 2023 when it was originally conceived and published (Veletsianos et al., 2022), co-authors were asked to approach it as "near future" as opposed to an exact date. By engaging multiple perspectives, the universality of what it means for futures to be "good" is problematised. This allowed us to highlight the messiness of speculative futures, and make visible the ways in which roles, values, identities, ideologies, and systems shape how learning futures are perceived to be "good".

The chapter is divided into three sections. The first section presents a summary of Magda's speculative future (readers interested in the original can refer to Veletsianos et al., 2022). The second section consists of co-authors' responses to the full version of the speculative future referenced above. The third section synthesises and summarises these responses.

Section 1: A summary of the story of Magda

In the original narrative we published, we described how Magda became interested in decentralised finance after learning about and exploring cryptocurrencies through a variety of resources such as online experts, a speaker series, and local university community programming. She decided to enrol in a degree at a local university as it would meet her diverse interests about this topic, which focused not just on the business sector but also on including the future of banking, government responses, climate change and the underlying technologies, as well as the political and social ramifications of the technologies underpinning decentralised finance.

To enrol in this degree program, Magda completes an online intake and evaluation form which generates data for an advisor to review before their meeting. Magda and her advisor develop a personalised learning program based on a variety of data, including input from a recommender system. Based on this, Magda is able to earn prior-learning credits for the equivalent of two courses and can begin her BSc in Cryptocurrency Studies program. Meetings with her advisor occur frequently, leading to updates and changes to her personalised learning plan.

At this university, Magda, faculty, and staff are supported by human and non-human resources. For example, Magda has access to a study plan available on her student portal. The student success professional she works with has access to a digital dashboard with relevant data that updates in real-time.

Magda's first course is online and has a mix of synchronous and asynchronous sessions. Courses in the program vary in duration, and this poses benefits (e.g., flexibility in course design) as well as challenges (e.g., scheduling difficulties often leading to inconsistent workloads). The courses she attends and the experiential learning opportunities she is able to take part in connect her with people in decentralised finance networks that reach across institutions and industries. As long as she is enrolled in her program, information and resources are available in her student portal, which automatically updates her digital learning passport whenever a learning action or outcome occurs.

Section 2: Responses to Magda's story

In this section, co-authors (Donahue, Leary, McLeod, and Scott) respond to the speculative future as captured in the narrative of Magda through their own HE experiences, their current roles and their positionality in that context. Some have approached this by taking up the narrative of Magda and building it forward, informing it as they do with insights from their own role and position to highlight opportunities and tensions. Others used the narrative as a reflective prompt resulting in a sharing of insights, wisdom, and raising questions for consideration.

Current online graduate student perspective: Donahue's response

Are algorithms and data determining Magda's future? Magda appreciates the convenience and flexibility of her local university and is glad her first course connects students to the instructor and each other through synchronous and asynchronous activities designed to foster a sense of community. Magda takes advantage of the opportunities to network with students, alumni, and professionals in the fields related to her areas of study. She is impressed by the information provided in her student portal and regularly logs in to review her progress, achievement, and future study plans. She observes that the university's technologies seem to be designed to tailor her experiences to her interests.

Throughout her first course, Magda develops personal relationships with other students. She is grateful for the networked connections she is making and the people who have become her support system. She is thrilled to discover a work-integrated learning opportunity in a blockchain start-up through her networks and eagerly dives in. Although Magda is quick to realise her work-integration experience is an effective pathway to gain experience and expertise in blockchain technologies, she begins to wonder if her university is too reliant on digital technologies. She is concerned that her future is being determined by algorithms and analytics, and she harkens back to a conversation between her and her advisor in which they confessed they did not understand the algorithms being utilised by the university's recommender system, but continued to rely on it, nonetheless.

Magda is troubled.

She logs in to her student portal and makes the unsettling discovery that the university's recommender has selected future courses for her that do not reflect the knowledge and competencies she is acquiring in her work-integrated learning which is based in a jurisdiction different from her local university. Instead, the recommender has drawn solely from data collected from profiles of other current students, which are not necessarily reflective of her unique experiences, to make suggestions and determine her future studies. This information and conversations she is having with her university friends in backchannel chats alerts Magda to the sobering realisation that when her work experience ends and she returns to regular studies at her university, she will not be continuing with the people in her circle. With each new course she takes, she will work with an entirely different group of classmates and instructors due to the organisational difficulties of the university's practice of varying course lengths based on course needs rather than a calendar.

It appears to Magda that the university exists in a paradoxical reality. On one hand, instructors and students engage in activities that are designed to create a human-centred sense of community. On the other hand, however, the university is totally reliant on the student dashboard and recommender system technologies. Magda is concerned that her forward-facing academic and professional pathways are being determined by algorithms and data collection. She is troubled by the level of data surveillance occurring and who may have access to the data the university is collecting. While Magda appreciates the opportunities she has been afforded by her university, she wonders about the ethical considerations of the technologies determining her future.

School of education and technology, school director perspective: Leary's response

The story of Magda offers both hope and concern for the future of higher education. There is hope reflected in the targeted online marketing initiatives, online scheduling app, online onboarding evaluation, and readily accessible program advisor outlined in the Magda story. Offering a prospective student easy access to the resources necessary for a seamless application, admission, and enrolment in the BSc in cryptocurrency studies is an effective and strategic enrolment initiative. Offering prior-learning assessment credits, a detailed and personalised program plan, access to an up-to-date student record, and credentialing alternatives reflect the university's student-centred approach to learning which offers much hope for future higher education processes and supports. Likewise, there is hope for prioritising the student experience with the intentional institutional pedagogy to develop community, connection, and support for the students. The university efforts to ensure Magda's studies align with and lead to career opportunities offer hope in addressing student and community expectations of a positive return on the ever-increasing tuition investment.

Less hopeful for the future of higher education is the robotic and transactional feel to Magda's university experience. The ever increasingly diverse student population across campuses requires leaders to critically reflect on current and future practices to ensure assumptions are not made about students' expectations, learning experiences, or about the meaning of "high touch". The learning needs and expectations of a highly motivated, technically savvy, and self-directed student like Magda differ from those of a student who is less familiar or comfortable with technology, uncertain of academic and career goals or requires more in-person interaction.

The services that the local university offers Magda are driven by the personal data she entrusts the university with from her first online interaction with it. The reference to Magda and the advisor not knowing how exactly the data is being used is a significant concern. The university's institution-wide recommender system raises concerns of privacy, profiling, and exerting institutional or societal bias. While technology has made it easier to collect and store students' personal data, it has also made it easier to misuse the information intentionally or accidentally.

The commitment to course content determining the length of the course is admirable but unrealistic. A university relies on fixed workflow processes and although systemic needs should not determine academic content or programming, there is no institution that can be all things to all people. Quality assurance may also be compromised if course content is frequently adjusted and if there are no standards for content or course duration. Typically, any organisational nightmare like that described in the vignette will negatively impact the student experience eventually and contribute to a negative work environment for staff and faculty.

The vignette offers hope for the future of higher education institutions in terms of students' equitable access to academic programming, seamless online administrative processes, current and flexible courses, and prioritised student learning experience. Points for further consideration include the need for a secure collection and storage of student data, holistic approach to administrative workflow processes, quality assurance measures, and an understanding of student engagement in the digital landscape.

Director, student services perspective: McLeod's response

Student services are generally described as services that support student academic achievement by reducing barriers to learning and providing opportunities for personal and professional growth. From the student services lens, there is a significant amount of "good" within the Magda future, where a student-centred approach promotes high-quality learning experiences that are supported through a combination of high-tech and high-touch services.

Technology is used to enable a high-touch personalised experience that integrates the best of digital and human services and support. There are several examples of this — the subscriber speaker series provides a low-risk opportunity for prospective students to engage with the university without requiring a significant commitment. The online appointment booking tool with data-gathering prompts allows prospective and current students to request the specific supports they need when they need them. Access to an academic advisor who can competently respond to student interests, and confidently discuss how to align these interests with relevant learning outcomes within courses and programs, helps to secure an appropriate "fit" between a student and their learning pathway. A customisable dashboard that includes courses, schedules, services, and resources, and that can be used on mobile devices is a very good service. This tool may also be useful to those who are concerned with student wellbeing and student success (student services) as they offer timely and relevant information about a student's level of engagement within their post-secondary community.

However, digital dashboards are not the future; at many institutions they are a current reality and quickly becoming a student expectation. Institutions who are not considering this type of technology-enabled student service may find themselves left behind. Digital dashboards are also becoming popular among post-secondary administrators who gather data for planning purposes. Information collected on these sites regarding student choices and student behaviour can feed directly into strategic enrolment management cycles and inform the design of programs and services.

There are some challenges within the university model shared in the Magda story. For example, the variations in course offerings, and in course length and credit load, could present scheduling difficulties for students. Though some course selections may be completed through self-service registration software, many decisions will require the ongoing support of academic advisors with an in-depth understanding of program requirements and completion options. This may result in unexpected (or undesirable) breaks within a study period. This could also become a very expensive model for an institution to support.

It should also be noted that though technology can increase accessibility of education for many, it does not guarantee access for everyone. Education models that rely too heavily on technology may facilitate the unintended consequence of limiting access to specific populations, particularly those who do not have access to either the technology hardware or the network infrastructure to support access. Finally, Magda's university appears to rely heavily on the use of technology for the collection of personal data (i.e. creating profiles of learners who share similar characteristics). There can be risks associated with the over-collection of personal data which should be minded.

Deputy provost, academic operations perspective: Scott's response

Overall, the future described in Magda's story has many characteristics that I believe are good. Beyond things which today we know to be important for learning (peer to peer networking, being seen and heard within the institution, and cared for in terms of aims and ambitions), there are a few key characteristics that stood out. The use of prior learning assessment and review (PLAR) to validate existing knowledge that Magda brought with her reflects a mature understanding that learning can happen in many contexts and across a lifetime. Magda appears to be quite self-directed and to have her prior learning validated formally is an acknowledgement of that trait, which could reinforce a sense that the local university is the right university for her. Magda is also studying a topic where knowledge is constantly emergent, and validated recognition of knowledge that comes from outside the institution while studying does "good" in terms of supporting the larger concept that knowledge can come from many places in many forms. The varied structure of the programme, the various additional learning opportunities, and the use of a portal and journal to help her structure and make sense of her learning reflect both the field itself and a commitment to continuing to support Magda as a self-directed learner. The use of automated advising and recommendation tools at various points might have the potential to box Magda in, but since they are most often used in conjunction with a personal conversation there is a reasonable degree of balance, and they are probably useful in terms of prompting and structuring a conversation.

The story notes that scheduling and managing workloads for this program are a challenge, and in my role as a senior administrator, I would be concerned about this. Making a program financially viable whilst keeping it affordable could be a challenge. The structure of a more traditional programme can be inflexible, but it also allows for a lot of predictability. Supporting the design and development of courses could also be challenging since there is a high degree of variability. Learning design could be an open-ended exercise since the time required to teach the course could be emergent within the design. This could also be an opportunity to shake up the design of courses in some interesting ways and there's likely some potential for reuse here over time.

The technology requirements of the program are also quite significant. A significant investment in technology ownership and maintenance is implied by this programme. That may not be a bad thing if it means that the university is in control of its own technological future. The amount of professional advising support that Magda receives is good, but I wonder again how sustainable it might be and still keep the programme tuition affordable.

Overall, there's a lot I like about this future, but I have worries about equity and inclusion. How will this program work for learners who are less self-directed? How can the cost of the programme be kept affordable in a way that means people from all walks of life can play a role in emergent industries? Without that, the diversity of perspective that Magda came to her local university to experience might not be possible.

Section 3: Synthesis

The narrative of Magda's speculative future was designed to prompt reflection. It is not an attempt to predict the future, imagine a utopian kind of institution, or instil hope or fear. Rather, its purpose is to say: What if this future, probable as it is with its connections to current systemic structures and processes, was our reality? What does it tell us about the present and about current choices we are making at our institutions? We undertook this effort to grapple with the question of "goodness" given a specific context and an imaginary scenario, rather than considering "goodness" in universal terms. The responses above highlight that any future we design for needs to be informed by a wide and diverse range of individuals, such that the tensions and opportunities of any future, and the tensions and opportunities of our current paths, are interrogated by those most heavily impacted. Below we explore some of the patterns that we see arising through the responses above and the questions that they raise for consideration. These are further discussed in the summary section.

Digital fluency

As the responses raised above, there is a tension, and perhaps an incongruence, between the technological infrastructure required and the personalised, caring approach aspired to in the speculative future that frames this chapter. Issues of data privacy, the need for a base level of digital fluency by the rights holders in the system, the requirement for digital accessibility (Kulkarni, 2019) and universal design for learning (CAST, n.d.), as well as the lack of integrated and seamless technology required to support the degree of system interconnectivity in this scenario are common threads through all responses. While the scenario describes a more responsive, easy-to-use student experience, the potential high barrier to entry imposed by the requirement for digital fluency, digital accessibility and universal design for learning brings equity and access questions to the forefront. This issue is aggravated by the fact that (a) the majority of K-12 and HE educators have little to no formal training in online and blended learning (Bates, 2021; Crichton & Childs, 2022; Johnson, 2021), and (b) definitions, policies, curricula, and outcomes surrounding K-12 digital literacy vary across educational systems (Hadziristic, 2017; McLean & Rowsell, 2020). The ripple effects of this impact the degree to which grade 12 (secondary school) graduates will have the degree of digital literacy and fluency required to participate in a future such as the one described above. Can higher education institutions provide the level of student support required, specifically among groups that traditionally struggle in the post-secondary context? How can institutions provide the supports and resources required to help faculty and staff build their capabilities to design, facilitate and support engaging learning experiences? What will count as quality, to whom, and who will "measure it" both internally and with the community partners that support the institution in offering quality education?

Agency, choice, and relationships

As highlighted in the responses above, digital platforms are not neutral, and indeed they are often biased. This reality has implications for the relevance of educational programming and exposure to meaningful learning opportunities selected for Magda, and thus cannot be overlooked. While significant and far-reaching work is being done to further justice, equity, inclusion, and diversity in learning contexts now replete with digital platforms (Beetham et al., 2022; Costanza-Chock, 2020), it may not yet be enough to assume that an AI system like the one Magda is engaging with will be fair, just, and equitable and that most of the population is going to feel comfortable relinquishing their agency and decision making on career pathways to AI. Further, there is also an assumption in the narrative that the information and insights generated by the AI reflect an agreed upon and recognisable body of knowledge that is known and fixed. However, in our ill structured, complex world, the knowledge required is transdisciplinary in nature, dynamic in composition, rapid in its evolution, and indeed plural: we should make no assumptions that a particular educational technology will be able to reflect multiple forms of knowledge (e.g. Indigenous knowledges) and account for epistemic justice, unless we took conscious steps to account for those in the design of such systems or in the training data that were used to develop them. What type of role should technology play in this future? Where does individual ownership, decision making and self-efficacy surface in Magda's narrative when decisions and pathways are established based on algorithms which prioritise certain values and knowledges but not others? What additional pressures does it place on the role of student support to be aware of programming at this level of detail? What risks does that pose to the institution as students follow the career guidance and programming direction provided?

It has been well established that humans are social beings who learn, grow, and thrive by connecting, developing, and maintaining relationships over time with diverse individuals. Being in community with others is not only a nice thing to do; it is the only thing that will enable us to address the challenging issues of our time (Corman & Cox, 2021; Cox, 2022). Balancing an individualised and personalised approach while also fostering, nourishing, and giving back to the larger community is increasingly seen as needing to be inherent in all our systems, including HE (Goodchild, 2021). In Magda's scenario, there is potential exposure to and recognition of a variety of ways of knowing and being, due to the multiple social interactions with students, alumni, and professionals in the field. Yet there is an anomaly between the rich social community being facilitated and the fact that the technologies that facilitate this community and network are created from a limited and biased vantage point. This disconnect underpins much of the discomfort expressed in the responses above. This is highlighted by our collective and contextual positionality as Canadian residents wrestling with the treatment of Indigenous peoples (Smith, 2012), the Truth and Reconciliation Commission calls to action (Truth & Reconciliation Commission of Canada, 2015), and the tragedies of residential schools. It caused us to raise questions such as: Where are the AI systems that are built on Indigenous ways of knowing and being, that make contextually relevant decisions, and that account for cultural protocols? In adopting digital systems that foster ease of use and connection, what inherent beliefs and values are being passed along as "good" by the institution based on the inherent bias in the code? What supports are needed for all rights holders as they navigate a HE system in transition?

Responsiveness

Increased frequency of large-scale climate events, pandemics, and geo-political instabilities are part of our shared global context. While Magda's story illustrates one approach to improving the student experience, this must be balanced with the needs of an ill-structured, uncertain, and complex world necessitating a transdisciplinary approach to address global problems. This requires that we consider the ways in which humans and machines can cooperate to valued ends. This is not as much a technological issue as a human limitation when it comes to thinking about diversity and design, what Staley (2019) calls a "poverty of imagination of what that innovation might be". Bayne et al. (2020) offer the following provocation:

> [W]e argue that if we do not feel ready at this point to actively welcome our robot colleagues, we should at least be prepared to open the door to them. To the extent that aspects of automation may prove to be genuinely beneficial to teachers, it seems important to remain open to the idea that it may allow us to explore new kinds of critical pedagogies, new creative possibilities, and new kinds of usefulness to our students. The key point we wish to make here is that for this to be the case, research and development of automation technologies in teaching should not be developed for teachers but by teachers. Teachers, the act of teaching, and the learning and well-being of students, not efficiency imperatives or fantasies of frictionless scaling up of education, should be placed at

the center of the way we think about automation. (pp. 111–12; Kindle loc 1495)

How can we build technologies that prompt, provoke, and otherwise help to build resilience and capacity? How can HE engage the student in co-creation and the development of iterative, responsive programming and institutions?

Conclusion

Those who choose to begin a higher education learning journey have given themselves the opportunity to learn from and with others who bring varied, diverse perspectives. Using a speculative future scenario allowed us to enter on our own learning journey and make visible some possibilities and gaps in the current HE system — a system in transition. As Harris (2014) states:

> It's in moments of mass change that our most constant qualities appear… It's in moments of translation that we learn what is indelible about us. We see what cannot pass forward into the new… but we also see what things [need to] remain. (p. 209)

Consistent with the values and beliefs captured in the Royal Roads University Learning, Teaching, and Research model, and evidenced in the responses to the Magda speculative future narrative, what counts as "good" in HE goes beyond preparing students to be labour market ready and beyond preparing the learning environment for them. It requires creating teaching and learning environments *with students* to address the needs and challenges that they are facing in the present and will face in the future. It requires critical awareness. It requires intentionality and an ongoing commitment to justice. And it requires a sort of radical acceptance that the status quo is neither desirable nor acceptable, so that we can turn our gaze to creating futures that are brighter.

Speculative future invites us to reflect on what would be left behind in creating a system that would support the experience of Magda or a version of it. In exploring its possibilities, it asks us to place a value on what would be lost and what would be gained as we move forward. This is not a decision that can be made in isolation or by a select few. It necessitates dialogue and discussion with all rights holders, and the building and maintaining of a multiplicity of relationships within and beyond the HE sector. It requires a connected, engaged, and committed community, as well as the courage to look beyond our current circumstances, and to acknowledge that there is nothing that is "normal" about current systems. They too were once speculative explorations.

References

Bates, T. (2021, December 16). Revising teaching in a digital age: The impact of Covid-19. *Online Learning and Distance Education Resources*.
https://www.tonybates.ca/2021/12/16/revising-teaching-in-a-digital-age-the-impact-of-covid-19/

Bayne, S., Evans, P., Ewins, R., Knox, J., & Lamb, J. (2020). *The manifesto for teaching online*. MIT Press.

Beetham, H., Collier, A., Czerniewicz, L., Lamb, B., Lin, Y., Ross, J., Scott, A-M. & Wilson, A. (2022). Surveillance practices, risks, and responses in the post pandemic university. *Digital Culture & Education, 14*(1), 16–37.
https://www.digitalcultureandeducation.com/volume-14-1

British Columbia. (n.d.). *Budget letters for post-secondary institutions.*
https://www2.gov.bc.ca/gov/content/education-training/post-secondary-education/institution-resources-administration/budget-letters?keyword=post&keyword=secondary&keyword=funding&keyword=formulae

British Columbia. (n.d.). *Post-secondary funding formula review.*
https://www2.gov.bc.ca/gov/content/education-training/post-secondary-education/post-secondary-funding-formula-review?keyword=post&keyword=secondary&keyword=funding&keyword=formulae

Canadian Broadcast Corporation. (2022, April 27). *StatsCan data indicates finding a place to live in B. C. is not about to get any more affordable.*
https://www.cbc.ca/news/canada/british-columbia/british-columbia-housing-census-2022-1.6433198

CAST (n.d). *Until learning has no limits.*
https://www.cast.org/impact/universal-design-for-learning-udl

Corman, I., & Cox, R. (2020) *Transdisciplinary: A primer* [PDF].
https://media.royalroads.ca/owl/media/macal/documents/MACAL_Transdisciplinary_Thinking03-31-21.pdf

Costanza-Chock, S. (2020). *Design justice: Community-led practices to build the worlds we need*. The MIT Press.

Cox, R. (2022, May 5). *Transdisciplinarity* [PowerPoint slides].
https://jamboard.google.com/d/1F7C1gA0uWeZxGYt4kiACS_KhY0xeV-fOYx45CNM5D00/viewer?f=0&pli=1

Crichton, S., & Childs, E. (2022). *Design principles for K-12 online learning: National validation study* [PDF]. Canadian eLearning Network.
http://canelearn.net/wp-content/uploads/2022/02/CANeLearn-Design-Principles-National-Validation-Study-Report.pdf

Goodchild, M., P., Senge, C., Scharmer, O., Longboat, R. D., Longboat, K. D., Hill, R., & Deer, K. K. (2021). Relational systems thinking: That's how change is going to come, from our Mother Earth. *Journal of Awareness Based Systems Change, 1*(1), 75–103.
https://jabsc.org/index.php/jabsc/article/view/577/696

Hadziristic, T. (2017). *The state of digital literacy in Canada: A literature review* [PDF]. The Brookfield Institute.
https://brookfieldinstitute.ca/wp-content/uploads/BrookfieldInstitute_State-of-Digital-Literacy-in-Canada_Literature_WorkingPaper.pdf

Harris, B., Childs, E. A., Axe, J., & Gorley, C. (2021). Developing a university learning, teaching and research framework through practice conversations. *Journal of Applied Research in Higher Education, 14*(2), 874–85.
https://doi.org/10.1108/JARHE-11-2020-0380

Harris, B., Walinga, J., Childs, E., Raby, J., Takach, G., Jorgenson, F., Mason, R., Zornes, D., Gorley, C., & Forssman, V. (2018). *Cultivating change leaders for a better world: RRU's learning, teaching and research model (LTRM)*. Royal Roads University.
https://oer.royalroads.ca/moodle/pluginfile.php/2485/mod_page/content/22/LTRM_Full_Sep_2018_final.pdf

Harris, M. (2014). *The end of absence: Reclaiming what we have lost in a world of constant connection*. HarperPerennial.

Henri, D. A., Provencher, J. F., Bowles, E., Taylor, J. J., Steel, J., Chelick, C., Popp, J. N., Cooke, S. J., Rytwinski, T., McGregor, D., Ford, A. T., & Alexander, S. M. (2020). Weaving Indigenous knowledge systems and Western sciences in terrestrial research, monitoring, and management in Canada: A protocol for a systematic map. *Ecol Solut Evidence, 2*(2), 1–9.
https://doi.org/10.1002/2688-8319.12057

Johnson, J. T., Howitt, R., Cajete, G., Berkes, F., Louis, R. P., & Kliskey, A. (2016). Weaving Indigenous and sustainability sciences to diversify our methods. *Sustainability Science, 11*, 1–11.
https://doi.org/10.1007/s11625-015-0349-x

Johnson, N. (2021). *2021 National report: Lessons from the COVID-19 pandemic* [PDF]. Canadian Digital Learning Research Association.
http://www.cdlra-acrfl.ca/wp-content/uploads/2022/05/2021_national_report_en.pdf

Kimmerer, R. (2002). Weaving traditional ecological knowledge into biological education: A call to action. *Bioscience, 52*(5), 432–38.
https://doi.org/10.1641/0006-3568(2002)052[0432:WTEKIB]2.0.CO;2

Kulkarni, M. (2019). Digital accessibility: Challenges and opportunities. *IIMB Management Review, 31*(1), 91–98. https://doi.org.10.1016/j.iimb.2018.05.009

Little, S. (2021, December 26). *Flooding, fires and heat: A year of unprecedented weather extremes in B. C.* Global News. https://globalnews.ca/news/8438007/bc-year-in-review-weather-extremes/

McLean, C. & Rowsell, J. (2019). Digital literacies in Canada. In J. Lacina, & R. Griffith (Eds), *Preparing globally minded literacy teachers: Knowledge, practices, and case studies* (pp. 177–98). Routledge.

Ross, J. (2017). Speculative method in digital education research. *Learning, Media and Technology, 42*(2), 214–29. https://doi.org/10.1080/17439884.2016.1160927

Ross, J. (2018). Speculative method as an approach to researching emerging educational issues and technologies. In L. Hamilton, & J. Ravenscroft (Eds), *Building research design in education* (pp. 197–210). Bloomsbury.

Royal Roads University. (2022). *Our vision.* https://www.royalroads.ca/about/our-vision

Smith, L. T. (2012). Colonizing knowledges. In, L. T. Smith (Ed.), *Decolonizing methodologies: Research and indigenous peoples* (pp. 117–43). Zed Books.

Staley, D. J. (2019). *Alternative universities: Speculative design for innovation in higher education.* JHU Press.

Truth and Reconciliation Commission (2015). *Truth and Reconciliation Commission: Calls to action* [PDF]. Government of Canada. https://publications.gc.ca/collections/collection_2015/trc/IR4-8-2015-eng.pdf

UN. (2020). *UN research roadmap for the COVID-19 recovery.* https://www.un.org/en/coronavirus/communication-resources/un-research-roadmap-covid-19-recovery

UNESCO. (2021). *Reimagining our futures together: A new social contract for education.* https://unesdoc.unesco.org/ark:/48223/pf0000379707.locale=en

Veletsianos, G. (2020). How should we respond to the life-altering crises that education is facing? *Distance Education, 41*(4), 1–3. https://doi.org/10.1080/01587919.2020.1825066

Veletsianos, G., Childs, E., Cox, R., Cordua-von Specht, I., Grundy, S. Hughes, J., Karleen, D., & Willson, A. (2022). Person in environment: Focusing on the ecological aspects of online and distance learning. *Distance Education, 43*(2), 318–24. https://doi.org/10.1080/01587919.2022.2064827

14. "Vibrant, open and accessible": Students' visions of higher education futures

Sharon Flynn, Julie Byrne, Maeve Devoy, Jonathon Johnston, Rob Lowney, Eimer Magee, Kate Molloy, David Moloney, Morag Munro, Fernandos Ongolly, Jasmine Ryan, Suzanne Stone, Michaela Waters, and Kyle Wright

Introduction

This chapter links past, present, and near-future perspectives to explore tensions in Ireland's higher education, emerging from a national-level student partnership research study focused on experiences of digital education across the sector. The chapter brings together student, academic, and other professional staff voices from various institutional contexts in a "future studies" approach (Daytor, 2002), building on work by Selwyn et al. (2020) and others. Student-articulated visions of the near future arising from a collaborative national teaching enhancement project are used as stimulus material here. The chapter explores how tensions between differing stakeholder perspectives on the near future of higher education in our context might be reconciled.

Our chapter develops around the following key questions:

- Why is student participation and student visioning of the future important in realising higher education for good (HE4Good)?

- What do students think an ideal learning future looks like, and how does this future align with the HE4Good concept?

The chapter first outlines and discusses the authors' commitment to students-as-partners (SaP) approaches in higher education (HE), and explores why it is crucial to draw on student perspectives when discussing potential pathways for higher education institutions. We then provide context and a project methodology underpinning a national sectoral collaboration, the Enhancing Digital Teaching and Learning (EDTL) project that informs the development of this chapter.

We move from reflecting on and documenting the EDTL project to articulating the methodological background justifying our use of speculative fiction as a mechanism for envisioning the near future of the Irish HE sector. Key themes arising from student-generated speculative fiction are discussed in terms of how they relate to higher education in our national context, and linking current reality with potential futures for the sector. We conclude by offering key points of reflection and recommendations to potentially impact positively on concepts of HE4Good as expressed elsewhere in this volume.

Contributors to this chapter include academic and academic-related staff, professional services and support staff, and perhaps most importantly, students whose lived experiences reflect and affect ongoing changes in society and HE. While our perspectives relate specifically to the Irish university context, we believe they will resonate with colleagues across HE more broadly. Student visions of change are woven together and explored to consider the potential for positive developments in Irish HE, navigating — potentially — towards a revised Irish higher education landscape in years to come. Taking a future studies approach to explore alternative futures for consideration — utopian and dystopian, likely and unlikely — we consider how best to move towards the most preferred visions of the future (Daytor, 2002; Sabzalieva et al., 2021). Data and student voice in the form of speculative fictional narratives gathered through the cross-institutional EDTL project provide the foundations for articulating these higher education futures.

Why are student participation and student visioning of the future important in realising HE4Good?

The Irish HE landscape is broad, varied, and includes traditional universities, technological universities, institutes of technology and a range of other public and private providers. Participation rates are among the highest in the world, and internationally domiciled students make up 12.4% of the student population (CSO, 2022). The Irish Universities Association (IUA) is the representative voice of Ireland's research intensive, enterprise engaged, public universities. A stated aim of the IUA Strategy 2022–2025 is to support member universities in increasing access for students with disabilities and from socially disadvantaged backgrounds.[1]

Navigating a pathway to HE4Good: Students as partners

Recent years have seen increasing recognition of the benefits of HE student-staff partnerships whereby "students are directly involved as change agents and partners within the system" (Collins et al., 2016, p. 16). As authors, we believe there is a real need for students and staff to engage as partners in learning. Such partnerships can generate benefits for all involved. Students are empowered to participate in shaping and improving the learning and teaching environment and supported in their development as critical thinkers and active citizens. For staff, partnering with students can offer an insight into what it is like to be a student today and can unearth and challenge existing assumptions about students and the student experience (Cook-Sather et al., 2014; Cook-Sather & Luz, 2015; Mathews et al, 2018; NStEP, 2021; USI, 2018).

The EDTL project, led by the IUA, commenced in January 2019 with the aim of enhancing the digital attributes and educational experiences of Irish university students. This was achieved by mainstreaming and integrating the use of digital technologies in teaching, learning and assessment, and by addressing the professional development of those who teach or support teaching and learning. Since its inception, the project has advocated that "[the] student voice will be built into all project activities at a local university level" (Flynn et al., 2020, p. 5), concretising a SaP ethos as one of the four key principles underpinning the project. In the context of EDTL, student partnership has evolved from the recruitment of a single student intern working directly with the project team to more than 20 student interns embedded within each

---

1   IUA Strategy 2022–2025 https://www.iua.ie/about/strategy/

of the partner universities contributing directly to the enhancement of staff and student digital skills. The EDTL amplification of student voice has provoked institutional and sector-wide discussion about where and how students desire change in Ireland's higher education (EDTL, 2022).

Student-generated speculative fiction and Irish higher education futures

Selwyn et al. (2020) describe the residual deep "grammar" of late twentieth-century schooling (e.g. its role in the post-industrial complex as preparatory for labour markets) as remaining mainly unchanged despite a surface-visible shift towards digital. The EDTL experience suggests that a lack of deep change applies similarly to Irish HE, where there is often a patchwork approach to digital teaching and learning, with compartmentalised knowledge silos and a "slow" renovation and updating of digital technologies in the context of existing HE custom and practice. "Good" higher education is perceived differently by various actors and stakeholders, e.g. "good" education as a personal and societal developmental process, or "good" education as a marketable product. These tensions are particularly prominent in the context of the Irish tertiary (e.g. higher education) sector, which only coalesces as a coherent system in the late twentieth century. Unlike more overtly marketised systems of higher education, Irish HE sees a "repositioning of higher education to prioritise more intensive engagement with industry and deployment of market mechanisms on a large scale for the first time' from the late 1990s onwards (Walsh, 2018, pp. 488–89). Topics of ongoing discussion in the Irish HE sector include values and priorities around universities as a public good, the role of research in generating "new" knowledge, the status of teaching and learning, and how university and other third-level institutional administrations respond to competing priorities (Loxley et al., 2014).

Speculative fiction has been one strategy used to articulate alternative futures to those seemingly inevitable futures arising from the current shift towards neoliberalism (Selwyn, 2020) and to explore how "the digital" can open up new avenues in educational thinking (Ross, 2017, 2018; Macgilchrist et al, 2020). The genre is described as offering an opportunity to allow the imagination to "run wild" in exploring possible futures (Kupferman, 2021). Suoranta et al. (2022) suggest that speculative fiction can "contribute to the development of a new normal where education will fulfil its mission to make the world a better place" (p. 228).

Speculative fiction is, perhaps inevitably, embedded in current experiences. We cannot predict or anticipate state of the art, without considering the state of the actual in embodied and localised lived experience (Selwyn, 2008). Who better, then, to provide insight into the state of the actual in higher education than current students? Student partners connected to the EDTL project were approached to develop responses in prose to questions around their vision of future higher education experiences. These visions are explored in greater detail and from a range of perspectives below.

Student perspectives on the near-future of higher education in Ireland

In March 2020, in the context of the rapid pivot to remote teaching and learning due to COVID-19, student-staff partnerships became even more important as a core value. The EDTL partnership ethos played a crucial role in enabling our cross-institutional project team to rapidly respond to the ongoing twists and turns of the pandemic context and in ensuring that our collaborative sectoral response was aligned to students' needs (EDTL, 2022; Ongolly & Flynn, 2022). Student interns collaborated to develop resources such as *The EDTL approach for students: A guide to remote learning — for students, by students*. At a local level, student-staff partnerships enabled the integration of existing staff knowledge about online learning and students' immediate experiences of remote learning due to the pandemic, into student-focused and staff-focused advice and supports (Johnston & Ryan, 2022; Kurz et al., 2022).

In April 2021, more than a year into the global pandemic, and at the end of a full academic year of remote learning, EDTL launched a social media campaign to ask Irish higher education students to articulate their aspirations for the post-pandemic-future of higher education. The *Your Education, Your Voice, Your Vision* campaign aimed to crowdsource a vision for university learning in an ideal world. Student responses from across Ireland were sought in response to questions co-developed with partner institutions.

The *Your Education, Your Vision, Your Voice* campaign was coordinated and managed in partnership with a team of student interns who analysed, coded and interpreted the results. More than 14,000 responses indicated that, for most HE students in Ireland, an on-campus experience is prized. The need for physical presence was tempered by the desire for flexibility, with 76% of respondents articulating a preference for no more than three days a week to be spent on the physical campus. Student preference for study location indicated a more divided range of opinions, with 58% of respondents opting to study from home if possible and 42% preferring to study from a university campus. The survey revealed a particularly high affinity for face-to-face interactions with staff and peers. Most students (80%) were explicit about not wanting face-to-face interactions with staff to be wholly replaced with online interactions. Student responses suggested that a preference for campus presence relates to engagement and interaction with peers, for social purposes and/or peer learning. This might broadly be summarised as "the college experience" (events, atmosphere, making friends etc.), campus facilities (access to institutionally provided digital tools and technologies, wifi, computer access, library resources etc.), and perhaps less obvious affordances of in-person interaction such as students' perceptions of enhanced focus/motivation (EDTL, 2021).

Overall, three key ideals for post-COVID-19 HE emerged from the national student voice campaign. First, there was a clear student demand for increased blended learning opportunities to provide access to, and support for, a more diverse range of students. Blended learning can potentially support students with differing circumstances, e.g. students with children or other caring responsibilities, those in full or part-time employment, students with disabilities, and/or those experiencing financial, time, or distance barriers to study. Second, there was a strong student demand to re-imagine the nature of assessment to more accurately reflect student learning and post-graduate application of skills and to remove the stress of exams. Four-fifths of respondents (81%) were critical of traditional exam-based assessment modalities and expressed preferences for open-book and/or continuous assessments. Finally, technological supports for learning such as the ability to review (pre)recorded lectures on grounds of convenience, flexibility, and inclusivity were perceived as essential in terms of providing a baseline of access for students who feel learning is negatively impacted by the realities of long-distance commutes.

This national level coordination of student preferences and visions of Irish higher education futures through the *Your Education, Your Voice, Your Vision* campaign, laid the foundations for a deeper exploration of some of these themes. Following on from this, and in preparation to write this chapter, current EDTL student partners were invited to respond to the following prompt: "What would a day in the life of a student look like in 2042"? This "medium-distance" future aimed to provide students with space to envision changes, radical or otherwise, to the lived experience of students in Irish higher education.

Articulating the future: Supporting students in a future-focused writing process

To support the writing process, student partners were encouraged to engage with a short online workshop led by a storyteller and writer. The workshop started with a group discussion about the future for learning in higher education, facilitating open discussion on how this might look in 2042. Students were encouraged to unpack their understanding of what might be required for the future of HE to be "good" and invited to teleport themselves into the future or, perhaps, to consider their children's future. An initial window of scaffolded free writing was followed by further discussion and sharing of ideas. Students were then asked to produce an individual written piece (approximately 500 words) on a day in the life of a student in 2042.

Five student partners representing both domestic and international student perspectives from across four different universities rose to the challenge. Three undergraduates and two postgraduate students from a range of disciplinary backgrounds articulated their own visions of a higher education future, bringing perspectives from business, politics, anthropology, biopharmaceutical engineering and creative digital media. Redefined power dynamics in HE, technological advancements, and calls to reconfigure the physical campus were common features in all five of the student contributions. There was a common acknowledgement of tensions between thinking about what they would like to see (i.e. utopian, imaginable, desirable), and considering what might be possible (e.g. achievable, implementable, doable) in their sculpting of the future.

"In the future, everybody can learn": Students' ideal visions of higher education futures

Student visions of the future are shared here and grouped thematically for discussion and analysis:

1. Curriculum, learning and assessment
2. A supportive environment for learning
3. Social and political change
4. The campus reimagined

1. Curriculum, learning, and assessment

Perhaps unsurprisingly, formal learning activities featured heavily in and across students' vignettes. Students conceive these learning activities in different ways. Some envision content and learning materials shifting towards more practical and vocational orientations. In doing so, students framed higher education in terms of employability and preparation for the world of work.

Imagined future curricula are closely aligned to students' perceptions of future employment opportunities. The alignment of curricula with employability has been a key feature of policy in Irish higher education for some time (Fortune et al., 2021; Frawley et al, 2020; HEA, 2020; NFTL, 2019). However, focusing solely on preparation for the world of work sits uncomfortably alongside wider ideas around the idea of the university and emerging narratives that counter employability discourse as the sole remit of higher education (NFTL, 2019):

> The type of courses offered by [university] have altered to provide a workforce for the evolving needs of business, technology and industry. The uptake of courses centred around sustainability, big data and analytics, automation, machine learning and artificial intelligence has risen, and this reflects the type of jobs available to graduates. Elements

of data science are integrated into more courses as the demands for data literacy expands.

This focus on data science, data, and technology affected how some students imagined future learning and teaching experiences:

> In 2042, the majority of teaching is online (live/recorded lectures, workshops), with value adding activities in person to facilitate group discussions (tutorials, labs). There is less prioritisation of being on campus. There is a general understanding that a physical presence does not equal effective learning.

The idea that being on campus is no longer prioritised, echoes Bayne et al.'s (2016, 2020) perspective on the need to move away from privileging on-campus presence. However, this speculative narrative is in tension with current practices in the Irish higher education sector, where a move to fully on-campus education has been widespread in the initial post-pandemic phase (Donnelly, 2022; MacKenzie et al., 2022).

In students' visions of the future, digital tools and practices are embedded in every aspect of teaching, learning, and assessment, and have met the long-held expectations to transform the university experience by creating a new sense of the university as a fluid space, beyond the campus. A key refrain is the presence of a desire for inclusive practice:

> Dedicated virtual machines give these remote students the opportunity to access all of the same technologies as those who attend in person, ensuring that no student is forgotten about and has an equal chance to learn and succeed.
>
> [...] module content is inclusive and suitable for diverse learner needs. Assistive digital tools are regarded as aids for all students. Exams are primarily online, with continuous assessment-based assignments Deadlines are spread out to relieve pressure on students. Alternative forms of assessment used, we are not focused on written exams suited for rote learners, instead creativity is appreciated e.g. poster, presentation, submit essay in video format, podcast, simulations, case studies, virtual reality.

The fluidity of the campus was extended to suggest potential cross disciplinary, cross institutional, and even global connection and cooperation:

> Teaching techniques and delivery methods have become more centralised across colleges, making content more interchangeable.

The incongruity between the perspectives of students on future curricula, learning and assessment with that of recent academic discourse, emphasises the importance of including students as partners when imagining higher education futures. This is particularly important for those involved in guiding and supporting the design and delivery of future curricula.

2. A supportive and inclusive environment for learning

Current students saw a commitment to inclusive teaching reflecting an enhanced and differentiated understanding of what it means "to be a student" in 2042. Universities in the future are likely to be tasked with providing a much higher level of student support, both in terms of explicit "supports" and also in how they negotiate the reality of a changing student profile:

> Mental Health services have become more accessible for students and counselling services are more readily available to students who need it. Improving student welfare has led to the creation of spaces in the student centre for meditation and yoga, offering an opportunity to switch off from digital demands.
>
> The demands of life, college, and work are accessible by student support and wrap-around services that are empathically run and responsibly funded.

Changes to student "face time" on site also impact on and flow from increased digital facilities. Current students expressed real concerns about commuting and accommodation, particularly in the context of Ireland's housing and cost-of-living crisis as well as the global climate crisis. To that end, virtual interactions were likely to be on the rise; physical interactions would be enabled through enhanced public transport provision:

> As prices of accommodation in [university] rose, the benefits offered by blended and virtual learning offered a solution for students struggling to meet high rent prices.
>
> The perfect day for a student on campus in 2042 is one where it's rent day, but there's no squabbling for money. They FaceTime their friend in

the next county whose online today because they're a commuter — but they commute by choice, not because of scarcity.

Learning will be less stressful as there will be no need for commuting and this will give the future student more opportunities to engage in hobbies and such as traveling etc.

The calls to improve public transport were heard and a Luas [tram] line now runs from the city centre to [university] and spans out to the outer suburbs of South Dublin, reducing the need for students to travel by car.

The reality of national tuition fee policy also impacted on student visions of change in the near future university as an issue connected with access, but also with societal and political change.

Understanding and prioritising students' needs must be central in developing a future HE4Good. Our focus on student voice and agency as articulating bottom-up visions from a community of scholarship resonates clearly with Bayne and Gallagher's (2021) account of Edinburgh University's top-down *Near Future Teaching* project, where they state that "universities need to get better at crafting their own, compelling counter-narratives concerning the future of technology in teaching, in order to assert the agency and presence of the academic and student bodies in the face of technological change" (p. 608). We suggest from our experience of partnership that students are particularly well placed to contribute to these narratives.

3. Social and political change

At the time of writing, accessing Irish higher education involves the highest fees for domestic tuition paid by individual students in the European Union. This is occluded as a rhetoric of "free fees" is offset by the presence of an annually levied "student registration charge". Given that financial circumstances profoundly affect students' access to and experience of HE, it is perhaps unsurprising that questions of access to education and sustainability in funding are reflected in writing about the university of the near future. Student narratives of the future demonstrate clear expectations for enhanced access and an assumption of greater governmental subsidy for third-level education:

> With the radical drop in tuition fees, even those on the lowest end of the income ladder can attend university, with the bulk of fees subsidised by the government, helping all students realise their dream and study the subject they have always wanted to.

Another feature that emerges strongly is a continuing trend towards "the digital university". National restrictions in response to COVID-19 accelerated uptake and integration of digital tools into everyday teaching and learning practices. Students suggest that in the future, the responsibility to support learning in the digital context will fall upon the institution rather than the individual:

> Colleges must supply technology more readily to students due to the heavy emphasis on digital technology in learning.

While our institutions collectively have done much to smooth the experience of remote learning, clearly there is still work to be done to advance and empower students to participate fully:

> The influence of the Irish Universities Association but, primarily, the impact of student partnership across departments, universities and sectors kicked everything into motion. In the background, students felt continually more empowered and acknowledged.

Visions of student empowerment suggest that student voice can influence future developments in HE.

> An ideal student outlook in 2042 is one wherein they (students) recognise and exercise their potential for positive change. Empowering students to provoke change, build relationships, and change perspectives in Irish universities lead to better resources, representation, and redistribution.

4. The campus reimagined

The physical college campus still holds a central place in students' visions of the future but their writing reveals a radical revision of space and a transformed college campus — collaborative, flexible, and accessible:

> The ideal campus in 2042 is one with a vibrant, open, and accessible campus that students stroll about

> Buildings have been adapted to maximise space for students and staff. Pods are offered for online meeting spaces. Lecture halls, tutorial rooms and the library are used as self-study areas when not in use.
>
> The dated library and [other] building have been replaced with buildings with more collaborative spaces, improved technology services and more study spaces. Books and archives have been digitalised and libraries have become more of a space for collaboration and study.

Improving campus facilities to facilitate collaboration, flexibility and accessibility for learners would seem to be natural enhancements to the current state, but it is unclear whether foundations are currently being laid for these enhancements. Scoping, planning and funding campus development is a multi-year process, so seeds for the campus of 2042 need to be planted today. Campus development and construction has increased significantly in HE in recent years (Wolff, 2019), and Ireland is no exception. Whether these facilities are future-focused or rooted in 20th century conceptions of a physical university, time will show. Additionally, and against an ongoing backdrop of systemic underfunding in comparison to similar tertiary education contexts, construction costs have risen significantly since COVID-19 lockdowns (O'Halloran, 2022). Whether innovative new facilities will be developed as students hope remains, yet, to be seen.

Irrespective of how campus development is planned and implemented, students are clear that their vision of the future campus is a pragmatic one. Echoing Brown's (2015) digital learning ecology model, the focus is on learning itself, supported by the affordances of physical campus in conjunction with the affordances of digital environment, leading to a shared understanding of the value of online and in person learning.

> There is less prioritisation of being on campus. There is a general understanding that a physical presence does not equal effective learning.
>
> Any in-person classes, tutorials and labs are organised on the same days (1–3 days a week). This offers greater flexibility to students and endeavours to make education more accessible for all, while still maintaining that level of face-to-face interaction that students value so highly.

Finally, some students envisage a shift away from the physical towards virtual infrastructure, with technology redefining the possibilities for how students learn:

> ... I see a future where more advanced technology such as virtual reality gadgets will be easily accessible to all with the possibility of experiencing touch (especially for technical/lab-based fields). This way, students will be able to see, hear, and feel in their virtual environments... universities will channel more funds towards improving virtual learning infrastructure and less on physical building.

Conclusion: Pathways to progress

Two key features have emerged clearly through our engagement with student-generated speculative fiction. First, these students' views of the future clearly respond to current anxieties and concerns. Students' writing suggests that broader solutions to the challenges they face in their current lives are there to be found: joined-up thinking about the affordability of accommodation, public transport and welfare supports are foundational features of these student visions of the future. Flexibility in study "mode" is identified as a desirable feature and being able to choose freely between in-person and remote learning modalities is a widely accepted feature of future scenarios.

Second, student visions of the future of higher education are strikingly positive: there is a hopeful future for the sector. Students see the (many) current challenges as not insurmountable, particularly when driven by a student partnership approach that aims to develop a culture of shared responsibility and high levels of trust between staff and empowered students.

We think it crucial to consider student participation when imaging the future of higher education: engaging in students-as-partners approaches has afforded us a renewed commitment to active staff-student collaboration when exploring next steps and looking ahead to the future of the Irish higher education sector. Student voice has been a key influencing factor on our practice and philosophies of higher education. We see student voice, agency, and partnership as crucial factors informing how to chart a path towards HE4Good and look forward to contrasting the reality of near-future teaching against the student visions of the future articulated in this chapter.

References

Bayne, S., Evans, P., Ewins, R., Knox, J., & Lamb, J. (2020). *The manifesto for teaching online.* MIT Press. https://doi.org/10.7551/mitpress/11840.001.0001

Bayne, S., & Gallagher, M. (2021). Near future teaching: Practice, policy and digital education futures. *Policy Futures in Education, 19*(5), 607–25. https://doi.org/10.1177/14782103211026446

Bovill, C., & Bulley, C. J. (2011). A model of active student participation in curriculum design: Exploring desirability and possibility. In C. Rust (Ed.), *Improving student learning (ISL) 18: Global theories and local practices* (pp. 176–88). Oxford Brookes University.

Brown, M. (2015). Looking over the horizon: New learning platforms, old technology debates. In B. Mooney (Ed.), *Education matters: Shaping Ireland's education landscape* (pp. 40–48). Education Matters.

Collins, T., Gormley, B., Purser, L., & O'Sullivan, D. (2016). *Enhancing student engagement in decision-making: Report of the working group on student engagement in Irish higher education* [PDF]. Higher Education Authority, Dublin. http://www.thea.ie/contentfiles/HEA-IRC-Student-Engagement-Report-Apr2016-min.pdf

Cook-Sather A., Bovill, C., & Fenton, P. (2014). *Engaging students as partners in learning and teaching: A guide for faculty.* Jossey-Bass

Cook-Sather, A., & Luz, A. (2015). Greater engagement in and responsibility for learning: What happens when students cross the threshold of student–faculty partnership. *Higher Education Research & Development, 34*(6), 1097–109. https://doi.org/10.1080/07294360.2014.911263

CSO. (2022). *Educational attainment thematic report 2022.* https://www.cso.ie/en/releasesandpublications/ep/p-eda/educationalattainmentthematicreport2022/

Daytor, J. A. (Ed.) (2002). *Advancing futures: Futures studies in higher education.* Greenwood Publishing Group.

Donnelly, K. (2022, August 30). *Full reopening of colleges as third level abandons the hybrid model.* Irish Independent. https://www.independent.ie/irish-news/education/full-reopening-of-colleges-as-third-level-abandons-the-hybrid-model-41945954.html

EDTL. (2021). *Your education, your voice, your vision: Report of the student campaign run by the Enhancing Digital Teaching & Learning project, April – May 2021* [PDF]. Irish Universities Association. https://edtl.blog/wp-content/uploads/2021/08/IUA-EDTL-Your-Education-Your-Voice-Your-Vision-Full-Report.pdf

EDTL. (2022). *Student partnership in teaching and learning: Lessons from the Enhancing Digital Teaching & Learning in Irish Universities project* [PDF]. Irish Universities Association.
https://edtl.blog/wp-content/uploads/2022/11/IUA-EDTL-Student-Participation.pdf

Flynn, S., Purser, L., Trench Bowles, N., Byrne, J., Hamill, D., O'Connor, K., Lowney, R., Stone, S., Molloy, K., Moloney, D., Munro, M., O'Connor, M., O'Reilly, M, O'Mara, T., & O'Callaghan, C. (2020). *Enhancing digital capacity in teaching and learning in Ireland: A national approach*. 2020 European Learning & Teaching Forum, Utrecht, Netherlands.
https://www.researchgate.net/publication/339377153_Enhancing_Digital_Capacity_in_Teaching_and_Learning_in_Ireland_a_national_approach

Fortune, N., Dippre, R., Dvorakova, L., Farrell, A., Weresh, M., & Yakovchuk, N. (2021). Beyond the university: Towards transfer. In M. Keane, C. McAvinia, & Í. O'Sullivan (Eds), *Emerging Issues IV: Changing times, changing contexts*. EDIN.
https://www.edin.ie/?page_id=540

Frawley, D., Harvey, V., Pigott, V., & Mawarire, M. (2020). *Graduate outcomes survey: Class of 2018* [PDF]. Higher Education Authority.
https://hea.ie/assets/uploads/2020/06/HEA-Graduate-Outcomes-Survey-Class-of-2018.pdf

Higher Education Authority (2020) *Human capital initiative*.
https://hea.ie/skills-engagement/human-capital-initiative/

Inayatullah, S. (2013). Futures studies: Theories and methods. In BBVA (Ed.), *There's a future: Visions for a better world* (pp. 37–63). BBVA.
https://www.bbvaopenmind.com/wp-content/uploads/2013/01/BBVA-OpenMind-Book-There-is-a-Future_Visions-for-a-Better-World-1.pdf

Johnston, J. M, & Ryan, B. (2022). From Students-as-Partners theory to Students-as-Partners practice: Reflecting on staff-student collaborative partnership in an academic development context. *All Ireland Journal of Higher Education (AISH-J)*, 14(1), 1–27.
https://ojs.aishe.org/index.php/aishe-j/article/view/637

Kupferman, D. W. (2021). Educational futures and postdigital science. *Postdigital Science and Education*, 4, 216–23.
https://doi.org/10.1007/s42438-021-00236-6

Kurz, K., Munro, M., Corr, E., Abraham, C., Gottlöber, S., Meyler, R., Nagi, J., & Waters, M. (2022). Learning together in, and about, student-staff partnership in higher education. *All Ireland Journal of Higher Education (AISH-J)*, 14(1), 1–19.
https://ojs.aishe.org/index.php/aishe-j/article/view/651

Loxley, A., Seery, A., & Walsh, J. (2014). *Higher education in Ireland: Practices, policies and possibilities*. Palgrave MacMillan.
https://doi.org/10.1057/9781137289889

Macgilchrist, F., Allert, H., & Bruch, A. (2020). Students and society in the 2020s. Three future 'histories' of education and technology. *Learning, Media and Technology, 45*(1), 76–89.
https://doi.org/10.1080/17439884.2019.1656235.

MacKenzie, A., Bacalja, A., Annamali, D., Panaretou, A., Girme, P., Cutajar, M., Abegglen, S., Evens, M., Neuhaus, F., Wilson, K., Psarikidou, K., Psarikidou, K., Koole, M., Hrastinski, S., Sturm, S., Adachi, C., Schnaider, K., Bozkurt, A., Rapanta, C., Gourlay, L. (2021). Dissolving the dichotomies between online and campus-based teaching: A collective response to the Manifesto for Teaching Online (Bayne et al. 2020). *Postdigital Science and Education, 4*, 271–329.
https://doi.org/10.1007/s42438-021-00259-z

Matthews, K. E., Dwyer, A., Hine, L., & Turner, J. (2018). Conceptions of students as partners. *Higher Education, 76*(6), 957–71.
http://www.jstor.org/stable/45116838

NFTL. (2019). *Understanding and enabling student success in Irish higher education*. National Forum for the Enhancement of Teaching and Learning in Higher Education.
https://hub.teachingandlearning.ie/resource/understanding-and-enabling-student-success-in-irish-higher-education/

NFTL. (2021). *Next steps for teaching and learning: Moving forward together* [PDF]. National Forum for the Enhancement of Teaching and Learning in Higher Education.
https://www.teachingandlearning.ie/wp-content/uploads/Next-Steps.pdf

NStEP. (2021). *Steps to partnership: A framework for authentic student engagement in decision making* [PDF]. National Student Engagement Programme.
https://studentengagement.ie/wp-content/uploads/2021/05/NStEP-Steps-to-Partner-ship-WEB-VERSION.pdf

O'Halloran, B. (2022, August 2). *Building costs to continue rising but at slower pace, surveyors predict*. Irish Times.
https://www.irishtimes.com/business/2022/08/02/building-costs-to-continue-rising-but-at-slower-pace-surveyors-predict/

Ongolly, F., & Flynn, S. (2022) Student staff collaboration in virtual and digital spaces: A case of the IUA EDTL students associate interns' experiences. *ALT annual conference*.
https://www.researchgate.net/publication/364314933_Student-staff_partnership_a_case_study_of_the_Enhancing_Digital_Teaching_and_Learning_in_Irish_Universities_Project_EDTL_internship_model

Pruvot, E. B., & Estermann, T. (2012). European universities diversifying income streams. In A. Curaj, P. Scott, L. Vlasceanu, & L. Wilson (Eds), *European higher education at the crossroads* (pp. 706–26). Springer.

Rasa, T., & Laherto, A. (2022). Young people's technological images of the future: Implications for science and technology education. *European Journal of Futures Research, 10*(1), 1–15.
https://doi.org/10.1186/s40309-022-00190-x

Ross, J. (2017). Speculative method in digital education research. *Learning, Media and Technology, 42*(2), 214–29.
https://doi.org/10.1080/17439884.2016.1160927

Ross, J. (2018). Speculative method as an approach to researching emerging educational issues and technologies. In L. Hamilton, & J. Ravenscroft (Eds), *Building research design in education* (pp. 197–212). Bloomsbury.

Sabzalieva, E., Chacón, E., Liu, B. L., Morales, D., Mutize, T., Nguyen, H., & Chinchilla, J. R. (2021). *Thinking higher and beyond perspectives on the futures of higher education to 2050* [PDF]. UNESCO.
https://www.iesalc.unesco.org/eng/wp-content/uploads/2021/05/Thinking-Higher-and-Beyond_EN-_Format_FINAL.pdf

Selwyn, N. (2008) From state-of-the-art to state-of-the-actual? Introduction to a special issue. *Technology, Pedagogy and Education, 17*(2), 83–87.
https:/doi.org/10.1080/14759390802098573

Selwyn, N. Pangrazio, L. Nemorin, S. & Perrotta, C. (2020) What might the school of 2030 be like? An exercise in social science fiction. *Learning, Media and Technology, 45*(1), 90–106.
https://doi.org/10.1080/17439884.2020.1694944

Suoranta, J., Teräs, M., Teräs, H., Jandrić, P., Ledger, S., Macgilchrist, F., Prinsloo, P. (2022). Speculative social science fiction of digitalization in higher education: From what is to what could be. *Postdigital Science and Educatio*n, *4*, 224–36.
https://doi.org/10.1007/s42438-021-00260-6

USI. (2018). *A vision for partnership: USI student engagement policy* [PDF].
https://usi.ie/wp-content/uploads/2018/02/Student-Engagement-Policy.pdf

Walsh, J. (2018). *Higher education in Ireland, 1922 – 2016: Politics, policy and power – A history of higher education in the Irish free state*. Palgrave.
https://doi.org/10.1057/978-1-137-44673-2

Wolff, J. (2019, April 9). Universities are in a building frenzy, but who is actually impressed? *The Guardian*.
https://www.theguardian.com/education/2019/apr/09/universities-building-frenzy-who-actually-impressed

15. Vulnerability and generosity: The good future for Australian higher education

Kate Bowles

Australia is closing its borders to all non-citizens and non-residents. (Media Release, Australian Prime Minister, 19 March 2020)

This tree is only a baby at the moment, but it will grow up to 35 metres tall. It will be seen for miles because of the beautiful red flowers it will have during the summer months, Professor Davidson said. The students expressed their excitement at being back in Australia (Media Release, University of Wollongong, 10 December 2021)

It's early in the summer, and staff are standing around in the courtyard of an Australian university building. The building is very new. The senior executive, campus staff and local media are masked and careful. There is a buffet table. Summer rain is falling lightly on and off. While the hosts make small talk, the guests are running late. They're still checking out of their isolation accommodation. It's been months of committee work and delicate negotiations with Australian state and federal governments to get everyone to this point.

Out in the rain, draped with a red ribbon, is a recently planted sapling. *Brachychiton acerifolius* is a rainforest tree that lives along the east coast of Australia, named by nineteenth century botanists for its maple shaped leaves and its seed clusters that resembled a short tunic (from the Greek: *brachys* and *chiton*). This tree is also known up and down the east coast of Australia by the name that it shares with the university's own region: the Illawarra flame tree. Its distinctive red flowers are in the university's crest and brand palette, the source of the red in the corporate PowerPoint templates and Zoom backgrounds. There's even a 1980s pub rock song that immortalises its place in Australian small-town culture (Delaney, 2015):

> the flame tree will blind the weary driver
> and there's nothing else could set fire to this town
> there's no change, there's no pace
> everything within its place

Finally, the visitors arrive. They are a very small group of international students who have returned to Australia in a government pilot program that might predict the end of pandemic border closures. They have been travelling and isolating for days and are tired and hungry. In a break in the rain, they assemble with the senior executives around the sapling that has been planted to commemorate their return, and the journalists take photographs of the scene.

This chapter reflects on the throwntogetherness (Massey, 2005) of this event in December 2021. It is a random start, an ordinary scene. Small events like these are marginal to the way we usually talk about universities, but they are core to the way a university presents itself to its local community. In this chapter, my aim is to pull apart some of the threads that are woven through this minor scene, to reflect on how Australian universities relate to the real estate they claim as their own, and to examine the enabling relations between governance, property and function that are overlooked when we focus only on what these relations have produced. These questions have come up during a period of global disruption that has left Australian universities and their staff (as with many of their colleagues across the globe) reeling from austerity, restructure, and burnout. We know (and if we did not realise this before, we have been relentlessly briefed) that the market vulnerability revealed by the pandemic did not originate with border closures. So now we have an opportunity to ask whether we really should try to return to how we did business before, or can we imagine a more courageous reform that addresses the provenance of our campuses and thinks differently about the standards by which we will measure a future that is good?

Doreen Massey's thinking about space has influenced this reflection, along with Australian Raewyn Connell's (2019) manifesto for the good university, Kathleen Fitzpatrick's (2019) call to save the (American) university through generous thinking, and ideas drawn from Arthur Frank's (2004) earlier call for the remoralisation of healthcare through the renewal of generosity. I have found Maria Puig de La Bellacasa's (2012) reading of Donna Haraway on "thinking with care" specifically helpful. Universities are places where pragmatism and idealism run up against each other all the time. I am inclined to hope for the efficacy of small generous acts that can be undertaken while it is still difficult to imagine wholesale reform; and at the same time, I am concerned that generosity can become a ruse. Like Connell (2019), I am an advocate for the good university that has a "modest demeanour in the world" (p. 175), and this means thinking about how generosity can proceed from uncertainty and extend in tentative action.

In choosing this scene as a starting point, I am drawn to its anxious conversation with what it is compensating for. It presents as a kind of neocolonial landscape painting: a sincere attempt to manage ambivalence about international student recruitment by planting a tree on stolen Aboriginal land. Ambivalence clearly did not start with the pandemic, nor with the business model that the pandemic interrupted; in this scene there are much older problems of moral legitimacy. So, this event contains what we need to think about whether and how Australian public education can now become a form of higher education that is for good, in three senses. Firstly, can Australian universities *come good*, and recover from the crisis imposed on them by the pandemic? Secondly, can Australian universities somehow *become good*, despite the morally untenable silence in the enabling Acts that established them? And finally, can Australian universities overcome their own currently demoralising habits of operation and be *for good*, in ways that are both enduring and worth saving?

I am conscious that in commencing with this scene, I am offering a hyperlocal response to the broadest possible questions about higher education in other places. I hope that the ideas raised here will be useful to readers in other contexts, particularly those where coloniality persists. When we generalise about higher education as a global phenomenon, whether as a set of business arrangements or a life stage, we overlook that all higher education takes place somewhere, quite literally. As universities around the world, and especially in colonised places, begin to engage with the challenge of decolonising their scholarly routines, it is timely to accept that this must also unsettle their sense of the proper in relation to land entitlement.

Universities as encounters

In thinking about universities as people meeting somewhere to do something (plant a tree, conduct research, enrol as students or work as teachers), I want to begin with Doreen Massey's (2005) well known proposition that we think about all space as relational, constituted by the stories that bring people together:

> Precisely because space on this reading is a product of relations-between, relations which are necessarily embedded material practices which have to be carried out, it is always in the process of being made. It is never finished; never closed. Perhaps we could imagine space as a simultaneity of stories-so-far. (p. 9)

To imagine higher education as an unfinished "simultaneity of stories-so-far" invites us to wind back some of the institutional stories that appear in the event of this tree-planting. Massey speaks specifically to spaces wrenched into action by colonial relations. She reads colonialism itself as a "story about space", a legitimising narrative that attempts

> a particular form of ordering and organising space which refused (refuses) to acknowledge its multiplicities, its fractures and its dynamism. It is a stabilisation of the inherent instabilities and creativities of space; a way of coming to terms with the great 'out there'. (p. 65)

As remnant colonial infrastructure, Australian universities are narrating machines for a reason: across strategic plans, annual reports and marketing their stabilising stories discipline the unstable "out there" of students, funders, donors, governments, and publics, while refusing just as many stories of their founding purpose and legitimising themselves as the solution to the problem of the future. This storytelling is relentless and smooth, and when it comes to events and occasions, the story is placed under pressure by the multiple storylines that show up when people and institutions meet.

Like Massey, Arthur Frank reflects on encounters, in his case, in health. He has written extensively about the muddled and ambiguous communication that occurs when people who are ill meet people who work in healthcare. In a 2020 essay on his blog, he asks a question that is relevant to our tree-planting: can occasions think? He suggests that occasions are special types of these encounters, choreographing persons, places, ideas, and things. As much as they are planned, occasions are always immediately disorganised by competing expectations and the pressure of their own temporal intensity. Multiple stories collide, always on the verge of derailment. Even when the logistics run like clockwork, the coming together of so many stories and witnesses means that the event's meaning cannot be contained. Frank notices that this draws up an obligation to recognise that coherence has its limits:

> The ethical question this raises — at least *ethical* is the best I can think to call it, although the word seems inadequate; should I just say *human*? — is whether the participants in this situation can each remain self-aware that the other participants do not share their perspective. Something beyond *empathy* (a word I seek to avoid) is involved here; it's rather an awareness of the limits of fellow-feeling, the limits of what George Herbert Mead called taking the role of the other. To return to Davis's metaphor, can we put ourselves inside a Cubist painting and live with the fracturing of the lines that, in normal perception, make the scene around us cohere?

I am using Frank's question about how we live with incoherence to look beyond the specific occasion of this tree planting ceremony and its many trajectories of feeling, one of which is my own. Past the period of emergency border closures in Australia, those of us who work in higher education are also trying to live within an incoherent scene, crisscrossed by many possible histories and futures, some of which are looking uncertain. To think about this fracturing, to ask what it is that *matters* about all this, we need to start with the recent backstories and then the further-back-stories of internationalisation in Australian higher education.

Backstories

The immediate story of this tree planting scene emerges from the way the Australian government responded to the pandemic in 2020. In March, the government abruptly closed Australian borders to non-citizens and non-residents (Hutchens, 2022; Murphy & Karp, 2020). For Australian businesses in travel, retail, hospitality and tourism, the sudden loss of foreign income resulted in widespread crisis. Australian universities were also caught out in their chronic dependency on the fees of international students coming to Australia to study. Only a month later, the prime minister announced that international students who had been living, working, paying taxes and making an extraordinary direct and indirect contribution to the Australian economy should think about leaving (Gibson & Moran, 2020): "As much as it's lovely to have visitors to Australia in good times, at times like this, if you are a visitor in this country, it is time… to make your way home," he said.

As it turned out, many international students were already caught outside Australia, due to the late summer timing of the border closure. Meanwhile others who made the brave and difficult decision to ride out the pandemic in Australia learned that as non-citizens they were excluded from all government assistance when they lost their casual jobs. Stories of international students relying on Australian university food banks were reported around the world, as the border closure stretched into a second year. Universities put in place emergency teaching measures to support international students to stay enrolled while at home, but the contraction of fee revenue converged with the controversial exclusion of universities from government support to affected businesses (Norton, 2021; Ross, 2020). By 2021, 40,000 higher education jobs were lost through a combination of early retirement incentives, restructuring of administrative teams, and slashing of casual positions (Littleton & Stanford, 2021).

After extensive sector lobbying, late in 2021 the Australian federal government allowed some state governments to trial the return of international students into quarantine from a restricted range of countries on managed flights (NSW Government, 2021). This was not a trial of public health measures so much as a test of electoral tolerance for allowing non-citizens to return when so many Australian families were still separated. Nevertheless, after the first pilot flights, change was relatively quick. By February 2022, borders opened fully, and government incentives appeared to encourage international students to return promptly (Jose, 2022; Study International, 2022). These were not trivial measures: changes to post-study visa conditions, visa fee refunds, and lifting the cap on casual work hours have all been significant policy adjustments. These efforts at incentive acknowledged that market confidence in Australia might have slipped after two years of government and universities blaming each other for international student recruitment as a business problem. Without a blush, the Prime Minister described this package as a "thank you for choosing Australia" and added that it would be "incredibly helpful" to have international students "filling some of these critical workforce shortages, particularly those who are working and being trained in health care, aged care, those types of sectors" (ICEF Monitor, 2022).

The back and forth between universities and government during the pandemic is a chapter in a long history of lobbying and dispute over the support of Australian public higher education. This hinges on the question of mission: whether Australian universities are some form of essential national infrastructure, or export business continually at risk of market failure at home. In reality, like the Australian creative industries, they are a combination of the two. Gwilym Croucher and James Wagner's (2020) commissioned history of Australian universities takes a snapshot of the problem: "In adapting themselves to serve their communities, local and national, universities have collectively been the partners of government and have worked in the service of the nation" (p. 172). This partnership gives Australian governments leverage over what universities do and how they manage themselves, and that continual pressure on purpose means that we often find ourselves back at the question Hannah Forsyth asks in the conclusion of her study of the Australian university: *what sort of university do we want*? (Forsyth, 2014).

The answers to this question are mixed. At one level we persist with a vague claim to moral purpose dating back to Bologna, and cling to the ideal of advancing knowledge and teaching students to become educated and successful citizens. We reject retail language on principle: we don't think students should be thought of as customers just because they pay to study. Nevertheless, while governments and lobbyists haggle over the mix of disciplines, student places, and who pays, dependence on what had appeared to be a stable pipeline of fee-paying non-citizen students has increased in jumps since the 1950s. Periodically, this business vulnerability has raised alarms (Moodie, 2011). Nevertheless, as Croucher and Wagner (2020) put it, by 2017 "almost one third of Australia's higher education students came on a student visa" (p. 169). This vulnerability to the risk of a shift in demand was not unique to Australia: when international travel stopped suddenly in 2020, the global supply chain logistics of international education revealed themselves in ugly ways. As Raewyn Connell (2019) argues succinctly, the reality of this trafficking will continue to inhibit our progress towards the good university system, "since the international market in fee-paying students sucks money out of developing countries to pay universities in richer ones" (p. 191).

This was the immediate challenge facing Australian universities as international recruitment pipelines slowly started functioning again. While trying to come good, the risk has been lapsing into the way we acted before, treating international students as revenue inputs, and Australian students in terms of their life goals and contribution to the nation's prosperity. As many observers of public higher education notice, universities draw on public funding to deliver selective private gain, even if public funding is not enough to sustain them. This problem is not resolved by cross-subsidising inadequate public funding with a partial privatisation strategy that leaves some students paying significantly more for the same experience as those they subsidise. We now have to be far more careful in the way we think, plan, and talk about why we want to invite international students back to our universities. At the very least, we need to challenge the longstanding enthusiasm for international education as Australia's extractive export winner alongside coal and iron ore (Moodie, 2011).

And this will need to be addressed with something more than tree planting. Of course, it feels generous, creative, and hopeful to plant a tree. It engages our humility and our confidence all at once: we expect trees to outlive us, and certainly to outlast our working lives, but here we are *doing something for the planet*, instead of just digging things out of it. In Australian universities, where we lead research into climate solutions, we landscape campuses and plant native trees in environmentally conscientious ways. But this ceremonial sapling, and the ground it has been planted into, are part of a much older problem, one that we have been trying both to ignore and talk our way out of.

All-the-way-back stories

Planting a tree on a university campus is an act of humility, but it is also an exercise of power. To plant a tree carefully and with whatever intentions is to stake a claim to the ground you're planting into. This entitlement is assured in the enabling legislation that awards each

Australian university its property rights. The enabling Act of the university where this tree was planted defines the university's object as "the promotion, within the limits of the University's resources, of scholarship, research, free inquiry, the interaction of research and teaching, and academic excellence" (AustLII, n.d.). Underneath this object, its principal functions are laid out, conceived in broad terms to unite knowledge and citizenship under the shade of good governance.

> (2) The University has the following principal functions for the promotion of its object:
>
> (a) the provision of facilities for education and research of university standard, having particular regard to the needs of the Illawarra region,
>
> (b) the encouragement of the dissemination, advancement, development and application of knowledge informed by free inquiry,
>
> (c) the provision of courses of study or instruction across a range of fields, and the carrying out of research, to meet the needs of the community,
>
> (d) the participation in public discourse,
>
> (e) the conferring of degrees, including those of Bachelor, Master and Doctor, and the awarding of diplomas, certificates and other awards,
>
> (f) the provision of teaching and learning that engage with advanced knowledge and inquiry,
>
> (g) the development of governance, procedural rules, admission policies, financial arrangements and quality assurance processes that are underpinned by the values and goals referred to in the functions set out in this subsection, and that are sufficient to ensure the integrity of the University's academic programs.

This is an uncontroversial summary of what a university is supposed to do, but from the Act the university acquires no obligations to think about where it is located. The Act presents its own *terra nullius*: it is silent on "Aboriginal", "Indigenous" and "Country". There are however 22 mentions of "land" and an entire division of the Act dealing with the question of property. The conferral of property rights enables the Australian public university to exercise itself somewhere, and on this basis to reach everywhere: "within or outside the State, including outside Australia" (AustLII, n.d.). It establishes the legal means to buy, sell, lease, and build; for Australian universities these are the underpinning rights to a portfolio of property that sustains landmark buildings, bright signage, landscaping and tree planting. Real estate assets are critical to branding, and what Connell calls "the process of turning universities into spectacle" (Connell, 2019, p. 131).

The provenance of real estate is a moral problem for all Australian universities. It is not our land, and it did not belong to the British crown when Australia's universities were legislated. This problem cannot be symbolically managed by Acknowledging Country, a far more common university practice than tree planting. Acknowledging Country is a ritual that we share with other major Australian institutions. Across public and corporate contexts, occasions of all kinds — ceremonies, committee meetings, sporting fixtures, social events begin with an Acknowledgement of the specific Aboriginal Country where the event is taking place, and a statement of respect both to the traditional owners of that Country, and to any Aboriginal people present. Australian universities acknowledge the Country on which our campuses have been built, our governance is managed, our business divisions do business, our servers are housed, our repositories are looked after, and our research and face-to-face teaching take place. Australian university staff acknowledge Country in conferences, presentations and Zoom meetings. An Australian university will generate several Acknowledgements of Country a day, one way and another. At the very least, this should cause us to notice that the object and functions of an Australian university depend on property that was seized in violent raids whose marks of harm remain.

This means that if Australia's universities are to become good, our symbolic actions need to raise our accountability to the true owners of our real estate. Of course, it is daunting for Western institutions to imagine doing this, but just as Raewyn Connell makes the bold suggestion of a Tobin tax to developing countries whose students we recruit (Connell, 2019, p. 191), we need to look closer to home, and as a first step consider how to address the back rent we owe for the land we occupy. While we imagine that extraordinary step, we do not need to sit on our hands. We can begin to align ourselves to that future possibility by asking of all our business decisions: how does this choice or this action represent our acknowledgement that we are on Country? What obligations are placed on our institutions, and how should we behave?

Thinking in the world

Here I find the work of Maria Puig de La Bellacasa (2012) on "thinking with care" very helpful. She distinguishes care from "hegemonic ethics", and secures care instead to the principle of acknowledging where you stand:

> Thinking in the world involves acknowledging our own involvements in perpetuating dominant values, rather than retreating into the secure position of an enlightened outsider who knows better. (p. 197)

The first step is here: we can acknowledge that public universities are currently designed to operate conservatively in relation to dominant values. Their mission is to keep operating. As people who work on campuses that are somewhere, we are not enlightened outsiders. We are inside the scene, holding tightly to the deeds, protecting the future of things going on as they do now. This is why it is much easier to imagine changing the form of words for an Acknowledgement of Country, to commit to supporting federal constitutional change in relation to national sovereignty and political agency, to fund cultural initiatives that will change how and what we teach and to transform ceremonial occasions to centre on Indigenous cultural practices (as this university has done). It is more difficult to develop meaningful reparations and figure out how to meet our obligations in other than symbolic ways.

Puig de La Bellacasa (2012), carefully surveying Donna Haraway's work on relational ontology, identifies two modes of operation that could help those of us who work in Australian universities, and indeed in the HE sector broadly to face these challenges. First, she addresses the practicalities of "thinking-with" that might help us to conceive of the identity of a public institution as neither fixed nor fluid but in action, "continuously in the making" (p. 199). We can be cynical about fluidity as the hallmark of privilege but thinking-with is an important step towards accepting our obligations to others (Fitzpatrick, 2019, p. 52), and admitting that our objects and functions matter because they have material impact. Of course, this is not a novel way to think, but dominant cultural habits of thinking-about have catching up to do, to acknowledge the sophistication of thinking-with, including thinking-with Country itself that pre-existed Australian public universities by tens of thousands of years (Wright et al, 2021).

Puig de La Bellacasa's second discovery within Haraway's writing is that thinking-with means dissenting-within. Dissenting-within is a stubbornness of attention to things that need fixing in small ways. It is not about big or public gestures, but about the continuous labour of scrutiny and refusal. "In sum", she writes, "thinking-with belongs to, and creates, community by inscribing thought and knowledge in worlds one cares about in order *to make a difference*—a diffraction" (pp. 204–5). This caring to make a difference, in both senses, lets us see the lines that tether the tree planting scene to its histories and that pull together its problematic effort at coherence. If we can let these entangled storylines become visible, we are taking a step to see past the staged present with its essential flaws to a future that can be imagined differently. So, this second step, beyond recognition that the dominant culture is catching up, is to invite the dominant culture to own its moral vulnerability, rather than just fixing its exposure to risk. Puig de La Bellacasa (2012) writes:

> *Dissenting-within* is openness to the effects we might produce with critiques to worlds we would rather not endorse. Caring for the effects this way can make us particularly vulnerable. Recognizing vulnerability has been reclaimed as an ethical stance; in the practice of thinking-with, it comes as a consequence of accepting one's thought as inheritor, even of the threads of thought we oppose. It might be also the inescapable price of commitment: if care is to *move* a situation, those who care will also be moved by it. (p. 206)

Again, apprehension about the dominant culture bringing moral attention back to itself is valid. Dominant cultures have a track record of flattering themselves that they have discovered humility without loosening their grip on power. But reconciliation to our shared and alarming future cannot commence without the dominant culture going through a few things. As Puig de La Bellacasa (2012) puts it, dissenting-within is to be dissented with — to have to live up to and live with the "effects of one's thinking" (p. 207) in a public way.

Future stories

In closing, I want to think about how a turn to vulnerability could change the assumptions we have held about generosity as both national benefit and community contribution, drawing on recent thinking about generosity as a critique of the philanthropic mission. It is difficult for universities with their roots in the mud of colonial history to contribute to a good future. Intentional vulnerability is not the way Australian universities were established, and it is not the way that they have evolved. We have awarded ourselves the contract to advance the good future through our research and our education of citizens. Knowledge and innovation assure our status; we have become so used to seeking approval by being internationally well-ranked that we have lost sight of the value of local modest action. Our idea of generosity involves big gestures in our communities, while making good against the international competition.

In the US context, Kathleen Fitzpatrick (2019) proposes a sharp criticism of the philanthropic understanding of generosity in universities. She sees in the idealisation of generous sharing the risk of moral burnout, and an excuse:

> to draw boundaries around our responsibilities to the communities in which our institutions are embedded... As a result, we create specific contexts for our generous behaviour that lie outside the center of our working lives. Nothing about that center need necessarily change: we do what we do, and then we bring the good of what we do to the world. Generosity in this model slips all too easily into a missionary project, in which we provide the understanding derived from our privileged position to the less fortunate around us. And, having done so, we can consider our obligations to the world to be fulfilled. (pp. 50–51)

Instead of engaging in generous acts that risk nothing of our own, Fitzpatrick advocates for radically generous thought that critiques philanthropic action itself. Arthur Frank (2004) also points out the limits of philanthropic attention. Both see the case for a renewed understanding of generosity: not the heroics of public giving while giving nothing up, but more in the everyday and reciprocal encounters between people who can make a small difference to each other. This is the modest, local scale at which generous reform of object and function can begin. But it is not an easy cultural shift. Fitzpatrick (2019) argues that this demands rigorous commitment to obligation, and a refusal to let ourselves off the hook. This generosity is necessarily uncomfortable, and inconcludable, an open-ended and open-minded determination "of which we cannot absolve ourselves" (p. 51). It is founded in vulnerable thinking rather than philanthropic hubris, and it pulls together thinking-with and dissenting-within. Of course, this kind of vulnerable generosity presents challenges to the business of universities, especially in the retail hothouse of international student recruitment, but it is within our reach to think intelligently about how we change the way we think and act, and to ask ourselves what this new modest demeanour means for every strategic choice.

So, do we still have time for universities to achieve change at small scale, become good at this slow pace, and having sorted out their own houses make a just contribution to a good future? Can public systems that depend on private revenue streams engage with the urgency of dissenting-within while still staying open for good outcomes? Universities don't have the privilege of downtime: all change has to happen live and incrementally, while workers depend on employment, students are enrolled and progressing through their degrees, and multinational research projects are underway. The perpetual activity of the public university means finding a way instead to think in the thick of the everyday choices, enactments, and routines that interpellate universities, their staff, and their students as themselves. It means allowing ourselves to become and remain uneasy when we know that something feels wrong, and to continue with patience to advocate for change.

In this chapter, I have been thinking about the ways in which, at any given ceremonial moment, a university can look like a scene in which "there's no change, there's no pace, everything within its place" (Delaney, 2015). To staff who are demoralised by living with misgivings about all of this, to students who facing an uncertain and expensive future, to communities who are not sure where their investment in higher education is taking them, to governments of all kinds, and above all to the true owners of the land universities are built on — to all these stakeholders, the way Australian universities have been operating, and the business risks they been taking, can make them seem out of touch with present realities and not fit for future purpose. Universities are easy to give up on. But sometimes a commitment to a good future begins with a simple refusal to give up trying.

A good future for higher education, and not just a future in which we're keeping the lights on, is a challenge that will involve new kinds of partnerships between universities and their communities. These partnerships, especially with true owners, will involve slow progress, significant mistakes, and the need for persistent, small scale, generous acknowledgement that this is hard. Locating generosity within vulnerability, we will have to ask for public and government support for an agenda of courageous reform over the long term. This kind of change is not a quick win. The courage to confront the provenance of our real estate would place the property portfolio at risk, as it should, and land back may not happen in any of our lifetimes. This is what makes it radical and worth cherishing as a dream.

Even to imagine such a move, let alone to lobby for it, is to plant a sapling in our imagination. And now that we have thought of it, it is already growing, and might yet come to be seen for miles.

Postscript

This is an essay written from a position of ambivalence, but not from bad faith. I work in internationalisation at the university where this sapling was planted, and I was the person who suggested planting it. The suggestion was met with warmth at every turn. Change is complex.

References

AustLII (n.d.). *New South Wales consolidated acts*. http://www8.austlii.edu.au/cgi-bin/viewdb/au/legis/nsw/consol_act/uowa1989316/

Connell, R. (2019). *The good university: What universities actually do and why it's time for radical change*. Zed Books.

Croucher, G., & Waghorne, J. (2020). *Australian universities: A history of common cause*. University of New South Wales Press.

Delaney, B. (2015, October 6). Cold chisel: Writing Australia's unofficial national anthems since 1973. *The Guardian*. https://www.theguardian.com/music/2015/oct/06/cold-chisel-writing-australias-unofficial-national-anthems-since-1973

Fitzpatrick, K. (2019). *Generous thinking: A radical approach to saving the university*. Johns Hopkins University Press.

Forsyth, H. (2014). *A history of the modern Australian university*. University of New South Wales Press.

Frank, A. W. (2004). *The renewal of generosity: Illness, medicine, and how to live.* University of Chicago Press.

Frank, A. W. (2020, June 9). *Can occasions think? Narrative, experience and ethics.* Arthur W. Frank.
https://arthurwfrank.wordpress.com/2020/06/09/can-occasions-think/

Gibson, J., & Moran, A. (2020, April 4). As coronavirus spreads, "it's time to go home" Scott Morrison tells visitors and international students. *ABC News online.*
https://www.abc.net.au/news/2020-04-03/coronavirus-pm-tells-international-students-time-to-go-to-home/12119568

Hutchens, G. (2022, February 9). The impact of Australia's closed borders: These four graphs tell the story. *ABC News online.*
https://www.abc.net.au/news/2022-02-09/four-charts-tell-the-story-of-australias-closed-borders/100813560

ICEF Monitor. (2022, January 26). *Australia further eases work rights and offers visa fee refunds for returning students.*
https://monitor.icef.com/2022/01/australia-further-eases-work-rights-and-offers-visa-fee-refunds-for-returning-students/

Jose, R. (2022, February 21). *Welcome back world! Australia fully reopens borders after two years.* Reuters.
https://www.reuters.com/world/asia-pacific/australia-fully-reopens-borders-shut-by-covid-pandemic-welcomes-back-tourists-2022-02-20/

Littleton, E., & Stanford, J. (2021, September 13). *An avoidable catastrophe: Pandemic job losses in higher education and their consequences.* Analysis and Policy Observatory.
https://apo.org.au/node/314011

Massey, D. (2005). *For space.* Sage Publications.

Moodie, A. (2011, March 6). *Australia: Long history of international higher education.* University World News.
https://www.universityworldnews.com/post.php?story=20110305121304874

Murphy, K., & Karp, P. (2020, March 19). Australian government moves to close borders as new coronavirus cases continue to rise. *The Guardian.*
https://www.theguardian.com/world/2020/mar/19/australian-government-moves-to-close-borders-as-new-coronavirus-cases-continue-to-rise

Norton, A. (2021, July 6). *Would universities have received JobKeeper under more favourable rules?* Andrew Norton.
https://andrewnorton.net.au/2021/07/06/would-universities-have-received-jobkeeper-under-more-favourable-rules/

NSW Government. (2021, September 24). *Pilot plan to return international students.*
https://www.nsw.gov.au/media-releases/pilot-plan-to-return-international-students

Puig de la Bellacasa, M. (2012). Nothing comes without its world: Thinking with care. *The Sociological Review, 60*(2), 197–216. https://doi.org/10.1111/j.1467-954X.2012.02070.x

Rezelska, A. (2021, December 10). *You are part of the University's DNA—UOW welcomes back international students*. University of Wollongong, Australia. https://www.uow.edu.au/media/2021/you-are-part-of-the-universitys-dna--uow-welcomes-back-international-students-.php

Ross, J. (2020, July 21). *Australian PM: no special deal for universities on bailouts*. Times Higher Education. https://www.timeshighereducation.com/news/australian-pm-no-special-deal-universities-bailouts

Study International. (2022, March 1). *Perks for international students who return to Australia*. https://www.studyinternational.com/news/australias-international-border-perks/

Wright, S., Lloyd, K., Suchet-Pearson, S, Burarrwanga, L., Tofa, M., & Bawaka Country. (2012). Telling stories in, through and with Country: Engaging with Indigenous and more-than-human methodologies at Bawaka, NE Australia. *Journal of Cultural Geography. 29*(1), 39–60. https://doi.org/10.1080/08873631.2012.646890

Section IV
Making Change through Teaching, Assessment and Learning Design

'Little Me' by Sheila MacNeill (CC BY 4.0)

Note from the artist

This work is based on a work which I created as part of a collaborative project for the NPA Lab 2021 Collaborative Online Exhibition. Our project was titled "Copped Out" and used the COP26 Climate Change Conference as its central theme.

Living in Glasgow, I was intensely aware of the impacts of the conference — both at local and global levels. One of the most profound experiences for me was a night time march with Little Amal, the 2m puppet who has walked from Syria to Europe. Watching and following

Little Amal as part of a torch lit parade was an intensely emotional experience. Hearing small children ask questions about the why and how of her reminded me of the importance of education and sharing lived experiences of the impact of our actions.

The puppet has an almost hyper real presence, embodying struggle, fear, resistance, hope but most importantly, humanity. Education is the key to all our futures, signifiers such as Little Amal bring the plight and stories of real people to those who are currently protected from the ravages of human cruelty and climate change. Her presence creates new empathy, understanding and new narratives, providing hope. I hope that this image provides some synergies with the narratives of hope being shared in this book.

16. A design justice approach to Universal Design for Learning: Perspectives from the Global South

Aleya Ramparsad Banwari, Philip Dambisya, Benedict Khumalo, and Kristin van Tonder

This chapter focuses on the issue of exclusion in higher education and how to promote inclusivity by implementing Universal Design for Learning (UDL) principles within a larger social and design justice context. The chapter critically analyses the strengths and challenges of a UDL approach within a Global South context, highlighting how social and design justice can be attained by focusing on broad conceptions of access and equity. The chapter documents the experiences of four postgraduate students in their roles as educational technology advisors (ETAs) at the University of Cape Town, outlining collaborative insights arising from the authors' varied positionalities and disciplinary backgrounds (Friedman, 1998; Kim, 2016). The chapter seeks to offer a challenge to established epistemological paradigms that regard the core nature of knowledge as impartial and absolute, as well as to catalyse more significant insights into inclusive, accessible, and socio-culturally responsive education practices in higher education.

Introduction

It is long established that formal education, in its role to meet the needs of the nations within which it is situated, can be as exclusionary as it can be liberating and empowering (Boughey, 2012; Khalid & Pedersen, 2016; Steyaert, 2005). Interwoven with the social, cultural, political, and economic dynamics of societies and the world at large, education and its exclusionary mechanisms extend beyond the physical structures of teaching and learning. Issues such as perpetuated language barriers and ableism permeate the fabric of higher education (HE). Educational exclusion impedes a student's learning experience, the direct consequence of socioeconomic conditions occurring outside of the academic realm (Sayed, 2003). Being unheard and underrepresented can cause students to feel alienated in their educational journey.

In this chapter, we consider UDL in the broader context of design justice and social justice. South Africa faces many challenges in the HE sector due to rising inequality, lack of stable access to electricity and other services, and high data costs, amongst many others. Historically, "the university" in South Africa as an institution of HE has been systemically exclusionary by perpetuating practices, values, and beliefs aimed at helping to further the interests of colonialists and, presently, the Global North (Brodkin et al., 2011). This extends into the realm of digital colonialism practices, in which institutions in the Global North develop much of the content that is utilised in the Global South. This is often done without consultation or contextualisation of who this content will be taught to and under what circumstances. The reasons that knowledge generated in the Global North is dominant are multiple, sometimes including the cost of materials and the lack of equivalent materials in the Global South; itself perhaps a by-product of the reach that material generated in the Global North has historically had. Unfortunately, the result remains the same: such practices implicitly privilege knowledge generated in the Global North instead of knowledge generated in the Global South (Adam, 2020). A social justice approach may aid in highlighting and then addressing these exclusionary practices.

Social justice, design justice, and Universal Design for Learning

Social justice can be framed as fairness in distributing wealth, resources, and opportunities (Fraser, 2005). The economic challenge of access to technology for some students, in conjunction with the aforementioned cultural issue of privileged epistemologies and the political issue of neo-colonialism, can be galvanising points to explore curriculum design and, by extension, design justice.

Understood as an "ethical praxis of world-making" (Escobar, 2018, p. 21), design is an integral feature in understanding the world around us. Design often reproduces existing hegemonic worldviews, which can silence marginalised communities and different ways of being (Escobar, 2018). There have been considerable strides made towards addressing this exclusion through better integration of technologies and more epistemologically driven means, such as Achille Mbembe's concept of the "decolonial pluriversity" (Reinders, 2019). A decolonial pluriversity is a space where a multitude of knowledge systems can exist on equal footing through dialogue, allowing for greater accessibility and a greater diversity of thought (Mbembe, 2015). It is impossible to achieve a decolonial pluriversity without addressing the underlying structures that prevent transformation from taking place (Luckett & Shay, 2017).

We argue that to achieve decolonial pluriversity, one must be cognisant of existing inequities, which manifest through curriculum design and dissemination in addition to socioeconomic and political equities. Only once we acknowledge existing inequities can we genuinely aim to combat ongoing disparities. The implementation of design justice can be used to bring this change about (Boidin et al., 2012).

Design justice brings to light how the design of objects, systems, and structures affect the production and distribution of risks, harms, and benefits among various people (Costanza-Chock, 2020). Design justice approaches can ensure a more equitable distribution of a design's benefits and burdens in a manner that promotes accessibility, thus allowing for more meaningful participation in design decisions and subsequent proceedings. Accessibility or the ease of access to information, services, or knowledge is critical to design justice in HE. A curriculum that empowers all people, strengthens societal dynamics, and addresses local needs should be the norm. Though a global commitment toward inclusive education exists, ways to actualise it are still being sought. UDL can be one step towards this commitment (Karisa, 2022).

Universal Design for Learning has gained international attention as a promising framework for reducing barriers to education and developing equitable, quality learning for all (McKenzie & Dalton, 2020; McKenzie et al., 2021; Zhang & Zhao, 2019). The goal of UDL is to design educational experiences that allow all students to match their unique ways of learning to varied modes of engagement, information representation, and expression of learning (CAST, 2018; McKenzie & Dalton, 2020).

Originating from disability accommodations in primary and secondary education settings, its proponents claim that it can also improve learning and inclusion for all students in HE settings (CAST, 2018). Inclusive practices are needed for all learners regardless of learning needs, socioeconomic status, and socio-political standing. It is envisaged that the UDL framework and its underpinning principles can enable design justice through intentionally redesigned courses for accessibility, equity, and inclusivity. Such an approach to course redesign may serve as a vehicle to actualise this. For example, providing well-described video lectures with closed captioning and transcripts ensures that students with hearing and visual impairments can engage meaningfully in lessons.

Our theoretical framework utilises Nancy Fraser's concept of social justice (2005), which contains three dimensions: economic, cultural, and political. These three dimensions speak to three key issues to help address injustice: redistribution (economic), recognition (cultural), and representation (political). In an educational context, redistribution refers to the equitable distribution of resources, including monetary resources for access to university. Recognition refers to ensuring equal access to a rich and intensive curriculum for students of all backgrounds. Representation refers to increased mechanisms for marginalised voices to be heard. For example, there should be a forum or platform for students who are differently abled to be heard (Fraser, 2005; Keddie, 2012).

Furthermore, recognition means that all stakeholders in the HE sector must be seen as "full partners in social interaction", allowing for increased participation (Fraser, 2000) of lecturers, students, external examiners, and representatives of government, industry, and civil society. Recognition and representation feed into one another. If we can provide recognition to marginalised communities in HE sectors, and give them a platform to be heard, we can enable representation (Caden, 2012). Social justice must be grounded in design justice. Design justice is defined by Costanza-Chock (2020) as:

a framework for analysis of how design distributes benefits and burdens between various groups of people.... Design justice is also a growing community of practice that aims to ensure a more equitable distribution of design's benefits and burdens; meaningful participation in design decisions; and recognition of community-based, Indigenous, and diasporic design traditions, knowledge, and practices. (p. 23)

UDL acts as a framework for a more equitable distribution of the design benefits of curriculum and learning design (see Figure 16.1).

Figure 16.1

Locating social justice within UDL, design justice, and cultural justice

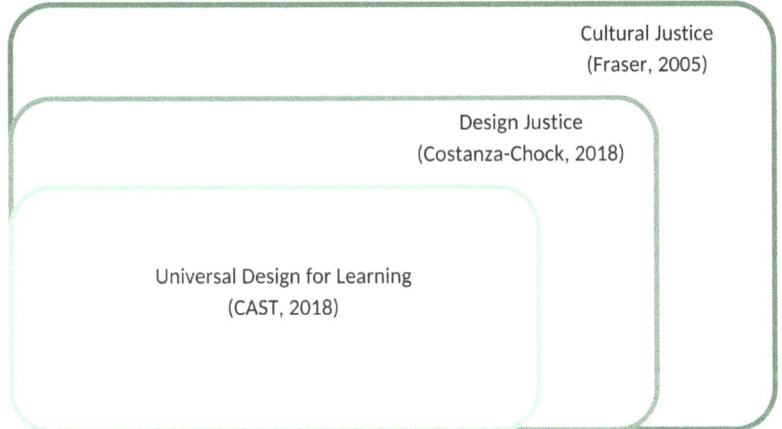

Considering UDL in a Global South context

Universal Design for Learning is a framework initially developed by the Center for Applied Special Technology (CAST) to provide a blueprint for a learning design process that will be equitable and inclusive (McKenzie & Dalton, 2020). Since its conception, UDL has been utilised as an increasingly popular framework in the education sector of countries in North America and Europe (McKenzie & Dalton, 2020). The UDL framework is built on the three pillars of "representation, action and expression, and engagement" (McKenzie & Dalton, 2020,

p. 4). These three principles are based on areas in the brain responsible for recognition, strategy, and affect (McKenzie & Dalton, 2020). They emphasise student diversity by advocating for multiple and appropriate forms of representation, action and expression, and engagement when designing a learning experience (McKenzie & Dalton, 2020). The principle of *multiple means of representation* refers to providing students with various ways of accessing learning material and the learning process. Practically, this can mean providing transcripts of voice recordings or videos or making infographics with alternative text on the content available to be accessible to students who are auditorily or visually impaired. Providing students with *multiple means of action and expression* will create opportunities for students to convey what they have learned in diverse ways. For instance, this can mean that some students will be assessed using a traditional written examination while others may opt for an oral examination. Finally, *multiple means of engagement* in UDL refer to how students learn and interact with the course material. By providing different methods of engagement, a more diverse range of students can be included in the learning experience.

UDL has become a central tenet in many North American and European HE institutions, where it is positioned as a paradigm for inclusivity that is premised on principles of sustainability (Fovet, 2020). This, in turn, allows for a reduced burden on accessibility services, as the needs of students can be addressed in the classroom itself, and can also lower the total expense while still revolutionising how we perceive education. These strong claims made about UDL motivated the writing of this section, which critically examines the successes of the implementation of UDL and addresses some of the barriers to learning that UDL unwittingly fails to consider.

UDL in the Global South

Since its inception, much has been written about UDL with most of the research centred on North America and Europe respectively (Cai & Robinson, 2021; Fovet, 2020; Olaussen et al., 2019). As UDL gains greater attention as a paramount inclusion in educational policy and practice, the need to understand how it is utilised in contexts outside the regions mentioned above becomes more crucial. As a result, this section explores the application of UDL in the Global South. The Global South broadly refers to the regions of Africa, Asia, Latin America, and Oceania.

There is a recognition that UDL has the potential to engage students, improve social inclusion, lead to higher achievement outcomes, and reduce the risk of stigma for marginalised students, including those with disabilities (Almumen, 2020; Lowrey et al., 2017; Mackey, 2019). The UDL framework recognises the individuality of learners and can facilitate more collaborative approaches and increased digital inclusion if support structures are implemented that enhance equity and accessibility. UDL's features of openness, flexibility, and foresight can enlighten teaching and learning practice, moving the focus of teaching methods from the curriculum and texts to the needs of and relevance to the learners.

Much like the broader concept of inclusive education, UDL has often been adopted as a way better to integrate learners with disabilities into the academic mainstream. Additionally, more focus is placed on the use of technology. Perspectives from the Global South appear to be breaking from this trend as they focus on how UDL can be used to enhance education and accessibility of all students, considering the barriers and different ways it can be applied. For example, Chiwandire (2019) explored how established UDL principles inform HE curricula in South Africa, while Al-Azawei, Parslow, and Lundqvist (2017) studied the direct application of UDL to strengthen e-learning acceptance at an institution in Iraq. Karr, Hayes, and Hayford (2020) posit that should educators in Ghana start receiving training in UDL, improved academic performances and a reduction in the stigma around people with disabilities may be seen. Zhang and Zhao (2019) share a similar sentiment and suggest that the autonomy and expressiveness that UDL seeks to cultivate may bolster Chinese education. However, the way it is currently being implemented is still deeply rooted in the instructor's pedagogy, indicating that instructors still need further support to change their traditional teaching philosophy and better utilise UDL technologies.

Across the literature, it is evident that the application of a UDL framework has generally failed to recognise the unequal power relations between the Global North and Global South (Fovet, 2020; Grech, 2011; Miles & Singal, 2010; Song, 2017). In low- and middle-income countries

(LMICs), there has been a limited amount of scholarship on UDL, and UDL experts and authors could be criticised for disregarding this geopolitical aspect of education (Benton Kearney, 2022). It is of utmost importance that the movement cultivates a culture where concepts such as power, privilege, and post-colonialism are critically examined and critiqued. The future of UDL in HE depends on the discourse consistently identifying the Global North/Global South divide and focusing more on embedding and magnifying perspectives from the South (Fovet, 2020).

There are significant barriers to implementing the UDL framework in the Global South. These include large class sizes, lack of resources, and lack of staff awareness regarding inclusive design (Ferguson et al., 2019; Maree, 2015; Song, 2016). A shortage of support professionals to guide educators in adapting their teaching, inaccessible environments, and an absence of effective screening and identification services exacerbates academic exclusion and implementation of interventions such as incorporating UDL into the teaching and learning space (McKenzie et al., 2021). Additionally, from our own experiences as education technology advisors (ETAs), it is evident that some educators may resist using UDL. For example, promoting accessibility and diverse learning environments is associated with a higher workload. One of the goals of UDL is to create expert learners (Rose et al., 2021). In other words, allowing learners to be the champion of their learning process.

Finally, there are other barriers that are barely addressed in the UDL guidelines. These are barriers that are faced by students who have been excluded, marginalised, or diminished because of their skin colour, language, ethnicity, gender, and/or sexual orientation. There is plenty of evidence that such students face barriers and low expectations. However, there is little evidence that the UDL guidelines are either relevant or attentive to these kinds of identity barriers they face (Griful-Freixenet et al., 2017; Rose et al., 2021). A scoping review by McKenzie et al. (2021) highlighted that UDL applications in LMICs tend not to utilise an intersectional lens well enough. For example, disability, gender, race, and socioeconomic status are not examined in consideration of each other.

Implementation of UDL

The COVID-19 lockdown pushed education sectors across the world to move teaching and learning to online platforms. The University of Cape Town (UCT) was no exception, as it encountered many challenges during the pivot to emergency remote teaching and learning. The UCT Centre for Innovation in Learning and Teaching (CILT) recognised that there was a gap in translating educational content into accessible online learning. As part of a Redesigning Blended Courses project in 2020, eight postgraduate students from various backgrounds were appointed to the roles of ETAs. The primary task of ETAs was to support teaching staff to design inclusive, digitally enabled education with a UDL-centred approach strategically aligned with UCT's Vision 2030. Recent findings suggest that the situatedness of those designing courses and curricula fundamentally affects the course released to students (Adam, 2020). ETAs were considered to be well-equipped to promote accessible and inclusive learning and teaching environments and materials because they are students and are more likely to understand the challenges that students may face. The ETAs underwent two weeks of training where they learnt about inclusivity and accessibility in relation to blended course design. Further topics covered were on student diversity and learning needs in HE, UDL, accessibility, disability and guidelines for accessible curriculum and educational content design, with reference to relevant tools and multimedia.

This chapter's four authors formed part of the ETA cohort. We hail from a diverse set of backgrounds academically (disability studies, public health, education, and anthropology), and personally in terms of race, gender, sexuality, abilities, and disabilities. All of us had been students during a time of significant change in South African HE, punctuated by movements such as Rhodes Must Fall (2015), Fees Must Fall (2016–2018), and the gender-based violence protests of 2018 and 2019.

Our primary role as ETAs was to offer support to teaching staff to create inclusive, accessible, and multimedia-rich learning materials and activities based on UDL principles and Web Content Accessibility Guidelines (WCAG). These efforts aimed to enhance student access and inclusion in blended courses for improved student learning outcomes.

This entailed working with lecturers and learning designers to ensure that any materials produced for learning complied with UDL and accessibility standards.

Our experiences as ETAs

In general, using UDL as a framework within a broader design justice approach was valuable in realigning focus on the diversity of our students in the university. Rather than creating a "one-size-fits-all" online learning experience, this approach to UDL allowed us to design different learning pathways. As noted earlier, the three core principles upon which the UDL framework is built are principles of representation, action and expression, and engagement (McKenzie & Dalton, 2020).

In our roles as ETAs, we ensured multiple means of engagement for students by providing video recordings of lectures with closed captions which were accompanied by transcriptions of the lectures. This allowed students to choose whether they would want to listen to the recording or read through the transcript. Another way in which engagement was fostered was by ensuring a streamlined design of the learning pathway on the learning management system (LMS), including detailed instructional text for all learning activities. This approach was especially helpful in supporting student engagement in short educational courses, as many students were unfamiliar with online learning. A more straightforward design allowed for easier site navigation. In disciplines such as accounting and health sciences, a checklist of learning outcomes was included at the end of each topic, encouraging students to engage with the content systematically. This was particularly helpful in a content-heavy discipline like accounting and self-paced courses for working students in the health sciences, promoting self-regulatory skills.

The UDL principle of multiple means of representation was accomplished by providing students with an array of text, audio, and visual representations of content. In some health sciences courses, infographics were created to simplify complex concepts. These infographics include alternative text for students using screen readers. Another visual enhancement added to course sites was introducing each topic with a flow chart, summarising the learning pathway for the topic. Each topic was also introduced with an introductory video (with closed captions) to give students a broad overview and the necessary background knowledge. ETAs from the science disciplines were especially adept at providing a student's perspective on what constitutes a conducive learning pathway, with one ETA creating such a user-friendly learning pathway for chemistry courses that they have been asked to provide the same treatment to other chemistry courses at UCT. In addition, the two ETAs in the education discipline provided theoretically grounded perspectives on improving students' learning experiences.

Multiple means of action and expression were enacted in various ways. First, several options for the physical act of responding to content were created. For instance, in using the comment tool on the LMS, students were able to post a written response, an audio or video clip, or a pictorial reply. Other tools in the LMS, such as the forum tool, allowed students to post their responses in diverse media. Additional communication tools were also incorporated such as Padlet and Twitter. Student expression was also guided by prompting questions on the content, helping to ensure meaningful engagement and expression.

The implementation of all three main principles of UDL using a design justice approach is perhaps best exemplified by a first-year course in the humanities that one of the chapter's authors worked on. This course was well-designed and extremely inclusive. The class comprised over one hundred students, the majority of whom were from low-income communities and were isiXhosa first language speakers. This course was designed to make the segue into academic writing, reading, and speaking easier. Keeping the demographic composition of the class in mind, the course convenor worked with the tutors to ensure that the course outline and instructional texts were provided in both English and isiXhosa. The tutors also created WhatsApp groups for their tutorial groups to check in with their students. Students who struggled with internet connectivity could conduct their tutorial discussions over WhatsApp. These actions helped to ensure that students were supported in terms of language (UDL Guidelines Checkpoint 2.4. Promote understanding across language), but also helped to ensure no students fell through the cracks by communicating with students through a less "formal" platform such as WhatsApp. This flexibility in learning methods (which is in line with UDL Guidelines Checkpoint

5.1. Use multiple media for communication) helped to ensure student success for students who may otherwise have fallen through the cracks because of their lack of connectivity, and ability to connect with tutors and classmates.

Key insights based on our experiences implementing UDL with a focus on design justice

Throughout this project, we realised that a design justice-focused implementation of UDL is complex and requires resources and sufficient time for planning and implementation. In terms of engagement, we noticed that an overemphasis on providing multiple pathways of engagement through many online activities could cause students to become overwhelmed and lose engagement. Another issue encountered was a lack of digital literacy from students, which inhibited meaningful engagement as students struggled to access many of the representations of content. Here, time and budget constraints also played a role. For instance, a visually impaired student had issues with accessibility in one course. Many concessions had to be provided manually, such as providing alternative text to graphics in the reading material or manually creating transcripts of video resources. This proved to be time-consuming. In addition, the physical action of expression proved challenging to some students, like accessing forum discussions or comment sections. Without allocating sufficient time and resources to developing competency in a UDL-adapted curriculum, the framework will fail due to the increased pressures and frictions that arise from adopting different pedagogies too rapidly.

Undertaking this work required awareness of challenges within our specific Global South context. Not all students have access to technology or a home environment conducive to studying. Approaches that minimise educational inequality in a digitally-enabled education must be taken. The challenge of promoting equitable education is further exacerbated by the growing diversity of the student body and resource inequalities. In the South African HE sector, resource inequalities have been at the forefront of the discussion through movements such as #FeesMustFall and, even more recently, during emergency remote teaching because of the digital divide becoming even starker (Czerniewicz et al., 2020).

For example, the cost of data in our context may prevent students from completing online learning activities such as quizzes and polls.

Another challenge we encountered was that while there was the intention to design courses that promoted accessibility and inclusion, there was room for improvement in the implementation of these guidelines in course design. Under the UDL principle of multiple means of action and expression, one checkpoint highlights the need to develop executive functions such as goal setting, strategy development and management of resources and information. This guideline is something we, as the ETA team, must consider. Hence, when designing courses on the LMS, the ETAs and broader learning design team included "checklists" on each lesson page so students could tick off tasks, and thus measure their progress through the course.

A significant challenge for one of our ETAs, who is visually impaired, was the lack of accessibility to build content on the LMS. The site is also often inaccessible for students depending on assistive devices for learning. Another challenge faced by one of the authors was lack of sufficient time to build a first-year archaeology site. This course focused heavily on the UDL principle of multiple means of action and expression, so there were many activities and exercises for the students to do. The setting up of these activities and exercises took a great deal of time because it required the creation of activity resources, such as images for the students to sort through. The setting up of such a course is highly beneficial for online students as it allows for options for physical action, and it is visually engaging. However, a total of three students registered for the course. While the content is valuable and can be reused in the future, it would have been more practical to design the course with fewer activities to suit a smaller class size, as some of the activities may have been better suited to a larger group of students. Our hope is that by identifying these challenges, barriers to inclusive education for all can be recognised and removed.

Principles of UDL to take forward in HE for good

In line with the core focus of this book, *Higher Education for Good*, we consider two questions in relation to our UDL project at UCT: What does learning for good look like? How could we re-imagine higher education futures for good?

The COVID-19 pandemic revealed multiple alternative teaching and learning futures. As a result of COVID-19 restrictions, universities had to adopt remote teaching strategies, which involved lecturers recording themselves teaching and adapting their teaching approaches and resources to be suitable for online use. The unanticipated pivot to remote online teaching and learning, at least in our UCT context, encouraged design approaches to accommodate different ways of knowledge being consumed and created.

However, these futures are still not yet realised, as we have gleaned through our dual roles as both students and ETAs. As we have discussed throughout this chapter, this process of transition between different teaching and learning modalities is difficult and uncomfortable. After teaching in-person on campus for many years, it was uncomfortable for lecturers who were being asked to teach online, often from their homes. It was uncomfortable for students who were trying to study and attend online lectures from home environments which may not be conducive to studying for several reasons. Also, it was uncomfortable because this shift to online learning requires more time, effort, and resources than the way teaching had traditionally been undertaken. Thus, a key theme that kept emerging when discussing our role was that of finding comfort in discomfort. How could we ease the discomfort during the transformation of pedagogical spaces such as the classroom?

We observed discomfort arise at many different intersections for students, teaching staff, and support staff. In addition to the personal toll of the pandemic, all these groups were experiencing heavy workloads, digital fatigue, and uncertainty — socially, economically, and politically. When considering teaching and learning futures, we must remember that "we cannot return to the world as it was before" (United Nations, 2020). The educational disruption caused by the pandemic has far-reaching consequences that we still do not fully understand. To prevent this crisis from causing further harm, it requires us to be resilient — not just as individuals, but systemically.

The United Nations (2020) highlighted the importance of building resilient education systems that can respond to immediate challenges but are also able to cope with unknown future crises. They emphasise that this can be made possible by focusing not just on access but also on inclusion and equity. To build resilient educational systems that can accommodate unforeseen changes, we need more than just technology. We need to share resources and teachings, reflect on past practices, consider how we can improve, and perhaps most importantly, we need to do all this with care and compassion. We are still at significant risk of creating a negative feedback loop of losing students through means of exclusion and a lack of accommodation.

So, how can we design and ensure alternative, inclusive, digitally enabled HE futures in which all students are encouraged and supported to reach their full learning potential? We have three recommendations, taken from our experiences, on how this future can be successfully achieved:

1. Student and faculty collaboration

An essential requirement under the UDL guideline of engagement is fostering community and collaboration. This does not simply apply to learners, but it applies to all involved in teaching and learning spaces. As ETAs, we can attest from our experience that the building of course sites is a collaborative task. There are many checks and balances in place when a course is being built. In our case, a course is usually built by an ETA who is supervised and assisted by a learning designer. Academic staff provide the content for the course and are there to offer feedback on the build and useability of the site. This process goes back and forth until both parties are happy. This whole process is overseen by a head learning designer who oversees the coordination of many courses within a discipline or faculty. Learning designers and educational technologists can teach lecturers how to engage students in online discussions to support learning. They can also collaborate with lecturers to determine how to best use technology for teaching and how to make the most of online/blended learning (Houlden & Veletsianos, 2020).

2. Focus on strategy, planning and resources for inclusive design

It is essential to remember that successful online education is not just about giving students information and expecting them to learn it. Ensuring that a digitally enabled education is accessible and inclusive requires careful planning and intelligent design. Such planning must take place at the conceptual level of course design to ensure that courses include rather than accommodate others into the learning process.

Based on our own experience, we found attending webinars and events about UDL and accessible education most valuable. This allowed us to learn from other educators and practitioners in the space about how they design and plan inclusive educational resources and content. Three of the authors of this chapter presented at a webinar panel titled "Promoting UDL principles and strategies for inclusive learning: The Redesigning Blended Courses Project at the University of Cape Town", hosted by INCLUDE and UCT in September 2021. Presenting on this panel provided a platform for us as ETAs to share our experiences with others from different HE institutions in other parts of the world who were also trying to implement UDL in their settings. More importantly, this webinar allowed us to learn from other attendees and improved how we implement UDL. We also found attending other webinars hosted by other universities, such as the Digitally Enhanced Education Webinars from the University of Kent to be particularly useful. We also noted that when learning about educational strategies used in the Global North, some recommendations would have to be adapted to suit our local context in the Global South.

3. Share resources and strategies

Institutions of HE should prioritise internal departmental collaboration as well as external collaboration with other HE institutions. These collaborations will ensure that departments and institutions benefit from each other's experiences. Within the CILT department, we hosted a weekly academic reading group which included both students and staff. These weekly sessions allowed for mutual learning and teaching between these two groups. These reading groups provided a forum for both groups to talk their way into and around scholarly topics, which allowed us to become familiar with discipline-specific terminology. As we were exposed to more literature, we were able to engage with various interpretations and approaches to educational pedagogy. Reading groups provide a great way for us to work with texts in the company of others, thus deepening our collective knowledge of scholarship on topics like UDL, social justice and blended learning, as well as (importantly) how we practise them (Thomson, 2021).

Furthermore, the integration of open education resources (OER) needs to be made an imperative. In collaborating and utilising OERs more readily, a practice of accessible information unhindered by physical and socioeconomic barriers becomes more of a reality (Butcher, 2015). These are beneficial strategies developed in one course. If these strategies could be shared with different departments at the university, others may benefit and ultimately help other students and teaching staff who may face a similar predicament.

Conclusion

The traditional pedagogical approach of "one-size-fits-all" cannot meet learner diversity in a contemporary academic milieu. As the student population in HE continues to diversify and the delivery of teaching changes (face-to-face, online, and blended), it is imperative to design curricula that effectively support and promote diversity and equity. UDL guidelines advocate for an inclusive instructional approach by minimising barriers and maximising learning for all students. University students can directly benefit from two major aspects of UDL: (a) its emphasis on a flexible curriculum and (b) the inclusion of a variety of instructional practices, materials, and learning activities. UDL is an educational framework that can effectively support university lecturers and learning designers in designing and developing curricula that are accessible to as many diverse learners as possible.

In this chapter, we have demonstrated as ETAs at UCT how design justice and UDL frameworks helped us to guide and support lecturers and learning designers as they attempt, during the COVID-19 pandemic and the overnight pivot, to untangle the social justice issues which surround online learning initiatives. We also have adopted decolonial theory as a lens to critically examine the practicability of UDL in shaping academic discourse from the Global South context. This contributes to the ongoing debates on transformation and inclusive pedagogies in the Global South. We conclude that UDL is a practical framework which can promote accessibility and include diversity if applied with a design justice lens. While the UDL framework cannot be treated as a catch-all solution to the challenges faced in HE institutions, especially those in the Global South, UDL has shown enough promise globally that it is likely to be a part of this solution. The use of UDL in a context in which its limitations and challenges are recognised will still provide means to create a truly equitable solution for the accessibility challenges within the Global South. Reflections within the Global South, like the experience of the authors of this chapter, have taken the theory of UDL and put it into practice. These provide a real way forward for UDL in the Global South and a new and more inclusive future of education. In doing so, we can start to ensure that the issue of education exclusion is less pronounced, and we move ever closer to true social justice.

Acknowledgements

Our chapter describes our experiences as Education Technology Advisors at the University of Cape Town, however, telling this story would not have been possible without the support of several key individuals. Firstly, a big thank you to the editors, Catherine and Laura for giving us the opportunity to be a part of this wonderful project. We are also most grateful to Nokthula Vilakati, Cheryl Hodgkinson-Williams, and the CILT team at UCT for their unwavering support. It has been incredible to be part of a broader project where young scholars such as ourselves are encouraged to contribute to the re-imagining of higher education futures with patience, kindness, and generosity. And lastly, thank you dear reader for wanting to re-imagine a different HE future alongside us.

References

Adam, T. (2020). *Addressing injustices through MOOCs: A study among peri-urban, marginalised, South African youth* [Doctoral dissertation, University of Cambridge].
https://doi.org/10.17863/CAM.56608

Al-Azawei, A., Parslow, P., & Lundqvist, K. (2017). The effect of universal design for learning (UDL) application on e-learning acceptance: A structural equation model. *International Review of Research in Open and Distributed Learning, 18*(6), 54–87.
https://doi.org/10.1177/2158244020969674

Almumen, H. A. (2020). Universal design for learning (UDL) across cultures: The application of UDL in Kuwaiti inclusive classrooms. *Sage Open, 10*(4). https://doi.org/10.19173/irrodl.v18i6.2880

Benton Kearney, D. (2022). *Universal design for learning (UDL) for inclusion, diversity, equity, and accessibility (IDEA)*. eCampus Ontario. https://ecampusontario.pressbooks.pub/universaldesign/

Boidin, C., Cohen, J., & Grosfoguel, R. (2012). Introduction: From university to pluriversity: A decolonial approach to the present crisis of western universities. *Human Architecture: Journal of the Sociology of Self-Knowledge, 10*(1), 1.
https://scholarworks.umb.edu/humanarchitecture/vol10/iss1/2/

Boughey, C. (2012). Social inclusion & exclusion in a changing higher education environment. *Multidisciplinary Journal of Educational Research, 2*(2), 133–51. https://hipatiapress.com/hpjournals/index.php/remie/article/view/244

Brodkin, K., Morgen, S., & Hutchinson, J. (2011). Anthropology as white public space? *American Anthropologist, 113*(4), 545–56.
https://doi.org/bf4nz6

Butcher, N. (2015). *A basic guide to open educational resources (OER)*. Commonwealth of Learning (COL).
https://doi.org/10.56059/11599/36

Cai, Q., & Robinson, D. (2021). Design, redesign, and continuous refinement of an online graduate course: A case study for implementing universal design for learning. *Journal of Formative Design in Learning, 5*(1), 16–26. https://doi.org/10.1007/s41686-020-00053-3

CAST. (2018). *Universal design for learning guidelines version 2.2.*
http://udlguidelines.cast.org

Cazden, C. B. (2012). A framework for social justice in education. *International Journal of Educational Psychology, 1*(3), 178–98.
https://hipatiapress.com/hpjournals/index.php/ijep/article/view/432

Chiwandire, D. (2019). Universal design for learning and disability inclusion in South African higher education curriculum. *Alternation Special Edition, 27,* 6–36.
https://doi.org/h7dw

Costanza-Chock, S. (2020). *Design justice: Community-led practices to build the worlds we need*. The MIT Press.
https://doi.org/10.7551/mitpress/12255.001.0001

Czerniewicz, L., Agherdien, N., Badenhorst, J., Belluigi, D., Chambers, T., Chili, M. et al. (2020). A wake-up call: Equity, inequality and covid-19 emergency remote teaching and learning. *Postdigital Science and Education, 2*(3), 946–67. https://doi.org/10.1007/s42438-020-00187-4

Escobar, A. (2018). *Designs for the pluriverse: Radical interdependence, autonomy, and the making of worlds: New ecologies for the twenty-first century*. Duke University Press Books.
https://doi.org/10.1215/9780822371816

Ferguson, B. T., McKenzie, J., Dalton, E. M., & Lyner-Cleophas, M. (2019). Inclusion, universal design and universal design for learning in higher education: South Africa and the United States. *African Journal of Disability, 8*(1), 1–7.
https://ajod.org/index.php/ajod/article/view/519/1100

Fovet, F. (2020). Universal design for learning as a tool for inclusion in the higher education classroom: Tips for the next decade of implementation. *Education Journal, 9*(6), 163–72.
https://doi.org/10.11648/j.edu.20200906.13

Fraser, N. (2000). Rethinking recognition. *New left review, 3*(3), 107–18.
https://newleftreview.org/issues/ii3/articles/nancy-fraser-rethinking-recognition

Fraser, N. (2010). Injustice at intersecting scales: On "social exclusion" and the "global poor". *European Journal of Social Theory, 13*(3), 363–71.
https://doi.org/10.1177/1368431010371758

Friedman, S. (1998). (Inter)disciplinarity and the question of the women's studies PhD. *Feminist Studies, 24*(2), 301–25.
https://doi-org.ezproxy.uct.ac.za/10.2307/3178699

Grech, S. (2011). Recolonising debates or perpetuated coloniality? Decentring the spaces of disability, development and community in the Global South. *International Journal of Inclusive Education, 15*(1), 87–100.
https://doi.org/10.1080/13603116.2010.496198

Griful-Freixenet, J., Struyven, K., Verstichele, M., & Andries, C. (2017). Higher education students with disabilities speaking out: Perceived barriers and opportunities of the universal design for learning framework. *Disability & Society, 32*(10), 1627–49.
https://doi.org/10.1080/09687599.2017.1365695

Houlden, S., & Veletsianos, G. (2020, March 12). *Coronavirus pushes universities to switch to online classes – but are they ready*? The Conversation.
https://theconversation.com/coronavirus-pushes-universities-to-switch-to-online-classes-but-are-they-ready-132728

Karisa, A. (2022). Universal design for learning: not another slogan on the street of inclusive education. *Disability & Society*, 1–7.
https://doi.org/10.1080/09687599.2022.2125792

Karr, V., Hayes, A., & Hayford, S. (2020). Inclusion of children with learning difficulties in literacy and numeracy in Ghana: A literature review. *International Journal of Disability, Development and Education*, 1–15.
https://doi.org/h7dz

Keddie, A. (2012). Schooling and social justice through the lenses of Nancy Fraser. *Critical Studies in Education, 53*(3), 263–79.
https://doi.org/10.1080/17508487.2012.709185

Khalid, M. S., & Pedersen, M. J. L. (2016). Digital exclusion in higher education contexts: A systematic literature review. *Procedia-Social and Behavioral Sciences, 228,* 614–21.
https://doi.org/10.1016/j.sbspro.2016.07.094

Kim, J. (2016). Locating Narrative Inquiry in the Interdisciplinary Context. In J. Kim, *Understanding Narrative Inquiry: The Crafting and Analysis of Stories as Research* (pp. 1–25). SAGE Publications, Inc.
https://dx.doi.org/10.4135/9781071802861

Lowrey, K. A., Hollingshead, A., & Howery, K. (2017). A closer look: Examining teachers' language around UDL, inclusive classrooms, and intellectual disability. *Intellectual and Developmental Disabilities, 55*(1), 15–24.
https://doi.org/f9xfvs

Luckett, K., & Shay, S. (2020). Reframing the curriculum: A transformative approach. *Critical Studies in Education, 61*(1), 50–65.
https://doi.org/h7d3

Mackey, M. (2019). Accessing middle school social studies content through universal design for learning. *Journal of Educational Research and Practice, 9*(1), 81–88.
https://doi.org/h7d5

Maree, J. G. (2015). Barriers to access to and success in higher education: Intervention guidelines. *South African Journal of Higher Education, 29*(1), 390–411.
https://hdl.handle.net/10520/EJC172780

Mbembe, A. (2015). *Decolonizing knowledge and the question of the archive* [PDF]. Wits Institute for Social and Economic Research, University of the Witwatersrand, Johannesburg.
https://wiser.wits.ac.za/system/files/Achille%20Mbembe%20-%20Decolonizing%20Knowledge%20and%20the%20Question%20of%20the%20Archive.pdf

McKenzie, J., Karisa, A., Kahonde, C., & Tesni, S. (2021). *Review of universal design for learning in low and middle-income countries.* Including Disability in Education in Africa (IDEA).

McKenzie, J. A., & Dalton, E. M. (2020). Universal design for learning in inclusive education policy in South Africa. *African Journal of Disability, 9.*
https://doi.org/10.4102/ajod.v9i0.776

Miles, S. and Singal, N. (2010). The Education for All and inclusive education debate: Conflict, contradiction or opportunity? *International Journal of Inclusive Education, Disability and the Global South, 14*(1), 1–15.
https://doi.org/10.1080/13603110802265125

Munro, P. (1998). *Subject to fiction: Women teachers' life history narratives and the cultural politics of resistance.* McGraw-Hill Education.

Ntombela, S. (2022). Reimagining South African higher education in response to covid-19 and ongoing exclusion of students with disabilities. *Disability & Society, 37*(3), 534–39.
https://doi.org/10.1080/09687599.2021.2004880

Olaussen, E. J., Heelan, A., & Knarlag, K. A. (2019). Universal Design for Learning–license to learn: A process for mapping a Universal Design for Learning process on to campus learning. In S. Braken, & K. Novak (Eds), *Transforming higher education through Universal Design for Learning* (pp. 11–32). Routledge.

Rao, K., & Torres, C. (2017). Supporting academic and affective learning processes for English language learners with universal design for learning. *Tesol quarterly, 51*(2), 460–72.
https://doi.org/gnbh5q

Reinders, M. B. (2019). *Decolonial reconstruction: A framework for creating a ceaseless process of decolonising South African society.* [LLM, University of Pretoria].
http://hdl.handle.net/2263/73485

Rose, D., Gravel, J. W., & Tucker-Smith, N. (2021). *Cracks in the foundation personal reflections on the past and future of the UDL guidelines* [PDF]. CAST.
https://www.cast.org/binaries/content/assets/common/news/cracks-foundation-whitepaper-20211029-a11y.pdf

Sayed, Y. (2003). Educational exclusion and inclusion: Key debates and issues. *Perspectives in education, 21*(3), 1–12.
https://digitalknowledge.cput.ac.za/handle/11189/5094

Small, J. (2020). *Redesigning blended courses project.* Center for innovation in learning and teaching.
http://www.cilt.uct.ac.za/cilt/projects/udl

Song, Y. (2017). To what extent is universal design for learning "universal"? A case study in township special needs schools in South Africa. *Disability and the Global South, 3*(1), 910–29.
https://disabilityglobalsouth.files.wordpress.com/2012/06/dgs-03-01-05.pdf

Staley, D. J., & Trinkle, D. A. (2011). The changing landscape of higher education. *Educause Review, 46*, 15–32.
https://er.educause.edu/articles/2011/2/the-changing-landscape-of-higher-education

Steyaert, J. (2005). Web-based higher education: The inclusion/exclusion paradox. *Journal of Technology in Human Services, 23*(1–2), 67–78.
https://doi.org/10.1300/J017v23n01_05

Thomson, P. (2021, 25 January). *Reading groups/journal clubs are a good idea*. Patter. https://patthomson.net/2021/01/25/reading-groups-journal-clubs-are-a-good-idea/#:~:text=Reading%20groups%20provide%20a%20forum,reading%20%E2%80%93%20here

United Nations. (2020). *Policy brief: Education during COVID-19 and beyond*. United Nations.

Zhang, H., & Zhao, G. (2019). Universal design for learning in China. In S. L. Gronseth, & E. M. Dalton (Eds), *Universal access through inclusive instructional design: International perspectives on UDL* (pp. 68–75). Routledge. https://doi.org/10.4324/9780429435515

17. Humanising learning design with digital pragmatism

Kate Molloy and Clare Thomson

As learning designers, we are often supported to discuss, reflect, and grapple with critical issues in learning technology within our personal learning networks. These networks outside of our daily work, like Special Interest Groups (SIGs), online communities, and conferences, afford us the freedom to reflect on power structures, inclusivity, privilege, accessibility, agency, surveillance technologies, and more. But then, we return to our daily work and our day jobs. We return to existing power structures. We return with our senses critically heightened and brimming with ideas, wondering how to reconcile our newly informed pedagogies with conventional institutional practice, whilst upholding our values.

The pandemic has further compounded this, with students being increasingly disadvantaged by lack of technical resources and exhausted staff with even less available time. Maintaining good mental health is a huge challenge for both groups, and self-care is often pushed further down the list (Campbell et al., 2022; Lee et al., 2021; Mofatteh, 2021; Morrish, 2019). This prompts our reflection on the word "good". If we are to aspire to a higher education for good, we need to explore who this good is for: students, staff, the institution, the sector and/or society. The care of these individuals and groups can be in tension with current demands for "excellence", understood as good quality education, and competitive individualistic approaches need to be problematised (Urbina-Garcia, 2020; Watermeyer & Tomlinson, 2022).

In this chapter we champion a pragmatic approach to critical instructional design. Educationalists John Dewey and George Herbert

Mead were known for their pragmatic philosophy, seeing each person as unique and working together on small, incremental changes to create solutions (Vanderstraeten & Biesta, 2006). Beyond practical problem solving, we draw on critical pragmatism to explore power relations and propose new ways of thinking and doing in the face of established historical approaches (Feinberg, 2015).

We set the theoretical considerations within the daily constraints that educators find themselves within. In Honeychurch's exploration of creative online spaces, an alternative term used for pragmatism is "satisficing" (Honeychurch, 2021). Satisficing, a combination of "to satisfy" and "to suffice" is viewed positively as a means of achieving forward motion rather than stagnating, trying to find the perfect solution to complex problems, accepting that good can be good enough. Those of us in support roles provide "good help" for colleagues and advocate for "good help" for students in our design consultations. This "good help" is generative, iterative and positive, guiding towards achievement in small steps, eventually leading "to transformational changes".[1]

As practitioners we are reflecting on our lived experiences pre and post COVID-19, with a combined experience of 30 years. We write from a position of supporting students and staff whilst occupying the third space which can be difficult to navigate with regards power structures, being neither senior management nor academic (Whitchurch, 2008). However, this unique third space can afford us an advantage as our strong networking abilities can position us well for collaborations and transformations (Veles et al., 2019). We are learning technologists situated in Ireland and the United Kingdom and, as with many in our position across the UK and Ireland, learning design is only one element of our complex roles. There is not one single framework that we draw on when designing for teaching and learning; rather we have a holistic approach that pays close attention to the complexities of each context. Inclusion and accessibility are at the heart of what we do, and Universal Design for Learning (Edyburn, 2005; Rose et al., 2006) informs that work.

---

1 https://www.nesta.org.uk/report/good-and-bad-help-how-purpose-and-confidence-transform-lives/

The chapter is structured into six sections, each corresponding to an element of adrienne maree brown's (2017)[2] *Emergent Strategy*. Using a biomimicry orientated lens, brown's framework facilitates an exploration of micro, meso and macro methods for changing and developing learning design culture. Whilst each of the six elements is distinct, their boundaries can blur and overlap in places, reflecting the complexities of policy and transformation. We identified with the aspiration of achieving transformation through a strategy which builds "complex patterns and systems of change through relatively small interactions" (brown, 2017, p. 2). To illustrate each of the elements, we use an example based on our experiences as learning technologists situated as we are within our respective institutional contexts, a broader sectoral context, and the global higher education community. In addition, we include an "educators' activity" in each section, so that interested readers can explore how these ideas might apply in their own context.

Our aim is to explore practical, humane solutions to digital problems related to teaching and learning in higher education — demystifying some of those challenges with creative and playful solutions. We focus on prevalent issues raised by staff and/or students in our own teaching settings and support sessions, as well as local and national surveys, literature, conferences, and community of practice settings over recent years.

---

[2] https://en.wikipedia.org/wiki/List_of_people_with_lower_case_names_and_pseudonyms

1. Fractals: The relationships between big and small

How we are at the small scale is how we are at the large scale. The patterns of the universe repeat at scale. (brown, 2017, p. 52)

We use the metaphor of fractals to consider the micro and macro relationship in teaching and learning practice. Fractals in nature replicate their micro elements numerous times, resulting in macro versions that are replicas of the micro. Small individual elements replicate again and again to create complex structures. As humans, we may feel we lack the agency to effect large scale change. However, as fractals, rethinking transformation as the result of multiple actions of individuals growing and growing until cultural change occurs.

Virtual learning environment (VLE)

One of the most significant online spaces in any higher education institution is the one which hosts the teaching and learning resources, usually the VLE. However, over the years a debate between using the VLE versus freely available third-party tools has persisted (Clay, 2019; Weller, 2007). Proposed benefits of the VLE when exploring uneven power dynamics in digital spaces are the safety of a contract agreement, adherence to FERPA regulations (GDPR for those of us in Europe), and student privacy and data concerns (UMW Division of Teaching and Learning Technologies, 2018). In contrast, projects that go "beyond the VLE" spaces such as DS106 and Domain of One's Own (DoOO) offer creative freedom and the chance for students to better hone their digital literacy skills (UMW Hurley Convergence Center, 2016). As instructional designers, these dichotomous positions may leave us with a sense of unease, of tension.

While understanding the ins and outs of an institutional VLE might not be the best avenue for developing transferable digital skills, a more in-depth understanding of the tools available could benefit students immensely and provide them with a more engaging learning experience. Local technologists or designers can likely offer some support and insight. There are also supportive communities and user groups associated with many VLE providers that will offer peer-led, practitioner-oriented support and shared practice.

In our work, we often see frustration arise during design work when the VLE does not do the thing that staff *really* want it to do. We understand this, but to avoid that level of frustration, it is important to understand how the VLE and external systems work, and what their strengths and limitations are. To start, there are many different settings behind the scenes that only administrators can see. Often, certain tools and functionalities are not enabled because information technology (IT) specialists within the institution cannot support them, or because they might impede other core functionality, such as security or student information system feeds. The same can apply to roles and privileges. If there is limited freedom to customise courses, there might be a technical reason for it. Clear communication between digital education, IT and academic teams can help alleviate these frustrations and work towards alternative solutions.

A wider understanding of how institutional systems interact with and feed into each other can also guide decision making at a course design level, such as how student data get to the VLE. If it is through registrations on a student information system (SIS), then changing a student's pronouns or name on the VLE might later be overwritten. There are likely workarounds if there is no way to change a name or pronouns on the VLE. In some cases, a student may be able to edit their profile pictures, so they might do that and add some text. They could include their pictures in their signatures on discussion board posts, or in the chat or profile names during online classes.

Another example is that curriculum management software may only be updated annually and if so, there may be only a single point in time during which to state course learning outcomes and assessment approach. Therefore, it is beneficial to find out when this takes place within the academic year to fit with course/programme design work.

> **Educators' activity**
>
> Jot down a VLE "wish list". What could the VLE do to create a better learning experience? Working with the local teaching and learning centre, information services or library or an online community, can generate possible solutions. There may be tips or workarounds to facilitate the items on the wish list. These will vary across the different VLE platform suppliers, but through different sources of support, there are sure to be answers to address the frustrations.

It is worth investigating how tools that are available can help to build a community of learners. Reflecting on hooks' (1994) thoughts on community, we are reminded that voice, presence, and excitement are crucial parts of the learning experience: "our capacity to generate excitement is deeply affected by our interest in one another, in hearing one another's voices, in recognising one another's presence." (p. 8).[3] Bowles provides practical advice for building safe online communities in spaces like the VLE,[4] offering tips around the timing of activities, allowing space to opt out, and involving students in the learning process. Within the functionalities of any VLE, it should be possible to provide safe options for personal stories, such as discussion boards (where posts are visible to the whole course) or an anonymous survey tool (ensuring a higher level of safety).

2. Intentional adaptation: How we change

> Change is definitely going to happen, no matter what we plan or expect or hope for or set in place. We will adapt to that change, or we will become irrelevant. (brown, 2017, p. 70)

We reflect here on the breath-taking murmurations created by starlings and how this concept can be applied to learning design. Thousands upon thousands of birds fly seamlessly together moving as a single entity. They work in sync, always communicating clearly, with collective

---

3 https://en.wikipedia.org/wiki/List_of_people_with_lower_case_names_and_pseudonyms
4 https://onehe.org/resources/some-safety-considerations-for-online-community-building/

leadership and deep trust with one another. Even when employing an institutional VLE, (learning) technology continually updates, new features are added, old ones disappear, connections to other systems change over time and may even be replaced. Keeping abreast of all these changes can be a time consuming and never ending job. Recognising where and when key knowledge is required by reaching out to colleagues across the institution, and working closely with advice and guidance can result in working intentionally for good — good for time constraints and good for students gaining from consistent and appropriate deployment of materials.

Video recordings

One specific activity that has frustrated many teachers we have worked with before and during the COVID-19 pandemic is video recording. Gone are the days when a video production expert was required to capture the footage, edit the takes together and then upload it to a server. Now teachers can use a range of tools to record, edit, upload directly to a streaming service, and embed the result in the VLE, whether a live session or an asynchronous recording of content. However, training and practice are required to become competent and confident to ensure that the finished product has both the correct visuals and sound. Frustration and work can rob the creator of precious energy and time.

Other crucial considerations include how provision of video affects those who are experiencing digital poverty, and the time required to caption content. Many systems now have machine-generated captions, but the accuracy of these vary considerably from speaker to speaker. It is essential to reflect on which course elements would benefit most from being presented as video and how design can encourage engagement

(Brame, 2016; Zhu et al., 2022). From our own student feedback and video analytics, students want short videos containing summaries, key assessment advice, demonstrations of practical skills, and to "meet" their teacher. The video tips we include here (see Table 1) are based on our experience supporting staff, but we encourage exploration and drawing inspiration from wider sources too (Boateng et al., 2016; Brame, 2016; Buchner, 2018; Harrison, 2020).

Table 1

Top video tips (for educators)

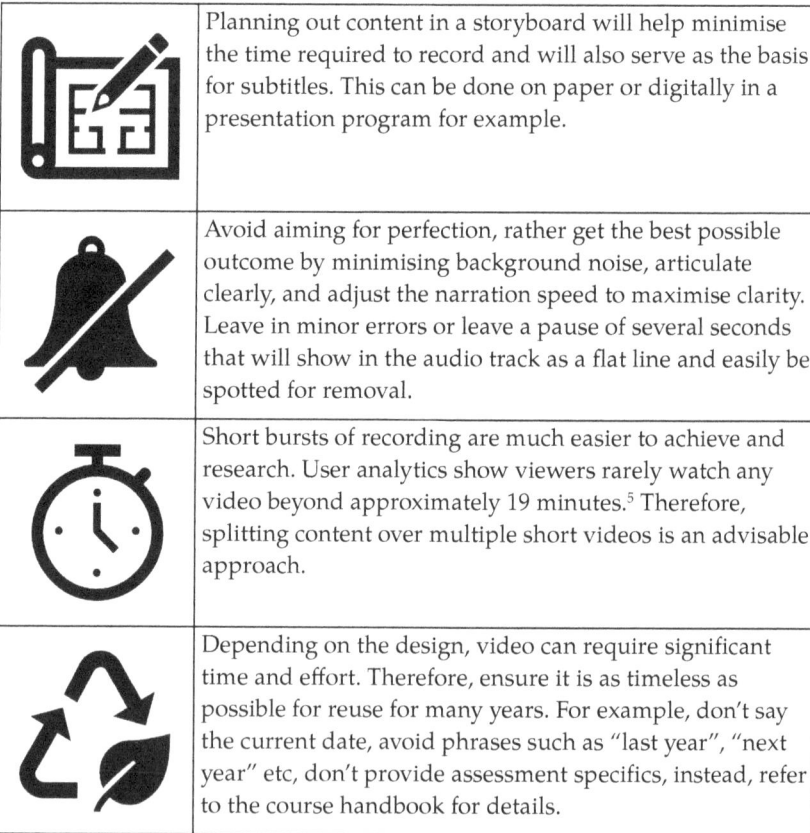

	Planning out content in a storyboard will help minimise the time required to record and will also serve as the basis for subtitles. This can be done on paper or digitally in a presentation program for example.
	Avoid aiming for perfection, rather get the best possible outcome by minimising background noise, articulate clearly, and adjust the narration speed to maximise clarity. Leave in minor errors or leave a pause of several seconds that will show in the audio track as a flat line and easily be spotted for removal.
	Short bursts of recording are much easier to achieve and research. User analytics show viewers rarely watch any video beyond approximately 19 minutes.[5] Therefore, splitting content over multiple short videos is an advisable approach.
	Depending on the design, video can require significant time and effort. Therefore, ensure it is as timeless as possible for reuse for many years. For example, don't say the current date, avoid phrases such as "last year", "next year" etc, don't provide assessment specifics, instead, refer to the course handbook for details.

---

5   https://www.techsmith.com/blog/video-statistics/

	This is not about having expensive high-tech equipment, rather a clean background, a solid surface for the recording device, good light, and a quality microphone.
	For simplicity and effectiveness, turn the camera on when doing a personable piece for human connection, but if talking to slides consider keeping it off. This decreases the cognitive load for both the creator and students as viewers.

Educators' activity

Record a 2–3-minute welcome to the course including a personal introduction, an overview of the course and why it is exciting or interesting. End with a prompt asking students to share why they are interested in taking the course or if it is a mandatory course, what apprehensions they may have. Give them a choice of where to share this: discussion forum thread, social media or at the start of a live session.

---

3. Interdependence and decentralisation: Who we are and how we share

> The idea of interdependence is that we can meet each other's needs in a variety of ways, that we can truly lean on others and they can lean on us. It means we have to decentralize our idea of where solutions and decisions happen, where ideas come from. (brown, 2017, p. 87)

Many organisms in nature are mutually reliant on one another, each flourishing because of the other. Spencer defines characteristics of co-operation, independence, and dependence between actors, rather than interdependence which is central to collaboration.[6] Further differences between collaboration and co-operation are long term

---

6   https://spencerauthor.com/can-you-force-collaboration/

visions and values (rather than short term goals), generation of ideas (rather than sharing of ideas), and empowerment (rather than engagement). Joining and collaborating with colleagues within and without the institution has a focus on partnerships, where individual contributions add together for learning at scale. The richest collaborations include student voices, not as a superficial add-on, but to truly integrate their views and experiences, with benefits such as enhanced literacies, increased motivation, and engagement, decreased dissonance (Bovill et al., 2011; Carless, 2020; Deeley & Bovill, 2017). In this section, we explore some of the open spaces for collaborations, both to learn from past work or to contribute to new ones.

Learning technology communities of practice

Conferences and events (online, in-person and hybrid) can serve as safe spaces to connect with others as we explore new ideas and approaches. When we step away from our everyday lives to participate in events, we are afforded space to reflect. There is an inherent value in the multiplicity of support we receive from these networks, ranging from technical support to emotional support. Beyond familiar communities of practice (Wenger, 2008), conferences and events can offer a support more akin to *affinity spaces* where diverse participants come together to act, learn, teach, create and problem solve around a common interest, "without regard to credentials, ages, outside status, or degrees of expertise" (Gee, 2017, pp. 28–29).

Every institutional setting is different, but finding local support and community is vital. Local learning technologists, instructional designers, librarians, and academic developers are a great place to start. Learning technologists can have a myriad of job titles, but the teaching and learning department can usually suggest appropriate contacts (Czerniewicz, 2021). Offering colleagues care-based support can afford them the agency and confidence to critically reflect on their teaching and learning designs, and perhaps implement small changes as a result.

Looking beyond institutions, across the sector and across the world, various organisations, projects, and initiatives can offer support. The range and scope of some are vast. For instance, the Association for Learning Technology (ALT)[7] in the UK has a network of over 3,500 educators in the UK and globally. In Ireland, groups such as the Irish Learning Technology Association (ILTA),[8] the Computers in Education Society of Ireland (CESI)[9] and the Irish Universities Association Enhancing Digital Teaching and Learning (IUA EDTL)[10] project (see Flynn et al., Chapter 14, this volume) have helped build a more comprehensive network of practitioners across Ireland. Beyond the UK and Ireland, TEL Advisors[11] is a community of practice in Australia and the Open/Technology in Education, Society, and Scholarship Association (OTESSA)[12] is based in Canada.

Other communities span across sectors and borders and are richer for their extensive reach. Initiatives like Virtually Connecting[13] and Equity Unbound[14] have helped to create and foster open networks of practitioners using the open web. Such open communities have developed learning opportunities, networking opportunities, and collaborations such as the #FemEdTech Quilt (see Bell et al., Chapter 10, this volume).[15]

Educators' activity

Opt-in! There may be hesitancy before signing up for new mailing lists or engaging in new activities or communities due to lack of time, and overflowing inboxes. However, selectively and intentionally opting-in to engage with new networks can pay dividends. Lurk at first, sit back and take in a webinar, or follow social media discussions or email/discussion forum threads. Evaluate the discourse before opting-in.

---

7   Association of Learning Technology (ALT): https://www.alt.ac.uk/
8   Irish Learning Technology Association (ILTA): https://ilta.ie/
9   Computers in Education Society of Ireland (CESI): https://www.cesi.ie/
10 EDTL Project: https://edtl.blog/
11 TEL Advisors: https://teledvisors.net/blog/
12 Open/Technology in Education, Society, and Scholarship Association (OTESSA): https://otessa.org/
13 Virtually Connecting: https://virtuallyconnecting.org/
14 Equity Unbound: http://unboundeq.creativitycourse.org/
15 FemEdTech Quilt: https://quilt.femedtech.net/

4. Nonlinear and iterative: The pace and pathways of change

> In a non-linear process, everything is part of the learning, every step. That includes constructive criticism, it is part of the feedback loop—experiment, gather feedback, experiment again. This is how we learn. (brown, 2017, p. 106)

The familiar adage of chaos theory is the butterfly who beats its wings, and the effects reverberate thousands of miles away. Problems are often considered *complicated* in higher education — linear, stable, following predictable patterns. Yet it may be beneficial to consider them as *complex* — networked, unpredictable, adaptable, evolving, uncertain and emergent (Hager & Beckett, 2020; Morrison, 2008). Educational technology is complex: entangled with capitalist, social, cultural, and human perspectives. For example, every device used by educators and learners has

different configurations. Rather than try to solve these at an individual level, it is important to design activities that will work in multiple modes and to give learners choices regarding how to interact with activities or resources.

Learning design frameworks

Considering accessibility and inclusion of resources across courses may seem a huge task. For example, to bring material up to appropriate accessibility standards such as the W3C Web Accessibility Initiative (WAI)[16] to meet disability legislation may take many hours of work. However, making one small change for each semester or academic year

---

16   https://www.w3.org/WAI/

will make an immediate impact (Bong & Chen, 2021). Frameworks can help map out the complexity such as Universal Design for Learning[17] (see Ramparsad Banwari et al, Chapter 16, this volume) or THRIVES.[18]

Learning design frameworks can provoke new ways of thinking about teaching and learning. In our support roles, we take care not to evangelise any one approach, but to distil meaning from these frameworks to create meaningful change in teaching and learning. By encouraging staff to adopt a plus-one approach, we help create achievable goals that are beneficial to all involved (Tobin & Behling, 2018). In this work, we often find when educators make one small change, for example permitting alternative format assignment submissions, we see benefits such as increased submission rates. They are then encouraged and inspired to build on those changes going forward, delving deeper into design frameworks.

Educators' activity

Set a "plus-one" challenge based on a framework of choice such as:

ABC Learning Design uses Diana Laurillard's learning types as the basis for quick course redesign (Laurillard, 1999). Quickly jot down which types of learning already take place in modules and re-balance activities, and tools used, to enhance student access and engagement.

Alternatively, examine the CAST Universal Design for Learning guidelines (see footnote 17) and arrive at one manageable change that may improve a course/programme design. For example, is there an assignment that could benefit from clearer instructions, could students submit the assignment in a different format or are there topics that might prove particularly difficult for students?

---

5. Resilience: How we recover and transform

Resilience is in our nature, and we recover from things that we would be justified in giving up over, again and again. (brown, 2017, p. 126)

---

17 https://www.cast.org/impact/universal-design-for-learning-udl
18 https://blogs.qub.ac.uk/digitallearning/accessibility/

Following the pandemic, we each have had to heal from the wounds it has inflicted — mental, emotional, and/or physical. If a starfish has a limb removed, it immediately seals over the damage, gradually building a tough callus over a few days for increased protection. Eventually, it may even extend fully as a replaced limb, though this may take some time. Likewise, as humans we have the capacity to heal damage to ourselves, if we have the time required. This healing often occurs within the supportive structures of communities and alongside colleagues, friends, and family.

The pandemic is not an isolated instance of a traumatic event. Crises such as climate change, global inequities, energy poverty and war will continue to affect education. Working together within our communities, alongside strong leadership, is crucial for recovery from wounds, seen and unseen.

It is necessary to acknowledge our own fragility, as well as that of our students. Support is manifest in designed interactions which ensure support, flexibility, and kindness by applying approaches such as Universal Design for Learning, pedagogy of care, community building activities, space for engagement and discourse.

Assessment and feedback

At the design stage of a course/programme, consider the digital skills required by teachers and students for the planned assessment. Discussions between designers, teachers and learning technologists can clarify the most appropriate approach to create assignment submission areas in the VLE, this will not only be a clear area for students to upload their work to but ensures a seamless

system for marking and feedback. Time spent at this stage will pay dividends: if multiple files are required, then ensure the submission box can accommodate this; if video files are required, check which system the institution uses for this. Additional setting choices may include individual versus group, peer marking, due dates if students can make more than one submission or submit after the due date. A significant number of support tickets we deal with regarding assignments are due to incorrect submission box settings.

Regardless of the chosen approach, it is crucial that guidance, support links and other aids are located above the submission box for students. This will reduce the number of queries received as well as reducing the stress on students. In addition, creating a discussion forum thread for the assignment allows answers to queries in a transparent space to avoid repeated questions in inboxes as well as the means for peer support.

Following institutional conventions or guidelines may result in tensions with personal values. Within design settings, there may be those with limited agency regarding assessment marking approaches. However, there may be opportunities to design in assignments without numerical scoring, referred to as ungrading (Blum, 2020; Flaherty, 2019). Many VLE platforms will be able to meet these needs, such as having "complete/incomplete" appear in the grade column to afford the ability to provide formative feedback without a number or percentage. Designing assessments such as this provides opportunities for students to learn and act on feedback across the course.

Feedback can be shared in multi-modal formats such as audio, video, or script annotations. This can potentially save time but can also add humanity and personalisation. Options for educators include recording a short podcast that highlights the most common feedback and comments emerging from an assignment, for example. This approach can help to lessen workload, whilst providing a unique opportunity for students to see that they are not alone in receiving this feedback (Gould & Day, 2013; Hennessy & Forrester, 2014). Students who internalise such feedback as criticism may be assured to hear others face the same issues, and the audio format is more personal than written feedback in which tone can be misinterpreted (Hayman, 2020; Parkes & Fletcher, 2017).

> **Educators' activity**
>
> Ask students to create a learning resource about a specific learning outcome and a specific target group and provide at least half a dozen formats/platforms for them to balance choice with scaffolding and guidance.
>
> Look to others for inspiration as redesigning assessment practice can be a daunting task. There is a wealth of experience across institutions, networks, and wider afield. One Irish example is the *History of Life* project by John Murray of the University of Galway.[19] Over several years, he supported students to produce their own video documentaries for the public domain, develop digital storytelling skills through guerrilla filmmaking, and contribute to the world of science.

6. Creating more possibilities: How we move towards life

Authentic, exciting unity takes time, and lots of experimenting. (brown, 2017, p. 156)

Looking toward the future of learning design, we can learn from water. A river can begin life as a small trickle, building and growing as it travels ever forward. It never stands still, constantly evolving and navigating around obstacles, such as rocks, changing with the weather and terrain. Bringing this generative and evolving ethos to learning design can result in experimentation and explorations to improve engagement with students. Remembering to accept that failure can open new possibilities, learning and successes.* As we move and flow forward as a sector, consideration of what is and is not sustainable for teaching and learning

---

19 https://media-and-learning.eu/type/featured-articles/filming-the-history-of-life-a-student-perspective/

is paramount to grow transformative justice cultures. As with other elements, the actions one builds and replicates numerous times results in transformative changes across higher education.

Rethinking the lecture

Face time is overvalued is one of the *Manifesto for Teaching Online* statements, which was written with specific reference to distance online education (Bayne et al., 2020). As learning technologists who went into the pandemic worried about how infrastructure would hold up, lack of access to internet connections and varying levels of digital skills, we initially advocated for a slow approach to the online pivot. "Use more asynchronous (non-live) activities and interactions, be intentional in your design", we repeated daily. However, again and again we saw teachers default to the synchronous norm and replicate the large didactic lecture theatre design in the online environment. The usage statistics for webinar systems soared beyond what was thought possible.[20]

After the early months of remote learning frustrations surfaced, teachers sought a connection to students through cameras, but students wanted privacy in their own chaotic, personal environments (Castelli & Sarvary, 2021; Leung et al., 2021). Soon after came the "Zoom fatigue", the continuous live interactions were exhausting for everyone unequally (Bailenson, 2021; Fauville et al., 2021). The physical, social, and emotional toll of live engagement was evident amongst so many of us, but particularly difficult for those who felt it imposed upon their personal space and agency, especially those who lacked appropriate learning spaces in digital poverty, anxious, lacking confidence etc (Curelaru et al., 2022; Li et al., 2022). The daily repetition of "you are on mute", "we can't hear you", "we lost you for a bit", "can you see my slides?" — a monotonous background to our daily lives.

Recording theory and information-heavy segments in short videos and making them available before the live session, referred to as flipped learning, frees up time in the session (refer to the video section above) (Eppard & Rochdi, 2017). Class time can then be better utilised

---

20 https://www.researchnester.com/reports/webinar-and-webcast-market-global-demand-growth-analysis-opportunity-outlook-2023/237

for tackling misinterpretations, clarifying difficult areas, and testing students' understanding. Small groups that retain the same student members throughout the course allow those important relationships to be built. Combining them with asynchronous activities such as discussion fora, reflective diaries, group blogs, photo logs, can ensure student-teacher interaction as well as with each other on their terms.

In addition, designing-in short but fun icebreakers or welcome activities bring presence lacking in didactic lectures. Emojis, GIFs and memes can contribute significantly to communication in these spaces, conveying meaning quickly and joyfully. Setting affective, hands-on tasks such as scavenger hunts, 3D metaphors, mapping exercises, sketchnoting give both relief from the screen and needed pauses for reflection, bringing in elements of emotion. Two rich sources of inspiration are the *OneHE* online community-building activities and the *Intention: Critical Creativity in the Classroom* book (Burvall & Ryder, 2019).[21]

Educators' activity

Oreo challenge. Ask students to come to the session with an Oreo cookie or similar two-layered cookie. Set a task that requires the student to create a poster/infographic/chart (whatever suits the context best) with the Oreo. They can use it whole, split it up, smash it, colour it — whatever they want, but the main element of their poster must be the cookie.

Conclusion

> We are excited by what we can create, we believe it is possible to create the next world.
> We believe. (brown, 2017, p. 16)

Taking a humanising, pragmatic approach in our learning design work enables us to vacillate between the practicalities of our on-the-ground work and the systemic change that is possible if we consider the big picture and work within trusting collaborations. Drawing on the tenets of emergent strategy, championing individual actions, which at scale

---

21   OneHE Community building activities: https://onehe.org/equity-unbound/

generate complex patterns. This collective and collaborative work can lead to transformative justice for ourselves and our students. Flexibility, time, and training are required to ensure high-quality education. Educating the educators to embrace the complex entanglement of pedagogy and technology is a necessity in a post-digital world (Fawns, 2022).

In an educational landscape that remains in a state of flux, heightened by the pandemic, emergent strategy frames our design approach between the micro and macro levels, and not only outlining how they intersect, but how cultural change can be driven (brown, 2017). Power imbalances can be addressed through collaborations and drive policy change for "good" such as inclusion, decolonisation, anti-surveillance, and wellbeing.

Ultimately, our reflections on nature-based metaphors, aim to empower colleagues to design for learning with increased attention to humanising it and ultimately "help students become more capable, self-managing participants in the processes" (Goodyear, 2015). We continue to believe in higher education for good, higher education for transformative justice.

References

Bailenson, J. N. (2021). Nonverbal overload: A theoretical argument for the causes of Zoom fatigue. *Technology, Mind, and Behavior, 2*(1), 1–16. https://doi.org/10.1037/tmb0000030

Bayne, S., Evans, P., Ewins, R., Knox, J., Lamb, J., Macleod, H., O'Shea, C., Ross, J., Sheail, P., & Sinclair, C. (2020). *The manifesto for teaching online*. The MIT Press.

Blum, S. D. (2020). *Ungrading: Why rating students undermines learning (and what to do instead)*. West Virginia University press.

Boateng, R., Boateng, S. L., Awuah, R. B., Ansong, E., & Anderson, A. B. (2016). Videos in learning in higher education: Assessing perceptions and attitudes of students at the University of Ghana. *Smart Learning Environments, 3*(1), 1–13.
https://doi.org/10.1186/s40561-016-0031-5

Bong, W. K., & Chen, W. (2021). Increasing faculty's competence in digital accessibility for inclusive education: A systematic literature review. *International Journal of Inclusive Education*, 1–17.
https://doi.org/10.1080/13603116.2021.1937344

Bovill, C., Bulley, C. J., & Morss, K. (2011). Engaging and empowering first-year students through curriculum design: Perspectives from the literature. *Teaching in Higher Education, 16*(2), 197–209.
https://doi.org/10.1080/13562517.2010.515024

Brame, C. J. (2016). Effective educational videos: Principles and guidelines for maximizing student learning from video content. *CBE—Life Sciences Education, 15*(4), 1–6.
https://doi.org/10.1187/cbe.16-03-0125

brown, adrienne maree. (2017). *Emergent strategy*. AK Press.

Buchner, J. (2018). How to create educational videos: From watching passively to learning actively. *Open Online Journal for Research and Learning, 12*, 1–10.
http://journal.ph-noe.ac.at/

Burvall, A., & Ryder, D. (2019). *Intention: Critical creativity in the classroom*. Blend Education

Campbell, F., Blank, L., Cantrell, A., Baxter, S., Blackmore, C., Dixon, J., & Goyder, E. (2022). Factors that influence mental health of university and college students in the UK: A systematic review. *BMC Public Health, 22*(1), 1–22.
https://doi.org/10.1186/s12889-022-13943-x

Carless, D. (2020). Longitudinal perspectives on students' experiences of feedback: A need for teacher–student partnerships. *Higher Education Research & Development, 39*(3), 425–38.
https://doi.org/10.1080/07294360.2019.1684455

Castelli, F. R., & Sarvary, M. A. (2021). Why students do not turn on their video cameras during online classes and an equitable and inclusive plan to encourage them to do so. *Ecology and Evolution, 11*(8), 3565–76.
https://doi.org/10.1002/ece3.7123

Clay, J. (2019, September 2). *The VLE is still dead… #altc*. eLearning Stuff.
https://elearningstuff.net/2019/09/02/the-vle-is-still-dead-altc/

Curelaru, M., Curelaru, V., & Cristea, M. (2022). Students' perceptions of online learning during COVID-19 pandemic: A qualitative approach. *Sustainability, 14*(13), 1–21.
https://doi.org/10.3390/su14138138

Czerniewicz, L. (2021). *Changing centres for teaching and learning: An analytical review*. University of Cape Town.
http://hdl.handle.net/11427/33848

Deeley, S. J., & Bovill, C. (2017). Staff student partnership in assessment: Enhancing assessment literacy through democratic practices. *Assessment & Evaluation in Higher Education, 42*(3), 463–77.
https://doi.org/10.1080/02602938.2015.1126551

Edyburn, D. L. (2005). Universal design for learning. *Special Education Technology Practice, 7*(5), 16–22.
https://www.ocali.org/up_doc/UDL_SETP7.pdf

Eppard, J., & Rochdi, A. (2017). A framework for flipped learning. In *Proceedings of the 13th international conference on mobile learning* (pp. 33–40). ERIC.
https://eric.ed.gov/?id=ED579204

Fauville, G., Luo, M., Queiroz, A. C. M., Bailenson, J. N., & Hancock, J. (2021). Nonverbal mechanisms predict Zoom fatigue and explain why women experience higher levels than men. *SSRN Electronic Journal*, 1–18.
https://doi.org/10.2139/ssrn.3820035

Fawns, T. (2022). An entangled pedagogy: Looking beyond the pedagogy—Technology dichotomy. *Postdigital Science and Education, 4*(3), 711–28.
https://doi.org/10.1007/s42438-022-00302-7

Feinberg, W. (2015). Critical pragmatism and the appropriation of ethnography by philosophy of education. *Studies in Philosophy and Education, 34*(2), 149–57.
https://doi.org/10.1007/s11217-014-9415-6

Flaherty, C. (2019, April 2). When grading less is more. *Inside Higher Ed*.
https://www.insidehighered.com/news/2019/04/02/professors-reflections-their-experiences-ungrading-spark-renewed-interest-student

Gee, J. P. (2017). Affinity spaces and 21st century learning. *Educational Technology, 57*(2), 27–31.
https://www.jstor.org/stable/44430520

Goodyear, P. (2015). Teaching as design. *HERDSA Review of Higher Education, 2*, 27–50.
http://www.herdsa.org.au/herdsa-review-higher-education-vol-2/27-50

Gould, J., & Day, P. (2013). Hearing you loud and clear: Student perspectives of audio feedback in higher education. *Assessment & Evaluation in Higher Education, 38*(5), 554–66.
https://doi.org/10.1080/02602938.2012.660131

Hager, P., & Beckett, D. (2020). *Emergence of complexity: Rethinking education as a social science*. Springer

Harrison, T. (2020). How distance education students perceive the impact of teaching videos on their learning. *Open Learning: The Journal of Open, Distance and e-Learning, 35*(3), 260–76.
https://doi.org/10.1080/02680513.2019.1702518

Hayman, R. (2020). First encounters of receiving summative assessment feedback in audio format: Expectations and experiences of final year undergraduate sport coaching students. *Practice and Evidence of Scholarship of Teaching and Learning in Higher Education 14*(1), 59–83.
https://www.pestlhe.org/index.php/pestlhe/article/view/218

Hennessy, C., & Forrester, G. (2014). Developing a framework for effective audio feedback: A case study. *Assessment & Evaluation in Higher Education, 39*(7), 777–89.
https://doi.org/10.1080/02602938.2013.870530

Honeychurch, S. L. (2021). *The emergence of participatory learning: Authenticity, serendipity, and creative playfulness* [Doctoral dissertation, University of Glasgow].
https://theses.gla.ac.uk/82365/

hooks, bell. (1994). *Teaching to transgress: Education as the practice of freedom.* Routledge.

Laurillard, D. (1999). A conversational framework for individual learning applied to the learning organisation and the learning society. *Systems Research and Behavioral Science, 16*(2), 113–22.
https://doi.org/10.1002/(SICI)1099-1743(199903/04)16:2<113::AID-SRES279>3.0.CO;2-C

Lee, J., Jeong, H. J., & Kim, S. (2021). Stress, anxiety, and depression among undergraduate students during the COVID-19 pandemic and their use of mental health services. *Innovative Higher Education, 46*(5), 519–38.
https://doi.org/10.1007/s10755-021-09552-y

Leung, H. T. T., Bruce, H., & Korszun, A. (2021). To see or not to see: Should medical educators require students to turn on cameras in online teaching? *Medical Teacher, 43*(9), 1099.
https://doi.org/10.1080/0142159X.2021.1873258

Li, N., Romera Rodriguez, G., Xu, Y., Bhatt, P., Nguyen, H. A., Serpi, A., Tsai, C., & Carroll, J. M. (2022). Picturing one's self: Camera use in Zoom classes during the COVID-19 pandemic. In *Proceedings of the ninth ACM conference on learning @ scale* (pp. 151–62). ACM Digital Library.
https://doi.org/10.1145/3491140.3528284

Mofatteh, M. (2021). Risk factors associated with stress, anxiety, and depression among university undergraduate students. *AIMS Public Health, 8*(1), 36–65.
https://doi.org/10.3934/publichealth.2021004

Morrish, L. (2019, May 23). Pressure vessels: The epidemic of poor mental health among higher education staff [PDF]. Higher Education Policy Institute.
https://www.hepi.ac.uk/wp-content/uploads/2019/05/HEPI-Pressure-Vessels-Occasional-Paper-20.pdf

Morrison, K. (2008). Educational philosophy and the challenge of complexity theory. In M. Mason (Ed.), *Complexity theory and the philosophy of education* (pp. 16–31). Wiley-Blackwell.

Parkes, M., & Fletcher, P. (2017). A longitudinal, quantitative study of student attitudes towards audio feedback for assessment. *Assessment & Evaluation in Higher Education, 42*(7), 1046–53.
https://doi.org/10.1080/02602938.2016.1224810

Rose, D. H., Harbour, W. S., Johnston, C. S., Daley, S. G., & Abarbanell, L. (2006). Universal design for learning in postsecondary education: Reflections on principles and their application. *Journal of Postsecondary Education and Disability, 19*(2), 135–51.
https://files.eric.ed.gov/fulltext/EJ844630.pdf

Tobin, T. J., & Behling, K. (2018). *Reach everyone, teach everyone: Universal design for learning in higher education*. West Virginia University Press.

UMW Division of Teaching and Learning Technologies. (2018, August 1). *Jade Davis – Ahead of the class: Frugal innovation and translatable skills* [Video]. YouTube.
https://www.youtube.com/watch?v=lo8eP94vANw

UMW Hurley Convergence Center. (2016, August 12). *Martha Burtis and Sean Michael Morris – Critical instructional design* [Video]. YouTube.
https://www.youtube.com/watch?v=lhlHKjtfjJ4

Urbina-Garcia, A. (2020). What do we know about university academics' mental health? A systematic literature review. *Stress and Health, 36*(5), 563–85.
https://doi.org/10.1002/smi.2956

Vanderstraeten, R., & Biesta, G. (2006). How is education possible? Pragmatism, communication and the social organisation of education. *British Journal of Educational Studies, 54*(2), 160–74.
https://doi.org/10.1111/j.1467-8527.2006.00338.x

Veles, N., Carter, M. A., & Boon, H. (2019). Complex collaboration champions: University third space professionals working together across borders. *Perspectives: Policy and Practice in Higher Education, 23*(2–3), 75–85.
https://doi.org/10.1080/13603108.2018.1428694

Watermeyer, R., & Tomlinson, M. (2022). Competitive accountability and the dispossession of academic identity: Haunted by an impact phantom. *Educational Philosophy and Theory, 54*(1), 92–103.
https://doi.org/10.1080/00131857.2021.1880388

Weller, M. (2007, November 8). *The VLE/LMS is dead*. The Ed Techie.
https://nogoodreason.typepad.co.uk/no_good_reason/2007/11/the-vlelms-is-d.html

Wenger, E. (2008). *Communities of practice: Learning, meaning, and identity*. Cambridge University Press.

Whitchurch, C. (2008). Shifting identities and blurring boundaries: The emergence of third space professionals in UK higher education. *Higher Education Quarterly, 62*(4), 377–96.
https://doi.org/10.1111/j.1468-2273.2008.00387.x

Zhu, J., Yuan, H., Zhang, Q., Huang, P.-H., Wang, Y., Duan, S., Lei, M., Lim, E. G., & Song, P. (2022). The impact of short videos on student performance in an online-flipped college engineering course. *Humanities and Social Sciences Communications, 9*(1), 1–10.
https://doi.org/10.1057/s41599-022-01355-6

Image Permissions

Chapter section	Image	Attribution
1	Fractals	Photo by sergio medina (2020), Unsplash, https://unsplash.com/photos/U4zohVXjQaE, Unsplash License
2	Starlings	Photo by Pete Godfrey (2023), Unsplash, https://unsplash.com/photos/jKNR--HDA_A, Unsplash License
3	Hummingbird	Photo by James Wainscoat (2021), Unsplash, https://unsplash.com/photos/Dku2qhI_s7I, Unsplash License
4	Butterfly	Photo by Boris Smokrovic (2018), Unsplash, https://unsplash.com/photos/3Od-27QTnKE, Unsplash License
5	Starfish	Photo by Serge Taeymans (2020), Unsplash, https://unsplash.com/photos/Xidkr8Ta3PI, Unsplash License
6	Water	Photo by Lina Loos (2017), Unsplash, https://unsplash.com/photos/04-C1NZk1hE, Unsplash License

18. Advancing 'openness' as a strategy against platformisation in education

Tel Amiel and Janaina do Rozário Diniz

> I am hopeful, not out of mere stubbornness, but out of an existential, concrete imperative.
>
> Paulo Freire (2014)

This chapter is a reflective, practice-based narrative on the experiences of emancipatory teaching to future educators regarding the platformisation of education. Drawing on experiences from teaching in Brazil, it aims to provide insight into the strategies and ideas created over time as we, two Brazilian educators, navigated the complex landscape of teaching in a novel, collaborative format during the pandemic. We believe that technocritique emerging from the field of education often fails (future) educators by only providing them with "critical perspectives", but no clear insight into strategies or tactics of resistance and collective action. Resisting the ever-growing techno-corporate mammoth in education and extractive surveillance demands: (1) having a critical consciousness, (2) learning to engage collectively, and importantly, (3) identifying possible alternatives and strategies to deploy when working as an educator. We believe that such resistance also can be enacted by students, and that the methods and possibilities discussed here can be used in a variety of different scenarios in higher education.

Introduction

After the 2020 COVID-19 outbreak in Brazil, schools and universities suspended their activities as a measure to curb the contagion. As elsewhere, educational institutions resumed operations via emergency remote teaching (ERT). This process took place at the institutions where we, the authors, teach — the State University of Minas Gerais (UEMG) and the University of Brasilia (UnB). Both are public, tuition-free, state-funded institutions that are widely respected in Brazilian higher education. At the respective ERT working groups, challenges were discussed, but surprisingly little attention was paid to identifying the services and tools that would best meet the emerging needs of students and teachers. Instead, we observed a proliferation of uncritical guides and suggestions of software, systems, and services particularly those identified as "free" that could "help" teaching in such uncertain times, and the de facto adoption of centralised educational services and platforms offered by large corporations.

The increased adoption of software platforms in education has led to the massive, top-down implementation of new services and software, with an unprecedented concentration of power in a handful of organisations offering "free" platforms to educational institutions around the world. For those countries and regions with reasonable internet access, cloud-based services in both school systems and higher education institutions have been advanced. Though this trend is not new, there is evidence of its increase during the COVID-19 pandemic (Amiel et al., 2021; Fiebig et al., 2023).

If platforms were once used in hybrid or distance education models, they had now become the mediators of access to formal education, in its broadest sense. We shared our critique of the adoption of these systems in ERT working groups in our respective universities but there was little response. Teachers and students did not participate in the needs analysis or choice of tools and platforms. In this context, we decided to develop projects with our students. As teachers in the field of education and technology, we felt an urgent need to clarify the importance of these decisions, particularly the risks and implications.

In keeping with the theme of this book, our goal is not simply to describe the projects we designed during our courses, spanning the COVID-19 pandemic. Rather, we aim to show the importance of moving beyond the rhetoric of technology as a tool at the service of education, and of simply adopting a "critical" stance to technology. Drawing on our own work with trainee teachers in the Brazilian higher education sector, we aim to show how this process was filled with doubt, insecurity, and precariousness, but also with resistance and hope.

We have organised the chapter as follows. We begin with a presentation of the main concepts that underlie recent debates on the rise of software platforms in education. We present the specific pedagogical projects we developed with our students during the pandemic. Next, our chapter takes a conversational tone as we detail the rationale and methods we used. Finally, we conclude the chapter with our reflections.

Data, platforms, and society

For some time, there has been a concerted effort to bring critical perspectives into the field of educational technology (Macgilchrist, 2021). Discussions about how to foster a critical outlook have taken many forms and names, including media literacy, digital literacy, and technology fluency (Amiel & Amaral, 2013). In Latin America, there is a strong tradition, borne out of critical perspectives, of examining information and communication technologies (ICT) through the lenses of politics and power imbalances, particularly in the analysis of mass media. Martín-Barbero (2003) had suggested that technologies for communication must be tools of expression and not just consumption. The critique also extends to questioning the purported neutrality of digital devices such as computers. Despite decades of discussion on the non-neutrality of technology and its tools (Dagnino, 2008), teacher education and professional development are still influenced by a rhetoric of technology as "tool" — choices to be purchased or used — based on whatever is offered by the market. However, if we continue to see technologies as a menu of tools and systems that teachers must learn about, choose, and deploy, all important decisions about technology will have been made without their participation (Borgmann, 1993).

Due to the prevalence of this consumer-oriented approach to technology, it is often difficult for educators to sensitise students regarding how these problems might impact them as they engage with educational technologies. There has been a recent rise of criticism of businesses such as Facebook (Meta) and Google (Alphabet), and punishments for violation of fair competition and privacy laws.[1] This, together with the massive move towards ERT provided fertile ground to renew our discussions of educational technologies not only in future lives of teachers but also current lives of students.

During the COVID-19 pandemic, we saw the growth of platform use in education through the widespread adoption of SaaS/PaaS[2] platforms, i.e. "(re-)programmable digital infrastructures that facilitate and shape personalised interactions among end-users and complementors, organised through the systematic collection, algorithmic processing, monetisation, and circulation of data" (Poell et al., 2019, p. 3). The platformisation of education is defined by Decuypere et al. (2021) as "how platforms take part in the assembling of education, connecting artefacts, actors, epistemologies, techniques and values into novel educational forms" (p. 2).

Surveillance capitalism, platform capitalism and data colonialism are concepts that shed light on understanding the role of big tech, platforms, and data in society and in education. Zuboff (2015) defined surveillance capitalism as a new economic order that has personal data as its main raw material. Human experience is raw material transformed into behavioural data that is processed, organised, and used to predict human behaviour (Zuboff, 2019). In a complementary vein, Srnicek (2017) defined platform capitalism as the new business model of 21st century capitalism where "the platform has data extraction built into its DNA" (Srnicek, 2017).

Two key points about the operation of platforms highlight their contribution to global inequality. First, the free flow of data mainly benefits platforms in the United States, since most of the data goes towards the databases of businesses that have headquarters in the US. Second, the offering of free or cheap services by platforms to countries in the Global South in exchange for the data provided by the populations of these countries can be considered "a modern system of forced underdevelopment in relation to data" (Srnicek, 2019), or data

---

1 See, for example:
https://www.nytimes.com/2019/03/20/business/google-fine-advertising.html and https://techhq.com/2021/08/amazon-slapped-with-biggest-gdpr-data-privacy-fine-ever/
2 Software and Platform as a Service.

colonialism (Couldry, 2020). Data colonialism has commonalities with historical colonialism, including resource appropriation, ideology, capital accumulation, and most importantly, broad changes in social relations (Couldry & Mejias, 2019a). Populations from across the globe, in both richer and poorer nations, become sources of data extraction, but the consequences of data colonialism are not symmetrical: the flow of data and profits almost always occurs from the Global South to the Global North (Cassino, 2021; Silveira, 2021). Furthermore, Cassino (2021) highlights the invisibility of subjects from the Global South who have historically had no voice. As in historical colonialism, what matters fundamentally are the extracted resources.

Based on these reflections, we observe the technological fragility of countries from the Global South, specifically Brazil. The transfer of data from Brazilian citizens to data centres operated by big tech, and the massive adoption of platforms from these corporations by public educational institutions in Brazil exacerbate the technological vulnerability of the country. Given the degree of dependence these platforms create, there is a concern that their adoption may also lead to a decrease in innovation and development of local technologies, and/or those that are in accordance with the needs, demands and perspectives of local users. It also compromises the training of skilled labour to develop their own solutions,[3] the freedom of citizens, and the sovereignty of the nation (Toledo, 2020).

Platformisation and pedagogy

As educators who study and teach about the intersection of education and technology, we are attuned to the emerging challenges of platformisation. Though we have discussed these topics as part of our courses, we believed that the pandemic made platformisation cardinal to the lives of students. Moreover, we felt that there was a general lack of understanding of these issues by educators in schools and in universities. We began tackling this issue through the Open Education Initiative (IEA; Iniciativa Educação Aberta), an initiative established in

---

3   One interesting development is the increasing value of platform and business-specific skills in traditional curricula (see for example, Foster et al., 2018).

2017, and co-led by one of us (Tel). Though the initiative's primary focus is on the broad topic of open education (OE), it positions digital rights as a central theme. In 2019, IEA began collecting and publishing data on the "partnerships" between public educational institutions in Brazil and GAFAM,[4] under the Education Under Surveillance Observatory (Observatório Educação Vigiada[5]). It is in the context of this group, that the authors of this chapter met online for the first time in August 2020, when Janaina shared a lesson plan on a course she was going to teach focused on issues of platformisation in education.

After connecting and finding common interests, we taught together, conducted three cross-disciplinary projects over three semesters, resulting in open educational resources (OER), and connecting students from both institutions. The first outcome of these projects was a "manifesto" focused on surveillance in education written collaboratively by students for students. The second, a series of online tutorials aimed at introducing FLOSS (Free/Libre and Open Source Software) that could be used by educators and students, and the third, a series of lesson plans on issues related to surveillance in education. In alignment with the principles we wanted students to learn about, we made use of FLOSS for communication and development of the projects, as detailed in Table 1 below.

---

4   Common acronym for some of the biggest information technology companies in the world: Google (Alphabet), Apple, Facebook (Meta), Amazon, and Microsoft.
5   https://educacaovigiada.org.br

Table 1

Project details

		Project 1: Manifesto Surveillance in Education	**Project 2:** Tutorials FLOSS platforms and software services	**Project 3:** Lesson plans digital rights in basic education
UEMG	Class	Society, Education and Technology; Mass Surveillance and Fake News	Society, Education and Technology	Society, Education and Technology
	Students	17	17[6]	28
UnB	Class	Introduction to Research (levels 1,2,3)	Education, Technology, and Communication	Education, Technology, and Communication
	Students	14	30	27
Period		Nov – Dec 2020	Feb – Mar 2021	Jul – Aug 2021
Software		Wikiversity; Etherpad; Telegram; Conferência Web (BigBlueButton fork)	Etherpad; Telegram; Conferência Web (BigBlueButton fork)	Wikiversity; Etherpad; Element; Conferência Web (BigBlueButton fork)
Output		aberta.org.br/portfolio/manifesto-sobre-a-vigilancia-na-educacao	escolhalivre.org.br/tutoriais	pilaresdofuturo.org.br/praticas

Our goal was to provide students with the opportunity to experiment with a variety of tools, and to understand the risks and implications of platformisation in education. We also aimed to build upon previous student work. Once the collective "manifesto" was published, we used it to demonstrate the potential of engaging with the principles and practical use of FLOSS to challenge the effects of platformisation.

---

6   Same students from the manifesto project.

We worked within the principles of open educational practices (OEP). There was also an emphasis on making the results of the work open and publicly available, both as future educational resources but also as assignments that could be revisited by future students for improvement (what some term "reusable assignments") (Clinton-Lisell, 2021). To foster collaboration, we connected students from different regions, experience levels and age, initially online in large groups (for discussions) and then small inter-institutional groups (for activities). Collaborative learning enables those involved working together, bringing in different perspectives, and thus understanding and solving problems and achieving goals collectively (Amiel, 2012). It also imposes challenges in that each participant must understand each other's limits and potentials. This was particularly strategic during the pandemic, as challenges to participation were exacerbated and unique to each student. In small groups, we believed, it would be easier for negotiations to take place that would provide opportunities of engagement for all, and effective participation (Bali et al., 2020). The use of messaging systems allowed students to look to each other and teachers as a source of support, in a horizontal fashion. Finally, regular feedback and group meetings were conducted as opportunities to check on well-being and to provide guidance on project development and group dynamics.

Project 1: Manifesto

A Manifesto on Surveillance in Education was collaboratively created by 31 students. We began by providing students with resources exploring platformisation, identifying themes which could be addressed in a student-led manifesto aimed at trainee teachers in education, i.e. data/metadata collection and analysis, behaviour prediction and fake news, user loyalty, technological autonomy, buying and selling of data and "big data", censorship and control, and concentration of power in a few companies (GAFAM). Students selected their topic of interest and formed groups. Synchronous meetings were held between the students and teachers in which texts prepared by the groups were shared and further reference materials were provided by the teachers. Students published their final drafts on Wikiversity.[7]

Students found drafting the manifesto to be very challenging. Educational platformisation was — and still is — a new subject, little discussed in the academic community, and in society at large. Even with the suggestion of materials for study and debates in class, students found it difficult to synthesise, through writing, their analyses and reflections. The use of FLOSS tools, most of which students had never experienced before, also provided a challenge. Accustomed to using proprietary software, students were surprised (and sometimes frustrated) with using something different. However, we believed that this was a safe space for experimentation that could lead to bringing forward insecurities and difficulties in ways that supported wider learning outcomes. Substantial text review was required by teachers. We aimed to limit our intervention on the text to preserve student voices. The final text of the manifesto was published in Wikiversity in October 2021.

Project 2: Tutorials

After developing a theoretical framework, the manifesto, and noticing the level of difficulty students had had with the use of FLOSS tools, we proposed the creation of tutorials about FLOSS for education. Students analysed closed/proprietary software and platforms used in education,[8] then researched free and open software and platforms that could substitute (or be used in tandem with) proprietary ones and presented comparisons to the larger group. Over a month-long period, 47 students created nine tutorials and a collaborative reflection. The tutorials were made available on the Escolha Livre (Free Choice) site.[9] This project occurred with greater fluidity than the development of the manifesto. Through dialogue between the authors and students, we noticed greater engagement. This was a more practical activity, beginning with an investigation of platforms with which students were familiar. Moreover,

---

7 https://pt.wikiversity.org/wiki/Educação_Aberta/A_vigilância_na_educação
8 A list of platforms were suggested, based on work done by previous students in 2019, which included WhatsApp, Netflix, Facebook, Instagram, among others. See: https://pt.wikiversity.org/wiki/Educação_Aberta
9 A website (escolhalivre.org.br) created in partnership with UNESCO Brazil and the Open Education Initiative.

students from UEMG had already participated in the design of the manifesto and had some familiarity with the collaborative methodology, themes, and tools.

Project 3: Lesson plans

In the third project, we sought a greater articulation of the theory of educational platformisation with teaching practice. We designed an activity that could serve as inspiration for other undergraduate students and teachers in basic education. The guiding questions were: how can we engage the school community with the issues you have studied regarding surveillance, privacy, and the platformisation of education? How can we contribute to the awareness of students, parents and/or teachers about digital citizenship? In a one-month period, 55 students developed or remixed lesson plans, resulting in eight lesson plans. To develop this activity, we relied in partnership with Pilares do Futuro (Pillars of the Future), a project that provides practice focused on digital citizenship developed by teachers of basic education.[10] The partnership provided the opportunity for students to engage in a workshop with the manager of the Pilares project. The lesson plans were subjected to the standard evaluation done by the Pilares curatorial team, and then made available on the platform,[11] providing meaningful visibility to student work.

The elaboration of lesson plans was challenging for many students, who had no prior experience with teaching or producing lesson plans. Some initial ideas proposed by students were broad, overly ambitious or misaligned with the context of Brazilian basic education. We had productive dialogues with students and noticed great efforts to reduce the scope to build feasible practices. Students presented to the larger group, providing possibilities for pointing out strengths, and providing encouragement for students to learn from and support one other. Our intervention, conversations with colleagues from other groups, and

---

10   The project is financed by NIC.br (The Brazilian Network Information Center) and has support from UNESCO Brazil. See: https://pilaresdofuturo.org.br
11   See, for example: https://pilaresdofuturo.org.br/praticas/buscando-alternativas-a-aplicativos-de-mensagens-proprietarios-reduzindo-o-impacto-da-vigilancia-na-educacao

discussions held during the workshop all contributed to the development of the work, and consequently to the learning and development of the students.

Autobiographical investigation: Our methodology

As teachers during the pandemic, we were dealing with a high level of daily uncertainty and shifting priorities — as was everyone, including our students. There was little time to document and reflect on the designs we created and how they were molded by contingencies and daily demands. At the end of this trajectory, we believed something unique had happened and felt the need to analyse this experience. To make sense of the paths taken, we engaged an autobiographical stance, enabling us as researchers to investigate our points of view and contribute to a process of professional development (Oliveira & Satriano, 2017). In an autobiographical methodology, it is accepted that there is no perfect recollection of events, and no amount of data and analysis would faithfully unearth what happened, was thought, and was devised. What one has is always a partial, evolving account based on recollection and selective memories. Thus, we aimed to provide an account of how we enacted a specific perspective on teaching about educational technology with our students, hoping to change how future basic education teachers might understand and think about education in pandemic and post-pandemic times.

We began by engaging in a text-based dialogue. One of us recollected salient aspects of our trajectory; the other wrote back. Based on these initial drafts, we met (online and then face-to-face) and made use of our records from the period (documents, text-based exchanges between teachers and student-teacher groups, outputs of projects) to "refine" these memories, but more importantly, to critically reanalyse the issues that emerged from this practice. The result of these conversations is systematised below, in the form of a dialogue.

Educating for autonomy: Dialogues on education, technology, and freedom

Tel: In our initial conversation, it was clear that the role of large software corporations in education was something that has disquieted each of us for some time. We have found that this is not something seen as problematic and urgent by university teachers in our schools of education. During the pandemic, bringing this topic up in discussions seemed even more fringe, as everyone seemed to be in a fast, problem-solving mode. It made me think about a sort of "Silicon Valley" narrative that education is "broken" (in this case, it wasn't ready to respond to pandemic demands) and needed to be fixed by market models (Weller, 2015). I got the sense we agreed that this only made the issues related to technology in education more imperative. Everyone was grappling with a host of concerns and emergencies. But it was amazing to me how little issues relating to technology were part of the discussion, and adoption of almost any software or platform was seen as positive. How did you begin your incursion into this topic?

Janaina: Since 2017, I had been researching mass surveillance with trainee teachers at my university (UEMG). The advancement of GAFAM in education during the pandemic brought me great concerns as a teacher, as I was aware of the risks and implications of adopting the educational platforms of large information technology corporations in the academic environment. Distress and frustration were recurring feelings for me. In order to alert those involved — management, professors, and students — I problematised the issue with co-workers and did some outreach directed to management and students. These activities were not enough to mobilise, even slightly, the academic community at my university. The reduced amount of resources and lack of preparedness to deal with the COVID-19 pandemic, in terms of technical infrastructure, provided the conditions for the adoption of Microsoft's platform. At that time, I intensified my studies about mass surveillance, surveillance in education and free software, and I had contact with the Education Under Surveillance Observatory.

Tel: I had a similar experience. I was already aware of general concerns with data collection, privacy, etc., and considered myself an activist for

FLOSS. My interest in surveillance in education became central for me when I learned that my university at the time, the University of Campinas (Unicamp), would be a pioneer in Brazil in the adoption of Google's services for education in 2016. This decision encouraged me and a small group of colleagues[12] to try and find out how this process was taking place, given that there was no publicity of this partnership. This led to the emergence of a small network of researchers and students who clustered around understanding this issue — interviewing researchers, professors, and staff at Unicamp, investigating university documents, watching recorded videos of meetings, and finally publicising these facts. When I arrived at my new institution in 2018 (University of Brasilia), I was faced with the same scenario: the university was in the process of adopting Microsoft's platform. Both, therefore, had already adopted the platforms before the onset of the COVID-19 pandemic. From the beginning, I was startled by the lack of criticism and awareness by those involved in moving the process forward, and the enthusiasm with which public institutions with great technical competence sought out (and were not co-opted by) these businesses to adopt their services. This became clear when I reviewed the recordings of meetings of the university's Council on Information and Communication Technology (Conselho de Tecnologia da Informação e Comunicação[13]). The adoption was not, as I had thought, only been the product of strong marketing action by the private sector — but an active search by the university for solutions to concrete problems (e.g. limited available storage for self-hosted e-mail), but also assumed problems (e.g. the perception that "everyone" was already using services such as Gmail, so no real issues were at stake) (Oddone, 2021; Parra et al., 2018). It scared me how easily issues associated with privacy, data collection, or the business model of these companies could be overlooked. Over time, this small cluster of researchers began engaging in systematic data collection to determine the scope of these partnerships, resulting in the Education Under Surveillance Observatory.

---

12   I was a researcher at NIED (https://www.nied.unicamp.br), and joined colleagues associated with LAVITS (https://lavits.org) in this initial investigation.

13   https://www.citic.unicamp.br/contic

Platforms, surveillance, and education

Janaina: When I first got in touch with the Observatory, I thought: "there are other people studying and worrying about this? I couldn't quite believe it! There is a light at the end of the tunnel." How did the Observatory begin?

Tel: The Education Under Surveillance Observatory began by providing a georeferenced system aimed at showing, on a map, the platformisation of public education in Brazil (Cruz et al., 2019). It expanded to include all countries in South America in 2021.[14] Current data shows that nearly 80% of higher education institutions in the continent make use of Microsoft and Google services. These corporations offer "free" access to Software and Platform as a Service (PaaS/SaaS) including e-mail, cloud file storage, videoconferencing, and teaching systems to tens of thousands of students and teachers in educational institutions across the country. However, what is touted as "free" has enormous costs (Amiel et al., 2021). The development of internal platforms by education systems or public higher education institutions requires considerable and sustained financial investment. In recent years, state investment in public education has dramatically decreased (Cruz & Venturini, 2020; Parra et al., 2018). These two factors were crucial in directing institutions to adopt platforms from large software corporations, which became de facto platforms that enabled remote learning, during the COVID-19 pandemic. As my colleagues Leonardo Cruz and Jamila Venturini (2020) have observed: "one cannot ignore the role of the neoliberal reforms undertaken in the last 30 years in the deterioration of the public technological and educational infrastructure" (p. 21).

Janaina: In education, I'm surprised by how big corporations occupy a space that, to me, should be the responsibility of the state. The education of millions of students in a country is in the hands of very few large corporations. The idea that surveillance capitalism thrives on people's ignorance of this phenomenon (Zuboff, 2019) was quite important for me, and it is something that we have mentioned as being evident to us at our institutions.

---

14   https://educacaovigiada.org.br

Tel: I think the platformisation of education as a phenomenon is qualitatively distinct from the large-scale adoption of proprietary software in education, which has happened for decades. The heavy use of data, centralisation/aggregation of multiple services, and network effects, make it possible for small players to participate in the market (collecting and aggregating data from multiple sources, including through APIs). But platformisation most definitely rewards a small number of very large players that have emphatically affected the effective governance of education.

Janaina: We are talking about the platformisation of education, but if we look around, we see that the issue is broader than that. We are living the platformisation of society, or of the most essential sectors of society, of the economy... when we discuss this topic with teachers, I find that it's important to contextualise this beyond the walls of school and the university.

Tel: Yes, it's important to expand beyond the realm of education to connect the issues that are sometimes known by the students and have been raised by popular media, such as fake news, social network addiction, and the like. I think we have an obligation to point out how platformisation also enhances and exacerbates traditional disparities, not only economic ones, but geopolitical.

Janaina: Poorer nations face great social inequalities and have basic issues such as food scarcity, lack of literacy, and limited housing. The extraction of data is yet another form of exploitation, deepening inequalities and increasing the concentration of wealth of these corporations and strengthening the governments of their parent countries. Examining the impact of data colonialism in poor countries, we can think of issues such as disinformation, for example, which has contributed to the rise of extreme right-wing governments in several countries around the world. In Brazil, the victory of a fascist government deepened social inequality in the country (Gennari, 2020). This is just one example of how the processing of data from populations in poorer nations — with limited technological autonomy — by companies that have profit as their ultimate goal, can contribute to the increase of the poverty of a nation. Technological autonomy, one of the strategic issues for the development of a country, is compromised and even made unfeasible by the technological, economic, and political domination that a few northern countries exert over those in the Global South.

Critical (and urgent) perspectives on educational technology

Janaina: We were aware of the problem: we saw platforms advancing in education, we tried to mobilise our fellow teachers and managers long before the COVID-19 pandemic. All this also changed my teaching, mainly because I work with teacher professional development. I found it impossible to teach without bringing forth, debating, and clarifying the platformisation of public education with my students. In my opinion, not taking this issue to class would be irresponsible. Students could not be unaware of a subject that directly impacts their daily lives today as students, and in the future as teachers. I organised the subjects I teach about technology and education in such a way that platformisation was the central subject. Having Paulo Freire as the canonical example of a teacher, I think that the educator, by choosing to be progressive, must contribute to overcoming the naive curiosity of the student towards a critical, epistemological curiosity; that is, promotion from naivete to criticality (Freire, 2018). Even in light of our university's determination for teachers to adopt the (Microsoft) Teams platform, for me, using it generated a conflict. "Teaching requires the embodiment of words by example... those who think right are tired of knowing that words lacking the embodiment of example are worth little or almost nothing"[15] (Freire, 2018, p. 35). I decided to adopt only free and open source software (FLOSS) in my classes, e.g. Jitsi, ConferênciaWeb, OnlyOffice,[16] Nextcloud,[17] Moodle and Telegram. I created a podcast channel about technologies, surveillance and education, and students developed

---

15 In the original: "Ensinar exige a corporificação das palavras pelo exemplo" [...] "quem pensa certo está cansado de saber que as palavras a que falta a corporiedade do exemplo pouco ou quase nada vale."

16 A free and open source productivity online platform, similar to other office suites (https://onlyoffice.com).

17 A suite for collaboration largely based on file/folder sharing (https://nextcloud.com).

podcasts about these subjects.[18] I continued to research surveillance in society, in education, free software, and also resistance initiatives to the surveillance and technology dependence sharpened by the IT monopolies during the pandemic.

Tel: My engagement with this topic as an academic grew much stronger during the first months of the pandemic. I was an open advocate of open education and publicly critical of the partnerships between higher education institutions and these businesses. Pre-pandemic changes in legislation, focused on distance education, already opened up avenues for the implementation of hybrid teaching.[19] I began to notice how the pandemic expanded interest not only in the idea of remote teaching but also hybrid education in Brazil. I felt like post-pandemic, pre-service teachers were unlikely to face a school system without demands for hybrid modes of teaching. There was no more pressing challenge to their activities as future teachers than discussing how this was not going to be a "simple" shift in spaces but a seismic shift in schooling. For quite a while, I had been openly aggregating class materials on distance and open education on a Wikiversity site, and in mid-2019 I began a project where trainee teachers had to critically analyse platforms such as WhatsApp and Instagram in regards to their educational uses and threats to privacy.[20] It was based on this effort that I made a call for educators to connect, and immediately found a possibility of connection between our themes and interests through the Observatory's Telegram group.

Janaina: These moments of initial conversations in 2020 gave me more hope for dealing with the situation posed by remote education. I realised that the advancement of GAFAM in education was not just my concern. Being aware of this, knowing that there are activists, teachers, technical analysts, and other professionals who share the same concerns and who act to problematise and understand the technological domination that we are exposed to, and that was imposed on us, gave me more courage to continue with actions that contribute to expanding my students'

---

18 https://archive.org/details/@tecnouemg
19 Law 13.415, enacted February 16, 2017: https://www.planalto.gov.br/ccivil_03/_Ato2015-2018/2017/Lei/L13415.htm
20 https://pt.wikiversity.org/wiki/Educa%C3%A7%C3%A3o_Aberta

knowledge about these issues. I know these are only local actions, but with possibilities of expansion through other fronts and collaborative practices.

Tel: There is limited time and engagement with students to discuss educational technology. There is also a disquieting feeling: while we advocate strongly against the use of these tools in our daily lives, work, and study, we also are aware of how difficult it is to not make use of these platforms.[21] So, in our discussions, I have come to realise that while I can pontificate about how much I avoid these platforms, this comes from a position of privilege, and does not always apply to my students. This, of course, has fallen apart during the pandemic, because within the realm of work we are required to use Microsoft and Google. Within the realm of family we need to use WhatsApp, to make a doctor's appointment or connect to our children's schools for example, and make use of social networks to navigate cultural activities, business agendas, an even public services.[22] Knowing of this "failure" to disengage, I wonder how useful it is to discuss these issues with future educators. Is this an unattainable goal that will only lead to some level of "consciousness" about the problem and promote anxiety?

Janaina: We criticise proprietary software, but we use it in our daily lives. Is this an inconsistency? I don't think so. We are discussing platforms developed by monopolies, and the main characteristic of a monopoly is market control. I am obliged to use Teams by my institution. I am often disobedient, but I can't always be. We should problematise this contradiction with students. I make my position clear, but I don't deny that I use these platforms and I explain the reasons that compel me to use them, and we reflect about the great political and economic power that these IT corporations have. I feel that transparent dialogue contributes to understanding the problem and contradictions that exist in our society.

---

21 See, for example: https://www.nytimes.com/2020/07/31/technology/blocking-the-tech-giants.html
22 Many private businesses and government now make use of platforms such as Instagram as "official" channels of communication. Thus, participation in civic life is limited without access to these systems. The local energy company in one of our cities recently announced power outages in their Instagram "stories", for example.

Tel: This makes me think about something we often criticise within the realm of the free software movement, where the use of any proprietary software is frowned upon. Simply suggesting that someone stop using WhatsApp to use an open-source alternative[23] does not actually address many of the issues we raise, most clearly those due to the network effect (who will you talk to?) but also more central issues like technical autonomy (the service is still hosted by a third party; having your own server is possible, but quite unreasonable for most people, including educators). In fact, this might lead to inflating the worth of individual decision-making (to abandon a platform, individually) in contrast to what actually might make a difference: collective action.

Janaina: Many education secretariats (spheres responsible for education at municipal and state levels) made mandatory the use of WhatsApp, Facebook and YouTube by teachers and students to enable formal education during the pandemic. One of the justifications given by education managers when adopting these platforms is that "everyone uses them" and that most students don't consume their pre-paid internet packages by accessing them through zero rating: the offer of "free" access to services, most common in mobile phone plans as part of packages offered to users, such as unlimited use of WhatsApp or other platforms (Rossini & Moore, n.d.). So, the network effect was determinant in the choice of these platforms by managers, and students were forced to use these platforms for learning. In this scenario, how can I criticise students for using the technologies of GAFAM? To act this way is to be insensitive to the socioeconomic reality of a good part of our students, the most affected by the practice of zero rating are the poorest ones, and to blame the individual for surveillance and control that is imposed on them. It is difficult to make changes to this scenario by acting as an isolated individual. There are no quick and easy ways out of the domination imposed by these oligopolies. Still, I think it is important to reflect on the problem of surveillance and platformisation with students and also to show possible ways to mitigate these problems, ways that only work if we act collectively. When I teach about free software, for example, there are students who continue to use it at university, at work, and in their

---

23 Matrix is often touted as an option — an open protocol for communication adopted by many platforms, including Element (https://element.io).

personal lives. When students know the implications and risks in using platforms, many take these discussions to other spaces. Likewise, I am sure that after all our discussions, most students look at and deal with GAFAM more critically. This is an important step, after all, it is necessary to know the problem in order to intervene. Our actions are limited when compared to the power of these companies. However, great changes in society do not happen overnight, the most important ones took centuries to consolidate and occurred through collective action. So, we are not going to change the world now, but I think we are contributing.

Tel: In class, I often try to demonstrate the possibility of the empowerment of the individual. For a while, I intended to become a living example of how one does not have to have social network accounts or proprietary methods of communication. I thought this stance would provide impact and inspiration in students (it usually does, in the form of an astonished question: "you don't have WhatsApp?") and lead them to reconsider their use of these systems. But I can see how this quite individualistic stance might send the wrong message. Individual emancipation is not only impractical, but impossible. It might lead one to think that sanitising your technical landscape might provide a higher moral ground, when it does very little to instil consciousness for collective action. Your perspective shows how even we, as public advocates against these systems, and university professors with a large level of operational autonomy also end up caught in this web. Demonstrating this vulnerability, and how we navigate this minefield collectively, might actually provide a more attractive and reasonable demonstration of a way forward. As teachers and future administrators, particularly in the public school system, forms of collective decision making already exist and can be leveraged, there is a real possibility that these future teachers might make this a realm for discussions.

Conclusion

Facing the advance of large software corporations in education, especially in the context of the pandemic, it is urgent to reflect in teacher professional development on the process, risks, and implications of the platformisation of education. Sensing a general lack of urgency around this issue, when we believed it would be seen as one of the most critical of our time, led us to enact teaching that was not only critical, but also joined theory and practice towards collective consciousness and action. We theorised about the problems together with students and framed strategies and practical possibilities for resistance, with concrete outputs that can be shared, modified, and improved as open resources. As we moved through this process, we found and discarded strategies that turned out to be radical and simplistic, such as promoting FLOSS as an alternative — ultimately reinforcing the rhetoric of technology as tool, and of tool "choice". Our realisation grew that the most useful strategies were slow and collective. There was frustration in dealing with this topic with our students, not only as we saw how the oligopolies grew, but also in realising how difficult it was to promote a sense of urgency on this topic.

However, we realised that these projects did indeed promote change, as when, for example, students informed us that they have continued to use FLOSS in academia and in their professional lives, or that they had discussed these issues in other spaces, such as work and with family members. We needed, as educators, to believe (and continually convince each other) that our teaching and our actions would, perhaps, contribute to mitigating the influence of these corporations in education. As we move forward, we will need to collectively maneuver to determine the future of educational technologies in our institutions and school systems. This cannot be done without the concerted effort of students and educators and continual reflection on an ever-changing landscape. We remain resolute.

References

Amiel, T. (2012). Educaçao aberta: Configurando ambientes, práticas e recursos educacionais. In B. Santana, C. Rossini, & N. D. L. Pretto (Eds), *Recursos Educacionais Abertos: Práticas colaborativas e políticas públicas* (pp. 17–34). Casa da Cultura Digital/Edufba.
http://www.aberta.org.br/livrorea/livro/home.html

Amiel, T., & Amaral, S. F. do. (2013). Nativos e imigrantes: Questionando a fluência tecnológica de alunos e professores. *Revista Brasileira de Informática Na Educação, 21*(3), 1–11.
http://dx.doi.org/10.5753/rbie.2013.21.03.1

Amiel, T., Pezzo, T. C., Cruz, L. R. da, & Oliveira, L. A. (2021). Os modos de adesão e a abrangência do capitalismo de vigilância na educação brasileira. *Perspectiva, 39*(3), 1–12. https://doi.org/10.5007/2175-795X.2021.e80582

Bali, M., Cronin, C., & Jhangiani, R. S. (2020). Framing open educational practices from a social justice perspective. *Journal of Interactive Media in Education, 2020*(1), 1–12. https://doi.org/10.5334/jime.565

Borgmann, A. (1993). *Crossing the post-modern divide*. University of Chicago Press.

Cassino, J. F. (2021). O sul global e os desafios pós-coloniais na era digital. In J. F. Cassino, J. Souza, & S. A. da Silveira (Eds), *Colonialismo de dados: Como opera a trincheira algorítmica na guerra neoliberal* (pp. 13–31). Autonomia Literária.

Clinton-Lisell, V. (2021). Open pedagogy: A systematic review of empirical findings. *Journal of Learning for Development, 8*(2), 255–68. https://doi.org/10.56059/jl4d.v8i2.511

Couldry, N. (2020). *Colonialismo de dados e esvaziamento da vida social antes e pós pandemia de covid-19*. http://www.ihu.unisinos.br/images/ihu/2020/eventos/simposio_homo_digitalis/conferencias_pdf/Nick_Couldry.pdf

Couldry, N., & Mejias, U. A. (2019a). Data colonialism: Rethinking big data's relation to the contemporary subject. *Television & New Media, 20*(4), 336–49. https://doi.org/10.1177/1527476418796632

Cruz, L. R. da, Saraiva, F. de O., & Amiel, T. (2019). *Coletando dados sobre o Capitalismo de Vigilância nas instituições públicas do ensino superior do Brasil*. LAVITS. https://repositorio.unb.br/handle/10482/36912

Cruz, L. R. da, & Venturini, J. R. (2020). Neoliberalismo e crise: O avanço silencioso do capitalismo de vigilância na educação brasileira durante a pandemia da Covid-19. *Revista Brasileira de Informática na Educação, 28*(0), 1060–85. https://doi.org/10.5753/rbie.2020.28.0.1060

Dagnino, R. (2008). *Neutralidade da ciência e determinismo tecnológico: Um debate sobre a tecnociência*. Unicamp.

Decuypere, M., Grimaldi, E., & Landri, P. (2021). Introduction: Critical studies of digital education platforms. *Critical Studies in Education, 62*(1), 1–16. https://doi.org/10.1080/17508487.2020.1866050

Fiebig, T., Gürses, S., Gañán, C. H., Kotkamp, E., Kuipers, F., Lindorfer, M., Prisse, M., & Sari, T. (2023). Heads in the clouds: Measuring the implications of universities migrating to public clouds. Proceedings on privacy enhancing technologies symposium (pp. 117–50). Cornell University. https://doi.org/10.56553/popets-2023-0044

Foster, D., White, L., Adams, J., Erdil, D. C., Hyman, H., Kurkovsky, S., Sakr, M., & Stott, L. (2018). Cloud computing: Developing contemporary computer science curriculum for a cloud-first future. In G. Rößling, & B. Scharlau (Eds), *Proceedings of the 23rd annual ACM conference on innovation and technology in computer science education* (pp. 130–47). ACM Digital Library. https://doi.org/ttps://doi.org/10.1145/3293881.3295781

Freire, P. (2014). *Pedagogy of hope: Reliving pedagogy of the oppressed.* Bloomsbury.

Freire, P. (2018). *Pedagogia da autonomia: Saberes necessários à prática educativa.* Paz e Terra. (Original work published in 1996).

Gennari, A. M. (2020). Brasil: Crise estrutural, pandemias, políticas sociais e a dura realidade conjuntural. *Revista Fim do Mundo, 3,* 18–49. https://doi.org/10.36311/2675-3871.2020.v1n03.p18-49

Macgilchrist, F. (2021). What is 'critical' in critical studies of edtech? Three responses. *Learning, Media and Technology, 46*(3), 243–49. https://doi.org/10.1080/17439884.2021.1958843

Martín-Barbero, J. (2003). Cultural change: The perception of the media and the mediation of its images. *Television & New Media, 4*(1), 85–106. https://doi.org/10.1177/1527476402239435

Oddone, A. C. (2021). *Alternativas ao capitalismo de vigilância: Uma análise do uso de software livre em instituições públicas de ensino superior brasileiras.* UnB. https://bdm.unb.br/handle/10483/29010

Oliveira, V. M., & Satriano, C. R. (2017). Narrativa autobiográfica do próprio pesquisador como fonte e ferramenta de pesquisa. *Linhas Críticas, 23*(51), 369–86. https://doi.org/10.26512/lc.v23i51.8231

Parra, H., Cruz, L., Amiel, T., & Marchado, J. (2018). Infraestruturas, economia e política informacional: O caso do Google suite for education. *Mediações, 23*(1), 63–99. https://doi.org/10.5433/2176-6665.2018v23n1p63

Poell, T., Nieborg, D., & Dijck, J. van. (2019). Platformisation. *Internet Policy Review, 8*(4), 1–13. https://doi.org/10.14763/2019.4.1425

Rossini, C., & Moore, T. (n.d.). *Exploring zero-rating challenges: Views from five countries.* Public Knowledge. https://web.archive.org/web/20190610203439/https://www.publicknowledge.org/assets/uploads/blog/ZeroRatingCombinedCR.pdf

Srnicek, N. (2019). Imaginar plataformas alternativas: Entrevista com Nick Srnicek [Interview].
https://digilabour.com.br/srnicek-capitalismo-de-plataforma-mudancas/

Silveira, S. A. da (2021). A hipótese do colconialismo de dados e o neoliberalismo. In J. F. Cassino, J. Souza, & S. A. da Silveira (Eds), *Colonialismo de dados: Como opera a trincheira algorítmica na guerra neoliberal* (pp. 32–50). Autonomia Literária.

Srnicek, N. (2017). *Platform capitalism*. John Wiley & Sons.

Toledo, D. G. C. de. (2020). Dependência e autonomia nas políticas externa e tecnológica do Brasil, 1951–79. *Monções: Revista de Relações Internacionais da UFGD, 9*(17), 476–505.
https://doi.org/10.30612/rmufgd.v9i17.10066

Weller, M. (2015). MOOCs and the Silicon Valley narrative. *Journal of Interactive Media in Education, 2015*(1), 1–7.
http://jime.open.ac.uk/articles/10.5334/jime.am

Zuboff, S. (2019). *The age of surveillance capitalism: The fight for a human future at the new frontier of power*. Public Affairs.

19. Imagination and justice: Teaching the future(s) of higher education through Africanfuturist speculative fiction

Felicitas Macgilchrist and Eamon Costello

The inequalities in higher education are palpable. For many observers, they are worsening as data-intense technologies are used more widely. Specific performance metrics generate hierarchical rankings of universities, causing uneven global access to essential infrastructure. Monitoring technologies of surveillance disproportionately penalise students of colour. Predictive analytics systems block the paths of those students with barriers to learning who the system predicts to be unlikely to succeed. The use of technologies within capitalist logics of profit and growth is stripping the planet of resources, with uneven impacts on people around the world. At the same time, hyperindividualism undergirds what can be seen as the colonial knowledge practices produced and reproduced in higher education, rendering individual students and educators responsible for their own success or failure. The structures and histories of disempowerment are made invisible.

Against this backdrop of "multi-layered digital inequalities" (Czerniewicz, 2022), this chapter responds to the call to elaborate on glimmers of alternative futures which foreground equity, social justice, care, and relational sustainability, by sketching a locally situated pedagogical opportunity that invites students to reflect on what 'good' can mean in higher education. The guiding idea is that by asking "what if?" with speculative fiction (Okorafor, 2017c), issues of power and transformation can be raised that will trouble most norms of higher education today. By inviting students to trouble these norms, educators invite them to open new possibilities for the future. Speculation is essential to imagining and creating alternatives to the current mess in this unequal and unjust planet.

To this end, this chapter presents a potential course (a 15-week seminar) in which students read speculative fiction and write their own stories about possible/potential/implausible futures for higher education. The course and this chapter aim to open generative spaces for students and lecturers to *reflect* on their (our) own positions in the academy, to *critique* the reproduction of classed, raced, gendered inequities in higher education through, e.g. digital technologies, automation or platformisation, and to *generate futures* that are oriented to justice. The course contributes to the growing movement in which re-thinking and re-imagining enable us to re-act in our contemporary entangled world in the reparative ways to which this crucial prefix "re" gestures (Facer, 2019a; Haraway, 2016).

The chapter begins by setting the scene, describing the context and key choices behind the course design. It then outlines how the course takes four steps towards "the good" in higher education: (1) by shaping an anti-racist, anti-classist storytelling and workshopping style of listening, respecting and giving generous feedback to one another; (2) by unpacking the power relations which make us who we are becoming (subjectivation, datafication); (3) by strengthening ways of becoming which are less hegemonic today (more-than-human sympoiesis, decolonised knowledge); and (4) by inviting students to write stories of higher education for good. In the conclusion, the chapter returns to the argument that higher education needs new ways of imagining the future otherwise, and that curating a blend of theory and speculative fiction is one way to open a space for shared imaginings. Finally, there is an afterword where the diary of a (fictional) student in the class is shared.

Setting the scene

The chapter took shape while having conversations about *how* and *what* to teach that addresses today's inequalities, but simultaneously imagines other futures. Perhaps due to the growing awareness of inequalities across society, including the long-standing critique of the "corporate" university, futures-making is generating a huge amount of interest today. Strategies for how to generate alternative futures draw on future workshops (Jungk & Müllert, 1987), empathy-based stories (Särkelä & Suoranta, 2020; Wallin et al., 2019), speculative story-writing sprints (Johnson 2019), pedagogical tools to "dig deeper" and "relate wider" inspired by Indigenous analyses and practices (Andreotti et al., 2019), critical design within an Afrofuturist aesthetic (Holbert et al., 2020), unpacking the conditions of possibility of current inequalities (C. Kelty, personal communication, May 5, 2022), or inviting students to write social science fiction (Lackey, 1994).

The following sketches out a seminar designed from and for a specific local context in Germany. Higher education in Germany remains predominantly white (which includes the authors of this chapter), most of the professors identify as cis-male (which one of us is not), and despite minimal or no tuition fees, students are largely from the middle or upper class. Imagine, therefore, a potential seminar, which as we write has not yet been put into action, for a large public university in Northern Germany. The group meets, as German seminars tend to, once a week for 90 minutes, for about 15 weeks. Imagine the course embedded in educational and cultural studies undergraduate courses, but open to all students across all faculties.

We were interested in reading beyond the region in which we live (Europe), and in teaching with authors beyond those (un)marked as white, and male who are so often read and cited more frequently than others (Dion et al., 2018). We came across *Binti*, a science fiction novella that speaks in a unique way to urgent issues facing higher education today (Okorafor, 2015). The author, Nnedi Okorafor, describes her work as "Africanfuturist". It is "concerned with visions of the future, is interested in technology, leaves the earth, skews optimistic, is centred on and predominantly written by people of African descent (black people) and it is rooted first and foremost in Africa" (Okorafor, 2019).

Thus *Binti*, which students can loan from the online Open Library, accompanies the class through the semester.[1] Binti is a young woman who has been awarded a place at the Oomza University. Oomza Uni is an elite institution, only 5% of the students are human. It is a planet in a

---

[1] Okorafor's Binti is available here for loan through the Open Library: https://archive.org/details/binti0000okor/mode/2up?view=theater

distant galaxy. Binti is the first in her family, and of the Himba people, to go to university. On the way to the launch pad, she finds herself among the light-skinned and wealthy Khoush. Some of them make fun of, or are repelled by Binti's thick hair. However, on the trip to Oomza Uni, on a *Miri 12* — a living spaceship like a shrimp, Binti befriends other first year students. The plot of the story revolves around events on the spaceship. The Meduse appear and kill everyone on board except Binti, who is protected by a particular technological device (*edan*), and her *otjize* which is a special paste she makes from red clay to cover her skin. Binti uncovers the purpose of the current Meduse killing spree: Khoush scholars stole the stinger of a Meduse chief for their research, and the Meduse want it back. At the end of the novella, Binti is able to forge peace using openness, communication and her *edan* to negotiate with the university on behalf of the Meduse chief. This 81-page novella thus touches on central issues of inequality and injustice in today's institutions of higher education.

Pedagogical approach: Anti-racist, anti-classist, generous workshopping

Students in this seminar read fiction and create stories. Storytelling offers a uniquely creative, open, and yet localised or grounded mode of:

> support[ing] our students to name and understand the troubles we are facing, to think with hope and with rigour about the sorts of futures that are being made today and to enable them to care for, imagine and make liveable futures in collective dialogue with others whose futures are also at stake. (Facer, 2019b, p. 4)

Storytelling as rehearsal, as playing, as never-quite-finished speculative practice tries to bring back "study" (as "the incessant and irreversible intellectuality" of activities like walking and talking, dancing and suffering) into universities from which it has been replaced by grading (Harney & Moten, 2013, p. 110).

The seminar encourages students to engage respectfully with each other's storytelling. It draws on Chavez's (2021) *The Anti-Racist Writing Workshop: How to Decolonize the Creative Classroom*, in which the author presents an approach to learning and teaching as a thoughtful, critical, and democratic mode of engaging with students and enabling students to engage with one another. Chavez's goal of identifying ways to align processes of critique with principles of creativity and justice are relevant to teaching across the disciplines. For this seminar, we imagine the first few sessions as reading sessions in which the class discusses and reflects on *Binti* and related research literature. In later sessions, students work on creating their own storied future(s), utopian, dystopian or otherwise speculative. These latter sessions have a more explicitly workshopping character in which students present and receive feedback on ongoing ideas or drafts.

Chavez offers ways to overcome the kind of feedback where the student only listens while their work is taken apart by others. Instead, she describes ways of "fostering engagement, mindfulness and generosity" (which includes removing competition), of "instituting reading and writing rituals" (including bringing putty to fidget with in class), of "promoting camaraderie and collective power". She draws on Liz Lerman's *Critical Response Process* in which students moderate their own feedback session, and students give their feedback in response to the moderator's priorities (Lerman & Borstel, 2003). This anti-racist workshop is also an anti-classist, anti-sexist and anti-ableist workshop. Thus, an incredibly powerful reworking of the hierarchies often reproduced in higher education.

It includes conversations in which students and professor explicitly deconstruct traditional hierarchies (hooks, 1994). This includes tapping into the discussions on #ungrading and providing student opportunities to co-design rubrics for receiving feedback. It means reflecting together on what makes good discussions (Brookfield & Preskill, 2005). For all the sharing and discussion activities noted below, the class uses strategies from "Equity Unbound" (Cronin et al., n.d.) and "liberating structures" (Lipmanowicz & McCandless, 2013) that aim to generate excitement collectively and equitably (hooks, 1994), such as "1–2–4–All", "9 Whys" and "Troika Consulting".

In the first session of the semester, we introduce ourselves. We watch a 10-minute TED Talk by Nnedi Okorafor from 2017 where she reads from the novella and reflects on Africanfuturist science fiction. We introduce the workshopping format and use it to discuss the current scholarly interest in futurity, and how the class can engage with the exciting questions that are currently being addressed by generatively critical research to imagine and make liveable futures together (Castellví et al., 2022; Facer, 2019a, Facer, 2019b; Muñoz, 2019; UNESCO, 2021).

By the second session, all students will have read the novella. We reflect on the story together. This may include Binti's gendered/classed/raced/heteronormative experiences at the beginning of her studies: she is Black, poor, rural and female. Students identify different aspects that point to potential university futures. If she were teaching, Felicitas would share her initial (daunting) experiences at a British university, and her personal "aha" moment towards the end of the first year when she first realised that the wealthy students from private schools, who seemed so knowledgeable, articulate, and superior did not actually know more about the specific issue being discussed than she did. Many of her (comprehensive school) friends had these aha moments, but only after months of being silent and feeling inferior in class. Eamon would talk about arriving just after the start of lectures, during his first year of university, so he would not have to meet fellow students, but also about learning to recognise and eventually even befriend social anxiety as a normal part of life. Any students who would like to, also share their own stories of starting university.

Unpacking power relations

The second phase of the seminar engages with central concepts and topics relevant to higher education. In each, we discuss an extract from *Binti* and selected academic publications which invite students to unpack hierarchical power relations in education.

Subjectivation

The first theme is subjectivation. Okorafor (2015) writes:

> "Stupid, stupid, stupid," I whispered. We Himba don't travel. We stay put. Our ancestral land is life; move away from it and you diminish. We even cover our bodies with it. *Otjize* is red land. Here in the launch port, most were Khoush and a few other non-Himba. Here, I was an outsider; I was outside. [...] I was by myself and I had just left my family. My prospects of marriage had been 100 percent and now they would be zero. No man wanted a woman who'd run away. However, beyond

my prospects of normal life being ruined, I had scored so high on the planetary exams in mathematics that the Oomza University had not only admitted me, but promised to pay for whatever I needed in order to attend. No matter what choice I made, I was never going to have a normal life, really. (p. 12f.)

How (as what or as whom) has Binti been addressed that leads to this train of thought? How does she enact herself as a particular subject of knowledge and power in this excerpt by refracting what others have said to her or acted towards her? Who had laughed at her for wanting to go to university? What did it do when one of her sisters told her to be rational and stop being selfish? Who congratulated her (and was anyone else moved to tears at that point in the story)? What is the power of scholarships? Who decides what a "normal life" is? Who benefits and who loses from these imaginations of normality? What tensions meet in this extract?

Students would have read some key texts in English on subjectivation in advance for this session (Butler, 1997; Foucault, 1982; Hall, 1997; Youdell, 2006), and in German (Reh & Ricken, 2012; Ricken et al., 2019). Linking the extract to this literature, we could tease out, for instance, the sections in the book in which Binti was addressed to see herself as a non-travelling, rooted Himba, as a cis woman with a good chance of a good marriage to a good cis man, as a runaway whom no Himba man will want to marry. And how she then sees herself differently when addressed by Oomza University as one of the best students in the galaxy, so good that they not only admit her, but will cover the costs of getting her to the university and enabling her to complete her degree there. The class could return to the gendered, raced, classed, heteronormative aspects that were mentioned in the first reading of the novella, and link them to theories of subjectivation. Students could find traces in the story of the norms and conventions that make her legible as a subject within the Himba frame in which she grew up.

One important idea will likely be "agency", and we could discuss the (powerful) idea of "discursive agency", i.e. that "[b]ecause the agency of the subject is not a property of the subject, an inherent will or freedom, but an effect of power, it is constrained but not determined in advance" (Butler, 1997, p. 139). This opens space for the different ways in which we are addressed to collide, mingle and lead to new openings and other foreclosures. We could discuss this questioning of the idea of a sovereign subject, this disruption of the idea of free will and autonomy, including how the agency of a post-sovereign subject makes space for Oomza Uni to address Binti in a different way that can lead to unexpected paths.

Datafication

The next session explores datafication, the transformation of ever more information about our lives into machine-readable data that can be stored, processed, aggregated, and accessed. Okorafor (2015) narrates:

> The travel security officer scanned my astrolabe, a full *deep* scan. Dizzy with shock, I shut my eyes and breathed through my mouth to steady myself. Just to leave the planet, I had to give them access to my *entire* life — me, my family, and all forecasts of my future. I stood there, frozen, hearing my mother's voice in my head. "There is a reason why our people do not go to that university. Oomza Uni wants you for its gain, Binti. You go to that school and you become its slave." I couldn't help but contemplate the possible truth in her words. I hadn't even gotten there yet and already I'd given them my life. I wanted to ask the officer if he did this for everyone, but I was afraid now that he'd done it. They could do anything to me, at this point. Best not to make trouble. (p. 13)

What kind of data about Binti's entire life could be stored on this astrolabe? How would Oomza Uni gain from these data? How would the forecasts about Binti's future be made? Who decides what data to store or what data to use to make predictions? Who acts on the forecasts? Who controls the data? Who can render it unavailable? What kind of protests might there have been in the past of this world (the future of ours)? Do we imagine the officer scanning everyone's astrolabe in the same way or are there hierarchies between Himba and Khoush in privacy and surveillance? Why was Binti afraid now that the security officer had seen the data? Does datafication inevitably lead people to think it is best not to make trouble?

The astrolabe is a hand-sized device built by Himba designers. Binti is an expert astrolabe maker. The Khoush pay a lot for a well-designed astrolabe (despite having little respect for Himba people). This scene can open up discussions about the datafication of the university: from the quantification of life and surveillance capitalism (Zuboff, 2019; Amiel et al., 2021), data colonialism (Anonymous, 2016; Couldry & Mejias, 2019) and the spaces of big data (Bernard 2021) through justice-oriented data literacy (Raffaghelli 2022), obfuscation tactics (Brunton & Nissenbaum, 2015), to the exploitation of people and the environment that occurs in the production of data-processing devices (Crawford & Joler, 2018).

With the help of excerpts from a selection of scholarly texts, we unpack the metaphor often used in discussions of higher education of data as the "new oil", and how this metaphor suggests that data are a resource lying around to be found and monetised (Bock et al., 2023; Iske et al., 2020; Jarke & Breiter, 2019; Macgilchrist et al., 2022; Parra et al., 2018; Williamson, 2018; see also Amiel & do Rozário Diniz, Chapter 18, this volume). With this literature, we discuss an alternative understanding of educational data as "made", constructed, produced. We discuss different critical positions in debates about datafication: a humanist critique which warns about the loss of human dignity in the way data are amassed and colonised (Couldry & Mejias, 2019; Kwet, 2017; Zuboff, 2019), critical analyses of the racialising and heteronormalising forces of datafication (Benjamin, 2019; Costanza-Chock, 2020; Dixon-Román et al., 2020; Prinsloo, 2020), and data activism and struggles for data justice (Daly et al., 2019; Gutiérrez, 2018; Milan & Treré, 2019). Students reflect on how they feel or how they would act in Binti's position, and thereby elaborate their position on datafication.

Becoming otherwise

A challenge of the datafication session could be that it pulls us too much towards the role of data today, rather than speculating about becoming otherwise in the future. The seminar's third phase turns towards this: where becoming "otherwise" refers to ways of living, learning, teaching that are outwith hegemonic hierarchies (Andreotti et al., 2020).

More-than-human

The next issue that we tackle is more explicitly in the realm of the speculative: the more-than-humans in/of higher education at Oomza Uni. First, there is connection to technological artefacts. Okorafor (2015) writes:

> I looked at my cramped hands. From within it, from my *edan*, possibly the strongest current I'd ever produced streamed in jagged connected bright blue branches. It slowly etched and lurched through the closed door, a line of connected bright blue treelike branches that shifted in shape but never broke their connection. The current was touching the Meduse. Connecting them to me. And though I'd created it, I couldn't control it now. (p. 41, 42)

With this blue current, Binti and the Meduse can understand each other even though they continue to speak their different languages. The *edan*'s current connected to Binti translates.

Second, there are multispecies beings. While negotiating with the Meduse chief, and before she can negotiate on behalf of the Meduse with Oomza Uni, Binti is stung by a Meduse in the back. Later, she realised what changed through this sting. Okorafor (2015) writes:

> My hair was rested against my back, weighed down by the *otjize*, but as I'd gotten up, one lock had come to rest on my shoulder. I felt it rub against the front of my shoulder and I *saw* it now. [...] I rubbed off the *otjize*. [The lock] glowed a strong deep blue like the sky back on earth on a clear day, like Okwu and so many of the other Meduse. [...] My hair was no longer hair. (p. 81)

Later, Binti looks at herself in the mirror, after washing off all her *otjize* and before applying new *otjize*. Okorafor (2015) writes:

> The *okuoko* were a soft transparent blue with darker blue dots at their tips. They grew out of my head as if they'd been doing that all my life, so natural looking that I couldn't say they were ugly. (p. 87)

What makes up a human? When Binti becomes connected with the *edan* through the current, does this make her a cyborg? What is a cyborg anyway, and in what way is it related to the military? How does connection lead to understanding? When does it lead to tension (both in the novel and beyond)? What happens to the idea of boundaries here, for example: boundaries of bodies or nations or "ethnic groups" or languages or capacities? Which interests are served if we imagine the body as bounded, and the human as only human? What difference does it make to our understanding of multispecies beings if we say Binti has become "part Meduse" or if we say she has become "also Meduse"? What "parts" are we made of? And can we split them up or are they entangled? Can any words in our vocabulary capture the idea of more-than-one thing being one? Why would Binti contemplate that the *okuoko* were "ugly"? In what way are they "natural looking"? What does it mean to look natural? Who decides, and on what basis? In what ways are our bodies today entwined and entangled with the more-than-human (e.g. materiality, animals, microbes, environment or technology like spectacles, smartphones, or the bacteria in our stomachs)?

The *edan* is a little stellated cube-shaped object covered by strange symbols, loops, swirls, and fractals that Binti found in the desert, but whose functions have been lost. Talking about this *edan* that merges with Binti, we discuss posthumanist and sociomaterialist theories in educational theory (Gourlay, 2021; Sørensen, 2009). We reflect on higher education initiatives which aim to "enact new, resistant ways of playing at the boundaries of the human and machine" by communicating with or (re-)programming bots (Bayne, 2015), and explore the interdependencies and responsibilities enacted. We also read Karen Barad (2007), Donna Haraway (2016) and Bayo Akomolafe (2017) for new vocabularies that try to capture relationality without resorting to words such as "hybrid", merging, blending, interaction or entwined (which still presuppose that at least two beings are separate before they merge, blend, interact or become entwined). For instance, with Barad, we have *intra-action*, becoming through action. With Haraway, we have *sympoiesis*, becoming-with (which has inspired work on the messy daily practices of "symmation" to contest fantasies of all-powerful "automation" in education; see Wagener-Böck et al. (2022). With Akomolafe, we have the urgency of slowing down and rejecting claims of independence, human superiority, or solutionism.

Decolonising knowledge

Decolonising knowledge sits at the heart of *Binti*. The world-making of this speculative fiction invites readers to see a university far beyond our contemporary colonial institutions of higher education. In the following extract, Binti has just reminded the assembled professors (human and other-than-human, including Haas, "like a spider made of wind") that the Meduse chief's stinger is in the university's weapons museum. She proposes that if they return the stinger, they will stop further bloodshed. Okorafor (2015) narrates:

> I was sure they would agree. These professors were educated beyond anything I could imagine. Thoughtful. Insightful. United. Individual. The Meduse chief came forward and spoke its piece as well. It was angry, but thorough, eloquent with a sterile logic. 'If you do not give it to us willingly, we have the right to take back what was brutally stolen from us without provocation,' the chief said.
>
> After the chief spoke, the professors discussed among themselves for over an hour. They did not retreat to a separate room to do this. They did it right before the chief, Okwu, and me. [...] Feet away from us, beyond the glass table, these professors were shouting with anger, sometimes guffawing with glee, flicking antennae in each other's faces, making ear-popping clicks to get the attention of colleagues. [...]
>
> Finally, the professors quieted and took their places at the glass table again. [...] The spiderlike Haas raised two front legs and spoke in the language of the Meduse and said, 'On behalf of all the people of Oomza Uni and on behalf of Oomza University, I apologize for the actions of a group of our own in taking the stinger from you, Chief Meduse. The scholars who did this will be found, expelled, and exiled. Museum specimen of such prestige are highly prized at our university, however, such things must only be acquired with permission from the people to whom they belong. Oomza protocol is based on honour, respect, wisdom, and knowledge. We will return it to you immediately'. (p. 76ff.)

Who profits from the stinger in the museum? Does this scene enact restorative justice? What makes someone seem educated? What difference to knowledge does it make to debate in front of guests and onlookers rather than retreating to a private room? What modes of knowing does retreating, when only the final decision is shared in public, legitimise? And which modes of knowing, which epistemologies, which ways of imagining are repressed in this process? What power does translation have? Which beings are speaking beings in *Binti*? Does this power of language destabilise ideas of human exceptionalism? How do Binti and the Meduse chief claim rights and redress here? What would happen in our local contexts if stolen artefacts were returned? How does Haas's statement shift understandings of who has the right to know and to ownership?

At this stage, we might read articles about Okorafor's work (Crowley, 2019; Davis, 2020; Hanchey, 2020). Some students may decide to read the second and third novellas in the *Binti* trilogy, which include further scenes of decolonising higher education. For example, when Binti learns more about the *edan* from the Indigenous "Desert People" than the university can teach her, or when animals inform people (Okorafor, 2017a, 2017b). We could consider the difference Halberstam proposes between "learning" as the consumerist mode of thinking that institutions require of students, and Harney and Moten's "study" — a "mode of thinking with others separate from the thinking that the institution requires of you" (Halberstam in Harney & Moten, 2013). We could then reflect on our role in this seminar, in which the educator-as-institution requires a particular mode of thinking from the students, and whether students can resist this within the institution. We could consider how Binti invites us to exceed that mode within the institution of higher education, or to rethink the future of higher education beyond specific modes of thinking. These considerations would be against the backdrop of decolonial thought (Escobar, 2007; Mignolo, 2009; Quijano, 2010).

Imagining futures

Engaging with selected publications on each of the four themes above, our hope is that students can connect with Binti and through her story relate to the theoretical literature in a more locally situated storied way. But by doing this through science fiction rather than through stories from our "own" lives, we can explore, experiment, reflect, refract, critique, share and generate ideas in new planetary or galaxy-wide ways.

After these initial weeks of intense reading and reflection on the key issues through Binti's story, the seminar becomes a workshop. We engage more thoroughly with Chavez's and Lerman's approach (see above). Students spend the rest of the semester working on projects. They develop ideas that reshape the future of higher education. These can be realistic or speculative social science fiction — they can be utopias, dystopias, or mixed forms. Students can work together on a shared idea or support each other to develop individual visions. They research, exchange ideas on how they envisage higher education for good and prepare their stories. Each week, the group hears from a small number of students, and "workshop" their ideas, with generous feedback as described above (Chavez, 2021). Staying in the storytelling mode, students write up these projects as social science fiction (Lackey, 1994).

We imagine student projects that are directly inspired by *Binti* to include *sustainability* (with technology which does not become obsolete, like the astrolabes built to last a lifetime) (Okorafor, 2015, p. 34), *commons* (which can be strengthened by designing for open, transparent platforms and spaces for debate in a knowledge commons in which everyone can participate or listen in, rather than today's confidential academic leadership meetings or publications behind paywalls; see the scene above), and ideas of *becoming planetary* or *becoming galactic* (when the connections among living beings on earth and across the galaxy become visible through, for example, Binti's *okuoko*, or biotechnology like the living *Miro 12* spaceship (Gabrys, 2018; Mbembe, 2022).

Further issues might include learning analytics and artificial intelligence which can range from dystopian visions of total surveillance to ethically designed convivial technologies, co-developed with participants, degrowth scenarios of slow scholarship with time for thinking and growing, design justice implemented across educational institutions, digital nomads who remove themselves from national solidarity systems, behaviourist futures, open science, or transhumanism (some of these futures are developed in Knox et al., 2019; Macgilchrist et al., 2020; Vetter, 2023).

Concluding thoughts

How does this seminar speak to higher education "for good"? Our aim was a classic one: to find new ways to invite students into conversations about urgent issues in higher education. The novella is short but rich in ideas for the future of higher education. With Binti, we have a character who is relatable. Without basing the seminar on "our own" experiences, we have a story to "support students to imagine and make liveable futures on their own terms" (Facer, 2019b, p. 3).

Stories in themselves are powerful entities. Lying outside current priorities in education to have "impact" beyond the classroom. Even if the stories remain in the classroom, the participants will have experienced themselves as having the agency to imagine concrete futures — utopian, dystopian or mixed — through their creation of speculative futures

(Rodriguez, 2001). They will have highlighted issues, delved into research, prioritised ways of living, learning, and teaching. Their own future decision-making will be affected. But these "what if" futures can also live beyond the classroom to influence other decision-makers in education, from lecturers to the university leadership or educational policymakers. We envisage exhibitions of student work in university buildings, near the management offices, or printed on banners, hanging from trees across the campus or city. We envisage students presenting their stories to senior academics in meetings at the edges of senate meetings or ministry events. We envisage podcasts, videos, press releases to influence public discourse on what is possible, what is impossible, and what is necessary to reshape a higher education for good.

The justice hinted at in the title of this chapter goes far beyond reforms such as making higher education more inclusive. Bayo Akomolafe has described the current crisis in which the world finds itself as a reproduction of the slave ship, with enslaved Africans chained in the hold, and European slavers on the top deck. Yet despite their different experiences of this ship, they were all on "a vessel of destruction" (reported in Dabiri, 2021, p. 73). Dabiri (2021) describes Akomolafe's position:

> [I]nclusion today can be understood as access to the top deck of the slave ship. Inclusion is access to power in a system that is ultimately a tool of destruction. It is not enough to make exploitative systems more 'inclusive'. Do we want to get on the top deck or do we want to destroy the goddamn ship? (p. 73)

This chapter set out a thought experiment to explore what might happen if theories important for higher education are brought together with the world-making of speculative fiction, in particular the kind of world-making seen in Africanfuturist, feminist or ecological science fiction that does not transfer today's norms and conventions into a future time, but instead reconfigures power relations. The goal is to open spaces for imagining the future otherwise. For instance, by reconfiguring subjectivation, reinventing data platforms, recalibrating justice to human and more-than-human entanglements, or decolonising knowledge practices.

As Le Guin (1976/2019) has said, science fiction is rarely about the future, it is about the present. It offers educators the means to delve deeply into today's imaginations of the future, and to support students to create stories about a liveable future. These "what if" futures may remain entirely speculative, and that would be fine. However, developing and sharing what-ifs is essential to reshape the discourse about higher education and to inspire those who are involved in making world-building decisions around the future of higher education, from presidents to students to educators.

Afterword: "Dear Diary" — Selected confessions of my study abroad year

What will students make of this seminar? As noted above, it has not yet been taught. Taking creative liberty, we imagine the following could occur:

> Dear Diary
>
> Started a new class.
>
> Completely over-prepared and read the required text Binti twice already. Okay, you got me. I cheated. It's on Audible. I read it with my *ears*, okay?
>
> The professor told us how she felt like an outsider starting in university once upon a time. This helped me a lot, but I still mumbled through my class introduction. Should have said something about coming here from Ireland, on Erasmus this year.
>
> In other news, a boy sat beside me who smelled really bad.
>
> Yours,
>
> C

> Dear Diary,
>
> Class today was about "subjectivation". I haven't tackled the readings yet beyond Binti itself. This is typical me. I start hyper-enthusiastic but fail to do the basics by week 2. I'm a bit disheartened.
>
> Smelly boy did not sit near me, which was a plus.
>
> Yours,
>
> C

Dear Diary,

Today's class blew my mind. Professor Mac G and the others in the class are bursting with ideas. My head is spinning. Datafication: that feeling the University is sucking your soul. Binti gives her whole self over to it when she decides to go there. And that's me! When I'm in, I'm all in. But I also feel datafication is a kind of complicity somehow, not always something being done to us.

Crashed in the evening and ate 5.5 chocolate biscuits — managed to spit the last half in the bin.

Yours,

C

Dear Diary,

Today was *more than human*. This was my favourite day so far. The red clay (otjize) that Binti puts on her skin I just love. Sometimes, I feel like going outside and clawing my hands into the earth. When everything feels disconnected, unreal. This world of ideas… It's like the university makes us more than human, but I want to get back to being merely human sometimes.

And Binti is honouring tradition too. She is literally smuggling the soil of her homeland into the academy, on her skin and in her hair. And it's also the dirt — the shit you can't leave behind — the stuff that follows you around. You can honour that too.

I took notes: "Why would Binti contemplate that the okuoko were 'ugly'? In what way are they 'natural looking'? What does it mean to look natural?"

Wow… what is natural? We are obsessed with physicalism — with beauty. We're wired that way, I guess. We see and dream in bodies and faces. But then, we make it worse, with the stories we spin around bodies, those more-than-human vapours.

Overcame sugar cravings this evening by drinking seven glasses of water. I will be up peeing all night (and a demon all day tomorrow).

Yours,

C

Dear Diary,

Notes from class:

"...Consider how Binti invites us to exceed that mode within the institution of higher education"

"...rethink the future of higher education beyond specific modes of thinking."

I felt like I was being spoken to directly, given the possibility that the forms of everything could be challenged, like we were being given a space for creativity and imagination.

We were split into pairs to work on our assignment. I chose my partner for the entire rest of semester... yep, you guessed it: smelly-boy.

Yours.

C

Dear Diary

I am really struggling with his highness of pong. He suggested we do a fanfiction of Binti for our assignment. I told him this could amount to cultural appropriation, but this was waaaay over his head. I find I am just explaining everything to him.

Renaming buildings after women, creating gender diversity in citation — are those necessary? *Hell yeah.* But is it sufficient? Will putting more women in STEM magically change boardroom cultures? How will we measure real change? How will we actually treat each other day to day?

Yours,

C

Dear Diary,

Today we learned about Felicia Rose Chavez. We are creating a democratic classroom. It's exciting! Also, it's terrifying. We can have a "mentor" that is any writing that inspires us — a book, a poem, a hip hop song, an anime comic. We choose whatever is right for us — a voice from home, from inside of us.

19. Imagination and justice

As you know dear diary, I am not much of a reader. I don't listen to anything cool music-wise, and I spend most of my time watching garbage on Netflix and YouTube that I WILL NOT be confessing to in class. So, I told s-b to get us a book. He brought in a book called "Dignity" by Donna Hicks (2011) (see Fig. 19.1). Under questioning he admitted to me that he has not actually read it and that he just took it from his parents' bookshelf. Reading between the lines, I think he is still living at home, which is interesting.

The book is good though. It has these principles based around affirming the dignity of another person. It would be perfect for our assignment actually. Recognising and upholding the dignity of others could be the underlying theme of a great story. We probably need a hero, a villain and… I guess a spaceship too. How hard can writing a story be?

Yours,

C

Figure 19.1

Dignity. Image by Liam Costello, CC BY 4.0

Dear Diary,

Affirming the dignity of another person... It sounds so inspiring, and it should be easy. It sounds like the right and good thing to do. But what does it actually mean?

Can I even uphold my own dignity?

This whole diary business — is it dignified? Or is it shameful? Would I let someone else read this?

Read about the white ceramic, coming closer, until I feel my head on the cold rim, fingers touching the back of my throat. Is it like that, just something compulsive?

And using unkind epithets, even here, where no-one sees, where everything is allowed to hurt... is that really okay?

Yours,

C

Dear Diary,

I had a weird dream. I was the dreamer but then I was also the one who dreamed of me. I was talking to Catherine Cronin, in London, about a book. The Good Book. It was actually many books, all full of the good. They were lined up on huge shelves in front of me. I was neither a man nor a woman and I was Binti too somehow (see Fig. 19.2). My dreadlocked hair flowed about me, pulsing luminous blue. Alive. And it was moving towards the books, reading the spines.

Yours,

C

Dear Diary,

We finally finished our story and read it to the class. I could hardly hear what was happening as my heart was pounding like a volcano. It went well! That's the main thing. Pure elation.

I couldn't smell him today which was weird.

Yours,

C

Figure 19.2

Dreamer. Image by Lily (Prajakta Girme), CC BY 4.0

Dear Diary,

I literally woke up today wondering how smelly boy lost his smell. Did he get the message and wash? Did I get covid? Am I immune to his pong now?

I leaned over closer to him during class, when he wasn't looking, and tried to sniff him. If anyone catches me doing this my life is over!

Yours,

C

Dear Diary,

I will miss Prof Mac G a lot I must say. And Binti too, who feels almost like a friend. At least I will be rid of smelly-boy. I am meeting him now to try and give him some last basic pointers on existence. He does not appear to have any friends — which is fine. I don't have ten zillion friends myself, but the problem is *he doesn't care* that he has no friends — which is just plain weird (and kind of liberating).

So, I'm trying to teach him some basic social skills. And, when he is not looking, maybe sniff him — ha ha!

Yours,

C

References

Amiel, T., Pezzo, T., Cruz, L. R. da, & Oliveira, L. A. (2021). Os modos de adesão e a abrangência do capitalismo de vigilância na educação brasileira. *Perspectiva*, *39*(3), 1–22.
https://doi.org/10.5007/2175-795X.2021.e80582

Andreotti, V. O. de, Stein, S., Suša, R., Čajkova, T., d'Emilia, D., Jimmy, E., Calhoun, B., Amsler, S., Cardoso, C., Siwek, D., & Fay, K. (2019). *Gesturing towards decolonial futures global citizenship* otherwise *study program*.
https://decolonialfutures.net.

Anonymous Author. (2016). Data colonialism: Critiquing consent and control in "Tech for social change". *Model View Culture*, *43*.
https://modelviewculture.com/pieces/data-colonialism-critiquing-consent-and-control-in-tech-for-social-change

Barad, K. (2007). *Meeting the universe halfway: Quantum physics and the entanglement of matter and meaning*. Duke University Press.

Bayne, S. (2015). Teacherbot: Interventions in automated teaching. *Teaching in Higher Education*, *20*(4), 455–67.
https://doi.org/10.1080/13562517.2015.1020783

Beer, D. (2018). *The data gaze: Capitalism, power and perception*. Sage.

Benjamin, R. (2019). *Race after technology*. Polity.

Bernard, T. (2021). From didactics to datafication: A critical reflection on virtual learning environments and the production of space. *Journal for Students Affairs in Africa*, *9*(1), 197–204.
https://doi.org/10.24085/jsaa.v9i1.1438

Bock, A., Breiter, A., Hartong, S., Jarke, J., Jornitz, S., Lange, A., & Macgilchrist, F. (Eds), (2023). *Die datafizierte Schule*. Springer.

Brookfield, S. D., & Preskill, S. (2005). *Discussion as a Way of Teaching: Tools and Techniques for Democratic Classrooms*. John Wiley & Sons.

Brunton, F., & Nissenbaum, H. (2015). *Obfuscation: A user's guide for privacy and protest*. MIT Press.

Butler, J. (1997). *Excitable speech: A politics of the performative*. Routledge.

Castellví, J., Escribano, C., Santos, R., & Marolla, J. (2022). Futures education: Curriculum and educational practices in Australia, Spain, and Chile. *Comunicar, 30*(73), 45–55.
https://doi.org/10.3916/c73-2022-04

Chavez, F. R. (2021). *The anti-racist writing workshop. How to decolonize the creative classroom*. Haymarket Books.

Costanza-Chock, S. (2020). *Design justice: Community-led practices to build the world we need*. MIT Press.
https://design-justice.pubpub.org/

Couldry, N., & Mejias, U. A. (2019). *The costs of connection: How data is colonizing human life and appropriating it for capitalism*. Stanford University Press.

Crawford, K., & Joler, V. (2018). *Anatomy of an AI system*.
https://anatomyof.ai/

Cronin, C., Zamora, M., & Bali, M. (n.d.). *Equity Unbound*.
http://unboundeq.creativitycourse.org/

Crowley, D. (2019). Binti's r/evolutionary cosmopolitan ecologies. *The Cambridge Journal of Postcolonial Literary Inquiry, 6*(2), 237–56.
https://doi.org/10.1017/pli.2018.54

Czerniewicz, L. (2022). Multi-layered digital inequalities in HEIs: the paradox of the post-digital society. *GUNI Report: New Visions for Higher Education towards 2030*, 1–8.
https://www.guni-call4action.org/article/multi-layered-digital-inequalities-heis-paradox-post-digital-society

Dabiri, E. (2021). *What white people can do next: From allyship to coalition*. Penguin.

Daly, A., Devitt, A. K., & Mann, M. (Eds), (2019). *Good data*. Institute of Network Cultures.

Davis, E. S. (2020). Decolonizing knowledge in Nnedi Okorafor's Binti trilogy. In A. S. Moore, & S. Pinto (Eds), *Writing beyond the state. Post-sovereign approaches to human rights in literary studies* (pp. 43–63). Springer.
https://10.1007/978-3-030-34456-6_3

Dixon-Román, E., Nichols, T. P., & Nyame-Mensah, A. (2020). The racializing forces of/in AI educational technologies. *Learning, Media and Technology, 45*(3), 236–50.
https://doi.org/10.1080/17439884.2020.1667825

Dion, M. L., Sumner, J. L., & Mitchell, S. M. (2018). Gendered citation patterns across political science and social science methodology fields. *Political Analysis, 26*(3), 312–27.
https://doi.org/10.1017/pan.2018.12

Escobar, A. (2007). Worlds and knowledges otherwise. *Cultural Studies*, 21(2), 179–210.
http://www.unc.edu/~aescobar/html/texts.html

Facer, K. (2019a). *Learning to live with a lively planet: Renewing the mission of the European University* [Video]. Youtube.
https://www.youtube.com/watch?v=3zHml2ySV2w

Facer, K. (2019b). Storytelling in troubled times: what is the role for educators in the deep crises of the 21st century? *Literacy*, 53(1), 2–13.
https://doi.org/10.1111/lit.12176

Foucault, M. (1982). The subject and power. In H. L. Dreyfus, & P. Rabinow (Eds), *Michel Foucault: Beyond hermeneutics and structuralism* (pp. 208–26). Harvester.

Gabrys, J. (2018). *Becoming planetary*. E-Flux.
https://www.e-flux.com/architecture/accumulation/217051/becoming-planetary

Gourlay, L. (2021). *Posthumanism and the digital university*. Bloomsbury Academic.

Gutiérrez, M. (2018). *Data activism and social change*. Palgrave.

Hall, S. (1997). The work of representation. In S. Hall (Ed.), *Representation: Cultural representations and signifying practices* (pp. 13–64). Sage.

Hanchey, J. N. (2020). Desire and the politics of africanfuturism. *Women's Studies in Communication*, 43(2), 119–24.
https://doi.org/10.1080/07491409.2020.1745589

Haraway, D. (2016). *Staying with the trouble: Making kin in the Chthulucene*. Duke University Press.

Harney, S., & Moten, F. (2013). *The undercommons: Fugitive planning and Black study*. Minor Compositions.

Hicks, D. (2011). *Dignity: Its essential role in resolving conflict*. Yale University Press.

Holbert, N., Dando, M., & Correa, I. (2020). Afrofuturism as critical constructionist design: building futures from the past and present. *Learning, Media and Technology*, 45(4), 328–44.
https://doi.org/10.1080/17439884.2020.1754237

hooks, b. (1994). *Teaching to transgress: Education as the practice of freedom*. Routledge.

Iske, S., Fromme, J., Verständig, D., & Wilde, K. (Eds), (2020). *Big data, Datafizierung und digitale Artefakte*. Springer VS.

Jarke, J., & Breiter, A. (2019). Special issue: Datafication of education. *Learning, Media and Technology*, 44(1), 1–6.
https://doi.org/10.1080/17439884.2019.1573833

Johnson, A. (Ed.), (2019). *Drones and dreams: A speculative sprint story collection*. Digital Asia Hub.
https://www.digitalasiahub.org/publications/drones-and-dreams-a-speculative-sprint-story-collection/

Jungk, R., & Müllert, N. R. (1987). *Future workshops: How to create desirable futures*. Institute for Social Inventions.

Knox, J., Williamson, B., & Bayne, S. (2019). Machine behaviourism: Future visions of "learnification" and "datafication" across humans and digital technologies. *Learning, Media and Technology*, 45(1), 31–45.
https://doi.org/10.1080/17439884.2019.1623251

Kwet, M. (2017). Operation Phakisa Education: Why a secret? Mass surveillance, inequality, and race in South Africa's emerging national e-education system. *First Monday*, 22(12).
https://doi.org/10.5210/fm.v22i12.8054

Lackey, C. (1994). Social science fiction: Writing sociological short stories to learn about social issues. *Teaching Sociology*, 22(2), 166–73.
https://doi.org/10.2307/1318562

Le Guin, U. K. (2019 [1976]). *The Left Hand of Darkness*. Penguin.

Lerman, L., & Borstel, J. (2003). Liz Lerman's Critical Response Process: A method for getting useful feedback on anything you make, from dance to dessert. *Liz Lerman Dance Exchange*.

Lipmanowicz, H., & McCandless, K. (2013). *The surprising power of liberating structures*. Liberating Structures Press.
https://www.liberatingstructures.com

Macgilchrist, F., Allert, H., & Bruch, A. (2020). Students and society in the 2020s: Three future "histories" of education and technology. *Learning, Media and Technology*, 45(1), 76–89.
https://doi.org/10.1080/17439884.2019.1656235

Macgilchrist, F., Hartong, S., & Jornitz, S. (2023). Algorithmische Datafizierung und Schule: kritische Ansätze in einem wachsenden Forschungsfeld. In K. Scheiter, & I. Gogolin (Eds), *Bildung für eine digitale Zukunft (Edition ZfE)* (pp. 317–38). Springer VS.

Mbembe, A. (2022, January 11). *How to develop a planetary consciousness* [Interview]. Noema.
https://www.noemamag.com/how-to-develop-a-planetary-consciousness

Mignolo, W. D. (2009). Epistemic disobedience, independent thought and decolonial freedom. *Theory, Culture & Society*, 26(7–8), 159–81.

Milan, S., & Treré, E. (2019). Big data from the South(s): Beyond data universalism. *Television & New Media*, 20(4), 319–35.
https://doi.org/10.1177/1527476419837739

Muñoz, J. E. (2019). *Cruising utopia: The then and there of queer futurity*. New York University Press.

Okorafor, N. (2015). *Binti*. Tor.

Okorafor, N. (2017a). *Binti: Home*. Tor.

Okorafor, N. (2017b). *Binti: The night masquerade*. Tor.

Okorafor, N. (2017c). *Sci-fi stories that imagine a future Africa*. https://www.ted.com/talks/nnedi_okorafor_sci_fi_stories_that_imagine_a_future_africa

Okorafor, N. (2019). *Africanfuturism defined*. https://nnedi.blogspot.com/2019/10/africanfuturism-defined.html

Parra, H., Cruz, L., Amiel, T., & Machado, J. (2018). Infraestruturas, economia e política informacional: o caso do google suite for education. *Mediações – Revista de Ciências Sociais, 23*(1), 63–99. https://doi.org/10.5433/2176-6665.2018v23n1p63

Pink, S., & Postill, J. (2019). Imagining mundane futures. *Anthropology in Action, 26*(2), 31–41. https://doi.org/10.3167/aia.2019.260204

Prinsloo, P. (2020). Data frontiers and frontiers of power in (higher) education: A view of/from the Global South. *Teaching in Higher Education, 25*(4), 366–83. https://doi.org/10.1080/13562517.2020.1723537

Quijano, A. (2010). Coloniality and modernity/rationality. In W. D. Mignolo, & A. Escobar (Eds), *Globalization and the decolonial option* (pp. 22–32). Routledge.

Raffaghelli, J. E. (2022). Alfabetización en datos y justicia social ¿Un oxímoron? Respuestas desde la contra-hegemonía. *Revista Izquierdas, 51*, 1–18. https://dialnet.unirioja.es/servlet/articulo?codigo=8361359

Reh, S., & Ricken, N. (2012). Das Konzept der Adressierung. Zur Methodologie einer qualitativ-empirischen Erforschung von Subjektivation. In I. Miethe, & H. R. Müller (Eds), *Qualitative Bildungsforschung und Bildungstheorie* (pp. 36–55). Barbara Budrich.

Ricken, N., Casale, R., & Thompson, C. (Eds), (2019). *Subjektivierung. Erziehungswissenschaftliche Theorieperspektiven*. Beltz Juventa.

Rodriguez, C. (2001). *Fissures in the mediascape: An international study of citizen's media*. Hampton Press.

Särkelä, E., & Suoranta, J. (2020). The method of empathy-based stories as a tool for research and teaching. *The Qualitative Report*. https://doi.org/10.46743/2160-3715/2020.4124

Selwyn, N., Hillman, T., Eynon, R., Ferreira, G., Knox, J., Macgilchrist, F., & Sancho-Gil, J. M. (2020). What's next for ed-tech? Critical hopes and concerns for the 2020s. *Learning, Media and Technology, 45*(1), 1–6. https://doi.org/10.1080/17439884.2020.1694945

Sørensen, E. (2009). *The Materiality of learning: Technology and knowledge in educational practice*. Cambridge University Press.
https://doi.org/10.1017/CBO9780511576362.

Suoranta, J., Teräs, M., Teräs, H., Jandrić, P., Ledger, S., Macgilchrist, F., & Prinsloo, P. (2021). Speculative social science fiction of digitalization in higher education: From what is to what could be. *Postdigital Science and Education*, 4(2), 224–36.
https://doi.org/10.1007/s42438-021-00260-6

UNESCO (2021). *Reimagining our futures together: A new social contract for education*.
https://unesdoc.unesco.org/ark:/48223/pf0000379707.locale=en

Vetter, A. (2023). *Konviviale Technik. Empirische Technikethik für eine Postwachstumsgesellschaft*. Transcript.

Wagener-Böck, N., Macgilchrist, F., Rabenstein, K., & Bock, A. (2023). From automation to symmation: Ethnographic perspectives on what happens in front of the screen. *Postdigital Science and Education*, 5(1), 136–51.
https://doi.org/10.1007/s42438-022-00350-z

Wallin, A., Koro-Ljungberg, M., & Eskola, J. (2019). The method of empathy-based stories. *International Journal of Research & Method in Education*, 42(5), 525–35.
https://doi.org/10.1080/1743727X.2018.1533937

Williamson, B. (2018). *Big data and education*. Sage.

Youdell, D. (2006). Subjectivation and performative politics: Butler thinking Althusser and Foucault: intelligibility, agency and the raced-nationed-religioned subjects of education. *British Journal of Sociology of Education*, 27(4), 511–28.

Zuboff, S. (2019). *The age of surveillance capitalism: The fight for a human future at the new frontier of power*. Profile Books.

20. One-one coco full basket — on the value of critical pedagogy of caring for learning and teaching in higher education

Carol Hordatt Gentles

Earlier this year I received a message from Pamela,[1] one of my students who had just completed her final course for her masters degree. She wrote:

> Good morning, Doc
>
> Thanks for being an awesome lecturer. I really appreciate the feedback and guidance. I think you are the best lecturer I had in my master's programme. I really like your teaching style and by and large your temperament. Your style has reframed my approach to teaching and learning. You treated us like humans. HONESTLY, you have impacted me greatly. Please continue to be that awesome lecturer. Your surname speaks a volume, GENTLE!!!!! (Pamela, personal communication, May, 23 2022)

This message was a highlight in my career because Pamela said I had treated students "like humans". It validated my life's work as an educator/teacher educator who has sought to be an advocate for humanising the experience of education. It was such a touching assertion of her own humanity because it demonstrated her confidence to express her opinions about me as her teacher. I was thrilled that she valued my style of teaching enough to consider it as a model for her own practice. Pamela's unsolicited affirmation strengthened my belief

---

[1] The name Pamela and all other names used are pseudonyms. All students have given me permission to share sentiments offered in private.

that there is value in practising pedagogy that is both critical and caring. It also built my own confidence as a teacher and academic to continue my work of theorising about the role of a critical pedagogy of caring in Jamaican higher education.

My premise that it is essential to consider critical, caring pedagogy as a means of improving teaching and learning in Jamaican higher education springs from my concern about the dominance of a neoliberal ideology in Jamaica and the world. I am unhappy with the dominant paradigms of higher education pedagogy (as explored throughout this book), that align with "the status quo discourse" and a culture of performativity. Such dominant discourse sees the work of teaching as "ahistorical and apolitical", "value-neutral" and identifies competencies through "process-product empirical research" (Marsh & Castner, 2017, p. 870).

There are many who would argue that higher education in Jamaica has historically positioned itself to support societal transformation from our colonial past. This is true, as is evident in its rich tradition of postcolonial research, and its commitment to making tertiary education accessible to all. Higher education at my institution has contributed much to the development of Jamaica and the Caribbean region in its production of stalwart Caribbean scholars (Chevannes, 2018; Miller, 2003; Nettleford, 2000; Shepherd & Hemmings, 2022) whose works have highlighted, questioned, and vociferously critiqued the lingering legacy of slavery and colonial hegemony. However, the language of current policy statements and strategic plans suggests the privileging of a business model approach focusing on accountability. For example, in its most recent strategic plan, students and faculty are described as "the main buyers of services", and faculty are seen as "the main suppliers of [its]core business offerings — Teaching, Learning and Research" (University of the West Indies [UWI], 2017, p. 6).

The same document describes using a "Porterian analysis (Five forces model of industry competition)" lens to guide the development of its mission and the way in which it rationalises this. To this end, it speaks to the urgency of "academic and entrepreneurial empowerment through teaching and learning and rekindling the agenda of applied research and professional training [which] are critical to building the region's resilience and promoting the praxis of relentlessly pursuing sustainable development" (UWI, 2017, p. 3). The document explains that evidence for this urgency is explained by "a clear reading of the regional context which shows the slow and sluggish economic recovery from the global financial recession" (UWI, 2017, p. 1).

As an educator who is passionately committed to an alternate critical discourse, this rhetoric seems contradictory to what I believe the ultimate purpose of higher education should be. Ideally, I see this purpose as a moral, ethical endeavour informed by a humanistic view of education. This does not reject the notion that economic development is crucial for improving the standard of living for humanity. However, as we look to the future, an alternate critical perspective speaks to the significance of reconceptualising how we understand development. This has become particularly urgent with the impact of climate change and the need for all of us to accept our responsibility to work for sustainability of the planet and the life it supports.

My views align with a growing discourse on re-establishing the commitment of universities to be socially responsible. Drawing on a variety of perspectives, there is an emerging consensus that universities have dual responsibilities at both global and local levels (Ali et al., 2021; GUNi, 2017; Hall & Tandon, 2021). They must figure out how to address "both the local demands of society based on the race for global competitiveness and the local and global demands to contribute to a more equitable and sustainable society" (GUNi, 2017, p. 37). There is a need for them to ensure that "students… fully develop their own abilities with a sense of social responsibility, educating them to become critical participants in a democratic society and promoters of changes that will foster equity and justice" (Coelho & Menezes, 2021, p. 2).

My way of contributing to this movement has been to adopt a Freirean (1970) humanistic perspective that aims to teach students to confront how schooling and society have objectified them. Freire challenges us as educators to teach our students to assert their humanity so they can become the *Subject* rather than the *Object* of their experiences, realities, and their future. To do this, I have, through my research and teaching (Gentles, 2018), advocated that as teacher educators and academic faculty, we should be committed to teaching with a critical and moral purpose that values and honours the humanity of teachers and students. I have focused my attention on trying to disrupt the technical rationality that erodes our capacity and confidence for professional autonomy. This is an ideology in which the purpose of teacher education is seen to be, according to Liston and Zeichner (1987):

> providing prospective teachers with that which will give them technical mastery of the teaching-learning environment... Prospective teachers are viewed primarily as passive recipients of teaching knowledge and skills and play little part in determining the substance and direction of their preparation for teaching and pedagogical practices. (pp. 26–27)

In this chapter, I share my experiences and insights gained over the course of my teaching career as an advocate for a different way of teaching. I consider what I have learned as instructive — possibilities for mainstreaming critical, caring pedagogy to improve the teaching and learning future of Jamaican higher education.

Methodology

As I begin, I declare that my aim is neither to moralise nor to prescribe. Rather, as I muse about the possibilities for changing the dominant pedagogy in my own environment, I simply wish to share and deconstruct my experiences as a teacher educator within the context of my beliefs and views about the role and purpose of university teaching and education. I am invoking the notion of "intimate scholarship" described by Hamilton and Pinnegar (2014) as:

> a subjective, relational, and up-close look [that can] expose those aspects of our lives. Intimate scholarship takes up ontological stance where recognition of the individual/collective relation has value, uncovers embodied knowing through autobiography and action, and explores the coming-to-know process in dialogue. (p. 153)

This is a form of educational inquiry that values the particular, vulnerability, and openness to interpretation. It allows for construction of knowledge about the practice of teaching and teacher education in ways that go against the grain of positivistic, empirical research (Hamilton & Pinnegar, 2015). What I share, therefore, are what I call learning moments in my eighteen-year journey as a teacher educator in a leading university in Jamaica. These are incidents and experiences I have documented in journal entries and notes to myself. Over the years, I have reflected and interrogated these to try and make sense of them, and to figure out what

I could have done differently. Some of these were watershed moments. Others were less momentous, yet instructive. I have been privileged to share my experiences with teaching colleagues and peers who have been willing to listen to my ruminations and whose feedback has been invaluable to the process of problematising my own insights into my practice. I have also benefited from feedback from my students over the years. Their responses to my teaching have been invaluable in motivating me to think deeply about my evolving identity as a teacher educator.

By documenting what I have learned from such critical interrogation, I have been using a self-study approach (LaBoskey, 2004; Loughran, 2004). Ritter (2016) suggests that self-study is acceptable as research practice because it is not a "prescriptive methodology" (p. 37). He explains that "rather than simply uncovering answers to research questions, self-study facilitates nuanced forms of learning that can be in relationship to others, with and through critical friends, or by seeing practice from the students' perspective." My reflections below highlight learning moments that have shaped my journey of advocacy for a critical, caring pedagogy in higher education. They show how my own understanding of a critical pedagogy of care has evolved. I discuss how these stories have been instructive for constructing a critically conscious understanding of the possibilities for using this approach in Jamaican higher education.

Learning moments

Yes — but how will you make a real difference?

The genesis of my advocacy began in the last five minutes of the oral defence of my doctoral thesis, when one of the examiners asked me how I planned to use what I had learned from my doctoral work. I was really taken aback. Wasn't it obvious? I had just finished sharing the results of six years of research on the pedagogical culture of a Jamaican teachers' college. This was the culmination of an intense life-changing journey through the theoretical discourse of critical pedagogy which I had used as a lens to examine teaching and learning in a teacher education institution. I had explained how important it was to disrupt the status quo of tradition and authoritarianism. I believed this could be accomplished by simply spreading the word about critical pedagogy. However, here was one of my examiners — a seasoned teacher educator and teacher education scholar saying: *"I hear you and like what you are saying, but how exactly will simply saying the words really change the way things are?"* This was the voice of reality intruding into the ideal world I had created in my mind. I realised that telling would not be enough. I would have to advocate through action. So, I responded: *"I really do believe I can promote the idea of critical pedagogy by encouraging critical consciousness of what is wrong with our education system. But I will also practise critical pedagogy by developing what Joan Wink (1996) calls a caring heart and a critical eye."*

With this declaration I made a commitment to what has defined my work as a teacher educator and academic — trying to construct a pedagogy that is critical and at the same time caring. I saw this as a way to contest traditional pedagogy by sharing and modelling a more humanistic type of teaching. But this came at a cost. I had been a high school teacher for many years prior to working in higher education. During this period, I had always tried to be a caring teacher by offering pastoral care: "supporting the well-being of students" (Mariskind, 2014, p. 309). I "cared about" and "cared for" (O'Connor, 2008) my students by trying to meet their emotional, developmental, and cognitive learning needs with patience, empathy, love and nurturing.

I took this pastoral approach to my new job in a university context because I saw it as the core of quality teaching. My doctoral engagement with the theoretical discourse of critical pedagogy had given me insights, and a new language and tools for strengthening this approach. So, as I began working with my higher education students, I added these ways of teaching and relating that explicitly showed and modelled respect. I devised strategies to help my students build a voice and a sense of self by making sure they always felt included, and develop the confidence and courage to participate equitably in class activities. No one was silenced. Everyone's ideas were welcomed and encouraged. No thought or query went unanswered or was judged. I also showed respect by making sure I was always fully prepared to teach by organising my content ahead of time and being punctual.

It was also important to teach my students to become critically conscious. I designed strategies to stimulate them intellectually by sharing my convictions about the significance of becoming critically conscious of the historical, social, political, and economic contexts of their daily lives as teachers and as graduate students. To do this in an engaging way, I integrated explanations of ideas and concepts with individual and group activities designed to challenge their thinking. I posed questions that encouraged them to deconstruct their personal and professional experiences and to recognise social injustice, oppression, marginalisation, silencing, and exclusion. I facilitated active thinking that strengthened their capacity to problematise issues. This included facilitating learning experiences designed to be stimulating and meaningful. We role played, we debated, we made charts, we envisioned ideal educational institutions. I assigned written coursework that required critical reflection on educational issues and on their own learning experiences.

It was plenty of work, but I believed it was worth the effort. My commitment to being a caring teacher reflected a Freirean view of good teaching as being caring enough to try to teach well in contextually relevant ways, with daring, expertise, and criticality (Anderson et al., 2019). Freire (2005) had argued that "educating involves a passion to know that involves us in a loving search for knowledge" (p. 7). By emphasising caring, I was adhering to the views of Noddings (2002; 2005) who believed that the "main aim of education should be a moral one, that of nurturing the growth of competent, caring, loving, and lovable persons" (Soltis, 2005, p. ix). Noddings proposed that this can be accomplished with "a curriculum organised around centers of care: care for oneself; for intimate others as well as strangers and distant others; for animals, plants, the earth; and for human instruments and ideas" (Soltis, 2005, p. ix). Another care theorist, Gilligan (1982) explained an "ethic of caring" as a "consciousness of the dynamics of human relationships… [which] becomes central to moral understanding joining the heart and eye in an ethic that ties the activity of thought to the activity of care" (p. 148). Thus, an ethic or ideology of caring supports the moral purpose of teaching and drives thinking into action. Caring becomes the "basis for thoughtful educational and moral decision making, and it requires action" (Rogers & Webb, 1991, p. 174).

Wise up or you will never get ahead!

I soon realised that what I was doing was not necessarily expected of me. I was advised by some colleagues to resist going overboard. They explained that at this level I was working with adults who were expected to take responsibility for their own learning. They told me I was "spoon-feeding" my students and creating too much work for myself. My head of department took me aside and pointed out the prospective "error of my ways". She explained my primary task was to publish research papers. I was expected to fulfil my teaching obligations and earn decent course evaluation scores because "in this system, little reward was given for teaching." She suggested I should wise up. This was food for thought.

In thinking this through, I realised that in this higher education context my caring work and pedagogy — a critical pedagogy of caring, was actually a form of subversion. What I was doing was caring-as-activism (McKamey, 2011). I was, as hooks (1994) characterised it, acting as "enlightened witness" for my students, "challenging power-as-domination and offering alternative models of interaction" (Mariskind, 2014, p. 309). However, my perspective and advocacy did not fit neatly into what was then the norm in higher education — an emphasis on requiring autonomous, self-directed learning from adult learners (Merriam et al., 2007). Caring was valued but was not regarded as a significant part of the duties of faculty (Goode et al., 2020). As Pranjic (2021) argues: "In the academic world, there is a common understanding that nurture is not the job of the university and that it is a matter of the family, primary and secondary school, while colleges [and universities] should deal exclusively with education" (p. 152). In higher education it was logical reasoning, objectivity, and empiricism that were regarded as most valuable. Caring was not discouraged but it was less highly regarded.

> The editor is rejecting your submission. You must have empirical evidence to inform your conclusions.

To do my job effectively, I had to figure out how to continue with my caring, critical activism, while also learning to play the game of publishing as expected by my university. One strategy has been to write reflective, conceptual papers that try to refine and defend my ideology and pedagogy to be more receptive in academic communities. This has not always been easy. In a positivistic higher education culture, reflective papers are often rejected because they are not based on statistical data. The devastating words I quote above were sent to me by the editor of a campus journal. She was rejecting a paper I had submitted in answer to a call for papers about the experiences of teaching at my university during the COVID-19 pandemic. I had written a critical interrogation of what it was like to try to enact critical, caring pedagogy while transitioning to online delivery. I had used critical theory to frame my experiences and ideas but included no numerical data to support the challenges I had described. Thankfully, for me, the same paper was accepted and published by another journal abroad. So, my efforts were not wasted.

I had a similar experience fourteen years earlier when I submitted a paper that described and interrogated the strategies I was developing to build student voice in a qualitative research methods course. At the time, I was trying to figure out how to create egalitarian, safe, learning spaces in a course with fifty-six students. Many were older students returning to higher education after teaching for many years. They had qualified as teachers in colleges which were very lecturer-centred and traditional. Students raised their hands when they wanted to speak. The lecturer decided if, when, and for how long the chosen student would speak. Correct answers were rewarded, incorrect answers were not. Discussion, dissent, dialogue were not encouraged. Thus, students came to my course with eroded confidence and silenced voices. They found it very difficult to speak freely. What they needed were opportunities to speak openly, with validation from me and their peers, so they could unearth their voices and gain confidence to participate in critical dialogue and discussion.

However, it was difficult to give each student the time they needed to do this in such a large group. I encouraged them to send me emails where they could say anything they wanted. I responded to each email as sensitively as I could. It turned out to be a wonderful experience where my students taught me so much. For example, I learned that not everyone liked this approach. They had come expecting to listen to me talk, take notes, study, memorise and regurgitate for a grade. As one student complained, "the dialogic stuff is too much work, I just want to get my 'A' and move on." I also learned that I was not as egalitarian as I thought when a female student wrote: "do you realise you address the men in the class as Mr, but you call us (women) by our first names??!!!" On the other hand, students reassured me that my critical pedagogy was working. Yet another shared: "At first, I was afraid to say anything.

I did not know anything about qualitative research, so I did not want to seem ignorant, but now I feel more comfortable." One more said: "I am beginning to feel a sense of community in the class. I feel more comfortable about talking out." At the end of the semester, we had a class party. I was deeply touched when the whole class got together to sing me a tribute and gave me a gift.

My aim in writing about this experience had been to share strategies for overcoming resistance to teaching in non-traditional ways. I wanted to celebrate how rewarding it was to help students construct their own knowledge and to "move out of their comfort zones into dangerous new places of critical thinking and reflection" (Gentles, 2007, p. 78). But the reviewers were concerned that I had no empirical data, no statistics or outcomes that were measurable. The validity of the paper was questioned. Thankfully, the editor decided to "take a chance" and published the paper despite the strong reservations of the reviewer. These experiences made me feel very sad. I felt my voice and the voices of my students had been silenced by my own university. They taught me about the tyranny of positivism in HE. It poses a challenge to faculty and students who want to write differently. It questions the integrity of their voice and the "findings" from their introspection and deep reflection. The system makes it more difficult for those who see the world of HE differently to express their views. Instead, writing that speaks to activism and alternate discourses must find different spaces in which to publish. Given that the work of publishing is already a difficult process, this marginalisation makes it even harder.

We have noticed a high percentage of A's on your grade sheet. Please justify in writing.

I have received this request from the office of graduate studies many times during my career, because more than 80% of my students had scored an "A". To many educators this is a reasonable request that conforms to the notion that student scores should align to the Bell Curve. For me, this expectation is problematic. It goes against the grain of how I see myself working with my students. My students' high performance is facilitated by the way I structure my courses. I provide a lot of feedback, guidance, and support to ensure they can all earn an

"A". I schedule special meetings with students who are not doing well on course assignments to teach them what they need to do to improve on previous assignments. In courses for doctoral students, I ask them to collaborate with me to design rubrics for assessing their papers. Students also benefit from receiving peer reviews, so they experience the value of collaboration and caring for each other. My critical, caring pedagogy aims to go the extra mile to ensure most, if not all succeed. I also require plenty of oral and written critical reflection from my students which become part of assessment for my courses. For example, in a course on teacher leadership, masters students are asked to design, implement, and report on a project that makes a change in their own students' lives. They work on this as a group and then submit individual reports.

This approach speaks to seeing the purpose of assessment differently from how it is understood in traditional, teacher-centred spaces. I am more interested in evaluating how much my graduate students have understood the work of becoming critically reflective. I consider the degree to which they have developed their voice and how strong it becomes. I want to see and hear their growing critical consciousness of the world of education. I believe this to be significant criteria for determining what and how they have learned in my courses. As Down and Ferguson (2022) suggest:

> we need... to be mindful of the larger purpose of assessment — that of clarifying the readiness of individuals to acknowledge self as part of the community of life... [it must be] part of teaching and learning that offers students a vision of a transformed life and world. (p. 85)

Your caring has made a difference.

A final learning moment I wish to share is one of affirmation. Recently, I was invited to a get-together by the newest graduates of my Masters in Teacher Education and Teacher Development programme. To my surprise, it was a party in my honour. Each of them gave a tribute which was touching and reassuring. However, there was one tribute from an articulate and excellent student that stood out. He said that while he appreciated my pedagogy and what he had learned about teaching, it was my caring that had inspired him. He explained that my caring had supported him and his fellow students through the programme.

Without this, many of them would not have found the motivation to continue the programme. Hearing this and witnessing his words, his voice, his confidence and sincerity was humbling. It reaffirmed there is value in advocating for incorporating critical, caring pedagogy into higher education in Jamaica.

Discussion

The picture that emerges from my reflections suggests it is possible to carve out a space for a critical, caring pedagogy within traditional higher education institutions. Over the years, my way of doing things has been enthusiastically accepted by students and tolerated within my institution because my activism occupies a small space that is not too dangerous. But the possibilities for mainstreaming such an approach seem slim. The reality is that teaching against the grain is hard work. Working from a space of critical, caring activism is difficult to do. Possibilities for educators to commit to advocacy for a critical, caring pedagogy are hindered by several realities.

First, while being a caring teacher educator is considered desirable, expressions of critical ideas based on being caring, or grounded in experiences of caring work, are less likely to gain the attention of university leaders and policy makers. One reason for this is that conceptualisations of caring in universities are often gendered and traditionally linked to women and femininity (Mariskind, 2014). Thus, academics who focus on caring for students are respected for their maternalism, and "are assumed to be nurturing, caring, emotional, irrational, empathetic and passive" (O'Neill, 2005). Those whose teaching is more masculine in orientation are seen as "independent, ambitious, competitive, objective, rational, and have good leadership and decision-making skills" (O'Neill, 2005). These masculine qualities align better with the business model approach and are thus more valued and respected. Faculty who espouse these qualities are seen to be more worthy of promotion to senior positions with influence and higher remuneration. Their opinions are more likely to be valued.

The reality is that as universities become more challenged by rising costs, economic recessions, competition for student enrolment, staffing shortages, and employee demands for decent remuneration, faculty may find themselves focusing more on economic survival than prioritising the social and ideological learning needs of their students. Staff redundancies in some universities and the COVID-19 pandemic have increased the workload of many faculty members, making it even harder to manage the job of teaching and conducting research. This minimises possibilities for faculty to take on a commitment to a critical, caring pedagogy that demands even more time and energy, even though they may agree with the urgency for contesting the status quo.

Ironically, a new trend of demanding that faculty engage in "care labour" is adding to that workload (Goode et al., 2020, p. 50). This requires them to "operate as a nexus of social and emotional support resources within the institutional contexts" of "best practices in serving students" as part of efforts to increase student retention and persistence of the most vulnerable students. Researchers are investigating the components of this care labour and theorising how to operationalise them so they can be taught to faculty (Mariskind, 2014; Walker-Gleaves, 2019). This development is disturbing. While it may lead to higher education environments where caring is part of the job description of faculty, the mindset that motivates "care labour" is not the same as teaching in critically caring ways. The concept of "care labour" serves the purposes of a business model and is informed by concerns for student/client satisfaction. This is different from caring work that is linked to activism aimed at repositioning higher education in a humanistic way.

The work of improving teaching and learning at my university by infusing a critical, caring pedagogy has been possible, but only on a small scale. It requires courage, confidence, and energy to sustain commitment to a critical, caring pedagogy, especially in contexts where the business model of higher education places high value on operationalising and standardising performance outcomes. As I have suggested, a critical, caring educator has to be willing to resist the system in every sphere of one's practice — planning, teaching, assessing, relationships with students. Critical, caring pedagogy is about encouraging student agency and changing mindsets. This can be difficult to evaluate and score objectively. When students feel comfortable and give generous feedback that validates your work, it is easy to believe that you have accomplished what you set out to do. But when a student writes a paper that shows they are speaking their minds and voicing what they really think, how do you score, in a standardised way, the awakening of self and critical consciousness? Teaching and assessing against the grain can be physically and emotionally exhausting. In today's high paced, frenetic systems of higher education, it is often difficult for educators to find the energy and the will to do things differently. This can diminish possibilities for mainstreaming critical, caring pedagogy into higher education.

Yet even as I consider the challenges of doing so, my vision remains steadfast — for a caring and critical mindset and pedagogy to be infused and mainstreamed into institutional cultures across Jamaican higher education. This means that the ideology underpinning a caring and critical pedagogy would become the core of university policies. This would be realised by a complete "disruption and reorientation of existing (curriculum, pedagogical and managerial) systems" (Evans et al, 2016, p. 66). I believe that this can be achieved by constructing understandings about these challenges and the ideologies they represent. This is how we build local small-scale knowledge we can leverage to strategise and implement meaningful educational change on a larger scale. This is what I have started to do in this chapter.

As a popular Jamaican saying goes: "one-one coco full basket". This refers to the reaping of coco, a root crop which is a staple Jamaican food. Poor subsistence farmers sometimes find it difficult to locate the root in their fields because they were planted on steep hillsides with tight, clay soils. Despite the challenges, they persist in digging for the coco. A testament to their resilience and faith that their efforts will eventually lead to filling a basket, one coco at a time. In keeping with the wisdom of my local context, I have faith that if I continue to consistently advocate for and model critical, caring pedagogy, I will produce some small measure of change. I am confident there is value in sharing experiences and insights with my peers, my students, and others, as ways of inviting them to "see" and "read" and understand the challenges they must overcome before they can effect meaningful pedagogical change. This approach, I suggest, is key to strengthening my position that a critical pedagogy of caring can help improve the teaching and learning future of higher education in Jamaica and beyond.

References

Ali, M., Mustapaha, I., Osman, S., & Hassan, U. (2021). University social responsibility: A review of conceptual evolution and its thematic analysis. *Journal of Cleaner Production, 286*.
https://doi.org/10.1016/j.jclepro.2020.124931

Anderson, V., Rabello, R., Wass, R., Golding, C., Rangi, A., Eteuati, E., Bristowe, Z., & Waller, A. (2020). Good teaching as care in higher education. *Higher education, 79*, 1–19.
https://doi.org/10.1007/s10734-019-00392-6

Chevannes, B. (2018). *Betwixt and between: Explorations in an African-Caribbean mindscape.* Ian Randle Publishers.

Coelho M., & Menezes I. (2021). University social responsibility, service learning, and students' personal, professional, and civic education. *Frontiers in Psychology, 12*.
https://doi.org/10.3389/fpsyg.2021.617300

Down, L., & Ferguson, T. (2022). *Education for sustainable development in the Caribbean: Pedagogy, processes and practices.* The University of the West Indies Press.

Freire, P. (2005). *Teachers as cultural workers: Letters to those who dare to teach.* Westview Press.

Freire, P. (1970). *Pedagogy of the oppressed.* The Seabury Press

Gentles, C. (2007). Using the internet to build student voice. *Institute of Education Publication Series, 4*, 71–82.
https://www.mona.uwi.edu/soe/publications/institute-education-publication-series/article/1523

Gilligan, C. (1982). *In a different voice: Psychological theory and womens' development.* Harvard University Press.

Global University Network for Innovation (GUNi) (2017). *Higher education in the World 6: Towards a socially responsible university: Balancing the global with the local* [PDF].
https://www.iau-hesd.net/sites/default/files/documents/download_full_report.pdf

Goode, J., Denker, K. J., Cortese, D., Carlson, L., & Morris. K. (2020). Intrusive teaching: The strain of care labor, identity, and the emerging majority in higher education. *Journal of Communication Pedagogy, 3*, 49–64.
https://doi.org/10.31446/JCP.2020.06

Hall, B., & Tandon, R. (Eds), (2021). *Socially responsible higher education: International perspectives on knowledge democracy.*
https://www.jstor.org/stable/10.1163/j.ctv1v7zbn5

Hamilton, M. L., & Pinnegar, S. (2015). Considering the role of self-study of teaching and teacher education practices research in transforming urban classrooms. *Studying Teacher Education, 11*(2), 180–90. https://doi.org/10.1080/17425964.2015.1045775

Hamilton, M. L., & Pinnegar, S. (2015). *Knowing, becoming, doing as teacher educators: Identity, intimate scholarship, inquiry.* Emerald Group Publishing.

Hordatt Gentles, C. (2018). Reorienting Jamaican teacher education to address sustainability: Challenges, implications and possibilities. *Caribbean Quarterly – A Journal of Caribbean Culture, 64*(1), 149–66. https://www.tandfonline.com/toc/rcbq20/64/1

LaBoskey, V. K. (2004). The methodology of self-study and its theoretical underpinnings. In J. J. Loughran, M. L. Hamilton, V. K. LaBoskey, & T. L. Russell (Eds), *International handbook of self-study of teaching and teacher education practices* (pp. 817–70). Kluwer Academic Publishers.

Liston, D. L., & Zeichner, K. M. (1987). Critical pedagogy and teacher education. *Journal of Education, 169*(3), 26–27.

Loughran, J. J. (2004). Learning through self-study: The influence of purpose, participants, and context. In J. J. Loughran, M. L. Hamilton, V. K. LaBoskey, & T. L. Russell (Eds), *International handbook of self-study of teaching and teacher education practices* (pp. 151–92). Kluwer Academic Publishers.

Mariskind, C. (2014). Teachers' care in higher education: contesting gendered constructions. *Gender and Education, 26*(3), 306–20. https://doi.org/10.1080/09540253.2014.901736

Marsh, M. M., & Castner, D. (2017). Critical approaches in making new space for teacher competences. In D. J. Clandinin, & J. Husu (Eds)., *The SAGE handbook of research on teacher education* (pp. 869–86). SAGE Publications Ltd.

McKamey, C. (2011). Restorying "caring" in education: Students' narratives of caring for and about. *Narrative Works: Issues, Investigations & Interventions, 1*(1), 78–94.
https://journals.lib.unb.ca/index.php/NW/article/view/18475

Merriam, S. B., Caffarella, R. S., & Baumgartner, L. M. (2007). *Learning in adulthood: A comprehensive guide.* Jossey-Bass.

Miller, E. (2003). *The prophet and the virgin: The masculine and feminine roots of teaching.* Ian Randle Publishers.

Nettleford, R. (2000). *Mirror, mirror: Identity, race and protest in Jamaica.* LMH Publishing.

Nettleford, R. (2003). *Caribbean cultural identity: An essay in cultural dynamics.* Ian Randle Publishers.

Noddings, N. (2002). *Starting at home: Caring and social policy.* University of California Press.

Noddings, N. (2005). *The challenge to care in schools: An alternative approach to education*. Teachers College Press.

O'Connor, K. E. (2008). You choose to care: Teachers, emotions and professional identity. *Teaching and Teacher Education, 24* (1), 117–26.
https://doi.org/10.1016/j.tate.2006.11.008

O'Neill, A. M. (2005). Gender and society. In P. Adams, R. Openshaw, J. Hamer (Eds), *Education and society in Aotearoa New Zealand* (2nd ed.) (pp. 65–100). Thomson/Dunmore Press.

Orr, D. (2004). *Earth in mind: On education, environment and the human prospect* (2nd ed.). Island Press.

Pranjić, S. S. (2021). Development of a caring teacher-student relationship in higher education. *Journal of Education Culture and Society, 12*(1), 151–63.
https://doi.org/10.15503/jecs2021.1.151.163

Ritter, J. K. (2016). The tension-fraught enterprise of teaching self-study. In D. Garbett, & A. Ovens (Eds), *Enacting self-study as methodology for professional inquiry* (pp. 37–43). Herstmonceux.

Rogers, D., & Webb, J. (1991). The ethic of caring in teacher education. *Journal of Teacher Education, 42*(3), 173–81.
https://doi.org/10.1177/002248719104200303

Shepherd, V., & Hemmings, G. D. L. (2022). *Introduction to reparation for secondary schools*. The University of the West Indies Press.

Soltis, J. F. (2005). Preface. In N. Noddings (Ed.), *The challenge to care in schools: An alternative approach to education* (2nd ed.) (pp. ix–x). Teachers College Press.

UNESCO (2015). *Rethinking education. Towards a global common good?*
https://www.sdg4education2030.org/rethinking-education-unesco-2015

University of the West Indies. (2017). *The UWI triple A strategy 2017–2022: Revitalizing Caribbean development* [PDF].
https://www.uwi.edu/uop/sites/uop/files/Full%20plan.pdf

Walker-Gleaves, C. (2019). Is caring pedagogy really so progressive? Exploring the conceptual and practical impediments to operationalizing care in higher education. In P. Gibbs, & A. Peterson (Eds), *Higher education and hope: Institutional, pedagogical and personal possibilities* (pp. 93–113). Palgrave Macmillan.

21. Critical data literacies for good

Caroline Kuhn, Judith Pete, and Juliana E. Raffaghelli

This chapter offers an illustrative and generative example of a local, social and pedagogical problem in a Global South context — students' engagement with open data for coming up with climate change solutions — to reflect on the importance of understanding the nuance and complex nature of data literacy, and to transform different aspects of their social reality. This, in turn, opens a discussion about how and why understanding the complexity of critical data literacy is the foundation of HE for good. Our work aims to contribute to demystifying the expectation that all solutions pre-exist the problems and that data literacy (particularly critical data literacy) stems from precise instructions or given frameworks that lead educational actions towards achieving data justice. The complex nature of critical data literacies asks for responsible action and concerted effort to deal with the unexpected and develop the expected through the best possible human condition in each context of life and development.

A vignette: Teaching and learning about climate change in Kenya

We begin this chapter with a story of a specific teaching and learning moment experienced at Tangaza University College in Nairobi, Kenya. A class of 32 students guided by Judith Pete, one of this chapter's authors, used open data to engage with the challenge of climate change in Kenya. In Judith's words:

I introduced a topic on models of social change in the 21st century for African organisations. I reminded the students what we have learned about open data for social innovation and open data as OER (open educational resources). One adult student interjected and asked: "Madam, can I suggest that we focus on simple models and strategies such indigenous tree planting campaigns, sensitisation of farmers about global warming to embrace modern agribusiness methods of farming etc. Such can help us reduce the impacts of climate change?" I immediately responded: "Sure, very good idea indeed". I then asked the groups to discuss local strategies they think could be implemented to help curb the climate change impacts in Kenya. This was the opportunity to use the skills they learned to work with open data to foster social change. The group presentations took place towards the World Open Data Day when a student shared that they all agreed, after doing their research, to buy 50 seedlings of indigenous trees to be planted as one of the simple but known strategies to reduce climate change impact in Kenya. This suggestion was supported by other groups, and we ended up planting 500 seedlings of different species of indigenous trees (see Figure 21.1). A list of names of various types of indigenous trees started, some in Swahili, and some in local languages. The student leader suggested the idea of educating the communities around Tangaza and beyond on the merits of planting these types of trees and what they can do to mitigate the effects of climate change. The decision was taken to transform this into an open educational resource further. I (Judith) learnt so much from this group and feel positively challenged by their catalytic approach to curbing climate change in Kenya. The spirit is still on in communities, and seedbeds with indigenous trees have been set up by some students in remote areas of the city.

21. Critical data literacies for good

Figure 21.1

Students undertaking a course on change management planted indigenous trees within the university and surrounding community, CC BY-NC

Who we are, and how this story came to happen

We are three female higher education educators with mixed backgrounds. Judith is a Kenyan with a passion for OERs, she has served in academic and regional non-governmental organisations in different managerial and leadership capacities for almost two decades. Juliana is an Argentinian living in Europe, her work has also been connected to education as an emancipatory instrument. Caroline emigrated to the UK from Venezuela, where she had experienced first-hand deep social inequalities. All three of us are educators widely interested in issues of social justice and equity. We believe that our backgrounds and concomitant values inform what we think is higher education for good.

In 2020, each of us was engaged in different activities dealing with openness in education, including the phenomenon of datafication. Our encounter was driven by a project, *DataPraxis*[1], whose goal was to foster educators' critical data literacy amongst four partner institutions including Tangaza University College, Nairobi, and in which we developed a critical pedagogical approach inspired by Freire's critical pedagogy principles and his ideas of problem posing, "critical consciousness", and generative themes (Kuhn & Raffaghelli, 2022). In the overall project, we learned that this critical pedagogical approach is powerful as it engages students in working on real problems in local contexts.

For Tangaza University College, with a longstanding trajectory in advocating for open education in Africa (Pete et al., 2017; Pete, 2019), the focus was on open data for social innovation and the extent to which the enthusiasm around this practice could become a catalyser for civic empowerment and innovation. We co-developed the materials and resources for the workshop.[2] We introduced the idea of data generated by local communities as 'post-academic' and 'co-liberational' as a generative theme, particularly reflecting on the work that has been done

---

1   This project was an international collaboration with the University de La Republica, Uruguay; University Oberta of Catalunya, Barcelona; University of Surrey, UK and Tangaza University College, Nairobi.

    The research team comprised: Juliana Raffaghelli, Leo Havemann, Javiera Atenas, Cristian Timermann, and Caroline Kuhn. The overall project can be accessed through https://datapraxis.net

2   https://datapraxis.net/chapter-narobi/the-open-data-for-empowerment-workshop-od4e/

already through the Environmental Justice Atlas initiative as a potential platform for them to explore. We consulted the participants to see if they could build their own maps of data. We were particularly interested in the possibility of addressing the problem of misrepresentation and misrecognition (Lambert, 2018; Onouha, 2018), i.e. the "no-data" case where some information is missed from the data set. As Onouha (2018) reminds us: "unsurprisingly, this lack of data typically correlates with issues affecting those who are most vulnerable in that [particular] context".[3] Data relations are often power relations. It was precisely these power relations that we wanted to scrutinise and explore. Arguably having a robust critical approach to data literacies is key to data justice, by which we mean the intersection of datafication and social justice, to explore pathways that can advance social justice in a datafied society (Dencik et al., 2022; Taylor, 2017). In Figure 21.2 the approach of students as catalysers of social change is depicted. Students explore meaningful situations of data injustice in the community engaging with data or the absence of it. Situations pertaining to the community are ideally brought into the classroom for discussion.

Figure 21.2

One of the slides used in our workshop: Students as catalysers of social change. We invited participants to uncover the "no data" situations through collaboration with the students as catalysers of social change

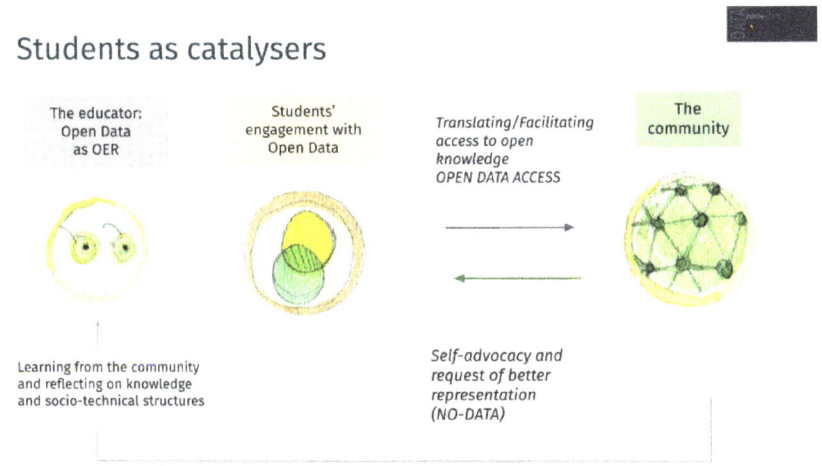

---

3   For more details of Onouha's work go to: https://mimionuoha.com/the-library-of-missing-datasets

In the remainder of this chapter, we explore critical issues related to data justice using the example of the vignette we have shared: the importance of local educators in identifying and engaging with urgent social issues, the need for meaningful participation, access, and the need to consider the material component of data literacy.

Local educators identify and engage with urgent social issues

In a recent report, UNESCO (2021) argues for a new contract for education where the purpose of education is defined as a common good involving everyone coming together to repair a damaged planet. UNESCO (2021) argues that to achieve this, a new social contract:

> grounded in human rights and based on principles of non-discrimination, social justice, respect for life, human dignity, and cultural diversity, is needed. It must encompass an ethic of care, reciprocity, and solidarity. It must strengthen education as a public endeavour and a common good (p. iii).

We see this new social contract aligned with the relational and communal values held by African thinkers (Biko, 2004; Mbiti, 1970; Fanon, 2005). This relational conception extends the notion of community agreeing that all human beings are related beyond the links of kinship and community by ties of reciprocity grounded on the interdependence of all human beings. Mbiti's maxim "I am because we are; and since we are, therefore I am" (1970, p. 141) is eloquent. Mbiti also talked of moral perfection as an understanding of what is good and evil leading to harmonious living in which the community's scarce resources are to be distributed equally at all times (Mbiti, 1970). We also see this social contract in line with our views and hopes for a more equal and inclusive HE system.

What struck us in this illustrative vignette is the fact that students selected the climate crisis to demonstrate change, the importance of access to information, and the urgency of action that takes into account not only the local university community but also students' rural communities. It is very real when, as we finalise writing this chapter, at least 18 million people in East Africa are food insecure due to one of the most severe droughts in recent history (Bechman, 2022). People needing humanitarian help are estimated to be 7 million in Ethiopia, 4 million in Kenya, and 5 million in South Sudan. In Kenya, the drought has impacted 20 out of 23 counties. Subsistence farmers are at risk of losing their cattle due to lack of food, as well as taking on debt and/ or fleeing to displacement camps. On a different scale, the increase in living costs and the lack of water that people used to rely on from the rainfall is confusing farmers, making them feel disoriented and helpless. They have no idea what to do or where to find guidance, as this reality feels very different from the one experienced by previous generations. Therefore, taking action is perceived as a considerable challenge despite the situation's urgency.

Returning to the issue of the alleged 'global' nature of the climate crisis, it is startling and revealing to read the same global drought observatory (GDO) analytical report (Toreti et al., 2022) about northern Italy's drought. In northern Italy, the reported impacts are not about millions of people being food insecure and needing humanitarian help, but how the ongoing drought is affecting the energy storage in the Italian hydropower system and the agricultural impacts in terms of the reduction of yield potential. It becomes clear that the consequences are not evenly distributed. On the contrary, the research shows that low and middle-income countries are highly climate vulnerable, and thus experience the worst collateral effects of climate change. For example, Kenya contributes less than 0.1 per cent of global greenhouse gas (GHG) emissions annually. The UN has warned of a "climate apartheid" as wealthy nations pay to escape hunger, overheating and conflict while the rest of the world, like Kenya, is left to suffer. A striking reminder is that fifty per cent of the global population (approx. 3.5 billion people) live in countries most vulnerable to climate change, bearing the impact of a crisis they did not cause.

Equitable critical data practices rely on access

The above example brings us to think about the benefits of accessing data, but at the same time, we reflect upon the fact that access is not a given; it is political. When we talk about access to data or information or knowledge the main feature is that it is openly accessible, usable, editable, and can be shared by anyone for any purpose, even commercially. Furthermore, open data and content must be in the public domain or provided under an open licence, promoting a robust commons in which anyone (with the proper social arrangements) may participate, and interoperability is maximised (Atenas et al., 2021). In contrast, closed data is data that someone owns and does not share in the public domain. Yet accessing data and content is more complex than being open and thus 'accessible'; it also needs to be discoverable. That is, it needs to show up when students search for it, and this is more political than it seems. Czerniewicz et al. (2016) demonstrate that "in the academic domains, indications are that knowledge patterns continue to reflect physically based geopolitical realities — where knowledge from the South is peripheral while knowledge from the North still dominates in terms of all the conventional metrics" (p. 1). There is a gap between the discoverability of data from the North in respect to data from the South. The existence of open data is not always the problem, but rather its discoverability and visibility via search engines (Czerniewicz et al., 2016). This is the case when it comes to research in climate change, where the USA is the dominant knowledge engine for publications (Czerniewicz et al., 2016). We agree with the authors that "citations also have their uneven geographies" (Czerniewicz et al., 2016, p. 3.). On the other hand, researchers in the Global South struggle to access research, and it is known that research works that are more likely to be found will be cited more often. The information found online shapes knowledge production and, thus, what comes to be known (Czerniewicz et al., 2016).

From this evidence, it is clear that the visibility and findability of data and in particular, open data is political, and never neutral. It is interesting that in our professional development experience, *DataPraxis*, the majority of the open data portals explored by participants were based in transnational institutions and non-governmental bodies with an overwhelming presence of Global North technicians and professionals, and of course, data sources. What we can infer from all of the above is that to access open data and content, one requires both the knowledge, understanding and skills to deal with the more technical side of it, but also the necessary social arrangements, e.g. meaningful connectivity. More broadly, it is essential that the knowledge, data, accessible and findable through search engines is not mainly from the Global North, but that it is more balanced between the North and the South.

Critical data practices are about access and participation

In our generative example, we could observe how the educator was able to provide the conducive social arrangements: openness in choosing the project, exposing critical social problems such as climate change in the local context, the knowledge educators gained through the broader project of *DataPraxis* that enabled students to do something they had reasons to value, namely addressing a local problem that affects their community. In short, the educator in collaboration with her students constructed a meaningful intervention that showed respect for and empowered real people, very much aligned with the key ideas of the Capability Approach (Nussbaum, 2011; Sen 1999; Robeyns, 2017) embodying the ethos of a higher education for good.

For data practices to be meaningful, it is critical that learners can meaningfully participate as agents in their development, i.e., enabling social arrangements so that students can make a significant epistemic contribution. In this case, the right combination of motivation, knowledge, understanding and skills, adequate scaffolding and the needed material infrastructure led the group to make a meaningful contribution to their local community, but also to other rural communities where indigenous trees were also planted. Students were empowered as they experienced the satisfaction of being agents of change in their local community (be it the immediate university surroundings or their local villages). Students' initiatives and own ideas make more sense than old models and approaches to social change, as one of the students shared with Judith. This, in turn, aligns with Fricker's (2007, 2015) idea that the wellbeing of a human person has an epistemic dimension that is not only about receiving knowledge but, what is more, giving and sharing knowledge with the local community. It is about epistemic reciprocity.

The meaningful participation of people as agents in development practice has been a central concern in capabilitarian scholarship — in the work of Walker, Sen, Fricker and others. For example, Fricker (2007, 2015) argues that making epistemic contributions, that is, contributing to the shared pool of knowledge is fundamental to human wellbeing, a dignified life, and expansive freedoms. Such contributions, the corresponding capabilities, and concomitant functionings can be fostered in and through education, and this endeavour surely will be for good.[4]

This vignette is an inspiring and generative example of what can be done by local people (students, teachers, and community members) who have agency and self-determination to contribute to local solutions in small and effective ways, partially through enacting a critical approach to data literacy. It materialises the fruitful combination suggested by Nussbaum (2011) of the internal capacities and dispositions of students and practitioners (motivation, aspirations, care and connection to their local context, knowledge, understanding, skills, self-determination), with conducive social arrangements: a suitable environment with a functioning digital and data infrastructure, access to resources and devices, and support from the lecturer that serve as enablers for people's agency to be enacted. The social conditions, in this case, served as the factors that transformed a desire, something students had reasons to value, into an action, a doing — planting indigenous trees around the university and local community and documenting that experience, creating an open educational resource (OER) that can be reused by others (see Figure 21.1). This example also shows how a group of students can make a meaningful contribution to the common pool of knowledge, i.e. in researching and listing those trees and showing how they can mitigate some effects of climate change and raise awareness in the community of small actions that can contribute to social change. We want to stress that given the relational conception of reality in African culture (Hord & Lee, 2016), being able to contribute to the local and shared epistemic pool of knowledge is hugely significant and can have a noteworthy impact on students' wellbeing.

One of the aims of HE4Good is to enable learners' meaningful participation as agents in their development. To do so, providing the enabling social arrangements so that students can make a meaningful epistemic contribution is key. Nonetheless, creating an educational

---

4   Given the scope of this chapter, we will not explain the Capabilities Approach in depth. Instead, we refer the interested reader to the work of Walker and Unterhalten (2007), Sen (1999), Nussbaum (2011), Robeyns (2017), and Witthaus (2022).

space for good that promotes these enabling conditions that can trigger students' ability to discover and develop their capabilities and transform them into functionings, can go beyond the educator's willingness and even professionalism.

Critical data literacy will not be strengthened by inserting more efficient technology in the classroom. Instead, becoming aware of the complexity inherent in any social context (a datafied society in this case), and finding what is appropriate to scrutinise and investigate concerning unjust data practices could be helpful. In the same vein, having data which is open is not good per se, especially when it gets appropriated by forces which are not good at all. However, while some have argued that there is a data divide that must be compensated through engagement with the local socio-technological ecosystem (Gurstein, 2011), we agree with others that marginal participation in the knowledge economy does not only depend on the researchers' and citizens' lack of skills and understanding, but on their position at geographic, linguistic, and epistemic margins (Czerniewicz et al., 2016). There are relevant initiatives developing in Latin America, e.g. in the field of femicides which came to be known by the international research community when they were "spoken" in English (see 'Feminicidios' in D'Ignazio & Klein, 2020). Working jointly with educators collecting local voices and data was an effort to go beyond the missed data and concomitant data (in)justices.

Whilst students expanded their freedoms and grasped the relevance of open data and open content to developing a specific local intervention, the ongoing understanding and engagement with open production and the interactions between academic and community knowledge could not be established in advance. Nonetheless, the critical understanding of open and open resources that is not produced 'about' the Kenyan society but 'with and by' the young, educated students in the Kenyan higher education system, is undoubtedly an enabler of agentic practices.

It is of note that the students in this example, studying in-person at an urban university, did have a generative combination of access to digital and data infrastructure, a suitable environment with appropriate guidance to realise the activity, and all the internal capacities that were needed to create this experience. Conversely, if there is no access to data and digital infrastructure, most people that live, study, and work in rural settings will not be able to participate in the knowledge economy, and their epistemic contribution is indirectly truncated. This brings an immediate consequence, amongst many others, that their capacity to be knowledge producers is severely curtailed. We know that the knowledge that counts is the knowledge that is produced and discoverable. Hence people in rural communities are excluded from that dynamic and vital process. This undoubtedly influences not only their participation in the (local) knowledge economy, but also in how they are (mis)represented in policy documents, government initiatives, and scholarship.

Data literacies are material

Our work stands in contrast to the tendency to think about data literacy with a Silicon Valley solutionist mindset, one that promotes the belief that data literacy is simply a matter of having the knowledge and skills to engage critically with data issues and data-driven technologies. What is often overlooked is that people can have the knowledge, skills, and motivation to collect and share data to solve local problems, but they might not have access to adequate infrastructure. By infrastructure, we mean, amongst other things, to have meaningful connectivity and access to electricity. In our view, the invisibilisation of the infrastructural problem is linked to the invisibilisation of the social reality of those at the margins, which entails injustice.

It is known that global connectivity and data innovation are fostering social change. Data shapes our daily lives and permeates the social and economic landscape of the different countries across the world. Yet, meaningful participation in today's digital age requires, amongst other things, access to data and information infrastructure, e.g. a high-speed broadband connection to the internet, moreover, *meaningful connectivity* (A4AI),[5] a new standard that measures not only if someone has access to the internet, but the quality of connection they have. The A4AI has defined meaningful connectivity by setting a minimum threshold across four dimensions:

- Regular internet use — minimum threshold: daily use.
- An appropriate device — minimum threshold: access to a smartphone.

---

5 Alliance for Affordable Internet. https://a4ai.org/meaningful-connectivity/

- Enough data — minimum threshold: an unlimited broadband connection at home or a place of work or study.
- A fast connection — minimum threshold: 4G mobile connectivity.

This more nuanced understanding of connectivity considers that not everyone connects to the internet similarly. Researchers and policymakers should not rely on a binary metric of have or have not. The A4AI argues that ignoring the huge disparities in how people connect will not only increase inequalities online but also offline. The report *Data for Better Lives* (2021) by the World Bank dedicates an entire chapter explaining how data infrastructure (lack of) is a source of inequality.

However, infrastructures are invisibilised if they serve to maintain power structures and metaphors that serve that purpose. The internet is a material infrastructure that mediates human interactions and socialisation. As Couldry and Hepp (2017) put it: "Communication, media and their infrastructures matter increasingly today in stating the whatness of what is" (p. 27). Infrastructures, particularly data and information infrastructures should be regarded as political, as Bowker, Mongili and Pellegrino (2014) argue:

> We all too rarely think about the ways in which our social, cultural, and political values are braided into the wires, coded into the applications and built into the databases, which are so much a part of our daily lives. (p. xiii)

Infrastructures not only have to do with wires and codes but how human values shape some elements of data and information infrastructure (see, for example, Chan et al., Chapter 4, this volume). Certainly, the symbolic dimension of data is important, but it is essential to integrate the material as a critical dimension of critical data literacy, given that it mediates any experience in and with the digital. The invisible nature of data infrastructures is political and easily overlooked despite its tangible and visible consequences on data literacy issues (Gray et al., 2018), data and social justice. Crawford (2020) eloquently points out how the metaphor of "cloud computing" which supports the supposed immateriality of artificial intelligence (AI) is possible only because data generation, maintenance, and circulation are realised through the hidden tubes, cables, and labour associated with these processes. In a similar vein, Starosielski (2015) in her book *The undersea network* states that:

> Manholes, such as the one beneath my feet [she refers to a picture taken by her in O'ahu beach in Hawaii, where a massive cable nexus is located that connects the island to the Internet] are some of the few sites where cable systems appear in public space. It is by looking down, rather than up to the sky, that we can best see today's network infrastructure. (p. ix)

Therefore, we argue that this material component is a key dimension of critical data literacy. Data justice requires it to be foregrounded and made visible. This aspect is critical when it comes to accessing and working with data. As mentioned above, the internet is mainly a material infrastructure that mediates human interactions and socialisation. In our example, the infrastructure was available to the students, together with other elements. Therefore, students could transform an opportunity into something tangible and real. They were able to do and be what they, as a group, had reasons to value, namely contribute to their local environment and the community by searching for adequate trees and planting them to curb some effects of climate change.

Conclusion

The purpose of education envisioned by UNESCO as a common good that involves everyone, everywhere coming together to repair a damaged planet, is possible. The potential of education as a route for sustainable collective futures, at least through this small example, is shown to be a reality. We can attest with this example how students enacted respect for life — human, but also non-human, by planting those trees. Education, as we have observed, encompasses an ethic of care, reciprocity, and solidarity. Conceptualizing education as a public endeavour and a common good aligns with data literacies for good and with higher education for good.

More generally, if, as educators, we understand literacy as a form of cultural politics (Freire & Macedo, 1987), a set of social practices that empower or disempower people, we will be in a better position to act. Moreover, this more nuanced understanding can enable educators to find strategies to articulate transforming practices that can mediate the relationship of learners to the world that takes place in the general milieu in which learners find themselves, as we could see in the generative example we presented. In addition to this still unaddressed wicked problem, educators are facing a frenzy of concern about what is being called "artificial intelligence literacy", which entails both popular fantasies around automata in a perfect world and the need for skills to meet the new jobs connected to them (Selwyn, 2022). In addition, there is a media discourse that portrays education as obsolete and soon replaced by these robots, making educators feel frustrated and ignored. There is still so much to do to fully understand and articulate fertile practices that foster and strengthen a critical approach to data literacy. It is important to be cautious and humble and not shy away from the unsolved wicked problem of how to address data literacy pedagogically. It can be tempting to jump to the next new EdTech trend so that we feel current and up-to-date with fancy and unsubstantiated media discourses.

Critical data literacies are arguably the most important literacy in an age of datafication, especially if HE is to be for good. We wish to end this chapter with a call to action by asking educators and students to do challenging work if the aim is to advance data justice and, more generally, social justice in such a convoluted and critical moment we are living in. If, as we argued earlier, data justice is the intersection of datafication and social justice, there is no way we can address any injustice if we cannot challenge, scrutinise, and problematise what seems natural and commonsensical, all of which is hard work! We are aware that these tectonic movements still entail new areas of chaos and uncertainty in the best understanding of Hannah Arendt's idea of "vita activa" where being "capable of action means that the unexpected can be expected" (Arendt, 1958, p. 178) recognising as she does that humans "live on the earth and inhabit the world" (p. 7). We hope that our vignette contributes to demystifying what is to be expected, embracing, in all its richness, the complexities of critical data literacies, navigating the unexpected through politically committed action.

References

Atenas, J., Bonina, C., Pane, J. and Belbis, J. (2021) *What is open data?* In: C. Kuhn, J. Atenas, & L. Havemann (Eds), Understanding data: praxis and politics. Human data interaction network (pp. 1–29). https://doi.org/10.5281/zenodo.4783601

Arendt, H. (1958). *The human condition.* University of Chicago Press.

Bechmann, I. (2022). *Providing water, food and shelter for people displaced on the horn of Africa.* UNHCR. https://www.unhcr.org/neu/86727-providing-water-food-and-shelter-for-people-displaced-on-the-horn-of-africa.html

Biko, S. (2004). *I write what I like.* Picador Africa

Bowker, G., Mongili, A., and Pellegrino, G. (2014). *Information infrastructure(s): Boundaries, ecologies, multiplicity.* Cambridge Scholars Publishing.

Couldry, N., & Hepp, A. (2017). *The mediated construction of reality.* Polity

Crawford, K. (2021). *Atlas of AI: Power, politics, and the planetary costs of artificial intelligence.* Yale University Press.

Czerniewicz, L., Goodier, S., & Morrell, R. (2016). Southern knowledge online? Climate change research discoverability and communication practices. *Information, Communication & Society, 20*(3), 386–405. https://doi.org/10.1080/1369118x.2016.1168473

Dencik, L., Hintz, A., Redden, J., & Treré, E. (2022). *Data justice.* Routledge

D'Ignazio, C., & Klein, L. (2020). *Data feminism.* The MIT Press.

Fanon, F. (2005). *The wretched of the earth.* Grove Press.

Freire, P. (2001). *Education for critical consciousness.* Penguin

Freire, P. & Macedo, D. (1987). *Literacy: Reading the word and the world.* Routledge

Fricker, M. (2007). *Epistemic injustice. Power and the ethics of knowing.* Oxford University Press

Fricker, M. (2015). Epistemic contribution as a central human capability, In G. Hull (Ed.), *The equal society: Essays on equality in theory and practice.* Lexington Books.

Gray, J., Gerlitz, C., & Bounegru, L. (2018). Data infrastructure literacy. *Big Data & Society, 5*(2), 1–13. https://doi.org/10.1177/2053951718786316

Gurstein, M. (2011, July 11). *A data divide? Data "haves" and "have nots" and open (government) data.* Gurstein's Community Informatics.
https://gurstein.wordpress.com/2011/07/11/a-data-divide-data-%E2%80%9Chaves%E2%80%9D-and-%E2%80%9Chave-nots%E2%80%9D-and-open-government-data/

Hord, F. L., & Lee, J. S. (2016). *I am because we are: Readings in Africana Philosophy.* University of Massachusetts Press.

Kitchin, R. (2014). *The data evolution: Big data, open data, data infrastructures & their consequences.* SAGE Publications.

Kuhn, C., & Raffaghelli, J. E. (2022). *Final report for Understanding data: Praxis and politics.*
https://doi.org/10.5281/zenodo.6482614

Lambert, S. R. (2018). Changing our (Dis)course: A distinctive social justice aligned definition of open education. *Journal of Learning for Development, 5*(3), 225–44.
https://jl4d.org/index.php/ejl4d/article/view/290

Mbiti, J. (1970). *African religion and philosophy.* Heinemann Educational Publishers.

Nussbaum, M. (2011). *Creating capabilities: The human development approach.* Harvard University Press

Onuoha, M. (2018). *The library of missing datasets 2.0.* MIMI ỌNỤỌHA.
https://mimionuoha.com/the-library-of-missing-datasets-v-20

Pete, J., Mulder, F., & Oliveira Neto, J. (2017). Differentiation in access to, and the use and sharing of (Open) Educational Resources among students and lecturers at Kenyan universities. *Open Praxis, 9*(2), 173–94.
http://doi.org/10.5944/openpraxis.9.2.574

Pete, J. (2019) *Open education resources differentiation: A cross-country study on differentiation in access, use and sharing of (open) educational resources at universities in Kenya, Ghana and South Africa* [Doctoral dissertation, Open University of the Netherlands].
https://research.ou.nl/en/publications/open-education-resources-differentiation-a-cross-country-study-on

Robeyns, I. (2017). *Wellbeing, freedom, and social justice.* Open Book Publishers.

Selwyn, N. (2022). The future of AI and education: Some cautionary notes. *European Journal of Education, 57*(4), 620–31.
https://doi.org/10.1111/ejed.12532

Sen, A. (1992). *Inequality reexamined.* Harvard University Press.

Sen, A. (1999). *Development as freedom.* Oxford University Press.

Spratt, S., & Baker, J. (2015). *Big data and international development: Impacts, scenarios and Policy options*. Institute of Development Studies.
https://opendocs.ids.ac.uk/opendocs/handle/20.500.12413/7198

Starosielski, N. (2015). *The undersea network*. Duke University Press.

Taylor, L. (2017). What is data justice? The case for connecting digital rights and freedoms globally. *Big Data & Society, 4*(2), 1–14.
https://doi.org/10.1177/2053951717736335.

Toreti, A., Bavera, D., Avanzi, F., Cammalleri, C., De Felice, M., De Jager, A., Di Ciollo, C., Gabellani, S., Maetens, W., Magni, D., Manfron, G., Masante, D., Mazzeschi, M., Mccormick, N., Naumann, G., Niemeyer, S., Rossi, L., Seguini, L., Spinoni, J., & Van Den Berg, M. (2022). *Drought in northern Italy – March 2022: GDO analytical report*. European Union.
http://doi.org/10.2760/781876.

Toreti, A., Bavera, D., Acosta Navarro, J., Cammalleri, C., de Jager, A., Di Ciollo, C., Hrast Essenfelder, A., Maetens, W., Magni, D., Masante, D., Mazzeschi, M., Meroni, M., Rembold, F., & Spinoni, J. (2022). *Drought in East Africa: August 2022*. European Union.
https://publications.jrc.ec.europa.eu/repository/handle/JRC130470

UNESCO (2021). *Reimagining our futures together: A new social contract for education*.
http://www.unesco.org/open-access/terms-use-ccbysa-en

Walker, M. (2016). *Higher education pedagogies*. Palgrave.

Walker, M. & Unterhalten, H. (2007). *Amartya Sen's capability approach and social justice in education*. Palgrave.

Williamson, B. (2018). The hidden architecture of higher education: Building a big data infrastructure for the 'smarter university'. *International Journal of Educational Technology in Higher Education, 15*(1), 1–26.
https://doi.org/10.1186/s41239-018-0094-1

Witthaus, G. (2022, April 15). *Exploring the capability approach as a social justice framework for researching higher education in 12 blog posts – now available as an OER*. Art of e-learning.
https://artofelearning.org/2022/04/15/exploring-the-capability-approach-as-a-social-justice-framework-for-researching-higher-education-in-12-blog-posts-now-available-as-an-oer/

22. Collaboratively reimagining teaching and learning

Flora Fabian, Jonathan Harle, Perpetua Kalimasi, Rehema Kilonzo, Gloria Lamaro, Albert Luswata, David Monk, Edwin Ngowi, Femi Nzegwu, and Damary Sikalieh

Introduction

In 2020, the African Regional Forum on Sustainable Development proclaimed Africa would only attain the Sustainable Development Goals (SDGs) if "universities in Africa collaborate in research, teaching and community or societal engagement" (Ligami, 2020). In 2022, the UNESCO World Higher Education conference called on universities to "reshape ideas and practices in higher education to ensure sustainable development for the planet and humanity" (UNESCO, 2022). While there are regular calls for African universities to improve their teaching, finding ways to do this within the resources and the available time in already stretched institutions, at the scale required, have proven elusive. This chapter is a reflexive exercise, discussing the work of an international partnership, *Transforming Employability for Social Change in East Africa* (TESCEA), that aimed to reshape habits of teaching and learning in institutions of higher education.[1] We, as TESCEA partners and authors of this chapter, hope that our example can make a significant contribution towards understanding how change can happen in higher education, and particularly in resource-constrained settings. We begin

---

1 See https://www.inasp.info/project/transforming-employability-social-change-east-africa-tescea

by presenting our approach and then offer reflections on the change we observed, the ways in which this was achieved, and the challenges we encountered along the way.

Context: problems and partnership

Higher education institutions in East Africa face multiple challenges, including: the quality and relevance of university learning; the challenge of graduate employability (McCowan, 2014; Nganga, 2014); how universities can more effectively and visibly serve their communities; and the ability of academics and university leaders to create the institutional environment for this to be possible — particularly enabling students to develop their critical thinking and problem-solving abilities (McCowan et al., 2022; Schendel, 2015, 2016) and addressing gender inequities. In response to these interconnected challenges, a group of academics, learning designers, social entrepreneurs and facilitators from East Africa and the UK gathered to identify shared goals and approaches. In 2017 the TESCEA partnership was formed, with funding from the Strategic Partnerships for Higher Education Innovation and Reform programme.[2]

The TESCEA partnership

The four universities in the TESCEA partnership are: Uganda Martyrs University (Uganda), Gulu University (Uganda), Mzumbe University (Tanzania), and University of Dodoma (Tanzania). The four universities are a diverse group. Three are public institutions (Dodoma, Gulu and Mzumbe) and one is private (Uganda Martyrs). They range in size from 4,000–5,000 students (Gulu, Mzumbe and Uganda Martyrs) to over 30,000 (Dodoma). Each institution has a clear commitment to serving its community and its nation, but conceives of and expresses this differently:

---

2   The Strategic Partnerships for Higher Education Innovation and Reform programme (SPHEIR) was funded by the UK Department for International Development (subsequently the Foreign, Commonwealth and Development Office), and operated by a fund management consortium led by the British Council with Pricewaterhouse Coopers and Universities UK International: see www.spheir.org.uk.

- Mzumbe University, in eastern Tanzania, traces its origins to a training school for local administrators established in the 1950s, becoming a higher learning institution in the 1970s and a full university in 2001. Mzumbe aims to serve the "socio-economic development of the people" (Mzumbe University, 2017).

- Uganda Martyrs University, based in central Uganda, was established in 1993 by the Catholic Church. Uganda Martyrs seeks to work "for the betterment of society guided by ethical values" (Uganda Martyrs University, n.d.).

- Gulu University, in northern Uganda, was established in 2001, admitting its first students in 2002, with a mission to help the region rebuild after a protracted and devastating conflict (Monk et al., 2020). Working "for community transformation" is at the heart of Gulu's mission (Gulu University, n.d.).

- University of Dodoma, the youngest of the four universities, was established in 2007 as a large multi-faculty institution in central Tanzania. Dodoma aims to contribute to the "economic growth, reduction of poverty, and improved social wellbeing of Tanzanians" (University of Dodoma, n.d.).

Notwithstanding their differences, change was to be achieved through redesigning established programmes in established institutions, not introducing new courses or establishing new centres. Across all four universities (as in so many places), most lecturers had received little, if any, preparation to teach. Most lecturers used a memorisation and exam model of teaching. Staff struggled to balance the competing pressures of teaching, research, and administrative duties, and had little time for professional development or additional student support.

Joining these universities in the TESCEA partnership were three organisations who support and facilitate change in higher education, each with their own histories. Established in 1992, INASP (UK)[3] has been working with East African universities to strengthen research and teaching for over 25 years. Ashoka East Africa (Kenya) was established

---

3   An original member of the partnership was Linking Industry with Academia (LIWA) based in Kenya. LIWA left the partnership during its second year.

in 2001 as a hub of the global network of social entrepreneurs. The Association for Faculty Enrichment in Learning and Teaching (AFELT, Kenya) emerged in the mid-2000s seeking to support improvements in teaching and learning across Kenya's higher education system (Brewis & McCowan, 2016).

INASP was the lead partner. Although a natural continuation of INASP's original convening role, it was also necessitated by funding requirements which stipulated grant management experience that was difficult for other partners to satisfy. Our efforts to counter the structural inequities that this introduced are discussed below.

Gathering evidence

Our evidence is drawn from several sources, the largest being a collaborative, utilisation-focused evaluation (Dooley et al., 2021). The evaluation sought to identify significant changes in the practices, knowledge, and attitudes of students, academics, and university stakeholders, from a baseline conducted in 2018. The evaluation employed quantitative surveys of lecturers and students and qualitative, open-ended questionnaires[4] amongst senior management, lecturers, students, and external stakeholders (totalling 766 individuals). It also drew on a body of data and evidence (including 40 documents) systematically gathered through partnership learning processes. Each university had a dedicated team member whose role was to ensure that evidence was gathered, synthesised, and learnt from. They coordinated quarterly learning reports which formed the basis of regular learning sessions. Additional evidence comes from project working documents, including student portfolios, interviews with students and lecturers, reflective blog posts, course outlines, site visits, interviews and focus groups with community stakeholders.

Our intention had been to test TESCEA's impact on teachers' practice through peer observations, and on student learning outcomes through a critical thinking assessment (Schendel, 2015). Both were thwarted by pandemic-initiated closures and subsequent pressures on teaching.

---

4   Qualitative, open-ended questionnaires were refashioned from planned interviews, because the pandemic and the additional pressures it created prevented interviews from being conducted.

Nevertheless, the systematic approach to data generation and learning throughout the project gave us a robust and diverse data set from which we can examine the effects of our work. To weave this evidence together the authors engaged in meta reflexive work. This was done by sifting through the evidence, and meeting for a series of cross-partnership reflective sessions, asking ourselves:

- What was significant in enabling change and motivating colleagues?
- What proved difficult and why?
- Where were we less successful?

TESCEA's approach, philosophy, and methodology

Our understanding of change

The TESCEA partnership worked to an overall theory of change. At the impact level, we wanted graduates to develop the skills, competencies, and dispositions that they needed to secure future opportunities and contribute to their societies.

We identified three mechanisms through which this change would be realised:

- Enable academics to teach for critical thinking and problem-solving, rather than for the acquisition of knowledge, and to redesign their courses in line with this new approach.
- Ensure degree programmes are relevant to the challenges that students would face beyond their studies.
- Enable active, real-time learning to enable the partnership to adjust its approach.

For this to occur, academics would:

- Need to be inspired and supported as individuals, be given the space to safely explore how to teach differently and have opportunities to engage with stakeholders beyond the university.

- Create appropriate learning environments, requiring input from students, communities, and employers.
- Observe the results of the changes they were making, and to learn from these, to maintain enthusiasm, momentum and maximise professional learning.
- Need to ensure that new practices could spread beyond the initial core of departments and academics, and that institutional processes and policies were revised. This would require a core pathway for all institutions, with the flexibility for each to adapt to their own needs and contexts.
- Embrace the challenges of facilitating significant change and adapt as we progressed through interrogating the efficacy of our work within the context of a strong learning framework and a culture of continuous learning.

Two further enabling factors were also central to our understanding of change:

- Change needed to emerge from a process that was rooted in East African universities, and the experiences and knowledge of African academics and their students.
- Educators themselves needed to be the ones leading that change.[5]

Our partnership approach: mutual trust and equitable governance

Three aspects were important to our approach to partnership. The first was an understanding that we could only achieve significant change by combining diverse talents and experience to generate new solutions to common problems. Partnership thus entailed an intentional effort to create something that neither organisation could achieve alone, and to develop an approach that if successful would draw greater validity,

---

5 This was a deliberate attempt to situate expertise within the region, rather than in academics of Northern universities who are commonly invited to train African peers through university partnership programmes, scholarship schemes or other externally funded initiatives.

because it had been tested in several institutional contexts. The second was a way of working together to achieve that change which centred on principles of mutual respect and trust, of valuing each other's knowledge and expertise, of collaborative working practices and consensus-based decision making.[6] The third was a commitment to learning, so that we could revise and adjust our approach, as we learnt what was effective, and what additional or alternative steps were needed to effect change (Nzegwu, 2018).

The grant required contracts with the funder, and between the lead and other partners, a process of financial due diligence, quarterly reports on expenditure and activities to claim funding in arrears, quarterly audits, and progress reports at six monthly intervals. These were taxing reporting and management processes, which strained all partners, and made it additionally difficult to facilitate change. Conscious of the hierarchy that the grant arrangements introduced, the problematic way in which one partner was placed in a position of contractual authority over others, and the power dynamics this could create, we sought to establish the most equitable governance structures that we could. We established a project leadership team, a monitoring and evaluation and learning (MEL) team, and a series of working groups, each composed of representatives from all partners. The latter included groups for communications, stakeholder engagement, finance, curriculum design and gender. Many team members were in several groups. The leadership and MEL teams came together in April 2018 to reassess, adjust, and agree on project plans. Subsequently the teams met online separately each month[7] and jointly every quarter, to discuss progress, consider new information, make decisions, and agree on any adaptations needed. Project leads came together each year for a deeper review meeting, initially in person and virtually during the pandemic. The summative evaluation was also undertaken by the MEL team (with external quality assurance) to ensure that it was a process owned by the universities.

---

6   While many of these were implicit in the ways in which we chose to work, they were also detailed in a "partnership framework document", developed during the planning process, and which became a useful touchstone to which we could return if necessary.

7   During the pandemic we met weekly or fortnightly for an extended period, to support each other and navigate the uncertainty and complexity that it introduced.

Our approach to teaching and learning

We approached transformative learning on multiple fronts: individually, structurally and culturally. We worked with academics to think about what it meant to teach for transformative learning, and we considered how universities could be transformed, by examining the wider learning environments, policies, and culture. We drew on established theorists to identify transformative learning as a process of critical self-reflection, reflective thinking, and meaning making (Fink, 2013; Freire, 2017; Mezirow, 1997, 2000). Our hope was that if academics and management were helped to think differently about learning, they would in turn provide a new type of environment for their students.

Rather than redesign whole programmes, we worked at the course level. Each institution identified four undergraduate programmes and selected courses within these, with the intention of building, testing, and refining an approach that would allow more rapid improvements to learning and provide a foundation to scale it in the future.[8] Selected programmes covered agriculture, medicine, education, business, social work, and IT. In each university, courses from additional programmes were redesigned as faculty embraced the process. To begin, we convened a series of workshops with lecturers and administrators to encourage them to formulate their own philosophies of learning and to explore how a transformative learning approach might offer new starting points. We argued that it was their role to facilitate a process of engagement and critical reflection with their students, rather than to transmit a body of knowledge. Workshops introduced critical readings on teaching and learning, exercises that engaged academics in reflective observation and active experimentation (TESCEA, 2021b). To ensure that local capacity to lead change was developed, we identified early enthusiasts and created a cadre of "multipliers"[9] (Mutonyi & Dryden,

---

8 This has since been published as "Transforming Higher Education for Social Change: A model from East Africa". See www.transformhe.org
9 Multipliers are members of university teaching staff who are trained in transformative learning and gender-responsive pedagogy, and can deliver course redesign workshops.

2021c) who initially took the role of co-facilitators and subsequently became lead facilitators, travelling to work with staff at other campuses.

This was followed by a process of programme alignment and in-depth sessions to redesign courses and create detailed lesson plans. To guide the development of learning outcomes, we consulted the relevant literature and key stakeholders to identify the skills, competencies, and dispositions that graduates needed, and mapped this to Fink's taxonomy of significant learning (Fink, 2013; Wild & Omingo, 2020). This process spanned several days of intensive workshops, a subsequent online course, and mentoring (Wild, 2022) during which lecturers mapped concepts and crafted their learning outcomes and teaching and assessment strategies (Laurillard, 2012, 2013; Mutonyi et al., 2021b, 2021a; Omingo et al., 2021b, 2021a; Wild, 2022). Lecturers were introduced to the digital Learning Designer[10] tool. The creation of teaching plans in the tool has allowed us to collect examples of designs representing a variety of pedagogic principles, including social learning, experiential learning, and active learning that can be used by others as inspiration for their teaching (TESCEA, 2021a).

In parallel we began to explore the ways in which gender intersected with learning. We first sought to build a common understanding of and commitment to gender equity — emphasising that it was not sufficient for women and men simply to be present in the classroom, they both needed to be involved in the learning process. We then developed an approach to gender-responsive pedagogy. We drew on a framework developed by African educators for schools (Doroba et al., 2015; Mlama et al., 2005) alongside other resources (Frei & Leowinata, 2014), to identify seven teaching and learning spaces and six dimensions of gender-responsive practice (Chapin et al., 2020; Chapin & Warne, 2020). Lecturers were encouraged to think about how to organise the classroom, ensure that all students were enabled to take on speaking and/or leadership roles, address any bias in case studies and content, and use language and tone to reinforce positive gender attitudes.

---

10   https://www.ucl.ac.uk/learning-designer/

Our approach to employability and community engagement

Employability was a central concern, but we wanted to avoid the sense that education was simply about preparing young people for the labour market. We used "employability" to explore the types of graduates that the universities wished to see emerging from their programmes, and the types of learning experiences that would require, defining it as "a person having the mindset, potential, attributes, skills, purpose, ability and agility to define their path and create their own future".

While each university had channels through which to engage stakeholders, these were often fragile and temporary. To create more enduring mechanisms for dialogue and collaboration, we established a series of Joint Advisory Groups (JAGs). These convened representatives from business, employer bodies, community groups and government in configurations determined by each university (Mutonyi & Dryden, 2021a; Wild & Nzegwu, 2022). An Ashoka fellow was identified to participate in each JAG, helping to introduce new ideas on learning for social entrepreneurship. The JAGs acted as regular forums for discussion between external stakeholders, university management, and academic and student representatives. JAG members participated in the course redesign processes, advising on the competences they felt were needed in professional settings, gave guest lectures, helped to prepare placements, and mentored students. In the process, our concept of partnership was expanded; as one Dodoma team member observed, they could not remain stakeholders, but needed to be recognised as partners too.

Navigating change — Successes and challenges

The overall results of the TESCEA partnership are clear. Academics and institutional managers have enthusiastically embraced the process. By December 2021, over 565 lecturers had participated in the programme, over 100 departments had introduced new teaching models, 212 courses had been redesigned, and universities had revised 39 university policies and process guidelines. Most importantly, 3,800 students had benefited from better teaching.

In this section, however, we reflect on *how* change happened in three domains: amongst academics, students, and institutions. While we present the experiences of the entire partnership, we also reflect on the nuances of change in each institution, and how it was enabled by specific cultures, environments, and histories.

Changing teaching practice

As academics prepared to teach their redesigned courses, we observed a growing wish to engage students in the learning process. In some cases, the process elicited particularly strong reactions: one academic at Uganda Martyrs suggested that the university should apologise to students for its previous teaching, while a brave lecturer in Dodoma wrote an open letter to his students, explaining that they were going to approach learning differently and inviting them to become partners in the process (Wild, 2022). Further testimonies from academics indicated similar sentiments.

> Students are not empty vessels; they have a lot in their minds, they have their assumptions, they have their imaginations. When you give them the opportunity to interact, to share what they have, they will learn how to solve problems themselves. (Lecturer 1, University of Dodoma)

> Students have now gotten used to (not sitting) in position for two hours or so in my class because I use blended learning activities […] one commented 'we don't sleep off because it is very interactive and we understand right from class'. (Lecturer 1, Gulu University)

Since institutional policies were still to be revised, this was evidently the result of personal changes made by lecturers, not changes enforced from above. It marked an emergent shift in teaching culture. Academics were engaging in a process of critical self-reflection that in turn opened new discussions with their colleagues and students (Mezirow, 2000). They came to reflect on both the content of what they taught, and how to assist students to make meaning from their learning. The proportion of academics who believed that lecturing was the most effective approach dropped by 21 percentage points, while those that believed that teaching for concepts and principles mattered more than conveying facts increased by 13 percentage points (Dooley et al., 2021). One lecturer explained:

> I have loved my experience. I have shifted my mental model about learning... I came in with the view that the lecturer would relay information and knowledge and that I would take it in and would then have learned what I was supposed to... It's very exciting! (Lecturer 2, University of Dodoma)

Multipliers proved particularly important. In Dodoma, they became a group of motivated champions who in turn trained and motivated fellow lecturers and middle level managers. Gulu was strategic in the selection of its team: the acting dean of education was enrolled as a multiplier and subsequently developed the teaching and learning centre. During the difficult months of 2020, multipliers also offered significant, informal support to their colleagues. At Uganda Martyrs they were tasked with training the whole university to adapt its teaching to online modes, allowing the university to remain open when it would otherwise have struggled to do so.

In addition to attitudinal shifts, we identified changes in teaching practices. The pandemic prevented significant observational work, but lecturers' own accounts indicated that their use of critical thinking and problem-solving techniques had increased by 43 percentage points, the use of active learning strategies (such as role plays, fishbowl debates and peer teaching) by 37 percentage points, the use of problem-based and team-based learning strategies by 15 percentage points, and the use of gender-responsive pedagogies by 45 percentage points. Conversely, the proportion of those who preferred students to listen and take notes had decreased by 21 percentage points, and the proportion who assumed that their students brought little knowledge of their own decreased by 26 percentage points. 94% of lecturers believed that the new approaches were more effective, enabling them to develop more relevant courses, more learner-centred teaching and assessment strategies, and provide better quality materials to their students (Dooley et al., 2021). One lecturer commented:

> When we are in class, let them think what we are teaching, think on the scenarios, think on the problems facing society, think on the problems facing their offices if they are employed in a company. (Lecturer 3, University of Dodoma)

A cross-partnership peer review team assessed lesson plans, looking for quality learning designs which demonstrated clear learning outcomes, realistic learning activities, clear assessment methods, a focus on key skills and were designed to foster dispositions such as social responsibility. They judged 72% to be good or very good, and one in three detailed learning designs was judged to be excellent, with a complete sequence of teaching and learning activities (Dooley et al., 2021).

Through carefully facilitated discussions about gender stereotypes and power, we encouraged significant shifts in attitude. Gender equity and responsiveness came to be appreciated as an integral part of teaching and learning (Mutonyi & Dryden, 2021b; Skovgaard et al., 2021). Academics reported that they guided the use of language in their classrooms, developed materials with gender in mind, adjusted classroom layouts and encouraged students to think about gender in their assignments. They also observed changes in the way students interacted, with greater respect for each other and with an observable increase in confidence amongst female students (Dooley et al., 2021). In a reflective session at Gulu, lecturers identified the practice of gender responsiveness as their most significant change. Dodoma identified a group of champions and brought them together to explore gender more deeply. While conversations on gender led to observable change, there was also resistance from some staff, often where gender was still perceived to be "about women", or where they were reluctant to initiate difficult conversations.

These significant changes generated discomfort for many academics, who pointed to the lack of time to absorb new ideas and insufficient support to embed them in their teaching. Some Dodoma staff felt that the new approach required too much time and that it wasn't possible to prepare detailed learning designs. At Mzumbe, the difficulties of trying to teach within lecture halls with fixed seating frustrated staff. Across all universities, the lack of infrastructure, particularly of internet connectivity was a common constraint, interrupting workshops and requiring creative approaches when power and internet connections failed. As facilitators, we found ourselves at times insufficiently prepared to deal with the range of needs presented and unable to provide sufficiently tailored support, including the digital skills needed to make effective use of tools such as Google Classroom and Learning Designer. These problems were heightened during the rapid, uneven digital shifts precipitated by the pandemic.

Changing student learning

Surveys of students, as well as observations made by their lecturers, suggested that students made shifts in their thinking, recognising their own agency, becoming more engaged in their learning, and using critical thinking and problem-solving approaches. There were positive increases in the proportion feeling equipped to: apply facts, theories, and methods in practice; examine their own views on issues and understand another's; change the way they thought about a concept; formulate their own questions; connect ideas from their studies to their own experience; clarify personal values and ethics; and understand the consequences of their actions (Dooley et al., 2021).

> …the classroom environment is free. You have the opportunity to express yourself and present ideas in a free manner […] I am used to the type of learning, where the teacher delivers, and students only listen. Getting used to open communication and guided classroom discussion really changed my academic perspectives and thinking. (Student 1, University of Dodoma)

> Me as a learner being involved made me feel like I am valued […] If I say something it can be listened to. I have a platform to air out my needs […] this is what I feel is lacking in the education system […] Every time you involve learners in the change making processes it makes them feel like they are valued. (Student 1, Gulu University)

> [It] made me more responsible with my own learning. I felt being empowered to manage my own learning. In the past, I felt that it is the responsibility of lecturers to teach us everything. But now I know that I have to contribute to my own learning. (Student 1, Mzumbe University)

Critical to managing this change and the disorientating effect it had on some students, there were efforts to involve students in the process (Mutonyi & Dryden, 2021e). Lecturers explained what would be changing and why, students were involved in JAG meetings, and they were encouraged to develop "student clubs" to explore issues themselves. A lecturer at Gulu noted initial resistance, with students complaining that they were asked to do the work of their teachers. But as the semester progressed, views began to shift. Although there was some discomfort, students played an important role in encouraging change through their response to new classroom practices. In some cases, they began to express a preference for lecturers who, as one student in Gulu explained, "allowed [students] to speak out, contest, argue, participate in our learning".

A significant obstacle was that assessment practices were difficult to change. Most students are still assessed predominantly through terminal exams, and while these can be altered to ask thinking questions or incorporate practical demonstrations, it can reinforce the sense that learning is to pass an exam, and not to contribute to society.

Changing institutions

While institutional change was a core strategic goal, we sought to shift cultures by demonstrating success, by actively engaging senior management, and using this to push for further structural and policy change (Mutonyi & Dryden, 2021d). Ultimately, universities were able to pass policies and develop guidelines covering safeguarding, whistleblowing, gender equity, quality assurance, effective teaching, and community-university engagement. Dedicated centres for teaching and learning, and gender began to emerge at Uganda Martyrs and Gulu. Gulu developed a new certificate course (completion of which provides merit for promotion at the university), and a focal point for gender-related concerns. University leaders recognised and encouraged their staff by awarding certificates in public ceremonies. Academics and university managers note that there is still a significant distance to travel if new approaches are to become fully embedded across institutions, but there are nevertheless signs that thinking has shifted, including at senior levels. Senior managers were positive about the changes underway, with 94% feeling they were very important to their institution, and two thirds very supportive of institutionalising changes.

Securing the support of senior managers was critical in all institutions. While Gulu's vice chancellor was directly involved in the partnership, a workshop on transformative learning with deans, directors, the academic registrar, and others proved important to engage other influencers on campus. Many became part of a core steering group, taking responsibility for specific areas such as students, community engagement, or policy review. Uganda Martyrs took a similar approach, running a transformative learning workshop for its management and deans; they were sufficiently impressed to ask the team to run it for the whole institution, and invited them to input into several strategic and policy processes.

At Dodoma, the inclusion of middle level managers in the core project team proved significant, creating a group who could influence colleagues at similar levels and work upwards to influence senior leadership. The team resolved early on that the directors of quality assurance and undergraduate studies should be invited to workshops, and it proved a decisive step, helping to ensure that changes were reflected in the redevelopment of core university processes, including efforts to understand the student learning experience through new feedback mechanisms. A direct alignment with the university's strategy, and a feeling TESCEA could help them respond to the "employment problem" helped to secure the support of Mzumbe's leadership.

Also, the JAGs played a vital role in fostering an environment for change. By asking university leaders to chair meetings, it drew them into the change process, while also giving them an opportunity to position their institutions as champions of employability and community engagement. Ashoka helped university teams think about how to facilitate the groups and leverage the expertise they brought. The JAG was Mzumbe's first framework for regularly engaging such a diverse group of stakeholders and helped to create a sense of a wider institutional project. At Dodoma, the JAG offered leaders a regular space to meet their stakeholders, who in turn encouraged leaders to do more. At Gulu, JAG members helped to identify gaps in graduate skills and suggested changes to classroom practices. By involving representatives of national regulators and ministries of education, JAGs also sought to open conversations that would enable wider policy change:

> It has been a dream to bring together in one room, students, employers, industries, and lecturers... Lecturers got to hear directly from employers about the challenges facing graduates and students at the same time heard what is expected from them... It was really an amazing experience. (Lecturer 1, Mzumbe University)

Changing policies and processes took time, and their misalignment with new teaching approaches created significant frustration and disincentives. At Mzumbe, policies were due for review, but it was either difficult to introduce new elements or the process took longer than anticipated. In contrast, Gulu found itself able to move more swiftly because key decision makers were already part of the project.

How we achieved change: Concluding reflections

Finally, through a process of collaborative reflection, we have identified several factors that shaped our successes and disappointments:

Beginning from aligned visions and a common purpose: From early conversations, the TESCEA partnership sought to respond to each university's vision and strategy, and to develop an approach which was anchored in their needs and concerns. Each university articulated these differently, but framed by broader East African concerns and strong social commitment, they found a clear alignment and complementarity. This foundation proved invaluable when we encountered difficulties because we could return to our common purpose. It was not always smooth, and at times we had to work hard to appreciate each other's knowledge and expertise. It took time for universities to appreciate the value of expertise from AFELT, for Ashoka to build relationships with universities, and for universities to appreciate the expertise Ashoka could bring. This required concerted encouragement and facilitation of the conversations that were needed, and a willingness to listen on both sides. We frequently returned to the principle that INASP, AFELT and Ashoka were not bringing solutions to the universities, but expertise and experience that could assist universities' own problem-solving efforts and enable the partnership to develop something new.

Trust and humility as the foundation of equitable partnership: Partnerships can be a powerful vehicle for initiating and facilitating change, despite the many inequities that they can bring. Innumerable guidelines and toolkits seek to guide those who would build better, more equitable partnerships, but simple acts of respect, of listening, and of humility are what underpin the creation of fairer governance and decision making structures. A commitment to listen and to learn, to recognise that each partner had expertise to bring, and to be open and transparent in decision making, all helped to foster a culture of respect and trust, a collaborative spirit that helped to resolve problems, and a willingness to challenge and be challenged. While trust was built within the partnership, the significant and regular scrutiny of expenditure by the funder was felt to be disproportionate and distrusting of the universities, and this was demotivating and fractured trust within extended university teams during an intense period of change.

If open and unfettered conversation enabled our successes, the converse was true for many of our challenges. The team experienced many pressures because of the complexities involved in the change process, the need to balance these alongside demanding jobs, and the co-dependencies of partners. Tensions emerged in roles and responsibilities, and there were sometimes disagreements, challenging discussions about budgets and resources, and dissatisfaction with the role that a partner was playing. It led to one partner leaving the partnership in 2020, but only after exhausting all avenues to repair relationships and support them to play their role. Leaders were called upon to steer their teams through institutional hierarchies and politics, to address gender-based inequities and dynamics of power, to manage expressions of discontent and frustration that threatened to damage relationships, and to resolve disagreements. Yet, even when there was contention, our capacity to retain a genuine respect for differing views enabled us to find ways through. Partners forged organisational and personal relationships, and these strong cross-institutional and interpersonal bonds allowed the partnership to adapt and thrive despite significant challenges, particularly those posed by COVID-19.

Rooting our models in East African practice and understanding: We all were determined that East African practice and expertise should be centred. All universities involved were East African, to ensure that ideas developed in very different HE contexts did not displace the knowledge, expertise, and confidence of East African academics. This did not mean that we dismissed expertise and scholarship from outside the region; these were incorporated throughout in the texts and theories which we drew on and through engagement with other experts. The partnership did benefit from the expertise of academics from beyond the region (alongside INASP's contributions to learning design), but this was mobilised through advisory roles and through each university's existing partnerships. The leadership of academics in each university, alongside AFELT's role, ensured this was possible, as did emphasising the central role of and expertise of the lecturers themselves: it was they who, by exploring new approaches and being bold enough to bring these into the classroom, would lead change, enable practice to shift, and transform the learning cultures of their institutions.

Only by learning and creating space to adapt and to adjust could we achieve our goals: We began with a collective recognition that we were on a journey: we did not know enough to predict how the outcomes would be achieved, but if we agreed to travel a "learning" rather than a "delivery" path, we were more likely to find our way to doing so. We recognised that a shared vision and a collective commitment were critical to this, to create a unifying sense of purpose; we returned to this regularly. Working across and between institutions was motivating and provided a frame of reference for institutions who knew they were not struggling in isolation, had the support of peers, and could learn from their successes and challenges. It was also important that each institution could adapt and adjust the approach to fit their own needs and to make the most of emerging opportunities. The rigidity of reporting, financial systems and payments in arrears made this harder to achieve, because it seeded uncertainty, and made institutions either reluctant or unable to initiate unplanned activities.

No doubt there are more lessons to be learnt in time. Understanding the underlying reasons for change and its real impact requires deeper and continued work. Nevertheless, we have successfully confronted outdated modes of teaching and learning, offered academics and institutions new approaches, seen significant changes in academics' and students' attitudes, knowledge and skills, visible changes in teaching methods, course materials and assessment methods, and greater engagement with communities. Despite strained resources and over-stretched teaching staff, we have demonstrated that change is possible when committed teams imagine and design together. We have seen that change happens when institutions empower academics in conjunction with their students and stakeholders to lead that change, by recognising and championing their professional abilities and tapping into their passion and commitment as educators. We offer this account in the belief there is much that the HE sector generally can learn from educators in East Africa, who are committed to change and to serving the social good.[11]

---

11 Our resources, toolkits, and other learning publications are available at www.transformHE.org

Acknowledgements

Although ten of us tell the story of TESCEA here, the work we describe was a collective achievement that depended on the imagination, energy and tireless commitment of dozens more colleagues in our four universities, joint advisory groups, and INASP, AFELT and Ashoka teams, and on the support of senior management at each university, who gave space and support for new ideas to flourish. We are also grateful to our students, who despite the many difficulties, embraced the possibilities that TESCEA offered, showed us what was possible, and encouraged us to do more. We are grateful to the UK Foreign, Commonwealth and Development Office (FCDO) which funded TESCEA from 2018–2021 through its Strategic Partnerships for Higher Education Innovation and Reform (SPHEIR) programme.

References

Africa Eye (2019, October 11). *Sex for grades: Undercover inside Nigerian and Ghanaian universities* [Video]. BBC.
https://www.bbc.co.uk/programmes/p07qtpbc

Brewis, E., & McCowan, T. (2016). *Enhancing teaching in African higher education: Perspectives of quality assurance and academic development practitioners in Ghana, Kenya, Nigeria and South Africa*. British Council.
https://www.researchgate.net/publication/340444030_Enhancing_teaching_in_African_higher_education

Chapin, J., Skovgaard, M., & Warne, V. (2020). *Integrating gender responsive pedagogy into higher education: Our approach*. INASP.
https://www.inasp.info/publications/gender-responsive-pedagogy-higher-education

Chapin, J., & Warne, V. (2020). *Gender responsive pedagogy in higher education: A framework*. INASP.
https://www.inasp.info/publications/gender-responsive-pedagogy-higher-education

Dooley, G., Luswata, A., Malagala, A., Milanzi, M., Ngowi, E., Nzegwu, F., Otieno, A. P., & Sikalieh, D. (2021). *Transforming employability for social change in East Africa: An evaluation*. INASP.
https://www.inasp.info/publications/transforming-employability-social-change-east-africa-evaluation

Doroba, H., Muhwezi, M., & Modungwa, B. (2015). *Tackling gender inequality in higher education institutions in Africa: From affirmative action to holistic approaches* [PDF]. Forum for African Women Educationalists and Association for the Development of Education in Africa.
http://www.adeanet.org/en/system/files/resources/policy_brief_gender_en.pdf

Fink, L. D. (2013). *Creating significant learning experiences: An integrated approach to designing college courses.* Jossey-Bass A Wiley Imprint.

Frei, S., & Leowinata, S. (2014). *Gender mainstreaming toolkit for teachers and teacher educators.* Commonwealth of Learning.
http://oasis.col.org/handle/11599/566

Freire, P. (2017). *Pedagogy of the oppressed.* Penguin Classics. (Original work published in 1970).

Gulu University. (n.d.). *Gulu University: For community transformation.*
https://gu.ac.ug/

Laurillard, D. (2012). *Teaching as a design science: Building pedagogical patterns for learning and technology.* Routledge.
https://doi.org/10.4324/9780203125083

Laurillard, D. (2013). *Rethinking university teaching: A conversational framework for the effective use of learning technologies.* Routledge.
https://doi.org/10.4324/9781315012940

Ligami, C. (2020, March 7). Forum calls for universities to take lead in achieving SDGs. *University World News.*
https://www.universityworldnews.com/post.php?story=20200303074939736

McCowan, T. (2014). *Can higher education solve Africa's job crisis? Understanding graduate employability in Sub-Saharan Africa* [PDF]. British Council.
https://www.britishcouncil.org/sites/default/files/graduate_employability_in_ssa_final-web.pdf

McCowan, T., Omingo, M., Schendel, R., Adu-Yeboah, C., & Tabulawa, R. (2022). Enablers of pedagogical change within universities: Evidence from Kenya, Ghana and Botswana. *International Journal of Educational Development, 90,* 1–10.
https://doi.org/10.1016/j.ijedudev.2022.102558

Mezirow, J. (1997). Transformative learning: Theory to practice. *New Directions for Adult and Continuing Education, 1997*(74), 5–12.
https://doi.org/10.1002/ace.7401

Mezirow, J. (2000). *Learning as transformation: Critical perspectives on a theory in progress.* Jossey-Bass A Wiley Imprint.

Mlama, P., Dioum, M., Makoye, H., Murage, L., Wagah, M., & Washika, R. (2005). *Gender responsive pedagogy (GRP): A teacher's handbook* [PDF]. Forum for African Women Educationalists.
https://www.wikigender.org/wp-content/uploads/2015/08/GRP-Booklet.pdf

Monk, D., Openjuru, G., Odoch, M., Nono, D., & Ongom, S. (2020). When the guns stopped roaring: Acholi ngec ma gwoko lobo. *Gateways: International Journal of Community Research and Engagement, 13*(1), 1–15.
https://doi.org/10.5130/ijcre.v13i1.7194

Mutonyi, H., & Dryden, J. (2021a). *The TESCEA approach to external engagement*. INASP.
https://www.inasp.info/publications/case-studies-about-transforming-employability-social-change-east-africa

Mutonyi, H., & Dryden, J. (2021b). *The TESCEA approach to gender equity*. INASP.
https://www.inasp.info/publications/case-studies-about-transforming-employability-social-change-east-africa

Mutonyi, H., & Dryden, J. (2021c). *The TESCEA approach to multipliers*. INASP.
https://www.inasp.info/publications/case-studies-about-transforming-employability-social-change-east-africa

Mutonyi, H., & Dryden, J. (2021d). *The TESCEA approach to senior management engagement*. INASP.
https://www.inasp.info/publications/case-studies-about-transforming-employability-social-change-east-africa

Mutonyi, H., & Dryden, J. (2021e). *The TESCEA approach to student engagement*. INASP.
https://www.inasp.info/publications/case-studies-about-transforming-employability-social-change-east-africa

Mutonyi, H., Sikalieh, D., Skovgaard, M., & Buchner. (2021a). Programme alignment: Facilitator resource pack. TESCEA.
https://www.transformhe.org/programme-alignment

Mutonyi, H., Sikalieh, D., Skovgaard, M., & Buchner. (2021b). Programme alignment: Participant handbook. TESCEA.
https://www.transformhe.org/programme-alignment

Mzumbe University. (2017). *Fourth corporate strategic plan: 2017/2018 – 2021/2022* [PDF].
https://www.mzumbe.ac.tz/site/images/FOURTH-CPS.pdf

Nganga, G. (2014, May 23). Survey finds most East African graduates "half-baked". *University World News*.
https://www.universityworldnews.com/post.php?story=20140523130246934

Nzegwu, F. (2018). *Using adaptive monitoring, evaluation and learning in programme design*. INASP.
https://www.inasp.info/publications/adaptive-MEL-programme-design

Nzegwu, F., Wild, J., Idraku, F., & Nkandu, J. (Forthcoming). *The roles and impact of joint advisory groups in educational transformation: The TESCEA case study.*

Omingo, M., Dennis, A., & Skovgaard, M. (2021a). *Course redesign: Facilitator resource pack.* TESCEA.
https://www.transformhe.org/transformative-learning

Omingo, M., Dennis, A., & Skovgaard, M. (2021b). *Course redesign: Participant handbook.* TESCEA.
https://www.transformhe.org/transformative-learning

Schendel, R. (2015). Critical thinking at Rwanda's public universities: Emerging evidence of a crucial development priority. *International Journal of Educational Development, 42*, 96–105.
https://doi.org/10.1016/j.ijedudev.2015.04.003

Schendel, R. (2016). Constructing departmental culture to support student development: Evidence from a case study in Rwanda. *Higher Education, 72*(4), 487–504.
https://doi.org/10.1007/s10734-016-0036-6

Skovgaard, M., Chapin, J., & Fabian, F. (2021). *Gender-responsive teaching improves learning outcomes for both women and men.* INASP.
https://www.inasp.info/publications/gender-responsive-teaching-improves-learning-outcomes-both-women-and-men

TESCEA. (2021a). *Pedagogical patterns.* TransformHE.
https://www.transformhe.org/other-resources

TESCEA. (2021b). *Transforming Higher Education for Social Change: A model from East Africa—Tools and Resources.* TESCEA.
https://www.transformhe.org/tools-and-resources

Uganda Martyrs University. (n.d.). *Our vision and mission.*
https://umu.ac.ug/about-us/our-vision-and-mission/

UNESCO. (2022). *UNESCO world higher education conference 2022.*
https://www.unesco.org/en/education/higher-education/2022-world-conference

University of Dodoma. (n.d.). *About UDOM.*
https://www.udom.ac.tz/about

Wild, J. (2022). *Transforming learning by rethinking teaching.* INASP.
https://www.inasp.info/publications/transforming-learning-rethinking-teaching

Wild, J., & Nzegwu, F. (2022). *How joint advisory groups have supported educational transformation in the TESCEA project.* INASP.
https://www.inasp.info/publications/how-joint-advisory-groups-have-supported-educational-transformation-tescea-project

Wild, J., & Omingo, M. (2020). *Graduate skills for employability in East Africa: Evolution of a skills matrix for course redesign*. INASP. https://www.inasp.info/publications/skills-matrix-TESCEA

23. The only way is ethics: A dialogue of assessment and social good

*Tim Fawns and Juuso Nieminen,
but not necessarily in that order*[1]

Assessment is so entangled with higher education that educators rarely ask fundamental questions about it. As students enter university, they not only attend lectures, engage with academic knowledge, and conduct group work, but are measured and assessed against academic standards. Similarly, teachers are measured through performance and achievement metrics that characterise the academic work in the "measured university" (Peseta et al., 2017). While assessment research has noted its potential for learning and sustainability (Boud, 2000; Carless, 2007; Hounsell et al., 2007), less attention has been given to questions of ethics, such as: what is *assessment for good* in the current higher education landscape?

We are two scholars of assessment and education from different fields, brought together by a sense of urgency to question and reshape assessment cultures. Assessment does not just "drive learning", as is often said. It also shapes students' orientations towards future learning, beyond any course, and beyond graduation. It shapes what is valued by students, teachers, and institutions — the kinds of knowledge and identity that hold legitimate status in disciplines and communities. It shapes power and trust relationships between junior and senior members of organisations, between those with different roles, between educational institutions and wider society.

---

1   Order of authorship is just one more example of the pervasive rank ordering of people that we argue against in our chapter.

Our different backgrounds of medical (Tim) and mathematics (Juuso) education form a basis for challenging each other about how assessment could be developed towards greater contribution to societal good. In both fields, disciplinary assessment cultures are steeped in traditions of individualism (Bleakley, Bligh & Browne, 2011; Nieminen & Atjonen, 2021). In medical education, strict accreditation of practitioners by professional bodies and academic structures is aligned with closely specified learning outcomes and tightly regimented methods of testing individual competence (Hodges, 2013). Yet, medical education also values authenticity, interdisciplinary teamwork, and immersion in complex clinical settings (Bleakley, 2010; Fawns et al., 2021; Hodges, 2013). Therefore, medical education is caught between abstract and standardised assessment, and structured observation of messy, situated practice (Rethans et al., 2002). Like medical education, post-secondary mathematics education has been characterised as exam driven (Iannone & Simpson, 2021), but this only reflects part of the reality. The authentic and messy forms of learning in this context, and the unpredictable outcomes that might follow, have received little interest in mathematics assessment research (Nieminen & Lahdenperä, 2021). Nonetheless, they have important implications for the assessment process and how it informs learning.

Although medical education is already focused on preparing future practitioners to contribute to social good (e.g. through healing others) in ethically sound ways, Tim's perspective brings an opportunity to reflect on broader considerations of "good-ness". Juuso's experience provides opportunities to rethink the role of assessment in test-driven STEM environments towards a more collective, societal benefit.

The rationale of our chapter

Assessment is an important and complex topic for research. It is disappointing that with some important exceptions (Govaerts & van der Vleuten, 2013; Henning et al., 2022; Hodges, 2013; McArthur, 2016; Montenegro & Jankowski, 2020; Nieminen, 2022), it is often insufficiently theorised, narrowly conceived, and focused on short-term, individual outcomes, technical methods, and objectivity in the form of validity, reliability, psychometrics and quantified measurement

(Biesta, 2009). We aim to build on more socially oriented studies that have supplemented and challenged the "measurement paradigm" by framing assessment as a social practice (McArthur, 2022), to exploring broader ethics of assessment, widening the focus beyond specific courses to social and future-oriented concerns.

We present an edited dialogue that explores how ethics are tightly interwoven into all assessments, whether implicitly or explicitly. Bringing the theme of the book into the field of assessment, we ask: how could we define "assessment for good"? What might this look like in practice? Our purpose is not to offer practical solutions, but to map out fruitful avenues for future exploration. Thus, we see our dialogue as part of a much broader conversation with multiple voices beyond our own.

We have organised our dialogue according to three key themes that formulate our idea of assessment for good as intrinsically communal, reflexive, and transformative.

Theme 1: Communality

The first theme concerns how assessment for good cannot rely solely on the assessment of individual students. We discuss how assessment steers higher education toward individualistic values instead of communal ones.

Assessment and the communal purpose of Higher Education

Tim: Given global problems such as climate change, war, and poverty, it no longer seems tenable to avoid connecting what we do in education to ideas of societal good. A lot of "good" is needed, quite urgently, at a global level. Nobody is going to sort out everything for us, we need to work collectively to contribute in whatever ways we can. Higher education seems like an important place to try to foster good and, within that, assessment is important because it shapes practices and orientations to learning. It shapes how we teach, how students perceive their subjects and disciplines, and what is valued.

Juuso: Assessment is a huge factor in education that causes barriers for producing social good, by focusing on individual students at the expense of collective endeavours. Educators and institutions need to consider the communal purposes of higher education, and how assessment either reflects those purposes or contradicts them. Currently, assessment in post-secondary mathematics and medical education is primarily focused on certifying individual students' skills and knowledge. This is an important but insufficient main purpose for something as important as assessment. Universities are significant actors in solving huge global problems — what is the role of assessment practice and research here? We need ways of helping students and educators realise that assessment is about more than individual skills certification: that it also prepares students to tackle the issues of today and the future. This work is never done only by individuals, but also by communities, and for the purposes of those communities. Assessment tasks that connect with real world issues can meaningfully provide *good* for communities in higher education and beyond (McArthur, 2022).

Tim: I have become increasingly frustrated by our emphasis on *heroic individualism* (Bleakley, 2010) which is deeply embedded in assessment cultures and practices, and in society, more generally. We base regimes of reward and recognition around individuals. But if we look at the COVID-19 pandemic, war, political unrest, climate change, poverty — these are collective problems that involve people working as communities. For these challenges, we need to find ways to value the combined efforts of people; that type of valuing is alien to systems of assessment predicated on individual achievement and contribution, and a culture of compliance over improvement (Ewell, 2009; Nieminen & Atjonen, 2022). Instead, higher education tends to emphasise ideas of heroic individuals who are very efficient and effective learners, assuming that their learning can be optimised and tested on an individual basis and that individuals are in competition. This implies assessment instruments can be fine-tuned to measure learning, as if each individual's thinking and contribution is independent of other people, and the cultures in which education and practice take place (Montenegro and Jankowski, 2017).

What about group assessment? Toward communal epistemologies

Juuso: It's fascinating how deeply individualistic assessment research is, even when it focuses on peer and group assessment. Both assessment research and practice predominantly deal with how to improve individual student outcomes. It's rarely about ideas such as "communal knowledge" or "shared cognition". After all, higher education provides grades and certificates for individual students, not for groups!

Tim: And if assessment research is based on individualism, the evidence base is likely to keep pinning us back to individualistic practices, thereby reinforcing the current system?

Juuso: Exactly! When knowing is considered an individual practice, and not a communal one. For example, the purpose of peer assessment might be seen as boosting the learning of individuals. This approach is limited if you think about the broader picture of what education is for: providing tools for both individuals and communities to *use* for various social purposes. While the main purpose of higher education is currently shifting towards economic rationales, another purpose of universities in providing *good* for societies is still mandated in the legislation of many countries (Yang, 2022). Assessment plays a role here by focusing on the individual rather than the social and the political. For example, educators and educational policymakers tend to demonstrate a widely accepted belief that mathematical skills reside in individuals. It is then possible to analyse, measure and track these skills in individualistic ways, as we often do. Mathematics skills are widely measured in testing regimes in most developed countries! It now seems radical to think about mathematical knowledge residing in groups and communities, or about how that knowledge might be wielded by groups of people. However, mathematical knowledge surely resides in cultures, and is passed from one generation to another. Why else would we see it as important to be taught in schools around the world? It is often stated that assessing groups is tricky, but I think this is mainly because we only approach this idea through the individualistic understanding of (mathematical) knowledge (Nieminen & Lahdenperä, 2021).

Tim: We might talk about epistemology here: what is considered knowledge, and how could that knowledge be learned? At the moment, when it comes to assessment in higher education, the dominant epistemology is that people only think or know as individuals. After all, we do not offer degrees or grades for groups or communities. This view of knowledge is quite limiting. For example, it makes it difficult to operationalise summative group assessment. You cannot extract an individual's contribution to group work as if it's independent of everything else. Every group work situation is, in a way, a complex system, with different individuals, their features and characteristics, working in a specific time and context — it can never be repeated! And, of course, neither individuals nor groups operate in isolation. There is an important difference between a view of humans as individual agents that are networked together, and a view of learning as beyond a given person or their "immediate network" to the "rich, complex, and meaningful ways that we belong to and contribute to multiple interlocking and distributed cultures" (Dron & Anderson 2022, p. 12). For me, this latter conception doesn't make epistemological sense alongside the allocation of numerical grades for individual contribution.

Authentic assessment: one answer to the call for communality?

Juuso: I really enjoyed Jan McArthur's (2022) article about authentic assessment which addresses the issue of authenticity in relation to whether we authentically contribute to society. There's a lot of potential there to rethink what we mean by assessment. Perhaps the idea of "authentic assessment" can help us to break the individualistic epistemic boundaries of assessment?

Tim: Jan argues for a shift from focusing on what tasks students are asked to do, to why those tasks matter. It is not just important that students do well in assessment and know how to apply their knowledge, but also that they understand the social value and implications of their work. This must go beyond subject-related knowledge and specific disciplinary competencies to the ways in which their learning can enrich the common good. Authenticity should be transformative. For McArthur, this social world of huge, urgent, global challenges is the "real world" to which authenticity should be connected. This offers an alternative to the common focus on validity and reliability. The common wisdom is that an exam must be reliable, in the sense that it must produce the same type of results across multiple contexts and trials. Validity is often seen as closely related: an assessment is only valid if it's reliable. This, again, is predicated on an individualistic conception of "objective" knowledge and performance (Govaerts & van der Vleuten, 2013), which closes down possibilities for collective assessment.

Juuso: This makes me think of Brown and Harris' (2016) study in which they talked about "intuitive test theories" as they discussed the assessment conceptions of non-professionals such as parents. I think that in higher education, we often draw on intuitive test theories as we design assessment. Assessment is rarely standardised or psychometrically solid, but we still conceptualise it through ideas of validity and reliability. Unfortunately, we might then forget what matters the most in assessment — not technical matters, but ethics and good education (Biesta, 2009). Issues of accessibility and social exclusion come to my mind when I think about what "intuitive test theories" produce in practice. For example, if we only understand fairness and equity in assessment through test theories, we might end up excluding and discriminating against students. We have to be careful that those concepts don't get in the way of something more meaningful. Do we actually value the diversity students bring to assessment? By answering such questions, we can reconsider how assessment might contribute to social good, not only for the students themselves, but for broader communities. To me, this makes "authentic assessment" an important aspect of assessment for good.

Theme 2: Reflexivity

Assessment for good requires constant consideration of social consequences that is *reflexive* and not just *reflective*. Whereas reflection often involves turning our gaze inward, reflexivity, for us, is outward facing, beyond individual humanism and individual development, toward the collective world (Bleakley, 1999). As Bleakley argues, this holistic view is an important ingredient for ethical and ecological sensitivity to the effects of what we do. It helps us go beyond immediate preoccupations with ourselves and our micro-level pressures, to look at a wider picture of what matters. Such reflexivity may be necessary for situating the learning and performance of individuals within collective endeavours.

Assessment as a way to divide populations

Tim: If we're honest, I think, our assessment systems are largely driven by a desire to label people in relation to ability.

Juuso: Absolutely. Testing systems around the world categorise children in terms of mathematical abilities, based on a cultural understanding of "ability" that shapes what we see as intelligent and productive. Mathematical abilities are seen as something that all modern citizens need in employment, and for participation in society as consumers. For example, people recognise that it's important for children in primary schools to learn about history, but history is not tested internationally in almost every single country of the world in the same way as is mathematics. Perhaps, this is partly because the relational aspects of history are widely acknowledged, whereas mathematics is seen as universal, as true and objective, and, thus, measurable. Education systems globally use mathematics assessment to divide children into different levels of society and jobs, according to their so-called "abilities".

Tim: This system gives the impression of providing clarity around what's right and wrong. It reduces people to single numbers that can be used to sort them into categories or trajectories, which is convenient from the viewpoint of accountability. History is a good example of how quickly things become complicated if we look below the surface. If there are multiple, alternative, possible histories — as there always are — then what is the right answer on an exam? Critical questions like this are inconvenient within our current assessment systems. They threaten the legitimacy of how we assess and, therefore, how we educate. It is both important and challenging to open up alternative possibilities for assessment and education when we're so entangled in closed and reductive systems.

Juuso: That's what's so fascinating about assessment! When I think about something seemingly simple, such as how to facilitate peer feedback in my classroom, it often leads to deep questions about epistemologies, preferred ways of educating, and being a modern citizen. This is particularly the case in higher education, where assessment helps students both to become productive parts of societies and to challenge and change societies!

Tim: It's interesting that exams are so prominent in primary and secondary school, and medical school. The argument is often made that exams are an efficient way of testing across a large range of domains. They capture a lot of subject content, and the results seem clear, though not necessarily meaningful for the learner or society. I suspect, though, that in both contexts, an important driver is also that education systems are set on categorising people in relation to each other. Relatedly, psychometrics as a way of measuring ability and assessment validity are prominent in medical education (Hodges, 2013). To me, this is really about a false reassurance that we can control outcomes in a messy, high stakes space. It also shows how higher education is not always a progressive space for critical appraisal. Some programmes can be constrained by links to professions and employment. For example, medical education programmes often set narrowly defined learning outcomes that conform to the requirements of accreditation bodies, but leave little room for exploration or attunement to situated or emergent social needs.

Reflexivity over what is good, and for whom?

Tim: Lining students up in competition through reductive metrics, I think, limits the claims we can make about assessment contributing to broader social good, at least in medical education. Our assessments are, technically, for good: they're aimed at making safer practitioners, and helping patient care. However, standardised ways of assessment in medical schools are also exclusionary, predicated on idealised models of medical students. We favour risk-averse, normative approaches, and I don't think we've sufficiently unpacked the harms they do to marginalised individuals and communities, and to the greater whole by missing out on important, diverse contributions.

Juuso: We could also take a wider view and ask who higher education is for. Who are our students in the first place? Here in Finland, very few people are talking about wider access to medical education in relation to disability, for example. We have a particular, ableist ideal of medical students.

Tim: This illustrates an important distinction between intentions of doing good and the actuality of different kinds of good. Intentions are insufficient. We live in a complex world with complex systems, and to understand the implications of educational practices, we need to trace the entanglements of the different components (Fawns, 2022). We need to look at students' actual experiences and try to understand the ongoing implications. For example, how do assessment experiences relate to how students and graduates view the world and the practices they develop?

Juuso: It's not an easy job to trace those entanglements, especially if you consider the potential diversity of how they might play out for different students. However, I think that we — as educators and assessors — have a responsibility to try. This can't be put aside as too hard, and it is not enough to follow the latest guidance and theory. To do good through assessment, we need to keep learning about the implications of what we do, and how things are connected. "Good" is not a fixed characteristic. It requires persistence, and ongoing learning and work, not only from students but from teachers as well.

Tim: One problem is, I suspect, that "good" is also not binary. Technologies, assessment formats, standards — they are good from some angles and not good from others, and only ever good in some ways for some individuals. We need tools for analysing the different and complex ways in which things are, or could be, good.

Good across different levels of education

Juuso: I believe that assessment for good is possible in higher education, perhaps more so than in lower levels of education, because there is more scope for interrogating and reshaping the focus on testing individual skills as part of a meritocratic system. There is more space to question myths of measurement and psychometrics. Do you think it may also be important for assessment at lower levels of education to contribute to the fostering of community and a valuing of social good?

Tim: Yes, I do. One of my worries, at any level of education, is that we create a distinction between learning the basics early on (e.g. retention of content), and addressing more nuanced and sophisticated ways of knowing later. This means students need to change gears suddenly and radically, after having been enculturated into narrower forms of education. This is particularly pronounced in medicine, where individualised, competitive knowledge retention at undergraduate level is suddenly replaced by teamwork, caring, discretion, and complex ethical judgement at postgraduate level. Once we've taught students to value exams, individual testing, grades, and right and wrong answers, it's hard to dismantle that. Students have developed certain values and habits, and neglected others. I think we want to start early with fostering patterns of reflection and action that are motivated by the desire to do collective good.

Juuso: Here, we might have different disciplinary perspectives. Mathematics is assessed from the very early stages of education in most societies. Its disciplinary assessment culture is strong and spans multiple levels of education, although it looks very different across those levels. In higher education, mathematics assessment is rarely as high stakes as it is at school. But when it comes to assessment practices, it's quite similar: test-driven (Iannone & Simpson, 2021). Students develop within cultures of testing. It must be quite different from medical education, because when medical students enter higher education, they wouldn't have a similar kind of assessment history, right?

Tim: Yes and no. Medical students have usually undergone traditional testing at school in maths, language and science. So, assessment in medical education is not independent of those contexts. And while medical education might be new to undergraduate medical students, those old ways of learning and being assessed are already embedded and embodied, which influences how they understand their new discipline. Where assessment in medical education resembles that mathematics testing culture you mentioned, I suspect it reinforces those ideas of right and wrong answers, individual ability, and so on.

Questioning and tweaking systems

Juuso: Earlier, you mentioned the need for confronting individualistic epistemologies. But this is tricky, as it requires us to think deeply about the system. We cannot simply provide a checklist for teachers to conduct assessment for good: "three easy steps toward assessment for good!" But we can certainly offer prompts for reflexivity, as we are trying to do with this chapter.

Tim: In some ways, medical education is already engaging with collective ideas, but these sit alongside a deeply entrenched, individualised system. Many teachers recognise the value of group work for example, but, pragmatically, they need to be able to transform collective work into individual marks. It is difficult to reconcile our assessment systems with the idea that being good at group work is different from being a good individual within a group. Yet, when graduates are employed, they become members of teams that are not just the sum of the individual parts, they are amalgams of people, processes and practices.

Juuso: Another challenge is that we can't just change assessment without changing teaching and the curriculum. On the other hand, many educators try to contribute to social good through their teaching and curriculum development, but without challenging assessment. Perhaps that's where formative assessment comes in?

Tim: For me, there's an important distinction between formative assessment that directly prepares students for summative assessment, e.g. practice exams, and that which compensates for gaps in summative assessment. This latter category includes things that teachers value but can't easily measure, e.g. complex practice, group, peer and self-assessment. These kinds of formative assessment might have forms and templates, but they often don't have grades. This frees them up to be more creative, which seems like more fertile ground for assessment for good.

Juuso: In the end, though, the division between assessment that leads to grades, and assessment that does not, is often quite clear for students and educators alike. This is why I think it is important for higher education to start certifying the "good" that assessment promotes. Perhaps digital badges or portfolios could be used to embed, say, authentic assessment projects in the curriculum? We need to start recognising the work teachers and assessors do towards social good. For example, while training mathematics teachers, I've seen many who are deeply interested in social justice and want to teach students to use mathematical knowledge for building better societies. Yet, teachers often struggle to connect these ideas to assessment. Why would they not, as testing systems around them do not exactly value "social good"? So, we might need concrete, tangible ways to value the "assessment for good" work of teachers in higher education and beyond.

Tim: Interesting idea. But could this valuing process avoid those same trivialising and individualising forces that we have discussed in relation to the assessment of students?

Theme 3: Transformation

To do good through assessment, reflexivity is not enough. Transformative practices are needed to move assessment closer to good in practice. Sustainable assessment change is never simple: we cannot simply rebuild the system while being entangled in it. Nor can we be content to say it is too hard. In this final theme, we search for a constructive message to tie up our dialogue.

The potential of higher education for transforming assessment

Tim: Reflexivity is a necessary but insufficient ingredient for assessment for good. Whether you are a clinician in a hospital or a mathematics teacher at university, you cannot contribute to social good in a meaningful way without both integrating into *and* shaping the systems that you are part of. Perhaps, we can imagine a future in which assessment practices modify the system rather than just complementing it or trying to co-exist with it!

Juuso: Higher education systems around the world have traditionally been seen as sites where students not only learn a predetermined set of skills, but also *become* someone new in the prevailing society

(Yang, 2022). These processes cannot be captured through traditional assessment practices. Might assessment projects be directed toward more sustainable higher education policies, perhaps by mobilising students and educators?

Tim: That's interesting. This might be another reason to revisit and expand our thinking about earlier ideas such as "sustainable assessment" and "authentic assessment". Sustainability, for example, seems like an important social value within higher education for good? For this, we need students to be involved in co-designing assessments and maybe even policy reform if we think this is where the need for transformation towards good is required. That way, we are less likely to impose our own *good* ideas on our students. We could collaborate with them to develop a more communal and sustainable conception of assessment for good. After all, we want systemic transformation rather than short-lived changes.

Juuso: The key issue with these earlier concepts is that they see context as something that surrounds assessment design. I don't think it is possible to separate assessment "practices" from their "context". This is the issue with technical approaches to assessment: we try to *implement* practices, such as formative assessment, just like we implement medical treatments for patients. Assessment is always partly about transforming the context, since educational practices are entangled with their environment. So, let us transform assessment and grading policies! It is easy to say that a cool, formative assessment practice from Finland cannot be used in the test-driven context of Hong Kong (having taught in both contexts). Less attention has been given to how certain assessment practices might transform their contexts and create more fruitful environments for sustainable learning.

Perhaps even one experience of assessment for good?

Juuso: I'd go so far as to say that every higher education student requires at least one experience of assessment for good — and preferably more than that! Does higher education meet its purpose if this promise cannot be fulfilled?

Tim: But is that how assessment for good works — "good" as a characteristic of a particular assessment? I am reminded of a quote in a recent paper by Coccia and Veen (2022) on *care* in healthcare education:

> If health care education is a cake, care is not just one of its ingredients, but the laws of chemistry that guide the baking process. It permeates everything else that happens there; it is essential rather than peripheral, and therefore a fundamental concept. (p. 342)

For me, goodness is not so much a quality, or characteristic, or feature, but an ethic that permeates not only our designs and practices, but the programmes and systems around them. It needs to be embedded at a deeper level in our cultures of assessment.

Juuso: Well said. I agree that good cannot simply be a characteristic of an assessment practice. However, students need *explicit* experiences of assessment for good. Perhaps, while we cannot transform our assessment contexts completely, assessment for good is all about creating "bolt-holes and breathing spaces" (Webb, 2018, p. 96) for students to really focus on what is important. Amidst the neoliberal ideologies that frame higher education—competition, individualism, and performativity—perhaps, once in a while, we could provide experiences of assessment for good. These experiences of using assessment for the purposes of broader communities might be something that students remember years later.

Tim: That sounds positive, but we should also keep in mind that "goodness" might be contextual. We have terms like "the greater good" which imply a sort of abstract goodness, but what is good for some can be bad for others. What's good in an overall sense can be bad for particular elements. An example in medical education is the normative nature of assessment, where we push students towards an idealised state to meet accreditation requirements, competencies, and standards. In theory, at least, this creates a safety net for future practice, but it marginalises those with different ways of learning, performing, and being (see, for example, Valentine et al., 2020 on fairness; and Zaidi et al., 2021 on racism). I wonder how much good we can do without also challenging some of these oppressive and discriminatory policies and systems?

The role of technology in transforming assessment for good

Tim: We sometimes think of digital education as distinct from "non-digital" education (Fawns, 2019). But all education, and all assessment, involves multiple technologies including computers, pens, paper, chairs, desks, rubrics, templates, etc. And technology — digital or otherwise — does make a difference, but that difference is entangled in the methods, purposes, values, and context of the assessment (Fawns, 2022). For example, in remote, online proctoring of a multiple choice question exam, the questions might be the same as a paper exam, but the experience is very different. The environment is different — learners might do the exam in their bedroom, and their agency is more heavily constrained (e.g. they must keep their eyes always focused on a screen in front of them). They are recorded, and their data is held by a third party commercial company that becomes part of the educational relationship (Fawns & Schaepkens, 2022). This is an extreme example of technology in assessment, but it raises questions about whether we really understand the contribution of technology to assessment and issues of ethics and social justice?

Juuso: The picture gets even more complex as we think about how digital technology might feed on individualisation, reductive quantification of complex learning, atomisation of knowledge via behaviourist principles, and so forth. And then I wonder: can digital technology also challenge the individualistic culture of assessment?

Tim: That's a very good question. Technology can never do this by itself, but it can be part of an approach. For example, wikis, social media platforms, and blogs all create design possibilities for opening up assessment beyond the course, or for creating and collaborating on work that can be shared with wider communities (e.g. Durand, 2016; Kohnke et al., 2021; Tay & Allen, 2011). An exam captures just a momentary snapshot, but these technologies create possibilities for broadening assessment out over time and space, and across social groupings. This may be messier, but it allows different options for going beyond testing, to generating new knowledge.

Conclusion

While an aim of higher education is to produce public good for societies, in-depth analyses of such "good" in assessment are lacking. Through this dialogue, we have contributed to a conversation about the ethics of assessment, and the various forms of social good it might produce. We have shared our "thinking out loud" and can offer no clear definitions, let alone solutions. Our tentative ideas and tensions around assessment for good cannot be resolved easily, and certainly not by the two of us on our own. More and diverse voices are needed to negotiate what it means to do "good" through assessment. However, we can offer some guiding thoughts.

For us, assessment for good means social, not just individual good. Whether in mathematics or medicine, to understand assessment in these terms seems, to us, to require an epistemological shift from the measurement of individual competencies and abilities against known standards, to collective and *communal* ways of knowing. We associate this with a shift in focus, from accrediting pre-specified outcomes to embracing uncertainty and complexity, such that we are better prepared, collectively, to adapt to, and shape, our uncertain futures. This is no simple feat: it means reframing fundamental principles of good assessment from its traditional basis on individual learning and achievement to societal values. All of this requires ongoing *reflexivity* around the social consequences of assessment practices, our own roles within them, and the relations between people, assessment practices, institutions, and wider society. Yet, reflexivity is not enough. We also need active, collective *transformation*, while recognising that earlier forms of education will also be critical to more deeply and sustainably embedding good habits and patterns.

Future work that delves deeper into definitions of "good" in assessment should, we think, challenge the usual idea of "social justice work" as a separate approach that might add something to assessment. Instead, we should place "good" in the centre of assessment. We particularly welcome wide definitions of good that consider something greater than a course, an individual student, or a closed system, instead connecting assessment to its social, cultural, and political contexts. As we have discussed, conversations about assessment for good take different shapes in different disciplines within higher education. There are also different kinds of public good to consider such as moral, health-related, or cultural good. Assessment is never simply "good" or "bad" but operates within complex and situational systems of ethics. Assessment always reflects what is seen as valuable and desirable in higher education (see Coccia & Veen, 2022, for a similar argument about care in healthcare). Furthermore, broader, societal conceptualisations might help us to unpack whether good would only be available to a minority of the population. Access to higher education is not equitable (Czerniewicz & Carvalho, 2022), and goodness should not be fostered according to privilege, or distributed via some flawed ideal of meritocracy.

There may be some benefit to introducing modest changes such as factoring goodness into the design of discrete assessments or integrating technologies that help us to expand assessment practices through creative, collaborative, iterative, and dialogic approaches that extend over longer periods of time. However, we think that more meaningful change will require threading goodness through programmes, policies, cultures, and systems of assessment. For this, we need to question and rethink some fundamental aspects of our assessment systems and, therefore, of higher education itself. In doing so, we must take care since intentions can be different from outcomes, and what can be good for some can be bad for others. A good starting point is to see all assessment as a social, reflexive, ethical, and transformative practice, for which we are all responsible.

Acknowledgements

Thanks to Paul Kleiman for his title suggestion "The only way is ethics: Reshaping assessment as a social good". It references British reality TV show "The only way is Essex", which itself references Yazz's 1980's pop song "The only way is up". Honourable mention to Karen Ray Costa for "Taking the a** out of assessment". Other great suggestions by David Carless, Kay Sambell, Karen Belnier, Anne-Marie Scott, Helen LH, Rachel Forsyth, Satu Piispa-Hakala, @MICRONANOPICO, Jim Luke, Simon Keily, and Kelly Galvin. Thanks to Catherine Cronin and Laura Czerniewicz for encouragement, guidance and support, and to Erik Montenegro for insightful comments.

References

Biesta, G. (2009). Good education in an age of measurement: On the need to reconnect with the question of purpose in education. *Educational Assessment, Evaluation and Accountability, 21*(1), 33–46.
https://doi.org/10.1007/s11092-008-9064-9

Bleakley, A. (2010). Blunting Occam's razor: Aligning medical education with studies of complexity. *Journal of Evaluation in Clinical Practice, 16*(4), 849–55.
https://doi.org/10.1111/j.1365-2753.2010.01498.x

Bleakley, A., Bligh, J., & Browne, J. (2011). *Medical education of the future: Identity, power and location.* Springer.
https://doi.org/10.1016/S0140-6736(00)70457-0

Carless, D. (2007). Learning-oriented assessment: Conceptual bases and practical implications. *Innovations in Education and Teaching International, 44*(1), 57–66.
https://doi.org/10.1080/14703290601081332

Czerniewicz, L., & Carvalho, L. (2022). Open, distance, and digital education (ODDE) – An equity view. In O. Zawacki-Richter, & I. Jung (Eds), *Handbook of open, distance and digital education* (pp. 1–20). Springer

Durand, S. (2016). Blog analysis: An exploration of French students' perceptions towards foreign cultures during their overseas internships. *Alberta Journal of Educational Research, 62*(4), 335–52.

Ewell, P. T. (2009). *Assessment, accountability, and improvement: Revisiting the tension* [PDF]. University of Illinois and Indiana University, National Institute for Learning Outcomes Assessment (NILOA).
https://www.learningoutcomesassessment.org/wp-content/uploads/2019/02/OccasionalPaper1.pdf

Fawns, T. (2019). Postdigital education in design and practice. *Postdigital Science and Education, 1*(1), 132–45.
https://doi.org/10.1007/s42438-018-0021-8

Fawns, T. (2022). An entangled pedagogy: Looking beyond the pedagogy – technology dichotomy. *Postdigital Science and Education, 4*, 711–28.
https://doi.org/10.1007/s42438-022-00302-7

Fawns, T., Mulherin, T., Hounsell, D., & Aitken, G. (2021). Seamful learning and professional education. *Studies in Continuing Education, 43*(3), 360–76.
https://doi.org/10.1080/0158037X.2021.1920383

Fawns, T., & Schaepkens, S. (2022). A matter of trust: Online proctored exams and the integration of technologies of assessment in medical education. *Teaching and Learning in Medicine, 34*(4), 444–53.
https://doi.org/10.1080/10401334.2022.2048832

Govaerts, M., & van der Vleuten, C. P. (2013). Validity in work-based assessment: Expanding our horizons. *Medical Education, 47*(12), 1164–74. https://doi.org/10.1111/medu.12289

Harris, L. R., & Brown, G. T. L. (2016). Assessment and parents. In M. A. Peters (Ed.), *Encyclopedia of educational philosophy and theory* (pp. 1–6). Springer.

Henning, G., Baker, G., Jankowski, N., Lundquist, A., Montenegro E. (2022). *Reframing assessment to center equity: Theories, models, and practices*. Stylus Publishing.

Hodges, B. D. (2013). Assessment in the post-psychometric era: Learning to love the subjective and collective. *Medical Teacher, 35*(7), 564–68. https://doi.org/10.3109/0142159X.2013.789134

Hounsell, D., Xu, R., & Tai, C. M. M. (2007). *Integrative assessment: Balancing assessment of and assessment for learning*. The Quality Assurance Agency for Higher Education. http://www.enhancementthemes.ac.uk/publications/

Jankowski, N. (2022). Reframing assessment to center equity: A resource to inform practice. *Assessment Update, 34*(2), 6–7. https://doi.org/10.1002/au.30294

Kohnke, L., Jarvis, A., & Ting, A. (2021). Digital multimodal composing as authentic assessment in discipline-specific English courses: Insights from ESP learners. *Tesol Journal, 12*(3).. https://doi.org/10.1002/tesj.600

McArthur, J. (2022). Rethinking authentic assessment: Work, well-being, and society. *Higher Education, 85*, (85–101). https://doi.org/10.1007/s10734-022-00822-y

McArthur, J. (2016). Assessment for social justice: the role of assessment in achieving social justice. *Assessment and Evaluation in Higher Education, 41*(7), 967–81. https://doi.org/10.1080/02602938.2015.1053429

Montenegro, E., & Jankowski, N. A. (2017). *Equity and assessment: Moving towards culturally responsive assessment* [PDF]. University of Illinois and Indiana University, National Institute for Learning Outcomes Assessment (NILOA). https://files.eric.ed.gov/fulltext/ED574461.pdf

Montenegro, E., & Jankowski, N. A. (2020). *A new decade for assessment: Embedding equity into assessment praxis* [PDF]. University of Illinois and Indiana University, National Institute for Learning Outcomes Assessment (NILOA). https://www.learningoutcomesassessment.org/wp-content/uploads/2020/01/A-New-Decade-for-Assessment.pdf

Nieminen, J. H. (2022). Assessment for inclusion: Rethinking inclusive assessment in higher education. *Teaching in Higher Education*, 1–19. https://doi.org/10.1080/13562517.2021.2021395

Nieminen, J. H., & Atjonen, P. (2022). The assessment culture of mathematics in Finland: A student perspective. *Research in Mathematics Education 19*(4), 1–20.
https://doi.org/10.1080/14794802.2022.2045626

Nieminen, J. H., & Lahdenperä, J. (2021). Assessment and epistemic (in) justice: How assessment produces knowledge and knowers. *Teaching in Higher Education*, 1–18.
https://www.tandfonline.com/doi/full/10.1080/13562517.2021.1973413

Peseta, T., Barrie, S., & McLean, J. (2017). Academic life in the measured university: Pleasures, paradoxes and politics. *Higher Education Research & Development, 36*(3), 453–57.
https://doi.org/10.1080/07294360.2017.1293909

Rethans, J., Norcini, J., Baron-Maldonado, B., Blackmore, D., Jolly, B., LaDuca, T., Lew, S., Page, G., & Southgate, L. (2002). The relationship between competence and performance: Implications for assessing practice performance. *Medical Education, 36*, 901–09.
https://doi.org/10.1046/j.1365-2923.2002.01316.x

Tay, E., & Allen, M. (2011). Designing social media into university learning: Technology of collaboration or collaboration for technology? *Educational Media International, 48*(3), 151–63.
https://doi.org/10.1080/09523987.2011.607319

Valentine, N., Durning, S., Shanahan, E. M., & Schuwirth, L. (2020). Fairness in human judgement in assessment: A hermeneutic literature review and conceptual framework. *Advances in Health Sciences Education, 26*, 713–38.
https://doi.org/10.1007/s10459-020-10002-1

Webb, D. (2018). Bolt-holes and breathing spaces in the system: On forms of academic resistance (or, can the university be a site of utopian possibility?). *Review of Education, Pedagogy, and Cultural Studies, 40*(2), 96–118.
https://doi.org/10.1080/10714413.2018.1442081

Yang, L. (2022). Student formation in higher education: A comparison and combination of Confucian Xiushen (self-cultivation) and Bildung. *Higher Education, 83*(5), 1163–80.
https://doi.org/10.1007/s10734-021-00735-2

Zaidi, Z., Partman, I. M., Whitehead, C. R., Kuper, A., & Wyatt, T. R. (2021). Contending with our racial past in medical education: A Foucauldian perspective. *Teaching and Learning in Medicine, 33*(4), 453–62.
https://doi.org/10.1080/10401334.2021.1945929

Section V
(Re)making HE Systems and Structures

'The Right to Flourish' by Niamh McArdle. All rights reserved: used with artist's permission.

Note from the artist

The word flourish has two meanings. The verb, to flourish means "to grow or develop in a healthy or vigorous way, especially as the result of a particularly congenial environment". I felt this encapsulated an ideal future for third-level education; the implementation of systems that create an environment to support, encourage and foster growth, learning and personal development regardless of gender, ethnicity, sexual orientation, age, religion and so on. An environment where minority groups do not have to work twice as hard to get half as far because the system itself is built on fairness, and equal opportunity, and prioritises the enjoyment of learning and creative thinking.

But secondly, flourish as a noun is "a bold or extravagant gesture or action, made especially to attract attention". For some reason however, I have a learnt definition of my own that some may see a flourish as a frivolous, feminine embellishment, as something unnecessarily over-the-top and vapid, something stupid and meaningless, without function, something vain that women would engage in: something unproductive. Using this word in this piece, I attempted to reclaim some of the feminine connotations of the word, embracing the power of the flourish through feminine colours, forms and typography. We all deserve the right to flourish in education and do so with our own individual flourishes, whatever they may be.

My name is Niamh McArdle and I am a graphic designer and occasional artist based in Dublin, Ireland. Originally from a very small village in Galway, I'm interested in emotive storytelling through the use of typography, language and image-making. I like to create work that will prompt an emotion from whoever happens to see it — whether it's amusement, sorrow or something else entirely depends on the viewer!

24. Cultivating sustainable blended and open learning ecosystems

Patricia Arinto, Primo Garcia, and Ana Katrina Marcial

Introduction

In recent years, blended, online, and open learning (BOL) have been heralded as the future of higher education. Face-to-face (f2f) instruction has limited reach and is often not accessible to those who are poor, geographically isolated, and/or differently abled. It is also characterised by uneven quality, with its dependence on the capability of individual teachers and their willingness to update their knowledge and skills (Lalima & Dangwal, 2017). In contrast, BOL can, in principle, cater to many and more diverse learners, increase student engagement using a range of digital tools and resources, and develop digital literacies and independent learning skills, which are essential to lifelong learning.

In the Philippines, Republic Act (RA) 10650 or the Open and Distance Learning (ODL) Act of 2014 and the Guidelines on the Implementation of Flexible Learning issued by the Commission on Higher Education (CHED) in 2020 encourage higher education institutions (HEIs) to implement BOL. The ODL Act (2014) declares:

> It is hereby declared the policy of the State to expand and further democratize access to quality tertiary education through the promotion of open learning as a philosophy of access to educational services, and the use of distance education as an appropriate, efficient and effective system of delivering quality higher and technical educational services in the country. (section 2)

During the COVID-19 pandemic, the relevance of distance education was further underscored as Philippine HEIs sought to maintain learning continuity amidst lockdowns and community quarantines. The CHED *Guidelines on the Implementation of Flexible Learning* (2020) issued at the height of the pandemic refer to "the urgent need to explore other innovative learning modalities that will.... allow customisation of delivery modes responsive to (sic) students' need for access to quality education" (p. 1). The CHED Guidelines (2020) define flexible learning as a pedagogical approach that addresses differences in learner needs and contexts through "the use of digital and non-digital technology and face-to-face or in-person learning, out-of-classroom learning... or a combination of modes of delivery" (p. 2).

Both the ODL Act and the Guidelines on Flexible Learning refer to the imperative to broaden access to quality higher education, consistent with the state's commitment to the protection and promotion of "the right of all citizens to affordable quality education at all levels" (Higher Education Act of 1994, section 2). Higher education is an important driver of economic and social development through poverty reduction and promotion of democratic values. It "leads to better jobs, stimulates economic growth, reduces vulnerability among the marginalised, and breaks patterns of poverty" (Pajayon-Berse, 2019). It can also help promote social cohesion through the development of "scientific" ways of thinking or "the capacity to analyse and understand complex socio-economic and political problems" (Leftwich, 2009, p. 23, quoted in Schweisfurth et al., 2017, p. 2), and social values such as tolerance, fairness, meritocracy, social responsibility, respect for the rule of law, and good governance (Schweisfurth et al., 2017). Higher education has an important role in achieving sustainable development goals, through the development of a "sustainability mindset" which includes "management ethics, entrepreneurship, environmental studies, systems thinking and self-awareness" (Žalėnienė & Pereira, 2021).

BOL can help improve access to higher education by providing learners flexibility regarding when and where to learn, and by facilitating access to more tools and resources for learning. It can also "optimiz[e] use of limited resources [such as classrooms], making these available to more individuals through proper... management" (Pajayon-Berse, 2019). Furthermore, BOL can stimulate new pedagogies that can transform learning. However, achieving quality higher education for all with the help of BOL requires a systems approach to building capacity in BOL among Philippine HEIs, as in HE sectors elsewhere. In this chapter, we explore the notion of a BOL *ecosystem*, composed of institutions interacting at different levels as a community of BOL providers in an environment with the resources and support mechanisms necessary for growth.

From ODL to BOL

BOL practice in the Philippines can be traced back to the adoption of open and distance learning (ODL) by several institutions in the 1990s. The Polytechnic University of the Philippines (PUP) claims to have pioneered the open university concept in the country with the establishment of its Open University called Pamantasang Bayan in the 1970s, and its revival in 1990. The University of the Philippines (UP) Los Baños implemented a project called Upgrading Science Teaching Using Distance Instruction (STUDI) in the mid-80s. In 1995, the UP Open University (UPOU) was established as a constituent university of the UP System, with the mandate to offer degree programs through distance education "to democratize access to quality higher education". Some of the other state universities (e.g. Benguet State University, Bicol University, and Central Luzon State University) followed suit and established their own DE units, adopting the nomenclature "open university"; although unlike UPOU they are not full-fledged universities operating autonomously. There are also private ODL institutions such as the Southeast Asia Interdisciplinary Development Institute (SAIDI) Graduate School of Organization Development and the Asian Institute for Distance Education (AIDE).

Until the end of the 1990s, distance education in the Philippines was print-based with occasional tutorial or study sessions held in learning centres. In 2001, UPOU adopted web-based or online distance education as a mode of delivery for some of its courses. Other universities were also taking an interest in e-learning and a national conference on e-learning was held in 2002. The Philippine eLearning Society was established in 2003 with the aim of "promoting substantive content, appropriate pedagogy, and appropriate use of technology for eLearning, guided by ongoing research activities."

By 2007, UPOU had shifted completely to online DE mode, and within five years (i.e. by 2012) began experimenting with offering its own massive open online courses (MOOCs) in partnership with organisations wanting to expand the reach of their continuing education programs. UPOU adopted the term MODeL, for "massive open distance e-learning" for its MOOC platform (Bandalaria, 2014). The term "open and distance e-learning" (ODeL) was coined by UPOU's administrators at the time to refer to "forms of education provision that use contemporary technologies to enable varied combinations of synchronous and asynchronous communication among learners and educators who are physically separated from one another for part or all of the educational experience" (Alfonso, 2012, n.d.). ODeL is an expansion of the term "open and distance learning" or ODL to include e-learning or online learning methodologies. Its coinage was consistent with the fact that only 17 Philippine higher education institutions were offering DE programs and many other academic institutions were expressing interest in offering courses in online or blended mode (Alfonso, 2014) as evidenced by the number of attendees in the conferences on ODeL that UPOU ran annually.

Still, it was not until the eruption of the COVID-19 pandemic in 2020 that Philippine universities really took DE and online learning seriously. Indeed, colleges and universities had no choice but to shift to DE or remote learning. The conventional HEIs pursued a type of remote learning characterised by a combination of synchronous and asynchronous online learning. This is a variant of blended learning (Cleveland-Innes & Wilton, 2018) called blended online learning (Power, 2008). The other two variants of blended learning are the blended block model, which combines blocks of independent online study and intensive f2f sessions, and the classical blended model, which alternates or rotates f2f sessions and asynchronous online learning (Cleveland-Innes & Wilton, 2018). When CHED allowed limited f2f sessions in programs in the medical and allied fields, the health sciences units in UP and other universities in Metro Manila adopted the blended block and classic blended models.

In the transition to a post-pandemic world, blended learning is seen as the better alternative to conventional classroom-based instruction and distance education. The draft guide to learning delivery modes in UP for academic year 2022–2023 notes that well designed blended learning can improve learning outcomes and provide flexibility for teachers and learners. Specifically, the guide refers to the potential of blended learning to foster learner engagement and active learning, expand opportunities for collaborative learning, enable learning anytime and anywhere, develop independent learning skills, and develop digital skills. The guide also notes that blended learning gives academic institutions greater flexibility in the scheduling of f2f sessions in different courses to avoid crowding on campus, and allows for learning continuity in case of changes in public health alert levels and other disruptions, through a rapid shift to fully remote or online learning. It can also allow academic institutions to plan for more optimal use of campus facilities and more strategic technology infrastructure development and support to ensure access for all learners, especially those with limited means.

The concern for ensuring access to learning for a diverse population of learners, the majority of whom come from low-income families and reside in areas with poor internet connectivity, underpins CHED's choice of the term "flexible learning" as the approach to higher education during and beyond the pandemic. The CHED Guidelines (2020) differentiate levels of technology use in teaching and learning and present three learning modalities for HEIs to consider: "off-line", blended, and "on-line". The Guidelines also suggest that flexible teaching and learning is not a temporary arrangement but a "paradigm shift" underpinned by the need to be "responsive to learners' needs for access to quality education".

A BOL ecosystem

For the realisation of the envisioned paradigm shift (to flexible higher education), it is important to consider the diversity of higher education provision in the Philippines, an archipelago of more than 7,000 islands and 182 ethnolinguistic groups living in a few crowded cities and regional centres, and many geographically isolated rural towns. There are at present close to 2,000 HEIs, including 112 public or state universities and colleges (SUCs) with 421 satellite campuses among them, 121 local universities and colleges, 13 "Other Government

Schools", and 1,729 private colleges and universities. Despite this relatively large number of tertiary education providers, the percentage of college students is small, given the low completion rate in basic and secondary education (only 55% of those who enrolled in Grade 1 finish high school). The Philippine education sector is confronted with the challenge of relevance and sustainability given the high levels of income inequality and poverty among the population, high dropout rates and poor academic achievement, and lack of funding for education, among others. How can BOL help address these systemic problems and how do "differently situated" HEIs come together to "converge and harmonize efforts" as the CHED Guidelines (2020) invite, to make quality higher education accessible to all learners through BOL?

To help address these questions, we use the metaphor of a BOL ecosystem composed of different types of institutions interacting as a community of BOL providers. Like a biological ecosystem, a BOL ecosystem has biotic (teachers, learners, institutions) and abiotic (educational technology, infrastructure) components and nodes interacting in a network of institutions (i.e. public and private colleges and universities and regulatory agencies). Figure 24.1 is a depiction of the current BOL ecosystem in the Philippines.

Figure 24.1

The current ecosystem, CC BY-NC

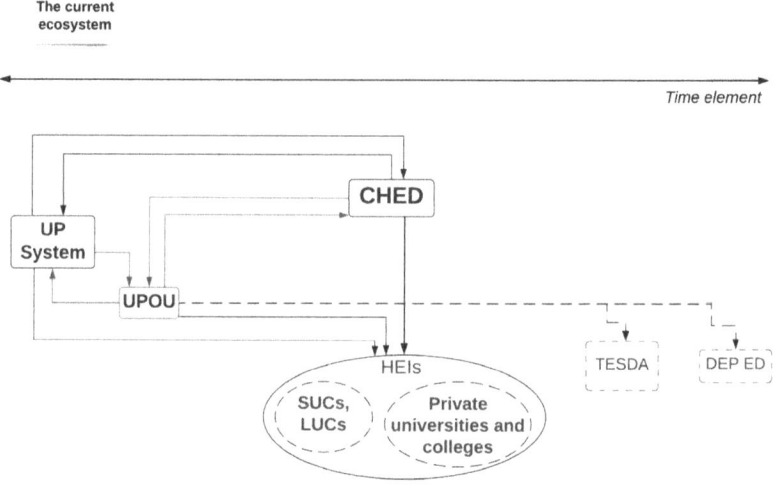

The key institutions in the current BOL ecosystem are the following:

- The Commission on Higher Education (CHED), which sets minimum standards for programs and institutions of higher learning as provided for in Republic Act No. 7722.
- The University of the Philippines (UP) System, composed of eight constituent universities including UPOU. As the national university, it is mandated to lead in higher education and development by setting academic standards and initiating innovations in teaching, research, and faculty development in various disciplines and professions, and by providing advanced studies to scholars and professionals, especially those who serve on the faculty of state and private colleges and universities (RA 9500).
- The UP Open University (UPOU), which is recognised as the leading provider of DE in the country and mandated by the ODL Act (RA 10650) to contribute to upgrading the quality of the Philippine education system by developing innovative instructional strategies and technologies, and sharing these with other colleges and universities through cooperative programs.
- State universities and colleges (SUCs), which are institutions of higher learning established by the Philippine congress, and are fully subsidised by the national government. At present there are 112 SUCs in the country.
- Private universities and colleges, which are incorporated as non-stock or stock educational corporations (BP Blg 232 as amended by RA 7798). There are currently more than 1,700.
- The Technical Skills Development Authority (TESDA), which aims to provide relevant, efficient, accessible, and high-quality technical education and skills development in support of the development of a globally competitive Filipino middle-level workforce (RA 7796).
- The Department of Education (DepEd) which is charged with "the establishment and maintenance of a complete, adequate, and integrated system of basic education relevant to the

goals of national development" through policy formulation, implementation, and coordination of basic education programs and projects and supervision of all elementary and secondary education institutions, including alternative learning systems, both public and private (DepEd, p)

There are various relationships or interactions between and among these primary actors in the ecosystem. CHED has a regulatory function over Philippine HEIs, which are classified by source of funding (i.e. as public or private) and by level of regulation (i.e. autonomous HEIs, deregulated HEIs, and regulated HEIs).[1] CHED sets higher education policies, standards and guidelines and ensures compliance through a system of accreditation of educational institutions and their academic offerings. CHED also facilitates access to higher education through scholarship programs and the promotion of flexible learning, and it provides competitive financial grants to these institutions to support teaching and research initiatives. CHED commissioners head the governing boards of all SUCs. In addition, senior academics from different universities who are recognised as leaders in their respective disciplines sit on CHED's technical panels.

UP as the national university occupies a unique position in the HE system. It is considered autonomous from CHED, although the CHED chairperson sits as the chairperson of the UP Board of Regents, and CHED disburses the tertiary education subsidy for UP students. UP provides technical expertise in higher education matters. It also applies for and receives financial grants from CHED for some of its educational and research initiatives. With regard to its interactions with other HEIs, UP has educated many of the country's leaders both in government and

---

1   Based on CHED's QA-based vertical typology, autonomous HEIs are those that exhibit exceptional institutional quality in terms of accreditation, recognition, certification, and remarkable graduate and research outcome; deregulated HEIs are those that demonstrate good quality through effective internal QA systems and good program outcomes; and regulated HEIs are those that still need to demonstrate good institutional quality and program outcomes. CHED's QA-based horizontal typology classified HEIs into professional institutions (which offer academic programs at the undergraduate and graduate level leading to professional practice), colleges (which develop adults with the skills needed for employment and other related roles); and universities (which provide specialised training in technical and disciplinary areas, with an emphasis on new knowledge generation).

industry, and many administrators and professors in other universities, particularly SUCs, receive their graduate training at UP. Its academic programs are considered the model for those of other institutions. Regarding BOL, given UP's status as well as the relative unfamiliarity of BOL to most educational institutions in the country, it is possible that the latter will find it safer to adopt or mimic (Cardona et al., 2020) the modes of teaching and learning in the national university.

UPOU is a primary node in the BOL ecosystem by virtue of its status as the leading institution in DE and online learning, its role as defined in the ODL Act, and its status as a constituent unit of the national university. The ODL Act stipulates that UPOU should provide technical advice to CHED in its regulatory functions related to distance and transnational education and in capacity building in open and distance learning. It also stipulates that CHED should provide funding to UPOU to support its capacity building programs for HEIs. The ODL Act also states that UPOU should provide technical assistance to TESDA in the delivery of their technical vocational courses via ODL. To fulfil this institutional mandate, UPOU has implemented a wide range of capacity building initiatives, including online and in-person seminars, MOOCs, workshops customised for specific organisations and groups, national and international conferences, and graduate certificate and Master's programs. Some of these initiatives are formal collaborations with CHED for large scale training, while others involve partnerships with specific institutions.

Public and private higher education institutions offer a range of curricular programs in different modes in keeping with their respective institutional mandates. In the post-pandemic context, many conventional institutions may be more likely to implement blended learning with a f2f learning component, while institutions catering to geographically dispersed learners would offer fully online programs with varying proportions of synchronous and asynchronous learning. Some of the more established universities may venture into offering MOOCs to the public, while others will limit their online offerings to students already enrolled in their regular programs or those whom they wish to attract into their programs.

Ecosystem resilience

Mars and Bronstein (2018) argue that in a biological ecosystem:

> not every node is linked to every other node; links may vary in strength and can impart positive, neutral, or negative effects… and… nodes grow and shrink over time; they can be lost, without the ecosystem as a whole necessarily failing. (p. 384)

Similarly, the BOL ecosystem can be seen as evolving with varying levels of interactions and types of collaboration among the different institutions comprising the network. At present, aside from participating in the training programs run by UPOU, SUCs and private HEIs connect with UPOU for benchmarking and research activities. But while these interactions are productive, there is an urgent need to make the BOL ecosystem more robust and resilient.

A robust and resilient ecosystem is better able to adapt to and recover from environmental change; it can withstand or respond to threats while maintaining diversity and important connections or links between members (Holling, 1973; Latham et al., 2021). Applied to the BOL ecosystem, developing resilience means cultivating diversity, vigour and adaptability, and stronger linkages among institutions. It is necessary to have different types of educational institutions (SUCs and private HEIs, conventional universities and distance education universities) offering a range of programs in different modes to diverse learners. And just as an ecosystem's resilience depends on links between and within habitats, partnerships and collaboration between BOL institutions will facilitate exchanges of ideas, practices, and economic and social capital that will strengthen each institution and the entire network.

Under the ODL Act, UPOU can help establish a robust and resilient BOL ecosystem by facilitating the development of zonal centres and nurturing a strong network of BOL leaders and practitioners. Section 13 of the ODL Act (2014) refers to "centers… one each in Metro Manila, Luzon, Visayas, and Mindanao, and eventually one in each region[2]… that shall take charge of the training of teachers for ODL programs." In the post-pandemic context, these zonal centres would support not only ODL programs but the whole range of BOL. This is the long-term aim

---

2   The Philippines has 17 regions.

of UPOU's Sustainable Institution Building for Open Learning (SIBOL) initiative, a pilot project under the "Advancing Equity and Access to Higher Education through Open and Distance Learning" project co-funded by the EU ERASMUS+ programme.

The acronym SIBOL is also a Filipino word that means "to sprout" or "to grow". Accordingly, the SIBOL program seeks to cultivate the capacity of academic institutions to plan, manage, and support effective BOL programs, and grow a network of BOL leaders and practitioners. The program has three phases. Phase 1 is a 14-week online training program composed of seven modules on systems for blended, online, and open learning; it combines independent and collaborative learning and features asynchronous and synchronous activities. Phase 2 is a mentoring and network-building program that aims to foster institutional collaboration in the implementation of different BOL initiatives. Active and meaningful participation in these two phases is expected to lead to Phase 3 where zonal centres will emerge to act as nodes of effective BOL practice in their respective regions.

SIBOL differs from UPOU's other capacity building initiatives in its application of a systems approach to fostering effective BOL practice within institutions and across the BOL ecosystem. For one, SIBOL participants are not individual practitioners, but teams of academic administrators tasked with overseeing BOL planning, program implementation, and monitoring and evaluation in their respective institutions (e.g. directors or coordinators of teaching and learning, DE or e-learning centres; coordinators for instructional materials development; systems administrators; students services coordinators; and QA officers). And instead of classroom or course level practice of BOL, the training curriculum focuses on the program and institution level components of BOL implementation: strategic planning, materials development, technology management, faculty development, learner support, and quality assurance.

At the time of writing this chapter, SIBOL was in its early phase. Nevertheless, some insights into cultivating a BOL ecosystem both within institutions and across the higher education sector can be gleaned from this initial stage of the program.

Within academic institutions, an ecosystem approach to BOL necessitates developing skills and capabilities in the following ways:

- Analysing the institutional context — i.e. the institution's mission and the communities it serves as well as national legislation, policies, and guidelines and global developments (e.g. the United Nations' Sustainable Development Goals) that provide the climate and weather conditions for BOL, and the available resources for BOL.
- Fostering and strengthening coordination among units in charge of different BOL subsystems.
- Calibrating the resources and effort needed for each BOL subsystem to develop, and the strategy for managing change within the institution.
- Anticipating the internal and external factors that may weaken the institution's BOL system and setting up healthy BOL subsystems that can keep the entire system from withering.

The issues and concerns articulated by the participants in SIBOL phase 1 show that planning for BOL is a highly complex process even where institutions have some experience of implementing BOL and willingness to institutionalise BOL. Aside from clear policies and adequate systems, BOL requires a collective rethinking of institutional thrusts and critical reflection on institutional culture and values and how these can inform as well as undermine the BOL strategy. Adopting a new instructional model is fraught with "daunting difficulties like change management" (as one participant put it), which require systems thinking and a long-term commitment to building trust among members of the institution before transformational outcomes (Lammert et al., 2018) can be achieved.

Across the higher education sector, an ecosystem approach to BOL calls for the following:

- Careful analysis of institutional backgrounds and capacities (i.e. organisational setup, human and technical resources, existing partnerships, and capacity building initiatives implemented) and levels of engagement in BOL based on institutional setups.
- Recognising the diversity of institutions and positioning each in a spectrum in terms of the assistance they need in

contextualising BOL frameworks and approaches and in stimulating interactions between institutions.

- Intentional design to deepen engagement, encourage interaction between institutions, and provide feedback; and
- Addressing environmental factors that impede growth, including a weak information technology (IT) infrastructure, policy gaps and tensions, lack of funding, and low levels of digital literacy, among others.

Infrastructure, including power supply, hardware (devices) and software, and connectivity, is a critical component of the environment for BOL in the Philippines. As the country's experience during the COVID-19 pandemic has shown, affordable as well as "reliable internet connectivity remains a challenge in many cities and municipalities across the country" (U.S. Embassy Manila, 2022, n.p.). In the Digital Quality of Life Index 2022, the Philippines ranked 98th out of 117 countries in internet affordability, 45th in internet quality[3] and 61st in mobile internet speed (Tan, 2022). These infrastructural challenges are beyond the control of the higher education sector and CHED (2020) has instead articulated a framework for flexible learning that includes a range of delivery modes, "depending on the levels of technology, availability of devices, internet connectivity, level of digital literacy, and approaches" to address "learners' unique needs". However, while the framework espouses a learner-centred perspective, the ability of HEIs to implement different learning delivery modes is circumscribed not only by infrastructural issues but also pressure from politicians, who approve the budget for higher education, to return to "100%" face-to-face classes (Fernandez, 2022).

---

3   Internet affordability is measured in terms of how much a 1 gigabyte (GB) mobile internet package costs in terms of amount of work measured in minutes. In the Philippines, a 1 GB package, which is roughly how much data is needed for a one-hour synchronous meeting or class session over Zoom, costs "4 minutes and 51 seconds of work per month in the Philippines, 59 times more than the 5 seconds of work needed to buy a 1 GB package in Israel, which has the most affordable mobile Internet in the world, based on the index" (Tan, 2022).

Concluding note

There is a long way to go in building a robust BOL ecosystem in Philippine higher education. And SIBOL is only one program among a host of interventions that are needed for establishing this ecosystem. What may be noted at this point is the value of an ecosystem perspective in adopting blended, online, and open learning as a strategy for providing quality higher education for all in the Philippines.

In the envisioned BOL ecosystem that SIBOL hopes to help cultivate (see Figure 24.2), the BOL centres mentor and support different types of academic institutions and associations or consortia of HEIs who are catering to different types of learners, including non-traditional learners and marginalised learners with little to no access to a post-secondary education, using various learning modalities. The diversity of institutions and the relationships among them (including collaborations and exchanges as well as healthy competition) would make individual members and the BOL ecosystem more responsive, adaptable, and productive (Hammer et al., 2018). In this robust and resilient ecosystem, quality higher education for all is possible.

Figure 24.2

The BOL ecosystem, CC BY-NC.

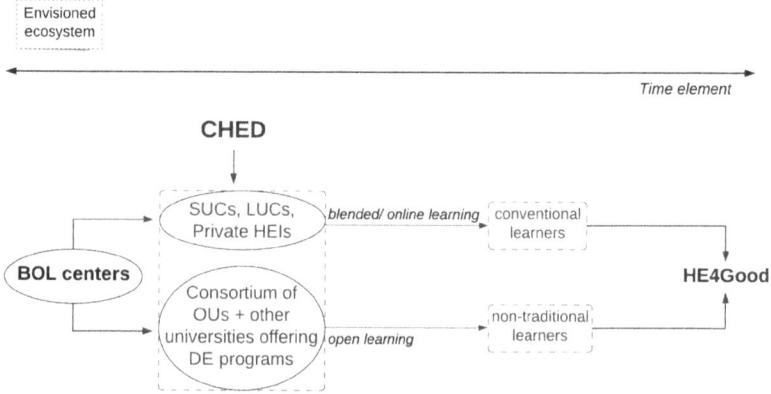

While this chapter focuses on the Philippines, we have aimed to illustrate how adopting an ecosystems perspective prompts us to think about how a healthy BOL ecosystem might be fostered. While natural ecosystems develop organically, building an education ecosystem is more intentional, involving a process of design (of capacity building programs, for example). Having an ecosystems perspective, however, means "analyzing how an educational ecology is functioning: how it is achieving what it achieves; how its internal processes generate its outcomes" (Ellis & Goodyear, 2019, p. 218), and adapting the approach through to development. The approach to be taken needs not only to be sensitive to internal dynamics and environmental factors promoting as well as limiting growth, but also developmental, collaborative, restorative, and reflexive, allowing individual members and the entire ecosystem to flourish.

References

Alfonso, G. J. (2012). Creating spaces and possibilities through open and distance e-Learning (ODeL): A worldview. In G. J. Alfonso, & P. G. Garcia (Eds), *Open and distance e-learning: Shaping the future of teaching and learning* (pp. 3–14). University of the Philippines Open University and Philippine Society for Distance Learning.

Antonacopoulou, E. (2004). The dynamics of reflexive practice: The relationship between learning and changing. In M. Reynolds, & R. Vince (Eds), *Organizing Reflection* (pp. 47–64). Ashgate.

Bandalaria, M. dela P. (2014). MODeLing: A search for an ideal MOOC framework. In G. J. Alfonso, & P. G. Garcia (Eds), *Open and distance e-learning: Shaping the future of teaching and learning* (pp. 111–24). University of the Philippines Open University and Philippine Society for Distance Learning.

Cardona, L., Pardo, M., & Dasi, A. (2020). The institutional isomorphism in the context of organizational changes in higher education institutions. *International Journal of Research in Education and Science (IJRES)*, 6(1), 61–73. https://doi.org/10.46328/ijres.v6i1.639

Commission on Higher Education (2020). *Guidelines on the implementation of flexible Learning* [PDF]. CHED Memorandum Order No. 4, series 2020. https://ched.gov.ph/wp-content/uploads/CMO-No.-4-s.-2020-Guidelines-on-the-Implementation-of-Flexible-Learning.pdf

Cleveland-Innes, M., & Wilton, D. (2018). *Guide to blended learning* [PDF]. Canada Commonwealth of Learning. https://oer4nosp.col.org/id/eprint/35/1/Cleveland-Innes-Wilton_Guide-to-Blended-Learning.pdf

Ellis, R. A. & Goodyear, P. (2019). *The education ecology of universities. Integrating learning, strategy, and the academy*. Routledge.

Fernandez, D. (2022, September 27). *UP, other schools' skipping of full face-to-face classes irks Pia Cayetano*. Inquirer.Net.
https://newsinfo.inquirer.net/1671434/up-other-schools-non-implementation-of-full-face-to-face-classes-irks-pia-cayetano#ixzz7lBkqZQS0

Garrett, H. M., & Ayling, S. (2020). *Ecosystem resilience in a nutshell 1. What is ecosystem resilience?* [PDF]. Natural Resources Wales.
https://cdn.cyfoethnaturiol.cymru/media/696279/ecosystem-resilience-in-a-nutshell-1-what-is-ecosystem-resilience.pdf

Hammer, D., Gouvea, J., & Watkins, J. (2018). Idiosyncratic cases and hopes for general validity: what education research might learn from ecology / Casos idiosincrásicos y expectativas de validez general: lo que la investigación en educación puede aprender de la ecología. *Journal for the Study of Education and Development, 41*(4), 625–73.
https://doi.org/10.1080/02103702.2018.1504887

Holling, C. S. (1973). Resilience and Stability of Ecological Systems. *Annual Review of Ecology and Systematics, 4*, 1–23.
https://doi.org/10.1146/annurev.es.04.110173.000245

Lalima & Dangwal, K. L. (2017). Blended learning: An innovative approach. *Universal Journal of Educational Research, 5*(1), 129–36.
https://doi.org/10.13189/ujer.2017.050116

Latham, J., Spode, S., Ayling, S., Thomas, R., Lindenbaum, K., & Bellamy, A. S. (2021). A framework for ecosystem resilience in policy and practice: DECCA. *Ecology and Society, 26*(4), 31.
https://doi.org/10.5751/ES-12865-260431

Mars, M. M., & Bronstein, J. L. (2018). The promise of the organizational ecosystem metaphor: An argument for biological rigor. *Journal of Management Inquiry, 27*(4), 382–91.
https://doi.org/10.1177/1056492617706546

Office of Planning, Research and Knowledge Management – Knowledge Management Division (2020). *Distribution of higher education institutions by region and sector, AY 2019–2020* [Data set]. Commission on Higher Education.
https://ched.gov.ph/wp-content/uploads/Distribution-of-Higher-Education-Institutions-by-Region-and-Sector-AY-2019-20.pdf

Pajayon-Berse, P. P. (2019, November 18). *Democratization of higher education and responsible internationalization: Bridging the gap towards an accessible and inclusive education*. BusinessWorld.
https://www.bworldonline.com/editors-picks/2019/11/18/264883/democratization-of-higher-education-and-responsible-internationalization-bridging-the-gap-towards-an-accessible-and-inclusive-education/

Power, M. (2008). The emergence of a blended online learning environment. *MERLOT Journal of Online Learning and Teaching, 4*(4), 503–14.
https://jolt.merlot.org/vol4no4/power_1208.pdf

Schweisfurth, M., Davies, L., Pe Symaco, L., & Valiente, O. (2017). Higher education, bridging capital, and developmental leadership in the Philippines: Learning to be a crossover reformer. *International Journal of Educational Development, 96,* 32–51.
https://doi.org/10.1016/j.ijedudev.2017.09.001

Tan, A. N. O. (2022, September 15). *PHL digital quality of life worsens.* BusinessWorld.
https://www.bworldonline.com/technology/2022/09/15/474576/phl-digital-quality-of-life-worsens/

U.S. Embassy Manila. (2022, October 7). *USAID, Philippine partners reaffirm support for reliable internet connectivity nationwide.*
https://ph.usembassy.gov/usaid-philippine-partners-reaffirm-support-for-reliable-internet-connectivity-nationwide/

USAID. (2021). *The impact of COVID-19 on opportunities for out-of-school youth in the Philippines* [PDF].
https://opportunity.org.ph/wp-content/uploads/USAID-EDC-Accenture-COVID-19-Impact-OSY-Philippines_v2021-11-08-Final-1.pdf

Žalėnienė, I. & Pereira, P. (2021). Higher education for sustainability: A global perspective. *Geography and Sustainability, 2*(2): 99–106.
https://doi.org/10.1016/j.geosus.2021.05.001

25. Making higher education institutions as open knowledge institutions

Pradeep Kumar Misra and Sanjaya Mishra

> The Open Courseware concept is based on the philosophical view of knowledge as a collective social product and so it is also desirable to make it a social property. (V. S. Prasad, quoted in UNESCO, 2002)

Higher education institutions (HEIs) and societies have a symbiotic relationship. Societies mould and shape HEIs as per their orientations and expectations, and in return, HEIs contribute to the societies' philosophical, social, political, cultural, and economic upliftment. By extending this relationship, it is obvious to ask, are HEIs a reflection of our society in terms of openness, specifically, openness in teaching and research? Here the word "open" denotes that one's policies, practices, resources, and achievements are visible to or immediately known to others. Openness in the context of HEIs is about freedom, flexibility, and fairness (Commonwealth of Learning, 2017), where the information and knowledge created by public funds are freely available to everyone and promote social justice. In a recent report, UNESCO (2022) suggests that HEIs become open institutions and aim for a more substantial social presence through proactive engagement and partnering with other societal actors.

In this chapter, we argue for transforming traditional face-to-face HEIs into Open Knowledge Institutions (OKIs). This chapter envisions OKIs as such institutions which aim to emerge as social welfare institutions by opening their policies, practices, and processes to welcome and support all those who aspire to enter and benefit from higher education. In this chapter, the arguments behind making HEIs as OKIs are guided by the authors' observations and experiences of the Indian higher education system, the second largest in the world, consisting of 1,113 universities, 43,796 colleges, 11,296 stand-alone institutions, 41.3 million students, and 1.5 million teachers (Government of India, 2021). Here, it must be mentioned that arguments and strategies emancipating in the background of Indian higher education may not be relevant to all, but may well be adaptable for many HEIs across the globe. The chapter presents in its first section sociological and developmental perspectives of HEIs as OKIs. The following sections outline the potential benefit of making HEIs as OKIs and the common issues and challenges. The final section provides the strategies for using technology as an enabler for transforming HEIs as OKIs.

Sociological and developmental perspectives on making HEIs as OKIs

Before discussing HEIs as OKIs, it is necessary to understand what HEIs do to benefit societies. Institutions approved by competent state authorities and imparting different types of studies, training, or training for research at the post-secondary level are referred to as institutions of higher education (UNESCO, 2019). HEIs mainly include universities, colleges, professional and technical institutions, and further education institutions. HEIs typically admit students after assessing them on various criteria, provide instruction for them in person for a specified time, and grant them degrees, diplomas, or certificates after the completion of their studies. The education imparted by such institutions is referred to as higher education. However, higher education is about the higherness in education and "is connected with not only the transmission of knowledge, but also its advancement through research, higher education has the task of legitimating society's cognitive structures" (Barnett, 1990, p. 8).

In the 21st century, HEIs have gained particular importance, carrying out three fundamental functions: instruction, research, and extension (Quitoras & Abuso, 2021). Higher education institutions are considered knowledge producers and providers in today's "knowledge economy" and "learning society" (Naidoo, 2008; Ozga, 2008; Scott, 2016; Snellman, 2015; Soysal & Baltaru, 2021). Higher education institutions contribute knowledge through research output and knowledge transfer, usually measured by research and development activities and output (Chen, 2012). HEIs are expected to fulfil a broad range of responsibilities. As noted by UNESCO (2022): "Higher education institutions are uniquely positioned to contribute to the social, economic and environmental transformations that are required to tackle the world's most pressing issues" (p. 3). Higher education also provides many personal benefits to individuals. A decennial review based on 1,120 estimates in 139 countries noted that private returns to higher education have increased over time, estimating a personal return on investment at 15.8% (Psacharopoulos & Patrinos, 2018).

The needs and realities of the 21st century require a shift in the purpose of education from developing human capital and bringing advances in science and technology for economic prosperity and development, to ensuring the wellbeing of individuals and societies. Wellbeing is not equated to material resources such as income, wealth, jobs, earnings and housing. The OECD (2018) explicates that:

> Education has a vital role to play in developing the knowledge, skills, attitudes and values that enable people to contribute to and benefit from an inclusive and sustainable future. Learning to form clear and purposeful goals, work with others with different perspectives, find untapped opportunities and identify multiple solutions to big problems will be essential in the coming years. Education needs to aim to do more than prepare young people for the world of work; it needs to equip students with the skills they need to become active, responsible and engaged citizens. (pp. 3–4)

The role of HEIs has become more critical considering the shift in the purpose of education. Now, HEIs have broader social and moral responsibilities to facilitate youths in forming such ideas and ideals that, in the future, will shape the fate and destiny of societies, as noted by Chankseliani et al. (2021):

> With the expansion of university participation beyond the elite, higher education has acquired a greater potential for contributing to societal development. Universities can educate citizens, statespersons, teachers, doctors, engineers, philosophers, lawyers, artists, and activists to support the development of peaceful, inclusive, and just societies. Universities can undertake basic and applied research to improve our understanding of life and to develop practical applications of scientific knowledge. (p. 110)

However, this is not yet reflected in reality. HEIs increasingly tend to adopt the characteristics of corporate entities (Jarvis, 2001; Ramos-Monge et al., 2017) due to a range of pressures, including the demands of technological developments and the need for jobs. As such, the focus on research, serving society as a change agent, and empowering people across different sections of society has taken a back seat. Kromydas (2017) noted that:

> the current policy focus on labor market-driven policies in higher education has led to an ever-growing competition transforming this social institution to an ordinary market-place, where attainment and degrees are seen as a currency that can be converted to a labour market value. Education has become an instrument for economic progress moving away from its original role to provide context for human development. As a result, higher education becomes very expensive and even if policies are directed towards openness, in practice, just a few have the money to afford it. (p. 1)

Over the past fifty years, HEIs have changed substantially. The changes have emerged in programmes, facilities, research priorities, teaching-learning methodologies, course content, resources, and approaches. In our knowledge society, the commodification of knowledge has given rise to the intellectual property regime and the race for ranking and power. Lyotard's (1984) claim has been borne out: "Knowledge in the form of an informational commodity indispensable to productive power is already, and will continue to be, a major — or perhaps *the* major — stake in the world-wide competition for power" (p. 5).

Some HEIs have also moved from offering education to the elite to massification (see Luke, Chapter 6, this volume). Nevertheless, the core nature and functions of HEIs have remained largely static. The unchanged aspect is that many HEIs are working independently focusing mainly on teaching and facilitating their students, working within protected boundaries, and not collaborating continuously with societies. Since HEIs have a mandate to nurture future leaders, it becomes prudent for them to take the lead to innovate and make efforts to further open their boundaries.

Usually, HEIs have a mandate to facilitate and nurture learners, conduct research for producing and disseminating knowledge, and carry out extension activities. These three prime activities of HEIs are directly related to the socioeconomic welfare of society and humanity and are aligned to the idea of the "ecological university" — focusing on its total environment and striving to work for global good in an ethical way (Barnett, 2011). However, there is a caveat. Despite advancements in the open education and open research movements in recent years, HEIs, generally, selectively share their research outcomes, techniques, products, knowledge, and resources with the wider world. These outcomes, often labelled in terms of proprietary items and patents, are only available to those willing to pay a fee or agree to share revenue of their profits.

In the Indian context, HEIs remain hesitant to collaborate with other institutions or sections of the society to share resources, conduct joint research, and produce common knowledge. Despite advances like the open access, open educational resources, and open research movements emerging in the past 20 years, the actions and activities of most HEIs in India are strictly guarded and protected, as there are increased expectations for patent filing and resource generation. Most surprisingly, those HEIs which run and thrive on public money (taxpayers' money) and those who run on their own money (but take different benefits and privileges from governments) have similar tendencies and patterns on this issue.

Possible benefits from making HEIs as OKIs

The world is currently facing unprecedented challenges such as climate change, rising inequalities, lack of adequate health services, exacerbating social fragmentation, increasing resource depletion, and widening economic crises (OECD, 2018). HEIs cannot remain isolated from these challenges and must focus on supporting the Sustainable Development Goals (SDSN Australia/Pacific, 2017). HEIs must take more responsibility, open their doors, and welcome anybody who wants their help or resources to find meaningful solutions for individual and societal benefits. A UNESCO (2022) report calls on higher education leaders and actors across the globe to push for transformations within their institutions and look for new alliances, incentives and propose viable solutions as a priority, considering the complexity of the issues at stake:

> Given this new reality in which the future of humans, along with other species, is at stake, it is time for HEIs and their stakeholders to systematically rethink their role in society and their key missions, and reflect on how they can serve as catalysts for a rapid, urgently needed and fair transition towards sustainability. (p. 18)

HEIs as OKIs give much hope to meet such demands and contribute to making this world a better place to live for all. The argument behind this proposition is that, as OKIs, the research and knowledge generated in HEIs will immediately be available to the public. In addition, as OKIs, HEIs would be more accessible for guidance, help, and consultancy to a broader range of people, diverse groups, and other institutions. As in many open universities globally, HEIs as OKIs can be places where senior citizens and working people can come at any time to improve and enhance their learning. This learning will ultimately help greater numbers of people to be happy, healthy, and employment-ready. The transformation of HEIs to OKIs, a timely and much-needed intervention, could bring socioeconomic benefits and sustainable development opportunities for societies. Following are some potential benefits of making HEIs as OKIs:

- There are HEIs (globally recognised, highly ranked, resource-rich, and credible among employers) where many students aspire to get admission, but only a few are selected to study. Making such HEIs as OKIs may offer possibilities, even to those who cannot enrol, to gain benefits of courses and programmes offered by those institutions.

- Research reveals that employability is a major concern in HEIs (Cheng et al., 2021) and what students learn in HEIs must continually be updated to remain relevant for employment (Alpaydın & Kültür, 2022). Students often look for different means to update their knowledge and skills to stay relevant and productive in their professions or engagements. HEIs as OKIs could offer students opportunities to return to their campuses (physically or virtually) to update their knowledge and skills.

- The world is moving towards an ageing society. The ageing population needs lifelong learning to remain mentally fit and active. Unfortunately, many elderly people lack opportunities for this purpose, as noted by a report from UNESCO Institute for Lifelong Learning that focused on the elderly in Europe, but also applicable globally (Ogg, 2021):

> although some practical and effective measures to include lifelong learning activities that address the needs of ageing societies have been put in place, there is growing need throughout Europe to focus on promoting lifelong learning in local and community settings and for all age groups. (p. 1)

- HEIs as OKIs can provide options to senior citizens to engage in needs-based lifelong learning programmes and activities, as well as suggest specific programmes and activities. Such initiatives are already in place in University of the Third Age (U3A, 2022) and similar programmes globally.

- HEIs are often involved in path-breaking and cutting-edge research. However, they often only share their results or findings with a specific community or for commercial gains. Some attempts, like open sharing of research, remain confined to a limited number of HEIs. HEIs as OKIs can commit to publicly sharing these results. Greater public sharing of research outputs may change the perception of higher education research and, most importantly, offer numerous opportunities for policymakers, practitioners, and citizens.

- HEIs carry out research on different issues and produce new knowledge but mainly from their perspectives. It is not a common practice in HEIs to survey or listen to society first, and conduct research accordingly. HEIs as OKIs could broaden their research circles by collaborating with and conducting research in consultation with society. Such a society-driven and socially-demanded research by HEIs would help to make this world a safer, better, and more sustainable place to live, for all.

Expected issues and challenges regarding making HEIs as OKIs

We contend that converting HEIs to OKIs is a much needed step. Nevertheless, doing it will not be easy as there are many challenges in the path of this noble venture. Besides policy shifts and attitudinal change in leadership, the ways and means to do it will be vital. We consider three main challenges in making HEIs as OKIs.

- **Changing mindset of faculty and leadership:** HEIs work, function, and carry out different roles and responsibilities according to their specified acts, ordinances, and policies within the regulatory framework in India. Several people in several capacities manage the functioning of HEIs. Those governing and running HEIs have a specific mindset and attitude to see the developmental needs and act upon them. Reimagining HEIs as OKIs would require a shift in thinking about the role and purpose of HEIs and would require a long-term engagement process with all faculty, staff, and students (including senior level staff) and, vitally, funding support.

- **Organisational changes regarding rules, regulations, and work culture:** Conversion of HEIs as OKIs is a novel concept, and HEIs would need to make several changes and adjustments to realise this vision. There will be many issues ranging from infrastructure to policies, plans, and guidelines to make HEIs as OKIs, and many HEIs do not have enough facilities and workforce to bring about this change. More than anything else, this shift will demand a substantial change in the working culture of the institutions. As per our experience in India, HEIs tend to deal with a largely homogeneous set of learners with similar profiles and expectations, but as OKIs, they would have to deal with varied groups of learners and focus on their needs to support them in pursuit of excellence in their chosen field.

- **Financial arrangements to accommodate more on campuses:** Another significant challenge would be ensuring financial resources for this change. The conversion of HEIs into OKIs would require additional financial support from government and other funding agencies. This conversion would also reduce the revenues generated and increase spending as HEIs would have to accommodate a greater number and diversity of students. HEIs may also be required to offer some educational programmes in a subsidised mode and share their educational and research resources with others, which would also cost additional maintenance.

It is clear that transforming HEIs into OKIs nationally would require bold steps and a clear policy framework. HEIs would need to change and adjust at cognitive, structural, and financial levels to embrace openness and perform their role as higher education institutions for the good of society, and for the future. Technology can be an enabler to help fulfil this promise. The following section details how HEIs may use technology to evolve as OKIs.

Technology as an enabler for making HEIs as OKIs

As OKIs, HEIs would offer various programmes to a broader range of people in society and share their resources and facilities, and would require appropriate technology to do so. Our advocacy for using technology to reimagine HEIs into OKIs is based on the argument that it can cater to people on a real time basis with affordable financial investment. Technology can increase access to quality higher education and promote inclusion and equitable opportunities for all by helping HEIs to identify and reach those in need of their services. Adopting relevant open tools and applications can promote the openness required for OKI. The development and acceptance of open educational resources in the higher education landscape is an innovative practice that could help educators in higher education to contribute to openness and make collective and collaborative contributions.

HEIs could consider using existing technology tools, i.e. web portals, learning management systems, MOOCs, and online databases, to make this mammoth task doable and manageable. The availability of a national government-supported MOOC platform, SWAYAM, as experienced in India could be leveraged to increase openness in teaching and learning. HEIs must combine intent with innovative ways to open HEIs to society. HEIs may devise specific strategies suiting their context, objectives, resources, and organisational priorities. In addition, any institution in any place, locality, or region in India could adopt and use the following technology-enabled strategies for evolving as OKIs.

- **Issuing a return to study pass to all registered students:** Students are the backbone of any education system. With the unprecedented explosion of knowledge and demand of emerging economies, today's higher education students will need to update their knowledge and skills regularly. As pointed out by O'Farrell (2017), preparing our students to cope with and succeed in an unpredictable world is arguably one of the most significant challenges universities face worldwide. However, HEIs are lacking in offering such support to those students who have graduated from their campuses. There tend to be few opportunities for students to return for further study or guidance. Of course, they can stay associated with these institutions as alumni, but there is a need to bring a change in this relationship. HEIs could provide a pass for students to return to their institutions for a specified time to update their knowledge and skills. This liberty and assurance for outgoing graduates to come back for study would make HEIs more open, caring, and inclusive. This would also foster belonging amongst students. Research shows that higher education students with a greater sense of belonging tend to have higher motivation, more academic self-confidence, higher levels of academic engagement, and higher achievement (Pedler et al., 2022). Technology could help, for example, in learning who would like to come back, and for what purposes, and supporting them accordingly. Existing models of this practice in global open universities and lifelong learning units can be drawn on as examples that may be adapted for local contexts.

- **Having a policy to offer lifelong learning programmes for senior citizens:** Surprisingly, most HEIs in India have no specific policy for welcoming senior citizens to their campuses for study and research. HEIs could implement policy in this area and create a dedicated portal to meet the lifelong learning needs of senior citizens. On this portal, HEIs could display the types of lectures, activities, and programmes that may interest senior citizens and record their preferences and preferred programmes. This open welcome of senior citizens, helping them to live a more engaged life, would undoubtedly contribute to making HEIs as OKIs. As above, existing models of this practice in global open universities and lifelong learning units can be drawn on as examples that may be adapted.

- **Reporting activities and functions of the institution to the public:** HEIs often report their achievements through their websites. However, most HEIs remain selective, usually publishing and advertising those activities and accomplishments that may help them to recruit students, obtain funding, and achieve higher rankings. There is a widespread perception that HEIs only show their better sides to the public, like businesses. HEIs could think about using their websites to report their activities, achievements, and even shortcomings in a fair, transparent, and easy-to-grasp manner. This approach could help to change society's perception of HEIs.

- **Identifying and inviting practitioners from different walks of life to conduct joint research:** HEIs may identify and invite practitioners not working in academic or research institutions to conduct collaborative research on chosen projects. HEIs could extend such invitations to those who are well versed in practices but do not have sufficient expertise and experience or lack the facilities to conduct research. A joint research effort between academic experts of HEIs and real life experiences and expertise of practitioners could bring highly fruitful results. HEIs can use technologies to identify such practitioners who are working silently in the fields or in remote areas to bring positive change to society. It is ironic that such people may not have academic degrees but have the potential to contribute substantially to joint research. The invitation for research to people at the grassroots would help HEIs to work in tandem with people across society to offer sustainable solutions to emerging problems of this complex world. Existing models of this practice in university-based community knowledge units, globally, can be drawn on as examples that may be adapted.

- **Releasing all institutional publications through an open repository:** As OKIs, HEIs could share their course content, publications, and research findings for free for broader dissemination and use. For this purpose, they could develop an institutional policy mandating the release of publications under an open licence. An open licence is a licence that respects the intellectual property rights of the copyright owner and provides permissions granting the public the right to access, reuse, repurpose, adapt and redistribute educational materials (UNESCO, 2018). Teaching and learning resources released under open licenses are known as open educational resources (OER). A commitment and a specific policy for releasing institutional resources as OER would be a welcome move for HEIs to emerge as OKIs. Existing institutional examples can be explored and adapted, e.g. University of Cape Town (2011) and University of Edinburgh (2021).

- **Offering different programmes in the form of MOOCs:** Massive Open Online Courses (MOOCs) are typically free, online courses designed for large numbers of geographically dispersed students. Due to the coronavirus pandemic, many undergraduate degree programs have implemented MOOCs as the new standard (Chai & Wigmore, 2022). MOOCs provide an affordable and flexible way for learners to learn new skills and for HEIs to deliver quality educational experiences at scale. Millions of people worldwide use MOOCs to learn for various reasons, including career development, changing jobs, college preparation, supplemental learning, lifelong learning, corporate training, and more (MOOC.org, 2021). HEIs may offer their popular programmes and courses as MOOCs, as many do already. As per the provisions of each country's higher education regulatory authority, HEIs can provide credit or non-credit MOOCs. If these courses are offered as credit-based courses, learners can use them for formal education purposes. In the case of non-credit courses, these can be used for lifelong learning and professional development purposes. MOOC provision could make HEIs accessible to all who aspire to study at any point in their life. The University Grants

Commission, India, has already made regulations to allow up to 40% of credits to be earned from MOOCs offered on the national MOOC platform (UGC, 2021). This is already an enabling environment to move towards becoming OKIs.

- **Developing an online portal to showcase and share facilities and resources:** In the present context, it is difficult to know the available facilities and resources in Indian HEIs. Publicising this information would help outside individuals and other institutions to approach those HEIs to access and use their resources and facilities for academic and research support. To make this happen, HEIs having excess or underutilised resources and facilities may think of developing an online portal to enlist their available facilities and resources. Such a portal would help individuals, community organisations and other institutions know the availability of facilities and request to use these services as per agreed terms and conditions. This simple use of technology could be effective in moving from closed to open educational institutions. This practice would bring institutions closer to society and help ensure the optimum utilisation of resources and staffing for the betterment of society.

Conclusion

This chapter advocates higher education for good and proposes that HEIs must evolve as OKIs. The authors consider higher education to be a public good that needs to be available for individual, social and economic gains. They argue that HEIs, especially in India, have to open their boundaries, become more accessible, and support individuals, societies, and industries. The chapter acknowledges that achieving this goal will be challenging, and HEIs will require structural and cultural change, organisational revisioning, and financial investments to evolve as OKIs. On a positive note, the chapter advocates that technology can be an enabler in materialising this vision and discusses the use of technology in this regard. The chapter finally suggests seven strategies to help HEIs emerge as OKIs, with hope that HEIs from India and other countries may use these strategies to emerge as mass welfare institutions, i.e. open knowledge institutions promoting inclusion, equity, social justice, and sustainable development.

References

Alpaydın, Y., & Kültür, K. (2022). Improving the transition from higher education to employment: A review of current policies. In B. Akgün, & Y. Alpaydın (Eds), *Education policies in the 21st Century* (pp. 103–29). Palgrave Macmillan.

Barnett, R. (1990). *The idea of higher education*. SRHE & OU Press.

Barnett, R. (2011). *Being a university*. Routledge.

Chai, W., & Wigmore, I. (2022). *Massive open online course (MOOC)*. TechTarget. https://www.techtarget.com/whatis/definition/massively-open-online-course-MOOC

Chankseliani, M., Qoraboyev, I. & Gimranova, D. (2021). Higher education contributing to local, national, and global development: New empirical and conceptual insights. *Higher Education, 81*, 109–27. https://doi.org/10.1007/s10734-020-00565-8

Chen, S. (2012). Contributing knowledge and knowledge workers: the role of Chinese universities in the knowledge economy. *London Review of Education, 10*(1), 101–12. https://doi.org/10.1080/14748460.2012.659062

Cheng, M., Adekola, O., Albia, J., & Cai, S. (2021). Employability in higher education: A review of key stakeholders' perspectives. *Higher Education Evaluation and Development, 16*(1), 16–31. https://doi.org/10.1108/HEED-03-2021-0025

Commonwealth of Learning (2017, n.d). *Openness to me is all about 3Fs* [Video]. YouTube. https://www.youtube.com/watch?v=94F6e-Aw6nc

Government of India. (2021). *All India survey on higher education 2020–21* [PDF]. Department of Higher Education, Ministry of Education. https://aishe.gov.in/aishe/viewDocument.action;jsessionid=58AB570C1AFE7BCF162E38A760E007F6?documentId=352

Jarvis, P. (2001). *Universities and corporate universities: The higher learning industry in a global society*. Kogan Page

Kromydas, T. (2017). Rethinking higher education and its relationship with social inequalities: Past knowledge, present state and future potential. *Palgrave Communication, 3*(1), 1–12. https://doi.org/10.1057/s41599-017-0001-8

Lyotard, J. F. (1984). *The postmodern condition: A report on knowledge*. University of Minnesota Press.

MOOC.org. (2021). *About MOOCs*. https://www.mooc.org/

Naidoo, R. (2008). Higher education: A powerhouse for development in a neo-liberal age? In D. Epstein, R. Boden, R. Deem, F. Rizvi, & S. Wright (Eds), *Geographies of knowledge, geometries of power: Framing the future of higher education: World yearbook of education* (pp. 248–65). Routledge.

O'Farrell, C. (2017). *Assessment for lifelong learning.* Trinity College, The University of Dublin.

OECD. (2018). *The future of education and skills education 2030.* OECD Publishing.

Ogg, J. (2021). *Embracing a culture of lifelong learning: Lifelong learning in ageing societies: Lessons from Europe.* UNESCO Institute for Lifelong Learning. https://unesdoc.unesco.org/ark:/48223/pf0000377820

Ozga, J. (2008). Governing knowledge: Research steering and research quality. *European Educational Research, 7*(3), 261–72. https://doi.org/10.2304/eerj.2008.7.3.261

Pedler, M. L., Willis, R., & Nieuwoudt, J. E. (2022). A sense of belonging at university: Student retention, motivation and enjoyment. *Journal of Further and Higher Education, 46*(3), 397–408. https://doi.org/10.1080/0309877X.2021.1955844

Psacharopoulos, G., & Patrinos, H. A. (2018). *Returns to investment in education: A decennial review of the global literature* [PDF]. World Bank. https://documents1.worldbank.org/curated/en/442521523465644318/pdf/WPS8402.pdf

Quitoras, M. C. L. & Abuso, J. E. (2021). Best practices of higher education institutions (HEIs) for the development of research culture in the Philippines. *Pedagogical Research, 6*(1), 1–7. https://doi.org/10.29333/pr/9355

Ramos-Monge, E. L., Audet, X. L., & Barrena- Martínez, J. (2017). Universities as corporate entities: The role of social responsibility in their strategic management. In O. L. Emeagwali (Ed.), *Corporate governance and strategic decision making.* IntechOpen. https://doi.org/10.5772/intechopen.69931

Scott, P. (2016). Higher education and the knowledge economy. In R. Barnett, P. Temple, & P. Scott (Eds), *Valuing higher education: An appreciation of the work of Gareth Williams* (pp. 195–213). UCL IOE Press

SDSN Australia/Pacific (2017). *Getting started with the SDGs in universities: A guide for universities, higher education institutions, and the academic sector* [PDF]. https://ap-unsdsn.org/wp-content/uploads/University-SDG-Guide_web.pdf

Snellman, C. L. (2015). University in knowledge society: Role and challenges. *Journal of System and Management Sciences, 5*(4), 84–113. http://www.aasmr.org/jsms/Vol5/No.4/JSMS-VOL5-NO4-5.pdf

Soysal, Y. N. & Baltaru, R. (2021). University as the producer of knowledge, and economic and societal value: The 20th and twenty-first century transformations of the UK higher education system. *European Journal of Higher Education, 11*(3), 312–28.
https://doi.org/10.1080/21568235.2021.1944250

UGC. (2021). *University Grants Commission (Credit Framework for Online Learning Courses through Study Webs of Active Learning for Young Aspiring Minds) Regulations, 2021-reg* [PDF].
https://www.ugc.ac.in/pdfnews/2702581_SWAYAM_letter_for_Regulations__2021.pdf

UNESCO. (2002). *Forum on the impact of open courseware for higher education in developing countries.*
https://unesdoc.unesco.org/ark:/48223/pf0000128515

UNESCO. (2018). *Open educational resources.*
https://www.unesco.org/en/communication-information/open-solutions/open-educational-resources

UNESCO. (2019). *Global convention on the recognition of qualification concerning higher education.*
https://www.unesco.org/en/legal-affairs/global-convention-recognition-qualifications-concerning-higher-education?hub=66535

UNESCO. (2022). *Knowledge-driven actions: Transforming higher education for global sustainability independent expert group on the universities and the 2030 agenda.*
https://unesdoc.unesco.org/ark:/48223/pf0000380519

University of Cape Town. (2011). *Intellectual property policy.*
http://www.rci.uct.ac.za/rcips/ip/policy

University of Edinburgh. (2021). *Open educational resources policy.*
https://www.ed.ac.uk/files/atoms/files/openeducationalresourcespolicy.pdf

University of the Third Age (U3A). (2022).
https://www.u3a.org.uk/

26. "It's about transforming lives!": Supporting students in post pandemic higher education

Vicki Trowler

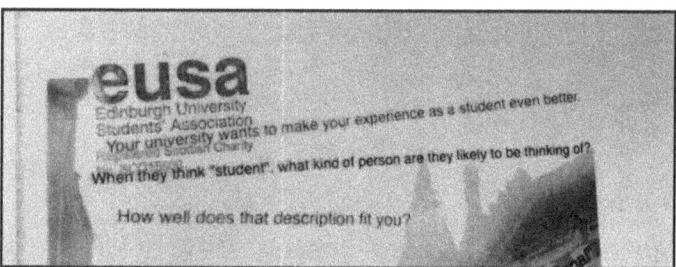

"When one thinks of 'a student', what springs to mind is often a young person from within the country, entering university directly from school with the appropriate school-leaving qualifications; this imagined student has no job or other responsibilities to distract them from their studies, no dependents or extended family to care for, and no disabilities. They identify unproblematically with the gender they were assigned at birth, and this predisposes them to select an appropriate programme of study and to participate in stereotypical student pursuits..." (Trowler, 2017.)

My PhD study challenged those assumptions. I enlisted 23 volunteers who were studying at universities in Scotland, who self-identified as "non-traditional" in their own study contexts, to explore how they perceived their own engagement as well as their universities' attempts to engage them, and tracked them over the course of a calendar year. Reasons for volunteering included age, socio-economic background, nationality/ ethnicity / "race", religion, caring responsibilities, gender, first-in-family to participate in HE, LGBTQIA+ identities, disability status, family estrangement, care experience, and non-standard entry qualifications - with students seldom presenting only a single reason.

This chapter revisits unpublished data from my PhD study, bringing it into conversation with current concerns to reflect on what makes HE "good?" When is HE "good?" How might we, working or studying in HE, help to ensure that it stays (or becomes) "good" - when there are so many challenges. Pseudonyms used in this chapter were chosen by the participants at the time, and images and objects used (e.g. the smiley mask chosen by Alex, or the meeting minutes covered in food chosen by Courtney) were selected by participants to characterise their engagement with their universities. To those students, and others I've interviewed and worked with since, my ongoing gratitude.

26. *"It's about transforming lives!"*   593

Students volunteered to participate in the study in response to posters in student areas on campuses in Scotland, seeking students who identified as "non-traditional" in their study contexts. The focus of the study was on student engagement, but conversations ranged widely. This chapter will bring their reflections on how universities could better meet the needs of students like themselves, into conversation with the post-pandemic HE landscape.

26. "It's about transforming lives!" 595

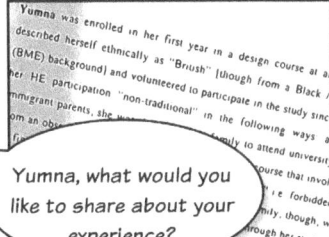

Yumna, what would you like to share about your experience?

The assumptions... the stereotypes. It's like they're not seeing me, they just see the veil. And then I'm either an object of pity, or an object of fear.

"There's an assumption that I'm not serious about my studies, that I just want a degree so I can get a better husband. And that because I dress modestly, I don't have opinions to share, so I never get asked in class. I'm quite shy, so I'm not going to shout out, like some, but it would be nice to be asked sometimes. And for people to listen properly when I speak, not assume what I'm going to say."

Some of the techniques we used during remote teaching allowed anonymity and facilitated participation. We mustn't lose that!

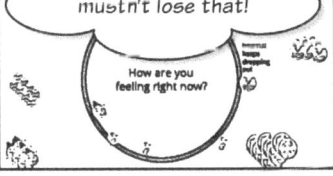

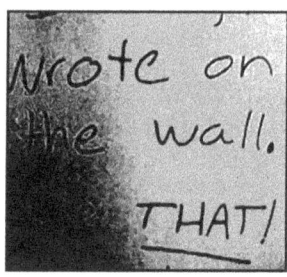

26. *"It's about transforming lives!"* 597

"In class, they treated us like kids! And the systems were so hostile to student parents. We had to campaign to get library hours extended. There is just always a tension between being a student, and being a parent. As a parent, you know what has to come first. But the uni doesn't see it that way. It would be much fairer to everyone if they could be more flexible."

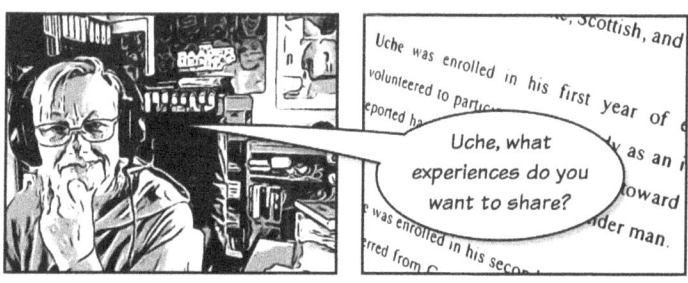

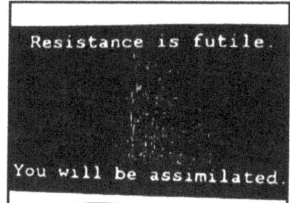
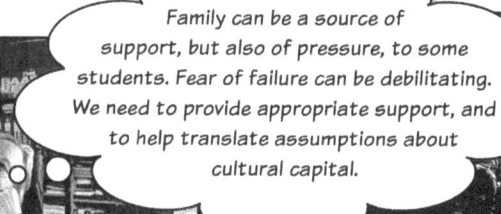

"In a sense you can't really go home, once you've left. You can visit, but the place you visit isn't really "home", not because it's changed, but you have. What you think is home now isn't that. It's something else, somewhere else. Or maybe... someplace you haven't gone yet, some place you still have to create."

26. "It's about transforming lives!"

References

Eringfeld, S. (2021). Higher education and its post-coronial future: Utopian hopes and dystopian fears at Cambridge University during Covid-19. *Studies in Higher Education, 46*(1), 146-157. https://doi.org/10.1080/03075079.2020.1859681

Freire, P. (2014). *Pedagogy of hope: Reliving pedagogy of the oppressed.* Bloomsbury Academic.

hooks, b. (1994). *Teaching to transgress: Education as the practice of freedom.* Routledge.

Peters, M. A., Rizvi, F., McCulloch, G., Gibbs, P., Gorur, R., Hong, M., Hwang,Y., Zipin, L., Brennan, M., Robertson, S., Quay, J., Malbon, J., Taglietti, D., Barnett, R., Chengbing, W., McLaren, P., Apple, R., Papastephanou, M., Burbules, N., Jackson, L., Jalote, P., Kalantzis, M., Cope, B., Fataar, A., Conroy, J., Misiaszek, G., Biesta, G., Jandrić, P., Choo, S., Apple, M., Stone, L., Tierney, R., Tesar, M., Besley,T. & Misiaszek, L. (2020). Reimagining the new pedagogical possibilities for universities post-Covid-19. *Educational Philosophy and Theory, 54*(6), 717-760. https://doi.org/10.1080/00131857.2020.1777655

Trowler, V. (2017). *Nomads in contested landscapes: Reframing student engagement and non-traditionality in higher education* [Doctoral dissertation, University of Edinburgh].

Trowler, V., Allan, R. L., & Din, R. R. (2019). "To secure a better future": The affordances and constraints of complex familial and social factors encoded in higher education students' narratives of engagement. *Widening Participation and Lifelong Learning, 21*(3), 81-98. https://doi.org/10.5456/WPLL.21.3.81

27. Who cares about procurement?

Anne-Marie Scott and Brenna Clarke Gray

The COVID-19 pandemic saw an exponential increase in the adoption of commercial educational technology across the globe (Williamson, 2021; Williamson & Hogan, 2020), and in many jurisdictions there have continued to be efforts to embed these educational technologies into the "new normal". With that in mind, it seems imperative not just to look more critically at educational technologies themselves, but also to interrogate and understand the procurement processes through which they come into being in our institutions.

In this chapter we explore the practices of procurement as we have experienced them within our respective roles in higher education. The format of the chapter is a slow conversation written over several months, a process which allowed us to expand our understanding of the topic by asking questions of each other, with pauses for reflection along the way. We come to this work with different roles and perspectives — Anne-Marie is a deputy provost, Brenna is a faculty coordinator of educational technologies — but with a shared belief that the practices of educational technology procurement in higher education are problematic and may actively work against ideas of what we think of as good in education. Amongst our concerns are that typical educational technology procurement practices do not centre educational expertise and ethical concerns (Whitman, 2021), do not account for the ways in which technology and pedagogy are entangled (Fawns, 2022), do not adequately capture the complexity and purpose of education (Biesta, 2015), that the profit motives (Facer, 2021) and increasingly extractive nature (Williamson, 2019) of commercial educational technology as a business may conflict with what we think of as "good". We have tried in our conversation to go beyond critique and identify opportunities for improvement, though we perhaps remain in a place where we believe that, even with improvement, current educational technology procurement practices may be fundamentally unfit for purpose.

Anne-Marie: Hey Brenna. So, it seems like we are co-writing a book chapter on procurement. I reckoned I always had a blockbuster keynote on edtech maintenance ahead of me, but nope. Procurement turns out to be the thing. So maybe it would be a good idea to explain to anyone reading this why we *do* care about educational technology procurement in higher education. I think we might both agree that procurement is one of those areas of higher education that is broken and in desperate need of disruption. So, maybe you could say a little bit more about the kinds of radical reinvention of procurement you'd like to see? I bet it involves blockchain…

Brenna: Ha! I use the brain cells I could spend on learning what blockchain is to ensure I never forget the words to any Lin-Manuel Miranda[1] songs. It is urgent work.

I first came to be curious — livid? — about procurement when I was a teaching faculty member. I considered myself engaged, I sat on all sorts of tech committees and so on, but still these technologies and services would be dropped into my lap, and I would be mandated to use them and I would think… where did this thing come from? Who asked for it? Have students used it? Do they like it? The studied disinterest with which these questions were met left me cold — it was impossible to get a meaningful answer.

Now that I have moved into faculty support on the education technologies side of the house, though, I find the work of procurement to be more important than only questions of consultation, like who is asked their opinion on a tool and how that opinion gets valued (though I still think that matters!). As I've learned more about tools like learning analytics, machine learning, facial recognition, and as I see how the

---

1   Lin-Manuel Miranda is a songwriter and playwright best known for the smash hit musicals *In the Heights* and *Hamilton*. If you are a parent to young children, you may better know him as the songwriter for films like Disney's *Moana* and *Encanto*. Brenna's joke about being "in the room where it happens" is a line from *Hamilton*; Alexander Hamilton is driven to become a legislator because he wants to be in that room. Brenna feels no similar compunction about becoming an academic administrator.

data from all of those things gets monetised, I have a lot of questions about how for-profit edtech products that employ such technologies are finding their ways into post-secondary classrooms. And I wonder whether the people signing the papers have a depth of knowledge of the ethical questions these technologies raise for many of us working in the field; can they see through the marketing lies of the people selling the tools? I know these tools and the way they are implemented is *legal*, but I am learning that legality is the floor of what we should expect of our technologies, and too often it is treated as the ceiling.

But alas, like a young Alexander Hamilton, I have never been in the room where it happens. You, intrepid administrator that you are, *have* been in the room. I'm wondering if your questions about procurement are the same (or more likely, much smarter) than mine?

Anne-Marie: Yeah — I've not just been in the room; I've driven the process on more than one occasion. I had the good fortune to have a Chief Information Officer (CIO) in my previous role who had crossed over from a commercial software company to run an enormous IT department in a large university, and he taught me all the tricks of the trade in terms of negotiation. I also learned a *lot* from him about how to drive out value from a procurement process (and I don't just mean cheapest price) and how to hold the balance of power. Every time a vendor offers you the opportunity to join a focus group to shape their product, never forget that this is actually free product development, that we are subject matter experts, and ask about what further discounts are on the table for that labour!

That's all to say that I think a lot of the problems we see in this space is because we cede our expertise as educators who work with technology far too easily and quickly. We cede it to IT departments because we let the technology become the dominant aspect in the process rather than the educational purpose, and IT departments in turn far too quickly cede expertise to edtech suppliers because of some sort of inherent belief that the market will provide and the expertise of suppliers outweighs our own. In reality, for many edtech products "little is known about how they work, whom they benefit and whether they work successfully" (Hillman, 2022). I'm talking in terms of broad generalisations here of course. Not all IT departments, not all edtech.

My own personal experience has also been that a certain set of instrumentalist and essentialist views of technology tend to persist in IT departments, along with an expectation to deliver on efficiency savings and value. Technology is simply a tool and is therefore neutral and any problems must be with our ability to use it; or that technology itself is the embodiment of the pedagogical principle, rather than what we do with it (Hamilton & Friesen, 2013). When one starts from that place philosophically then the marketing speak can be highly seductive and perhaps dilutes the chances of some of the critical ethical questions that we are both concerned about being asked.

Beyond the problematic specific technologies that you have already identified (analytics, machine learning, facial recognition etc), I believe that there has also been a broader move towards higher education as a site of value and ongoing wealth extraction (Hall, 2016, Komljenovic, 2021, Williamson, 2019). Edtech platforms and the stories that edtech companies tell are increasingly designed to exert a form of governance over user behaviours, which in turn begins to extend into influence over policy and decision making within universities. Educational technologies today, and the speculative stories about educational technologies tomorrow are tools through which the institution can be influenced and directed in order to safeguard and expand lucrative sources of revenue into the future (Facer, 2021, Komljenovic, 2021, Williamson & Hogan, 2020)

In my view this starts to represent an existential threat to higher education, and it reaches its zenith in some of the recent issues we've seen around proctoring technologies. When Proctorio (an online proctoring company that many universities pay for service) pursued legal action against a university employee who offered a critical analysis of the service (Corbyn, 2022), ostensibly to protect its business, it had a chilling effect on research activity (Selwyn et al., 2021). That cuts absolutely to the heart of our educational mission. If technology and pedagogy and research are connected, and we are unable to critically assess our own digital education practices, then our claim to having any kind of quality assurance capability starts to fall apart. How can we make any claims to providing "Good" education in those circumstances?

Since I am not an academic, but in fact a senior administrator, the tools in my kit bag tend to be policy and process. So, I am interested in how we can improve procurement practices to ensure that the right questions are asked up front such that we don't admit companies and products into our institution that do harm. And I believe we can do this for educational technology because I've seen procurement policies for other kinds of purchasing in higher education that privilege ethical trading practices, or ethical working conditions for employees. It is not uncommon to have modern slavery policies, or favour Fairtrade products for example, and indeed I often joke that we spend more time thinking about the ethics of buying teabags in universities than we do technology. I believe that the same instrumentalist views of technology that I've already mentioned are what make procurement practices weak. If technologies are neutral, then there's no ethical issues to be concerned about. So, how do we change?

Brenna: I like this word "instrumentalist" because it's useful. Often, I think technology procurement has been seen as a fixtures and fittings issue, e.g. not in need of academic governance, but part of the business function of the university. And yet, as you rightly point out, universities *do* draw ethical lines around procurement practice all the time. Maybe not as often as we hope, but I vividly remember the Cola Wars on North American campuses in the 90s where student unions, starting with Carleton University in Ottawa in 1992, vociferously fought exclusivity agreements between campuses and PepsiCo due to Pepsi's continued trade in what was then Burma; when PepsiCo divested from Burma in response, many student unions turned their focus to Coca-Cola's human rights abuses in Nigeria (Klein, 2009). The quest for the least evil purveyor of sugary drinks seems a quite apt comparison.

You ask how we change that, and I wonder if the pandemic moment will have moved the needle at all when we are able to look back. I think it's suddenly become very clear for lots of instructors who may never have really thought about it before that the choice of technology is a choice that impacts teaching and learning. As people moved en masse to large-scale adoption of these tools out of necessity, it became more obvious how they shape, circumscribe, and transform pedagogy. And how they have continued to do so. This is a lesson borne out of moments of frustration and moments of possibility both, and it's not as easy as framing out a good and a bad.

Maybe it's just wishful thinking on my part because I want to kill the concept of "don't let the technology shape the pedagogy" — of course it does! Access to a pen and paper shapes pedagogy!

So, my hope is that teaching staff who have had the experience of seeing the effects of these tools on their teaching might want more of a say. As you note, we cede expertise too quickly, and while administrators certainly have the really important policy expertise in question, there is also teaching and learning expertise. Addressing the teaching and learning piece is hard for institutions, because it's unlikely that a single solution will work for the needs of every discipline — particularly at the regional comprehensives I am most familiar with where you might have a law school and a trade school and a nursing school on the same campus.

I'm also glad you brought up the chilling effect of research and critique. How often are the people who know most about the ethics of these tools from a research perspective — librarians, education faculty, sociologists, media studies educators, software engineers — invited to offer feedback on procurement processes? A common complaint in our institutions is that in-house expertise isn't respected — ask your resident organisational behaviourists how they feel about things down in the old salt mine — and I think this is a key example of where the pooled expertise of the institution is typically laid aside. But we also, as people who care about these issues, do have a responsibility to build and share expertise and explain why this is something that we should care about, and why those of us who are in a position to use our voices should be loud about it.

Since you have driven these processes, and since you know about the business decision calculus, I wonder if you've got some insights on where we go from here. Like, maybe the starting line is: what questions do you think should be asked that aren't, typically?

Anne-Marie: Well, I would like to think that in the procurements that I've run, the questions that did need to be asked were asked, but more important is *how* the questions are asked and weighted. Hold that thought as I'll come back to it in a moment…

In terms of any procurement process I have been involved with, the outcomes almost always failed to make everyone happy, so I think the point that you raised above about whether single solutions can work for institutions that teach a wide variety of disciplines is key. Combine that with austerity measures and only the very richest institutions can afford multiple technologies with overlapping functionality, and even that doesn't always sit well with students who wonder why they have to learn so many specialist systems and question whether we are cohesive as an institution. Given that the large majority of us have to live in systems of constrained resources, for me the calculation starts with an acceptance that perfection isn't possible, and we're looking for best / least bad. I've spoken in a few places before about viewing a lot of this work through the lens of harm reduction as a useful way to view it and still stay sane.

The first question in my mind is who is out there in the market today, and what does the landscape look like? Knowing the market is key, because you need to know what the differentiators in the market are and you need to know a bit about risks. You also need to know what the market offers and what it doesn't in order to write a request for proposals (RFP) that will get you detailed enough information back on which to make a decision. So, whilst I absolutely believe that crowdsourcing requirements from across the institution to gather as much of that learning and teaching expertise as possible is crucial, *someone* needs to do some initial work of looking at just how many of those requirements are actually supported today.

As an example, in a lecture recording procurement I led, we all agreed that Learning Tools Interoperability (LTI) integration with the Learning Management System (LMS) was a very important feature. Our early research showed that every major vendor already supported it, so although it was important to us as an institution, it wasn't going to be a differentiator in our RFP and therefore didn't deserve a high weighting. We also knew a bit from other colleagues about how various projects had gone elsewhere, so we knew we might want to ask some specific questions about implementation methodology, vendor project team / resources etc. We also crowdsourced functional requirements that seemed to be more future looking from academic and professional colleagues, and knowing that nobody had them in products today, we asked questions about roadmaps, and how we can influence development. Once technology is in an institution it tends to stick around, so the quality of the relationship is almost as important as the feature set at any point in time.

What begins to emerge from that for me, is that there needs to be a high degree of pedagogical and technical knowledge and skill within a procurement team from the start. Just inviting your local learning technologist to score the solutions won't cut it. They need to be in from the ground building the procurement strategy based on their knowledge of the institution, the field, and the sector.

I'm highlighting this because most procurements involve giving some notion of weighting to the questions that you ask, and I have seen too many procurements result in a cheap product that is functionally a bad fit winning as the outcome because this weighting has been done badly or the wrong questions have been asked. Knowing not just what's important to you as an institution, but what is in the market, and crafting the right questions and weightings so that you drive out a decision based on the points that really matter is crucial.

One other group that I would say are rarely involved in procurement and should be are students (and we should pay them for their time). Nobody has the authentic experience of being a student today except a student today, and whilst no single student can speak for the entire student body, I have seen everybody involved lift their game and not default to lazy stereotypes when students are in the room. Vendors included. I've argued that if we can co-design our curriculum with our students, then we should also be co-designing the edtech used to deliver that curriculum (Scott & Nanfeldt, 2018), because, as we've said a few times now, pedagogy and technology are connected. Successful co-design of technology requires an investment of time into building trust and levelling out power relations (Dollinger & Lodge, 2018), and RFP processes typically are bounded by short timelines and dates.

That's all to say that knowing the right questions to ask *and* how to use the mechanisms of a procurement process to get the best decisions go hand in hand, and I think there are probably loads of examples out there where all the right questions *were* asked, and it produced the wrong decision.

That still doesn't answer your question about what questions should be asked that often aren't, but hopefully it helps explain that deciding how to ask questions in a procurement is a real skill and one that I think is sadly missing in many cases.

If I was to make a hit list of questions beyond the specific features of any piece of edtech, these are some of the things I would include:

- Describe your process for product development, including how you involve your user community, how you carry out horizon scanning, and to what extent you draw upon best practice and research to inform this work. Include details of any beta testing programmes, product development committees etc.
- What percentage of revenue is re-invested into product development?
- What data does your system collect and what is it used for? Include details of how this is made visible to end users.
- Provide your product Voluntary Product Accessibility Template (VPAT) detailing your accessibility compliance. How is the accessibility of your product validated? Provide details of testing done as part of regular release cycles as well as within product development.

There are many other questions I would ask in addition to these, but they would be more product specific. For example, if there was some automated decision making within the product, I would want to ask for a description of algorithms used, data factors that are important, and details of how any testing has been carried out to ensure that the potential effects of bias have been accounted for.

I'm interested in what you think about the above. What other questions would you ask? And as someone who has been a teacher and is now a learning technologist, where do you think those roles would fit in the above? And do you feel you've ever been well equipped in either of those roles to play a useful part? Or ignore these questions and take us in a different direction if something else stood out for you there!

Brenna: If I start with the last question first: no. Not even just do I not feel like I've been well-equipped, I've never been invited into a procurement process, either as teaching faculty or as a learning technologist, or even as a student or graduate student. (I agree with you that everyone defaults to lazy stereotypes about students less frequently when students are in the room; now that I serve on a lot of committees as the faculty rep when people don't remember I'm faculty myself, I get to see a little bit of how lazy stereotypes are used about faculty, too. I am also very guilty of stereotyping senior management!) I can't overstate the extent to which these processes have always seemed like alchemy to me — and I am, most of the time, a pretty keyed-in, clued-in community member who sits on a lot of relevant committees and asks a lot of questions. I'm interested in how many people share the sense that all of this happens *somewhere else* that we are simply not able to access.

Obfuscation, it seems to me, is often the name of the game here. And that obfuscation often comes from vendors, but it isn't always easy to get meaningful answers out of our own institutions, either. I had some questions for my university, for example, about how our institutional [redacted cloud-based office suite and communication tool] was dealing with data and what features (behavioural trackers and reporting functions) were enabled. The response to my question was that I should file a Freedom of Information Act request. So I did, after baulking a little. And when the document that came back, months later, it didn't answer my questions. But I evidently don't have the expertise to know what I should be asking for at this point, because I thought I was asking a clear question and what I got back was… not. But then again, why should I need to have expertise beyond my functional and relatively high-level knowledge of both the tool and the basics of edtech ethics? Should I even have to have that? Especially in a publicly funded institution that deals with large amounts of data from individuals who have limited to no ability to meaningfully opt-out, and when these software contracts are paid for by taxpayers… What the heck justification is there for all of this being so shrouded in secrecy?

Ah, I see I have stepped away from the question of procurement with a wee rant. Anyway…

I'm grateful for your explanations of the kinds of questions that need to be asked and the high-level expertise needed to do this work well. It's not a reason to limit community consultation, of course — after all, ordinary faculty and staff sit on, say, the budget committee of senate and other complex, nuanced conversations. Collegial governance — the process of governance by shared relationships — is supposed to support all members of the community having a "look in" at all aspects of the

27. Who cares about procurement?   613

university. But I do get that this isn't as simple as an open consultation process and then buying the tool most people want.

That said, I use these tools extensively as one who builds resources and one who supports those who use them; my unique position as both the end user *and* the person most likely to be yelled at by the end user means that I do wish the user experience was something more institutional consideration went into. I use so few tools — and it's almost none of the institutionally sanctioned tools — in my day to day working life that bring me joy or pleasure. And I am one who takes joy and pleasure in using technology! The enterprise email, the LMS, the video platform, the videoconferencing tool, the word processor: at best they are all merely fine, and it's a good day when they don't actively impede my workflow. I know stuff has got to scale, and stuff that scales has to work a little bit for a lot of people, and stuff that works a little bit for a lot of people is going to be clunky at best. But it's also 2023, and we live our lives and do our learning in these spaces, and they still are so much more likely to bring frustration than pleasure.

And maybe there's no way to glean that in the procurement process. But I do often find myself wondering whether anyone who was in the room at the signing of the deal ever tried to use this [redacted] thing.

And I get what you say about harm reduction: I really do. I think that some work could be done around roll-out and messaging, often — okay, I'm leaving procurement again — but, like, if a suite was picked because it is the best on accessibility metrics A, B, and C, I would like to know that! It would absolutely frame my own usability critiques to know that. But usually that information — in my experience at the 6 or so places I've worked or learned, so not at all exhaustive — is not forthcoming.

I alluded to this before, but I do wonder about how much of the disconnect happening here stems from the massive sea-change we've experienced over the few years that have made the learning management system at most universities, and other learning technologies, move from a "nice to have" or even, as it has been at most places I have worked, a fringe interest, to absolutely central to the practice of teaching and learning. As such, I think more folks are more aware of how these tools circumscribe our options for teaching but the processes that govern them are mostly still designed for when it was the niche interest of the few. And the truth is that as individuals and institutions, we have values, and yet the technology we have doesn't always align with those values. It seems like a problem to me.

I guess the question here is: is there a solution? I'm seeing the following critical points emerging over our conversation in terms of what we might call "must-dos":

- Involve key stakeholders, including students, staff, and faculty, not just in a blanket consultation but in the selection process itself. Pay the students for their time! And give the people in the room who are there as users time to develop an understanding of the scope of the questions to be asked.

- Establish a core procurement team that has a lot of pedagogical *and* technological expertise, including people who can speak to data ethics and privacy; accessibility; and diversity, equity, and inclusion.

- Tell people what you're doing and why, to the extent that it's helpful and meaningful, and keep this transparency and clarity into the roll-out period.

At least that's what I'm taking home from this discussion. How about you?

Anne-Marie: I think in those 3 points above you're pretty much nailed my entire approach to procurement when I get to drive the process! Let me see if I can add a little more to the bones of it from my experience in case someone might be looking for a list of steps to follow:

1. **Know the market before you start.** Ask your friends, ask your colleagues, read the marketing rags, ask companies to come and show you their wares. Invite a range of colleagues into those product demos including faculty, learning technologists, students, IT colleagues. Procurement processes usually have some kind of pre-RFP process that you can use to get some show and tell sessions.

2. **Know what's important to you.** Canvas for requirements from as many stakeholder groups as possible. Synthesise and analyse those to develop an RFP that really drives out quality on the points that are both important to the institution, and differentiators.

3. **Involve your community.** Beyond consultation per above, construct an RFP process that allows different stakeholder groups to score the areas in which they have most expertise. Yes — like you say above, let faculty and students score the actual procurement. I like to give a percentage of the overall score to demos of the products and that's where I've often found it easiest to engage faculty as it involves least preparation on their part, and you can provide a light rubric to ensure you get the key points you need input on. That said I wouldn't exclude anyone from the formal scoring, but a key tactic of suppliers is to bombard you with masses of information in written answers, so I always want to be mindful of asking for academic engagement on fair terms. I'd also have data protection officers scoring, digital security colleagues, service desk colleagues etc. in the areas of an RFP where their expert judgement is required. Essentially anyone who's going to have to use / support / be responsible for the thing should be represented.

4. **Communicate.** Hopefully it's clear that by doing the things above in the order outlined you're actually building knowledge within the institution about what you're doing and why. Ideally, I would have the team scoring the RFP review and sign off the various question sets that they are scoring before the RFP is issued. It's important to take the time to prepare them for scoring by explaining the rationale behind why these are the questions (e.g. "we're not asking about XYZ feature because nobody does it, but we are asking about R&D and product development"). For anyone in Q&A sessions with the supplier it will equip them to participate actively. One of my proudest professional moments has been when I empowered a student in a procurement process to the extent that she took the supplier (nicely) to task and really nailed a concrete answer out of them rather than marketing-speak.

5. **Communicate again.** You raise an excellent point that the rationale behind the choice needs to be part of the rollout communications. When a choice is made, I like to write up some kind of news article or announcement for internal consumption.

>   I usually take it round various committees / councils and answer questions colleagues might have. Through the magic of re-use, such a thing can then be used by the rollout project as a first communication! I also like to share lists of who has been involved in all the activities listed above because it's really helpful both to properly recognise the effort that colleagues put into these processes, but also to be transparent about how the decision was made and who made it.

I liked your phrase "open consultation process" because I think that whilst there's definitely a place for expertise in this process — and I believe learning technologists sitting at the nexus of technology and pedagogy are crucial — I absolutely agree with you that our colleagues are plenty smart enough to cope with complicated matters. The clue is that we all work in universities. I also fundamentally believe that universities are collections of labour (kudos to Raewyn Connell here) and that the best outcomes are always going to come from working together. Why would we not want to run open and transparent processes as far as we are able and involve a wide range of colleagues (and I include students in that definition)? Does it not strengthen our institutional capacity? Bluntly, an institution that doesn't see a process like procurement as an opportunity to build knowledge and capacity isn't really thinking about what learning is and how it happens. Let's take a bet on how many of the same institutions have "lifelong learning" in their strategies and are engaged in some kind of digital transformation though...

One last point from me is that procurement isn't the end — it's just the start. You are completely right that rollout is a thing that happens after a procurement and the two things should be connected in ways that are obvious. So, I'll push your point on further and say that once rollout is complete, this stuff is then in our institutions, and it tends to hang around and evolve and grow over time. So, somebody has to do an ongoing job of liaising with suppliers, influencing product development, communicating change inside the institution, and holding suppliers to account. Supplier management is another subject in the digital education Dark Arts curriculum though, and so maybe that's another chapter for another book.

Seriously though, in a little over 4,600 words we've been able to explain the frustrations and impacts of these processes when not done well. We've also identified a number of activities and common questions that could be widely adopted as some kind of standard practice in ways that we think would do good in higher education. So, my final question is, how do we get this change to happen? Do we need to start doing presentations at IT conferences to explain this stuff? Maybe a session titled "Learn these 3 cool hacks to unlock lifelong learning and digital transformation!" because I worry that we're talking in our own echo chamber sometimes.

Brenna: Well, I think the good news is that more people might be interested in the conversation now than ever before, for all the reasons we've discussed. So maybe this is the moment to try to do some professional development around these issues. IT conferences: yes! And I think, too, wherever it is that Provosts and Presidents hang out. I think there are good reputational risk management reasons to make the most senior leaders more aware of why they should care about this — but I guess probably a university is going to have to get sued before that happens. The lawsuit over Turnitin at McGill in 2004 (Rosenfeld v. McGill University) offers one such case; the student won his argument against compelled usage of Turnitin by making an argument that invoked the Canadian Charter of Rights and Freedoms, and that decision perhaps explains why text-matching software is somewhat less ubiquitous in Canadian higher education than in the US, for example (Eaton & Christiansen Hughes, 2022). But I would like to know these kinds of risks are imagined before these cases end up in the courts.

But also, we need to engage these questions in teaching and learning circles and student unions, to talk about strategy and activism and key issues so that when consultation processes do come around, people are ready, and they know what to ask.

I think the process in general would be strengthened by more people having an understanding of it. I have to believe that once we understand the stakes, most of us, regardless of institutional role, probably want the same things: functional tools, good privacy protections, and ethical data use. More information — and conversations like this one! — are the place to start.

Anne-Marie: So, we took a break after writing the above, and got some good and helpful peer review feedback. One question that a reviewer challenged us to consider is the extent to which the RFP decision making process itself is a problem? Public sector procurement practices use scoring/weighting mechanisms for some sense of transparency and accountability e.g. that a decision has been reached by a competitive process that gives suppliers a fair chance, and that there's a clear rationale for spending public money (OECD, 2015). But our reviewer challenges the extent to which these kinds of decisions can realistically be automated given that those involved in an RFP will be trying to make a decision about strategic fit, based on imperfect information, and a pre-determined set of scorings and weightings. We've talked a lot about how to make the existing decision-making process work better by asking better questions and having a wider range of people involved, but we've not really tackled the bigger question of whether we are just measuring what's easy to measure, rather than what we truly value?

It seems to me that our RFP processes force us to reduce a set of pedagogical contexts, purposes, and values (Fawns, 2022) into a set of (more neutral?) functional requirements that can be scored and weighted easily. In that sense we are already consigned to working with poor proxies for what we are really trying to achieve before we even begin. There is a very real chance then that our edtech procurement process is an exercise in trying to minimise the "crapshoot" effects of such a scored/weighted process (because we are working with inaccurate proxies for what we want), or an exercise in creative scoring to game the system after the fact, or a bit of both. Ultimately this all sounds like we're primarily trying to minimise the possibility of being sued for unfair practices, or slapped for spending public money badly, rather than ensuring we buy edtech that could underpin "Good" education. I might define that broadly as edtech that liberates knowledge and learning, allows agency, and opens up possibilities, rather than locks down information, extracts value from the labour of students and teachers, or creates harm through bias. That doesn't feel very ethical at all, now that I think about it.

What're your thoughts? Is it the case that we're trying to force a set of procurement processes into producing better quality outcomes when in fact they're fundamentally and not at all designed to do so because it's very hard to score something like a set of values?

Brenna: We really are back at this question of whether we are measuring what is important or what we can measure. It seems to me that you're asking: are the rubrics we can imagine currently for procurement processes really up to the task? I have to conclude not, given the kinds of tools that are ending up on our desks. If I'm right in my Pollyanna-ing above, that we all really do want the same outcome, then it's clear to me that we need a new process. And maybe we need to give up on the idea that there's a way to capture values and ethics on a scorecard from one to ten.

Of course, there's also the issue that every teacher experiences in their life — that rubrics, well, they kind of suck. Or at least they flatten differences between key priorities. If ethics score a 4 out of 10 and usability scores a 10 out of 10, the pure math might make this a 7 out of 10 tool — but I don't weight ethics and usability equally. The rubric needs to be carefully set up to determine how we demonstrate our values, and those are the hard conversations that need to happen before the procurement process gets underway.

Conclusions

Our peer reviewers cannily noted that we were lacking some of the "good" expected in a collection titled "HE for Good". Where, they asked, is the hopefulness in our chapter? The truth is that procurement is a difficult nut to crack — it seems boring from the outside, it's not well-understood by the vast majority of staff and students in higher education, and the opacity of the narratives about it don't make for engaging reading. And yet it's the genesis of how all tech tools — the good and the bad — find their way to our desks.

We hope that this chapter has made clear the pressing urgency of all of us engaging with processes of procurement. We offer here suggestions on how to bring ethic of care thinking to the procurement process. The "good" in this chapter comes from our overarching belief and hope that when we know better, we will do better, and that, at a minimum, we all ultimately want the same things from the technologies we offer to our colleagues and students: safety, privacy, accessibility, and equity. The work of centring those values in our procurement practices is not the scope of one essay; it is the practice of a lifetime for all of us. Let us undertake this work together and ensure that the HE of the future is one where technology truly serves as a net good for everyone.

Acknowledgements

My heartfelt gratitude and love go to all the friends and peers that I continue to learn from every day, too numerous to list which is in itself a blessing. The opportunity to talk with and think with you all in community makes this work doable and even enjoyable. And to Brenna, when we should both have stopped and given ourselves grace, but didn't. Thanks pal. Many thanks, Anne-Marie.

References

Biesta, G. (2015). What is education for? On good education, teacher judgement, and educational professionalism. *European Journal of Education, 50*(1), 75–87. https://www.jstor.org/stable/26609254

Corbyn, Z. (2022, August 26). I'm afraid: Critics of anti-cheating technology for students hit by lawsuits. *The Guardian*. https://www.theguardian.com/us-news/2022/aug/26/anti-cheating-technology-students-tests-proctorio

Dollinger, M., & Lodge, J. M. (2018). Co-creation strategies for learning analytics. In *Proceedings of the 8th International Conference on Learning Analytics and Knowledge* (pp. 97–101). ACM Digital Library. https://doi.org/10.1145/3170358.3170372

Eaton, S., Christensen Hughes, J. (2022). Academic integrity in Canada: Historical perspectives and current trends. In S. E Eaton, & J. Christensen Hughes (Eds), *Academic integrity in Canada: An enduring and essential challenge* (pp. 3–24). Springer, Cham. https://doi.org/10.1007/978-3-030-83255-1

Facer, K. (2021). *Futures in education: Towards an ethical practice*. UNESCO. https://unesdoc.unesco.org/ark:/48223/pf0000375792.locale=en

Fawns, T. (2022). An entangled pedagogy: Looking beyond the pedagogy—technology dichotomy. *Postdigital Science and Education, 4*(3), 711–28. https://doi.org/10.1007/s42438-022-00302-7

Gray, B. C. (2021, January 22). *Digital detox #2: The LMS, tech-driven pedagogy, and making bad choices too easy*. Tru Digital Detox. https://digitaldetox.trubox.ca/digital-detox-2-the-lms-tech-driven-pedagogy-and-making-bad-choices-too-easy/

Hamilton, E., & Friesen, N. (2013). Online education: A science and technology studies perspective/Éducation en ligne: Perspective des études en science et technologie. *Canadian Journal of Learning and Technology/La Revue Canadienne de l'apprentissage et de La Technologie, 39*(2), 1–21. https://doi.org/10.21432/T2001C

Hillman, V. (2022). *Edtech procurement matters: It needs a coherent solution, clear governance and market standard*. LSE Department of Social Policy. https://www.lse.ac.uk/social-policy/Assets/Documents/PDF/working-paper-series/02-22-Hillman.pdf

Klein, N. (2009). *No logo*. Vintage.

Komljenovic, J. (2021). The rise of education rentiers: Digital platforms, digital data and rents. *Learning, Media and Technology, 46*(3), 1–13. https://doi.org/10.1080/17439884.2021.1891422

OECD. (2015). *OECD Recommendation of the council on public procurement*. https://www.oecd.org/gov/public-procurement/recommendation/

Scott, A. Nanfeldt, K. (2018). #ETConf18: *Lecture recording: A student co-creation case study*. A placid island of ignorance. https://ammienoot.com/brain-fluff/etconf18-lecture-recording-a-student-co-creation-case-study/

Selwyn, N., O'Neill, C., Smith, G., Andrejevic, M., & Gu, X. (2021). A necessary evil? The rise of online exam proctoring in Australian universities. *Media International Australia, 186*(1), 149–64. https://doi.org/10.1177/1329878X211005862

Whitman, M. (2021). Modeling ethics: Approaches to data creep in higher education. *Science and Engineering Ethics, 27*(6), 1–18. https://doi.org/10.1007/s11948-021-00346-1

Williamson, B. (2019). *The platform university: A new data-driven business model for profiting from HE*. Wonkhe. https://wonkhe.com/blogs/the-platform-university-a-new-data-driven-business-model-for-profiting-from-he/

Williamson, B. (2021). Education technology seizes a pandemic opening, *Current History, 120*(822), 15–20. https://doi.org/10.1525/curh.2021.120.822.15

Williamson, B., & Hogan, A. (2020). *Commercialisation and privatisation in/of education in the context of Covid-19*. Education International. https://issuu.com/educationinternational/docs/2020_eiresearch_gr_commercialisation_privatisation/1

Afterword: Higher education for good

Raewyn Connell

I'm very pleased to add a few words at the end of this remarkable collection. By the time you get to my words — assuming you are an excellent student and have read straight through the whole text, you will have travelled to many parts of the world, from Ireland to Brazil, from Jamaica to India, from South Africa to Germany to the United States. You will have explored and debated many methods of teaching and learning, age-old and ultra-modern. You will have been terrified by fierce computers and calmed by meditation. And your mind will have been expanded by multiple media: plain text, science fiction, visual art, dialogue, poetry, and even quilting.

We know, comprehensively, what has happened to higher education in the last generation. There's now a formidable literature: higher education studies is now a research field in its own right.

The main points are not hard to summarise. The whole sector has expanded massively on a world scale, and that is a democratic gain. But it has also become more unequal, ranging from Ivy League universities with assets in the tens of billions of dollars to underfunded rural campuses in the poorest regions of the world. Higher education has always been a site of struggle to overcome privilege. Now, its context and rationale have changed. What was a generation or two ago, essentially a public sector serving public purposes has been half privatised on a world scale.

In the course of that change, higher education has become a bonanza for entrepreneurs, corrupt politicians, and corporations in publishing, ICT and business services. Right-wing governments have concluded it is possible and even desirable to shrink real public funding to higher education, by shifting the costs onto students and their families. Within university and college walls, power has increasingly been centralised in the hands of corporate-style managers. Students are increasingly placed in the status of consumers. The higher education workforce is increasingly precarious, and subject to remote control by surveillance, performance management, and audit from above.

And all that was before COVID-19.

If we are paying attention, we know what is wrong. But how do we know what is right? If we are concerned about these troubles, what alternatives are possible for the future? These are the main themes of this book, and I think they are very important questions indeed. They have consequences not just for the sector itself, but for the whole of human society. We need to understand not just the ills and weaknesses of higher education, but also its possibilities. These are grounded in the strengths and resilience of the higher education workforce — which were formidably on display during the COVID-19 crisis.

I have been a university worker since the early 1970s, and I was involved in university reform even before my first job in the sector. As a graduate student, I was part of a group who set up an experimental, student-controlled Free University in Sydney. Then, working in the mainstream system, with many colleagues I was involved in creating new curricula, exploring student-centred pedagogies, and designing research agendas with greater social relevance.

As managerial power increased, income inequalities in higher education rose and more of the workforce was outsourced or precariously employed. I had always been a union member, and now union action had become vital in defending employee rights and wage levels. Finally, at the university where I was working, we had to go on strike. In discussions on the picket line, I concluded that we needed a more ambitious analysis and agenda for the future; that thinking eventually became *The Good University*. Since that book was published, I have been deeply impressed, but not surprised, by the creative and cooperative responses of university workers to the pandemic.

We have many practical examples of reform. There is a much richer history of democratic, radical and experimental colleges and universities than we usually think. There have been labour colleges, folk high schools (adult education centres, despite the name), women's universities, anti-imperialist and multi-civilisational colleges and universities, Indigenous colleges and universities, student-run free universities, popular research movements, illegal underground universities, and many democratic innovations and experiments within mainstream higher education systems. We don't lack for models and inspiration.

In making alternatives real in current conditions, there will certainly be struggle in the realm of ideas. One illusion we must overcome is that it's all a matter of individual inspiration and effort — an idea that provides some justification for the growing inequality within our institutions. Certainly, personal commitment matters for good work in any role in higher education. But a close look at teaching, research, community service, or the other functions that universities and colleges perform show that the basic effects are a matter of cooperative work and shared effort.

We celebrate star researchers and have even given some of them Nobel prizes. But their good work always builds on a mass of work by other researchers, by teachers and colleagues, professional and administrative and maintenance workers, and is inspired and ultimately enabled by generations of students. The advance of knowledge is fundamentally a collective undertaking. I think of the higher education workforce as the modern collective intellectual. And it's the welfare of that whole workforce, and the capacity of the collective intellectual to work effectively, that are now at stake, in decisions being made today.

We can imagine paths into the future, and it is useful to do that — as many chapters in this book do. Utopian thinking is important, and we could do with more of it! Yet it's not enough on its own. We also need to think about practicalities: about governance, about budgets, about the steps towards institutional reform. This kind of thinking too is found in this book. Since the current controllers of higher education are well entrenched, a reform agenda will need powerful support. So, it is necessary to think carefully about the alliances and resources that an actual reform process will require.

There are considerable assets for a democratic reform agenda. Public support for good, public higher education remains strong, despite the political ascendancy of market agendas and the high-profile attacks on science and education in recent years. The social need for advanced education and new knowledge remains; indeed, in the perspective of the coming climate catastrophe, that need is growing. The coming decades will not be easy but change for good is possible. The ideas found in this book are much needed.

Sydney, Australia, 1 November 2022

The last word:
"Making noises through our work"

Jyoti Arora

I have recently encountered the profound concept of "triquetra" used in the German science fiction thriller series on time travel titled *Dark*. Triquetra is the symbol used in ancient Nordic, Celtic, German, and Japanese cultures; composed of three interlaced arcs, it has many interpretations. It often represents the interconnectedness of past, present and future and sometimes of different worlds. It also reflects unity, protection and eternity of life. This is where this book has transfixed me with interconnectedness in the higher education sector (with its own past, present and future) and its interdependence on other sectors. Higher education, especially the public sector, is facing crises in the form of austerity, inequality, inertia and lack of quality education. The COVID-19 pandemic has unfolded disturbing truths about higher education and reminded us that nothing exists in isolation and "everything is connected with everything else" — also referred to as the first law of ecology. The uncertainty and crisis were exacerbated by the war between Ukraine and Russia as well as severe climate changes witnessed by different parts of the world, resulting in exploration of more and alternative resources. None of us, the stakeholders in HE, remain indifferent or untouched by these events. The crisis which HE was already experiencing in pre-COVID-19 times turned into giant waves in the last few years, some demanding immediate routes to navigate. This is where we must learn from history — that human species can transform the crisis for human emancipation and must break deadlocks.

This book has investigated the crisis of HE by critically discussing a wide range of themes: critical pedagogy, reflexive pedagogy, public good, common-community good, commodification of HE, internationalisation of HE, digital pedagogy, ICT and AI in HE, inclusive education, ethics, pedagogy of care and more, connecting markets, state and academic oligarchy.[1] The book has opened a Pandora's box of the higher education sector, looking at HE as a whole more than its parts.

The book has raised important questions about the aim and role of HE which I think should centre around the well-being and happiness of youth, enabling them to strive towards their higher potential[2] and empowering each life as "life-long learners" to explore and innovate solutions for the problems (micro and macro) that humanity is grappling with at large. However, when it centres around the narrow goal of receiving credentials based on the "skills" to gain employment, the transformation of critical minds for human emancipation remains dubious. This reflection is pertinent in these times when markets and new public management (NPM) are guiding the outcomes of HE and we, the students, are considered as "products". What worries me as a young scholar is not the opportunity cost of pursuing higher education, but the uncertainties in HE, the dynamic and newer demands of HE and the trade-offs between global, national, and local aspirations in HE. These all create pressures on us young scholars to make ourselves "visible" in the academy, visible enough to get placed with permanent tenure (rather than working as adjunct faculty or researchers) and to "deliver" the expectations of the HE market. Who sets these expectations or targets? Who is "capable" of achieving these targets? Do these targets acknowledge and respect my social reality? Do we have a level playing field for everyone in the HE sector? Is the role of faculty or researcher just to teach enough and publish to meet time-bound targets? Once we are conscious of the broader aims of higher education, it will take us to the next step to discover new possibilities and alternatives for sustainable futures by understanding our roles and responsibilities as educators, researchers, and students.

Another central concern which the book has invoked is the crisis of public universities and "publicness" in HE. Around the world, including in India, austerity in HE has created tensions between expanding access and universalising HE, especially for public HEIs which are dependent

---

1   The three vertices of Burton Clark's Triangle
2   Based on the principles of Soka Education

on the state for resources. There is pressure on public HEIs in India to initiate self-financed courses and collaborations to generate revenues. The bigger question is who will lose more or who will get "pushed out of the system?" Which institutions will thrive, and which will perish? Also, the austerity experienced by the sector is impacting students who are in genuine need and demotivating them to enter or continue HE. In India, there are cuts and delays in scholarships for students from disadvantaged sections of society. Moreover, New Education Policy (NEP) 2020 proposed education financed through loans, disregarding the socioeconomic inequalities in India and lessons derived from developed countries like the USA. While scholars like me who are working in the disciplines of social sciences and humanities struggle to get funding and other support, STEM programs are relatively well funded (for both teaching and research) as they are perceived (by state and markets) to contribute directly to "knowledge production".

One of my takeaways from this book is about creating inclusive spaces for voices of the powerless, minorities, and disadvantaged. We need to co-create structures for discourses which are not elite or even mainstream as what is widely accepted by the majority is not the only marker of "knowledge". If we succeed in embracing the diversity of people and perspectives, I think HE will provide us opportunities to come together to collaborate and learn the facets which are still hidden beneath the commonly accepted domains of knowledge. This would help us to challenge and enrich already accepted knowledge. We also must prepare ourselves to deal with classrooms having learners with diverse needs and contexts — a learner who could be a refugee, differently-abled, transgender, first-generation, Black, and/or poor. This diversity is more nuanced for developing countries like India where dimensions of caste, religion and language are added. India is struggling to understand these needs and diversity and possible approaches to restructuring institutions. However, the process is very slow. As faculty, I would reimagine myself as a reflexive agent and have empathy and compassion for my companions who do not have the opportunity to negotiate, in order to meet their needs. In addition, we must develop flexible forms of learning as well as learning environments and assessments to embrace inclusivity in our systems. This is certainly very demanding terrain. I think "assessment and evaluation" as an area has received less attention than needed in the discourse of HE. It is critical to question here, as this book has, the purpose of assessment: What do we want to assess? Why do we want to assess? What do we want to achieve through this assessment? Is it possible to objectively assess the subjective realities of learners?

Technology and AI have emerged as powerful tools in the 21st century to create flexible structures in HE. It has helped to break the physical barriers of distance and expand learning and collaboration, especially for first-generation learners and students who are at the margins. Many of my friends, including me, could attend lectures, webinars and conferences organised by reputed institutions almost for free or relatively less cost during the pandemic lockdowns. In this way, technology opened paths to access and tapped into opportunities, especially for scholars in developing countries. Moreover, open and online distance learning has emerged as one of the alternatives for continuing life-long learning and has the potential to address inequalities to some extent, thus contributing to SDG 4, the sustainable development goal to ensure inclusive quality education.[3] It has certainly widened access to digital resources although at the same the digital market is differentiated by quality and cost. Furthermore, revenue generation may be based on the branding of the service providers rather than the quality of the resources.

This book has provoked me to ask these questions — this is also good! Who can access technology and who cannot? Who has the power or control over its design, availability, and usage? Should knowledge be free? Is technology inclusive? Are we focusing on building digital capabilities embedded in ethics, care, and justice? Are faculty trained to meet changing roles and expectations given digital and 'glonacal'[4] interfaces? What's happening with edtech — mergers and acquisitions — moving towards oligopoly and monopoly rather than having a competitive market? How to ensure quality and credibility? How are state policies pushing edtech recklessly and what is its impact

---

3   Sustainable Development Goal 4 (SDG 4) aims to "ensure inclusive and equitable quality education and promote lifelong learning opportunities for all."
4   The term 'glonacal' [glonacal = global + national + local] (p. 177) is borrowed from Marginson, S. (2004). Competition and Markets in Higher Education: A 'Glonacal' Analysis. *Policy Futures in Education*, 2(2), 175–284, https://doi.org/10.2304/pfie.2004.2.2.2

on sustainability in HE? Certainly, there is no "one" concrete answer to each of these questions. There are great opportunities and scope in the domain of technology in HE, but there is no escape from the need to regulate it. This is where the role of a nation state is crucial — to regulate the "bull" of technology for credible, quality, and affordable online education which can be accessed by all. Moreover, with rampant increases in technology in HE, the boundaries between the private and public sector are blurring. This will impact the future and "publicness" of HE.

I have no intention of saying that technology is a substitute for a university. For instance, many of my friends could not afford to buy a laptop or access the internet during the COVID-19 lockdowns and could not access educational resources from their homes. There was significant time lost on their research since they were dependent on university premises to access digital infrastructure. Also, most of us missed interacting with our peers or colleagues and literally prayed for lockdowns to end. Human interaction beyond virtual boundaries is important for us as social animals and no level of AI can replace this essence. The university has its own life and culture beyond classrooms and the "expected learning outcomes" of our academic program, like discussions over coffee and tea, students' elections, cultural programs and fests, conferences, seminars, etc. The transformations that we experience over time by being in the university are the lessons which were never deliberately taught nor explicitly learned, but which shape us — our personality, thoughts, aspirations. This is where this book has questioned the extent to which technology and AI can support lifelong learning and why the very existence of the university is crucial. There is a need to use these tools wisely and cautiously to empower educators and learners, and not pose threats to their privacy and rights.

Furthermore, this book has also made me, a student of economics, doubt (and yeah "doubting" is good!) some of the basic assumptions of economics — the belief that we can determine or develop a path with the highest possible equilibrium, balancing resources, political culture, policies, and other factors. Clearly, there is no one future but alternative futures which are not deterministic, and we all aspire towards better combinations over time. These combinations are different for different individuals and groups, and no one set of parameters can clearly define or assess "the ideal" or "the best" — which is what ranking agencies try to do. Higher education for good, unlike any other commodity, cannot be replicated. Human capital is embedded, and the best is always in process of evolution — from its own past, towards its own future in its own world. Hence, imitating successful strategies and confining them in an index of scores ignores the untold success stories of people and systems who evolved them. Every ranking agency follows its own perception of a good institution and best outcomes. But what is missed is the "process" which is unique to its own context. The best itself is in process, unforeseen and evolving. There could be lessons, different models to strive towards better systems, but rankings cannot be ends in themselves. Such myopic ideas of higher education and university are detrimental rather than striving to improve quality.

I think there is a need to "open" or reopen the democratic spaces within the universities where non-formal talks among peers and students have their own mandates or urgency, but which has become lost in universities' neoliberal processes. Formal spaces in universities have been captured by research outputs, and formal and regulated conversations in the "managed" universities. It is the non-formal deliberations, dialogues or talks which also shape and ignite ideas and creativity in young scholars. This reminds me of John Nash (from the movie *A Beautiful Mind*) who had the thirst to find "path-breaking" ideas in game theory. He found this by observing real patterns and conversing with his friends in the classroom. This book has provided us, the authors, and readers precisely this: the freedom to choose these non-formal spaces to freely express our thoughts and reflections through different genres (articles, poetry, stories, reflective cases, etc.), provocations and a range of ideas centring around the broader theme of HE for good that embarks on or ignites creativity.

So where is the *hope*? Borrowing from another interpretation of triquetra, hope is in finding union and harmony when faced with opposing forces (global, national, local) and dualistic manifestations in higher education from within or outside. Hope is right here. In other words, 'hope' is in resistance, resilience and reimagination, as this book argues. To me, it lies in the resistance from the past (opposite forces), resilience in the present (towards recovery) and reimagination of the future. It is in reimagining the idea of university transcending "infrastructures of extraction" to that of "infrastructures of care" without which we will not be able to take care of people and the planet. It is in reexamining the mission and futures of the university and not surrendering the public good, community good and global good character of HE. I agree that we must imagine futures that people do not know but need to know and have the right to know. When we, young scholars, talk of hope we must remind ourselves that we owe responsibility and debt towards future generations to hand over the planet at least better than what it is at the present. Every possible effort should be made to make the world a better place. I think we must safeguard the "publicness" of HE by creating noises for policy makers and managers of HE, and we must continue making these noises through our work as this book has done, especially when there are attacks on democratic spaces to suppress our voices. Let's continue striving with such endeavours with even more vigour and let's continue shaking the universe of HE through our ideas and the power of words to explore more pathways towards HE for good.

Acknowledgements: I extend my gratitude to the editors of the book, Prof. Laura and Dr. Catherine; copy editor, Larry Erhuvwuokhene Onokpite; Prof. Saumen Chattopadhyay and Dr. Binay Kumar Pathak for their guidance and valuable comments.

New Delhi, India, 1 October 2022

Index

Aboriginal 240, 355, 361–362
Aboriginal Country 362
abyssal line 101, 150
access 41, 47, 60, 65, 67, 118, 128, 147, 149, 151, 153, 161–163, 167, 170–172, 175–178, 206, 211, 213, 218–220, 244, 255, 298–299, 304–305, 310–312, 318, 320, 322–325, 328, 337, 340–341, 343, 345, 373–376, 381, 384, 386, 409, 413, 422, 434, 438–439, 445, 452, 459, 496–502, 542, 557–559, 561, 564, 570, 579, 583, 586–587, 612, 628, 630–631
accessible, accessibility 112, 123, 213, 221, 240, 243, 298, 304, 310, 312, 323, 325, 328, 335, 344, 346–348, 373, 375–376, 378–382, 384–385, 387–390, 397–398, 408–409, 474, 497–498, 539, 557, 562–563, 580, 586–587, 611, 613–614, 619
Acknowledging Country 362–363
Adivasi 140
Adorno, Theodor W. 103
Africa 57, 63, 152, 203, 207, 209, 212, 217, 220, 227–229, 257, 307, 379, 447, 494, 496, 509–511, 516, 527
African 145–146, 152–153, 203, 207, 217–218, 226–229, 304–305, 309, 447, 459, 492, 496, 500, 509, 511, 514, 517, 525–526
Africanfuturist science fiction 46, 445, 447, 449, 459
Afrofuturist 447
Afropolitanism 138, 152

Akesson, Jimmie 70
America 55, 63, 67–68, 70, 216, 227, 309, 377–378, 434
American 57, 59, 61, 68–69, 71, 118, 227, 354, 378, 607
Americanization 57
Angola 200, 206, 208–209, 212–215, 218, 228–229
Anthropocene 153
Arendt, Hannah 96–97, 505
Arendtian 98
Aristotle 142
artificial intelligence (AI) 42, 126–127, 239–250, 252–259, 329–330, 503, 628, 630–631
Ashoka East Africa 511, 518, 524–525, 528
Asia 36, 63, 217, 253, 379, 559
Asian Institute for Distance Education (AIDE) 559
assemblage 245, 267, 270–273, 276–277, 279–287
assessment 43, 112, 139–141, 148–149, 175, 183–184, 195, 239, 243, 246, 259, 323, 326, 337, 340, 342–344, 401, 404, 410–412, 483, 512, 517, 520–521, 523, 527, 533–550, 629–630
Association for Faculty Enrichment in Learning and Teaching (AFELT) 512, 525–526, 528
Association for Learning Technology (ALT) 275, 284, 407
Athabasca University 255

Auckland, University of 115
austerity 41, 53, 56–57, 59, 62, 65–66, 92, 97–98, 243, 354, 609, 627–629
Australia 48, 56, 63, 69, 216, 240, 253, 256, 276, 353–354, 357–362, 407, 579, 626
Australian 114, 240, 245, 256–257, 353–363, 365–366
authoritarianism 69–70, 94, 98, 144, 189, 477

Baldwin, James 40, 53–54, 72
Becker, Gary 174
Binti 447–458, 460–462, 464–465
biomimicry 399
Black 60, 71, 117–118, 140, 204, 450, 629
Black Lives Matter 117
blended learning 328, 340, 387, 389, 519, 560–561, 565
blended, online, and open learning (BOL) 557–559, 561–563, 565–571
Bolsonaro, Jair 70
borders, crossing borders 42, 49, 280, 297, 353–354, 357–358, 407
Brazil 69, 200, 209, 215, 229, 421, 425–426, 429–430, 432, 434–435, 437, 623
Brazilian 204, 213, 421–422, 425, 430
British 117, 318, 362, 450, 510, 550
Brod, Max 95
Brown University 68
Butler, Octavia 45, 50, 102–104, 451

Caffentzis, C. G. 165, 167
California 219
California at Berkeley, University of 60–61, 172
Cambodia 69
Canada 48, 56, 71, 115, 119, 144, 276, 317–318, 330, 407
Canadian 114, 119, 319, 330, 617
Cape Town, University of (UCT) 38, 204–205, 220, 373, 381, 383, 385–386, 388–390, 586
capitalism 44, 50, 58, 59, 63, 65, 67, 100, 111, 116, 117, 121, 124, 125, 161, 172, 176, 179, 190, 191, 192, 194, 196, 200, 203, 271, 287, 408, 424, 434, 445, 452. *See also* surveillance capitalism
care 43–44, 47–51, 55, 59, 72, 84, 87, 111, 113, 116–117, 121, 125–130, 208, 225–226, 230, 239–240, 243, 252, 267, 272, 278–281, 287, 292, 296, 298–299, 302, 319, 326, 328, 340, 355, 359, 363–364, 387, 397, 406, 409–410, 445, 448, 466, 473–474, 476–481, 483–486, 496, 500, 504, 541, 543, 547, 550, 584, 603–604, 608, 617, 619, 628, 630, 633
CARE principles 126
Caribbean 118, 474
caring pedagogy 474, 476–477, 481, 483–486
Center for Applied Special Technology (CAST) 328, 376–377, 409
Central Florida, University of 68
Chandler, Alfred 172
ChatGPT 205, 241, 243–244, 246, 259
Chicago, University of 174
Chile 34, 58
China 61, 119, 168, 214–215, 217–218
Chinese 201, 218, 379
Christian 68, 200
City University of New York (CUNY) 62
climate crisis 99, 344, 496–497
coalition 49, 69
Codrington, Christopher 118
Cold War 68, 213–214
collaboration 37, 129, 178, 249, 259, 284, 308, 336, 339, 347–348, 387–389, 398, 405–407, 414–415, 428, 436, 483, 494–495, 499, 518, 548, 565–567, 570, 578, 581, 629–630
colonialism 41, 46, 125, 144–147, 150, 356, 374–375, 380, 424–425, 435, 452
coloniality 41, 355
Commission on Higher Education (CHED) 557–558, 560–565, 569
commodification 100, 113, 118–119, 151, 154, 183, 188, 190, 196, 578, 628
common good 44, 98, 138, 141, 146, 152–154, 184, 187, 303, 310–313, 496, 504, 538

common pool resource (CPR) 166–167, 169, 175
commons 44, 63, 161–162, 164–170, 172–173, 175–180, 188–190, 196, 286, 458, 498
communality 49, 538
community 44–46, 48–50, 55, 60–62, 85, 88, 98, 114–117, 125–127, 129–130, 138, 142–143, 147, 151, 162, 166–169, 171, 176, 185–186, 189–190, 218, 221, 241, 273, 282, 286, 298, 301, 303, 306, 308–313, 319–323, 325, 328–330, 332, 345, 354, 359, 361, 364–367, 375–377, 383, 387, 397, 399, 401–402, 406–408, 410, 414, 429–430, 432, 480, 482–483, 492–496, 499–502, 504, 509–512, 514, 518, 523–524, 527, 533, 536–539, 541, 543, 547–548, 558–559, 562, 568, 581, 585, 587, 611–612, 615, 620, 625, 628, 633
competition 49, 96, 116, 119, 121, 169, 175, 178, 365, 424, 449, 474, 484, 536, 541, 547, 570, 578
ConferênciaWeb 436
Connell, Raewyn 45, 48, 146, 149–150, 354–355, 359, 362, 616, 623–626
Conservative Party (UK) 57
control 58, 70, 86, 98, 111, 115–116, 123–128, 179, 183–184, 192, 225, 267, 327, 428, 438–439, 454, 541, 569, 624, 630
Cottom, Tressie McMillan 60, 73
COVID-19 31–32, 55–56, 65, 92, 111, 121, 183, 202, 215, 219–220, 225, 239, 269, 272, 276, 284–286, 308, 317, 339–340, 346–347, 381, 386, 389, 398, 403, 421–422, 424, 432–436, 481, 485, 526, 536, 558, 560, 569, 603, 624, 627, 631
critical 38, 91–92, 137–142, 147, 154, 202, 209, 221, 241, 244, 247–248, 278, 308, 317, 319, 340, 398, 421, 423, 437, 440, 447–448, 450, 453, 475, 477–486, 494, 496, 499, 501, 504–505, 516, 519, 523, 540–541, 568, 606, 614, 628
  approach 41, 50, 101, 125, 138–139, 148, 151–152, 154, 246, 268, 331, 397, 421–423, 436, 475, 481, 495, 497, 500, 505, 516
  literacies 72, 491, 494, 501, 503–505
  pedagogy 92, 154, 330, 473–474, 476–478, 480–481, 483–486, 494, 627
  thinking 54, 92, 151, 195, 207, 246, 259, 303, 337, 510, 512–513, 520, 522
Croucher, Gwilym 359
curriculum 41, 63, 68, 70, 121, 137–143, 145, 148–154, 189, 215, 217, 227, 307, 312, 328, 342, 344, 375–377, 379, 381, 384, 389, 401, 425, 479, 486, 515, 544–545, 565, 567, 610, 616, 624
cursing 42, 91, 95–96

darkness 42, 68, 90–95, 98–100, 104–105, 196, 217, 294
Dartmouth, University of 67
data collection 124–125, 217, 257, 322, 432–433
data colonialism 125, 424–425, 435, 452
data extraction 41, 124–125, 424–425
data justice 41–42, 239–241, 250, 252–253, 259, 453, 491, 495–496, 505
data literacies 33, 41, 343, 453, 491, 494–496, 500–505
decolonisation 41, 93, 100–102, 128, 137–138, 141, 143–145, 147–148, 150–154, 227, 318, 355, 375, 389, 415, 457, 459
decolonising knowledge(s) 137–138, 147–148, 152, 459
democratic 45, 62, 69, 93, 97, 99, 101–102, 104–105, 139, 151, 172, 195, 449, 462, 475, 558, 623–625, 632–633
design justice 43, 47, 373–377, 382–384, 389, 458
de Sousa Santos, B. 47, 101, 145–146, 150
Dewey, J. 97–98, 397
digital education 42, 121, 335, 401, 548, 606, 616
digital literacies 328, 384, 400, 423, 557, 569
digital pragmatism 397
digital transformations 317–318, 609, 616

disciplinary contexts 42, 98, 115, 124, 130, 141, 149, 152, 224, 309, 341, 343, 373, 426, 534, 538, 543, 564
distance education (DE) 559–560, 563, 565, 567
Dodoma, University of 510–511, 518–522, 524
Douglass, Frederick 118

East Africa 496, 509–511, 516, 527
ecosystem 297, 299–300, 302, 501, 557, 559, 561–568, 570–571
educational technology advisors (ETAs) 373, 380–383, 385–389
educational technology/ies 243, 250, 268, 317, 329, 373, 423–424, 431, 435–437, 441, 562, 603–604, 606–607
Eltahawy, Mona 96
emergence, emergent 39, 57, 89, 117, 125, 128, 144, 152, 162, 164, 171, 174, 179, 191, 199, 206, 218–219, 223, 241, 256–257, 268, 270, 272–273, 276, 306, 317, 326–327, 335, 340, 342, 348, 386, 399, 408, 411, 414–415, 421–422, 431–433, 475, 512, 518–519, 526–527, 541, 578–579, 584–585, 614, 630
emergency remote teaching (ERT) 422, 424
England 36, 146, 217, 269
English 36, 48, 53–54, 206, 215, 305, 383, 451, 501
Enhancing Digital Teaching and Learning 336–341, 407
Enlightenment 99, 144
epistemic pluralism 113, 118, 126, 128
epistemology 44, 116, 150, 538
equality 97, 104, 189, 220
equity 43, 47, 57, 82, 101, 118, 149, 151, 227, 239–240, 242, 244, 247–248, 305, 327–329, 373, 376, 379, 386, 389, 414, 445, 475, 494, 517, 521, 523, 539, 587, 614, 619
ethics 41, 44, 49, 99, 102, 116–117, 126–127, 140, 142, 145, 147, 153–154, 221, 239–240, 242, 246, 248, 250, 252–253, 255–258, 276, 278–279, 287, 309, 312, 322, 357, 363–364, 375, 475, 511, 522, 533, 535, 539, 543, 548–550, 558, 579, 603, 605–608, 612, 614, 617–619, 628, 630
ethics of care 44, 116, 239–240, 252
Eurocentrism 152
Europe 63, 69, 144, 151, 168, 215–216, 228, 276, 371, 377–378, 400, 447, 494, 581
European 115, 119, 128, 144, 215, 227, 345, 378, 459
exclusion 41, 46–47, 100, 112, 139–140, 143, 145–147, 154, 203, 208, 252, 311, 358, 373–375, 380, 387, 390, 479, 502, 539, 615
extractive, extraction 41–42, 72, 101, 111–114, 116–119, 121–125, 127–130, 144, 146, 360, 421, 424–425, 435, 603, 606, 633

Facebook 423, 426, 429, 439
fascism 69, 101, 435
FastTrain College 69
#FeesMustFall 381, 384
FemEdTech 49–50, 267–277, 279–284, 286–287, 407
  Quilt of Care and Justice in Open Education 49, 267–269, 279, 281, 407
feminism 49, 96, 268–269, 271–273, 275, 278–279, 286–287, 459
Filipino 563, 567
Finland 69, 542, 546
First Nation, First Nations 71, 240
Fitzpatrick, Kathleen 354, 363, 365
Flagler College 68
Fleming, Peter 91, 93–94, 99
Florida 68
FLOSS (Free/Libre and Open Source Software) 426–427, 429, 432, 436, 440–441
Forsyth, Hannah 359, 550
France 69, 215, 217
Frank, Arthur 354, 356–357, 365
Franklin, Ursula 112, 128–129
Fraser, Nancy 117, 275, 374, 376
Free and Autonomous University of San Francisco 190

Freirean 475, 479
Freire, Paulo 50, 72, 195–196, 421, 436, 475, 479, 494, 504, 516
future, futures 38–39, 43, 45–47, 50, 63, 72–73, 81, 91, 94, 96–97, 99, 124, 147, 152, 174, 179, 189, 195, 201, 204, 206–207, 210–212, 216, 224–226, 228, 230, 241, 271, 275, 277, 291, 303–313, 317–329, 331, 335–336, 338–339, 341–348, 353–354, 356–357, 362–366, 372, 380, 385–387, 390, 412, 421, 424, 427–428, 431, 436–438, 440–441, 445–450, 452–453, 457–460, 462, 475–476, 486, 504, 513, 516, 518, 533–536, 545, 547, 549, 556–557, 577–578, 580, 583, 606, 609, 619, 624–625, 627–628, 630–633

GAFAM 426, 428, 432, 437, 439
Galway, University of 412
generosity 44, 189, 353, 355, 364–367, 390, 449
Georgetown University 118
German 67, 447, 451, 627
Germany 253, 447, 623
Ghana 227, 379
gift, gifting 44, 60, 68, 92, 95, 102, 104, 113–114, 116, 183–188, 191, 193, 196, 482
Gilliard, Chris 124, 243, 247
Giroux, Henry 59, 98, 196
Glaude Jr, Eddie S. 53
globalism 91
Global North 31, 48, 138, 257, 307, 374, 379–380, 388, 425, 498–499
Global South 31, 307, 373–374, 377–380, 384, 388–390, 424–425, 435, 491, 498
Google 202–203, 205, 213, 228, 257, 423, 426, 432, 434, 438, 521
governance 44, 111, 118, 121, 123, 126–127, 139, 164, 166, 169, 176, 178, 189–190, 241, 243–244, 246, 253–255, 257–259, 307, 354, 361–362, 435, 514–515, 525, 558, 606–607, 612, 625
Gramsci, Antonio 195
Grawe, Nathan D. 64–65
Greek 35–36, 142, 353
Gulu University 510–511, 519–525

haiku 39, 46, 199, 201
Haraway, Donna 355, 363–364, 446, 455
Harvard University 56, 118, 226
Harvey, Caitlan 115–116
#HE4Good 43, 81, 240, 267, 285, 287, 292, 297–300, 335–337, 345, 348, 500
Heaney, Seamus 92, 105
higher education institutions 43, 49, 111–114, 120–121, 123–124, 163–165, 168–179, 557–562, 564–566, 569–570, 575–587, 628–629
Hillsdale College 68
Himba 448, 450–452
historically Black colleges and universities (HBCUs) 71
Hong Kong 253, 546
Honig, Bonnie 97–99, 104–105
hope 35–37, 39, 42, 45–46, 50, 53–54, 71–72, 82–83, 85–86, 91–93, 95, 100, 104–105, 140, 183–184, 195–196, 210, 228–229, 278–280, 285, 287, 292, 302, 323–324, 327, 347, 355, 372, 385, 402, 423, 437, 448, 457, 505, 509, 516, 580, 587, 607–608, 619, 632–633
hospitality 113, 128, 357
human capital theory (HCT) 174–175, 177
Hyde, Lewis 185–186, 193, 196

identity 112, 130, 142, 221, 275, 304, 320, 363, 380, 477, 533
Illinois, University of 60
imagination 38–40, 42, 44–47, 50–51, 68, 82, 87–88, 100, 137, 162–163, 176, 184, 189, 191, 195–196, 201, 206, 221, 223, 230, 279, 295, 298, 302, 306, 308–310, 313, 327, 330, 338, 340, 354–356, 362–363, 367, 385, 390, 448–452, 454, 456, 458, 460, 462, 519, 527–528, 545, 619, 625, 633
INASP 511–512, 525–526, 528
inclusion, inclusivity 43, 118–119, 128, 146, 202, 227, 254, 305, 327, 329, 341, 373, 376, 378–379, 381, 385–386, 389, 397, 408–409, 524, 583, 587, 614, 629
India 56–57, 61, 69, 119, 139–140, 168, 576, 579, 582–584, 587, 623, 628–629, 633

Indian 61, 115, 217, 575–576, 579, 587
Indigenous knowledge systems, ways of knowing, philosophies 44, 48, 116, 126–127, 143, 146, 278, 308–309, 312, 318–319, 329–330, 447
Indigenous land, sovereignty 102, 114–115, 125–126, 361, 492–493, 499–500
Indigenous peoples, communities, cultures 44, 48, 71, 114–118, 125–127, 245, 279, 304–305, 330, 363, 377, 457, 625
individualism 49, 93, 174, 397, 440, 534–539, 544, 547–548
  hyperindividualism 445
Industrial Revolution 162, 170
inequality, inequity 41, 92, 97, 103, 121, 144, 165, 176, 194, 199, 219, 224, 250, 257, 304, 312, 374, 384, 424, 435, 448, 503, 562, 625, 627
infrastructure 41, 58, 67, 111–115, 117–123, 126–130, 177, 202, 209, 214, 298, 325, 328, 347–348, 356, 359, 413, 424, 432, 434, 445, 499–504, 521, 561–562, 569, 582, 631–633
infrastructures of care 111, 113, 117, 126–129, 633
Instagram 112, 429, 437–438
instructional design 173, 175, 397
intellectual property (IP) 174–175, 177, 258
Intergovernmental Panel on Climate Change (IPCC) 194, 207
international students 119–120, 128, 341, 354–355, 357–360, 366
intersectionality 37
intimate scholarship 476
Ireland 38, 96, 155, 335, 337–340, 344, 347, 398, 407, 460, 556, 623
Irish 47, 105, 336–339, 341–343, 345–346, 348, 407, 412
Irish Universities Association (IUA) 337, 346, 407
isiXhosa 235, 383
Islamic 168
Italian 297, 497

Italy 69, 294, 297, 497
Ivy League 60, 67, 623

Jamaica 474, 476, 484, 486, 623
Jamaican 474, 476–477, 486
Jansen, Jonathan 27–30, 203–204
Japan 69, 168, 199
Japanese 199, 627
Jesuit 118
Jewish 272
Jhangiani, Rajiv 65, 73
Jitsi 436
Joint Advisory Groups (JAGs) 518, 522, 524
justice 37, 40–43, 46–47, 51, 55, 58–59, 69, 85, 87, 117, 128, 145, 147, 151, 153, 194, 239–241, 250, 252–255, 259, 272, 275, 278–279, 281, 305, 312, 329, 331, 373–377, 382–384, 389–390, 413, 415, 445–446, 449, 453, 456, 458–459, 475, 491, 494–496, 503–505, 545, 548–549, 575, 587, 630

Kafka, Franz 95
Kantian 142
Keatsian 100
Kent, University of 388
Kenya 57, 491–492, 497, 511–512
Kenyan 494, 501
Kerr, Clark 172, 202
Keynesian 98
Khoush 448, 450, 452
Klein, Naomi 65, 125, 501, 607
Knight, Phil 68, 286
knowledge commons 44, 63, 161–162, 164, 167–170, 172, 175–179, 458
knowledge factory 162, 171, 173–179
Korea 168

La Bellacasa, Maria Puig de 355, 363–364
Labour Party (UK) 57
landscape 46, 49, 64, 70, 293–297, 301–302, 324, 336, 355, 360, 415, 421, 440–441, 502, 533, 583, 609
large language models (LLMs) 241
Latin 200, 272
Latin America 58, 117, 150, 379, 423, 501

Latin American 70
learning analytics (LA) 241–242, 245, 250, 255
learning design 326, 377, 385, 397–398, 402, 408–409, 412, 414, 526
Learning Management Systems (LMS) 111, 121–124, 243, 382–383, 385, 609, 613
Learning, Teaching and Research model (LTRM) 318–319, 331
Le Guin, Ursula 292, 459
Lerman, Liz 449, 457
Lorde, Audre 46
low- and middle-income countries (LMICs) 380
Lowe, Roy 162–164, 168
Lula (Luiz Inácio Lula da Silva) 70

manifesto 39, 50, 354, 413, 426–429
Māori 126, 278–280
Markov Chain poem 269–270, 277, 279, 286
Marxian 189
Marxist 44, 188, 275
Massey, Doreen 354, 356
massification (of higher education) 239, 241, 249, 578
massive open distance e-learning (MODeL) 560
massive open online courses (MOOCs) 560, 565, 583, 586–587
Mauritius 200, 204, 206, 208, 216–218
Mbembe, Achille 41, 44, 98, 145, 152–153, 375, 458
Mead, George Herbert 357, 398
Meduse 448, 454–456
Microsoft 202, 256, 426, 432–434, 436, 438
Moodle 121, 436
Morgan, Edwin 279
Morrill Act 1862 71
Murray, John 412
Mussolini, Benito 195
Mzumbe University 510–511, 521–522, 524

Nairobi 491, 494
neoliberalism 40–41, 57–60, 65, 67–71, 81, 91–93, 95–100, 102–103, 105, 141, 144, 151, 174–175, 191, 199, 267, 271, 276, 285, 338, 434, 474, 547, 632
Netherlands, the 69, 217
New Education Policy (NEP) 629
New Public Goods theory 101
New Zealand 114–115, 276
Nextcloud 436
Ngati Awa people 115
Nike 68
Nike, University of 68

Oceania 379
Okorafor, Nnedi 46, 445, 447, 449–450, 452–454, 456–458
Online Program Management (OPM) 67
OnlyOffice 436
Oomza University 447–448, 451–454, 456
open access 33, 162, 178, 213, 220, 579
OpenAI 244
open and distance e-learning (ODeL) 560
open and distance learning (ODL) 557–560, 563, 565–566
open educational practices (OEP) 427
open educational resources (OER) 162, 175, 178, 281, 389, 426, 492, 494, 500, 586
open education (OE) 426
open knowledge institutions (OKIs) 49, 575–576, 579–587
open learning 557, 567, 570
openness 42, 44, 49–50, 210, 243, 275, 364, 379, 421, 448, 476, 494, 499, 575, 578, 583
open pedagogies 162, 178, 275
Oregon, University of 60, 68
Ostrom, Elinor 165–167, 176, 188–189

Padlet 383
Papa Reo project 126
pedagogy, pedagogies 44, 48, 91, 92, 93, 99, 100, 116, 152, 162, 178, 183,

184, 186, 189, 190, 191, 196, 204, 205, 220, 225, 226, 275, 318, 323, 330, 379, 384, 388, 389, 397, 410, 415, 425, 473, 474, 476, 477, 478, 480, 481, 483, 484, 485, 486, 494, 516, 517, 520, 558, 559, 603, 606, 607, 608, 610, 616, 624, 627, 628. *See also* teaching pedagogies; *See also* open pedagogies
  pedagogy of care 48, 225–226, 410, 477, 628
  pedagogy of hyperlinkages 204
Persia 168
Philippine 558–560, 562–564, 570
Philippines, the 69, 557, 559, 561–563, 566, 569–570
Philippines, University of the (UP) 559–561, 563–565
Platform as a Service (PaaS) 424, 434
platformization 243, 421, 424–428, 430, 434–436, 439–440, 446
podcast 46, 286, 293, 343, 411, 436, 459
poetry 39, 46, 51, 54, 82, 86, 199–200, 208, 269–270, 277–281, 286, 462, 623, 632
Polytechnic University of the Philippines (PUP) 559
populism 69
positionality 142, 206, 321, 330
post-colonialism 141
postcolonialism 100, 137, 305, 380, 474
postdigital 415
power structures 37, 85, 168, 170, 184, 397–398, 503
prior learning assessment and review (PLAR) 326
privatisation 57–58, 65–66, 98, 177, 188, 360, 623
procurement 603–605, 607–616, 618–619
public good 44, 57–59, 62, 91–93, 98–103, 124, 128, 139, 142, 153, 188, 250, 308, 310, 338, 549–550, 587, 627, 633

Quacquarelli Symonds Ltd (QS) 120

Raworth, Kate 176
reciprocity 113, 123, 193, 308, 365, 496, 499, 504

reflexive, reflexivity 151, 268, 509, 513, 535, 539–540, 544–545, 549–550, 571, 627, 629
refugees 35–36, 125, 128, 204, 240, 629
reparations 100, 113, 125, 128, 363
resistance 39–40, 42–43, 45, 81, 83, 86, 95–96, 102–103, 118–119, 127, 138, 150, 196, 271, 285–287, 372, 380, 421, 423, 436, 440, 457, 479, 482, 485, 521–522, 632
#RhodesMustFall 117–118, 217, 381
Rich, Adrienne 53–54, 71–72
Rosa, Hartmut 191–193
Royal Roads University (RRU) 317–319, 331
Russia 128, 627

scholarship of teaching and learning (SoTL) 240
Schultz, Theodore 174
Silicon Valley 42, 432, 502
Skinner, B. F. 242
slavery 117–119, 474, 607
social good 162, 165, 170, 527, 533–534, 536, 539, 541, 543–545, 549–550
social imaginaries 102, 162, 163
social justice 37, 69, 85, 153, 194, 241, 253, 255, 259, 275, 305, 312, 374, 376–377, 389–390, 445, 494–496, 503, 505, 545, 548–549, 575, 587
Software as a Service (SaaS) 424, 434
South Africa 38, 47, 61, 92, 116, 138–140, 144, 151, 200, 203–204, 207–212, 217, 219, 276, 303–305, 312, 374, 379, 623
South African 151, 203–204, 207, 209–212, 220, 228, 305, 381, 384
Southeast Asia Interdisciplinary Development Institute (SAIDI) 559
Spain 69
Special Interest Groups (SIGs) 397
speculative futures 318–321, 327–328, 331, 458
speculative methods 46, 317
Spinoza, Baruch 272

state universities and colleges (SUCs) 561, 563–566
State University of Minas Gerais (UEMG) 422, 427, 429, 432
storytelling 223, 356, 412, 446, 448, 457, 556
Strategic Partnerships for Higher Education Innovation and Reform programme (SPHEIR) 510, 528
student information system (SIS) 401
students 38–39, 41–42, 46–48, 51, 54–56, 58–69, 71–72, 86–87, 90, 94, 100, 102–103, 112, 114, 118–125, 127–129, 140–142, 145, 148–149, 151–154, 171, 173, 179, 183–184, 186–191, 195, 199–202, 204–213, 215–228, 239–255, 258–259, 287, 293, 298–299, 303–304, 307–309, 312–313, 318, 320–325, 328–331, 335–348, 353–360, 362, 366, 373–374, 376, 378–389, 397–406, 409–412, 414–415, 421–441, 445–451, 456–460, 473–475, 477–478, 480–486, 491–492, 494–496, 498–501, 504–505, 510–514, 516–524, 527–528, 533, 535–539, 541–547, 549, 557–558, 562, 564–565, 567, 576–578, 580, 582–586, 591, 604, 607, 609–611, 614–619, 623–625, 628–632
subjective, subjectivation 193, 251, 446, 450–451, 459–460, 476, 630
surveillance 41–42, 94, 98, 111–112, 121–122, 124–125, 240, 247–248, 250–251, 253, 258, 322, 397, 415, 421, 424, 426, 430, 432–434, 436, 439, 445, 452, 458, 624
surveillance capitalism 125, 424, 434, 452
sustainability 37, 40, 43–45, 50, 66, 166–167, 170, 176–177, 179, 191, 196, 276, 279, 298–299, 319, 327, 342, 345, 378, 412, 445, 458, 474–475, 504, 509, 533, 546, 557–558, 562, 577, 580–581, 585, 587, 628, 630–631
Swahili 48, 492
Sweden 69–70
Swiss 297
Switzerland 58, 69
Syria 371
systemic change 414

Tangaza University College 491, 494
Tanzania 510–511
teaching pedagogies 183–184, 196
Teams (Microsoft) 436, 438
Technical Skills Development Authority (TESDA) 563, 565
techno-corporate 421
technocritique 421
Telegram 427, 436–437
terra nullius 125, 361
Thailand 69
theory 44, 92, 96, 101, 123–124, 141–142, 174–175, 185–186, 242, 249, 277, 319, 389–390, 408, 413, 430, 440, 446, 455, 481, 513, 542, 547, 632
Times Higher Education (THE) 120, 218
Transforming Employability for Social Change in East Africa (TESCEA) 509–513, 516–518, 524–525, 528
tree, tree-planting 35–36, 38, 48, 50, 90, 228, 297, 353–357, 360–362, 364, 367, 492, 500, 504
Trump, Donald 70
Twitter 201–202, 273, 276, 278, 383

Ubuntu 309
Uganda 57, 510–511, 519–520, 523
Uganda Martyrs University 510–511, 519–520, 523
Ukraine 128, 627
Ukrainian 128
UNESCO 139, 163, 240, 243, 304–307, 312, 317, 429–430, 450, 496, 504, 509, 575–577, 579, 581, 586
Sustainable Development Goals (SDGs) 144, 509, 568, 579
United Kingdom (UK) 36, 47, 56–57, 183, 190–191, 200, 218, 253, 398, 407, 494, 510–511, 528
United Nations (UN) 317, 386, 497, 568
United States of America (USA) 48, 54, 56–60, 62, 64, 67, 70–71, 99, 114–115, 118, 144, 162, 171–172, 175, 190–191, 200, 203, 209, 218, 220, 228, 243, 276, 365, 424, 498, 617, 623, 629

Universal Design for Learning (UDL) 47, 373–385, 387–390
University of Brasilia (UnB) 422, 427
University of Campinas (Unicamp) 432–433
Upgrading Science Teaching Using Distance Instruction (STUDI) 559
UP Open University (UPOU) 559–560, 563, 565–567

virtual learning environment (VLE) 400, 401, 402, 403, 410, 411
visioning process 303–304, 306–307, 311, 313

Wagner, James 359

Wallace, David Foster 163
Watters, Audrey 242
Weber, Max 172
West Indies, University of the (UWI) 474–475
WhatsApp 383, 429, 437–440
Wikimedia 278
Wikipedia 206, 222, 278
Wikiversity 427–429, 437

Xenofeminists 278–279

Yasuhara, Yoshihito 162–164, 168
YouTube 278, 281, 439, 463

Zoom 353, 362, 413, 569

About the Team

Alessandra Tosi was the managing editor for this book.

Larry Erhuvwuokhene Onokpite copyedited this manuscript; Maria Eydmans and Maria Teresa Renzi Sepe proofread it. Lucy Barnes produced the index.

Jeevanjot Kaur Nagpal designed the cover. The cover was produced in InDesign using the Fontin font.

Laura Rodriguez Pupo distributed and marketed this book.

Jeremy Bowman typeset the book in InDesign and produced the paperback and hardback editions. The text font is Tex Gyre Pagella; the heading font is Californian FB.

Cameron Craig produced the EPUB, PDF, HTML, and XML editions — the conversion was made with open-source software such as pandoc (https://pandoc.org/), created by John MacFarlane, and other tools freely available on our GitHub page (https://github.com/OpenBookPublishers).

This book has also been peer-reviewed anonymously by experts in their field. We thank them for their invaluable help.

This book need not end here...

Share

All our books — including the one you have just read — are free to access online so that students, researchers and members of the public who can't afford a printed edition will have access to the same ideas. This title will be accessed online by hundreds of readers each month across the globe: why not share the link so that someone you know is one of them?
This book and additional content is available at:
https://doi.org/10.11647/OBP.0363

Donate

Open Book Publishers is an award-winning, scholar-led, not-for-profit press making knowledge freely available one book at a time. We don't charge authors to publish with us: instead, our work is supported by our library members and by donations from people who believe that research shouldn't be locked behind paywalls.
Why not join them in freeing knowledge by supporting us:
https://www.openbookpublishers.com/support-us

Follow @OpenBookPublish

Read more at the Open Book Publishers BLOG

You may also be interested in:

Dire Straits-Education Reforms
Ideology, Vested Interests and Evidence
Montserrat Gomendio & José Ignacio Wert (authors)

https://doi.org/10.11647/OBP.0332

Learning, Marginalization, and Improving the Quality of Education in Low-income Countries
Daniel A. Wagner, Nathan M. Castillo & Suzanne Grant Lewis (editors)

https://doi.org/10.11647/OBP.0256

Shaping the Digital Dissertation
Knowledge Production in the Arts and Humanities
Virginia Kuhn & Anke Finger (editors)

https://doi.org/10.11647/OBP.0239

Milton Keynes UK
Ingram Content Group UK Ltd.
UKHW020155141223
434308UK00003B/10